Readings in
SOCIAL PSYCHOLOGY

W9-AAK-496

BOOKBROKERS

Readings in
SOCIAL PSYCHOLOGY

General, Classic, and Contemporary Selections

WAYNE A. LESKO
Marymount University

J. Vaveris

ALLYN AND BACON
Boston ■ London ■ Toronto ■ Sydney ■ Tokyo ■ Singapore

Managing Editor: Susan Badger
Editorial Assistant: Dana Lamothe
Production Administrator: Annette Joseph
Production Coordinator: Susan Freese
Editorial-Production Service: Karen Mason
Cover Administrator: Linda K. Dickinson
Cover Designer: Suzanne Harbison
Manufacturing Buyer: Megan Cochran

Copyright © 1991 by Allyn and Bacon
A Divison of Simon & Schuster, Inc.
160 Gould Street
Needham Heights, Massachusetts 02194

All rights reserved. No part of the material protected by this copyright notice may be reproduced or utilized in any form or by any means, electronic or mechanical, including photo-
copying, recording, or by any information storage and retrieval system, without the written
permission of the copyright owner.

Library of Congress Cataloging-in-Publication Data

Lesko, Wayne A.
    Readings in social psychology: general, classic, and contemporary
selections / Wayne A. Lesko.
        p.   cm.
    Includes bibliographical references and index.
    ISBN 0–205–12698–7
    1. Social psychology.   I. Title.
HM251.L4723   1990
302 — dc20   90–47113
                                                                              CIP

Printed in the United States of America

10 9 8 7 6 5 4 3 2 1   95 94 93 92 91 90

To my son,
Matthew,
who is an inspiration to me always

Brief Contents

Contents

Preface

THE TYPICAL SOCIAL PSYCHOLOGY class ranges from sophomore through graduate levels, and the audience may include majors who are required to take the course as well as nonmajors who have elected to do so. Regardless of the level or the audience, many instructors—myself included—feel that a collection of readings is a valuable means of promoting an understanding of the discipline.

Current collections of readings typically fall into two categories: professional articles from journals in the field or popular articles reprinted from such magazines as *Psychology Today*. The category of professional readings may include contemporary articles, classic articles, or a combination of the two. These articles provide excellent insight into the core of social psychology by describing not only the research outcomes but also the detailed methodology for how the results were obtained. Popular articles, on the other hand, lack the scientific rigor of journal articles but often present a broad overview of a number of findings pertaining to a particular topic. Clearly, both types of readings have advantages and disadvantages associated with them, depending on the particular level at which or the students to whom the course is taught.

In more than 15 years of teaching social psychology at both the undergraduate and graduate levels, I have found that students seem to respond best to a variety of reading formats. Popular articles are easy to understand and provide a good overview, while also generating critical thinking about an issue. Research articles provide insight into the methodological issues in social psychology and help the student develop a critical attitude in evaluating research contributions and conclusions. Classic research articles familiarize the student with early research that has had a lasting impact on social psychology, while contemporary work illustrates issues currently being studied and the methods used to investigate them. *Readings in Social Psychology: General, Classic, and Contemporary Selections* is intended to provide exactly this breadth of exposure to the different sources of information available in the field.

Each chapter begins with an introduction to the topic, which is followed by three articles: one general (popular), one classic, and one contemporary. Each article begins with a short introduction that sets the stage, or provides a context for the article. Each article is followed by a set of "Critical Thinking Questions," which ask the student to examine critically some part of the article presented, to speculate about generalizations and implications of the research, and in some cases to suggest new studies based on the information in the article. The classic articles are also followed by a list of "Additional Related Readings" for students who may wish to examine more contemporary articles on the same topic.

The topical organization of *Readings in Social Psychology: General, Classic, and Contemporary Selections* directly parallels Baron and Byrne's *Social Psychology: Understanding Human Interaction* (6th edition). However, the book can be readily adapted for use with any other text or, depending on how the course is taught, used in lieu of a text. Likewise, the book can be used with audiences of varying levels by structuring which articles will be emphasized and in how much detail they will be examined. All articles are presented verbatim, in their entirety, since it is my firm belief that one valuable skill gained by students from reading research articles is the ability to abstract pertinent information from an original source. The Note to the Reader that follows this Preface offers some suggestions on how to get the most out of the book. It is especially recommended for students who do not have an extensive background in reading research articles.

At this point, perhaps some notice is in order about several of the articles. Understandably, everything is representative of the time in which it was written, both in terms of the ideas presented and the language used. Some of the classic articles in this collection were written some 30 to 40 years ago and are out of step with current usage, employing racial labels such as *Negro*. Moreover, some of the descriptions made and observations offered would be considered condescending and even offensive by today's standards. Please keep this in mind, and consider the context in which each of the articles was written.

ACKNOWLEDGMENTS

I owe thanks to a number of people who either directly helped with the production of this book or who provided much needed support. First and foremost, I would like to thank the authors and publishers of the reprinted articles for their permission to use their work.

At Allyn and Bacon, I would like to thank Susan Badger, Managing Editor, and Dana Lamothe, Editorial Assistant, for their guidance and help with the format of the book. Thanks also go to the reviewers who provided suggestions about the book at various stages: Robert A. Baron, Rensselear Polytechnic Institute; Donn Byrne, State University of New York—Albany; Victoria Esses, University of Toronto; Robert W. Holt, George Mason University; Elizabeth Hough, Rutgers University; Thomas Jackson, Fort Hays State University; Jack Powell, University of Hartford; Steven Prentice-Dunn, University of Alabama; Nicholas R. Santilli, John Carroll University; and Michael J. White, Ball State University.

Personal thanks go to several individuals. Frank McAndrew, Knox College, and Rebecca Pliske, Marymount College, provided me with some useful ideas and support for my project, for which I am in their debt. My two graduate assistants, Amy Kurylas and Maria Tatis, were of invaluable help in getting production off the ground.

W. L.

A Note to the Reader

AS YOU EMBARK upon your study of social psychology, you will soon discover that the field is broad indeed. Many different topics will be encountered, but they all are related by the common thread that defines social psychology: namely, the study of individual behavior in social situations.

As a collection of readings, this book is designed to expose you to some of the most important areas of study within social psychology. Just as the topics found in the area of social psychology are diverse, so, too, are the ways in which social psychological knowledge is disseminated. If you are new to the field, most likely you have encountered one common source of information: articles in nonprofessional sources. For example, newspaper and magazine articles may present the information from some study in social psychology. Typically nontechnical pieces directed to the general public, these articles summarize a number of studies on a given topic and are fairly easy to comprehend. Each of the fourteen chapters that comprise this book begins with such an article, what I have termed a *general* reading.

A second source of information is actually the backbone of social psychology: articles that appear in professional journals of the field. These articles are the primary means by which new ideas and the results of research are shared with the professional community. While they tend to be more technical and difficult to read compared to the general works, professional articles have the advantage of providing the readers with sufficient detail to draw their own conclusions, rather than be forced to rely on someone else's interpretation of the information. Some of these articles represent research that has stood the test of time and are generally regarded as *classics* in the field; the second reading found in each chapter is such an article.

Finally, the last type of article found in each chapter is labeled *contemporary*. These articles are fairly recent examples of research currently being conducted in social psychology.

The format of each chapter is the same. Each opens with a brief introduction to the chapter topic; following, one general, one classic, and one contemporary article are presented, in that order. Each article begins with an introduction written by me, which serves to focus your perspective before reading. Each article is followed by a section labeled "Critical Thinking Questions." In some cases, these questions directly refer to information contained in the articles; in others, the questions are more speculative, asking you to go beyond the data presented. Finally, the classic articles contain an additional section of "Additional Related Readings." The references included here are either recent articles that address the same issues discussed in the classic article (a way of updating the current status of research on the topic) or a topic similar to the one discussed in the original. In either case, the interested student can use these references to find more information on the topic.

All of the articles in this collection are reprinted in their entirety. Not a word has been abridged or altered. For the general articles, this should not be a problem for anyone. However, if this is the first time that you are reading journal articles from their primary source, some assistance might be in order. First of all, do not allow yourself to be overwhelmed or intimidated. New students often are confused by some of the terminology that is used and are left totally dumbfounded by the detailed statistics that are usually part of such articles. Approached in the right way, these articles need not be intimidating and should be comprehensible to any reader willing to expend a little effort.

In reading a research article, I would like to make the following suggestions. Most articles begin with an Abstract or end with a Summary. If these are provided, begin by carefully reading them; they will give you an overview of why the study was conducted, what was done, and what the results were. Next, read the Introduction fairly carefully; this is where the authors describe previous research in the area and develop the logic for why they are conducting the experiment in the first place. The Methods section describes in detail the techniques used by the researchers to conduct their study; read this section thoroughly in order to understand exactly what was done. The next section, Results, is where the authors describe what was found in the study. This is often the most technically difficult part of the article; from your standpoint, you might want to skim over this part, focusing only on the sections that verbally describe what the results were. Don't worry about the detailed statistical analyses that are presented. Finally, you might want to read the Discussion section in some detail; here, the authors discuss the findings and implications of the study and perhaps suggest some avenues for further study.

To summarize: Each article is fairly straightforward to comprehend, provided that you don't allow yourself to get too bogged down in the details and thus frustrated. The journey may seem difficult at times, but the end result—an appreciation and understanding of the complex issues of human social behavior—will be worth it. Enjoy!

W. L.

Readings in
SOCIAL PSYCHOLOGY

Chapter One

RESEARCH ISSUES

AN INTRODUCTION TO a course such as social psychology often includes a section on research methods. Nonmajors confronting this topic often wonder why they need to know about research methods when in all likelihood they will never actually conduct research. Whether you are majoring in psychology or not, familiarity with research methods will benefit you, for several reasons.

First, it will help you understand the studies that make up the knowledge base of social psychology. Familiarity with methodology will allow you to make informed decisions about the conclusions drawn by various studies. Second, and perhaps more important, some knowledge of research issues will allow you to be an intelligent consumer of research information. Results of studies often are reported to the general public in newspapers and magazines. Knowing something about the methods used to produce these results will better prepare you to decide whether the conclusions drawn are warranted. For these reasons, Article 1, "The Sample with the Built-in Bias," is about issues of particular concern to survey studies, but they apply to other types of research studies, as well.

A second, related topic is the role of theory in research. Are theories really necessary? is a question often asked by beginning students. Article 2, "Social Psychology and Science," addresses the role of theory in understanding and predicting social behavior. In addition, the article addresses a question often raised in social psychology: namely, Can social psychology develop theories that can actually predict behavior, or is it impossible to do so given the unique subject matter of the discipline? The article represents a classic response to this issue.

Finally, values and ethics are certainly a part of the study of research methods in social psychology. Besides the ethical issues involved in research, such as protecting the well-being of the subjects, another question is the extent to which researchers' biases influence the studies they conduct and the conclusions they draw. We hope that scientists seek the truth and do not bias their research studies, at least not intentionally. However, are researchers always unbiased, or do their own particular values sometimes intrude on the scientific process? The final reading in this chapter, Article 3, "Pornography, Social Science, and Politics," addresses this issue in the context of a recently released government report on the effects of pornography.

ARTICLE 1 _____

At the heart of all of the articles you will read in this book is research methodology. Given a question that you want to investigate, how do you go about actually collecting the data?

There are a number of different ways of conducting social psychological research. One broad distinction is between *experimental methods* and *correlational (nonexperimental) methods.* A set of potential advantages and disadvantages is associated with each. One is not necessarily better than the other; it depends on what you are investigating.

Students encountering research methods literature for the first time are often surprised at the difficulty of designing and conducting a good piece of research. It isn't as easy as it might seem on the surface. Numerous artifacts that can affect the outcome of a study need to be accounted for and controlled. An examination of the introductory chapter of most social psychology texts will give you a better understanding of some of these issues.

One issue that is central to a number of methods, whether experimental or correlational, is that of *sampling.* Specifically, who are the subjects in the study? How were they selected? Can you generalize the findings obtained on these subjects to other groups of people? The following article is the opening chapter of the book, *How to Lie with Statistics,* by Darrell Huff. It provides a good overview of the issues concerning sampling. In particular, you might want to focus on the types of bias, both intentional and unintentional, that may operate in research, as well as the question of how generalizable the results may be. Although the article examines primarily survey (questionnaire) research, the same concerns apply to experimental studies.

The Sample with the Built-In Bias
■ Darrell Huff

"The Average Yaleman, Class of '24," *Time* magazine noted once, commenting on something in the New York *Sun,* "makes $25,111 a year."

Well, good for him!

But wait a minute. What does this impressive figure mean? Is it, as it appears to be, evidence that if you send your boy to Yale you won't have to work in your old age and neither will he?

Two things about the figure stand out at first suspicious glance. It is surprisingly precise. It is quite improbably salubrious.

There is small likelihood that the average income of any far-flung group is ever going to be known down to the dollar. It is not particularly probable that you know your own income for last year so precisely as that unless it was all derived from salary. And $25,000 incomes are not often all salary; people in that bracket are likely to have well-scattered investments.

Furthermore, this lovely average is undoubtedly calculated from the amounts the Yale men *said* they earned. Even if they had the honor sys-

"The Sample with the Built-In Bias" is reprinted from *How to Lie with Statistics* by Darrell Huff, pictures by Irving Geis, by permission of W. W. Norton & Company, Inc. Copyright 1954 by Darrell Huff and Irving Geis. Copyright renewed 1982 by Darrell Huff and Irving Geis.

Some of the language used and views presented are indicative of the time in which the article was written. The reader should consider the article in that context.

tem in New Haven in '24, we cannot be sure that it works so well after a quarter of a century that all these reports are honest ones. Some people when asked their incomes exaggerate out of vanity or optimism. Others minimize, especially if it is to be feared, on income-tax returns; and having done this may hesitate to contradict themselves on any other paper. Who knows what the revenuers may see? It is possible that these two tendencies, to boast and to understate, cancel each other out, but it is unlikely. One tendency may be far stronger than the other, and we do not know which one.

We have begun then to account for a figure that common sense tells us can hardly represent the truth. Now let us put our finger on the likely source of the biggest error, a source that can produce $25,111 as the "average income" of some men whose actual average may well be nearer half that amount.

This is the sampling procedure, which is the heart of the greater part of the statistics you meet on all sorts of subjects. Its basis is simple enough, although its refinements in practice have led into all sorts of by-ways, some less than respectable. If you have a barrel of beans, some red and some white, there is only one way to find out exactly how many of each color you have: Count 'em. However, you can find out approximately how many are red in much easier fashion by pulling out a handful of beans and counting just those, figuring that the proportion will be the same all through the barrel. If your sample is large enough and selected properly, it will represent the whole well enough for most purposes. If it is not, it may be far less accurate than an intelligent guess and have nothing to recommend it but a spurious air of scientific precision. It is sad truth that conclusions from such samples, biased or too small or both, lie behind much of what we read or think we know.

The report on the Yale men comes from a sample. We can be pretty sure of that because reason tells us that no one can get hold of all the living members of that class of '24. There are bound to be many whose addresses are unknown twenty-five years later.

And, of those whose addresses are known,

many will not reply to a questionnaire, particularly a rather personal one. With some kinds of mail questionnaire, a five or ten per cent response is quite high. This one should have done better than that, but nothing like one hundred per cent.

So we find that the income figure is based on a sample composed of all class members whose addresses are known and who replied to the questionnaire. Is this a representative sample? That is, can this group be assumed to be equal in income to the unrepresented group, those who cannot be reached or who do not reply?

Who are the little lost sheep down in the Yale rolls as "address unknown"? Are they the big-income earners—the Wall Street men, the corporation directors, the manufacturing and utility executives? No; the addresses of the rich will not be hard to come by. Many of the most prosperous members of the class can be found through *Who's Who in America* and other reference volumes even if they have neglected to keep in touch with the alumni office. It is a good guess that the lost names are those of the men who, twenty-five years or so after becoming Yale bachelors of arts, have not fulfilled any shining promise. They are clerks, mechanics, tramps, unemployed alcoholics, barely surviving writers and artists . . . people of whom it would take half a dozen or more to add up to an income of $25,111. These men do not so often register at class reunions, if only because they cannot afford the trip.

Who are those who chucked the questionnaire into the nearest wastebasket? We cannot be so sure about these, but it is at least a fair guess that many of them are just not making enough money to brag about. They are a little like the fellow who found a note clipped to his first pay check suggesting that he consider the amount of his salary confidential and not material for the interchange of office confidences. "Don't worry," he told the boss. "I'm just as ashamed of it as you are."

It becomes pretty clear that the sample has omitted two groups most likely to depress the average. The $25,111 figure is beginning to explain itself. If it is a true figure for anything it is one merely for that special group of the class of '24 whose addresses are known and who are willing to stand up and tell how much they earn. Even that requires an assumption that the gentlemen are telling the truth.

Such an assumption is not to be made lightly. Experience from one breed of sampling study, that called market research, suggests that it can hardly ever be made at all. A house-to-house survey purporting to study magazine readership was once made in which a key question was: What magazines does your household read? When the results were tabulated and analyzed it appeared that a great many people loved *Harper's* and not very many read *True Story*. Now there were publishers' figures around at the time that showed very clearly that *True Story* had more millions of circulation than *Harper's* had hundreds of thousands. Perhaps we asked the wrong kind of people, the designers of the survey said to themselves. But no, the questions had been asked in all sorts of neighborhoods all around the country. The only reasonable conclusion then was that a good many of the respondents, as people are called when they answer such questions, had not told the truth. About all the survey had uncovered was snobbery.

In the end it was found that if you wanted to know what certain people read it was no use asking them. You could learn a good deal more by going to their houses and saying you wanted to buy old magazines and what could be had? Then all you had to do was count the *Yale Reviews* and the *Love Romances*. Even that dubious device, of course, does not tell you what people read, only what they have been exposed to.

Similarly, the next time you learn from your reading that the average American (you hear a good deal about him these days, most of it faintly improbable) brushes his teeth 1.02 times a day—a figure I have just made up, but it may be as good as anyone else's—ask yourself a question. How can anyone have found out such a thing? Is a woman who has read in countless advertisements that non-brushers are social offenders going to confess to a stranger that she does not brush her teeth regularly? The statistic may have meaning to one who wants to know only what people say about tooth-brushing but it does not tell a great

deal about the frequency with which bristle is applied to incisor.

A river cannot, we are told, rise above its source. Well, it can seem to if there is a pumping station concealed somewhere about. It is equally true that the result of a sampling study is no better than the sample it is based on. By the time the data have been filtered through layers of statistical manipulation and reduced to a decimal-pointed average, the result begins to take on an aura of conviction that a closer look at the sampling would deny.

Does early discovery of cancer save lives? Probably. But of the figures commonly used to prove it the best that can be said is that they don't. These, the records of the Connecticut Tumor Registry, go back to 1935 and appear to show a substantial increase in the five-year survival rate from that year till 1941. Actually those records were begun in 1941, and everything earlier was obtained by tracing back. Many patients had left Connecticut, and whether they had lived or died could not be learned. According to the medical reporter Leonard Engel, the built-in bias thus created is "enough to account for nearly the whole of the claimed improvement in survival rate."

To be worth much, a report based on sampling must use a representative sample, which is one from which every source of bias has been removed. That is where our Yale figure shows its worthlessness. It is also where a great many of the things you can read in newspapers and magazines reveal their inherent lack of meaning.

A psychiatrist reported once that practically everybody is neurotic. Aside from the fact that such use destroys any meaning in the word "neurotic," take a look at the man's sample. That is, whom has the psychiatrist been observing? It turns out that he has reached this edifying conclusion from studying his patients, who are a long, long way from being a sample of the population. If a man were normal, our psychiatrist would never meet him.

Give that kind of second look to the things you read, and you can avoid learning a whole lot of things that are not so.

It is worth keeping in mind also that the dependability of a sample can be destroyed just as easily by invisible sources of bias as by these visible ones. That is, even if you can't find a source of demonstrable bias, allow yourself some degree of skepticism about the results as long as there is a possibility of bias somewhere. There always is. The presidential elections in 1948 and 1952 were enough to prove that, if there were any doubt.

For further evidence go back to 1936 and the *Literary Digest's* famed fiasco. The ten million telephone and *Digest* subscribers who assured the editors of the doomed magazine that it would be Landon 370, Roosevelt 161 came from the list that had accurately predicted the 1932 election. How could there be bias in a list already so tested? There was a bias, of course, as college theses and other post mortems found: People who could afford telephones and magazine subscriptions in 1936 were not a cross section of voters. Economically they were a special kind of people, a sample biased because it was loaded with what turned out to be Republican voters. The sample elected Landon, but the voters thought otherwise.

The basic sample is the kind called "random." It is selected by pure chance from the "universe," a word by which the statistician means the whole of which the sample is a part. Every tenth name is pulled from a file of index cards. Fifty slips of paper are taken from a hatful. Every twentieth person met on Market Street is interviewed. (But remember that this last is not a sample of the population of the world, or of the United States, or of San Francisco, but only of the people on Market Street at the time. One interviewer for an opinion poll said that she got her people in a railroad station because "all kinds of people can be found in a station." It had to be pointed out to her that mothers of small children, for instance, might be underrepresented there.)

The test of the random sample is this: Does every name or thing in the whole group have an equal chance to be in the sample?

The purely random sample is the only kind that can be examined with entire confidence by means of statistical theory, but there is one thing wrong with it. It is so difficult and expensive to obtain for many uses that sheer cost eliminates it. A more economical substitute, which is almost universally used in such fields as opinion polling and market research, is called stratified random sampling.

To get this stratified sample you divide your universe into several groups in proportion to their known prevalence. And right there your trouble can begin: Your information about their proportion may not be correct. You instruct your interviewers to see to it that they talk to so many Negroes and such-and-such a percentage of people in each of several income brackets, to a specified number of farmers, and so on. All the while the group must be divided equally between persons over forty and under forty years of age.

That sounds fine—but what happens? On the question of Negro or white the interviewer will judge correctly most of the time. On income he will make more mistakes. As to farmers—how do you classify a man who farms part time and works in the city too? Even the question of age can pose some problems which are most easily settled by choosing only respondents who obviously are well under or well over forty. In that case the sample will be biased by the virtual absence of the late-thirties and early-forties age groups. You can't win.

On top of all this, how do you get a random sample within the stratification? The obvious thing is to start with a list of everybody and go after names chosen from it at random: but that is too expensive. So you go into the streets—and bias your sample against stay-at-homes. You go from door to door by day—and miss most of the employed people. You switch to evening interviewers—and neglect the movie-goers and night-clubbers.

The operation of a poll comes down in the end to a running battle against sources of bias, and this battle is conducted all the time by all the reputable polling organizations. What the reader of the reports must remember is that the battle is never won. No conclusion that "sixty-seven per cent of the American people are against" something or other should be read without the lingering question, Sixty-seven per cent of which American people?

So with Dr. Alfred C. Kinsey's "female volume." The problem, as with anything based on sampling, is how to read it (or a popular summary of it) without learning too much that is not necessarily so. There are at least three levels of sampling involved. Dr. Kinsey's samples of the population (one level) are far from random ones and may not be particularly representative, but they are enormous samples by comparison with anything done in his field before and his figures must be accepted as revealing and important if not necessarily on the nose. It is possibly more important to remember that any questionnaire is only a sample (another level) of the possible questions and that the answer the lady gives is no more than a sample (third level) of her attitudes and experiences on each question.

The kind of people who make up the interviewing staff can shade the result in an interesting fashion. Some years ago, during the war, the National Opinion Research Center sent out two staffs of interviewers to ask three questions of five hundred Negroes in a Southern city. White interviewers made up one staff, Negro the other.

One question was, "Would Negroes be treated better or worse here if the Japanese conquered the U.S.A.?" Negro interviewers reported that nine per cent of those they asked said "better." White interviewers found only two per cent of such responses. And while Negro interviewers found only twenty-five per cent who thought Negroes would be treated worse, white interviewers turned up forty-five per cent.

When "Nazis" was substituted for "Japanese" in the question, the results were similar.

The third question probed attitudes that might be based on feelings revealed by the first two. "Do you think it is more important to concentrate on beating the Axis, or to make democracy work better here at home?" "Beat Axis" was the reply of thirty-nine per cent, according to the Negro interviewers; of sixty-two per cent, according to the white.

Here is bias introduced by unknown factors. It seems likely that the most effective factor was a tendency that must always be allowed for in reading poll results, a desire to give a pleasing answer. Would it be any wonder if, when answering a question with connotations of disloyalty in wartime, a Southern Negro would tell a white man what sounded good rather than what he actually believed? It is also possible that the different groups of interviewers chose different kinds of people to talk to.

In any case the results are obviously so biased as to be worthless. You can judge for yourself how many other poll-based conclusions are just as biased, just as worthless—but with no check available to show them up.

You have pretty fair evidence to go on if you suspect that polls in general are biased in one specific direction, the direction of the *Literary Digest* error. This bias is toward the person with more money, more education, more information and alertness, better appearance, more conventional behavior, and more settled habits than the average of the population he is chosen to represent.

You can easily see what produces this. Let us say that you are an interviewer assigned to a street corner, with one interview to get. You spot two men who seem to fit the category you must complete: over forty, Negro, urban. One is in clean overalls, decently patched, neat. The other is dirty and he looks surly. With a job to get done, you approach the more likely-looking fellow, and your colleagues all over the country are making similar decisions.

Some of the strongest feeling against public-opinion polls is found in liberal or left-wing circles, where it is rather commonly believed that polls are generally rigged. Behind this view is the fact that poll results so often fail to square with the opinions and desires of those whose thinking is not in the conservative direction. Polls, they point out, seem to elect Republicans even when voters shortly thereafter do otherwise.

Actually, as we have seen, it is not necessary that a poll be rigged—that is, that the results be deliberately twisted in order to create a false impression. The tendency of the sample to be biased in this consistent direction can rig it automatically.

CRITICAL THINKING QUESTIONS

1. Nearly every day, newspapers and magazines report the results of one survey or another to their readerships. Find such an example in a paper or magazine. Based upon the information given with the data, how accurate are the findings presented? What possible sources of bias may have influenced the results? Does the article mention or address any potential problems with the data?

2. Design a survey on some topic of interest to be administered on your campus. Based upon the reading, what factors should you consider in designing and implementing the survey instrument? Could any methods be used to minimize sources of bias that may be present?

3. Do you think that people ever intentionally design a biased survey instrument? Find an example of such a study where you might be suspicious of the accuracy of the results, given the biases of the researchers.

4. One central issue in the article was the generalizability of results to the entire population given the use of a sample. A great deal of research in psychology is conducted on volunteers obtained from students enrolled in general psychology classes. How reliable is such a sample of subjects for the generalizability of findings to other populations? For example, are college students a representative subset of the general population, or are they somehow different? For that matter, are students enrolled in general psychology necessarily representative of college students in general? What other issues may have an impact on the interpretation and generalization of research findings?

ARTICLE 2 _____

In Chapter 9 of this book, you will read about a classic line of research in social psychology concerning when people help (or don't help) in emergency situations. One finding from this research is that people are less likely to help in emergency situations in which many people are present.

Now imagine that some time after reading the article, you come across a building on fire, and a large number of people are standing around. There is no evidence that the fire department has arrived yet. What do you do? Specifically, now that you know there is less likelihood of someone helping when a large number of people are present, would you be more likely to do something to help? Or do you think that what you study has no impact on how you act?

"Social Psychology as History," a paper discussed in the following reading, essentially suggested that when social psychology phenomena were understood by people, they would change their behavior and thus invalidate the theory. As such, social psychology could not *predict* behavior but rather could only *describe* behavior (hence, a historical inquiry). The next article, "Social Psychology and Science," is a response to that assertion. The author, Barry R. Schlenker, discusses the "history" article in detail and clearly demonstrates why he feels that social psychology actually is a science.

Besides addressing whether social psychological research is truly a scientific enterprise, the article also is of value because it illustrates the role of theory in any science. While reading, pay attention not only to the arguments given establishing social psychology as a science but also issues such as free will versus determinism, pure versus applied science, and facts versus theories.

Social Psychology and Science

 Barry R. Schlenker[1]

Critical attacks challenging the scientific status of the social disciplines have been with us as long as the disciplines themselves. Periodically such challenges resurface, and it again becomes necessary to clear the air and reaffirm the scientific stature of the social disciplines. Gergen recently has contended that "social psychology is primarily an historical inquiry" incapable of generating scientific principles and general theories. Many of his contentions demonstrate a myopic focus on particulars, a misconception of the nature of science, and an unjustifiable pessimism. Additionally, his arguments merely resurrect older challenges which have been hurled at social scientists for decades and which fail to fundamentally distinguish the natural from the social sciences. The present article attempts to demonstrate why Gergen's contentions are logically and empirically incorrect. In so doing, it hopefully will provide a needed affirmative statement concerning the scientific status of social psychology and other social disciplines. Humanistic principles are not challenged by such an affirmative declaration. Rather, it is argued that social behavior (including the ex-

Reprinted from the *Journal of Personality and Social Psychology*, 1974, *29*, 1–15. Copyright 1974 by the American Psychological Association. Reprinted by permission.

ercise of "free" choice) is understandable and ex-plainable within the context of inquiry we call science.

A recurring theme in the philosophy of science is the degree to which psychology, or for that matter any social discipline, possesses the requisite characteristics to be considered a science (for discussions of some of the issues, see Bergmann, 1953; Brown, 1963; Cohen, 1953; Grünbaum, 1953, 1956; Hempel, 1965; Kaplan, 1964; Kemeny, 1959; Nagel, 1953, 1961; Zilsel, 1953). Those who insist that the subject matter of the social disciplines is sufficiently different from the subject matter of the natural sciences to disqualify the former from scientific stature typically enumerate several timeworn arguments. These include (a) the capriciousness and flux of social phenomena, making regularities impossible to uncover; (b) the existence of free will, oftentimes confused with indeterminism, which allows people to decide their own fate rather than "obey" scientific "laws"; (c) the cultural relativity of laws, making universal or nomic laws unobtainable; (d) the temporal relativity of laws, making any social statement a mere transient phenomenon; (e) the value aspects of social phenomena, coloring the social scientist's selection, interpretation, and presentation of facts; (f) the difficulty of social experimentation and control of necessary variables; (g) the open system problem, in which new information constantly affects individuals' behaviors in an apparently unpredictable fashion; and (h) the ability of the public to become aware of social hypotheses and modify their behavior to validate otherwise false hypotheses and invalidate otherwise true hypotheses. Each of these arguments has been the topic of classic debates on the status of the social disciplines, with the overwhelming majority of philosophers of science coming to the conclusion that there is really nothing fundamentally different about the social sciences as compared to the natural sciences which would preclude the attachment of the "honorific" label "science" to both branches of knowledge equally. Nevertheless, Gergen (1973) has reopened the is-

sue and resurrected many of the above arguments in an attempt to conclude that

social psychology is primarily an historical inquiry. Unlike the natural sciences, it deals with facts that are largely nonrepeatable and which fluctuate markedly over time. Principles of human interaction cannot readily be developed over time because the facts on which they are based do not generally remain stable. Knowledge cannot accumulate in the usual scientific sense because such knowledge does not generally transcend its historical boundaries (p. 310).

Therefore, "the continued attempt to build general laws of social behavior seems misdirected . . . (p. 316)."

Gergen's thesis contains two convergent lines of thought. First, he considers the impact of social science upon society as a whole and the effects of the dissemination of knowledge on behavioral predictions. He contends that "social science can fruitfully be viewed as a protracted communications system (p. 310)" in which the social observer describes behaviors and communicates them back to the public through mass-media channels. However, social scientists have value commitments which are "almost inevitable by-products of social existence, and as participants in society we can scarcely dissociate ourselves from these values in pursuing professional ends (p. 312)." These values and other types of information can be communicated to subjects during an experiment, and "such communication can have a vital impact on behavior (p. 313)," causing a subject to behave in a reactive and otherwise unanticipated fashion. Additionally, since "psychological principles pose a potential threat to all those for whom they are germane," subjects "may strive to invalidate theories that ensnare us in their impersonal way (p. 314)." Thus, either through mass-media dissemination and/or through the experimenter's unintentionally communicated value commitments, subjects modify their behaviors to show that they are not perfectly predictable. Gergen contends that such a process would threaten not only the immediate results of a particular study but produce widespread changes in public behaviors. Therefore, the existence and propagation of theories is itself a social variable which "increases alternatives to action, and previous patterns of behavior are modified or dissolved (p. 313)," thereby invalidating the theory and relegating it to the status of a description of social behavior which might have been valid at a particular historical moment.

The second arm of Gergen's contention derives from his hypothesis that "If we scan the most prominent lines of research during the past decade, we soon realize that the observed regularities, and thus the major theoretical principles, are firmly wedded to historical circumstances (p. 315)." If all our theories can only be phrased to hold in only a few places at particular moments in time, then they obviously would not possess the kind of universality necessary to serve as the foundations of a science.

Gergen's arguments typify several popular misconceptions about the nature of science and exhibit some undue pessimism. One purpose of the present article is to examine Gergen's arguments and try to demonstrate why his conclusion is justified neither by his logic nor his evidence. In so doing, a second purpose should be accomplished — to provide a positive statement concerning the applicability of scientific explanation to social phenomena. Since Gergen's second argument rests on several quite elementary ideas, it is considered first.

CULTURAL AND TEMPORAL RELATIVITY

Gergen's second contention, that existing theoretical principles are culturally and temporally bound, is challenged by several fundamental considerations, specifically: (a) the nature of theoretical abstractness; (b) the nature of the search for regularity; (c) the nature of open systems; (d) the conditional nature of scientific propositions; and (e) the essential uniqueness of all events.

Theoretical Abstractness

One of the necessary conditions for the formulation of universal theories and laws, whether in the natural or social sciences, is that they be phrased in sufficiently abstract form as to allow for (a) the insertion of specific objects, cases, places, events, and times as variables and/or (b) the deduction and explanation of specifics from higher-order and more abstract theoretical principles. If a theory incorporates specifics, it would not possess the generality to satisfactorily explain the required diversity of phenomena. For example, Kaplan (1964) noted that a statement of a relationship such as "The Japanese people perceive the neck region to be a highly erogenous zone" might well serve as a fact or empirical generalization but could hardly be considered a universal proposition which would be unaffected by future cultural changes. However, a statement such as "Infants who are carried on their mother's back facing the neck will subsequently perceive that region as an erogenous zone" would meet the universality requirement. Similarly, the statement, "A promise of a lollipop will get a child to finish his spinach at suppertime," lacks the universality of the statement, "Expectations of positive reinforcement will increase the probability of a contingent response."

It is the case in the social sciences that many contemporary principles formulated through social research are empirical generalizations which incorporate numerous specifics. Naturally, there is nothing wrong with this state of affairs since social psychology needs all of the facts and empirical generalizations it can muster. Without the compilation of systematic information about social behavior, construction of higher-order theories would be rendered near impossible. However, a myopic focus on such particulars only promotes undue pessimism and does not imply that underlying abstract regularities cannot and have not been formulated. In fact, it is argued below that numerous principles have been formulated in sufficiently abstract terms and have been supported by a sufficiently wide range of data to establish a claim for their universality and transhistoricality.

Freeing ourselves from the everyday concrete conceptualizations of social processes and human behavior which have been instilled in us since childhood is a difficult feat at best. As Nagel (1961) commented,

the possibility must . . . be recognized that in comparison with the variables employed in the past in proposed transcultural laws, the concepts required for this purpose may have to be much more "abstract," may need to be separated by a greater "logical gap" from the familiar notions used in the daily business of social life, and may necessitate a mastery of far more complicated techniques for manipulating the concepts in the analysis of actual social phenomena (pp. 465–466).

However, a difficult task should not be confused with an impossible one, and empirical generalizations should not be confused with abstract universal propositions.

The Search for Regularity

The search for abstract underlying regularities in social phenomena is reminiscent of early similar attempts in the physical sciences. One can imagine the dismay of some ancient Greeks on first realizing that their hypothesized four basic elements in the universe — earth, air, fire, and water — sometimes changed forms, with water evaporating into air, earth eroding in water, and fire producing ashes.[2] The abandonment of this conceptual characterization of the universal properties of the world did not occur because earth, air, fire, and water do not exist, but because the schema was inadequate in allowing further understanding and explanation of physical phenomena. Failures to find underlying regularities in natural and social phenomena speak more about our ability to understand than they do about the phenomena in question. Many of the great advances in science have come when phenomena that appear inconsistent and irregular are abstractly interpreted as consistent and regular, and when phenomena that are apparently consistent and regular are abstractly interpreted as inconsistent and irregular; success in this conceptual task determines in large measure the ability of a discipline to advance.

At least a portion of Gergen's (1973) skepticism about the social scientist's ability to formulate universal theories can be accounted for by his focus on particular research examples which include specifics in their formulation and which were never intended to serve as abstract transhistorical principles. For example, he notes that "Variables that successfully predicted political activism during the early stages of the Vietnam war are dissimilar to those which successfully predicted activism during later periods (p. 315)." Given the specificity of many of these empirical generalizations (e.g., attitudes toward the Johnson administration versus attitudes toward the Nixon administration), there is no reason to expect universality. (An additional problem with the example is that the situation changed radically and introduced unforeseen variables during these periods, a consideration to be discussed below under the topic of the conditional nature of scientific propositions.) Or consider another finding cited by Gergen — that women are more persuasible than men (Janis & Field, 1959). Unless one theorizes that the difference is produced solely by genetic determinants (and almost no one does), then there is absolutely no reason not to believe that in another situation, culture, or time, males would be found to demonstrate more conformity than females. An explanation of the finding might be obtained through deductions from a theory which hypothesizes that susceptibility to external influence is inversely related to perceptions of one's own ability to interpret complex events. If females have been subjected to social learning experiences which reduce their confidence in some of their abilities, then an explanation of the particular result would be accomplished. Any number of other higher-order theories could be developed to deduce this particular phenomenon. To claim that the phenomenon itself is an historically bound fact and therefore invalidates the search for universal theories is analogous to claiming that no universal theories could have been developed in the natural sciences because ice changes into water, or water boils at different temperatures (depending upon atmospheric pressure), or dinosaurs are no longer with us while other species are. As Homans (1967, p. 56) stated, the "claim" of social scientists is not that "human nature is the same the world over," and, it might be added, at all times. Rather, it is "that a relatively few general propositions hold good of human behavior, from which, under a variety of given conditions, . . . a great variety of different forms of concrete behavior follows (Homans, 1967, p. 56)."

Existing Regularities

There is no a priori reason why surface dissimilarities in the social sciences are any greater than surface dissimilarities in the physical sciences. For example, prior to Newton, it was "obvious" to most people that the phenomena described by Galileo's law of free fall, the motions of the planets depicted by Kepler, and the rise and fall of the tides were unrelated phenomena. Newton showed that all three could be related within a single theoretical perspective. Later, Einstein showed that these phenomena, along with other phenomena such as the motion of light rays, could all be explained from the General Theory of Relativity.

There unquestionably are untold surface disparities between different people and cultures, yet a great many similarities exist between all known societies. For example, all possess incest taboos, have some form of family organization, provide some types of care for their young, and have some provisions for maintaining order. Men in all societies share other things in common: the physiological nature of the species, the ability to process and interpret information about the physical and social world, the ability to learn from experience, the necessity to maintain effective transactions of one form or another with the physical and social environment, the tacit or explicit formulation of social rules and interaction patterns, etc. Whether or not these similarities will lend themselves to truly adequate social theories of a universal quality is anyone's guess at the moment, but there is reason for optimism.

Many general social theories have been developed, at least in crude form, and it is not at all as apparent as Gergen would have us believe that they do not possess the requisite characteristics to be considered universal. Social learning phenomena (e.g., Bandura & Walters, 1963), "social facilitation" effects (cf. Zajonc, 1965, 1972), unequivocal behavior orientations (Jones & Gerard, 1967), social comparison processes (Festinger, 1954), the effects of mere exposure on liking toward social and nonsocial objects (Zajonc, 1968), the existence, functioning, and maintenance of status and dominance hierarchies (Brown, 1965), and numerous other phenomena have received theoretical attention and should, if they have not already done so, generate theories which can validly claim universal, transcultural properties. For example, social facilitation effects, that is, that the presence of others produces general arousal patterns which affect learning and performance in a predictable fashion, have been demonstrated in lower animals as well as in man (Zajonc, 1965). Remarkable similarities in status and dominance hierarchies and their effects on social organization exist not only between cultures but in lower animals as well (Brown, 1965). It would be difficult to demonstrate greater "transcultural" effects.

Evidence for certain transhistorical social regularities also abounds. If social processes were as transient as Gergen believes, it would be difficult to explain why the writings of Aristotle, Plato, Marcus Aurelius, Kant, Locke, Rousseau, Hobbes, and other philosophers and social commentators of more or less "ancient" origin still affect contemporary conceptualizations of man. Many of their hypotheses concerning human social behavior and cognitive processes appear as applicable today as the time they were made. Spinoza's *Ethics* contains numerous insights, some of which serve as fundamental postulates in Heider's (1958) balance theory. Machiavelli's sixteenth-century advice to his prince has served as the basis for theoretical work and systematic investigations of Machiavellianism as a personality trait in twentieth-century society (Christie & Geis, 1970). The listing could continue almost indefinitely.

Gergen's reactions to the probability that some contemporary theories are transcultural and trans-historical are puzzling. For example, he dismisses such a claim for the theory of social comparison processes (Festinger, 1954) with little more than a wave of his hand. The theory hypothesizes that people have a need to evaluate their beliefs and themselves accurately and that they use others for comparison purposes when nonsocial criteria are unavailable. It would be possible to further explain these particular hypotheses by deducing them from high-order hypotheses concerning effectance motivations present in men and lower animals (cf. White, 1959), since to maintain effective social commerce one must accurately assess the world and one's self, or social exchange concepts in which men must be aware of the characteristics they and others possess in order to enter into social transactions (cf. Kelley & Thibaut, 1969). However, Gergen concludes that "There is scant reason to suspect that such dispositions are genetically determined, and we can easily imagine persons, and indeed societies, for which these assumptions would not hold (p. 315)." "Imagining" a society which does not employ social comparison processes brings back images of Anselm's ontological argument for the existence of a supreme and perfect being—if we can imagine it, it exists. I have great difficulty imagining a person (much less a whole society) who does not use other people to aid him in evaluating his beliefs and abilities when direct nonsocial evidence is unavailable. The self-concept presumably develops through such social comparison and reflected appraisals (cf. Jones & Gerard, 1967; Mead, 1934; Sullivan, 1953). A foundation of the scientific method relies on intersubjective reliability, the use of several observers and replications, to insure that particular facts about the world are interpreted accurately. However, in the final analysis, whether or not hypotheses about social comparison processes are truly transcultural and transhistorical is an empirical question which will not be resolved through idle speculation.

Gergen also dismisses the possibility that social learning theory could serve as a fundamental theory in social psychology. He notes that since

it has been argued [by him] that the stability in interaction patterns upon which most of our theories rest is dependent on learned dispositions of limited duration . . . [it] implicitly suggests the possibility of a social learning theory transcending historical circumstances (p. 316).

However, he feels such a conclusion unwarranted primarily because of the ramifications of the definition of a reinforcer. Since a reinforcer is defined as that which increases the probability of a particular response class, "the theory seems limited to post hoc interpretation (p. 316)." Although a particular reinforcer such as social approval might be inductively identified, "it is also apparent that reinforcers do not remain stable across time (p. 316)"; he notes that social approval might have been a less potent reward several decades ago than it is today. The latter hypothesis is an empirical question of dubious validity. However, assume for the moment that social approval was worth more then than now. First, the mere assertion that a reinforcer must be determined inductively does not present logical problems for the status of the concept or distinguish the concept from those employed in the natural sciences (cf. Meehl, 1950). Whether or not a specific object or event meets the requirements for inclusion in a particular construct class must always be determined inductively. If a chemist is testing an hypothesis about the combinatorial effects of pure oxygen with other gases, he first must determine whether or not he has pure oxygen. Second, whether or not the class inclusion and value of such an object or event changes over time also does not present logical difficulties. The container of pure oxygen might develop a leak over the course of several weeks and no longer fall into the class of pure oxygen. As another example, a particular rock might be tested to determine its radioactive content prior to an experiment designed to assess the effects of a radioactive substance on a particular physiological process in a laboratory rat. If another researcher used the same rock in a similar experiment several centuries from now, he might fail to obtain similar effects due to radioactive disintegration which would render the rock harm-less. The fact that the value of a particular variable or its inclusion in a particular class changes over time as a consequence of intervening events in no way distinguishes the social sciences from the natural sciences. It would do so only if the changes which occurred in the social variables appeared chaotic and not subject to explanation. The biologist conducting the experiment on radioactivity effects could make specific predictions about the radioactive disintegration process on the basis of theoretical explanations of such processes developed by physicists. In the social sciences, changes in reinforcement values also have been shown to follow regular patterns, and themselves become the subject of scientific explanation. For example, social approval acts as a more potent reinforcer following social deprivation than social satiation (e.g., Gewirtz & Baer, 1958). There is every reason to believe that such changes therefore can be made the subject of universal theories and laws which complement the theories and laws which relate reinforcement value to behaviors. Thus, Gergen's grounds for dismissal of a social learning theory as a fundamental universal theory in social science are totally invalid.

The Nature of Open Systems

Many of Gergen's points implicitly or explicitly argue that since we cannot predict precisely what will happen tomorrow, social flux precludes the establishment of a social science. Nagel (1961) noted that the argument is a "common source of skepticism toward the prospects for transcultural social laws . . . (p. 460)." He traced the view to Beard (1934), who held that if social science

> were a true science, like that of astronomy, it would enable us to predict the essential movements of human affairs for the immediate and indefinite future, to give pictures of society in the year 2000 or the year 2500 just as astronomers can map the appearance of the heavens at fixed points of time in the future. Such a social science would tell us exactly what is going to happen in the years to come

> and we should be powerless to change it by any effort of will (Beard, 1934, p. 29).

Nagel (1961) responded to the argument by pointing out that "Inability to forecast the indefinite future is . . . not unique to the study of human affairs, and is not a certain sign that comprehensive laws have not been established or cannot be established about the phenomena (p. 461)." Few systems in science are for all practical purposes isolated systems as is the subject matter of astronomy. Any nonisolated or open system is subject to the intrusion of unforeseen events which serve to disconfirm specific predictions without serving to invalidate the theories from which the predictions are derived. A sudden gust of wind or a sneeze by a scientist observer would disconfirm specific predictions about the movements of a pendulum. Of course, if the intruding forces were known in all relevant detail, accurate predictions could be made by taking into account the effects of these variables. The specific place at which a falling leaf would touch the ground could be perfectly predicted by the laws of physics if specifications of all relevant variables were known in advance; this is never the case when one is observing the leaf fall in one's front yard. That these ideal knowledge states are rarely realized in any open system recommends the use of controlled experiments where as many factors as possible which are not of direct interest to the investigator are controlled to a greater or lesser degree to allow the test of specific predictions. However, the difficulties associated with intruding variables and their effects on predictions present problems only in specifically testing predicted effects; these difficulties are logically irrelevant to the status of universal theories and do not distinguish the natural sciences from the social sciences.

The Conditional Nature of Scientific Propositions

The conditional nature of scientific propositions is pertinent to any discussion of scientific predictions. Laws and hypotheses are formulated, either explicitly or implicitly, in a logical implicative, if–

then form; if particular antecedent conditions are realized, then particular consequences should follow. If the antecedent conditions are not realized, either because of improper methodology, a change in the values of parameters, the intrusion of unforeseen events, etc., then there is no reason to expect the consequents to follow.

For example, learning theorists would hypothesize that if a reinforcement is contingently applied to a particular class of responses under a particular set of stimulus conditions, then the future presentation of the stimuli should increase the probability of the occurrence of the contingent response. Suppose that an individual has learned the relationship and we produce the necessary stimulus conditions; however, now we immediately follow the presentation of the stimuli with the administration of a potent electric shock to the subject's foot. No one would claim that the hypothesis is incorrect simply because the subject screams in pain rather than producing the expected response to the discriminative stimuli. Yet analogous situations are repeatedly described by Gergen to support his claim that transhistorical theories are impossible to develop in the social sciences. For example, Gergen (1973, p. 316) argues that if an individual becomes aware of an attempt to manipulate his behavior through the application of social reinforcements, the person will "resent" the threat to his autonomy and might behave to invalidate the manipulator's expectations and social learning theory. Gergen's argument presents difficulties for the social scientist in terms of measuring the unforeseen variables of knowledge and resentment, predicting when such knowledge and resentment occur, relating these variables to their antecedents, relating these variables to any change in reforcement value which might occur, and deriving additional hypotheses concerning the effects of such resentment on behavior; however, it does not produce any unique difficulties in terms of the logic of scientific inquiry, explanation, or prediction.[3]

As another example of the conditional nature of scientific propositions, examine the following statement by Gergen: "knowing that persons in trouble are less likely to be helped when there are large numbers of bystanders . . . may increase one's desire to offer his services under such conditions . . . and previous patterns of behavior are modified or dissolved (p. 313)." Gergen's implication is that the theory which deduced the fact therefore becomes only a historical description of the way people once behaved. Several misconceptions permeate the argument. First, the results of previous studies are facts, not theories, and therefore might be historically bound. As with previous examples, there is no reason to believe that these particular behaviors (i.e., less helping behavior in a crowd) will be observed everywhere and at all times. However, the theories which deduce them may or may not be historically bound. Species change, but a theory of evolution is transhistorical. Second, the mere observation of apparently opposite behaviors at different times might either (a) be irrelevant to the validity of the theory because of the conditional nature of the hypothesis or (b) actually support the theory. To illustrate the latter, suppose that the altruism researcher framed the following hypothesis: Helping behavior is directly related to a bystander's perception that his help is needed. One bystander might feel that when many other people are present, they will offer aid and his personal assistance is not required. A second bystander might read that fewer people give help when many people are present and realize that his personal assistance is most needed by a victim when a crowd is present. These two individuals might behave in exactly opposite ways (the latter giving help and the former not giving help) and still provide support for the hypothesized relationships.

Essential Uniqueness of All Events

Gergen's statement that social science is unlike natural science in part because "it deals with facts that are largely nonrepeatable (p. 310)" fails to take into account the essential uniqueness and nonrepeatability of all events, whether physical or social. All texts on the philosophy of science devote some attention to the fact that every event is unique in one way or another: It is impossible to perfectly replicate an event in all details. One value of a theory is that it tells us whether the differences which do exist between past and present events are important and if so, in what ways. However, the mere assertion that events are nonrepeatable in no way distinguishes the natural sciences from the social sciences.

PUBLIC AWARENESS

Gergen's claim that no transhistorical theories have or can be developed because of the cultural specificity of existing theories and the nature of cultural change is not warranted on the basis of the arguments he presents. The other, and possibly more important, basis for his claim is derived from the argument that social science has an impact upon society which serves to invalidate all possible universal theories of behavior. His argument essentially consists of these points: (a) an open communication system exists in the social sciences which allows researchers to communicate either directly to their subjects or to future subjects information about social theories and (b) that this information might produce behavior designed to invalidate the theory. Transcending even the laboratory situation, such dissemination of knowledge might affect a whole segment of society and produce fundamentally different types of behaviors than existed prior to public awareness of a theory. The misconceptions underlying the argument include several which have already been discussed along with some yet to be considered. These include (a) the nature of open systems; (b) the conditional nature of scientific propositions; (c) the nature of suicidal predictions and self-fulfilling prophecies; (d) the degree to which people can change behaviors by desiring to do so; and (e) the nature of free will and determinism. It has already been shown that (a) above does not distinguish the natural from the social sciences and presents no unique difficulties for the development of universal theories.

The Conditional Nature of Scientific Statements

While the conditional nature of scientific statements has already been discussed, it is worth re-

considering in a slightly different context. Gergen (1973) notes that it is "common research practice in psychology to avoid communicating one's theoretical premises to the subject either before or during the research (p. 312)," because of the recognition that such cues might alter subjects' behaviors. He therefore feels,

Herein lies a fundamental difference between the natural and social sciences. In the former, the scientist cannot typically communicate his knowledge to the subjects of his study such that their behavioral dispositions are modified. In the social sciences such communication can have a vital impact on behavior (p. 313).

One problem with this conclusion should be apparent: Information concerning the hypotheses in question in a study is withheld for the reason that such information might introduce contaminating variables into a controlled test of a specific hypothesis; information is not withheld simply because knowledge would demonstrate that man's behavior is unpredictable or unexplainable. A specific if-then hypothesis cannot be assessed if intruding variables alter the antecedent conditions necessary to conduct the test. A physicist would not demonstrate a law of free fall by dropping a feather from the top of a multi-storied Chicago office building on a windy day. Similarly, a social researcher interested in investigating the methods subjects use to ingratiate under conditions where they expect that their target and all bystanders will be unaware of their ingratiation would not tell the subjects beforehand that he is interested in how they manipulate other people. The introduction of such information, clearly antithetical to the test, would change the necessary antecedent conditions for the test and allow other variables which are of no immediate concern (e.g., subjects' resentment) to further complicate the picture. The statement that a stone does not care what is done to it in a laboratory while people do is trivially correct in this context; it does not alter the fundamental logic of the process of inquiry nor demonstrate that universal theories are impossible in principle. It only requires changes in the specific techniques and methods employed by the social scientist in dealing with his subject matter.

Suicidal Predictions and Self-Fulfilling Prophecies

In general, there are two different types of predictions whose truth value is affected by public reactions. *Suicidal predictions* involve predicting future events which appear likely to occur given present theories and information concerning relevant variables but which are disconfirmed as a consequence of public disclosure of the prediction. Nagel (1961) employed the example of the prediction of a recession in 1947 which was made by economists on the basis of relevant and apparently valid economic data. The warning allowed businessmen to lower prices on strategic goods which increased the demand for these goods and circumvented the predicted recession. The *self-fulfilling prophecy* involves a prediction which is not justified by relevant information at the time it is made and would turn out to be disconfirmed by ensuing events; however, knowledge of the prediction produces actions taken to confirm it. For example, a financially sound bank might be put out of business if an inaccurate rumor of bank difficulties produced a public response of lack of confidence and transfer of funds from the bank. Given (a) the conditional form of scientific statements and (b) the ability to explain such effects through other scientific principles, there is little reason for the concern frequently devoted to the topic.

Nagel (1961, pp. 469–470) illustrated situations involving suicidal predictions and self-fulfilling prophecies drawn from the physical sciences which do "not differ in essential respects" from these types of predictions in the social sciences. He has us imagine an anti-aircraft gun which can be fired solely through purely physical mechanisms and which contains radar for target location, a computer for calculating direction and for pointing the gun, an adjusting device for the physical pointing process, and some device for co-ordinating and transmitting messages between the systems.

Let us suppose that, were the gun fired in accordance with the calculations of the computer on a given occasion, the target would be hit; but let us also suppose that the signals transmitting these calculations have disturbing effects (whether on the adjusting apparatus or on the target) for which the computer has made no allowance. Accordingly, although the gun is set and fired in accordance with calculations that were correct at the time they were made, it nevertheless fails to hit the target because of the changes introduced by the process of transmitting these calculations (Nagel, 1961, p. 469).

To translate the above suicidal prediction into a self-fulfilling prophecy, we only have to assume

that either the radar equipment or the computer suffers from some "defect," such that if the gun were pointed and fired in accordance with the calculations of the computer on a given occasion, the gun would in fact fail to hit the target. It is nevertheless obviously possible that, though the gun is fired according to calculations that were incorrect at the time they were made, the target is successfully hit because of the perturbations produced by the process of transmitting those calculations (pp. 469–470).

The existence of suicidal predictions and self-fulfilling prophecies present no unique logical difficulties which would distinguish the social sciences from the natural sciences. Unforeseen behaviors which do occur as a consequence of the public's awareness of a particular theory or a particular set of findings are usually found to be explainable within the context of the same or some other set of hypotheses. The propositions used to explain these behaviors will probably turn out to be general ones which reflect particular types of perceptions, awarenesses, or particular induced motive states. Thus, the changes in helping behavior noted previously might result from a change in the subjects' perceptions of the value of the help needed and can be interpreted within the context of the same theory which would predict other behaviors given different perceptions.

The only way suicidal predictions and self-fulfilling prophecies would present unique difficulties for the social sciences would be if subjects' behaviors seemed to follow no perceptible pattern. Given such indeterminism, no social science or even social history would be feasible. Every regularity uncovered in the social sciences supports the opposite assumption—that behaviors do follow perceptible patterns and are explainable.

The "Cause" of Invalidation

It is evident from Gergen's article that he considers the crucial flaw in the social scientist's ability to discover transhistorical laws to be the mass-media dissemination of knowledge which would serve to invalidate social theories.[4] Yet none of the reasons so far considered has served to support his conclusion or fundamentally distinguish the natural from the social sciences. Gergen introduced a new and rather simple twist to explain why he feels there is cause for concern.

> *Valid theories about social behavior constitute significant implements of social control. To the extent that an individual's behavior is predictable, he places himself in a position of vulnerability. Others can alter environmental conditions or their behavior toward him to obtain maximal rewards at minimal costs to themselves . . . Investments in freedom may thus potentiate behavior designed to invalidate the theory . . . The more potent the theory is in predicting behavior, the broader its public dissemination and the more prevalent and resounding the reactions. Thus, strong theories may be subject to more rapid invalidation than weak ones (Gergen, 1973, pp. 313–314).*

Gergen's reasoning strikes me as odd. He is arguing that *no* transhistorical, universal propositions can be found in social science precisely because of the transhistorical, universal, and social reason that people do not want to appear overly predictable. Whether or not his proposition could serve as the basis for a theory of social behavior rooted

in the nature of the social interaction process is a matter for future theoretical and empirical refinement. However, his suggestion indicates that he does believe, contrary to his other conclusions, that at least one universal proposition about social behavior is available.

Reactions to Theories That Predict Reactions to Theories

After arguing that all theories will be invalidated primarily because of his predictability hypothesis, Gergen contends that "a theory that predicts reactions to theory is also susceptible to violation or vindication (p. 314)." While the mind-boggling infinite sequence of theory-reaction-theory-reaction-etc. might prompt one to throw up one's arms and beg for mercy at the hands of an ever changing universe, his conclusion is again unjustified for reasons previously considered. First, it is unlikely that it would be necessary to formulate a theory which does nothing more than predict people's reactions to another theory or set of theories. Hence, the reactive theory link in the sequence is unlikely ever to occur. Second, if principles are formulated in sufficiently abstract terms, there is absolutely no a priori reason why adequate universal theories could not be developed which explain a variety of behaviors, both reactive and nonreactive. Third, the conditional nature of scientific laws allows for the fact that new information added to an open system does not necessarily invalidate a basic proposition even though it alters a particular behavior.

The Ability to Change

A pragmatic consideration, raised by Gergen's contention that people immediately alter their behaviors as a consequence of the awareness of a particular theory, is the degree to which people can, simply by desiring to change their behaviors, actually do so. Habits are powerful controllers of actions, and wishing to behave in a certain way will not necessarily make it so. If it did, psychotherapists would have few clients and a great deal of time on their hands. As McGuire (1969) observed, results obtained by flagrant disregard of the principles of keeping subjects unaware of experimental hypotheses are often replicated surprisingly well with naive subjects. In any event, the issue is one which is best pursued by vigorous theory based on empirical research and not with speculation that the problems might be unsolvable in principle.

Humanistic Principles and Free Will

An implicit theme in Gergen's article is the notion that people can, within reason, do anything they want anytime they want and there is nothing that a scientist or his theories can do to stop them. And if this is the case, how can universal theories of behavior be possible? Many students of social psychology feel compelled to dismiss the possibility that psychology could ever be a "real" science because people make decisions and behave in accord with their "free will." People are not mechanistic automatons, and consequently it "feels right" for many people concerned with humanistic principles to conclude that no science of human affairs is possible.[5]

In actuality, there is nothing contradictory between the concepts of free will and scientific determinism, although determinism and indeterminism sit on opposite sides of the scientific fence. This is not the place to reopen in its entirety the free will versus determinism issue, and many excellent expositions are available (e.g., Kaplan, 1964; Kemeny, 1959). However, a few words are in order. By free will, most people mean that they can and do make choices between alternatives based upon what they want at the time; and no scientific law is going to tell them that they cannot. The basic confusion derives from the notion that behavioral laws compel or coerce people to behave against their will; these laws fatalistically determine what a person (and even a whole society) will do and nothing can be done to escape the consequences. If such laws cannot be found, any type of science is impossible. While this fatalistic determinism position is what many people regard to be the basis of science, it is a complete misunderstanding of the nature of scientific

explanations. Laws and theories are not physical things which lie hidden beneath bushes waiting for us to serendipitously trip over them. They are not "ultimate truths" which have been strewn about by a great cosmic force and which can be picked up like jewels and shown to our friends. They are man-made abstractions and interpretations of the world around and within us; they are conceptualizations which are the basis of explanations. Laws and theories always possess a lack of finality, since we are always laboring to make them more complete and adequate in performing their explanatory function. If nature behaves in a way which cannot be accounted for by our laws, she has not broken them—they are inadequate. Kemeny (1959) described the situation as it applies to human behavior by first restating the false fatalistic argument which would conclude that

> we cannot have a free choice because the Law of Nature says what the outcome of our choice will be. If it is already "written," then we have no real choice. [However the] Law [of Nature] is not something binding, but a simple description of all events, past, present, and future. Among other things it describes how we choose. This is the only reason why our decision must be in accordance with it. It would be just as correct, and perhaps less misleading, to say that the Law of Nature depends on our choice, instead of the reverse (pp. 225–226).

To maintain that given certain knowledge about the individual (e.g., his past learning history, his attitudes and values, his genetic constitution, etc.) we can make predictions about his behavior is not to maintain that the person could not help behaving the way he did. Modifying an example from Kemeny (1959), suppose that you know that your best friend was invited to a party this weekend. You know your friend's preferences for parties compared to other activities, you know who will be at the party and how your friend feels about each of them, you know whether or not your friend was planning another affair on the evening in question, etc. To be able to predict whether or not your friend will actually go to the party does not in the least imply that he had no choice about attending or not attending. All that it means is that you know how your friend goes about making decisions. You have conceptualized the kinds of things which he takes into consideration, you have "guessed" how he weighs each one, and you know a little bit about the mechanisms of the decision. In short, you have developed a naive theory useful in understanding, explaining, and predicting behavior. Thus, to state that social psychology is indeed a science is not to claim that humans are pushed around by inexorable forces which they are helpless to counter. Rather, it is to affirm that human actions are understandable and explainable — the context and methods flowing from these assertions are what is called science. The notion of *determinism* in science really means nothing more than this. *Indeterminism,* on the other hand, refers to a situation where events appear to be in a constant state of flux and man's ability to understand is sufficiently limited that understanding explanation is impossible. Our present state of knowledge is an indication that an assumption of indeterminism probably is incorrect.

IMPLICATIONS

In summary, Gergen's (1973) two-pronged attack on the scientific status of social psychology is philosophically unsound, and none of the issues raised by him serve to fundamentally distinguish the natural from the social sciences from a philosophy-of-science standpoint. Additionally, many of his apparently philosophical arguments against the present existence of certain transcultural and transhistorical social theories are really empirical issues, and the available evidence fails to support his claims.

Some of the implications of Gergen's thesis are nonetheless worth consideration.

Expanded Sensitivities

Gergen states that one implication of his thesis is that

[since the] field can seldom yield principles from which reliable predictions can be made. . . . [it should provide] research informing the inquirer of a number of possible occurrences, thus expanding his sensitivities and readying him for more rapid accommodation to environmental change (p. 317).

The conclusion is a desirable one, but it does not follow exclusively from the premises of Gergen's thesis. One of the practical benefits of any type of scientific inquiry is the gathering of information about the world which will help us to perceive alternatives accurately and behave in a personally and socially rewarding fashion. The potential application of social scientific findings through any type of technological or prescriptive use is a very real motivation for many scientists.

Interdisciplinary Activity

Another implication Gergen considers is that interdisciplinary approaches should be encouraged; the "historically bound" disciplines of political science, sociology, economics, social psychology (and other branches of psychology), and history should share knowledge of facts and methods and complement one another in their common goal. Again, the conclusion is a valid one which follows irrespective of whether one perceives social inquiry to be science or history. The pursuit of knowledge is a cumulative public endeavor; even the most parochial intradisciplinarians find a great deal of value in the findings and advancements of other social scientific disciplines.

Pure versus Applied Science

Gergen also believes that since the "knowledge that pure research bends itself to establish is transient (p. 317)," it follows that we should abandon the distinction between pure and applied research and concentrate on "an intensive focus on contemporary social issues, based on the application of scientific methods and conceptual tools of broad generality (p. 317)." The present article makes it clear that the distinction between pure and applied research is a valid one. Applied research typically begins by selecting a particular problem area or "contemporary issue" and directs attention toward possible immediate solutions. Pure research focuses on more general explanations of phenomena which might one day serve as the theoretical basis for the solution of some problem, but understanding and explanation is the focus and goal. These different goals often serve to complement one another; many advances in basic science were preceded by technological advances and vice versa (cf. Hofstadter, 1962). Yet the empirical generalizations often sought by applied researchers are often not the kind which can serve as general principles useful in laying the foundations of social science and from which other explanations of behavior can be deduced.

The Mind–Body Problem Revisited

One of the most important implications of Gergen's thesis is the idea that a "continuum of historical durability (p. 318)" should be contemplated in which phenomena are classified in accordance with their transiency. The continuum is anchored at one end by "physiological givens" and irreversible acquired characteristics and at the other end with easily modifiable learned behaviors. Presumably, some behaviors we cannot control by our cognitive processes and modify at will, and these behaviors might serve as the basis for relatively long-enduring and probably universal, transhistorical, general theories.

At first glance, the continuum appears to serve an heuristic function of focusing our attention on processes which are more or less enduring (basic?). Under closer scrutiny it appears that an essential separation is being proposed. At the extreme end of the continuum are processes which are so intrinsic—"physiological givens," genetic processes, biological functions, biochemical events—that Gergen would admit them to the stature of things which can be subjected to scientific explanation. These processes become abruptly separated from cognitive processes, most

learned behaviors, and environmental influences which are the bases of psychological and social theory and which are not considered by Gergen to be proper subjects for scientific explanation. If pushed to the extreme, the argument resurrects the ancient mind–body duality problem, in which biological processes can be considered the subject matter of scientific inquiry and theorizing while the mind, our cognitive processes and ability to understand the world, can never be considered an appropriate topic for scientific explanation. In milder form, the position resurrects the nature–nurture issue with a slight twist. The problem becomes one of determining which processes and behaviors are a function of the innate or instinctual propensities of the organism and therefore might be explainable in terms of scientific theories and which behaviors are largely learned and therefore can be modified by cognitive processes and are not subject to scientific explanation. Either form of interpretation serves to thwart the basic process of inquiry and can serve no function other than giving solace to those who find social science sometimes frustrating in its complexity.

Several inconsistencies are raised by Gergen's continuum. It is well known that social psychological events are related to physiological changes. For example, environmental conditions and cognitive states produce profound effects on physiological and motivational processes (cf. Zimbardo, 1969); such changes frequently serve to justify seemingly irrational actions. After choosing to go without food for an unanticipated additional time, already hungry individuals not only report less hunger but also show fewer physiological signs of hunger than do people who are given less choice and more justification in the matter (Brehm, Back, & Bogdonoff, 1964). Are these physiological changes capable of explanation through universal laws or are they subject only to historical interpretation? Another question concerns the social behavior of lower animals. Is a rat colony in one area of the world fundamentally different from one in another area of the world or one in the same place at a different time? From Gergen's perspective the answer might appear to be an obvious no, since the behavior of rats would seem tied more closely to physiological givens than the behavior of man. What about different groups of lower primates? It has been claimed that chimps possess a rudimentary self-concept (Gallup, 1968); therefore, it is possible that their social behaviors could be affected by their constructions of themselves and others and hence be only historical phenomena. Or consider that macaque monkeys have been observed to display "remarkable innovations in social behavior . . . that anthropologists would consider equivalent to profound cultural changes (Zajonc, 1972, p. 2)." Some of the younger macaques in a particular group began to wash potatoes and wheat grains before consuming them, learned to season the food with salt, and began swimming and diving. These behaviors were imitated by the younger monkeys while watched with caution by the elders. Are these behaviors the subject of only historical interpretation? Or can their interpretation be based on a sufficiently sound and universal theory which would not be fundamentally different from other scientific theories? Zajonc's (1972) conclusion is sound:

> To be sure, physical events appear less capricious than social behavior, but it is important to stress that phenomena appear capricious only when there are no concepts that abstract from them regularities and constancies. These abstractions are what make phenomena seem simple and obvious. Order is not a feature of the universe and of nature but of the conceptions of the universe and of nature (p. 2).

A different interpretation of the "continuum" can be accomplished which serves to integrate it within the framework of scientific explanation. Instead of a continuum, envision pyramids lined up side by side. Each pyramid represents a basic theoretical superstructure imposed on a particular subject matter in the natural and social sciences. At the top of each pyramid are the fundamental universal postulates of a basic theory. From these can be deduced the general hypotheses of the theory which serve to construct the middle of the pyramid. These hypotheses can be related through rules of correspondence to the conceptual repre-

sentations of specific objects, cases, and events which serve as the subject matter of the theory and form the base of each pyramid. The specific phenomena depicted at the bottom of each pyramid may change with time and circumstances and, if they are not adequately related to the upper structures, may cause a full or partial collapse of the pyramid. The specifics in many of the natural sciences seem to change less rapidly than the specifics in the social sciences because they can be interpreted more readily from the superior construction of the higher-order theories. In the natural sciences new phenomena are added and old are reinterpreted, and instead of causing a total collapse of a whole structure, pyramids are redesigned and merged into a large pyramid as these branches of knowledge converge and more and more phenomena become interpreted within a superior theoretical framework. Construction was begun later in the social sciences, and the higher-order structures are less adequate: many times it appears as if there is no top of a pyramid and hence no pyramid at all. Nevertheless, the construction process is well under way and will not be abandoned simply because the stones are heavy and the construction difficult.

REFERENCES

Bandura, A. *Principles of behavior modification.* New York: Holt, Rinehart & Winston, 1969.

Bandura, A., & Walters, R. H. *Social learning and personality development.* New York: Holt, Rinehart & Winston, 1963.

Beard, C.A. *The nature of the social sciences.* New York: Scribners, 1934.

Bergmann, G. On some methodological problems of psychology. In H. Feigl & M. Brodbeck (Eds.), *Readings in the philosophy of science.* New York: Appleton-Century-Crofts, 1953.

Brehm, M. L., Back, K. W., & Bogdonoff, M. D. A physiological effect of cognitive dissonance under stress and deprivation. *Journal of Abnormal and Social Psychology,* 1964, 69, 303–310.

Brown, R. *Explanation in social science.* Chicago: Aldine, 1963.

Brown, R. *Social psychology.* New York: Free Press, 1965.

Christie, R., & Geis, F. L. *Studies in Machiavellianism.* New York: Academic Press, 1970.

Cohen, M. R. Reason in social science. In H. Feigl & M. Brodbeck (Eds.), *Readings in the philosophy of science.* New York: Appleton-Century-Crofts, 1953.

Festinger, L. A theory of social comparison processes. *Human Relations,* 1954, 7, 114–140.

Gallup, G. G. Mirror-image stimulation. *Psychological Bulletin,* 1968, 70, 782–793.

Gergen, K. J. Social psychology as history. *Journal of Personality and Social Psychology,* 1973, 26, 309–320.

Gewirtz, J. L., & Baer, D. M. The effect of brief social deprivation on behavior for a social reinforcer. *Journal of Abnormal and Social Psychology,* 1958, 56, 49–56.

Grünbaum, A. Causality and the science of human behavior. In H. Feigl & M. Brodbeck (Eds.), *Readings in the philosophy of science.* New York: Appleton-Century-Crofts, 1953.

Grünbaum, A. Historical determinism, social activism, and prediction in the social sciences. *British Journal for the Philosophy of Science,* 1956, 7, 236–240.

Heider, F. *The psychology of interpersonal relations.* New York: Wiley, 1958.

Hempel, C. G. *Aspects of scientific explanation.* New York: Free Press, 1965.

Hofstadter, R. *Anti-intellectualism in American life.* New York: Vintage, 1962.

Homans, G. C. *The nature of social science.* New York: Harcourt, Brace & World, 1967.

Janis, I. L., & Field, P. B. Sex differences and personality factors related to persuasibility. In C. I. Hovland & I. L. Janis (Eds.), *Personality and persuasibility.* New Haven: Yale University Press, 1959.

Jones, E. E., & Gerard, H. B. *Foundations of social psychology.* New York: Wiley, 1967.

Kaplan, A. *The conduct of inquiry: Methodology for behavioral science.* San Francisco: Chandler, 1964.

Kelley, H. H., & Thibault, J. W. Group problem solving. In G. Lindzey & E. Aronson (Eds.), *The handbook of social psychology.* Vol. 4. (2nd ed.) Reading, Mass: Addison-Wesley, 1969.

Kemeny, J. G. *A philosopher looks at science.* New York: Van Nostrand, 1959.

McGuire, W. J. The nature of attitudes and attitude change. In G. Lindzey & E. Aronson (Eds.), *The handbook of social psychology.* Vol. 4 (2nd ed.) Reading, Mass.: Addison-Wesley, 1969.

Mead, G. H. *Mind, self and society.* Chicago: University of Chicago Press, 1934.

Meehl, P. E. On the circularity of the Law of Effect. *Psychological Bulletin,* 1950, 47, 52–75.

Nagel, E. The logic of historical analysis. In H. Feigl & M. Brodbeck (Eds.), *Readings in the philosophy of science.* New York: Appleton-Century-Crofts, 1953.

Nagel, E. *The structure of science: Problems in the logic of scientific explanation.* New York: Harcourt, Brace & World, 1961.

Sullivan, H. S. *Conceptions of modern psychiatry.* New York: Norton, 1953.

White, R. W. Motivation reconsidered: The concept of competence. *Psychological Review,* 1959, 66, 297–334.

Zajonc, R. B. Social facilitation. *Science,* 1965, 149, 269–274.

Zajonc, R. B. The attitudinal effects of mere exposure. *Journal of Personality and Social Psychology Monograph Supplement,* 1968, 8(2, Pt. 2).

Zajonc, R. B. *Animal and social behavior.* Morristown, N.J.: General Learning Press, 1972.

Zilsel, E. Physics and the problem of historico-sociological laws. In H. Feigl & M. Brodbeck (Eds.), *Readings in the philosophy of science.* New York: Appleton-Century-Crofts, 1953.

Zimbardo, P. G. *The cognitive control of motivation.* Glenview, Ill.: Scott, Foresman, 1969.

NOTES

1. Thanks are extended to Marvin E. Shaw and Lawrence J. Severy for their helpful comments on an earlier draft of the manuscript and to Patricia Schlenker for her comments and contributions throughout.

2. Anaximander suggested an ingenious solution: The ultimate proportions of each of the elements in the universe was fixed by natural law, and while each of the elements was constantly attempting to enlarge its empire by changing other elements, the justice of the universe served to restore the balance.

3. In developing the argument that social learning theory could not serve as a transhistorical theory and that resentment and invalidation would be produced should a subject become aware of the manipulation, Gergen (1973) misrepresents the nature of the concept of reinforcement. "The notion that behavior is wholly governed by external contingency is seen by many as vulgarly demeaning (p. 316)," and therefore would be reacted against. Few social learning theorists hold this straw-man position. Social learning theorists (e.g., Bandura, 1969) explicitly recognize the control over behavior exerted by internal factors.

4. To combat the public's reaction to theories, Gergen (1973) at one point suggests that a possible solution to the problem would require hiding the theories from the public. "To preserve the transhistorical validity of psychological principles, the science could be removed from the public domain and scientific understanding reserved for a selected elite (p. 314)."

Naturally, such a solution was recognized as "repugnant" by Gergen. However, it might be noted that his suggestion implies that the knowledge of theories makes scientists somehow fundamentally different from the rest of humanity. While some might like to believe this, my personal unsystematic observations indicate to me that social psychologists' behaviors are remarkably similar to those of other "less informed" mortals.

5. The mechanistic conceptualization of the universe derives from Newtonian physics, which was seen as the paradigm for scientific theories until Einstein's General Theory of Relativity and his Unified Field Theory drastically altered physicists' conceptualizations. Many early psychologists and a good number of contemporary ones have drawn mechanistic analogies from Newton's theories. Because of this early precedent in psychology, the terms Newtonian mechanics and science have been confused and treated synonymously by psychologists who are skeptical of the scientific explanation of human behavior. For example, Gergen (1973) states that a psychology aimed at establishing general scientific principles

is, of course, a direct descendant from eighteenth century thought. At that time the physical sciences had produced marked increments in knowledge, and one could view with great optimism the possibility of applying the scientific method to human behavior . . .(p. 309).

To make these assertions is to miss completely the basic advances made by Einstein. Einstein, who was an exceptional philosopher of science, reaffirmed the necessity for general theories capable of abstractly explaining events and relationships. To Einstein, science was not the process of exposing basic truths which had a physical existence and which compelled phenomena to do their bidding. Rather, science is the process of comprehensive and systematic theorizing which can be checked for correspondence with sensory impressions of the world (i.e., tested) and is desirable for its explanatory prowess. Thus, to state that social science is indeed a science is not to ascribe to a mechanistic conceptualization of man and the universe. In fact, those who assert that no science of human behavior is possible are usually found to be referring only to the application of the old mechanistic view of science; it is they who do not fully appreciate the more recent advances in the philosophy of science.

CRITICAL THINKING QUESTIONS

1. Do you agree with the author of the article that social psychology is actually a science? Or did he say that social psychology has the potential to be a science? In order to more fully understand the positions taken by Schlenker, find and read the original article by Gergen.

2. Do you think that a theory developed today to explain some aspect of social behavior (how we form impressions of people, for example) would also be able to explain how people a thousand years ago acted? Do you think that fundamental human nature and processes have remained relatively stable over time?

3. Prior to taking social psychology, you most likely had at least one other course in psychology, such as an introductory course. Could anything you encountered in the course have influenced your subsequent behavior, so that you now act differently than you might have had you not taken the course and encountered the information? Give an example. How does this relate to what Schlenker is saying?

4. Some sort of deception is commonly used in social psychological research. Why? According to Schlenker, is it really necessary? Although not covered in the article, what ethical issues are involved in the use of deception?

5. As you progress through this course in social psychology, have you encountered any theories in social psychology that are sufficiently abstract to be universally applicable? Or are most studies not at that level of abstraction?

ARTICLE 3 _____

When the U.S. Attorney General's Commission on Pornography report was released in 1987, there was a flurry of controversy regarding its findings. Many scientists protested the conclusions that were drawn, arguing that they were unwarranted, while others hailed the report as evidence of the harmfulness of pornography.

At the heart of the issue are the data that were selected for review by the commission and the conclusions that were drawn from the research. Critics of the report claimed that committee members were biased and that not all were scientists. The first claim centers around the issue of values in research. Did the values of the committee members influence what was studied and how the results were interpreted? The second claim centers on the conclusions that were drawn by the committee. Were the conclusions sound, or did the report make unwarranted assumptions and inferences?

In the following article Wilcox comments on these two issues by examining the composition of the committee and the conclusions that were drawn. It also makes an interesting comparison between this most recent commission and a 1970 commission that examined the same topic. The article raises some important issues concerning the role of values in research. Additionally, it suggests the possibility that the members, even if not intentionally biased, were nonetheless unprepared to properly interpret the data. As an example of how the same basic data can be interpreted differently by two different groups, read the report on the effects of pornography written by Surgeon General C. Everett Koop that can be found in the *American Psychologist* (1987, vol. 42, pp. 944–945).

Pornography, Social Science, and Politics
When Research and Ideology Collide

■ Brian L. Wilcox

In ceremonies associated with the signing of the Child Protection Act of 1984, President Reagan announced his intention to establish a national commission to study the effects of pornography on society. This announcement led to the appointment of an 11-member panel by Attorney General Edwin Meese in the spring of 1985 to serve as the Attorney General's Commission on Pornography.

The work of the commission was surrounded by controversy from its inception. Critics argued that many of the commissioners lacked the cre-

dentials and experience necessary to evaluate the scientific and legal literatures relevant to the commission's broad mandate. Only three of the commissioners, psychologist Judith Becker, psychiatrist Park Dietz, and law professor Frederick Schauer, had written extensively on subjects related directly or indirectly to social, behavioral, and psychological consequences of exposure to pornography. Other critics noted that many, though not all, of the commissioners seemed to have been selected because of their ideological compatibility with the Attorney General, who has

Reprinted from the *American Psychologist*, 1987, *42*, 941–943. Copyright 1987 by the American Psychological Association. Reprinted by permission.

been very outspoken in his attacks on pornography and in his calls for more effective means of containing the spread of pornography. Six of the commissioners had publicly called for increased government action against pornographic materials (Hertzberg, 1986). The chair of the commission, Henry Hudson, had achieved a certain notoriety as a county prosecutor for his successful campaign against adult theaters and bookstores. Finally, critics argued that the commission lacked the resources and time necessary to competently fulfill its mandate. Indeed, it is instructive to compare the circumstances surrounding the conduct of the Attorney General's Commission on Pornography with those of the 1970 Commission on Obscenity and Pornography appointed by President Johnson.

The 1970 commission had two years to fulfill its mandate to study the effects of pornography and obscenity on the public, analyze obscenity law, and make recommendations, if deemed necessary, to regulate the flow of pornographic materials (Commission on Obscenity and Pornography, 1970). To carry out this task, the commission had a budget of 2 million dollars, a staff of 22, and 18 appointed commissioners. Only three of the members had publicly stated their positions on pornography. The 1970 commission used its funds not only to conduct hearings and support its staff, but also to fund empirical studies and literature reviews by psychologists and legal scholars. In contrast, the 1986 commission was given 12 months, $400,000, and a staff of nine to complete its mandate. No original research was funded. Few social scientists were called on as expert witnesses. In fact, the major source for social science input came from the Workshop on Pornography and Public Health organized by Surgeon General C. Everett Koop and described in his article in this issue (pp. 944–945). It is instructive to note that although this excellent workshop was requested by the Attorney General, members of the commission did not attend, with the exception of Hudson, and the final report of the workshop was not delivered until August 4, 1986, some 25 days after the release of the final report of the Attorney General's Commission.

It is probably inappropriate to compare, as some critics have done, the interpretations of the social science literature made by the two commissions. As any perusal of social science literature on pornography clearly indicates, this field of research has matured significantly during the past decade (cf. Donnerstein, Linz, & Penrod, 1987; Malamuth & Donnerstein, 1984). The 1970 commission can be seen as having provided the impetus for the development of a large yet limited body of empirical research dealing with the social and psychological consequences of exposure to pornography. The more appropriate comparison lies between the conclusions drawn by the Meese Commission's interpretation of the social science literature and those drawn by the participants in the Surgeon General's Workshop. Both groups had access to the same body of work, yet the differences in interpretation are significant.

As noted in the article in this issue by Linz, Donnerstein, and Penrod [*American Psychologist*, 1987, *42*, 946–953], the 1986 commission conducted an extensive review of the literature examining the relationship between exposure to pornography and social attitudes and behavior. As Linz et al. indicate, the fatal flaw of the Meese Commission was not that the commissioners misread or misinterpreted these findings; rather, the conclusions they drew were based on overgeneralizations from social psychological studies that were largely laboratory based. Linz et al. detail several of the problems inherent in generalizing from such studies. This overgeneralization is particularly problematic in light of the wide-ranging legislative and legal remedies recommended by the commission. Although such social science research was only one of several sources of information relied on by the commission, it is clear from the commission's report (U.S. Department of Justice, Attorney General's Commission on Pornography, 1986) and from the public comments of commission officials that the credibility of the final report was in large part tied to the inclusion of scientific evidence.

Compare the conclusions drawn by the Attorney General's Commission, as described by Linz et al. (this issue) with those drawn by the participants in the Surgeon General's Workshop (Mulvey & Haugaard, 1986). The consensus statements, described in Surgeon General Koop's article, are much more circumspect and delimited in nature than those drawn in the final report of the Attorney General's Commission. Participants in the Surgeon General's Workshop struggled to achieve consensus on five statements. Several of these statements contain important qualifiers. This cautious approach, according to participants, was justified by the limitations in the state of our knowledge:

> These bits of knowledge . . . do not yet form a totally coherent picture of the real world effects of exposure to pornography. We still know little about actual patterns of use or the power of attitudes in precipitating sexually aggressive behavior. Much research is still needed in order to demonstrate that the present knowledge has significant real world implications for predicting behavior. Pornography is one of many potential influences on behavior and it must be assessed in conjunction with some of these other factors in order for more global statements about effects to be warranted. (Mulvey & Haugaard, 1986, pp. 56–57)

THE RESPONSE TO MISREPRESENTATION

Misrepresentation of scientific findings is an all-too-common occurrence. Misrepresentation stems from a number of causes, but most commonly from a misunderstanding of the findings or the limitations associated with a study or series of studies. Occasionally, misrepresentation is ideologically motivated. Whatever the reasons, the credibility of science is threatened when inappropriate characterizations of findings go unchallenged.

In the case of the misrepresentation of social psychological findings by the Attorney General's Commission, several of the social scientists whose work was heavily cited in the final report of the commission spoke out when a draft copy of the final report was leaked to the press. In statements to the press, psychologists Edward Donnerstein and Neil Malamuth and sociologist Murray Straus objected to the inferential leaps made by the commission and attempted to more accurately portray the limitations and realistic implications of their work (Kurtz, 1986). Media coverage of this issue was quite extensive.

Additionally, Ellen Levine, editor of *Woman's Day,* and psychologist Judith Becker, both members of the commission, authored a dissenting opinion in which they criticized the final report for inaccurately characterizing the available scientific evidence.

> It is essential to state that the social science research has not been designed to evaluate the relationship between exposure to pornography and the commission of sexual crimes. Efforts to tease the current data into proof of a causal link between these acts simply cannot be accepted. (U.S. Department of Justice, Attorney General's Commission on Pornography, 1986, p. 129)

Furthermore, the two commissioners noted in their dissent that visual materials presented to the commissioners during hearings were heavily skewed toward the exceptionally violent and degrading, which may have given the commissioners a distorted impression of the prevalence of such materials. As Linz et al. (this issue) note, the available research on this point does not support the contention by the authors of the final report that extremely violent and degrading pornography represents the largest share of pornographic materials.

THE DEFINITION DILEMMA

The debate on the effects of pornography and obscenity has continually been plagued by the fact that these two terms have often been used loosely, with some writers using them interchangeably. Certainly, the final report of the Meese Commission uses these terms in a confusing fashion, sometimes treating them as synonyms and sometimes drawing distinctions in their use. This definitional problem continues to trouble both legal scholars and scientists. According to the U.S. Supreme Court, the term *pornography* includes all materials that can be considered erotic; such materials may have constitutional protection. Obscenity is a more limited term; obscene materials do not enjoy constitutional protection (*Miller* v. *State of California*, 1973). Courts attempting to regulate obscene materials rely on the *Miller* standard, with a few minor modifications.

> *The basic guidelines of the trier of fact must be: (a) whether "the average person, applying contemporary community standards" would find that the work, taken as a whole, appeals to the prurient interest; (b) whether the work depicts or describes, in a patently offensive way, sexual conduct specifically defined by the applicable state law; and (c) whether the work, taken as a whole, lacks serious literary, artistic, political, or scientific value.* (Miller v. California 1973, p. 23)

Thus, this standard requires that for a piece of pornography to be classified as legally obscene and therefore unprotected, it must be clear "beyond a reasonable doubt" that the material is patently offensive and would be condemned by "contemporary community standards." Furthermore, the work must be completely (not largely) devoid of "serious literary, artistic, political, or scientific value."

These definitions provide little assistance to the researcher attempting to study the relationships among various types of sexually explicit materials, attitudes, and social behavior. The term pornography, as used by the courts, is far too broadly defined to guide the researcher. Donnerstein (1984) noted that "the long-standing issue of how to define pornography will be with us for some time. Yet an examination of its effects on aggression must begin with a closer look at the term itself" (p. 79). Earlier in the same work, Donnerstein suggested that "the issue of whether or not pornography is related to aggression against women might best be served by doing away with the term *pornography*" (p. 79, emphasis in original). The legal definition of obscenity is similarly useless for the researcher. A term whose definition changes with time (the standard is "contemporary") and place (it is a "community standard") does not readily lend itself to operationalization in a fashion that would encourage replication of studies.

PSYCHOLOGY'S CONTRIBUTION TO THE DEBATE

Further progress toward answering the sorts of questions posed to the Attorney General's Commission and the Surgeon General's Workshop may require the development of a more refined taxonomy of sexually explicit materials. Investigators such as Donnerstein (Donnerstein & Linz, 1986), Malamuth (1984), and their colleagues have begun this process by differentiating between violent and nonviolent sexually explicit materials. Additional operational refinements, such as development of a definition of coercive versus consenting sexual activity, will allow researchers to pursue other important distinctions.

Psychologists' ability to contribute to this debate in a more direct fashion awaits the conduct of significant longitudinal research on a range of topics. Questions concerning the stability of behavioral and attitudinal effects of pornography can only be addressed by studies using longer time frames than has typically been the case. Likewise, psychologists' ability to document the hypothesized effects of attitudinal changes brought about by exposure to pornography on behaviors such as sexual aggression is limited in the absence of longitudinal studies similar to those conducted by Eron and his colleagues in studying the effects of television on the development of aggressive attitudes and behaviors (Huesmann, Eron, Lefkowitz, & Walder, 1984).

With time, many of the gaps in knowledge on this topic may be filled. Nevertheless, even the clearest and least ambiguous research findings can be misunderstood or intentionally distorted, leading to a misrepresentation of those findings. It remains incumbent on psychologists to carefully scrutinize the uses to which psychological data are put, especially when the subject matter deals with issues around which our society has deep moral and ideological divisions. Direct, frank participation in such policy debates is one of the best means of preventing such misuses, especially when we portray the research in a complete and honest fashion, spelling out limitations as well as strengths. In the debate on pornography, psychology has acquitted itself well.

REFERENCES

Child Protection Act of 1984, 18 U.S.C. 2251.

Commission on Obscenity and Pornography. (1970). *Report of the Commission on Obscenity and Pornography.* New York: Bantam.

Donnerstein, E. (1984). Pornography: Its effect on violence against women. In N. M. Malamuth & E. Donnerstein (Eds.), *Pornography and sexual aggression* (pp. 53–81). Orlando, FL: Academic Press.

Donnerstein, E., & Linz, D. (1986). Mass media sexual violence and male viewers: Current theory and research. *American Behavioral Scientist, 29,* 601–618.

Donnerstein, E., Linz, D., & Penrod, S. (1987). *The question of pornography: Research findings and policy implications.* New York: Free Press.

Hertzberg, H. (1986, July 14 & 21). Big boobs: Ed Meese and his pornography commission. *The New Republic,* pp. 21–24.

Huesmann, L. R., Eron, L. D., Lefkowitz, M. M., & Walder, M. O. (1984). The stability of aggression over time and generations. *Developmental Psychology, 20,* 1120–1134.

Koop, C. E. (1987). Report of the Surgeon General's Workshop on Pornography and Public Health. *American Psychologist, 42,* 944–945.

Kurtz, H. (1986, May 30). The pornography panel's last controversial days, *Washington Post,* p. A13.

Linz, D., Donnerstein, E., & Penrod, S. (1987). The findings and recommendations of the Attorney General's Commission on Pornography: Do the psychological "facts" fit the political fury? *American Psychologist, 42,* 946–953.

Malamuth, N. M. (1984). Aggression against women: Cultural and individual causes. In N. M. Malamuth & E. Donnerstein (Eds.), *Pornography and sexual aggression* (pp. 19–52). Orlando, FL: Academic Press.

Malamuth, N. M., & Donnerstein, E. (Eds). (1984). *Pornography and sexual aggression.* Orlando, FL: Academic Press.

Miller v. State of California, 413 U.S. 15 (1973).

Mulvey, E. P., & Haugaard, J. L. (1986, August 4) *Report of the Surgeon General's Workshop on Pornography and Public Health.* Washington, DC: U.S. Department of Health and Human Services, Office of the Surgeon General.

U.S. Department of Justice, Attorney General's Commission on Pornography (1986, July). *Attorney General's Commission on Pornography: Final report.* Washington, DC: Author.

CRITICAL THINKING QUESTIONS

1. For many, pornography is a very emotional topic. Given that, personal feelings and biases have a strong potential for coloring how data on the topic are viewed. Identify other issues that pertain to social psychology that likewise can be very emotional for a large number of people.

2. Should decisions of law be based upon research findings? Suppose that research someday clearly demonstrates no causal link between pornography and negative behaviors, such as violence toward women and children. Would this be a compelling reason not to regulate pornography? Or should factors other than the research findings be considered? What other factors should be examined?

3. Examine the composition of the membership of the Meese commission mentioned in the article. In your opinion, who would be best suited to sit on such a committee? Only scientists? Lay people? Legal experts? Defend your position.

4. One major implication of the article was that the conclusions drawn by the Meese commission may not be warranted, given the actual data at hand. For example, the commission tended to draw cause-and-effect conclusions from purely correlational data. In a free society such as that of the United States, how important is it

for the average person to be able to make an intelligent, informed judgment on issues such as pornography? Would it be desirable to ensure that everyone had at least some exposure to research methodology and data interpretation so that he or she could make more informed decisions?

5. Do you think that the commission members could charge that the people who disagree with their conclusions also are biased? Do you think that the values of researchers inevitably intrude on their findings, even if they are trying to be objective? Is it possible to be totally objective?

Chapter Two

SOCIAL PERCEPTION

HOW DO WE form impressions of other people? How important are first impressions? How accurate are the impressions we form? How good are we at knowing what types of impressions we make on other people? These are some of the questions addressed by the readings in this chapter on social perception.

Part of the information that we use in making judgments about other people involves social stereotypes. As a type of mental shortcut, stereotypes are often used by people to help make sense of the world by simplifying it. Stereotypes allow us to make generalizations, however inaccurate, about people based upon knowing just a few things about them. For example, people often associate physical attractiveness with a variety of positive traits; thus, people who dress well are viewed differently than their less-well-dressed counterparts. But what about the types of food people eat? Do we have stereotypes about people based upon their diets? Is it possible that people actually choose diets based upon their personalities? "Profiles in Eating," Article 4, examines these questions and presents some interesting findings about diet-based stereotypes.

When we meet a person for the first time, we are presented with an array of information about him or her. We may notice, for example, what he or she looks like and what type of personality he or she seems to have (friendly, shy, and so on). Are all of these pieces of information equally important in forming an initial impression of the person? Article 5 — "The Warm-Cold Variable in First Impressions of Persons" — suggests that some factors may be more important than others and that initial impressions, formed before the person is actually met, influence judgments about as well as future interactions with him or her. The article provides a fine example of the power of first impressions and the impact that they have on how we relate to others.

Finally, Article 6 — "Accuracy of Person Perception" — asks: Do people know what kinds of impressions they convey? We have an obvious interest in knowing how other people see us. To the extent that we are accurate in making such judgments, we are more likely to successfully use "impression management" to give people the impression of ourselves that we want. This article discusses how accurate people normally are and the conditions that seem to affect this perception.

ARTICLE 4 _____

What information do we use in forming impressions of other people? When meeting people, we might first of all notice what they look like. Considering physical features, we then may make some judgments based upon our stereotypes of people who look like that. Likewise, we may use stereotypes of occupations, age, and even clothing to give us information about what type of person they are.

But what about food? Do we make judgments about people (such as assessing personality characteristics) based upon what they eat? Is it possible that what people choose to eat is not just a matter of simple taste preference but rather an extension of how they view themselves?

The following article, by Sadalla and Burroughs, examines the role of diet both in our perception of other people as well as in our own self-perception. The article may give the phrase, "you are what you eat" a new meaning. Additionally, the study reports on a series of experiments that investigate different aspects of the topic.

Profiles in Eating
Sexy Vegetarians and Other Diet-Based Social Stereotypes
■ Edward Sadalla and Jeffrey Burroughs

There is plenty of casual evidence that people choose food not only for taste and nourishment but also because it bolsters their self-image and sends strong messages about them to the rest of the world.

Consider the prizefighter who wolfs down a bloody steak before the title fight: photographers and reporters are usually summoned to capture the ferocious spectacle of the contender rending and tearing his dinner, steer blood trickling out of the corners of his mouth.

The late Bernarr McFadden, a health-food enthusiast whose missionary zeal would be hard to surpass, went skydiving in his 80s and skinny-dipping in the dead of winter. The press was inevitably present for McFadden's incredible geriatric feats, which were fueled, as he reminded one and all, by wheat germ and black-strap molasses.

Human beings are an omnivorous species, able to survive on a wide variety of foods. Nonetheless, the diets that particular individuals or groups ac-

tually choose may be quite limited. Even today, many Eskimo eat little but great hunks of meat, yet return home after a day of seal hunting in the numbing cold with enough energy left for a night of partying.

By contrast, George Bernard Shaw, a lifelong and militant vegetarian, continued to write and rail with energy to burn when his white beard was down to his breastbone.

Intrigued by the psychological implications of human eating behavior, our team at Arizona State University set out to determine whether food choices are indeed linked to self-image and to the way others regard us.

We divided foods into five categories: *vegetarian, gourmet, health food, fast food,* and *synthetic food.* We asked an initial group of 500 subjects to list the foods they associated with each category. From their lists, we picked 14 specific dishes to typify each category. Vegetarian dishes included broccoli quiche, avocado sandwiches

Reprinted from *Psychology Today,* 1981 (October), *15,* 51–57. Reprinted with permission from *Psychology Today Magazine.* Copyright © 1981 (PT Partners, L.P.).

with bean sprouts, and brown rice with snow peas. Typical gourmet foods were fresh oysters, lobster Newburg, Indonesian roast lamb, and caviar. The health-food list included granola with dried fruit, wheat germ, yogurt, and carob cake. The synthetic-food category included such high-tech items as Lean Strips (processed bacon), Egg Beaters (processed eggs), Carnation Instant Breakfast, and Cheez Whiz. At the top of the fast-food list were Whoppers and Big Macs, Kentucky Fried Chicken, hot dogs, and submarine sandwiches.

We presented 150 subjects in a second group with a list of typical foods from each category and asked them to think of the traits that described people who would prefer such foods. This procedure resulted in a list of 65 descriptions such as hypochondriac, unworried about health, executive, blue collar, late, punctual, callous, sensitive, worrier, emotionally stable.

Using our lists of specific foods and descriptions, we performed three separate studies to examine the relationship between food preferences and personality. In our first experiment, 75 college students evaluated a hypothetical person with specific dietary preferences by rating that person on each of the 65 items on our list. We were initially surprised at the alacrity and confidence with which subjects paired food preferences with descriptions. If a person was said to like bean sprouts, for example, our subjects described him without hesitation as anti-nuclear power and pro-solar energy.

Our subjects not only "knew" which character traits went with what foods but also were in considerable agreement when we asked them to characterize someone with a specific food preference. They saw fast-food lovers as patriotic, pronuclear, conservative, antidrug, and dressed in polyester suits. They saw vegetarians as pacifist, hypochondriacal, drug-using, weight-conscious, liberal, and likely to drive foreign cars.

That first experiment was designed to assess the inferences people make about others based on food preferences. If people prefer foods that communicate an "appropriate" social identity, then the social inferences of those who observe them should show some agreement. Thus observers should be able to "read" the social information present in food preferences, and their reading should show some consensus with that of other observers. The results we obtained provided strong support for that assumption. The question that follows quite naturally from that finding concerns the validity of the observers' inferences.

In a second experiment, we examined the extent to which inferences made about a person based on his or her eating preferences correspond to that person's self-image. In order to test that, we screened about 2,000 students at Arizona State University and found 352 whose food preferences fell clearly within one of our five categories. We then asked them to rate themselves—in terms of the identity they project—on traits we had developed in our first experiment. Then we compared their self-descriptions with the stereotypes that others had constructed about people with those food preferences.

The resulting data indicated substantial agreement between stereotypes and self-descriptions for people whose food preferences fell in the health-food, vegetarian, or gourmet categories, less agreement for those in the fast-food or synthetic-food categories.

The Vegetarian

Self-Description	Highest Correlations
Noncompetitive	.22
Uses drugs	.20
Serious	.17
Sexual	.16
Pacifist	.15
Drives foreign car	.14
Artistic	.14

Hobbies: Crafts—ceramics, painting, sewing, jewelry making, jigsaw puzzles, collecting, folk dancing

Favorite Foods: broccoli quiche, brown rice with snow peas, avocado sandwich with bean sprouts, eggplant parmigiana

The Gourmet	
Self-Description	*Highest Correlations*
Uses drugs	.41
Lives alone	.35
Liberal	.34
Atheist	.33
Cultured	.31
Sensual	.27
Self-oriented	.25
Sophisticated	.23

Hobbies: Glamour Sports—sailing, boating, riding, mountain climbing, skiing, motorcycling, tennis, scuba diving
Fast Living—gambling, going to nightclubs, horse races

Favorite Foods: fresh oysters, lobster Newburg, caviar, freshly ground French-roast coffee

The Health-Food Fan	
Self-Description	*Highest Correlations*
Uses drugs	.36
Lives alone	.27
Antinuclear	.26
Democrat	.22
Prosolar	.21
Drives foreign car	.20
Atheist	.20
Hypochondriac	.19

Hobbies: Intellectual—acting, attending concerts and plays, civic organizations, photography, playing music, reading, traveling

Favorite Foods: protein shake, wheat germ, granola with dried fruit, carob cake, organic honey, yogurt

Those two experiments indicated that a relationship exists between perceived social identity and patterns of food preference. But to what extent are food preferences related to objective measures of personality and life-style?

To find out, we undertook a third experiment: we gave another group of subjects a battery of well-validated personality tests: the Future Events Test, the Social Readjustment Rating Scale, items from the Rotter External Locus of Control Scale, the Work and Family Orientation Questionnaire, and the Leisure Activities Blank.

All of those tests are designed to assess thought patterns, behavior, or lifestyle variables related to social identity. We had 275 volunteers—students and nonstudents—complete the battery of tests; they then rated their preferences for specific dishes in each food category.

The data we obtained suggested a significant correlation both between food preferences and objective personality tests and between food preferences and self-ratings of personality. In other words, the foods people prefer can—to some extent—be used to predict their personalities.

The personality portraits related to the food preferences in our sample were quite distinctive. For example, vegetarians emerged as relatively noncompetitive, with a taste for handicrafts and for difficult, challenging tasks of an intellectual nature. They claim to be weight-conscious, "sexy," and to use recreational drugs.

Health-food enthusiasts projected themselves as noncompetitive, intellectual, and mechanically inclined; also hypochondriacal, antinuclear, prosolar, likely to use recreational drugs, and, by their own admission, "weird" and individualistic.

Gourmets who admitted to an even higher "fun" drug use than the veggies, tended to be atheist, liberal, and live alone; they also reported feeling that marriage is more vital to happiness than a job. They enjoy fast living (gambling, nightclubs, etc.) and engage both in glamour sports and in neighborhood athletics. They consider themselves sensual and sophisticated.

To the extent that a fast-food portrait emerged, the preference seems related to a desire to work hard at one's job, a need to win, and the urge to have children. Fast-food people described themselves as religious, conservative, family-oriented, pronuclear, antidrug. The synthetic-food fans also showed themselves to be conservative and home-oriented as well as practical and competitive.

To the best of our knowledge, our project was the first systematic attempt to link social symbolism and specific food categories, examining the hypothesis that food preferences are part of the complex system of attitudes and behavior that define social identity.

Many undeveloped or unverified theories about food have been advanced over the years: for example, that "we are what we eat" or that familiar foods represent security; that milk and milk-based products have a tranquilizing effect thanks to nursery memories; that wine and gourmet cooking are attempts to gain some control over eating.

In his classic anthropological work, *The Golden Bough,* James Frazer wrote extensively of the ritual use of food, concluding that "among primitive tribes, there is a universal belief that by eating the flesh of a man or an animal, an individual acquires the physical, moral, and intellectual qualities of that man or animal."

The Creeks and Cherokee of North America thought the man who dined on venison swifter and smarter than the one who fed on the meat of the clumsy bear, the slow-footed cattle, or the wallowing swine. Similarly, the Zaparo Indians of Ecuador tried to avoid meat from heavy animals such as tapirs and pigs; they preferred birds, monkeys, deer, or fish. And in Central Africa, young men seeking instant courage ate the flesh and hearts of lions, while would-be lovers desiring sexual strength dined on the testicles of goats. Before the Zulu warriors went into battle, they would often eat meat smeared with dried powder made from the flesh of leopards, lions, and elephants in hopes of acquiring the strength and aggressiveness of those creatures.

The magic that primitive hunters and warriors saw in their food is not so different from the symbolic messages contemporary men and women believe their eating patterns convey. Accordingly, we think that our research helps shed light on the problem of why some people choose diets that are nutritionally poor or linked with medical problems. Medical research has begun to suggest that Americans as a group tend to overeat and to eat foods too rich in animal fat and sugar. It is possible that the patterns of American food preferences

---

The Fast-Food Devotee

Self-Description	Highest Correlations
Religious	.26
Logical	.25
Conservative	.24
"Polyester"	.23
Competitive	.23
Wears business suit	.21
Family-oriented	.21
Antidrug	.18

Hobbies: none frequently mentioned

Favorite Foods: Whopper, Kentucky Fried Chicken, hot dog, Big Mac, milk shake, submarine sandwich, pizza

---

The Synthetic-Food User

Self-Description	Highest Correlations
Logical	.29
"Polyester"	.27
Religious	.24
Family-oriented	.21
Wears business suit	.20
Competitive	.20
Masculine	.20
Antidrug	.19
Conservative	.19

Hobbies: none frequently mentioned

Favorite Foods: Squeeze Parkay (liquid margarine), Egg Beaters (processed eggs), Carnation Instant Breakfast, Lean Strips (artificial bacon), Cheez Whiz (cheese spread)

stem from the symbolism inherent in certain foods—red meat symbolizing status, success, power, achievement; sugar-laden foods representing pleasure, self-reward, and playfulness.

Our study, confined to middle-class Americans able to choose what they eat, suggests that the symbolism of food must also be taken into account in trying to get people to change their eating habits. Madison Avenue understands that very well, of course: witness the number of ad campaigns linking this or that food with success, status, or romance. While the particular personality portraits associated with given food preferences may change with time or geographical region, we assume that some food-identity linkages will be present even if the specific relationship changes.

Our experiments in Arizona make it clear how the diner who orders Indonesian roast lamb and asparagus with hollandaise sauce, washing it down with a '65 Bordeaux, is reinforcing his sense of self—and sending a message about himself to others.

Doing the same is the pretty girl in bare feet and granny glasses who calls for comfrey tea with clover honey, granola with dried fruit, and carob cake. Likewise feeding a sense of self (as well as his face) and sending out a message is the teenager who shouts for a Big Mac, fries, and a chocolate shake to go.

CRITICAL THINKING QUESTIONS

1. The article indicated that food may serve a symbolic function and be tied to a person's sense of identity. If this is true, how might a person's self-identity change if he or she improved a poor (nutritionally unsound) diet? What factors would need to be considered to make such an attempt more likely to succeed?
2. According to your understanding of the article, does our self-identity influence our choice of food? Or is the reverse possible: Does our selection of food influence our view of ourselves? If the latter is possible, would a marked change in diet influence our view of ourselves? How could you test this possibility?
3. Let's suppose that self-identity is related to selection of diet. Given that, are there other external ways in which we project our self-image? Design a study testing these factors.
4. Does your own experience confirm the descriptions of the types of people who select various diets? If so, how? If not, what differences can you cite?

ARTICLE 5 _____

A variety of sources of information may be available for use in forming an impression of a person. However, that does not mean that all of the information will be used or hold equal value. Some sources of information may carry more weight than others. For example, you may notice how the person acts, or you may have heard something about him or her from someone else. How do you use this information to develop an impression of the person?

Building on the classic work of S. E. Asch, Harold H. Kelley examines what can be called a *central organizing trait,* one that is important in influencing the impressions that we form. By examining the effect of changing just one adjective in describing a person (*warm* versus *cold*), the study demonstrates that this initial difference influenced how the subjects actually rated the person. Even more interesting is that these differences in initial impression carried over into how the subjects interacted with the person. The implication is that perhaps our initial impressions lead us to act in certain ways toward others, perhaps creating a self-fulfilling prophecy by giving us what we expected to see in the first place.

The Warm-Cold Variable in First Impressions of Persons

■ Harold H. Kelley

This experiment is one of several studies of first impressions (3), the purpose of the series being to investigate the stability of early judgments, their determinants, and the relation of such judgments to the behavior of the person making them. In interpreting the data from several nonexperimental studies on the stability of first impressions, it proved to be necessary to postulate inner-observer variables which contribute to the impression and which remain relatively constant through time. Also some evidence was obtained which directly demonstrated the existence of these variables and their nature. The present experiment was designed to determine the effects of one kind of inner-observer variable, specifically, *expectations* about the stimulus person which the observer brings to the exposure situation.

That prior information or labels attached to a stimulus person make a difference in observers' first impressions is almost too obvious to require demonstration. The expectations resulting from such preinformation may restrict, modify, or accentuate the impressions he will have. The crucial question is: What changes in perception will accompany a given expectation? Studies of stereotyping, for example, that of Katz and Braly (2), indicate that from an ethnic label such as "German" or "Negro," a number of perceptions follow which are culturally determined. The present study finds its main significance in relation to a study by Asch (1) which demonstrates that certain crucial labels can transform the entire impression of the person, leading to attributions which are related to the label on a broad cultural basis or even, perhaps, on an autochthonous basis.

Asch read to his subjects a list of adjectives which purportedly described a particular person. He then asked them to characterize that person.

Reprinted with permission of the publisher from *Journal of Personality,* Vol. 18, pp. 431–439. Copyright 1950, renewed 1978, by Duke University Press.

He found that the inclusion in the list of what he called *central* qualities, such as "warm" as opposed to "cold," produced a widespread change in the entire impression. This effect was not adequately explained by the halo effect since it did not extend indiscriminately in a positive or negative direction to all characteristics. Rather, it differentially transformed the other qualities, for example, by changing their relative importance in the total impression. Peripheral qualities (such as "polite" versus "blunt") did not produce effects as strong as those produced by the central qualities.[1]

The present study tested the effects of such central qualities upon the early impressions of *real* persons, the same qualities, "warm" vs. "cold," being used. They were introduced as preinformation about the stimulus person before his actual appearance; so presumably they operated as expectations rather than as part of the stimulus pattern during the exposure period. In addition, information was obtained about the effects of the expectations upon the observers' behavior toward the stimulus person. An earlier study in this series has indicated that the more incompatible the observer initially perceived the stimulus person to be, the less the observer initiated interaction with him thereafter. The second purpose of the present experiment, then, was to provide a better controlled study of this relationship.

No previous studies reported in the literature have dealt with the importance of first impressions for behavior. The most relevant data are found in the sociometric literature, where there are scattered studies of the relation between choices among children having some prior acquaintance and their interaction behavior. For an example, see the study by Newstetter, Feldstein, and Newcomb (8).

PROCEDURE

The experiment was performed in three sections of a psychology course (Economics 70) at the Massachusetts Institute of Technology.[2] The three sections provided 23, 16, and 16 subjects respectively. All 55 subjects were men, most of them in their third college year. In each class the stimulus person (also a male) was completely unknown to the subjects before the experimental period. One person served as stimulus person in two sections, and a second person took this role in the third section. In each case the stimulus person was introduced by the experimenter, who posed as a representative of the course instructors and who gave the following statement:

> *Your regular instructor is out of town today, and since we of Economics 70 are interested in the general problem of how various classes react to different instructors, we're going to have an instructor today you've never had before, Mr. ____. Then, at the end of the period, I want you to fill out some forms about him. In order to give you some idea of what he's like, we've had a person who knows him write up a little biographical note about him. I'll pass this out to you now and you can read it before he arrives.* Please read these to yourselves and don't talk about this among yourselves until the class is over so that he won't get wind of what's going on.

Two kinds of these notes were distributed, the two being identical except that in one the stimulus person was described among other things as being "rather cold" whereas in the other form the phrase "very warm" was substituted. The content of the "rather cold" version is as follows:

> *Mr. ____ is a graduate student in the Department of Economics and Social Science here at M. I. T. He has had three semesters of teaching experience in psychology at another college. This is his first semester teaching Ec. 70. He is 26 years old, a veteran, and married. People who know him consider him to be a rather cold person, industrious, critical, practical, and determined.*

The two types of preinformation were distributed randomly within each of the three classes and in such a manner that the students were not aware that two kinds of information were being given out. The stimulus person then appeared and led the class in a twenty-minute discussion. During this time the experimenter kept a record of how often each student participated in the discussion. Since the discussion was almost totally leader-centered, this participation record indicates the number of times each student initiated verbal interaction with the instructor. After the discussion period, the stimulus person left the room, and the experimenter gave the following instructions:

> Now, I'd like to get your impression of Mr. _____. This is not a test of you and can in no way affect your grade in this course. This material will not be identified as belonging to particular persons and will be kept strictly confidential. It will be of most value to us if you are completely honest in your evaluation of Mr. _____. Also, please understand that what you put down will not be used against him or cause him to lose his job

> or anything like that. This is not a test of him but merely a study of how different classes react to different instructors.

The subjects then wrote free descriptions of the stimulus person and finally rated him on a set of 15 rating scales.

RESULTS AND DISCUSSION

1. *Influence of warm-cold variable on first impressions.* The differences in the ratings produced by the warm-cold variable were consistent from one section to another even where different stimulus persons were used. Consequently, the data from the three sections were combined by equating means (the S.D.'s were approximately equal) and the results for the total group are presented in Table 1. Also

TABLE 1 / Comparison of "Warm" and "Cold" Observers in Terms of Average Ratings Given Stimulus Persons

Item	Low End of Rating Scale	High End of Rating Scale	Average Rating Warm N = 27	Cold N = 28	Level of Significance of Warm-Cold Difference	Asch's Data: Per Cent of Group Assigning Quality at Low End of Our Rating Scale* Warm	Cold
1	Knows his stuff	Doesn't know his stuff	3.5	4.6			
2	Considerate of others	Self-centered	6.3	9.6	1%		
3†	Informal	Formal	6.3	9.6	1%		
4†	Modest	Proud	9.4	10.6			
5	Sociable	Unsociable	5.6	10.4	1%	91%	38%
6	Self-assured	Uncertain of himself	8.4	9.1			
7	High intelligence	Low intelligence	4.8	5.1			
8	Popular	Unpopular	4.0	7.4	1%	84%	28%
9†	Good natured	Irritable	9.4	12.0	5%	94%	17%
10	Generous	Ungenerous	8.2	9.6		91%	08%
11	Humorous	Humorless	8.3	11.7	1%	77%	13%
12	Important	Insignificant	6.5	8.6		88%	99%
13†	Humane	Ruthless	8.6	11.0	5%	86%	31%
14†	Submissive	Dominant	13.2	14.5			
15	Will go far	Will not get ahead	4.2	5.8			

*Given for all qualities common to Asch's list and this set of rating scales.
†These scales were reversed when presented to the subjects.

in this table is presented that part of Asch's data which refers to the qualities included in our rating scales. From this table it is quite clear that those given the "warm" preinformation consistently rated the stimulus person more favorably than those given the "cold" preinformation. Summarizing the statistically significant differences, the "warm" subjects rated the stimulus person as more considerate of others, more informal, more sociable, more popular, better natured, more humorous, and more humane. These findings are very similar to Asch's for the characteristics common to both studies. He found more frequent attribution to his hypothetical "warm" personalities of sociability, popularity, good naturedness, generosity, humorousness, and humaneness. So these data strongly support his finding that such a central quality as "warmth" can greatly influence the total impression of a personality. This effect is found to be operative in the perception of real persons.

This general favorableness in the perceptions of the "warm" observers as compared with the "cold" ones indicates that something like a halo effect may have been operating in these ratings. Although his data are not completely persuasive on this point, Asch was convinced that such a general effect was *not* operating in his study. Closer inspection of the present data makes it clear that the "warm-cold" effect cannot be explained altogether on the basis of simple halo effect. In Table 1 it is evident that the "warm-cold" variable produced differential effects from one rating scale to another. The size of this effect seems to depend upon the closeness of relation between the specific dimension of any given rating scale and the central quality of "warmth" or "coldness." Even though the rating of intelligence may be influenced by a halo effect, it is not influenced to the same degree to which considerateness is. It seems to make sense to view such strongly influenced items as considerateness, informality, good naturedness, and humaneness as dynamically more closely related to warmth and hence more perceived in terms

of this relation than in terms of a general positive or negative feeling toward the stimulus person. If first impressions are normally made in terms of such general dimensions as "warmth" and "coldness," the power they give the observer in making predictions and specific evaluations about such disparate behavior characteristics as formality and considerateness is considerable (even though these predictions may be incorrect or misleading).

The free report impression data were analyzed for only one of the sections. In general, there were few sizable differences between the "warm" and "cold" observers. The "warm" observers attributed more nervousness, more sincerity, and more industriousness to the stimulus person. Although the frequencies of comparable qualities are very low because of the great variety of descriptions produced by the observers, there is considerable agreement with the rating scale data.

Two important phenomena are illustrated in these free description protocols, the first of them having been noted by Asch. *Firstly,* the characteristics of the stimulus person are interpreted in terms of the precognition of warmth or coldness. For example, a "warm" observer writes about a rather shy and retiring stimulus person as follows: "He makes friends slowly but they are lasting friendships when formed." In another instance, several "cold" observers described him as being "... intolerant: would be angry if you disagree with his view. . .."; while several "warm" observers put the same thing this way: "Unyielding in principle, not easily influenced or swayed from his original attitude." *Secondly,* the preinformation about the stimulus person's warmth or coldness is evaluated and interpreted in the light of the direct behavioral data about him. For example, "He has a slight inferiority complex which leads to his coldness," and "His conscientiousness and industriousness might be mistaken for coldness." Examples of these two phenomena occurred rather infrequently, and there was no way to evaluate the relative strengths of these countertendencies. Certainly some such evaluation is necessary to determine the conditions under which behavior which is contrary to a stereotyped label resists distortion and leads to rejection of the label.

A comparison of the data from the two different stimulus persons is pertinent to the last point in so far as it indicates the interaction between the properties of the stimulus person and the label. The fact that the warm-cold variable generally produced differences in the same direction for the two stimulus persons, even though they are very different in personality, behavior, and mannerisms, indicates the strength of this variable. However, there were some exceptions to this tendency as well as marked differences in the *degree* to which the experimental variable was able to produce differences. For example, stimulus person A typically appears to be anything but lacking in self-esteem and on rating scale 4 he was generally at the "proud" end of the scale. Although the "warm" observers tended to rate him as they did the other stimulus person (i.e., more "modest"), the difference between the "warm" and "cold" means for stimulus person A is very small and not significant as it is for stimulus person B. Similarly, stimulus person B was seen as "unpopular" and "humorless," which agrees with his typical classroom behavior. Again the "warm" observers rated him more favorably on these items, but their ratings were not significantly different from those of the "cold" observers, as was true for the other stimulus person. Thus we see that the strength or compellingness of various qualities of the stimulus person must be reckoned with. The stimulus is not passive to the forces arising from the label but actively resists distortion and may severely limit the degree of influence exerted by the preinformation.[3]

2. *Influence of warm-cold variable on interaction with the stimulus person.* In the analysis of the frequency with which the various students took part in the discussion led by the stimulus person, a larger proportion of those given the "warm" preinformation participated than of those given the "cold" preinformation. Fifty-six per cent of the "warm" subjects entered the discussion, whereas only 32 per cent of the "cold" subjects did so. Thus the expectation of warmth not only produced more favorable early perceptions of the stimulus person but led to greater initiation of interaction with him. This relation is a low one, significant at between the 5 per cent and 10 per cent level of confidence, but it is in line with the general principle that social perception serves to guide and steer the person's behavior in his social environment.

As would be expected from the foregoing findings, there was also a relation between the favorableness of the impression and whether or not the person participated in the discussion. Although any single item yielded only a small and insignificant relation to participation, when a number are combined the trend becomes clear cut. For example, when we combine the seven items which were influenced to a statistically significant degree by the warm-cold variable, the total score bears considerable relation to participation, the relationship being significant as well beyond the 1 per cent level. A larger proportion of those having favorable total impressions participated than of those having unfavorable impressions, the biserial correlation between these variables being .34. Although this relation may be interpreted in several ways, it seems most likely that the unfavorable perception led to a curtailment of interaction. Support for this comes from one of the other studies in this series (3). There it was found that those persons having unfavorable impressions of the instructor at the end of the first class meeting tended less often to initiate interactions with him in the succeeding four meetings than did those having favorable first impressions. There was also some tendency in the same study for those persons who interacted least with the instructor to change least in their judgments of him from the first to later impressions.

It will be noted that these relations lend some support to the autistic hostility hypothesis proposed by Newcomb (7). This hypothesis suggests that the possession of an initially hostile attitude toward a person leads to a restriction of communication and contact with him which in turn serves to preserve the hostile attitude by preventing the acquisition of data which could correct it. The present data indicate that a restriction of interaction is associated with unfavorable preinformation and an unfavorable perception. The data from the other study support this result and also indicate the correctness of the second part of the hypothesis, that restricted interaction reduces the likelihood of change in the attitude.

What makes these findings more significant is that they appear in the context of a discussion class where there are numerous *induced* and *own* forces to enter the discussion and to interact with the instructor. It seems likely that the effects predicted by Newcomb's hypothesis would be much more marked in a setting where such forces were not present.

SUMMARY

The warm-cold variable had been found by Asch to produce large differences in the impressions of personality formed from a list of adjectives. In this study the same variable was introduced in the form of expectations about a real person and was found to produce similar differences in first impressions of him in a classroom setting. In addition, the differences in first impressions produced by the different expectations were shown to influence the observers' behavior toward the stimulus person. Those observers given the favorable expectation (who, consequently, had a favorable impression of the stimulus person) tended to interact more with him than did those given the unfavorable expectation.

REFERENCES

1. Asch, S. E., Forming impressions of personality. *J. abnorm. soc. Psychol.*, 1946, **41**, 258–290.
2. Katz, D., and Braly, K. W. Verbal stereotypes and racial prejudice. In Newcomb, T. M. and Hartley, E. L. (eds.), *Readings in social psychology.* New York: Holt, 1947, Pp. 204–210.
3. Kelley, H. H. First impressions in interpersonal relations. Ph.D. thesis, Massachusetts Institute of Technology, Cambridge, Mass. Sept., 1948.
4. Krech, D., and Crutchfield, R. S. *Theory and problems of social psychology.* New York: McGraw-Hill, 1948.
5. Luchins, A. S. Forming impressions of personality: a critique. *J. abnorm. soc. Psychol.*, 1948, **43**, 318–325.
6. Mensch, I. N., and Wishner, J. Asch on "Forming impressions of personality": further evidence. *J. Personal.*, 1947, **16**, 188–191.
7. Newcomb, T. M. Autistic hostility and social reality. *Hum. Relations.*, 1947, **1**, 69–86.
8. Newstetter, W. I., Feldstein, M. H., and Newcomb, T. M. *Group adjustment: a study in experimental sociology.* Cleveland: Western Reserve University, 1938.

NOTES

1. Since the present experiment was carried out, Mensch and Wishner (6) have repeated a number of Asch's experiments because of dissatisfaction with his sex and geographic distribution. Their data substantiate Asch's very closely. Also, Luchins (5) has criticized Asch's experiments for their artificial methodology, repeated some of them, and challenged some of the kinds of interpretations Asch made from his data. Luchins also briefly reports some tantalizing conclusions from a number of studies of first impressions of actual persons.
2. Professor Mason Haire, now of the University of California, provided valuable advice and help in executing the experiment.
3. We must raise an important question here: Would there be a tendency for "warm" observers to distort the perception in the favorable direction regardless of how much the stimulus deviated from the expectation? Future research should test the following hypothesis, which is suggested by Gestalt perception theory (4, pp. 95–98): If the stimulus differs but slightly from the expectation, the perception will tend to be *assimilated* to the expectation; however, if the difference between the stimulus and expectation is too great, the perception will occur by contrast to the expectation and will be distorted in the opposite direction.

CRITICAL THINKING QUESTIONS

1. Reread the information that was presented to the subjects to manipulate the warm-cold variable. The manipulation obviously produced a significant effect on the subjects' subsequent evaluation of the teacher. Do you feel that the manipulation was realistic? For example, how realistic is it to have a guest teacher described as "rather cold" in a brief biographical sketch? Could this particular manipulation

have resulted in any experimental demand characteristics? Address the issue of the relative importance of experimental versus mundane realism as it pertains to this study.

2. How long lasting do you think these first impressions are? For example, would they persist over the course of a semester or even longer? How could you test this?
3. What are the practical implications of this study? If you were working in a setting where you were interviewing and hiring applicants for a job, how could you use this information to help you make better, more accurate decisions?
4. The warm-cold information was provided by the instructor of the course, a person who presumably had high credibility. Do you think the credibility of the source of the information would affect how influenced the individuals were? How could you test this?

ADDITIONAL RELATED READINGS

Fisk, S. T., and Taylor, S. E. (1984). *Social Cognition*. Reading, MA: Addison-Wesley.

Wishner, J. (1960). Reanalysis of "Impressions of Personality." *Psychological Review*, *67*, 96–112.

ARTICLE 6 _____

Impression formation is a two-way street: While we are busy forming impressions of the people we meet, they are busy forming impressions of us. This social reality leads to two questions. First of all, how accurate are we in forming impressions of other people? Article 5 discussed some of the factors that may influence the impressions that we form. The second question falls under the general heading of *impression management:* How good are we at knowing what type of impression we convey? The answer to this question has obvious practical implications: Since our self-concept is partly defined by how we think other people see us, the accuracy of such perceptions is crucial. If we aren't accurate, for example, then our self-perceptions, based upon these inaccurate assessments, also will be inaccurate.

The study by DePaulo and colleagues that follows examines how accurate people are in knowing what types of impressions they convey to others. The design of the study allows several types of accuracy to be examined simultaneously. The results provide some interesting insights into this issue, since people were accurate in certain situations but not in others.

Accuracy of Person Perception
Do People Know What Kinds of Impressions They Convey?

■ Bella M. DePaulo, Claudia W. Hoover, William Webb, David A. Kenny, and Peter V. Oliver

Do people know what kinds of impressions they convey to other people during particular social interactions? In a study designed to answer this question, subjects interacted individually with three partners on each of four different tasks. After each interaction, participants reported their impressions of the other person's likability and competence. They also postdicted the impressions they believed they conveyed to the other person along the same dimensions. Accuracy was computed as recommended by Cronbach (1955) and by Kenny's (1981) Social Relations Model. Subjects could tell to a significant degree how the impressions they conveyed to their partners changed over time (time accuracy) and how they changed over time in different ways with different partners (differential accuracy). They could also tell how their competence was differentially perceived by different partners (dyadic accuracy).

However, they were not very accurate at discerning which partners perceived them as most competent or most likable across all interactions (person accuracy). Subjects believed that they conveyed similar impressions of themselves to all of their partners, although actually partners evidenced little agreement with each other in their impressions of a given subject. The implications of these findings for symbolic-interactionist theories of the development of the self and impression-management perspectives on social behavior are described.

There are many contexts in which it is important to people to know what kind of impression they created on another person. Job interviews, first dates, or any evaluative interactions with potentially significant consequences would all qualify. In many more mundane interactions, too,

Reprinted from the *Journal of Personality and Social Psychology,* 1987, *52,* 303–315. Copyright 1987 by the American Psychological Association. Reprinted by permission.

people are often interested in knowing how they are viewed by others. The question of accuracy in perceiving conveyed impressions is one that interests people not only as it applies to themselves but also as it applies to others (e.g., "Does she have any idea how she is coming across?").

The importance to social interactants of understanding the impressions of themselves that they have conveyed to others is underscored by several major theoretical perspectives on human behavior. First, theories of the self in social interaction—most notably symbolic-interactionist theories (e.g., Cooley, 1902; Mead, 1925, 1934; see also Shrauger & Schoeneman, 1979)—argue that the self is socially constructed. In Mead's (1925) words, "we are in possession of selves just insofar as we can and do take the attitudes of others toward ourselves and respond to those attitudes" (p. 273). Cooley's (1902) notion of the looking-glass self is probably the most widely known expression of this idea. Three sequential components contribute to the construction of a reflected self: "the imagination of our appearance to the other person; the imagination of his judgment of that appearance; and some sort of self-feeling, such as pride or mortification" (p. 184). According to Cooley, then, the judgments (or perceived judgments) of others are essential to the development of the self, and they have immediate affective consequences as well. If people do indeed develop selves in part by assuming the attitudes of others toward themselves, then it is important to know the degree to which their perceptions of those attitudes are accurate. The implicit assumption made by the symbolic interactionists is that such perceptions are accurate (Kinch, 1963). Clearly, though, this is an empirical question.

Accuracy in perceiving conveyed impressions is also important to impression-management formulations (e.g., Baumeister, 1982; Goffman, 1959; Jones, 1964; Schlenker, 1980, 1985; Snyder, 1979; Tedeschi, 1981), which posit that people are often concerned about the impressions they are conveying to others. One way of determining whether they are creating their

intended impressions is to monitor the targets of their impression management attempts for feedback. To the extent that the impression they believe they conveyed is discrepant from the impression they intended to convey, they can alter their behavioral strategies in an attempt to attain a closer match. If people are in fact altering their strategies in accord with their perceptions of the impressions they have created on others, then again it is important to determine the extent to which such perceptions are accurate.

There are many different ways to conceptualize and operationalize people's accuracy at understanding the impressions they have conveyed. We will emphasize two that we believe are among the most important. The first, which we will call *individual accuracy,* describes people's ability to understand how they are generally viewed by others. It is their ability to know how they are perceived by a group of people as a whole, apart from their ability to discern how they are differentially perceived by specific members of the group. For example, if Pam, more so than Sue Ellen or Donna, believes that she is liked by a group that includes Bobby, J. R., and Ray, and if Bobby, J. R., and Ray do indeed like Pam relatively more than they like Sue Ellen or Donna, then Pam has achieved individual accuracy.

Dyadic accuracy describes people's ability to discern how they are viewed differentially by specific others. To continue the example: If (a) Pam believes that Bobby likes her more than he likes Sue Ellen or Donna, and if she believes that Bobby likes her more than J. R. or Ray likes her, and if (b) Bobby really does like Pam more than he likes Sue Ellen or Donna, and if he likes her more than J. R. or Ray likes her, then Pam has achieved dyadic accuracy.

People who are individually accurate might know, for example, that they are popular, but they will not necessarily know which specific persons like them the most; therefore, they may not be dyadically accurate. In contrast, those who are dyadically accurate can distinguish their friends from their enemies, but they may not necessarily know how they are regarded by a group as a whole. The attainment of individual accuracy might be important to people deciding whether to pursue or maintain membership in various formal or informal groups, whereas the achievement of dyadic accuracy might be useful to people deciding which particular relationships to pursue.

We are not the first to propose separating individual and dyadic components of accuracy. For example, Ausubel, Schiff, and Glaser (1952) and Israel (1958) have separately measured individual and dyadic accuracy, and Swann (1984) has distinguished between two types of accuracy that he calls global accuracy and circumscribed accuracy. However, these perspectives partially confound the two types of accuracy, either statistically (Ausubel et al., 1952) or conceptually (Swann, 1984); see Kenny and Albright (1986).

There are numerous informational bases of both individual and dyadic accuracy. For example, people might have a sense of the types of personalities that are valued by the culture, by the particular group in question, or by specific individuals, and they might also have a sense of whether they fit one of those valued types to a greater or lesser degree than do other group members. People can also learn about their standing in the group, as well as the ways in which they are differentially regarded by different individuals, by direct communications from relevant others and by indirect communications from third parties. Objective evidence is available, too (e.g., the crowdedness of one's social calendar). Finally, people can learn about how they are regarded by observing other people's reactions to them during social interactions. The question of the degree to which people's perceptions, based on all of this information, are accurate is the one that has been addressed by almost all of the previous research.

PREVIOUS RESEARCH

Several decades ago, the study of accuracy in person perception was an extremely popular topic. However, the result of the methodological critiques published in 1955 by Cronbach and by Gage and Cronbach was to bring research on this topic nearly to a standstill. Although a few peeps have been heard since then (e.g., Bronfenbrenner, Harding, & Gallwey, 1958; DePaulo, 1978; Harackiewicz & DePaulo, 1982; Snodgrass, 1985), the topic has not nearly regained the status or excitement that it once enjoyed (Funder, 1987).

The butt of the Cronbach critiques was the discrepancy or difference scores used to calculate accuracy. These scores were computed simply by finding the difference (unsigned or signed) between the postdiction and the criterion. The scores are problematic in that they reflect not just one kind of accuracy but a series of rating biases and different kinds of accuracies. Cronbach's analysis indicates that accuracy results based on such scores are essentially uninterpretable.

Studies relevant to individual and dyadic accuracy at understanding conveyed impressions are those in which subjects postdicted the impressions of either multiple targets or of a group as a whole. Studies with only a single target (such as those in the marital-interaction literature) simultaneously measure individual and dyadic accuracy and therefore will not be considered. Also excluded are studies that report uninterpretable measures of accuracy and studies with problematic methodological or reporting procedures

Individual Accuracy

Studies of individual accuracy are summarized in Table 1. These studies included as participants nurses, football players, Peace Corps trainees, members of military work groups and sensitivity-training groups, and classmates of many different ages. Participants reported their impressions of each other and their postdictions of how they were perceived by others on a wide variety of dimensions. In some studies, participants rated the group as a whole, whereas in others (Anderson, 1984; Ausubel et al., 1952; Israel, 1958; Norman & Goldberg, 1966; Passini & Norman, 1966) they rated each individual member of the group. In these studies, the ratings made of specific others were summed to produce a measure of how the participants believed they were perceived by others in general. That measure was then correl-

TABLE 1 / Studies of Individual Accuracy

Study	Subjects	Type of Judgment	Accuracy Correlations
Anderson (1984)	65 men and 56 women from 3 fraternities and 2 sororities	Intellect, humor, defensiveness, and considerateness	.52, .73, .40, and .42 for the respective judgments
Ausubel, Schiff, & Glaser (1952)	245 third, fifth, seventh, eleventh, and twelfth graders	Desirability as a friend	.68, .76, .72, .79, and .89 for the respective grades
Bohrnstedt & Felson (1983)	411 sixth, seventh, and eighth graders	Liking, academic ability, and athletic ability (for boys)	.36, .50, and .48 for the respective judgments
Felson (1981)	72 college football players	Performance during the current season	.19
Israel (1958)	29 student nurses	Orderliness, intelligence, leadership, and appearance	Only intelligence and leadership accuracy were significantly better than chance
Norman & Goldberg (1966)	73 Peace Corps trainees (groups of approximately 10 people each)	Extraversion, agreeableness, dependability, emotional stability, and culture	.62, .41, .56, .33, and .54 for the respective judgments
Orpen & Bush (1974)	14 high school students	Rating scales and CPI scales of sociability and responsibility	.27 and .09 for rating and CPI measures of responsibility; .24 and .05 for sociablity
Passini & Norman (1966)	84 undergraduates (first day of class)	Extraversion, agreeableness, dependability, emotional stability, and culture	.37, .15, .50, .26, and .26 for the respective judgments
Reeder, Donohue & Biblarz (1960)	54 men in military work groups	Excellence as a leader and worker	Specific scores were not reported, but accuracy appeared to be substantial
Sherwood (1965)	34 men and 34 women in 6 sensitivity-training groups	22 different dimensions	Mean correlation was approximately .58
Walhood & Klopfer (1971)	13 master's students	Rank-orderings and scores on Leary's (1957) Interpersonal Checklist of affection and dominance	.37 and .47 for ranking and checklist scores of affection; .80 and .58 for dominance

ated with actual impressions to produce an individual-accuracy score. Individual-accuracy scores in the studies reported in Table 1 were typically between-subjects correlations.

Although a few of the individual-accuracy correlations were very small, most were of moderate magnitude and several were quite high. In the types of groups that have been studied—usually small, intact groups of people who have known each other for at least a few months and often much longer—people are reasonably accurate in their assessments of how they are regarded by the group as a whole.

Dyadic Accuracy

Studies of dyadic accuracy are summarized in Table 2. Typically, the accuracy scores are within-subjects correlations of participants' postdictions of how they were perceived by every member of the group, with the actual impressions of the participants reported by the other group members. Several studies reported both individual and dyadic accuracy scores and therefore appear in both Table 1 and Table 2. Again, a wide variety of participants were included in these studies, and the participants rated each other on a variety of dimensions.

A comparison of the Table 2 results with the Table 1 results shows that studies of dyadic accuracy generally have reported less impressive levels of accuracy than those reported in studies of individual accuracy. However, with the exception of the Bronfenbrenner et al. (1958) study, dyadic accuracy was always positive and occasionally significantly so.

TABLE 2 / Studies of Dyadic Accuracy

Study	Subjects	Type of Judgment	Accuracy Correlations
Anderson (1984)	65 men and 56 women from 3 fraternities and 2 sororities	Intellect, humor, defensiveness, and considerateness	.13, .23, .15, and .23 for the respective judgments
Ausubel & Schiff (1955)	44 high school juniors	Desirability as a friend	.38
Bronfenbrenner, Harding, & Gallwey (1958)	72 undergraduates in 12 mixed-sex discussion groups	6 positive and 6 negative traits	"Essentially zero"
Israel (1958)	29 student nurses	Orderliness, intelligence, leadership, and appearance	Intelligence and leadership accuracy were significantly better than chance; orderliness and appearance accuracy were worse than chance
Tagiuri (1952)	16 fraternity members	Liking	Specific scores were not reported, but accuracy appeared to exceed chance
Tagiuri, Bruner, & Blake (1958)	47 different groups (e.g., naval crews, seminars, summer campers, therapeutic groups)	Liking	Specific scores were not reported, but accuracy appeared to exceed chance

PRESENT EXPERIMENT

Social interactions provide the raw data for person perception. We want to assess the degree to which people can tell how they are viewed by others on the basis of data that are available to them during ongoing social interactions and apart from any information from other sources that might be relevant (e.g., past histories, communications from third parties).

To determine the degree of individual accuracy and dyadic accuracy that can be gleaned from the raw data of social interactions, it is necessary to study subjects who are initially strangers to each other, each of whom interacts with several different persons in separate face-to-face interactions. It is important that subjects be unacquainted so that they have access to no other information that could aid them in their assessments of how they are being perceived. Each subject should be paired with several different partners so that dyadic accuracy can be assessed, and the interactions should be dyadic rather than group interactions so that the partners' reactions are likely to pertain to the subject. In a study such as the Bronfenbrenner et al. (1958) study of 6-person groups, subjects could at any point be reacting to any of the group members or to the group as a whole.

In the study we designed, each subject interacted individually with 3 other subjects on each of four different tasks. Dyad members rated each other on each of six different scales after each task and also indicated how they believed they would be perceived by their partner on each of the six dimensions.

We first analyzed these data using the procedures described by Cronbach (1955),[1] which are described more fully in the Results section. From these analyses, we computed what we will call person accuracy (the ability to tell which partners were impressed most favorably and which were impressed least favorably across time), time accuracy (the ability to discern how the impressions being conveyed change over time, averaging across partners), and differential accuracy, or Person × Time Accuracy (the ability to discern how the impressions being conveyed change differentially over time with different partners). One limitation of the Cronbach analysis, however, is that it is a fixed-effects model. Partners are considered fixed rather than random, and therefore it is not possible to generalize beyond the particular partners involved in the experiment. A second limitation is that it ignores the interactive nature of the situation. Therefore, we also analyzed the data using Kenny's Social Relations Model (Kenny, 1981; Kenny & La Voie, 1984; Warner, Kenny, & Stoto, 1979), which is a component model of accuracy similar to other component models such as Cronbach's (Cronbach, 1955; see also Cronbach, Gleser, Nanda, & Rajaratnam, 1972). However, it is a random-effects model. Also, it provides a variety of other measures that are informative about the processes that might lead to accuracy or inaccuracy in social perception.

Finally, in this study we also examined individual difference correlates of Cronbach scores and also scores from the Social Relations Model. The individual difference measures we included were measures of public self-consciousness and social anxiety (Fenigstein, Scheier, & Buss, 1975),[2] need for approval (Crowne & Marlowe, 1964), and self-monitoring (Snyder, 1974). Although persons high on these dimensions differ in numerous theoretically predicted and empirically documented ways, they share a concern with their public self-images. The developers of the Public Self-Consciousness Scale linked the construct directly to Mead's symbolic-interactionist perspective. As they noted, "the essence of public self-consciousness is the self as a social object" (Fenigstein et al., 1975, p. 525). Persons who are high in this dimension are believed to be especially aware of how they are perceived by others (Scheier & Carver, 1981). People high in need for approval are highly motivated to be favorably evaluated by others, and high self-monitors are especially concerned with the appropriateness of their interpersonal behaviors. However, it does not necessarily follow that the motivation to create a desirable or appropriate impression will result in a more accurate reading of feedback from others. It is equally plausible that these types of persons will instead show a pattern of interpretations that is better characterized as biased than as accurate; that is, they might believe, or want to believe, that they are conveying positive impressions even when they are not. This bias interpretation is particularly pertinent to persons with a high need for approval, for whom positive self-descriptions are hypothesized to be largely defensive. Using the Cronbach scores and the scores from the Social Relations Model, we can test both the accuracy and the bias alternatives.

Like people high in need for approval, self-monitoring, and public self-consciousness, socially anxious people are motivated to convey just the right impression during social interactions; however, they are also especially insecure about their ability to do so (Schlenker & Leary, 1982, 1985). Their insecurity should translate directly into a tendency to believe that they have not succeeded in conveying a desirable impression. If their anxiety interferes with their reading of social cues, then their perceptions of the impressions they have conveyed may be inaccurate.

The Social Relations Model

The Social Relations Model posits that a person's behavior is a function of an actor, a partner, and a relationship effect. The *actor effect* represents consistency in a person's behavior across partners. The *partner effect* represents consistency in the behavior of the person's partner. The *relationship effect* represents the unique way that a person behaves with a given partner.

Consider the two variables of central interest in this study: the *impressions* that people form of each other during social interactions, and their *postdictions* of the impressions they conveyed to each other (i.e., their perceptions of how they came across to each other). In the Pam and Bobby example, we might pose the questions "what kind of impression does Pam make on Bobby?" (Bobby's impression of Pam) and "what kind of impression does Pam think she has made on Bobby?" (Pam's postdiction of the impression she made on Bobby).

Bobby's impression of Pam has a number of components: (a) an actor effect: Bobby's general impression of others (e.g., his impression of Pam, Sue Ellen, and Donna); (b) a partner effect: other people's general impression of Pam (e.g., Bobby, J. R., and Ray's view of Pam); and (c) a relationship effect: Bobby's particular impression of Pam, controlling for his general impressions of everyone and everyone's general impression of Pam.

Pam's postdiction of the impression she made on Bobby is composed of a similar set of components: (a) an actor effect: Pam's postdiction of how other people (e.g., Bobby, J. R., Ray) generally view her; (b) a partner effect: the kind of impression that people (e.g., Pam, Sue Ellen, Donna) generally think they make on Bobby; and (c) a relationship effect: the particular impression that Pam postdicts that she made on Bobby, controlling for the kind of impression she thinks she makes on everyone, and the kind of impression everyone thinks they make on Bobby.

Accuracy is defined by the links between the appropriate components of the Social Relations Model. The link between the partner component of impressions and the actor component of postdictions indicates whether people know how they are generally viewed. This link describes individual accuracy. The link between the two relationship components describes dyadic accuracy. Although the dyadic components include measurement error, the individual accuracy correlations do not.

Method

Subjects   Subjects were 42 unacquainted female undergraduates who signed up for a study of impressions. They received experimental credit for their participation in partial fulfillment of course requirements.

Procedure   Subjects participated in groups of 6, and the sessions lasted 2 hr. While subjects were waiting for the session to begin, they completed the individual-difference measures. When all subjects had arrived, they were randomly assigned a number from 1 to 6. The odd-numbered subjects interacted with the 3 even-numbered subjects and vice versa. A total of nine different dyads were formed from each set of 6 persons.

The experiment was conducted in three phases. During Phase 1, each subject interacted with her first partner on each of four tasks; during Phase 2, she interacted with her second partner on those tasks; and during Phase 3, she interacted with her third partner on the four tasks. All phases were openly videotaped with the subjects' knowledge and consent. The videotapes are not relevant to this report and will not be further discussed.

Three female experimenters were assigned to each of three rooms. At the beginning of the first phase, Subjects 1 and 2 were assigned to the first experimenter's room, Subjects 3 and 4 were assigned to the second experimenter's room, and Subjects 5 and 6 were assigned to the third experimenter's room. During the two subsequent phases, subjects switched partners and rooms, so that each experimenter ran each subject through each of the four tasks.

The four tasks were chosen for diversity, and the first three were similar to those used by Snodgrass (1985). The first task was a teaching task. In four of the seven sessions, randomly determined, Subjects 1, 3, and 5 were assigned to the role of teacher, and Subjects 2, 4, and 6 were assigned to the role of learner. (Subjects remained in those roles when participating in the task with all three of their partners.) In the other three sessions, subjects took turns serving as teacher and as learner, with Subjects 1, 3, and 5 serving first as teachers.

The teaching task consisted of four minilessons on attitudes. In the sessions in which just one of the dyad members served as teacher, the teacher-subject read the four one-paragraph minilessons to her partner. She was instructed to read the lessons in a way that would hold her partner's attention and was given time to read through the lessons before beginning. After reading the four lessons, she administered a 4-item quiz without giving any feedback about the accuracy of her partner's answers. In the sessions in which subjects served as both teachers and learners, the subjects alternated reading the minilessons to each other, then alternately quizzed each other about the lessons.

Three sets of lessons were prepared so that subjects could work with different materials with each of their partners.

The order in which the subjects completed the next three tasks was counterbalanced using a Latin square design. One of the tasks was a competitive task called Blockhead, in which subjects take turns placing odd-shaped blocks on top of each other. If a subject places a block in a way that makes the stack of blocks topple, that subject loses. The goal, then, is to place one's own block in a precarious position, so that the partner will topple the stack when she tries to place her block. A cup of nickels was left in the room and subjects were instructed to take a nickel (which they were allowed to keep) every time they won a round. The subjects were allotted exactly 4 min in which to complete as many rounds as possible.

Another task was a cooperative task based on the game show Password. Each subject was given a set of cards, each of which had one word printed on it. Subjects were instructed to give one-word clues to their partner, who would then try to guess the key word from the clues. Subjects took turns giving the clues. The dyads were allowed 4 min to complete as many rounds as possible. Subjects were given different sets of word cards to use during the three phases of the experiment.

The other task was a discussion task (e.g., coming to an agreement about which of 10 needy people should be given access to the only three available kidney machines). Again, three different versions were used, and subjects were allotted 4 min for each discussion.

After each task, subjects moved to different ends of the room, facing away from each other, and completed a set of 20-point rating scales. They first indicated their impressions of their partner during the task they just completed on six scales with the high endpoints labeled *very friendly, very dominant, very sincere, very confident, very intelligent,* and *I like her very much.* These scales were selected to represent two basic dimensions of person perception (Rosenberg & Sedlak, 1972): social good-bad (friendly, sincere, liking) and intellectual good-bad (dominant, confident, intelligent). Subjects then answered the question "what was your partner's impression of *you* during the task that you just completed?" on six scales with analogous end labels. All questionnaires were completed anonymously, and accuracy was emphasized. Subjects were assured that their responses were confidential and that their partner would never see them. As soon as the subject completed a questionnaire, she put it in a manila envelope and sealed the envelope. The experimenter then collected those envelopes before the subjects proceeded to the next task. After completing all 12 interactions (3 partners × 4 tasks), subjects were debriefed and thanked for their participation.

Results

There are two major sets of variables: the impressions subjects formed of each other (their actual ratings of each other) and their postdictions of the impressions they conveyed to each other (their perceptions of the ratings they received).[3] On the basis of the correlations, we constructed two composite variables from the impressions and the postdictions: the mean of friendly, sincere, and liking, and the mean of dominant, confident, and intelligent. We will use the terms *liking* and *competence* for these composite variables.

Because dyad members interacted with each other four times on four different tasks (three of which were counterbalanced), the four different interactions could be represented as a time factor (Time 1, 2, 3, and 4) or as a task factor (teaching, competitive, cooperative, discussion). We conducted all analyses both ways: by time, controlling for task, and by task, controlling for time. Although the results were similar, the time-ordered analyses, which we will present, were somewhat more straightforward.

Table 3 shows the means of the liking and competence variables for impressions and postdictions for each of the four time periods. In all sets of ratings, it was the Time 1 rating that was most noticeably lower than all other ratings. Also, subjects seemed to feel that they made a worse impression than they actually did make, as indicated by the fact that the postdictions means were always lower than the impressions means. This difference was more striking for liking than for competence.

Cronbach Analyses For each of the two variables, liking and competence, a 3 (partners) × 4 (time periods) matrix of impressions and a corresponding 3 × 4 matrix of postdictions was constructed for each subject. Person accuracy was measured by the correlation between the marginal means for the partner variable in the impressions matrix with the corresponding marginal means in the postdictions matrix. Time accuracy was computed analogously. The marginal means for the four time periods in the impressions matrix were correlated with the corresponding means in the postdictions matrix. Differential accuracy (Person × Time Accuracy) was calculated by first computing the interaction residuals (the effects remaining after the row and column effects and the grand mean were subtracted out) of the two matrices. A correlation was then computed between these two sets of 12 residuals.[4] We controlled for task by subtracting the task mean from each score.

Mean accuracy scores. All six accuracy scores were positive (see Table 4). The two person-accuracy scores, however, were small and not sig-

TABLE 3 / Mean Ratings of Impressions and Postdictions

	Liking				Competence			
	Time 1	Time 2	Time 3	Time 4	Time 1	Time 2	Time 3	Time 4
Impressions	14.65	15.89	16.35	16.43	13.98	15.05	15.50	15.66
Postdictions	13.82	15.09	15.67	15.70	13.86	15.03	15.17	15.49
Difference	.83	.80	.68	.73	.12	.02	.33	.17

TABLE 4 / Cronbach Accuracy Correlations

Type of Accuracy	Liking	Competence
Person	.01	.14
Time	.61*	.50*
Differential	.17*	.13

*$p < .05$

nificantly different from zero. Thus, subjects could not accurately differentiate which partners liked them most or least across all time periods considered together, nor could they tell which partners viewed them as more or less competent.

Subjects' time accuracy was much more impressive. Both correlations were significant. This substantial degree of time accuracy was due largely to the fact that subjects generally believed that they came across more favorably as the sessions progressed, and they were right (as indicated in Table 3).

Differential accuracy was not as high as time accuracy, but it was significantly better than chance for liking. Thus, subjects did show some sensitivity to the most specific and differentiating types of distinctions summarized by these various

Cronbach scores: They were able to tell, at least to some degree, how the impressions they conveyed changed over time in different ways with different partners.

Individual differences. We correlated the six Cronbach scores with the seven individual-difference measures: need for approval, the full Self-Monitoring Scale and its three subscales (Briggs, Cheek, & Buss, 1980), public self-consciousness, and social anxiety. Scores on the Acting subscale of the Self-Monitoring Scale correlated negatively with the liking measure of person accuracy, and scores on the Extraversion subscale correlated negatively with the competence measure of person accuracy. Social anxiety was negatively correlated with the liking measure of differential accuracy. Because these were the only 3 significant correlations in a total of 42, it is possible that these results represent chance findings.

Analyses Derived from the Social Relations Model

Variance partitioning. Table 5 shows the partitioning of the variance in ratings of impressions

TABLE 5 / Variance Partitioning of Impressions and Postdictions

Variance Component	Liking			Competence		
	Actor	Partner	Relationship	Actor	Partner	Relationship
Impressions						
Time						
1	.37	.11	.52	.26	.18	.56
2	.49	.09	.43	.52	.00	.48
3	.50	.06	.44	.43	.10	.47
4	.43	.00	.57	.48	.02	.50
Stable	.37	.05	.28	.37	.07	.20
Unstable	.07	.01	.22	.06	.01	.31
Postdictions						
Time						
1	.66	.02	.32	.58	.02	.40
2	.72	.03	.25	.57	.03	.40
3	.71	.03	.26	.65	.00	.35
4	.69	.00	.31	.61	.02	.37
Stable	.64	.01	.14	.56	.03	.10
Unstable	.05	.01	.15	.04	.00	.28

and postdictions into actor, partner, and relationship components. The variance partitioning is presented separately for each time period. Also reported are variance partitionings in which time periods are treated as replications. In those analyses, stable variance indicates the amount of variance that is stable across time, whereas unstable variance is time specific. For impressions, the patterning of the partitioning for liking is similar to the patterning for competence. The actor effect accounts for a substantial proportion of the variance (between 26% and 52%) at each time period for liking and competence. Thus, subjects formed general impressions of their partners' likability that were fairly consistent across their three partners, and they similarly viewed their set of partners as having a certain consistent degree of competence. These general impressions that subjects formed of their set of partners were stable across time.

The partner component for both liking and competence was very small for impressions (ranging from 0% to 18% of the variance). Thus, the impressions conveyed by a given subject to a set of partners were not consistent at all; different partners formed different impressions of the same subject. For liking especially, the largest amounts of partner variance occurred early in the interactions.

Overall, the relationship effect was a large component of the impressions ratings for both liking and competence. The amount of variance that it accounted for at each time period ranged from 43% to 57%. Thus, a substantial proportion of the variance in subjects' impressions of each other is accounted for by the unique impression that subjects form of particular other persons. In the Social Relations Model, error variance is assigned to the relationship components; nonetheless, the amount of relationship variance that is stable across time is still substantial for both liking and competence.

The patterning of the variance partitioning for postdictions was similar to the patterning for impressions except that the actor effect, relative to the relationship effect, accounted for an even greater proportion of the variance, particularly for liking. Thus, for liking, between 66% and 72%

of the variance in subjects' postdictions of how they came across was accounted for by their tendency to assume that they conveyed a consistent level of likableness across all of their partners. This perception of consistency across partners in the liking that was conveyed was also stable across time. For postdictions of competence, too, the actor effect was large (ranging from 57% to 61%). Thus, subjects believed that they came across as having a certain level of competence to all of their partners; this perception was also stable over time.

Comparison of the large actor variance for postdictions (the consistency of the impressions that subjects thought they made across partners) with the small partner effect for impressions (the consistency across different partners in their actual impressions of a given subject) indicates that subjects believed that they made a much more consistent impression across partners than they really did.

The amount of variance in postdictions accounted for by the partner effect was again small for both liking and competence. This means that there was little consistency in the impressions that different subjects thought they had made on a given partner.

Even allowing for error variance, the relationship component of postdictions was substantial. Thus, a sizable proportion for the variance in subjects' postdictions of the impressions they made was accounted for by the unique impressions they thought they had made on specific partners.

Given the large amount of actor variance in both impressions and postdictions, we might ask whether the same response set influenced the two components. The correlations between the actor effect for impressions and the actor effect for postdictions were .72, .88, .90, and .83 for the four time periods, respectively, for liking and .46, .83, .81, and .83, respectively, for competence. (These correlations have been disattenuated for measurement error.) Although there is considerable overlap between the two components, they do not share all of their variance. The Time 1 correlations were the lowest of the set. As further evidence of the discriminant validity of the two components, the personality variables correlated much more strongly with the actor effect in postdictions than with the actor effect in impressions (see discussion to follow).

High correlations between actor effects are not necessarily indicative of a response-set bias. Instead, these correlations can be regarded as indicative of a theoretically meaningful construct, that is, perceived reciprocity at the individual level. A positive correlation between the actor effect for impressions and the actor effect for postdictions indicates that subjects who generally have favorable impressions of their partners tend to believe that their partners have favorable impressions of them. This perceived-reciprocity effect at the individual level has been reported previously (Kenny, 1981). It is not possible on the basis of this data set to choose definitively between the response-set and the perceived-reciprocity interpretations.

Individual differences. Actor effects in impressions and postdictions can be correlated with the individual difference measures. Those correlations were computed separately for each of the four time periods. Because the partner effects were so tiny, correlations with those variables were not computed. Correlations of individual difference measures with relationship effects cannot be computed either, because the relationship components described the dyads rather than the individual dyad members.

Only 2 of the 56 correlations with actor effects in impressions were significant. The correlations of the individual difference measures with the actor effects in postdictions are shown in Table 6.

The strongest set of findings was the negative correlations between social anxiety and postdictions of both liking and competence. Thus, socially anxious subjects believed that they came across as unlikable and incompetent. These negative postdictions tended to become even more negative over time.

Extraverts and actors also showed consistent effects in their postdictions across all four time periods. Both extraverts and actors postdicted that they conveyed a consistently positive impression of their likability and competence. For their postdictions of competence in particular, extraverts' and actors' confidence in their impression-management success became even greater over time.

The only other significant correlations were with need for approval, and again these correlations were stronger for postdictions than for impressions. Subjects high in need for approval tended to postdict that their partners liked them, though their positivity seemed to ebb a bit over time. These subjects also tended to report that they liked their partners, but only the Time 1 correlation was significant.

Individual accuracy. Individual accuracy is a measure of sensitivity to one's general standing in the group. Therefore, it is an especially appropriate ability to assess when there is some consensus among group members in their regard for a particular individual. In this study, there was some consensus among partners in their impressions of a given subject (partner effect in impressions), but the percentage of variance accounted for by this effect was small. We will report the accuracy correlations only for Time 1, when the amount of partner variance was highest. For liking, individual

TABLE 6 / Correlations of Individual Difference Variables with Actor Effects in Postdictions

Individual Difference Variable	Liking				Competence			
	Time 1	Time 2	Time 3	Time 4	Time 1	Time 2	Time 3	Time 4
Need for approval	.46*	.44*	.29	.29	.31	.23	− .02	.00
Self-monitoring	.04	.09	.20	.10	.10	.17	.38	.29
Other-directedness	− .22	− .20	− .14	− .25	− .19	− .13	.09	− .09
Extraversion	.28	.34	.46*	.41*	.24	.29	.36	.42*
Acting	.22	.29	.41*	.37	.34	.42*	.50*	.55*
Public self-consciousness	− .02	.03	.02	− .01	− .07	− .04	− .05	− .16
Social anxiety	− .39	− .42*	− .55*	− .51*	− .48*	− .53*	− .53*	− .63*

*$p < .05$

accuracy was .26 and for competence it was .57. These disattenuated correlations should be interpreted with caution, because the partner effect was relatively small (Malloy & Kenny, 1986). Neither of these correlations was statistically significant.[5]

Dyadic correlations. Dyadic-accuracy correlations for liking and competence at each of the four points in time are shown in Table 7. Seven of the eight accuracy scores are positive, and four of them—including three of the competence correlations—are significant. Thus, subjects did show some significant degree of sensitivity to the unique impressions they were creating on particular other people, especially for impressions of competence.

Table 7 also shows the dyadic-level correlations summarizing subjects' perceptions of reciprocity of impressions. These scores answer such questions as "if Pam has a favorable impression of Bobby, does she think that Bobby has a favorable impression of her?" All eight perceived-reciprocity scores are positive, and six—including all four liking scores—are significant. Perceived reciprocity of liking is uniformly high and increases over time to a peak of .81 at Times 3 and 4. Perceived reciprocity of liking is higher than perceived reciprocity of competence at every time period.

Correlations indicating actual reciprocity of impressions at the dyadic level answer such questions as "if Pam has a favorable impression of Bobby, does Bobby have a favorable impression of Pam?" The eight correlations measure actual reciprocity for liking and competence at each of the four time periods (see Table 7). Although seven of these eight correlations are positive, they are consistently and substantially smaller in magnitude than the corresponding perceived-reciprocity correlations. Thus, subjects believed that their unique impressions of specific partners were reciprocated more than they really were reciprocated.

Correlations summarizing actual reciprocity of postdictions at the dyadic level answer such questions as "if Pam thinks that she is making a good impression on Bobby, does Bobby think that he is making a good impression on Pam?" There is very little evidence of actual reciprocity of postdictions except for the liking scores at Times 1 and 4 (see Table 7). Dyad members seemed to be affectively in synch during their first and last interaction with each other. During those times, subjects believed that their liking for each other was shared, and furthermore, their feelings of liking toward each other and their perceptions of whether they really were liked by each other actually were shared.

Discussion

How Much Accuracy? We were interested in the degree of accuracy that people could achieve at determining how they were viewed by others when their primary source of data came from their social interactions with those other persons. Thus the task we constructed for our subjects was in many ways more difficult than that faced by participants in many previous accuracy studies. Our

TABLE 7 / Dyadic Accuracy and Reciprocity Correlations

Type of Dyadic Relationship	Liking				Competence			
	Time 1	Time 2	Time 3	Time 4	Time 1	Time 2	Time 3	Time 4
Accuracy	.24*	.04	−.06	.40***	.30**	.34***	.34***	.22
Perceived reciprocity of impressions	.53***	.63***	.81***	.81***	.14	.33**	.24*	.34***
Actual reciprocity of impressions	.32*	.19	.04	.39**	.06	.04	−.00	.09
Actual reciprocity of postdictions	.28	−.20	−.03	.38**	−.01	.01	−.04	.22

*p < .10. **p < .05. ***p < .01

subjects interacted with partners whom they had never met and about whom they had no other information. Still, they achieved some level of accuracy, and sometimes a significant degree of accuracy, on almost every measure.

Scores on the Cronbach measures indicated that subjects could tell to a significant degree how the impressions they conveyed to their partners changed over time (time accuracy), and they could also tell how the impressions they conveyed changed over time in different ways with different partners (differential accuracy). Only person accuracy failed to reach statistical significance. Thus, subjects could not tell to any notable degree which partners liked them the most across all interactions, nor could they tell which partners thought they were most competent.

We did not anticipate that subjects would be least successful at person accuracy. In fact, we were surprised that for liking, person accuracy (a main effect) proved to be more difficult than differential accuracy (an interaction effect). Therefore, we can only speculate about the reasons for these results. Success at determining which partners have formed the most favorable impressions across all interactions may depend on the expressiveness of the partners. Some partners may be characteristically open in expressing their feelings, whereas others may be more inhibited and reserved (e.g., Buck, 1979). Furthermore, some partners may be much more likely than others to try politely to convey positive affect, regardless of their actual feelings (e.g., Rosenthal & DePaulo, 1979a, 1979b). Therefore a partner who appears generally to be responding more favorably than another partner may instead be characteristically more expressive than the other, or more eager to try to convey positive reactions, regardless of her true feelings (cf. Ickes, Patterson, Rajecki, & Tanford, 1982). To be accurate at determining the partner's actual reactions, subjects would have to be adept at knowing when to take a message at face value and when to look for more covert meanings. These are difficult tasks at which people are rarely highly successful (e.g., DePaulo, Stone, & Lassiter, 1985). It follows, then, that person accuracy might not be very high. Characteristic levels of ex-

pressiveness, however, can be distinguished from variations in expressiveness within the same individual (Buck, 1979). That is, a particular individual may be generally inhibited but still show more inhibition in some situations than in others. These intraindividual differences in expressiveness may be apparent to observers; if so, such legibility may account for the significant degree of differential accuracy that subjects are able to achieve.

Because partners did not agree in their impressions of a given subject during any of the last three time periods, individual accuracy could be computed only for the teaching task. For both liking and competence, individual accuracy was positive, and it was especially high for competence; however, neither of these correlations was significant. As in previous research, subjects attained a small to moderate degree of dyadic accuracy. The liking measure of dyadic accuracy peaked during the first and the last interactions. The competence measure was positive for every time period and significantly better than chance for each of the first three. Thus, subjects had some inkling of which particular partners liked them most, and they were significantly successful at determining which particular partners perceived them as most competent.

Of course, this investigation represents just one kind of context for assessing accuracy. It is possible to construct and construe other conditions in which different degrees and patternings of accuracy result and in which individual differences are related to accuracy, impressions, and postdictions in different ways than they were in this study.

As we noted previously, the task of understanding how one is perceived by others has been accorded a significant status in several major social psychological theories. The symbolic-interactionist perspective, for example, posits that the development of the self involves a process of perceiving the attitudes of others toward oneself and then internalizing those attitudes. Subjects in our research did attain some degree of accuracy at perceiving other people's opinions of them. However, their accuracy was far from perfect. Does this mean that the attitudes toward themselves that people ascribe to others, and which they then internalize, are often different from the attitudes that those others really do hold? We think the answer to this question is likely to be yes. However, there are other sources of data about other people's perceptions of oneself besides the raw data of social interactions. For example, people might learn to infer how others perceive them on the basis of third-party communications. The implication for the interpretation of our research is that the level of accuracy that people achieve on the basis of the data available to them in face-to-face interactions may be different from the level they might attain when other information is also available. We think that additional information will ordinarily enhance accuracy (especially individual accuracy), but this awaits empirical confirmation.

We also argued earlier that the accuracy question is relevant to the impression-management perspective on social behavior. According to this perspective, people often try to convey a particular impression of themselves to others. While interacting, they monitor the reactions of others. If those reactions deviate from the reactions they would like to elicit and believe they can elicit, then they will alter their self-presentation strategies in an attempt to attain a closer fit. Once again, the fact that subjects in our research achieved a level of accuracy that was respectable, but far from perfect, raises an interesting question: Are people often altering their self-presentational strategies on the basis of reactions to themselves that they have misperceived? We think the answer to this question also is yes. However, we also want to acknowledge that an impression-management perspective does not necessarily assume that people are constantly monitoring the reactions of others. Rather, the motivation to monitor depends on both the desire to make a particular impression and the confidence that one can succeed at doing so. When individuals are unconcerned about the opinions of their interaction partner, they will not bother to monitor that person's reactions. They will also neglect to monitor when they are confident that they will succeed at conveying exactly the impression they wish to convey. It is only when the motivation to convey a particular impression is high,

but the confidence in succeeding at doing so is not high, that careful monitoring of the reactions of others is likely to occur (Schlenker, 1984; Schlenker & Leary, 1985).

In the experimental setting we constructed, we believe that the desire to convey a favorable impression was heightened by the fact that subjects knew they were being evaluated. In addition, the fact that their partners were persons with whom they had no prior acquaintance is likely to have dampened their confidence in their ability to convey just the right impression. Because subjects presumably experienced the appropriate combination of high motivation to create a particular impression and low or moderate confidence in their ability to do so, we believe that they monitored the reactions of their interaction partners and that some of the accuracy they achieved was a function of that monitoring. However, we also believe that even in this context, in which we tried to make subjects highly dependent on specific behavioral feedback from others as a source of information as to how they were coming across, subjects could have attained some accuracy without paying any attention at all to the reactions of their partners. We address this issue next.

Mechanisms for Achieving Accuracy   Of the numerous mechanisms subjects may have used to attain accuracy without attending to the specific reactions of their partners, one in particular has been underscored in earlier critiques of accuracy research: the mechanism of assumed similarity (e.g., Cronbach, 1955). As applied to our research, the assumed-similarity interpretation is that subjects may have used their impressions of their partners as a guide to postdicting the impressions of themselves that they conveyed to their partners. Specifically, subjects may have assumed that their partners formed the same impressions of the subjects as the subjects formed of their partners. As Tagiuri, Blake, and Bruner (1953) have pointed out, if subjects assume reciprocity, and reciprocity does indeed occur, then subjects' judgments will be accurate. Because we can measure both actual reciprocity and perceived reciprocity, in addition to accuracy, the possibility that assumed similarity might have accounted for subjects' accuracy can be directly assessed. The dyadic liking accuracy that subjects attained at Times 1 and 4 could indeed have resulted from the assumed-similarity mechanism. Subjects believed that their liking for their partners was reciprocated at every time period, and at Times 1 and 4 it really was reciprocated. Dyadic competence accuracy, however, which was even higher than liking accuracy for three of the four time periods, could not have been attained in the same way because impressions of competence were not significantly reciprocated at any time period.

In addition to the assumed-similarity mechanism, there are other processes that people can use to achieve accuracy without attending at all to the specific behavioral reactions of their interaction partners. For example, subjects might observe their own behavior and consider how that behavior might be interpreted by the other person. People sometimes realize instantly and accurately, and without looking to others for feedback, that a particular thing they just said or did made them look unlovable or inept. Another mechanism might be one in which subjects assume that most people view others as likable and competent. If they then guess that regardless of how they behave their partners will view them as likable and competent, and if their partners do indeed regard them in those ways, then subjects' postdictions will be accurate. Still another possibility is that subjects might assume that their personalities are immediately apparent to others. If partners' impressions of the subjects match subjects' own self-theories, then individual accuracy will result.

Central to most of the mechanisms just described is the hypothesis that subjects assume substantial correspondence between their own theories and perceptions and the theories and perceptions of others. And in fact, in research derived from a symbolic-interactionist perspective, one of the strongest relations is between subjects' self-perceptions and their perceptions of how they are viewed by others (Shrauger & Schoeneman, 1979). In contrast, the links involving the actual views of others (i.e., the links between self-perceptions and the actual views of others, and between the perceived views of others and the ac-

tual views of others) are demonstrably weaker. If people do indeed assume strong correspondence between their perceptions and others', then perhaps they habitually fail to attend closely to the ongoing reactions of others and ultimately fail to learn as much as they might about how to interpret those reactions. Consistent with these speculations are the individual difference findings from this study, in which even those subjects hypothesized to be especially attuned to the responses of others (e.g., subjects high in public self-consciousness) showed no special skill at understanding those reactions.

Inflated Impressions of Consistency in Impressions Conveyed: Can We Account for Them? The two largest variance components in the ratings of both impressions and postdictions were actor effects and relationship effects. Partners' impressions of subjects were primarily accounted for by their tendency to see all subjects as characterized by a certain level of likability and competence (actor effect) and by their tendency to form unique impressions of the likability and competence of particular subjects (relationship effect). Similarly, subjects' postdictions of the impressions they conveyed were accounted for primarily by their strong tendency to postdict that they conveyed similar impressions of likability and competence to all their partners, and by a somewhat less striking tendency to postdict that they conveyed unique impressions of likability and competence to particular partners. For both types of ratings, impressions and postdictions, partner effects were remarkably small. Thus, it was not the case that different subjects believed they conveyed similar impressions to a given partner. More interestingly, there was little consistency in the impressions that different partners formed of the same subject.

Why is it that partners did not agree in their impressions of a given subject, and under what conditions might they be expected to agree? Perhaps most important is the fact that subjects and partners interacted one-on-one. Different partners may have elicited different behaviors from the same subject; they then would have had different data bases to inform their judgments. In contexts in which partners have available to them a common store of information about the subject (e.g., group interviews), agreement among partners in their evaluations of a given subject might increase. Kenny and La Voie's (1984) review of partner effects in previous research is consistent with this suggestion.

Partners might also be especially unlikely to agree in their reactions to a given subject when the subject's behavior is highly scripted and therefore uninformative about his or her personality. In this research, the behavior of the participants assigned to the role of teacher was much more highly scripted than that of the participants assigned to be learners. Teachers were told exactly what to say during the lesson, and they were not allowed to give individuating feedback even when administering the quiz at the end of the lesson. Learners, in contrast, were not told what to say; their behavior during the teaching task was therefore more highly informative about their likability and especially their competence. Because the division of participants into teachers, learners, and participants assigned to no special role results in a very small number of subjects for each category, we did not report results separately for each of these groups. However, the trends that occurred in those data were consistent with the hypothesis under consideration. Specifically, there was some agreement among different teachers in their perceptions of a given learner, particularly in their assessments of the learner's competence during the teaching task. However, there was virtually no agreement at all among learners in their perceptions of a given teacher.

Agreement among partners might also be increased by increasing the duration of their interactions with the subject or by recruiting partners who have known the subject for a longer period of time and who share their impressions of the subject with each other. A final possibility is that genuine cross-situational consistencies in behavior are nonexistent or exceedingly rare (e.g., Mischel & Peake, 1982); therefore, it is inappropriate to expect partners who have observed different samples of a person's behavior—especially such brief samples—to agree in their assessments of that person.

In this experiment, the low level of consistency among partners in their reactions to a given subject, regardless of its causes, is especially interesting in light of the high level of consistency that subjects believed characterized the impressions they conveyed to different partners (cf. Reeder, 1985). Why did subjects believe that they conveyed such similar impressions to all of their partners, when their partners in fact agreed hardly at all in their impressions of the subjects?

One possibility is that subjects' behaviors were consistent across all of their partners, but different partners' interpretations of those behaviors differed markedly. Subjects could have made mistaken postdictions of consistency if they attended primarily to their own behavior or if they failed to attend to, or understand, the differences in the reactions of the different partners.

The most plausible explanation, we believe, is related to the layperson's firmly held belief in personality consistency. Armed with this theory of personality consistency, along with their well-developed self-schemata, subjects may have simply assumed that their true personalities, as they perceived them, would be readily apparent to whomever they interacted with, no matter how briefly.[6]

A Paradigm for Studying Accuracy   In their analysis of theory and research on the concept of accuracy in social judgment, Hastie and Rasinski (in press) conclude by recommending that research on accuracy should include a criterion of accuracy, measured independently of subjects' judgments, against which subjects' judgments can be compared. They also recommend the use of accuracy scores that can be decomposed into conceptually meaningful components. We concur with their suggestions and have followed them in this study. By use of the Social Relations Model, the outcomes of social perception can be studied (levels of individual and dyadic accuracy) as well as some of the processes that might mediate these outcomes (e.g., assumed similarity). We think that the paradigm we used can be adapted to the study of other types of accuracy (e.g., accuracy of self-perceptions and of other perceptions) in addition to the type of accuracy we investigated in this study.

REFERENCES

Anderson, R. D. (1984) *Measuring social self-perception: How accurately can individuals predict how others view them?* Unpublished doctoral dissertation, University of Connecticut, Storrs.

Ausubel, D. P., & Schiff, H. M. (1955). Some intrapersonal and interpersonal determinants of individual differences in socioempathic ability among adolescents. *Journal of Social Psychology, 41,* 39–56.

Ausubel, D. P., Schiff, H. M., & Glaser, E. B. (1952). A preliminary study of developmental trends in socioempathy: Accuracy of perception of own and others' sociometric status. *Child Development, 23,* 111–128.

Baumeister, R. F. (1982). A self-presentational view of social phenomena. *Psychological Bulletin, 91,* 3–26.

Bohrnstedt, G. W., & Felson, R. B. (1983). Explaining the relations among children's actual and perceived performances and self-esteem: A comparison of several causal models. *Journal of Personality and Social Psychology, 45,* 43–56.

Briggs, S. R., Check, J. M., & Buss, A. H. (1980). An analysis of the Self-Monitoring Scale. *Journal of Personality and Social Psychology, 38,* 679–686.

Bronfenbrenner, U., Harding, J., & Gallwey, M. (1958). The measurement of skill in social perception. In D. C. McClelland, A. L. Baldwin, U. Bronfenbrenner, & F. L. Strodtbeck (Eds.), *Talent and society* (pp. 29–111). Princeton, NJ: Van Nostrand.

Buck, R. (1979). Individual differences in nonverbal sending accuracy and electrodermal responding: The interalizing–externalizing dimension. In R. Rosenthal (Ed.), *Skill in nonverbal communication* (pp. 140–170). Cambridge, MA: Oelgeschlager, Gunn, & Hain.

Cooley, C. H. (1902). *Human nature and the social order* (rev. ed.). New York: Scribner's.

Cronbach, L. J. (1953). Correlations between persons as a research tool. In O. H. Mowrer (Ed.), *Psychotherapy: Theory and research* (pp. 376–389). New York: Ronald Press.

Cronbach, L. J. (1955). Processes affecting scores on "understanding of others" and "assumed similarity." *Psychological Bulletin, 52,* 177–193.

Cronbach, L. J. (1958). Proposals leading to analytic treatment of social perception scores. In R. Tagiuri & L. Petrullo (Eds.), *Person perception and interpersonal behavior* (pp. 353–379). Stanford, CA: Stanford University Press.

Cronbach, L. J., & Gleser, G. C. (1953). Assessing similarity between profiles *Psychological Bulletin, 50,* 456–474.

Cronbach, L. J., Gleser, G. C., Nanda, H., & Rajaratnam, N. (1972). *The dependability of behavioral measurements: Theory of generalizability for scores and profiles.* New York: Wiley.

Crowne, D. P., & Marlowe, D. (1964). *The approval motive: Studies in evaluative dependence.* New York: Wiley.

DePaulo, B. M. (1978). Accuracy in predicting situational variations in help-seekers' responses. *Personality and Social Psychology Bulletin, 4,* 330–333.

DePaulo, B. M., Stone, J. I., & Lassiter, G. D. (1985). Deceiving and detecting deceit. In B. R. Schlenker (Ed.), *The self and social life* (pp. 323–370). New York: McGraw-Hill.

Felson, R. B. (1981). Self- and reflected appraisal among football players: A test of the Meadian hypothesis. *Social Psychology Quarterly, 44,* 116–126.

Fenigstein, A., Scheier, M. F., & Buss, A. H. (1975). Public and private self-consciousness: Assessment and theory. *Journal of Consulting and Clinical Psychology, 43,* 522–527.

Funder, D. C. (1987). Errors and mistakes: Evaluating the accuracy of social judgment. *Psychological Bulletin, 101,* 75–90.

Gage, N. L., & Cronbach, L. J. (1955). Conceptual and methodological problems in interpersonal perception. *Psychological Review, 62,* 411–422.

Goffman, E. (1959). *The presentation of self in every day life.* Garden City, NY: Doubleday.

Harackiewicz, J. M., & DePaulo, B. M. (1982). Accuracy of person perception: A component analysis according to Cronbach. *Personality and Social Psychology Bulletin, 8,* 247–256.

Hastie, R., & Rasinski, K. A. (in press). The concept of accuracy in social judgment. In D. Bar-Tal & A. Kruglanski (Eds.), *The social psychology of knowledge.* Cambridge, England: Cambridge University Press.

Ickes, W., Patterson, M. L., Rajecki, D. W., & Tanford, S. (1982). Behavioral and cognitive consequences of reciprocal versus compensatory responses to preinteraction expectancies. *Social Cognition, 1,* 160–190.

Israel, J. (1958). Self-evaluation in groups. *Acta Sociologica, 3,* 29–47.

Jones, E. E. (1964). *Ingratiation.* New York: Appleton.

Kenny, D. A. (1981). Interpersonal perception: A multivariate round robin analysis. In M. B. Brewer & B. E. Collins (Eds.), *Knowing and validating in the social sciences: A tribute to Donald T. Campbell* (pp. 288–309). San Francisco: Jossey-Bass.

Kenny, D. A., & Albright, L. (1986). *Accuracy in interpersonal perception: A social relations analysis.* Unpublished manuscript, University of Connecticut, Storrs.

Kenny, D. A., & La Voie, L. (1984). The social relations model. In L. Berkowitz (Ed.), *Advances in experimental social psychology* (Vol. 18, pp. 141–182). Orlando, FL: Academic Press.

Kinch, J. W. (1963). A formalized theory of the self-concept. *American Journal of Sociology, 68*, 481–486.

Leary, T. F. (1957). *The interpersonal diagnosis of personality.* New York: Ronald Press.

Malloy, T. E., & Kenny, D. A. (1986). The Social Relations Model: An integrative method for personality research. *Journal of Personality, 54*, 101–127.

Mead, G. H. (1925). The genesis of the self and social control. *International Journal of Ethics, 35*, 251–273.

Mead, G. H. (1934). *Mind, self, and society.* Chicago: University of Chicago Press.

Mischel, W., & Peake, P. K. (1982). Beyond déjà vu in the search for cross-situational consistency. *Psychological Review, 89*, 730–855.

Norman, W. T., & Goldberg, L. R. (1966). Raters, ratees, and randomness in personality structure. *Journal of Personality and Social Psychology, 4*, 681–691.

Orpen, C., & Bush, R. (1974). The lack of congruence between self-concept and public image. *Journal of Social Psychology, 93*, 145–146.

Passini, F. T., & Norman, W. T. (1966). A universal conception of personality structure. *Journal of Personality and Social Psychology, 4*, 44–49.

Reeder, G. D. (1985). Implicit relations between dispositions and behaviors: Effects on dispositional attribution. In J. H. Harvey & G. Weary (Eds.), *Attribution: Basic issues and applications.* Orlando, FL: Academic Press.

Reeder, L. G., Donohue, G. A., & Biblarz, A. (1960). Conceptions of self and others. *American Journal of Sociology, 66*, 153–159.

Rosenberg, S., & Sedlak, A. (1972). Structural representations of implicit personality theory. In L. Berkowitz (Ed.), *Advances in experimental social psychology* (Vol. 6, pp. 235–297). New York: Academic Press.

Rosenthal, R., & DePaulo, B. M. (1979a). Sex differences in accommodation in nonverbal communication. In R. Rosenthal (Ed.), *Skill in nonverbal communication.* Cambridge, MA: Oelgeschlager, Gunn, & Hain.

Rosenthal, R., & DePaulo, B. M. (1979b). Sex differences in eavesdropping on nonverbal cues. *Journal of Personality and Social Psychology, 37*, 273–285.

Scheier, M. F., & Carver, C. S. (1981). Private and public aspects of the self. In L. Wheeler (Ed.), *Review of personality and social psychology* (Vol. 2, pp. 189–216). Beverly Hills, CA: Sage.

Schlenker, B. R. (1980). *Impression management.* Monterey, CA: Brooks/Cole.

Schlenker, B. R. (1984). Identities, identifications, and relationships. In V. J. Derlega (Ed.), *Communication, intimacy and close relations* (pp. 71–104). New York: Academic Press.

Schlenker, B. R. (Ed.). (1985). *The self and social life.* New York: McGraw-Hill.

Schlenker, B. R., & Leary, M. R. (1982). Social anxiety and self-presentation: A conceptualization and model. *Psychological Bulletin, 92*, 641–669.

Schlenker, B. R., & Leary, M. R. (1985). Social anxiety and communication about the self. *Journal of Language and Social Psychology, 4*, 171–192.

Sherwood, J. J. (1965). Self-identity and referent others. *Sociometry, 28*, 66–81.

Shrauger, J. S., & Schoeneman, T. J. (1979). Symbolic interactionist view of self-concept: Through the looking glass darkly. *Psychological Bulletin, 86*, 549–573.

Snodgrass, S. E. (1985). Women's intuition: The effect of subordinate role on interpersonal sensitivity. *Journal of Personality and Social Psychology, 49*, 146–155.

Snyder, M. (1974). The self-monitoring of expressive behavior. *Journal of Personality and Social Psychology, 30*, 526–547.

Snyder, M. (1979). Self-monitoring processes. In L. Berkowitz (Ed.), *Advances in experimental social psychology* (Vol. 12, pp. 85–128). New York: Academic Press.

Swann, W. B., Jr. (1984). Quest for accuracy in person perception: A matter of pragmatics. *Psychological Review, 91*, 457–477.

Tagiuri, R. (1952). Relational analysis: An extension of sociometric method with emphasis upon social perception. *Sociometry, 15*, 91–104.

Tagiuri, R., Blake, R. R., & Bruner, J. S. (1953). Some determinants of the perception of positive and negative feelings on others. *Journal of Abnormal and Social Psychology, 48*, 585–592.

Tagiuri, R., Bruner, J. S., & Blake, R. R. (1958). On the relation between feelings and perception of feelings among members of small groups. In E. E. Maccoby, T. M. Newcomb, & E. L. Hartley (Eds.), *Readings in social psychology* (3rd ed.). New York: Holt, Rinehart & Winston.

Tedeschi, J. T. (Ed.). (1981). *Impression management theory and social psychological research.* New York: Academic Press.

Walhood, D. S., & Klopfer, W. G. (1971). Congruence between self-concept and public image. *Journal of Consulting and Clinical Psychology, 37*, 148–150.

Warner, R. M., Kenny, D. A., & Stoto, M. (1979). A new round robin analysis of variance for social interaction data. *Journal of Personality and Social Psychology, 37*, 1742–1757.

NOTES

1. Cronbach has contributed numerous articles on the analysis of accuracy data (e.g., Cronbach, 1953, 1955, 1958; Cronbach & Gleser, 1953; Gage & Cronbach, 1955). We will draw primarily from his 1955 work, in which he presented this more influential terms for this.

2. Private self-consciousness, which is one of the subscales of the Self-Consciousness Scale, was also assessed. However, we did not believe this construct was relevant to the issues in our study, and all correlations with the subscale were nonsignificant.

3. The distributions of all raw variables were negatively skewed; therefore the variables were recoded. Ratings of 11 through 20 on these 20-point scales were left unchanged. Ratings of 9 were recoded to 10; ratings of 5 through 8 were recoded to 9, and ratings of 1 through 4 were recoded to 8. We chose this recoding strategy instead of a transformation for the following reasons: First, common transformations (e.g., square root) remove positive skew, and second, we wanted to avoid creating noninteger values.

4. Cronbach (1955) did not actually recommend the procedure of correlating the interaction residuals. Instead, he suggested the computation of separate time-accuracy scores (or item accuracies, in his example) for each partner, which could then be averaged. However, such a method would confound time accuracy with differential accuracy.

5. Because these correlations were for Time 1 only, we did not need to control for task. Therefore we computed the correlations for each group and tested whether the mean was significantly different from zero.

6. David Funder (personal communication, March 11, 1986) has offered a different interpretation of these results. He suggests that "the reason people overestimate the agreement others will have about them is that the people most important to them in daily life, those who know them well, generally *do* tend to agree with each other very well. And even with first acquaintants, it is reasonable to expect that they will eventually come to agree with each other well as they come to know the subject better. So the subject is overgeneralizing in an appropriate way by acting as if these acquaintances agree. They either will, eventually, or else they won't have any lengthy contact with the subject anyway—so who cares what they think?" Still another perspective has been contributed by Cronbach (1955), who has argued that statistically, under conditions of uncertainty, perceivers will do better to make predictions that are less variable rather than more differentiated.

This article was written while Bella M. DePaulo was visiting at the University of Florida and David A. Kenny was visiting at Arizona State University. We thank these universities for their support. Thanks are also due to the National Institute of Mental Health for grant support to Bella M. DePaulo and David A. Kenny and to the National Academy of Education for grant support to Bella M. DePaulo. In addition, we thank Mark Alicke, Lee Cronbach, David Funder, Thomas Malloy, Glenn Reeder, Barry Schlenker, and William Swann for helpful comments on an earlier version of this article, Sally Snodgrass for sharing unpublished data, and Carol Litowitz and Kerry Marsh for their help with this research.

William Webb is currently at Texas A&M University.

CRITICAL THINKING QUESTIONS

1. This study was a laboratory experiment that examined the initial interaction of two strangers. How could a study be conducted that would examine the same questions by using friends in a more natural setting (e.g., the changes that take place during the development of friendship)?

2. What are the implications of the findings of this study? Should we be confident of our ability to judge the impressions that we convey to other people? How can we increase the reliability of the impressions that we actually give to others?

3. Do you have a general impression of how people see you? Or does it depend on the specific situation you are in (in a class, at work, with friends, at home with family)? Have you ever been aware of a change in the impression you made based upon some experience you have had?

4. What factors do you feel may influence the accuracy of the impressions that a person conveys to others? For example, do you think that one's level of self-esteem may have an impact? Is there any way to test this or any other factors that you feel may be important?

Chapter Three

SOCIAL COGNITION

THE WORLD AROUND us presents a complex array of information. It is humanly impossible to pay attention to all the information available to us due simply to sheer volume. So, given all of this information, how do we make sense of it? This chapter on social cognition examines some of the ways that people process information about themselves and others in order to make judgments.

A major interest of social psychologists is how we mentally process the information that we receive. Decisions are not always based on an impartial evaluation of all the information presented. Instead, due to time constraints or information overload, we may use a set of techniques called *cognitive strategies* (or mental shortcuts) to process the information. These commonly used shortcuts help us to make sense of our world, but unfortunately, they are often prone to error. Article 7, "Seven Quick Ways to Kid Yourself," discusses some of the common strategies people use to evaluate their world and the consequences of using them.

Social cognition also deals with how we make sense of ourselves. One interesting line of research has addressed the relationship between cognition and emotion. Specifically, do our mental processes influence what we feel, or is it the other way around: that is, Do our feelings shape our mental processes? Article 8, "Cognitive, Social, and Psychological Determinants of Emotional State," is a classic investigation of the relationship between thought processes and emotion. The methods and findings of the study make interesting reading, but its implications are even more important: Is it possible to change the emotions we experience simply by changing the cognitive labels that we attach to them?

One final issue addressed in this chapter is the difficulty of changing social cognitions once they have been formed. Given that we may use various mental strategies to process information and form beliefs, does it follow that these beliefs are hard to change? Or do we constantly revise our beliefs based upon new information that we encounter? The final reading in this section, Article 9, "Persistence of Inaccurate Beliefs about the Self," provides an experimental demonstration of how difficult it is to change initial, inaccurate beliefs even when clear evidence contradicts them. The study, conducted in a school setting, provides some interesting (and disquieting) implications as to how this process may affect students' beliefs about their academic abilities.

ARTICLE 7 _____

We are constantly making decisions. Some are important, and some are trivial. Very often, we must make decisions under less than ideal circumstances. Sometimes, we simply don't have the time to sit down and methodically work through all of the pros and cons involved. At other times, we don't have all of the facts and must make a decision based on less than perfect information. At still other times, we simply use mental shortcuts to help make a complex situation a little easier to handle.

In "Floundering in Fallacy," Offir presents several of these shortcuts (or cognitive strategies) that people use to help them make decisions. While using these strategies makes it easier to make decisions, they often lead to incorrect or poor decisions, which have some serious consequences. To the extent that these ineffectual strategies can be eliminated or reduced, better, more informed decisions may result.

Floundering in Fallacy
Seven Quick Ways to Kid Yourself
■ Carole Wade Offir

What a piece of work is man! How noble in reason! How infinite in faculties! in form and moving how express and admirable! in action, how like an angel! in apprehension, how like a god! the beauty of the world! the paragon of animals!

Hamlet's paean to man is so stirring, one is tempted to believe it. But real men and women; though capable of being noble and reasonable, are finite in faculty. Faced with the task of judging the past or predicting the future, they frequently bog down in biases and flounder in fallacies, revealing themselves to the flawed gods.

Baruch Fischhoff has demonstrated that when we have to judge a decision made in the past, we scrutinize it through the clarifying spectacles of hindsight. We're apt to condemn decision makers who made mistakes instead of trying to understand why their decisions seemed right at the time. This self-deceiving habit of hindsight makes us less realistic in assessing future events than we should be.

Several of Fischhoff's colleagues have studied other psychological screens that make us see the future dimly. They are concerned with how we arrive at generalizations and how we decide that one event is very likely to happen while another is not. Despite our best efforts to be rational, we consistently make certain kinds of errors without realizing it. Some examples:

THE GAMBLER'S FALLACY

Suppose you toss a coin four times. Each time it comes up heads. What are the odds that it will come up tails if you throw it again?

Many people think the likelihood of getting tails on the fifth toss is greater than 50 percent. But that is impossible: if the coin is fair, the probability of tails (or heads) is one half, no matter what happened on previous tosses. Of course, over the very long run, 50 percent of the tosses will result in heads, but that need not be true in the short run.

Reprinted from *Psychology Today*, 1975 (April) *8*, 66–68. Reprinted with permission from *Psychology Today Magazine*. Copyright © 1975 (PT Partners, L.P.).

Similarly, if you ask people which random sequence of heads and tails is more likely, HTTHTH or HHHTTT, they usually choose the first one. In fact, the sequences are equally likely. To those who make the error, "random" seems to mean "without apparent pattern."

As psychologists Amos Tversky and Daniel Kahneman put it, "The gambler feels that the fairness of the coin entitles him to expect that any deviation in one direction will soon be cancelled by a corresponding deviation in the other. Even the fairest of coins, however, given the limitations of its memory and moral sense, cannot be as fair as the gambler expects it to be."

Misunderstanding about the laws of chance can dominate a gambler's betting strategy. A person at the roulette wheel may feel confident that red will win after black has won two or three times in a row, and feel cheated if, after he bets on red, the ball lands once again on black.

The gambler's fallacy has many consequences outside the casino. For example, the parents of three boys may decide to have another child only because they're sure they're due for a girl. Subjectively, the odds may seem to be 80 or 90 percent. Statistically, though, the likelihood of a girl is the same as it always was—about 50 percent. Anytime you feel that it's time for a turn in luck, either way, better see if you're caught in the gambler's fallacy.

FAITH IN SMALL NUMBERS

The gambler's fallacy is really one variation of a more general misconception, that a small random sample of things or events will have all the characteristics of the large population from which it was drawn. This belief is sometimes justified; often it is not.

When we blindly assume that a small group is representative of a larger one, we may reach unwarranted conclusions on the basis of what we know about the small group. Thus, after hearing only a few man-on-the-street interviews, we may go around proclaiming that "most people" hold such and such a view. Scientists, who are supposed to know better, also sometimes generalize after studying only a handful of subjects. They may be too quick to accept positive results from a small study, only to find later that their results can't be replicated by anyone else. Or, they may become needlessly discouraged when they fail to find what they expected, and decide not to pursue what could turn out to be a worthwhile line of research. And many an executive reaches for "mother-in-law data" and makes decisions on the basis of a sample of one in his own tight little environment.

FORGETTING REGRESSION

If you compile a list of the tallest men in your community (using some arbitrary cutoff point), and then list the heights of their sons, you'll find that the sons are, *on the average,* shorter than the fathers. Similarly, if you compare the shortest men in the community with their sons, the sons will be, on the average, taller than the fathers. This statistical phenomenon is called "regression toward the mean."

There are many everyday instances of regression toward the mean, but most people don't recognize them. For example, a teacher may expect students who get very high grades on an exam to score just as well on the next test, and expect students who did very poorly to do just as poorly the next time. But because of regression toward the mean, after the second test the teacher is likely to be a bit disappointed in the first group and pleasantly surprised by the second. Keep in mind that we're talking here about group averages, not the score of each individual.

Tversky and Kahneman relate this problem to people's belief that a predicted outcome (e.g., scores on the second test) must be representative of, or similar to, the factor we use to make the prediction (e.g., scores on the first test). When the prediction turns out to be wrong, we search for the cause. In our classroom example, the teacher may conclude that she's doing something right with the dull group (praising or punishing them) and something wrong with the bright group, when actually, her efforts may have had little to do with the results.

THE AVAILABILITY TRAP

People overestimate the probability of an event when it's easy to think of relevant examples or imagine plausible scenarios. Tversky and Kahneman call this the problem of availability.

Consider a simple question. If a word is selected at random from an English text, which alternative is more likely: that it will start with the letter *k* or that it will have *k* as its third letter? Tversky and Kahneman found that most people think *k* is more likely to be in the first position. In truth, a typical text contains twice as many words with *k* in the third position as it does words beginning with *k*. Apparently, people fail to recognize this fact because it's easier to think of words starting with *k*.

In everyday life, this sort of error may be quite common. Thus, no matter how many times we hear that statistically speaking, airplane travel is safer than car travel, none of us really quite believes it. We can all remember specific airplane disasters, but it's hard to recall a series of automobile accidents involving a large number of victims. So airplane fatalities seem more likely. You may have noticed that after an airplane crash occurs, you feel particularly uneasy about flying, because subjectively, the odds of your dying in an airplane seem to be extremely high.

People who practice a profession requiring them to make intuitive predictions about the future ought to be aware of this bias. Physicians, clinical psychologists, sportscasters, and political analysts may base a prediction on a past event that is salient, while ignoring others that are important but less memorable. The late Sewell Avery, while head of Montgomery Ward, kept the company stagnant for decades while waiting for another depression.

ILLUSIONS OF CORRELATION

Suppose you want to know whether marijuana use by teenagers is related to delinquency. A statistician would tell you to consider four kinds of students: marijuana users who are delinquents, marijuana users who aren't delinquents, delinquents who don't use marijuana, and nondelinquents who don't use marijuana. If you take a random sample of students and tally the number of cases in each of these categories, you can apply a very simple mathematical formula to find out if there is a relationship between delinquency and pot.

Unfortunately, when people deal with problems of this sort, they tend to rely on the first category alone, looking at positive instances but not negative ones. Consequently, they may see an association where none exists. This bias is probably traceable to the availability trap; confirming instances are more noticeable or easier to recall than disconfirming ones. Much of our unconscious conditioning in everyday life invites us into illusions of correlation; the conventional wisdom of every profession is loaded with such confusion.

OVERESTIMATING COMPOUND PROBABILITIES

This psychological screen is a little harder for the layperson to understand, but can be explained with an example used by psychologist Paul Slovic. Suppose we wish to know the probability that a nuclear power plant will have a nuclear accident. The plant uses a multiple safeguard system; an accident can occur only if several components of the system break down all at once or in rapid succession.

If we assume that these component breakdowns are independent of each other, we can calculate the probability of an accident by *multiplying* all the component probabilities. Thus, if there were only two components and the probability of each breaking down was 1/100, the probability of an accident would be only one in 10 thousand ($1/100 \times 1/100 = 1/10,000$).

But researchers find that people seem to estimate the probability of an event as if they're *adding* component probabilities, not multiplying them. That means they overestimate the likelihood of the event. When the possible outcome is a nuclear disaster, this bias may be a good thing. But there are other situations where it is not. Much of the caution that binds us into drab lives can be traced to adding the probabilities of disaster.

MISUSING INFORMATION

There are many ways in which we fail to evaluate information correctly when we make predictions or decisions. In one study, Kahneman and Tversky found that people who had to guess which field a graduate student was in relied on a phony "personality sketch" and ignored what they knew about the relative number of students enrolled in each field. The sketch was purportedly based on a psychologist's evaluation of the student's responses to a projective test given several years earlier. It depicted him as intelligent, lacking in true creativity, with a need for order and clarity. More than 95 percent of the subjects said the student was more likely to be in computer science than in the humanities or education.

Apparently the judges in this study matched the description to their stereotyped preconceptions about the kinds of students enrolled in computer science and the humanities. They did not realize that even if most of the computer-science students had these characteristics and most of the humanities and education students did not, the odds that the student in question was in the humanities or education could still be high, simply because there are many more people enrolled in those fields.

The participants later indicated that they held projective tests in very low esteem. But that did not prevent them from using information supposedly derived from such a test. Information that appears to be specific in nature has an influence on us that is out of proportion to its true value.

If the mental pitfalls that show up in psychological experiments also snare us in ordinary situations, it is clear why we often make faulty decisions when serving on juries, buying a car, advising a patient, gambling in Las Vegas, or investing money. Our shortcomings have prompted some social scientists to suggest that we turn certain problems over to a more reliable decision maker—the computer. There is persuasive evidence that a computer, working with a mathematical model of decision-making, can make some kinds of predictions more accurately than human beings. The computer lets us reject the standard psychological screens.

Most decisions, though, will remain in human hands, if only because we enjoy the sense of responsibility and power we derive from making them. Therefore, we ought to learn what our biases are, and try to overcome them.

CRITICAL THINKING QUESTIONS

1. Think of examples based on your own experience or that of people you know that illustrate each of the fallacies discussed in the article.
2. Have you encountered any other sources of bias in addition to the ones discussed in the text? Give examples.
3. Given that many of these biases are quite common, are there ways to reduce their effects? Would simply educating people about their existence and how they operate help? Or would something else be needed? Is it the case that maybe people can't be changed after all, that these biases are part of human nature? Defend your position.

ARTICLE 8 _____

How do you know what emotion you are experiencing? Ask that question of someone who has just learned that he or she has won the lottery, and the answer would undoubtedly be "thrilled," "excited," "overjoyed," or some such adjective to describe a very positive emotional state. Ask if it is actually anger that the winner is feeling, and he or she probably would look at you as if you were crazy. But how does that person *know* what emotion he or she is feeling?

The work that follows by Schachter and Singer is a classic study that addresses what determines a person's emotional state. Briefly, the authors' findings suggest that what we call *emotion* is partly due to some sort of physiological arousal. However, what we feel is also determined by the cognitive label that we attach to that physiological arousal. According to this approach, a person who experiences some sort of physiological arousal might subjectively experience one of two very different emotional states, either anger or euphoria, depending on how he or she labeled the experience. The article discusses the process as well as some of the conditions that result when this process occurs.

While reading the article, think of its implications: Is cognition a necessary part of emotion? Without it, what (if anything) would we feel? What about newborn children? Since their cognitive abilities are not yet fully developed, does that mean that they don't experience emotions?

Cognitive, Social, and Physiological Determinants of Emotional State[1]

■ Stanley Schachter and Jerome E. Singer

The problem of which cues, internal or external, permit a person to label and identify his own emotional state has been with us since the days that James (1890) first tendered his doctrine that "the bodily changes follow directly the perception of the exciting fact, and that our feeling of the same changes as they occur *is* the emotion" (p. 449). Since we are aware of a variety of feeling and emotion states, it should follow from James' proposition that the various emotions will be accompanied by a variety of differentiable bodily states. Following James' pronouncement, a formidable number of studies were undertaken in search of the physiological differentiators of the emotions. The results, in these early days, were almost uniformly negative. All of the emotional states experimentally manipulated were characterized by a general pattern of excitation of the sympathetic nervous system but there appeared to be no clear-cut physiological discriminators of the various emotions. This pattern of results was so consistent from experiment to experiment that Cannon (1929) offered, as one of the crucial criticisms of the James-Lange theory, the fact that "the same visceral changes occur in very different emotional states and in non-emotional states" (p. 351).

More recent work, however, has given some indication that there may be differentiators. Ax (1953) and Schachter (1957) studied fear and anger. On a large number of indices both of these states were characterized by a similarly high level of autonomic activation but on several indices

Reprinted from *Psychological Review*, 1962, 69, 379–399.

they did differ in the degree of activation. Wolf and Wolff (1947) studied a subject with a gastric fistula and were able to distinguish two patterns in the physiological responses of the stomach wall. It should be noted, though, that for many months they studied their subject during and following a great variety of moods and emotions and were able to distinguish only two patterns.

Whether or not there are physiological distinctions among the various emotional states must be considered an open question. Recent work might be taken to indicate that such differences are at best rather subtle and that the variety of emotion, mood, and feeling states are by no means matched by an equal variety of visceral patterns.

This rather ambiguous situation has led Ruckmick (1936), Hunt, Cole, and Reis (1958), Schachter (1959) and others to suggest that cognitive factors may be major determinants of emotional states. Granted a general pattern of sympathetic excitation as characteristic of emotional states, granted that there may be some differences in pattern from state to state, it is suggested that one labels, interprets, and identifies this stirred-up state in terms of the characteristics of the precipitating situation and one's apperceptive mass. This suggests, then, that an emotional state may be considered a function of a state of physiological arousal[2] and of a cognition appropriate to this state of arousal. The cognition, in a sense, exerts a steering function. Cognitions arising from the immediate situation as interpreted by past experience provide the framework within which one understands and labels his feelings. It is the cognition which determines whether the state of physiological arousal will be labeled as "anger," "joy," "fear," or whatever.

In order to examine the implications of this formulation let us consider the fashion in which these two elements, a state of physiological arousal and cognitive factors, would interact in a variety of situations. In most emotion inducing situations, of course, the two factors are completely interrelated. Imagine a man walking alone down a dark alley; a figure with a gun suddenly appears. The perception-cognition "figure with a gun" in some fashion initiates a state of physio-logical arousal; this state of arousal is interpreted in terms of knowledge about dark alleys and guns and the state of arousal is labeled "fear." Similarly a student who unexpectedly learns that he has made Phi Beta Kappa may experience a state of arousal which he will label "joy."

Let us now consider circumstances in which these two elements, the physiological and the cognitive, are, to some extent, independent. First, is the state of physiological arousal alone sufficient to induce an emotion? Best evidence indicates that it is not. Marañon[3] (1924), in a fascinating study, (which was replicated by Cantril & Hunt, 1932, and Landis & Hunt, 1932) injected 210 of his patients with the sympathomimetic agent adrenalin and then simply asked them to introspect. Seventy-one percent of his subjects simply reported their physical symptoms with no emotional overtones; 29% of the subjects responded in an apparently emotional fashion. Of these the great majority described their feelings in a fashion that Marañon labeled "cold" or "as if" emotions, that is, they made statements such as "I feel *as if* I were afraid" or *"as if* I were awaiting a great happiness." This is a sort of emotional "déjà vu" experience; these subjects are neither happy nor afraid, they feel "as if" they were. Finally a very few cases apparently reported a genuine emotional experience. However, in order to produce this reaction in most of these few cases, Marañon (1924) points out:

> One must suggest a memory with strong affective force but not so strong as to produce an emotion in the normal state. For example, in several cases we spoke to our patients before the injection of their sick children or dead parents and they responded calmly to this topic. The same topic presented later, during the adrenal commotion, was sufficient to trigger emotion. This adrenal commotion places the subject in a situation of "affective imminence" (pp. 307–308).

Apparently, then, to produce a genuinely emotional reaction to adrenalin, Marañon was forced to provide such subjects with an appropriate cognition.

Though Marañon (1924) is not explicit on his procedure, it is clear that his subjects knew that they were receiving an injection and in all likelihood knew that they were receiving adrenalin and probably had some order of familiarity with its effects. In short, though they underwent the pattern of sympathetic discharge common to strong emotional states, at the same time they had a completely appropriate cognition or explanation as to why they felt this way. This, we would suggest, is the reason so few of Marañon's subjects reported any emotional experience.

Consider now a person in a state of physiological arousal for which no immediately explanatory or appropriate cognitions are available. Such a state could result were one covertly to inject a subject with adrenalin or, unknown to him, feed the subject a sympathomimetic drug such as ephedrine. Under such conditions a subject would be aware of palpitations, tremor, face flushing, and most of the battery of symptoms associated with a discharge of the sympathetic nervous system. In contrast to Marañon's (1924) subjects he would, at the same time, be utterly unaware of why he felt this way. What would be the consequence of such a state?

Schachter (1959) has suggested that precisely such a state would lead to the arousal of "evaluative needs" (Festinger, 1954), that is, pressures would act on an individual in such a state to understand and label his bodily feelings. His bodily state grossly resembles the condition in which it has been at times of emotional excitement. How would he label his present feelings? It is suggested, of course, that he will label his feelings in terms of his knowledge of the immediate situation.[4] Should he at the time be with a beautiful woman he might decide that he was wildly in love or sexually excited. Should he be at a gay party, he might, by comparing himself to others, decide that he was extremely happy and euphoric. Should he be arguing with his wife, he might explode in fury and hatred. Or, should the situation be completely inappropriate he could decide that he was excited about something that had recently happened to him or, simply, that he was sick. In any case, it is our basic assumption that emotional states are a function of the interaction of such cognitive factors with a state of physiological arousal.

This line of thought, then, leads to the following propositions:

1. Given a state of physiological arousal for which an individual has no immediate explanation, he will "label" this state and describe his feelings in terms of the cognitions available to him. To the extent that cognitive factors are potent determiners of emotional states, it could be anticipated that precisely the same state of physiological arousal could be labeled "joy" or "fury" or "jealousy" or any of a great diversity of emotional labels depending on the cognitive aspects of the situation.

2. Given a state of physiological arousal for which an individual has a completely appropriate explanation (e.g., "I feel this way because I have just received an injection of adrenalin") no evaluative needs will arise and the individual is unlikely to label his feelings in terms of the alternative cognitions available.

   Finally, consider a condition in which emotion inducing cognitions are present but there is no state of physiological arousal. For example, an individual might be completely aware that he is in great danger but for some reason (drug or surgical) remain in a state of physiological quiescence. Does he experience the emotion "fear"? Our formulation of emotion as a joint function of a state of physiological arousal and an appropriate cognition, would, of course, suggest that he does not, which leads to our final proposition.

3. Given the same cognitive circumstances, the individual will react emotionally or describe his feelings as emotions only to the extent that he experiences a state of physiological arousal.[5]

PROCEDURE

The experimental test of these propositions requires (a) the experimental manipulation of a state of physiological arousal, (b) the manipulation of the extent to which the subject has an appropriate or proper explanation of his bodily state, and (c) the creation of situations from which explanatory cognitions may be derived.

In order to satisfy the first two experimental requirements, the experiment was cast in the framework of a study of the effects of vitamin supplements on vision. As soon as a subject arrived, he was taken to a private room and told by the experimenter:

In this experiment we would like to make various tests of your vision. We are particularly interested in how certain vitamin compounds and vitamin supplements affect the visual skills. In particular, we want to find out how the vitamin compound called "Suproxin" affects your vision.

What we would like to do, then, if we can get your permission, is to give you a small injection of Suproxin. The injection itself is mild and harmless; however, since some people do object to being injected we don't want to talk you into anything. Would you mind receiving a Suproxin injection?

If the subject agrees to the injection (and all but 1 of 185 subjects did) the experimenter continues with instructions we shall describe shortly, then leaves the room. In a few minutes a physician enters the room, briefly repeats the experimenter's instructions, takes the subject's pulse and then injects him with Suproxin.

Depending upon condition, the subject receives one of two forms of Suproxin—epinephrine or a placebo.

Epinephrine or adrenalin is a sympathomimetic drug whose effects, with minor exceptions, are almost a perfect mimicry of a discharge of the sympathetic nervous system. Shortly after injection systolic blood pressure increases markedly, heart rate increases somewhat, cutaneous blood flow decreases, while muscle and cerebral blood flow increase, blood sugar and lactic acid concentration increase, and respiration rate increases slightly. As far as the subject is concerned the major subjective symptoms are palpitation, tremor, and sometimes a feeling of flushing and accelerated breathing. With a subcutaneous injection (in the dosage administered to our subjects), such effects usually begin within 3–5 minutes of injec-

tion and last anywhere from 10 minutes to an hour. For most subjects these effects are dissipated within 15–20 minutes after injection.

Subjects receiving epinephrine received a subcutaneous injection of ½ cubic centimeter of a 1:1000 solution of Winthrop Laboratory's Suprarenin, a saline solution of epinephrine bitartrate.

Subjects in the placebo condition received a subcutaneous injection of ½ cubic centimeter of saline solution. This is, of course, completely neutral material with no side effects at all.

Manipulating an Appropriate Explanation

By "appropriate" we refer to the extent to which the subject has an authoritative, unequivocal explanation of his bodily condition. Thus, a subject who had been informed by the physician that as a direct consequence of the injection he would feel palpitations, tremor, etc. would be considered to have a completely appropriate explanation. A subject who had been informed only that the injection would have no side effects would have no appropriate explanation of his state. This dimension of appropriateness was manipulated in three experimental conditions which shall be called: Epinephrine Informed (Epi Inf), Epinephrine Ignorant (Epi Ign), and Epinephrine Misinformed (Epi Mis).

Immediately after the subject had agreed to the injection and before the physician entered the room, the experimenter's spiel in each of these conditions went as follows:

Epinephrine Informed. I should also tell you that some of our subjects have experienced side effects from the Suproxin. These side effects are transitory, that is, they will only last for about 15 or 20 minutes. What will probably happen is that your hand will start to shake, your heart will start to pound, and your face may get warm and flushed. Again these are side effects lasting about 15 or 20 minutes.

While the physician was giving the injection, she told the subject that the injection was mild and harmless and repeated this description of the symptoms that the subject could expect as a consequence of the shot. In this condition, then, subjects have a completely appropriate explanation of their bodily state. They know precisely what they will feel and why.

Epinephrine Ignorant. In this condition, when the subject agreed to the injection, the experimenter said nothing more relevant to side effects and simply left the room. While the physician was giving the injection, she told the subject that the injection was mild and harmless and would have no side effects. In this condition, then, the subject has no experimentally provided explanation for his bodily state.

> Epinephrine Misinformed. *I should also tell you that some of our subjects have experienced side effects from the Suproxin. These side effects are transitory, that is, they will only last for about 15 or 20 minutes. What will probably happen is that your feet will feel numb, you will have an itching sensation over parts of your body, and you may get a slight headache. Again these are side effects lasting 15 or 20 minutes.*

And again, the physician repeated these symptoms while injecting the subject.

None of these symptoms, of course, are consequences of an injection of epinephrine and, in effect, these instructions provide the subject with a completely inappropriate explanation of his bodily feelings. This condition was introduced as a control condition of sorts. It seemed possible that the description of side effects in the Epi Inf condition might turn the subject introspective, self-examining, possibly slightly troubled. Differences on the dependent variable between the Epi Inf and Epi Ign conditions might, then, be due to such factors rather than to differences in appropriateness. The false symptoms in the Epi Mis condition should similarly turn the subject introspective, etc., but the instructions in this condition do not provide an appropriate explanation of the subject's state.

Subjects in all of the above conditions were injected with epinephrine. Finally, there was a placebo condition in which subjects, who were injected with saline solution, were given precisely the same treatment as subjects in the Epi Ign condition.

Producing an Emotion Inducing Cognition

Our initial hypothesis has suggested that given a state of physiological arousal for which the individual has no adequate explanation, cognitive factors can lead the individual to describe his feelings with any of a diversity of emotional labels. In order to test this hypothesis, it was decided to manipulate emotional states which can be considered quite different—euphoria and anger.

There are, of course, many ways to induce such states. In our own program of research, we have concentrated on social determinants of emotional states and have been able to demonstrate in other studies that people do evaluate their own feelings by comparing themselves with others around them (Schachter 1959; Wrightsman 1960). In this experiment we have attempted again to manipulate emotional state by social means. In one set of conditions, the subject is placed together with a stooge who has been trained to act euphorically. In a second set of conditions the subject is with a stooge trained to act in an angry fashion.

Euphoria

Immediately[6] after the subject had been injected, the physician left the room and the experimenter returned with a stooge whom he introduced as another subject, then said:

> Both of you have had the Suproxin shot and you'll both be taking the same tests of vision. What I ask you to do now is just wait for 20 minutes. The reason for this is simply that we have to allow 20 minutes for the Suproxin to get from the injection site into the bloodstream. At the end of 20 minutes when we are certain that most of the Suproxin has been absorbed into the bloodstream, we'll begin the tests of vision.

The room in which this was said had been deliberately put into a state of mild disarray. As he was leaving, the experimenter apologetically added:

> *The only other thing I should do is to apologize for the condition of the room. I just didn't have time to clean it up. So, if you need any scratch paper or rubber bands or pencils, help yourself. I'll be back in 20 minutes to begin the vision tests.*

As soon as the experimenter had left, the stooge introduced himself again, made a series of standard icebreaker comments, and then launched his routine. For observation purposes, the stooge's act was broken into a series of standard units, demarcated by a change in activity or a standard comment. In sequence, the units of the stooge's routine were the following:

1. Stooge reaches for a piece of paper and starts doodling saying, "They said we could use this for scratch, didn't they?" He doodles a fish for some 30 seconds, then says:
2. "This scrap paper isn't even much good for doodling" and crumples paper and attempts to throw it into wastebasket in far corner of the room. He misses but this leads him into a "basketball game." He crumples up other sheets of paper, shoots a few baskets, says "Two points" occasionally. He gets up and does a jump shot saying, "The old jump shot is really on today."
3. If the subject has not joined in, the stooge throws a paper basketball to the subject saying, "Here, you try it."
4. Stooge continues his game saying, "The trouble with paper basketballs is that you don't really have any control."
5. Stooge continues basketball, then gives it up saying, "This is one of my good days. I feel like a kid again. I think I'll make a plane." He makes a paper airplane saying, "I guess I'll make one of the longer ones."
6. Stooge flies plane. Gets up and retrieves plane. Flies again, etc.
7. Stooge throws plane at subject.
8. Stooge, flying plane, says, "Even when I was

a kid, I was never much good at this."
9. Stooge tears off part of plane saying, "Maybe this plane can't fly but at least it's good for something." He wads up paper and making a slingshot of a rubber band begins to shoot the paper.
10. Shooting, the stooge says, "They [paper ammunition] really go better if you make them long. They don't work right if you wad them up."
11. While shooting, stooge notices a sloppy pile of manila folders on a table. He builds a tower of these folders, then goes to the opposite end of the room to shoot at the tower.
12. He misses several times, then hits and cheers as the tower falls. He goes over to pick up the folders.
13. While picking up, he notices, behind a portable blackboard, a pair of hula hoops which have been covered with black tape with a few wires sticking out of the tape. He reaches for these, taking one for himself and putting the other aside but within reaching distance of the subject. The stooge tries the hula hoop, saying, "This isn't as easy as it looks."
14. Stooge twirls hoop wildly on arm, saying, "Hey, look at this—this is great."
15. Stooge replaces the hula hoop and sits down with his feet on the table. Shortly thereafter the experimenter returns to the room.

This routine was completely standard, though its pace, of course, varied depending upon the subject's reaction, the extent to which he entered into this bedlam and the extent to which he initiated activities of his own. The only variations from this standard routine were those forced by the subject. Should the subject originate some nonsense of his own and request the stooge to join in, he would do so. And, he would, of course, respond to any comments initiated by the subject.

Subjects in each of the three "appropriateness" conditions and in the placebo condition were submitted to this setup. The stooge, of course, never knew in which condition any particular subject fell.

Anger

Immediately after the injection, the experimenter brought a stooge into the subject's room, introduced the two and after explaining the necessity for a 20 minute delay for "the Suproxin to get from the injection site into the bloodstream" he continued, "We would like you to use these 20 minutes to answer these questionnaires." Then handing out the questionnaires, he concludes with, "I'll be back in 20 minutes to pick up the questionnaires and begin the tests of vision."

Before looking at the questionnaire, the stooge says to the subject,

> I really wanted to come for an experiment today, but I think it's unfair for them to give you shots. At least, they should have told us about the shots when they called us; you hate to refuse, once you're here already.

The questionnaires, five pages long, start off innocently requesting face sheet information and then grow increasingly personal and insulting. The stooge, sitting directly opposite the subject, paces his own answers so that at all times subject and stooge are working on the same question. At regular points in the questionnaire, the stooge makes a series of standardized comments about the questions. His comments start off innocently enough, grow increasingly querulous, and finally he ends up in a rage. In sequence, he makes the following comments.

1. Before answering any items, he leafs quickly through the questionnaire saying, "Boy, this is a long one."
2. Question 7 on the questionnaire requests, "List the foods that you would eat in a typical day." The stooge comments, "Oh for Pete's sake, what did I have for breakfast this morning?"
3. Question 9 asks, "Do you ever hear bells? _____ How often? _____" The stooge remarks, "Look at Question 9. How ridiculous can you get? I hear bells every time I change classes."
4. Question 13 requests, "List the childhood dis-

eases you have had and the age at which you had them" to which the stooge remarks, "I get annoyed at this childhood disease question. I can't remember what childhood diseases I had, and especially at what age. Can you?"

5. Question 17 asks "What is your father's average annual income?" and the stooge says, "This really irritates me. It's none of their business what my father makes. I'm leaving that blank."
6. Question 25 presents a long series of items such as "Does not bathe or wash regularly," "Seems to need psychiatric care," etc. and requests the respondent to write down for which member of his immediate family each item seems most applicable. The question specifically prohibits the answer "None" and each item must be answered. The stooge says, "I'll be damned if I'll fill out Number 25. 'Does not bathe or wash regularly'—that's a real insult." He then angrily crosses out the entire item.
7. Question 28 reads:
   "How many times each week do you have sexual intercourse?" 0–1 _____ 2–3 _____ 4–6 _____ 7 and over _____. The stooge bites out, "The hell with it! I don't have to tell them all this."
8. The stooge sits sullenly for a few moments then he rips up his questionnaire, crumples the pieces and hurls them to the floor, saying, "I'm not wasting any more time. I'm getting my books and leaving" and he stamps out of the room.
9. The questionnaire continues for eight more questions ending with: "With how many men (other than your father) has your mother had extramarital relationships?"
   4 and under _____: 5–9 _____: 10 and over _____.

Subjects in the Epi Ign, Epi Inf and Placebo conditions were run through this "anger" inducing sequence. The stooge, again, did not know to which condition the subject had been assigned.

In summary, this is a seven condition experiment which, for two different emotional states, allows us (a) to evaluate the effects of "appropriateness" on emotional inducibility and (b) to begin to evaluate the effects of sympathetic activation on emotional inducibility. In schematic form the conditions are the following:

Euphoria	*Anger*
Epi Inf	Epi Inf
Epi Ign	Epi Ign
Epi Mis	Placebo
Placebo	

The Epi Mis condition was not run in the Anger sequence. This was originally conceived as a control condition and it was felt that its inclusion in the Euphoria conditions alone would suffice as a means of evaluating the possible artifactual effect of the Epi Inf instructions.

Measurement

Two types of measures of emotional state were obtained. Standardized observation through a one-way mirror was the technique used to assess the subject's behavior. To what extent did he act euphoric or angry? Such behavior can be considered in a way as a "semiprivate" index of mood for as far as the subject was concerned, his emotional behavior could be known only to the other person in the room—presumably another student. The second type of measure was self-report in which, on a variety of scales, the subject indicated his mood of the moment. Such measures can be considered "public" indices of mood for they would, of course, be available to the experimenter and his associates.

Observation

Euphoria　For each of the first 14 units of the stooge's standardized routine an observer kept a running chronicle of what the subject did and said. For each unit the observer coded the subject's behavior in one or more of the following categories:

Category 1: Joins in activity. If the subject en-

tered into the stooge's activities, e.g., if he made or flew airplanes, threw paper basketballs, hula hooped, etc., his behavior was coded in this category.

Category 2: Initiates new activity. A subject was so coded if he gave indications of creative euphoria, that is, if, on his own, he initiated behavior outside of the stooge's routine. Instances of such behavior would be the subject who threw open the window and, laughing, hurled paper basketballs at passersby; or, the subject who jumped on a table and spun one hula hoop on his leg and the other on his neck.

Categories 3 and 4: Ignores or watches stooge. Subjects who paid flatly no attention to the stooge or who, with or without comment, simply watched the stooge without joining in his activity were coded in these categories.

For any particular unit of behavior, the subject's behavior was coded in one or more of these categories. To test reliability of coding two observers independently coded two experimental sessions. The observers agreed completely on the coding of 88% of the units.

Anger　For each of the units of stooge behavior, an observer recorded the subject's responses and coded them according to the following category scheme:

Category 1: Agrees. In response to the stooge the subject makes a comment indicating that he agrees with the stooge's standardized comment or that he, too, is irked by a particular item on the questionnaire. For example, a subject who responded to the stooge's comment on the "father's income" question by saying, "I don't like that kind of personal question either" would be so coded (scored + 2).

Category 2: Disagrees. In response to the stooge's comment, the subject makes a comment which indicates that he disagrees with the stooge's meaning or mood; e.g., in response to the stooge's comment on the "father's income" question, such a subject might say, "Take it easy, they probably have a good reason for wanting the information" (scored -2).

Category 3: Neutral: A noncommittal or irrelevant response to the stooge's remark (scored 0).

Category 4: Initiates agreement or disagreement. With no instigation by the stooge, a subject, so coded, would have volunteered a remark indicating that he felt the same way or, alternatively, quite differently than the stooge. Examples would be "Boy I hate this kind of thing" or "I'm enjoying this" (scored $+2$ or -2).

Category 5: Watches. The subject makes no verbal response to the stooge's comment but simply looks directly at him (scored 0).

Category 6: Ignores. The subject makes no verbal response to the stooge's comment nor does he look at him; the subject, paying no attention at all to the stooge, simply works at his own questionnaire (scored -1).

A subject was scored in one or more of these categories for each unit of stooge behavior. To test reliability, two observers independently coded three experimental sessions. In order to get a behavioral index of anger, observation protocol was scored according to the values presented in parentheses after each of the above definitions of categories. In a unit-by-unit comparison, the two observers agreed completely on the scoring of 71% of the units jointly observed. The scores of the two observers differed by a value of 1 or less for 88% of the units coded and in not a single case did the two observers differ in the direction of their scoring of a unit.

Self Report of Mood and Physical Condition

When the subject's session with the stooge was completed, the experimenter returned to the room, took pulses and said:

Before we proceed with the vision tests, there is one other kind of information which we must have. We have found, as you can probably imagine, that there are many things beside Suproxin that affect how well you see in our tests. How hungry you are, how tired you are, and even the mood you're in at the time—whether you feel happy or irritated at the time of testing will affect how well you

see. To understand the data we collect on you, then, we must be able to figure out which effects are due to causes such as these and which are caused by Suproxin.

The only way we can get such information about your physical and emotional state is to have you tell us. I'll hand out these questionnaires and ask you to answer them as accurately as possible. Obviously, our data on the vision tests will only be as accurate as your description of your mental and physical state.

In keeping with this spiel, the questionnaire that the experimenter passed out contained a number of mock questions about hunger, fatigue, etc., as well as questions of more immediate relevance to the experiment. To measure mood or emotional state the following two were the crucial questions:

1. How irritated, angry or annoyed would you say you feel at present?

I don't feel at all irritated or angry (0)	I feel a little irritated and angry (1)	I feel quite irritated and angry (2)	I feel very irritated and angry (3)	I feel extremely irritated and angry (4)

2. How good or happy would you say you feel at present?

I don't feel at all happy or good (0)	I feel a little happy and good (1)	I feel quite happy and good (2)	I feel very happy and good (3)	I feel extremely happy and good (4)

To measure the physical effects of epinephrine and determine whether or not the injection had been successful in producing the necessary bodily state, the following questions were asked:

1. Have you experienced any palpitation (consciousness of your own heart beat)?

Not at all (0)	A slight amount (1)	A moderate amount (2)	An intense amount (3)

2. Did you feel any tremor (involuntary shaking of the hands, arms or legs)?

Not at all (0)	A slight amount (1)	A moderate amount (2)	An intense amount (3)

To measure possible effects of the instructions in the Epi Mis condition, the following questions were asked:

1. Did you feel any numbness in your feet?
2. Did you feel any itching sensation?
3. Did you experience any feeling of headache?

To all three of these questions was attached a four-point scale running from "Not at all" to "An intense amount."

In addition to these scales, the subjects were asked to answer two open-end questions on other physical or emotional sensations they may have experienced during the experimental session. A final measure of bodily state was pulse rate which was taken by the physician or the experimenter at two times—immediately before the injection and immediately after the session with the stooge.

When the subjects had completed these questionnaires, the experimenter announced that the experiment was over, explained the deception and its necessity in detail, answered any questions, and swore the subjects to secrecy. Finally, the subjects answered a brief questionnaire about their experiences, if any, with adrenalin and their previous knowledge or suspicion of the experimental setup. There was no indication that any of the subjects had known about the experiment beforehand but 11 subjects were so extremely suspicious of some crucial feature of the experiment that their data were automatically discarded.

Subjects

The subjects were all male, college students taking classes in introductory psychology at the University of Minnesota. Some 90% of the students in these classes volunteer for a subject pool for which they receive two extra points on their final exam for every hour that they serve as experimental subjects. For this study the records of all potential subjects were cleared with the Student Health Service in order to insure that no harmful effects would result from the injections.

Evaluation of the Experimental Design

The ideal test of our propositions would require circumstances which our experiment is far from realizing. First, the proposition that: "A state of physiological arousal for which an individual has no immediate explanation will lead him to label this state in terms of the cognitions available to him" obviously requires conditions under which the subject does not and cannot have a proper explanation of his bodily state. Though we toyed with such fantasies as ventilating the experimental room with vaporized adrenalin, reality forced us to rely on the disguised injection of Suproxin—a technique which was far from ideal for no matter what the experimenter told them, some subjects would inevitably attribute their feelings to the injection. To the extent that subjects did so, differences between the several appropriateness conditions should be attenuated.

Second, the proposition that: "Given the same cognitive circumstances the individual will react emotionally only to the extent that he experiences a state of physiological arousal" requires for its ideal test the manipulation of states of physiological arousal and of physiological quiescence. Though there is no question that epinephrine effectively produces a state of arousal, there is also no question that a placebo does not prevent physiological arousal. To the extent that the experimental situation effectively produces sympathetic stimulation in placebo subjects, the proposition is difficult to test, for such a factor would attenuate differences between epinephrine and placebo subjects.

Both of these factors, then, can be expected to interfere with the test of our several propositions. In presenting the results of this study, we shall first present condition by condition results and then evaluate the effect of these two factors on experimental differences.

RESULTS

Effects of the Injections on Bodily State

Let us examine first the success of the injections at producing the bodily state required to examine the propositions at test. Does the injection of epinephrine produce symptoms of sympathetic discharge as compared with the placebo injection? Relevant data are presented in Table 1 where it can be immediately seen that on all items subjects who were in epinephrine conditions show considerably more evidence of sympathetic activation than do subjects in placebo conditions. In all epineprine conditions pulse rate increases significantly when compared with the decrease characteristic of the placebo conditions. On the scales it is clear that epinephrine subjects experience considerably more palpitation and tremor than do placebo subjects. In all possible comparisons on these symptoms, the mean scores of subjects in any of the epinephrine conditions are greater than the corresponding scores in the placebo conditions at better than the .001 level of significance. Examination of the absolute values of these scores makes it quite clear that subjects in epinephrine conditions were, indeed, in a state of physiological arousal, while most subjects in placebo conditions were in a relative state of physiological quiescence.

The epinephrine injection, of course, did not work with equal effectiveness for all subjects; indeed for a few subjects it did not work at all. Such subjects reported almost no palpitation or tremor, showed no increase in pulse and described no other relevant physical symptoms. Since for such subjects the necessary experimental conditions were not established, they were automatically excluded from the data and all further tabular presentations will not include such subjects. Table 1, however, does include the data of these subjects. There were four such subjects in euphoria conditions and one of them in anger conditions.

In order to evaluate further data on Epi Mis subjects it is necessary to note the results of the "numbness," "itching," and "headache" scales also presented in Table 1. Clearly the subjects in the Epi Mis condition do not differ on these scales from subjects in any of the other experimental conditions.

Effects of the Manipulations on Emotional State

Euphoria   Self-report. The effects of the several manipulations on emotional state in the euphoria conditions are presented in Table 2. The scores recorded in this table are derived, for each subject, by subtracting the value of the point he checks on the irritation scale from the value of the point he checks on the happiness scale. Thus, if a subject

TABLE 1 / The Effects of the Injections on Bodily State

Condition	N	Pulse		Self-rating of				
		Pre	Post	Palpitation	Tremor	Numbness	Itching	Headache
Euphoria								
Epi Inf	27	85.7	88.6	1.20	1.43	0	0.16	0.32
Epi Ign	26	84.6	85.6	1.83	1.76	0.15	0	0.55
Epi Mis	26	82.9	86.0	1.27	2.00	0.06	0.08	0.23
Placebo	26	80.4	77.1	0.29	0.21	0.09	0	0.27
Anger								
Epi Inf	23	85.9	92.4	1.26	1.41	0.17	0	0.11
Epi Ign	23	85.0	96.8	1.44	1.78	0	0.06	0.21
Placebo	23	84.5	79.6	0.59	0.24	0.14	0.06	0.06

TABLE 2 / Self-Report of Emotional State in the Euphoria Conditions

Condition	N	Self-report scales	Comparison	p
Epi Inf	25	0.98	Epi Inf vs. Epi Mis	< .01
Epi Ign	25	1.78	Epi Inf vs. Epi Ign	.02
Epi Mis	25	1.90	Placebo vs. Epi Mis, Ign, or Inf	ns
Placebo	26	1.61		

All *p* values reported throughout paper are two-tailed.

were to check the point "I feel a little irritated and angry" on the irritation scale and the point "I feel very happy and good" on the happiness scale, his score would be + 2. The higher the positive value, the happier and better the subject reports himself as feeling. Though we employ an index for expositional simplicity, it should be noted that the two components of the index each yield results completely consistent with those obtained by use of this index.

Let us examine first the effects of the appropriateness instructions. Comparison of the scores for the Epi Mis and Epi Inf conditions makes it immediately clear that the experimental differences are not due to artifacts resulting from the informed instructions. In both conditions the subject was warned to expect a variety of symptoms as a consequence of the injection. In the Epi Mis condition, where the symptoms were inappropriate to the subject's bodily state the self-report score is almost twice that in the Epi Inf condition where the symptoms were completely appropriate to the subject's bodily state. It is reasonable, then, to attribute differences between informed subjects and those in other conditions to differences in manipulated appropriateness rather than to artifacts such as introspectiveness or self-examination.

It is clear that, consistent with expectations, subjects were more susceptible to the stooge's mood and consequently more euphoric when they had no explanation of their own bodily states than when they did. The means of both the Epi Ign

and Epi Mis conditions are considerably greater than the mean of the Epi Inf condition.

It is of interest to note that Epi Mis subjects are somewhat more euphoric than are Epi Ign subjects. This pattern repeats itself in other data shortly to be presented. We would attribute this difference to differences in the appropriateness dimension. Though, as in the Epi Ign condition, a subject is not provided with an explanation of his bodily state, it is, of course, possible that he will provide one for himself which is not derived from his interaction with the stooge. Most reasonably he could decide for himself that he feels this way because of the injection. To the extent that he does so he should be less susceptible to the stooge. It seems probable that he would be less likely to hit on such an explanation in the Epi Mis condition than in the Epi Ign condition for in the Epi Mis condition both the experimenter and the doctor have told him that the effects of the injection would be quite different from what he actually feels. The effect of such instructions is probably to make it more difficult for the subject himself to hit on the alternative explanation described above. There is some evidence to support this analysis. In open-end questions in which subjects described their own mood and state, 28% of the subjects in the Epi Ign condition made some connection between the injection and their bodily state compared with the 16% of subjects in the Epi Mis condition who did so. It could be considered, then, that these three conditions fall along a dimension of appropriateness, with the Epi Inf condition at one extreme and the Epi Mis condition at the other.

Comparing the placebo to the epinephrine conditions, we note a pattern which will repeat itself throughout the data. Placebo subjects are less euphoric than either Epi Mis or Epi Ign subjects but somewhat more euphoric than Epi Inf subjects. These differences are not, however, statistically significant. We shall consider the epinephrine-placebo comparisons in detail in a later section of this paper following the presentation of additional relevant data. For the moment, it is clear that, by self-report manipulating appropriateness has had a very strong effect on euphoria.

Behavior. Let us next examine the extent to which the subject's behavior was affected by the experimental manipulations. To the extent that his mood has been affected, one should expect that the subject will join in the stooge's whirl of manic activity and initiate similar activities of his own. The relevant data are presented in Table 3. The column labeled "Activity index" presents summary figures on the extent to which the subject joined in the stooge's activity. This is a weighted index which reflects both the nature of the activities in which the subject engaged and the amount of time he was active. The index was devised by assigning the following weights to the subject's activities: 5—hula hooping; 4—shooting with slingshot; 3—paper airplanes; 2—paper basketballs; 1—doodling; 0 does nothing. Pretest scaling on 15 college students ordered these activities with respect to the degree of euphoria they represented. Arbitrary weights were assigned so that the wilder the activity, the heavier the weight. These weights are multiplied by an esti-

mate of the amount of time the subject spent in each activity and the summed products make up the activity index for each subject. This index may be considered a measure of behavioral euphoria. It should be noted that the same between-condition relationships hold for the two components of this index as for the index itself.

The column labeled "Mean number of acts initiated" presents the data on the extent to which the subject deviates from the stooge's routine and initiates euphoric activities of his own.

On both behavioral indices, we find precisely the same pattern of relationships as those obtained with self-reports. Epi Mis subjects behave somewhat more euphorically than do Epi Ign subjects who in turn behave more euphorically than do Epi Inf subjects. On all measures, then, there is consistent evidence that a subject will take over the stooge's euphoric mood to the extent that he has no other explanation of his bodily state.

Again it should be noted that on these behavioral indices, Epi Ign and Epi Mis subjects are somewhat more euphoric than placebo subjects but not significantly so.

Anger Self-report. Before presenting data for the anger conditions, one point must be made about the anger manipulation. In the situation devised, anger, if manifested, is most likely to be directed at the experimenter and his annoyingly personal questionnaire. As we subsequently discovered, this was rather unfortunate, for the subjects, who had volunteered for the experiment for extra points on their final exam, simply refused to endanger these points by publicly blowing up, admitting their irritation to the experimenter's face or spoiling the questionnaire. Though as the reader will see, the subjects were quite willing to manifest anger when they were alone with the stooge, they hesitated to do so on material (self-ratings of mood and questionnaire) that the experimenter might see and only after the purposes of the experiment had been revealed were many of these subjects willing to admit to the experimenter that they had been irked or irritated.

This experimentally unfortunate situation

TABLE 3 / Behavioral Indications of Emotional State in the Euphoria Conditions

Condition	N	Activity index	Mean number of acts initiated
Epi Inf	25	12.72	.20
Epi Ign	25	18.28	.56
Epi Mis	25	22.56	.84
Placebo	26	16.00	.54

p value

Comparison	Activity index	Initiates
Epi Inf vs. Epi Mis	.05	.03
Epi Inf vs. Epi Ign	ns	.08
Plac vs. Epi Mis, Ign, or Inf	ns	ns

Tested by χ^2 comparison of the proportion of subjects in each condition initiating new acts.

pretty much forces us to rely on the behavioral indices derived from observation of the subject's presumably private interaction with the stooge. We do, however, present data on the self-report scales in Table 4. These figures are derived in the same way as the figures presented in Table 2 for the euphoria conditions, that is, the value checked on the irritation scale is subtracted from the value checked on the happiness scale. Though, for the reasons stated above, the absolute magnitude of these figures (all positive) is relatively meaningless, we can, of course, compare condition means within the set of anger conditions. With the happiness-irritation index employed, we should, of course, anticipate precisely the reverse results from those obtained in the euphoria conditions; that is, the Epi Inf subjects in the anger conditions should again be less susceptible to the stooge's mood and should, therefore, describe themselves as in a somewhat happier frame of mind than subjects in the Epi Ign condition. This is the case; the Epi Inf subjects average 1.91 on the self-report scales while the Epi Ign subjects average 1.39.

Evaluating the effects of the injections, we note again that, as anticipated, Epi Ign subjects are somewhat less happy than Placebo subjects but, once more, this is not a significant difference.

Behavior. The subject's responses to the stooge, during the period when both were filling out their questionnaires, were systematically coded to provide a behavioral index of anger. The coding scheme and the numerical values attached to each of the categories have been described in the methodology section. To arrive at an "Anger index" the numerical value assigned to a subject's responses to the stooge is summed together for the several units of stooge behavior. In the coding scheme used, a positive value to this index indicates that the subject agrees with the stooge's comment and is growing angry. A negative value indicates that the subject either disagrees with the stooge or ignores him.

The relevant data are presented in Table 5. For this analysis, the stooge's routine has been divided into two phases—the first two units of his behavior (the "long" questionnaire and "What did I have for breakfast?") are considered essentially neutral revealing nothing of the stooge's mood; all of the following units are considered "angry" units for they begin with an irritated remark about the "bells" question and end with the stooge's fury as he rips up his questionnaire and stomps out of the room. For the neutral units, agreement or disagreement with the stooge's remarks is, of course, meaningless as an index of mood and we should anticipate no difference between conditions. As can be seen in Table 5, this is the case.

For the angry units, we must, of course, anticipate that subjects in the Epi Ign condition will be angrier than subjects in the Epi Inf condition. This is indeed the case. The Anger index for the Epi Ign condition is positive and large, indicating that these subjects have become angry, while in the Epi Inf condition the Anger index is slightly negative

TABLE 4 / Self-Report of Emotional State in the Anger Conditions

Condition	N	Self-Report scales	Comparison	p
Epi Inf	22	1.91	Epi Inf vs. Epi Ign	.08
Epi Ign	23	1.39	Placebo vs. Epi Ign or Inf	ns
Placebo	23	1.63		

TABLE 5 / Behavioral Indications of Emotional State in the Anger Conditions

Condition	N	Neutral units	Anger units
Epi Inf	22	+ 0.07	− 0.18
Epi Ign	23	+ 0.30	+ 2.28
Placebo	22[a]	− 0.09	+ 0.79

Comparison for anger units	p
Epi Inf vs. Epi Ign	< .01
Epi Ign vs. Placebo	< .05
Placebo vs. Epi Inf	ns

[a]For one subject in this condition the sound system went dead and the observer could not, of course, code his reactions.

in value indicating that these subjects have failed to catch the stooge's mood at all. It seems clear that providing the subject with an appropriate explanation of his bodily state greatly reduces his tendency to interpret his state in terms of the cognitions provided by the stooge's angry behavior.

Finally, on this behavioral index, it can be seen that subjects in the Epi Ign condition are significantly angrier than subjects in the Placebo condition. Behaviorally, at least, the injection of epinephrine appears to have led subjects to an angrier state than comparable subjects who received placebo shots.

Conformation of Data to Theoretical Expectations

Now that the basic data of this study have been presented, let us examine closely the extent to which they conform to theoretical expectations. If our hypotheses are correct and if this experimental design provided a perfect test for these hypotheses, it should be anticipated that in the euphoria conditions the degree of experimentally produced euphoria should vary in the following fashion:

$$\text{Epi Mis} \geq \text{Epi Ign} > \text{Epi Inf} = \text{Placebo}$$

And in the anger conditions, anger should conform to the following pattern:

$$\text{Epi Ign} > \text{Epi Inf} = \text{Placebo}$$

In both sets of conditions, it is the case that emotional level in the Epi Mis and Epi Ign conditions is considerably greater than that achieved in the corresponding Epi Inf conditions. The results for the Placebo condition, however, are ambiguous for consistently the Placebo subjects fall between the Epi Ign and the Epi Inf subjects. This is a particularly troubling pattern for it makes it impossible to evaluate unequivocally the effects of the state of physiological arousal and indeed raises serious questions about our entire theoretical structure. Though the emotional level is consistently greater in the Epi Mis and Epi Ign conditions than in the Placebo condition, this difference is significant at acceptable probability levels only in the anger conditions.

In order to explore the problem further, let us examine the experimental factors identified earlier, which might have acted to restrain the emotional level in the Epi Ign and Epi Mis conditions. As was pointed out earlier, the ideal test of our first two hypotheses requires an experimental setup in which the subject has flatly no way of evaluating his state of physiological arousal other than by means of the experimentally provided cognitions. Had it been possible to physiologically produce a state of sympathetic activation by means other than injection, one could have approached this experimental ideal more closely than in the present setup. As it stands, however, there is always a reasonable alternative cognition available to the aroused subject—he feels the way he does because of the injection. To the extent that the subject seizes on such an explanation of his bodily state, we should expect that he will be uninfluenced by the stooge. Evidence presented in Table 6 for the anger condition and in Table 7 for the euphoria conditions indicates that this is, indeed, the case.

As mentioned earlier, some of the Epi Ign and Epi Mis subjects in their answers to the open-end questions clearly attributed their physical state to the injection, e.g., "the shot gave me the shivers." In Tables 6 and 7 such subjects are labeled "Self-informed." In Table 6 it can be seen that the self-informed subjects are considerably less angry than are the remaining subjects; indeed, they are not angry at all. With these self-informed subjects eliminated the difference between the Epi Ign and the Placebo conditions is significant at the .01 level of significance.

Precisely the same pattern is evident in Table 7 for the euphoria conditions. In both the Epi Mis

TABLE 6 / The Effects of Attributing Bodily State to the Injection on Anger in the Anger Epi Ign Condition

Condition	N	Anger index	p
Self-informed subjects	3	− 1.67	ns
Others	20	+ 2.88	ns
Self-informed vs. Others			.05

TABLE 7 / The Effects of Attributing Bodily State to the Injection on Euphoria in the Euphoria Epi Ign and Epi Mis Conditions

	N	Epi Ign Activity Index	p
Self-informed subjects	8	11.63	ns
Others	17	21.14	ns
Self-informed vs. Others			.05

	N	Epi Mis Activity Index	p
Self-informed subjects	5	12.40	ns
Others	20	25.10	ns
Self-informed vs. Others			.10

and the Epi Ign conditions, the self-informed subjects have considerably lower activity indices than do the remaining subjects. Eliminating self-informed subjects, comparison of both of these conditions with the Placebo condition yields a difference significant at the .03 level of significance. It should be noted, too, that the self-informed subjects have much the same score on the activity index as do the experimental Epi Inf subjects (Table 3).

It would appear, then, that the experimental procedure of injecting the subjects, by providing an alternative cognition, has, to some extent, obscured the effects of epinephrine. When account is taken of this artifact, the evidence is good that the state of physiological arousal is a necessary component of an emotional experience for when self-informed subjects are removed, epinephrine subjects give consistent indications of greater emotionality than do placebo subjects.

Let us examine next the fact that consistently the emotional level, both reported and behavioral, in Placebo conditions is greater than that in the Epi Inf conditions. Theoretically, of course, it should be expected that the two conditions will be equally low, for by assuming that emotional state is a joint function of a state of physiological arousal and of the appropriateness of a cognition we are, in effect, assuming a multiplicative function, so that if either component is at zero, emo-

tional level is at zero. As noted earlier this expectation should hold if we can be sure that there is no sympathetic activation in the Placebo conditions. This assumption, of course, is completely unrealistic for the injection of placebo does not prevent sympathetic activation. The experimental situations were fairly dramatic and certainly some of the placebo subjects gave indications of physiological arousal. If our general line of reasoning is correct, it should be anticipated that the emotional level of subjects who give indications of sympathetic activity will be greater than that of subjects who do not. The relevant evidence is presented in Tables 8 and 9.

As an index of sympathetic activation we shall use the most direct and unequivocal measure available — change in pulse rate. It can be seen in Table 1 that the predominant pattern in the Placebo condition is a decrease in pulse rate. We shall assume, therefore, that those subjects whose pulse increases or remains the same give indications of sympathetic activity while those subjects whose pulse decreases do not. In Table 8, for the eupho-

TABLE 8 / Sympathetic Activation and Euphoria in the Euphoria Placebo Condition

Subjects whose:	N	Activity index	p
Pulse decreased	14	10.67	ns
Pulse increased or remained same	12	23.17	ns
Pulse decrease vs. pulse increase or same			.02

TABLE 9 / Sympathetic Activation and Anger in Anger Placebo Condition

Subjects whose:	N[a]	Activity index	p
Pulse decreased	13	+ 0.15	ns
Pulse increased or remained same	8	+ 1.69	ns
Pulse decrease vs. pulse increase or same			.01

[a] N reduced by two cases owing to failure of sound system in one case and experimenter's failure to take pulse in another.

ria condition, it is immediately clear that subjects who give indications of sympathetic activity are considerably more euphoric than are subjects who show no sympathetic activity. This relationship is, of course, confounded by the fact that euphoric subjects are considerably more active than non-euphoric subjects—a factor which independent of mood could elevate pulse rate. However, no such factor operates in the anger condition where angry subjects are neither more active nor talkative than calm subjects. It can be seen in Table 9 that Placebo subjects who show signs of sympathetic activation give indications of considerably more anger than do subjects who show no such signs. Conforming to expectations, sympathetic activation accompanies an increase in emotional level.

It should be noted, too, that the emotional levels of subjects showing no signs of sympathetic activity are quite comparable to the emotional level of subjects in the parallel Epi Inf conditions (see Tables 3 and 5). The similarity of these sets of scores and their uniformly low level of indicated emotionality would certainly make it appear that both factors are essential to an emotional state. When either the level of sympathetic arousal is low or a completely appropriate cognition is available, the level of emotionality is low.

DISCUSSION

Let us summarize the major findings of this experiment and examine the extent to which they support the propositions offered in the introduction of this paper. It has been suggested, first, that given a state of physiological arousal for which an individual has no explanation, he will label this state in terms of the cognitions available to him. This implies, of course, that by manipulating the cognitions of an individual in such a state we can manipulate his feelings in diverse directions. Experimental results support this proposition for following the injection of epinephrine, those subjects who had no explanation for the bodily state thus produced, gave behavioral and self-report indications that they had been readily manipulable into the disparate feeling states of euphoria and anger.

From this first proposition, it must follow that given a state of physiological arousal for which the individual has a completely satisfactory explanation, he will not label this state in terms of the alternative cognitions available. Experimental evidence strongly supports this expectation. In those conditions in which subjects were injected with epinephrine and told precisely what they would feel and why, they proved relatively immune to any effects of the manipulated cognitions. In the anger condition, such subjects did not report or show anger; in the euphoria condition, such subjects reported themselves as far less happy than subjects with an identical bodily state but no adequate knowledge of why they felt they way they did.

Finally, it has been suggested that given constant cognitive circumstances, an individual will react emotionally only to the extent that he experiences a state of physiological arousal. Without taking account of experimental artifacts, the evidence in support of this proposition is consistent but tentative. When the effects of "self-informing" tendencies in epinephrine subjects and of "self-arousing" tendencies in placebo subjects are partialed out, the evidence strongly supports the proposition.

The pattern of data, then, falls neatly in line with theoretical expectations. However, the fact that we were forced, to some extent, to rely on internal analyses in order to partial out the effects of experimental artifacts inevitably makes our conclusions somewhat tentative. In order to further test these propositions on the interaction of cognitive and physiological determinants of emotional state, a series of additional experiments, published elsewhere, was designed to rule out or overcome the operation of these artifacts. In the first of these, Schachter and Wheeler (1962) extended the range of manipulated sympathetic activation by employing three experimental groups—epinephrine, placebo, and a group injected with the sympatholytic agent, chlorpromazine. Laughter at a slapstick movie was the dependent variable and the evidence is good that amusement is a direct function of manipulated sympathetic activation.

In order to make the epinephrine-placebo comparison under conditions which would rule out the operation of any self-informing tendency, two experiments were conducted on rats. In one of these Singer (1961) demonstrated that under fear inducing conditions, manipulated by the simultaneous presentation of a loud bell, a buzzer, and a bright flashing light, rats injected with epinephrine were considerably more frightened than rats injected with a placebo. Epinephrine-injected rats defecated, urinated, and trembled more than did placebo-injected rats. In nonfear control conditions, there were no differences between epinephrine and placebo groups, neither group giving any indication of fear. In another study, Latané and Schachter (1962) demonstrated that rats injected with epinephrine were notably more capable of avoidance learning than were rats injected with a placebo. Using a modified Miller-Mowrer shuttle-box, these investigators found that during an experimental period involving 200 massed trials, 15 rats injected with epinephrine avoided shock an average of 101.2 trials while 15 placebo-injected rats averaged only 37.3 avoidances.

Taken together, this body of studies does give strong support to the propositions which generated these experimental tests. Given a state of sympathetic activation, for which no immediately appropriate explanation is available, human subjects can be readily manipulated into states of euphoria, anger, and amusement. Varying the intensity of sympathetic activation serves to vary the intensity of a variety of emotional states in both rats and human subjects.

Let us examine the implications of these findings and of this line of thought for problems in the general area of the physiology of the emotions. We have noted in the introduction that the numerous studies on physiological differentiators of emotional states have, viewed en masse, yielded quite inconclusive results. Most, though not all, of these studies have indicated no differences among the various emotional states. Since as human beings, rather than as scientists, we have no difficulty identifying, labeling, and distinguishing among our feelings, the results of these studies have long seemed rather puzzling

and paradoxical. Perhaps because of this, there has been a persistent tendency to discount such results as due to ignorance or methodological inadequacy and to pay far more attention to the very few studies which demonstrate *some* sort of physiological differences among emotional states than to the very many studies which indicate no differences at all. It is conceivable, however, that these results should be taken at face value and that emotional states may, indeed, be generally characterized by a high level of sympathetic activation with few if any physiological distinguishers among the many emotional states. If this is correct, the findings of the present study may help to resolve the problem. Obviously this study does *not* rule out the possibility of physiological differences among the emotional states. It is the case, however, that given precisely the same state of epinephrine-induced sympathetic activation, we have, by means of cognitive manipulations, been able to produce in our subjects the very disparate states of euphoria and anger. It may indeed be the case that cognitive factors are major determiners of the emotional labels we apply to a common state of sympathetic arousal.

Let us ask next whether our results are specific to the state of sympathetic activation or if they are generalizable to other states of physiological arousal. It is clear that from our experiments proper, it is impossible to answer the question for our studies have been concerned largely with the effects of an epinephrine created state of sympathetic arousal. We would suggest, however, that our conclusions are generalizable to almost any pronounced internal state for which no appropriate explanation is available. This suggestion receives some support from the experiences of Nowlis and Nowlis (1956) in their program of research on the effects of drugs on mood. In their work the Nowlises typically administer a drug to groups of four subjects who are physically in one another's presence and free to interact. The Nowlises describe some of their results with these groups as follows:

At first we used the same drug for all 4 men. In those sessions seconal, when compared with placebo, increased the checking of such words as expansive, forceful, courageous, daring, elated, and impulsive. In our first statistical analysis we were confronted with the stubborn fact that when the same drug is given to all 4 men in a group, the N that has to be entered into the analysis is 1, not 4. This increases the cost of an already expensive experiment by a considerable factor, but it cannot be denied that the effects of these drugs may be and often are quite contagious. Our first attempted solution was to run tests on groups in which each man had a different drug during the same session, such as 1 on seconal, 1 on benzedrine, 1 on dramamine, and 1 on placebo. What does seconal do? Cooped up with, say, the egotistical benzedrine partner, the withdrawn, indifferent dramamine partner, and the slightly bored lactose man, the seconal subject reports that he is distractible, dizzy, drifting, glum, defiant, languid, sluggish, discouraged, dull, gloomy, lazy, and slow! This is not the report of mood that we got when all 4 men were on seconal. It thus appears that the moods of the partners do definitely influence the effect of seconal (p. 350).

It is not completely clear from this description whether this "contagion" of mood is more marked in drug than in placebo groups, but should this be the case, these results would certainly support the suggestion that our findings are generalizable to internal states other than that produced by an injection of epinephrine.

Finally, let us consider the implications of our formulation and data for alternative conceptualizations of emotion. Perhaps the most popular current conception of emotion is in terms of "activation theory" in the sense employed by Lindsley (1951) and Woodworth and Schlosberg (1958). As we understand this theory, it suggests that emotional states should be considered as at one end of a continuum of activation which is defined in terms of degree of autonomic arousal and of electroencephalographic measures of activation. The results of the experiment described in

this paper do, of course, suggest that such a formulation is not completely adequate. It is possible to have very high degrees of activation without a subject either appearing to be or describing himself as "emotional." Cognitive factors appear to be indispensable elements in any formulation of emotion.

SUMMARY

It is suggested that emotional states may be considered a function of a state of physiological arousal and of a cognition appropriate to this state of arousal. From this follows these propositions:

1. Given a state of physiological arousal for which an individual has no immediate explanation, he will label this state and describe his feelings in terms of the cognitions available to him. To the extent that cognitive factors are potent determiners of emotional states, it should be anticipated that precisely the same state of physiological arousal could be labeled "joy" or "fury" or "jealousy" or any of a great diversity of emotional labels depending on the cognitive aspects of the situation.
2. Given a state of physiological arousal for which an individual has a completely appropriate explanation, no evaluative needs will arise and the individual is unlikely to label his feelings in terms of the alternative cognitions available.
3. Given the same cognitive circumstances, the individual will react emotionally or describe his feelings as emotions only to the extent that he experiences a state of physiological arousal.

An experiment is described which, together with the results of other studies, supports these propositions.

REFERENCES

Ax, A. F. Physiological differentiation of emotional states. *Psychosom. Med.*, 1953, *15*, 433–442.
Cannon, W. B. *Bodily changes in pain, hunger, fear and rage.* (2nd ed.) New York: Appleton, 1929.
Cantril, H., & Hunt, W. A. Emotional effects pro-

duced by the injection of adrenalin. *Amer. J. Psychol.* 1932, *44*, 300–307.

Festinger, L. A theory of social comparison processes. *Hum. Relat.*, 1954, *7*, 114–140.

Hunt, J. McV., Cole, M. W., & Reis, E. E. Situational cues distinguishing anger, fear, and sorrow. *Amer. J. Psychol.*, 1958, *71*, 136–151.

James, W. *The principles of psychology.* New York: Holt, 1890.

Landis, C., & Hunt, W. A. Adrenalin and emotion. *Psychol. Rev.*, 1932, *39*, 467–485.

Latané, B., & Schachter, S. Adrenalin and avoidance learning. *J. comp. physiol. Psychol.*, 1962, *65*, 369–372.

Lindsley, D. B. Emotion. In S. S. Stevens (Ed.), *Handbook of experimental psychology.* New York: Wiley, 1951. Pp. 473–516.

Marañon, G. Contribution à l'étude de l'action émotive de l'adrénaline. *Rev. Francaise Endocrinol.*, 1924, *2*, 301–325.

Nowlis, V., & Nowlis, H. H. The description and analysis of mood. *Ann. N. Y. Acad. Sci.*, 1956, *65*, 345–355.

Ruckmick, C. A. *The psychology of feeling and emotion.* New York: McGraw-Hill, 1936.

Schachter, J. Pain, fear, and anger in hypertensives and normotensives: A psychophysiologic study. *Psychosom. Med.*, 1957, *19*, 17–29.

Schachter, S. *The psychology of affiliation* Stanford, Calif.: Stanford Univer. Press, 1959.

Schachter, S., & Wheeler, L. Epinephrine, chlorpromazine, and amusement. *J. abnorm. soc. Psychol.*, 1962, *65*, 121–128.

Singer, J. E. The effects of epinephrine, chlorpromazine and dibenzyline upon the fright responses of rats under stress and non-stress conditions. Unpublished doctoral dissertation, University of Minnesota, 1961.

Wolf, S., & Wolff, H. G. *Human gastric function.* New York: Oxford Univer. Press, 1947.

Woodworth, R. S., & Schlosberg, H. *Experimental psychology.* New York: Holt, 1958.

Wrightsman, L. S. Effects of waiting with others on changes in level of felt anxiety. *J. abnorm. soc. Psychol.*, 1960, *61*, 216–222.

NOTES

1. This experiment is part of a program of research on cognitive and physiological determinants of emotional state which is being conducted at the Department of Social Psychology at Columbia University under PHS Research Grant M-2584 from the National Institute of Mental Health, United States Public Health Service. This experiment was conducted at the Laboratory for Research in Social Relations at the University of Minnesota.

   The authors wish to thank Jean Carlin and Ruth Hase, the physicians in the study, and Bibb Latané and Leonard Weller who were the paid participants.

2. Though our experiments are concerned exclusively with the physiological changes produced by the injection of adrenalin, which appear to be primarily the result of sympathetic excitation, the term physiological arousal is used in preference to the more specific "excitation of the sympathetic nervous system" because there are indications, to be discussed later, that this formulation is applicable to a variety of bodily states.

3. Translated copies of Marañon's (1924) paper may be obtained by writing to the senior author.

4. This suggestion is not new for several psychologists have suggested that situational factors should be considered the chief differentiators of the emotions. Hunt, Cole, and Reis (1958) probably make this point most explicitly in their study distinguishing among fear, anger, and sorrow in terms of situational characteristics.

5. In his critique of the James-Lange theory of emotion, Cannon (1929) also makes the point that sympathectomized animals and patients do seem to manifest emotional behavior. This criticism is, of course, as applicable to the above proposition as it was to the James-Lange formulation. We shall discuss the issues involved in later papers.

6. It was, of course, imperative that the sequence with the stooge begin before the subject felt his first symptoms for otherwise the subject would be virtually forced to interpret his feelings in terms of events preceding the stooge's entrance. Pretests had indicated that, for most subjects, epinephrine-caused symptoms began within 3–5 minutes after injection. A deliberate attempt was made then to bring in the stooge within 1 minute after the subject's injection.

CRITICAL THINKING QUESTIONS

1. In order to conduct the experiment, the researchers deceived the subjects. What ethical issues are involved in this type of research? The obvious deception was not telling the subjects the true nature of the experiment. Does the use of injections of a drug that had a physiological impact on the subjects prompt additional ethical considerations?

2. This study examines the effects of just one drug, epinephrine, which has excitatory effects on people. Would you expect a similar pattern of results for other classes of drugs? Which ones might be interesting to study?

3. What might the implications of this study be for people who use drugs in a social setting? Would the feelings that they associate with using drugs be due to how others around them responded? How could you test this possibility?

4. Do you think it is possible to change the emotion you are experiencing by changing the label of the emotion? For example, if you were afraid of public speaking, could you change your emotion from a negative one (fear) to a positive one (excitement) by changing the label given to your physiological arousal? Have you had any personal experience with this: examples of when something like this may have occurred or a situation when you were aware of how other people influenced how you interpreted the situation?

ADDITIONAL RELATED READINGS

Lazarus, R. S. (1984). On the primacy of cognition. *American Psychologist, 39,* 124–129.

Zajonc, R. B. (1984). On the primacy of affect. *American Psychologist, 39,* 117–123.

ARTICLE 9 _____

The processes involved in social perception also are used in evaluating ourselves. How do we perceive ourselves? For example, how do you see yourself in the social psychology class you are taking? Very capable of doing the work? Lucky if you pass the course?

When we talk about our beliefs about the self, how accurate are they? If we find out that our initial beliefs were wrong, do we change them? Or do we tend to discount the new, inconsistent information? Although objectively it would seem that we should change our erroneous beliefs when confronted with conflicting information (especially when our initial belief was negative), the fact is that we do not. We are prone to use many cognitive strategies, such as the ones discussed in Article 7, that often render our self-judgments inaccurate. We may ignore or discredit the contradictory information, for example.

This article, by Lepper, Ross, and Lau, presents an interesting examination of what happens when people are confronted with information that contradicts their initial beliefs about themselves. The article is of particular interest not only because of its important implications but also because of where it was conducted: in a real-world high school setting, not in a laboratory.

Persistence of Inaccurate Beliefs about the Self
Perseverance Effects in the Classroom

■ Mark R. Lepper, Leę Ross, and Richard R. Lau

The perseverance of erroneous self-assessments was examined among high school students. Subjects were first exposed to either highly effective or thoroughly useless filmed instruction, leading, respectively, to their consequent success or failure. No-discounting subjects received no assistance in recognizing the relative superiority or inferiority of their instruction. Discounting subjects, by contrast, were subsequently shown the opposite *instructional film, highlighting the obvious differences in instructional quality. Subsequent measures revealed that all subjects recognized the effectiveness or ineffectiveness of their instruction, although this contrast was clearer for discounting subjects. Nevertheless, both discounting and no-discounting subjects continued to draw unwarranted inferences—in line with their initial outcomes—about their personal capacities, immediately afterward. Dissociated and disguised measures of academic preferences and perceptions completed weeks later produced even more dramatic results: The continuing impact of initial outcomes was generally greater for discounting than no-discounting subjects.*

The beliefs we hold about our skills and abilities have profound personal and social consequences. In academic contexts, variations in perceived competence have been repeatedly shown to influence an individual's choices among tasks, willingness to invest effort in task accomplishment, and persistence in the face of subsequent failure (e.g.,

Reprinted from the *Journal of Personality and Social Psychology*, 1986, *50*, 482–491. Copyright 1986 by the American Psychological Association. Reprinted by permission.

Bandura, 1977, 1982; Deci, 1980; Lepper & Greene, 1978; Weiner, 1974, 1979). Understanding the conditions under which erroneous self-assessments may initially be formed and the processes by which they may survive or be modified in the face of further experience is thus an issue of practical as well as theoretical significance.

Impressions about one's academic abilities are presumably influenced by one's initial encounters with novel tasks or new subjects. Individuals who experience initial success or failure in some new undertaking tend to infer that they possess relatively high or low aptitude in the pertinent domain of endeavor. Often such first impressions may be quite accurate and may be bolstered as we gain more experience and sophistication. Sometimes, however, the first impressions we form about ourselves may be inaccurate or unfounded—a reflection of our failure to appreciate the difficulty or ease of the task confronting us or, more generally, of our reliance on biased, irrelevant, or invalid information (Nisbett & Ross, 1980). Under such circumstances we will be challenged to update our impressions in the light of subsequent outcomes and subsequent insights about the circumstances attending our original outcomes (Abelson, 1974, 1976; Fischhoff, 1976; Kelley, 1967, 1971; Ross & Lepper, 1980). Failure to assimilate new evidence appropriately or failure to discount old evidence sufficiently in the face of challenges to its probativeness would obviously promote erroneous self-assessments and potentially dysfunctional decisions.

In recent years educational researchers have expressed concern about the destructive, and often unwarranted, negative self-assessments that many students form on the basis of initial academic failures and then seem to retain in the face of subsequent experiences and strenuous attempts by teachers and counselors to change them. Failures in the early school years—failure that may result not from a lack of ability but from inadequate personal preparation, from exposure to ineffective or insensitive instruction, or from motivational deficits—have been cited as a primary cause of children's early defeatist reactions to school and their devaluation of academic performance (e.g.,

Glasser, 1969; Holt, 1964; Silberman, 1970). Studies of college attrition have led educators to hypothesize that college students' first-semester successes or failures influence the probability of their eventual graduation far more than can be accounted for by differences in measured aptitudes (Pantages & Creedon, 1978). Researchers concerned with math phobia have suggested that students' initial impressions of their lack of aptitude or ability, which often are based less on actual evidence of incompetence than on expectations and beliefs unrelated to measurable aptitude, may prove strikingly resistant to educational or therapeutic attempts to alter those beliefs (e.g., Betz, 1978; Fox, Brody, & Tobin, 1980).

Little evidence currently exists to corroborate, or to challenge these speculations. Two recent social-psychological literatures, however, add some credence to such claims. There is, first, a wide array of evidence consistent with the proposition that people forming impressions about their own abilities are prone to commit the "fundamental attribution error" (Ross, 1977)—that is, that they fail to make appropriate allowances even for situational determinants of their performance that they recognize to be highly significant.

Similarly, evidence from a variety of sources documents the considerable capacity of initial impressions and beliefs to survive subsequent logical or empirical challenges. At least in the experimental laboratory, people's first impressions tend to be lasting and new evidence that appears to disconfirm previously formed beliefs is apt to be given little weight (e.g., Asch, 1946; Jones & Goethals, 1971; Kelley, 1950; Lord, Ross, & Lepper, 1979; Luchins, 1942, 1957). More recently, a second and rather different line of research on belief perseverance has begun to emerge. This research examines people's responses not to new evidence, but to the discrediting or negating of old evidence—that is, to the discrediting of the very evidence that initially led them to form particular beliefs. Thus, even thoroughly debriefing subjects about deceptive initial feedback or inauthentic data may not suffice to undo the effects of the deceptive information (Anderson, Lepper, & Ross, 1980; Fleming & Arrowood, 1979; Jennings, Lepper, & Ross, 1981; Ross, Lepper, & Hubbard, 1975; Valins, 1974; Walster, Berscheid, Abrahams, & Aronson, 1967). This line of research, with its broader suggestion that people might similarly show less belief change than would logically be warranted in the face of many other forms of evidential discrediting, seems particularly germane to the educational questions at issue here. It implies that students who have formed an initial assessment of their abilities on the basis of their previous performance may persevere in such assessments even after they have been provided with compelling evidence that the performance in question was an invalid reflection of their aptitude.

A primary purpose of the present investigation, therefore, was to examine the relevance of these debriefing experiments in an ecologically representative educational setting that would answer criticisms concerning the use of an artificial debriefing paradigm. It might be suggested, for example, that the results obtained in earlier studies depended importantly upon subjects' perception that the experimenter had previously lied to them in providing false feedback, or their perception that the experimenter had intentionally attempted to manipulate their initial self-assessments. One might further be concerned that subjects in these studies were responding to demand characteristics of an experimental setting that presented initial outcomes, discrediting of outcomes, and subsequent self-perception measures in close proximity to each other. More generally, it is important to show that previous demonstrations of perseverance effects were not hot-house products of an exotic methodology, but rather were reflective of processes and mechanisms that are apt to produce significant and enduring instances of unwarranted belief persistence in everyday social interaction (see Nisbett & Ross, 1980; Ross & Lepper, 1980).

These general issues were addressed through the use of a design in which students were initially led to succeed or to fail through exposure to either a highly effective or a totally worthless method of instruction in a new subject area. Later, in the *discounting* conditions (but not in *no-discounting*

conditions), subjects had an opportunity to see the alternative method of instruction, a procedure designed to help them to recognize the dependence of their initial performance on their prior instruction and to discount the significance of that performance vis à vis their personal aptitudes. Immediately following these manipulations, subjects' assessments of their ability at the task were obtained, along with direct measures of subjects' cognizance of the probable impact of the different methods of instruction. Roughly 3 weeks later, in a setting divorced from the previous experimental sessions, these immediate measures were supplemented with a disguised measure of students' assessments of their general ability at and liking for academic activities similar to the experimental task. Our primary concerns were the extent to which students' assessments of their personal aptitudes would reflect their situationally determined initial outcomes rather than their real ability levels and the extent to which any such erroneous assessments would survive the relevant discounting manipulations.

METHOD

Overview

High school students were presented with either a highly effective instructional film teaching them how to solve seemingly complex reasoning problems through the use of a simple matrix (*success condition*) or a highly ineffective film purporting to teach them to solve these same problems with a confusing and generally unhelpful set of exhortations (*failure condition*). All of the subjects then attempted to solve four such problems. Prior to any dependent measures involving the subjects' assessments of their abilities, subjects in the discounting condition were additionally presented with the teaching film initially shown to subjects in the other condition, thus providing them with some explicit evidence about the relative efficacy of their initial instruction and the need to discount their initial success or failure accordingly. In the no-discounting conditions, subjects did not see the alternative film or receive any other information to help them recognize the extent to which their initial outcome had been situationally rather than dispositionally determined. Direct measures of subjects' perceptions of the impact of the initial teaching film and their perceptions of their abilities were obtained immediately after the performance test (and, where appropriate, the subsequent discounting procedure). To provide delayed and dissociated measures of the persistence of these initial beliefs, students later took part in a survey being conducted by the school's mathematics department. This survey, completed in class 3 weeks after the end of the experiment, asked students to assess their relative competence at and preferences among several possible units allegedly being considered for inclusion in the regular math curriculum. One unit featured problems identical to those encountered previously in the experimental sessions.

Subjects

Subjects were 52 high school freshmen and sophomores enrolled in basic math courses at Awalt High School in Mountain View, California. Subjects were recruited by their teachers, who solicited volunteers to participate in an experimental study of teaching techniques in math. The sample (which included all volunteers with parental permission to participate) totaled 29 female and 23 male subjects, distributed equally across conditions. Three subjects were not present during the subsequent posttest; their data, however, are included for measures taken immediately after the initial experimental session.[1]

Experimental Task

The study required a task at which few untutored subjects would succeed, but for which a brief instructional procedure could be devised to guarantee their success. These requirements were met through the use of a set of deductive-reasoning problems of a sort common in recreational mathematics, problems that require the student to match a number of individuals with their appropriate occupations, actions, possessions, or the

like by extracting information from a collection of *clues* that, in combination, serve to eliminate incorrect pairings.[2] Extensive pretesting indicated that although such problems were generally unfamiliar and rather difficult for our subject population, students could be taught to solve such problems in a relatively short time through the use of a simple matrix to keep track of the information contained in the different clues.

Procedure

Subjects participated in the study in individual sessions conducted in a research trailer parked on school grounds. Upon arrival, subjects were seated at a desk in front of a movie screen. They were told that the study involved evaluations by the math department of different techniques for solving mathematical reasoning problems and that the particular type of problem to be considered in that day's session involved deductive reasoning. Each student also received a sample problem to be solved in conjunction with the two training films.

Success-Failure Manipulation At this point, subjects were shown one of two 10-min instructional films featuring an experienced teacher presenting either a highly effective or a thoroughly ineffective technique for solving the deduction problems. Both films included a general introduction to the method being taught and subsequent illustrations of the use of that method. At the end of both films, the sample problem provided to subjects was addressed, and students used the method they had been taught to solve this problem.

In the success conditions, the film presented subjects with the *matrix method* for solving these problems. These subjects were taught how to generate a matrix, to enter the information gleaned from different clues, and ultimately to solve the problem by systematically eliminating incorrect alternatives. This procedure made the solution of the problems a relatively routine matter, and its value became evident to subjects as they worked through a sample problem. In the failure conditions, by contrast, subjects were presented with the *affirmation-negation method,* which consisted largely of a series of exhortations to reason logically and to be sure to keep in mind all of the information contained in previous clues as each new piece of information was encountered. Although the teacher frequently extolled the value of this method, her explication of its use was more confusing than helpful. Frequently, in fact, the links she made between clues and their implications depended on her advance knowledge of the correct answer.

After viewing one film or the other, subjects were asked to solve a series of four problems. The first of these was quite easy (and ultimately solved by all participants), but the last three were fairly difficult. Students were given 20 min to work on these problems, and it was casually suggested that three correct answers would be a "good score." No specific information was given, however, concerning the average number correct. After subjects had worked on the problems for the allotted time (or had completed all four of them correctly), the experimenter went over the answers to each of the problems with the subject, providing immediate performance feedback.

Discounting Manipulation   At this point, within both the success and failure conditions, half of the subjects were exposed to the discounting procedure designed to make clear to them, in a vivid and compelling fashion, the extent to which their initial performance had been determined by the type of instruction they had received. Specifically, subjects in the discounting conditions were now exposed to the film demonstrating the alternative teaching technique, that is, the technique to which subjects in the *opposite* condition had initially been exposed.

In viewing this second film, subjects, as before, were required to solve the sample problem using the method they had just been taught. This insured that subjects would have an opportunity to use the alternative method and recognize clearly its benefits or deficits. This second film, then, presented both success and failure subjects in the discounting condition with explicit evidence concerning the causes of their prior performance. For failure-condition subjects, who had not solved many of the problems, the second film made it clear that the problems would be much easier to solve using the matrix method and, presumably, helped them recognize that their prior performance had reflected a lack of effective instruction rather than a lack of aptitude. For success-condition subjects, the second film served to emphasize the extent to which their initial outcome had been influenced by the specific techniques they had been taught and thus served to help them recognize that less effective instruction might well have led to less stellar performance.

The remaining subjects, those assigned to the no-discounting conditions, were not exposed to the alternative film. Instead they proceeded to complete the immediate dependent variable measures without receiving any evidence about the relative effectiveness of the problem-solving techniques they had been taught. These subjects were nevertheless free to reach their own conclusions about the relative quality and impact of their own instructional film. Their data, accordingly, allow us to determine whether situationally determined successes or failures were, in fact, attributed to personal aptitudes. They also provide a baseline against which the effectiveness of the explicit discounting manipulation can be assessed.

Immediate Dependent Measures   After subjects had finished working on the four problems (and, in the discounting conditions, after they had viewed the second film), they were asked to answer a series of questions ostensibly created to assist the math department in evaluating the effectiveness of the teaching techniques to which they had been exposed. The questionnaires included items asking subjects to estimate their probable future performance at the task, given a set of 10 further problems of comparable difficulty; to assess the effectiveness of the techniques they had been shown; and to rate their own ability, relative to that of their peers, at "solving problems of this sort," at "working puzzles," at "making logical deductions," and at mathematics and school work in general. Following the completion of these questionnaires, the experimental session was terminated and subjects were thanked for their participation and returned to class.

Dissociated Dependent Measures To investigate the persistence and probe the potential behavioral implications of the self-perceptions formed by subjects during the experimental session, additional dependent measures were collected 3 weeks later in subjects' regularly scheduled math classes. Students were told by their own teachers that the math department was conducting a survey to assess their reactions to three proposed mini-units under consideration for inclusion in the regular curriculum. To enhance the plausibility of this survey, all of the students in each classroom were asked by their teachers to take part.

The units presented for possible adoption into the regular math program included "deductive reasoning," "sequential decision making," and "probabilistic reasoning." The survey included, for each, a brief description of the skills the unit was designed to teach and examples of the types of problems to which these skills might be applied. The sample "deductive-reasoning" problem was highly reminiscent of those previously encountered by subjects who had participated in the experiment; the others were novel. For each unit, students were asked to rate how well they thought they might do on the unit and how much they would like to see the unit included in the program. They were also asked to make parallel ratings concerning the probable abilities and preferences of their peers. Comparisons of subjects' responses to the three units, then, produced an index of their attitudes toward and perceived competence at the experimental task relative to other comparable tasks. Finally, subjects were asked specifically to rank order the three units in terms both of their own perceived competence and the preferences and probable responses of their peers. At no time, it should be emphasized, did the teachers ever mention the prior experimental sessions.

Final Debriefing After these measures had been obtained, students in each classroom were given a thorough debriefing concerning the aims and purposes of the study and the necessity for the various deceptions that had been employed. This debriefing was patterned after the process-debriefing technique, shown in previous research (Ross et al., 1975) to be effective in greatly reducing or eliminating the effects of false performance feedback. Hence, this final debriefing included both a discussion of perseverance effects and the processes underlying them and a more pointed discussion of the personal relevance of this line of research to the students' current perceptions about their academic performance.

RESULTS

Preliminary Analyses, Manipulation Checks, and Perceptions of Instructional Effectiveness

Preliminary Analyses Preliminary analyses including sex of subject as a factor in the design of this study yielded no evidence of significant interactions of sex of subject with treatment condition. The data were therefore collapsed across this factor for further analysis.

Success–Failure Manipulation It is clear from subjects' performance on the four test problems that the success–failure manipulation was generally, but not universally, effective in producing the intended performance differences. Subjects in the success conditions solved significantly more problems ($M = 3.04$) than did subjects in the failure conditions ($M = 1.74$), $F(1, 48) = 28.20 < .0001$.[3] Only 3 of 26 failure-condition subjects solved as many as three problems (11 subjects solved only the one easy problem, 12 solved it and one other problem, 2 solved three problems, and 1 solved all four problems), whereas only 7 of 26 success-condition subjects solved fewer than three problems (2 subjects solved only the single easy problem and an additional 5 solved only two problems, but 9 solved three problems and 10 solved all four problems). Thus, despite the overall success of the manipulation, a small minority of subjects succeeded or failed despite instruction designed to produce the opposite outcome; these exceptional subjects, of course, can be expected to weaken mean differences between the relevant success and failure conditions (but they obviously must be included in our analyses because their exclusion would virtually guarantee a difference in the mean aptitude levels of the two outcome groups).

Perceptions of Instructional Effectiveness Several measures were included to determine whether subjects recognized the difference in the quality of their instructional method and its probable impact on their performance. (The results from some of these are summarized in Tables 1 and 2.) Within the discounting conditions, where subjects saw both methods, success subjects rated their own matrix method as far superior (M = 8.77) to the opposite affirmation–negation method (M = 3.92), $t(12)$ = 7.22, p < .001; conversely, failure subjects rated their own method as decidedly inferior (M = 5.75) to the opposite method (M = 8.63), $t(11)$ = 6.95, p < .001. Consistent with these assessments, success subjects predicted that an average student would score a mean of 3.2 correct with their matrix method and only 2.4 with the opposite method, $t(12)$ = 7.58, p < .001, and failure subjects predicted that an average student would score 3.1 correct with the opposite method and only 2.1 with their own method, $t(11)$ = 5.42, p < .001. In assessing the impact of the methods on their own performance, success-condition subjects who had scored a mean of 3.2 correct with their own method estimated that they would have scored 2.4 with the opposite method; failure subjects who had actually scored a mean of 1.9 estimated that they would have scored 3.0 correct with the opposite method. In short, both success- and failure-condition subjects who experienced the discounting procedures were well aware of the relevant difference in instructional quality between the two techniques, and subjects in both conditions (particularly subjects in the failure condition) seemed quite accurate in estimating the probable impact of the two techniques on their own performance and that of their peers.

The perceptions of subjects in the two no-discounting conditions are more difficult to assess, largely because they never had an opportunity to compare the quality and impact of their own instruction to that offered in the opposite condition. Nevertheless, several between-subject comparisons seem highly revealing. First, success subjects rated their instructional method

TABLE 1 / Perceived Impact of Instructional methods on Average Student Performance

Outcome condition	No. correct with own method	No. correct with opposite method	Difference (own − opposite)
Discounting conditions			
Success	3.15	2.35	+ 0.80
Failure	2.13	3.13	− 1.00
Difference (success − failure)	+ 1.02	− 0.78	+ 1.80
No-discounting conditions			
Success	3.38	1.88	+ 1.50
Failure	2.46	1.50	+ 0.96
Difference (success − failure)	+ 0.92	+ 0.38	+ 0.54

TABLE 2 / Perceived Impact of Instructional Methods on Own Performance

Outcome condition	Actual no. correct	No. correct if opposite method	Difference (actual − opposite)
Discounting conditions			
Success	3.15	2.45	+ 0.70
Failure	1.92	3.00	− 1.08
Difference (success − failure)	+ 1.23	− 0.55	+ 1.78
No-discounting conditions			
Success	2.92	1.75	1.17
Failure	1.57	1.64	− 0.07
Difference (success − failure)	+ 1.35	+ 0.11	+ 1.24

more highly (M = 8.96) than did failure subjects (M = 6.29), $t(25)$ = 4.37, p < .001—a difference (D = 2.67) almost as great as that seen for discounting-condition subjects (D = 3.02) who had been given the opportunity to contrast their method with the opposite one. Estimates of perceived impact further reveal the extent to which no-discounting subjects, even in the absence of any opportunity to view the other method, were aware of the relative effectiveness or ineffectiveness of the method they had been taught. Success subjects predicted that average students would score 3.4 correct with the matrix method but only 1.9 correct if they received no instruction at all; they also estimated that with no prior instruction they personally would have scored only 1.8 correct instead of the 2.9 correct they actually scored after learning the matrix method. It is interesting that failure subjects seemed to make a distinction between themselves and others in assessing the instructional method they had received. Although they thought that they personally had gained nothing from the affirmation–negation method—in fact, they estimated on average that their performance would have been slightly better without such instruction (M of 1.64 vs. 1.57)—they estimated that an average student's performance would be boosted from 1.5 correct to 2.5 correct. Thus, no-discounting subjects, like discounting subjects, seemed generally insightful about the quality and probable impact of the instruction they had received, although failure subjects seemed to believe that the instruction they received might have served others less poorly than themselves.

Immediate Postexperimental Measures

At the conclusion of the experimental sessions, subjects were asked to complete a brief questionnaire assessing their perceptions of their abilities. The results are summarized in Table 3. Our primary objectives were (a) to determine whether the (largely) situationally determined outcomes achieved by subjects in the success and failure conditions exerted an initial impact on their perceptions of their personal aptitudes and (b) to

TABLE 3 / Immediate Dependent Measures

Condition	Discounting	No discounting
Expected no. correct on 10 new trials		
Success	7.84	7.23
Failure	5.67	4.25
Difference (success – failure)	+ 2.17	+ 2.98
Ratings of own ability on 3 related tasks		
Success	6.67	6.72
Failure	6.25	5.93
Difference (success – failure)	+ 0.42	+ 0.79

determine whether any such impact was reduced by the vivid and compelling discounting procedure of having subjects actually see the opposite instructional method.

As a direct index of subjects' perceptions of their ability at the specific deduction task, subjects were asked to estimate how many problems they thought they could solve if presented with a set of 10 new problems of comparable difficulty. The results, displayed in Table 3, indicate that failure subjects expected to do less well than success subjects under both no-discounting and discounting conditions. In fact the relevant difference between success and failure subjects was roughly 70% as large for discounting subjects (D = 2.71) who ultimately were exposed to both instructional methods, as it was for no-discounting subjects (D = 2.98) who were exposed only to their own method. Indeed, when a simple two-way analysis of variance is performed, we find a highly significant main effect for the success–failure manipulation, $F(1, 48)$ = 25.88, p < .0001, but no significant interaction between the outcome and discounting manipulations, $F(1, 48)$ = .62. When discounting-condition subjects are considered separately, the postdiscounting impact of the initial outcome manipulation remains significant, $F(1, 48)$ = 8.53, p < .01; that is, the failure-condition subjects continue to predict significantly poorer performance for themselves than do success-condition subjects, even after they have ultimately viewed the same instructional materials as the success-condition subjects.

Additional items dealt with subjects' perceptions of more general abilities related to the deduction task—that is, "this sort of problem solving," "doing puzzles in general," and "making logical deductions." Despite the fact that subjects in both success and failure conditions seemed to recognize that their initial outcome had been heavily, and perhaps even completely, the result of superior or inadequate instruction, a composite measure combining these three items suggested some generalization of the initial outcome manipulation. Here, however, the main effect of the outcome manipulation only approached statistical significance, $F(1, 48) = 3.69$, $p < .10$. Again, there was no evidence of any significant interaction between the discounting and outcome manipulations, $F(1, 48) = .35$. This time the difference between success-condition means and failure-condition means were slightly more than 50% as great in the discounting conditions (D = 0.42) as it was in the no-discounting conditions (D = 0.79), and in neither no-discounting nor discounting conditions was the effect of the outcome manipulation individually significant, $Fs(1, 48) = 1.42$ and 1.22, respectively.

Finally, it is worth noting that additional items assessing subjects' global perceptions of their school performance in various subjects showed no differences among conditions. Thus, the results for the measures relevant to our manipulation do not appear to have resulted simply from some difference in the subjects' mood state or some general set to respond positively or negatively about their abilities.

Delayed and Dissociated Dependent Measures

The second set of dependent measures was collected 3 weeks after the experimental sessions had concluded by teachers in the school's regular math classes. As part of a survey ostensibly designed by the math department, subjects were asked to assess their own abilities and preferences, and those of other students, with regard to three prospective units being considered for inclusion in the math curriculum. One proposed unit (i.e., deductive reasoning) was described featuring examples highly reminiscent of the prior experimental task. The other two proposed units (i.e., sequential decision making and probabilistic reasoning) were described in a way that made the prior experimental task irrelevant to them. Ratings on these two novel units were eventually averaged and subtracted from their ratings on the critical deductive-reasoning unit to provide an index that reduced variance resulting from individual differences in scale usage.[4] The resulting means for each treatment condition are presented in Table 4.

For subjects' perceptions of their own ability at deductive reasoning relative to other tasks, the results seem fairly clear and, in at least one respect, quite surprising. Once again we find a significant main effect for prior success or failure, $F(1, 46) = 4.50$, $p < .05$, and again we find no significant interaction between success–failure and the discounting manipulation, $F(1, 46) = .51$. However, unlike the immediate measures, the effects of prior success versus failure seem to be somewhat stronger in the discounting conditions than in the control conditions. These effects are illustrated in Figure 1. Considering subjects in the discounting condition alone, the effect of the prior success–failure manipulation remains individually significant, $F(1, 46) = 4.04$, $p = .05$.

For measures of subjects' liking for the deductive-reasoning unit relative to the other units under consideration for inclusion in the regular curriculum, the pattern of results is even more striking. We see an impact of prior success or failure only in the discounting conditions, $F(1, 46) = 6.71$, $p < .025$, although both the relevant main effect of prior outcome and the interaction effect between outcome and discounting manipulations reach only marginal significance, $F(1, 46) = 3.49$ and 3.19, $ps < .10$, respectively.

A generally similar picture emerges from a consideration of subjects' explicit rankings of the three units, with the relevant "perseverance" effects again appearing to be stronger in discounting than in no-discounting conditions. Analyses

TABLE 4 / Delayed, Dissociated Dependent Measures

Condition	Discounting	No discounting
Perceived ability of self at relevant versus irrelevant units		
Success	+4.96	+5.32
Failure	−0.29	+2.71
Difference (success − failure)	+5.25	+2.59
Liking for relevant versus irrelevant units		
Success	+5.19	+1.82
Failure	−1.13	+1.68
Difference (success − failure)	+6.32	−0.14
Perceived ability of others at relevant versus irrelevant units		
Success	+3.15	+3.36
Failure	−0.58	+2.32
Difference (success − failure)	+3.73	+1.04
Rankings of relevant units: own ability		
Success	+1.23	+1.55
Failure	+1.83	+1.85
Difference (success − failure)	+0.60	+0.30
Own liking		
Success	+1.15	+1.18
Failure	+1.83	+1.46
Difference (success − failure)	+0.68	+0.28

of variance considering the discounting conditions alone revealed significant main effects of the initial outcome measure both for ability rankings, $F(1, 46) = 8.13$, $p < .01$, and preference rankings, $F(1, 46) = 6.19$, $p < .02$. In neither case, however, was there a significant interaction between the outcome and discounting manipulations, $Fs(1, 46)$ of 1.39 and 0.45, respectively.

Finally, ratings and rankings of the probable abilities and preferences of peers suggests that the subjects' own responses reflected, at least in part, their inferences about the inherent difficulty and likeability of the proposed units. Thus, the overall pattern of results of ratings of *peers' ability*, is similar to that seen for *own ability*, although both the main effect within the discounting conditions, $F(1, 46) = 3.72$, $p < .10$, and the interaction between outcome and discounting manipulations, $F(1, 46) = .96$, are weaker for peer assessments than for self-assessments. Ratings of probable peer preferences, similarly, are reminiscent of own preferences. Here, however, neither the magnitude of the relevant main effect within the discounting conditions, $F(1, 46) = 1.32$, nor the interaction effect between outcome and discounting manipulations, $F(1, 46) = .78$, approaches significance.

Taken together, these results provide substantial evidence that the discounting manipulation failed to eliminate the impact of the students' initial outcomes. This failure, it should be emphasized, occurred despite the fact that the subjects seemed to have recognized the role that superior versus inferior instructional films played in determining their initial outcomes. Indeed, the delayed and dissociated measures employed in this study suggest that subjects' longer-term perceptions of their abilities and corresponding preferences regarding future courses of study may have been more influenced by initial outcomes among students who received the discounting manipulation than among no-discounting subjects who never had the opportunity to see the opposite instructional film (see Figure 1). At the very least, we can conclude that long-term consequences were no less among the subjects in the discounting conditions than among subjects in the no-discounting condition.

DISCUSSION

In the present study, participants in all experimental conditions made inferences about their abilities that failed to discount adequately the role of superior versus inferior instruction in determining their performances. Half of these students did so under conditions where no explicit

FIGURE 1 / Postdiscounting effects of success versus failure: Comparison of immediate and delayed/dissociated responses of high school students.

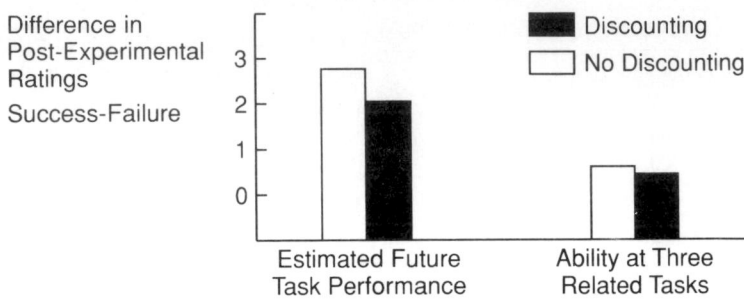

Immediate Dependent Measures

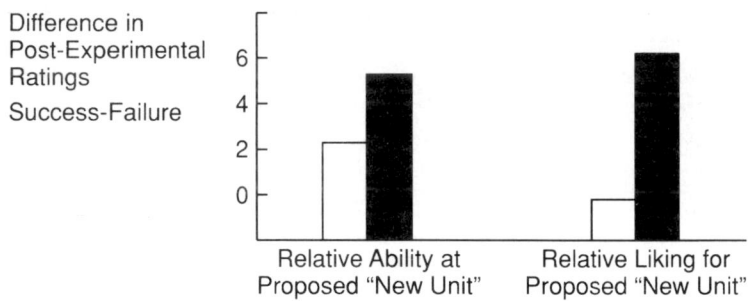

Delayed/Dissociated Dependent Measures

information or evidence was provided to prompt such discounting. Half of them did so even after seeing their own instruction explicitly contrasted with the far superior, or far inferior, instruction received by a group of their peers. Thus, students persevered in erroneous self-perceptions and attributions even after the initial basis for such beliefs was discredited in a fashion that was representative of, but probably more decisive and compelling than, any procedures likely to be employed by well-meaning peers or counselors in real-world educational contexts. The students, we should note, were no doubt familiar with the notion that good teachers often help us learn things we might otherwise have difficulty with and that bad teachers often confuse us about things that we might otherwise have mastered easily. But the message had probably never been presented to them so

concretely or pointedly. Nevertheless, although subjects in general and unsuccessful subjects in particular recognized the impact that their prior instruction had exerted on their performance, they showed no corresponding adjustment of their beliefs concerning their own abilities, even in delayed and dissociated posttest measures. Subjects who had initially succeeded after receiving excellent instruction continued to see themselves as highly competent and expressed corresponding academic preferences; conversely, subjects who had initially failed after exposure to inadequate instruction continued to see themselves as incompetent and to express relatively little liking for or optimism regarding subsequent course work that might tap the abilities in question. In fact, on delayed and dissociated measures the perseverance effect was at least as marked, and perhaps more marked, among the subjects who had received the explicit discounting manipulation as it was among subjects who had been given no explicit evidence or information to deter erroneous personal attributions.

These findings demonstrate the relevance of the fundamental attribution error and of belief perseverance phenomena to educational contexts in which students' decisions are influenced by their perceptions concerning their abilities. Although we might have expected failing students, in particular, to grasp at any exculpatory explanation for their seemingly poor performance, they did not do so. Moreover, in both success and failure conditions, students' subsequent self-evaluations remained heavily influenced by their outcomes, even when they were subsequently exposed to concrete evidence designed to make salient a plausible alternative interpretation for their performance.

Elsewhere (e.g., Ross & Lepper, 1980) we have speculated about some of the cognitive mechanisms that underlie belief perseverance, including assimilation biases (Lord et al., 1979) and the formulation of supportive causal scenarios (Anderson et al., 1980). In the present case, for example, students should be prone to recall past experiences or outcomes congruent with their performance at the experimental task. Those who initially failed, for example, might be likely to recall previous failure in mathematics, on problem-solving exercises, or in playing games of logic — items of evidence congruent with their feelings of low ability at the task. Students should be likely, in addition, to postulate or recall factors that are not only consistent with their initial outcome, but serve to explain that outcome. Initially successful subjects might, for instance, trace their success at this new task to their high tested aptitude in mathematics or their childhood obsession with games of strategy and logic. Indeed, the presumed relevance of ambiguous past events is likely to be determined, in part, by their congruence with the outcome at hand. As a result, subjects in each condition are provided with additional, and seemingly independent, evidence that their recent outcome was,

in fact, indicative of their abilities and aptitudes. This additional evidence may not only bolster impressions prior to debriefing; it can also help to sustain the belief after it has been attacked. When, as in the present case, that attack is less than totally decisive (as opposed, for example, to a complete debriefing about bogus outcomes), subjects may minimize the significance of the challenge precisely because they seem to possess other evidence that suggests the wisdom of their prior conclusions.

These findings also extend previous laboratory research on the perseverance of unwarranted self-assessments in several respects. First, they suggest that the perseverance of discredited initial beliefs may occur even when subjects are demonstrably aware of the fact that their performance had been determined largely by a factor other than their own ability at the task. Second, they suggest that such perseverance effects are not limited to contexts in which subjects perceive the experimenter to have lied to them or to have deliberately manipulated their beliefs. They also cast doubt on the possibility that demonstrations of unwarranted belief perseverance result solely from the demand characteristics of experimental settings. Such arguments could hardly explain why the subjects continued to evaluate their competence in line with their previous performance and to express corresponding degrees of enthusiasm and optimism for new, proposed curricular materials, when tested several weeks later in a classroom setting explicitly divorced from their prior participation in the experiment. In short, these results strongly suggest that belief perseverance effects are not merely artificial and short-lived products of either the psychological laboratory or specific features of the debriefing paradigm.

We should address a potential difficulty with the present results: the possibility that stipulating the nature of a good performance (i.e., telling subjects that getting 3 of 4 right would constitute good performance) may have discouraged some subjects, in both discounting and no-discounting conditions, from attributing their poor performance solely to the inadequacy of their instruction. In context, the remark was deliberately ambiguous about whether the good performance would reflect the merits of the student or the instructional techniques.[5] Although we cannot determine with certainty what role these procedural details played in producing the present results, there is some evidence that such a procedure does not provide a sufficient explanation of our findings. In a preliminary pilot study at the same research site (which omitted several other procedural niceties eventually employed, including, significantly, the use of delayed and dissociated dependent measures), we were able to show post-discounting perseverance on the immediate post-test measures, despite the absence of any information about what would constitute either a good or average performance (cf. Lau, Lepper, & Ross, 1976).

Although the data are generally consistent with our hypotheses, one result deserves additional attention: the apparent finding (on the dissociated classroom measures) that subjects who had been shown a second instructional film, thereby making explicit their prior advantage or handicap, seemed to show more impression perseverance (certainly no less) than did subjects who had not been exposed to this additional information. How can we account for the fact that the information-discounting procedures that seemed, a priori, to be quite compelling and potent proved, a posteriori, to be so utterly ineffective and perhaps even counterproductive? With hindsight, it is not difficult to suggest a variety of possibilities, some of which relate to specific procedural details of our study, some of which relate to basic theoretical assumptions. For example, the consecutive presentation of the two films in our discounting procedure may have heightened rather than attenuated subjects' feelings of success or failure—that is, by making success-condition subjects feel that the puzzles were really quite difficult if one went about solving them in a muddle-headed fashion, or, alternatively, by making failure-condition subjects feel that the puzzles that initially had seemed so difficult were actually quite easy if one attacked them properly. (Such an account, however, leaves one with the task of ex-

plaining why such enhancement effects were apparent only when the dependent measures were delayed and dissociated.) A more general and perhaps more interesting possibility may be that many different types of discounting or debriefing procedures will prove counterproductive because they make the outcome more salient and memorable, or because they make subjects ponder the outcome more deeply—perhaps even heightening the tendency for subjects to generate additional evidence or to postulate causes and explanations for the outcome that is being reconsidered, or otherwise engage in precisely the cognitive activities previously postulated to underlie postdiscounting belief perseverance (cf. Ross & Lepper, 1980; Ross et al., 1975; Ross, Lepper, Strack, & Steinmetz, 1977).

It is important to make clear that it is neither our thesis nor our conclusion from the present data that initial assessments of our abilities cannot be changed or even reversed. Indeed, the present paradigm itself provided direct evidence of changes in subjects' self-assessments, in the sense that subjects' perceptions of competence were clearly influenced by their initial success or failure. By selecting an experimental task that pretesting had suggested would be new to most, if not all, of our subjects, we attempted to create a situation—like that encountered when students are confronted with a new topic or subject—in which subjects would not have well-formed prior beliefs about their aptitudes. By contrast, had we selected a task or topic on which subjects had strong prior beliefs, especially beliefs linked to more encompassing world views (cf. Lord et al., 1979), even our success–failure manipulation might have exerted minimal impact on subjects' self-assessments.

We have no reason to doubt that some more powerful or extensive discrediting procedures might have eliminated the perseverant effects of initial performance. Various types of process-debriefing techniques, wherein subjects are made familiar with the phenomena and proposed underlying mechanisms, might have proven fruitful (cf. Lord, Lepper, & Preston, 1984; Ross et al., 1975). Another possibility might be the use of reenactment procedures, whereby subjects in the discounting condition were allowed to fully repeat their previous experience (ideally with different outcomes) after exposure to the second instructional film (cf. Massad, Hubbard, & Newtson, 1979). Nevertheless, although such procedures might enhance the impact of discounting or discrediting techniques, we would not be surprised if even their application proved disappointing. Readers who have encountered math-phobic students in their own classes, for example, may recall instances in which even demonstrably successful performances seem not to guarantee changes in students' basic assessments of their abilities. The story is not unfamiliar. First, such students, convinced that they do not possess the ability to understand or do math, are dismayed to discover that their social science programs include a required statistics course. They arrive at the instructor's door the first week of the course to throw themselves on the mercy of the court, confessing a total inability to deal with mathematical concepts. Many such students complete the course and, in fact, earn a high grade. Suggestions to these students, at this point, that their original self-perceptions of inability might have been inaccurate are, in our experience, rarely met with assent. Instead, the students reply that they have learned that statistics is not like *real* math (which remains impenetrable), that it is sometimes possible to fake it through a course when one understands nothing, or that it was only by dint of egregious effort and considerable luck that they managed to get through the course. Such justifications, obviously, leave intact the students' potentially unwarranted self-impressions.

Obviously, illusions about the self eventually can be reversed by a mounting record of consistent successes or failures. The present study, however, addresses the more common and more clinically challenging situation in which it is not possible to arrange for the individual to reenact previous experiences or undertake new ones with different outcomes. Under such circumstances, the relevant issue remains whether there are other ways of overcoming inaccurate self-assessments. (cf. Valins & Nisbett, 1971). Part of the difficulty posed by

such situations, of course, lies in the fact that discrediting procedures or therapeutic techniques short of complete reenactment typically will be less vivid and concrete, and less affectively involving, than the experiences that engendered the subjects' initial beliefs. What is noteworthy about the present study, in this regard, is that the discounting procedure employed was probably as vivid and involving as it could be without a full reenactment of subjects' previous experience. Not only were experimental subjects shown precisely the same instructional film afterward as their counterparts had seen initially, they were asked, in addition, to employ the newly learned techniques in solving a specific sample problem that illustrated concretely and personally the benefits (or deficiencies) of those techniques. Relative to previous literature in this area, the present study would seem to provide rather compelling evidence of the difficulties inherent in overcoming prior direct, and affectively loaded, experiences with cooler informational manipulations.

In either case, the practical implications of the present studies seem relatively clear. Overcoming the pernicious effects of early school failures on students' self-perceptions and attitudes may indeed prove a difficult assignment (cf. Glasser, 1969; Silberman, 1970). Simply demonstrating to a child, even in a clear and concrete fashion, that his or her poor performance may well have been the consequence of an inept or biased teacher, a substandard school, or even prior social, cultural, or economic disadvantages may have little impact on his or her feelings of personal competence or potential. If the student's beliefs are translated, as well, into a selective avoidance of related subjects or tasks in the future—as in the present experiment where failure subjects showed less optimism and enthusiasm about the inclusion of related materials in the curriculum—opportunities for subsequent enlightenment may be precluded, and negative views about one's abilities may become self-fulfilling.

How such self-defeating cycles of failure and fear can be overcome remains an important issue for further field research. We are convinced, however, that recognizing the biases inherent in social and personal judgments, and beginning to study the processes underlying them (see Nisbett & Ross, 1980), is a necessary first step in discovering the means for combatting them.

REFERENCES

Abelson, R. P. (1974). Social psychology's rational man. In G. W. Mortimore & S. I. Benn (Eds.), *The concept of rationality in the social sciences* (pp. 58–89). Boston: Routledge & Kegan Paul.

Abelson, R. P. (1976). Script processing in attitude formation and decision making. In J. S. Carroll & J. W. Payne (Eds.), *Cognition and social behavior* (pp. 33–45). Hillsdale, NJ: Erlbaum.

Anderson, C. A., Lepper, M. R., & Ross, L. (1980). The perseverance of social theories: The role of explanation in the persistence of discredited information. *Journal of Personality and Social Psychology, 39,* 1037–1049.

Asch, S. E. (1946). Forming impressions of personality. *Journal of Abnormal and Social Psychology, 41,* 258–290.

Bandura, A. (1977). Self-efficacy: Toward a unifying theory of behavioral change. *Psychological Review, 84,* 191–215.

Bandura, A. (1982). Self-efficacy mechanism in human agency. *American Psychologist, 37,* 122–147.

Betz, N. E. (1978). Prevalence, distribution, and correlates of math anxiety in college students. *Journal of Counseling Psychology, 25,* 441–448.

Deci, E. L. (1980). *The psychology of self-determination.* Lexington, MA: D. C. Heath.

Fischhoff, B. (1976). Attribution theory and judgment under uncertainty. In J. H. Harvey, W. J. Ickes, & R. F. Kidd (Eds.), *New directions in attribution research* (Vol. 1, pp. 421–452). Hillsdale, NJ: Erlbaum.

Fleming, J., & Arrowood, A. J. (1978). Information processing and the perseverance of discredited self-perceptions. *Personality and Social Psychology Bulletin, 5,* 201–205.

Fox, L. H., Brody, L., & Tobin, D. (Eds.). (1980). *Women and the mathematical mystique.* Baltimore, MD: Johns Hopkins University Press.

Glasser, W. (1969). *Schools without failure.* New York: Harper & Row.

Holt, J. (1964). *How children fail.* New York: Dell.

Jennings, D. L., Lepper, M. R., & Ross, L. (1981). Persistence of impressions of personal persuasiveness: Perseverance of erroneous self-assessments outside the debriefing paradigm. *Personality and Social Psychology Bulletin, 7,* 257–263.

Jones, E. E., & Goethals, G. R. (1971). Order effects in impression formation: Attribution context and the nature of the entity. In E. E. Jones, D. E. Kanouse, H. H. Kelley, R. E. Nisbett, S. Valins, & B. Weiner (Eds.), *Attribution: Perceiving the cause of behavior* (pp. 27–46). Morristown, NJ: General Learning Press.

Kelley, H. H. (1950). The warm–cold variable in first impressions of persons. *Journal of Personality, 18,* 431–439.

Kelley, H. H. (1967). Attribution theory in social psychology. In D. Levine (Ed.), *Nebraska Symposium on Motivation* (Vol. 15, pp. 192–246). Lincoln, NE: University of Nebraska Press.

Kelley, H. H. (1971). Attribution in social interaction. In E. E. Jones, D. E. Kanouse, H. H. Kelley, R. E. Nisbett, S. Valins, & B. Weiner, (Eds.), *Attribution: Perceiving the causes of behavior* (pp. 151–174). Morristown, NJ: General Learning Press.

Lau, R. R., Lepper, M. R., & Ross, L. (1976, April). *Persistence of inaccurate and discredited personal impressions: A field demonstration of attributional perseverance.* Paper presented to the meeting of the Western Psychological Association, Los Angeles.

Lepper, M. R., & Greene, D. (Eds.). (1978). *The hidden costs of reward.* Hillsdale, NJ: Erlbaum.

Lord, C. G., Lepper, M. R., & Preston, E. (1984). Considering the opposite: A corrective strategy for social judgment. *Journal of Personality and Social Psychology, 47,* 1231–1243.

Lord, C. G., Ross, L., & Lepper, M. R. (1979). Biased assimilation and attitude polarization: The effects of prior theories on subsequently considered evidence. *Journal of Personality and Social Psychology, 37,* 2098–2109.

Luchins, A. S. (1942). Mechanization in problem solving: The effect of Einstellung. *Psychological Monographs, 54,* 1–95.

Luchins, A. S. (1957). Experimental attempts to minimize the impact of first impressions. In C. I. Hovland, W. Mandell, E. H. Campbell, T. Brock, A. S. Luchins, A. R. Cohen, W. J. McGuire, I. L. Janis, R. L. Feierabend, & N. H. Anderson (Eds.), *The order of presentation in persuasion.* New Haven, CT: Yale University Press.

Massad, C. M., Hubbard, M., & Newtson, D. (1979).

Selective perception of events. *Journal of Experimental Social Psychology, 15,* 513–532.

Nisbett, R. E., & Ross, L. (1980). *Human inference: Strategies and shortcomings.* Englewood Cliffs, NJ: Prentice-Hall.

Pantages, T. J., & Creedon, C. F. (1978). Studies of college attrition: 1950–1975. *Review of Educational Research, 48,* 49–101.

Ross, L. (1977). The intuitive psychologist and his shortcomings. In L. Berkowitz (Ed.), *Advances in experimental social psychology* (Vol. 10, pp. 173–220). New York: Academic Press.

Ross, L., & Lepper, M. R. (1980). The perseverance of beliefs: Empirical and normative considerations. In R. A. Shweder & D. Fiske (Eds.), *New directions for methodology of behavioral science: Fallible judgment in behavioral research* (pp. 17–36). San Francisco: Jossey-Bass.

Ross, L., Lepper, M. R., & Hubbard, M. (1975). Perseverance in self-perception and social perception: Biased attributional processes in the debriefing paradigm. *Journal of Personality and Social Psychology, 32,* 880–892.

Ross, L., Lepper, M. R., Strack, F., & Steinmetz, J. (1977). Social explanation and social expectation: The effects of real and hypothetical explanations upon subjective likelihood. *Journal of Personality and Social Psychology, 35,* 817–829.

Silberman, C. (1970). *Crisis in the classroom.* New York: Random House.

Valins, S. (1974). Persistent effects of information about internal reactions: Ineffectiveness of debriefing. In H. London & R. E. Nisbett (Eds.), *Thought and feeling: Cognitive modification of feeling states.* Chicago: Aldine.

Valins, S., & Nisbett, R. E. (1971). Attribution processes in the development and treatment of emotional disorders. In E. E. Jones, D. E. Kanouse, H. H. Kelley, R. E. Nisbett, S. Valins, & B. Weiner (Eds.), *Attribution: Perceiving the causes of behavior* (pp. 137–150). Morristown, NJ: General Learning Press.

Walster, E., Berscheid, E., Abrahams, D., & Aronson, V. (1967). Effectiveness of debriefing following deception experiments. *Journal of Personality and Social Psychology, 6,* 371–380.

Weiner, B. (Ed.). (1974). *Achievement motivation and attribution theory.* Morristown, NJ: General Learning Press.

Weiner, B. (1979). A theory of motivation for some

classroom experiences. *Journal of Educational Psychology, 71,* 3–25.

NOTES

1. Data for these 3 subjects are omitted, however, from Figure 1, which presents a direct comparison of immediate versus delayed dependent measures.

2. Problem 2 in the set of four, which was similar to Problems 3 and 4 in terms of complexity and difficulty, was presented as follows: There are only five passengers on a bus bound for San Francisco, and each passenger was born in a different country. The five countries are Arabam and Elsala (both of which are hot), Beshubar and Dugoland (both of which are cold), and Cetostan (which has many rivers). Two of the passengers, Jani and Gora, are women, and three of them, Mala, Jessar, and Pesso, are men. Furthermore, Jani, Mala, and Jessar are very tall, whereas Gora and Pesso are very short. Upon careful observation, we learn the following facts: (a) Both of the women are sorry that they were not born in hot countries; (b) in Cetostan, it is considered improper to give a child a name beginning with the letter *J*. Nobody ever disobeys this custom; (c) Mala quickly made friends with the two passengers who came from the hot countries; (d) the tallest passenger on the bus is from Elsala; (e) Gora moved from her native country to neighboring Arabam when she had a child, and she has never been in the faraway lands of Beshubar and Dugoland; and (f) Mala left his native country to become a foreign student at the University of Dugoland. In what country was Mala born? Who is the Beshubarian? (A complete set of the problems employed is available from the authors.)

3. All p values reported in this article are based on two-tailed tests of significance.

4. We believe that the use of such difference scores is justified on both conceptual and empirical grounds. On a conceptual level, the measures obtained in the delayed testing situation were clearly designed to be inherently comparative; thus, the task presented to subjects explicitly involved assessments of their relative liking for and abilities at the three different proposed units. Empirically, moreover, there proved to be relatively substantial correlations between subjects' responses to the target and filler units (rs of .52 for both the liking and the perceived ability measures). Alternative analyses, in which responses to irrelevant units are employed as covariates and responses to the relevant unit as dependent measures, yielded results similar to those reported here. For perceptions of ability, a significant main effect of success–failure remained apparent, $F(1, 45) = 5.78$, $p < .025$, and this difference proved nearly significant within the discounting conditions alone, $F(1, 45) = 3.92$, $p < .06$. For preference ratings, however, both the main effect for success–failure, $F(1, 45) = 2.99$, $p < .10$, and this difference within the discounting conditions $F(1, 45) = 3.24$, $p < .10$, proved only marginally significant.

5. The present results may also be compared to previous findings reported by Ross, Lepper, and Hubbard (1975). In the first of two reported experiments, subjects in success and failure conditions provided with no explicit information about average performance persevered in their post-debriefing perceptions of the difficulty of that task, as well as in their perceptions of their own ability at the task. When explicit in-

formation about average performance was provided in the second of the two experiments reported, success and failure subjects did not differ in perceptions of task difficulty, but differed only in their perceptions of their own abilities. The present procedure, which was designed primarily to motivate students in all experimental conditions to keep working until they had solved all of the problems, probably fell somewhere between the contrasting procedures employed in the two earlier Ross et al. (1975) experiments.

This research was supported in part by Research Grants MH-26736 from the National Institute of Mental Health and BNS-78-01211 from the National Science Foundation to Mark R. Lepper and Lee Ross.

The authors wish to express their gratitude to Leslie Cooley, William Easton, Barbara Finn, Julie Kaplan, and Julia Steinmetz for their assistance in conducting these studies; to Teresa Amabile for her excellent performance as the teacher in our instructional films; and to Mark Zanna for his helpful and perceptive comments on an earlier draft of this article. These studies would not have been possible without the cooperation and assistance of Al Baker, principal; John Highland, guidance counselor; and the staff of the mathematics department at Awalt High School in Mountain View, California. Their support for and interest in these studies is greatly appreciated.

CRITICAL THINKING QUESTIONS

1. The findings of the study seemed to suggest that it is difficult to change a person's initial beliefs about himself or herself. Suppose that a person strongly believes that he or she is not good at math. What sort of long-term intervention strategy could change this self-perception? Or are we doomed to keep our sometimes inaccurate beliefs about ourselves?

2. If it is difficult to change established beliefs, what does this suggest about our educational system? Specifically, when should the greatest effort be made to detect and change any negative self-images that students might have? Is there some practical way that this could be accomplished?

3. Many studies in social psychology manipulate some aspect of the subject's belief system without his or her knowledge. For example, low self-esteem might be induced to observe the impact that this factor might have on some other measure of interest. What implications does this study have for experiments that involve such manipulations? Would a thorough debriefing of the subjects following the study be enough to eliminate these experimentally induced effects? Why or why not?

4. Think about yourself or someone you know. Can you give an example of an inaccurate belief that you or your acquaintance have about yourself in spite of evidence to the contrary?

Chapter Four

ATTITUDES AND
ATTITUDE CHANGE

THE STUDY OF attitudes is considered by many social psychologists to be the core issue in understanding human behavior. How we act in any given situation is the product of the attitudes that we have formed, which in turn are based upon the experiences we have had.

Whether or not we believe that attitudes constitute the core of social psychology, the study of attitudes and attitude change has been prominent in social-psychological research from the beginning. Part of this interest has been theoretically driven. How attitudes are formed and how they can be changed, as well as what factors make some attitudes so resistant to change, are but a few of the topics that theorists have studied. However, there is also a more pragmatic, applied reason for this interest in attitudes: Principles of attitude change and attitude measurement have a direct bearing on several major industries. For example, survey organizations and advertising agencies focus on attitudes, measuring what they are, how they change over time, as well as how best to change them. Theoretical research often has provided the foundation for the applied principles used by advertisers and surveyors.

The readings in this chapter relate to three major subfields in the area of attitudes and attitude change. Article 10, "The Great American Values Test," examines how attitudes are formed: What influences the formation of an attitude? Once an attitude already exists, how can it be changed? Article 11, "Social Forces: Attitudes vs. Actions," deals with the consistency between attitudes and behavior: Do we always act in accordance with our attitudes? Or do we sometimes do things that contradict what we say we believe? Finally, Article 12, "Cognitive Dissonance and Energy Conservation," considers the process of *cognitive dissonance,* a special process of self-justification (and hence attitude change) that is employed when an inconsistency between our behaviors and our attitudes is recognized: Under what conditions is a state of cognitive dissonance aroused? How is the inconsistency typically resolved?

ARTICLE 10

How are attitudes formed? Obviously, they are formed in a great variety of ways. Some attitudes are a result of direct experience: We meet someone from a certain country and, based upon that limited experience, form an attitude (or stereotype) about people from that particular country. In other words, we generalize our experience to form an attitude. In many other cases, however, we don't experience the person, situation, or event directly but rather indirectly. For example, so-called *second-hand attitudes* are the result of information that we got from someone else, such as our parents or friends, and form a major source of our beliefs.

One aspect of this indirect formation of attitudes that has received increased attention and concern over the years is the role of the media—and television, in particular—in influencing attitudes. The evidence is growing that some aspects of television have a direct impact on the viewers' behavior. Chapter 10 addresses these issues, which center around the influence of televised aggression on the subsequent behaviors of the audience. However, a more basic question is whether television actually affects specific attitudes of viewers, and if it does, to what extent?

"The Great American Values Test," by Ball-Rokeach, Rokeach, and Grube, describes an interesting and unusual experiment that was done to investigate the impact of the media on the attitudes and subsequent behavior of television viewers. This experiment involved the creation of a 30-minute television program that the researchers arranged to have broadcast simultaneously on all three channels in a part of Washington state. In effect, the entire population of one community was the subject pool; another city that did not receive the broadcast was the control group.

Most studies on the impact of the media usually involve bringing subjects into a laboratory where they are exposed to some attitude manipulation and then evaluated for attitude change. This field study overcomes the problems associated with studies where the subjects know they are being investigated (i.e., *reactive research*) by reproducing what media effects might occur in the real world. Some limitations to the findings of the study are also discussed in the article. Comments on the changes in attitudes and behaviors that were found are included, as well as speculation on the underlying causes of the changes.

The Great American Values Test

■ Sandra J. Ball-Rokeach, Milton Rokeach, and Joel W. Grube

Ever since Peterson and Thurstone's pioneering effort to measure the impact of D. W. Griffith's *Birth of a Nation* in 1933, social scientists have been struggling to assess how film and television influence attitudes and behavior. Today, the average American spends more than six hours a day watching television, and as advertisers—political and otherwise—increasingly make use of TV, important questions arise. Many envision TV as a medium with enormous potential for encouraging greater self-knowledge, better health and constructive changes in basic values, attitudes and

Reprinted from *Psychology Today,* 1984 (November) *18,* 34–41. Reprinted with permission from *Psychology Today Magazine.* Copyright © 1984 (PT Partners, L.P.).

behavior. Others worry about the sinister effects of programming. Both views assume that TV can have powerful effects on what people believe and do. But can it?

The fact is that even after years of research there is little firm proof of TV's power to persuade. One of the problems is that the studies have been rather artificial: People are invited into laboratories where they watch commercial programming; they are observed, questioned and paid for their efforts. These experiments, while important, tend to obscure the natural self-selection that plays an important part in the influence process.

We have designed and conducted an experiment that overcomes the major problems plaguing past research. We have studied voluntary viewers: people who choose to watch a particular program in the privacy of their own homes, alone or with friends or family, with their normal level of attention; people who retain the option of turning the set off, who might be interrupted by any number of everyday incidents and who, finally, are not worried about being observed.

We also wanted to test an idea of ours—that people change their values, attitudes and ultimately their behavior when they are forced to confront themselves—to honestly assess whether or not their values are consistent. If people recognize inconsistencies in their belief system, we believe, they experience a sense of dissatisfaction with themselves—a condition for reassessment and change. To test this idea in as natural a setting as possible, we designed an elaborate experiment involving thousands of viewers who, one day in 1979, sat down in their own homes and tuned in a show called *The Great American Values Test.*

The Great American Values Test is a program we had produced especially for this experiment. It is cohosted by Ed Asner, former star of *The Lou Grant Show,* and Sandy Hill, the former anchor of ABC's *Good Morning America.* In the course of this 30-minute program Asner and Hill discuss values, generally at first, and then with an emphasis on three basic ones—freedom, equality and a world of beauty. They gently prod viewers to examine their own commitment to these values, which we as researchers wanted to influence.

The first 15-minute segment of our TV program is purely introductory in nature, designed to capture and then to hold the viewer's interest. Asner and Hill discuss what human values are and how social scientists measure them. They also talk about various findings from a national survey of American values conducted several years ago by the National Opinion Research Center, which showed differences in values between blacks and whites, men and women, young and old, rich and poor and between citizens of Israel and citizens of the United States.

The latter part of the program focuses upon the three target values. By needling viewers to examine their own commitment to these values, we hoped to make them satisfied or dissatisfied, depending on how well they thought they measured up to their ideal conceptions of themselves as moral citizens in a democratic society. For instance, Asner attempts to influence viewers' value priorities for freedom and equality by drawing attention to certain findings from the national survey:

"Americans feel that freedom is very important. They rank it third. But they also feel that equality is considerably less important. . . . They rank it 12th. Since most Americans value freedom far higher than they value equality, the question is: What does it mean? Does it suggest that Americans as a whole are much more interested in their own freedom than they are in freedom for other people? Is there a contradiction in the American people between their love of freedom and their lesser love for equality?"

All this was designed to arouse the TV viewer's feelings about his own consistency or lack of it. Viewers who recognized a discrepancy between their notion of an ideal moral citizen and their own value priorities for freedom and equality would experience consternation, causing them—we theorized—to reexamine their beliefs. Viewers who examined their values and found them consistent would also be aroused—satisfied in this case—reinforcing (perhaps even increasing) their commitment.

Asner and Hill then discuss the national survey results further, pointing out to viewers that equality rankings, but not freedom rankings, had a lot to do with attitudes toward racism and with differences in emotional reaction to the assassination of the Rev. Martin Luther King Jr. They noted that the higher people rank equality, the more favorable are their attitudes toward civil-rights issues and the more antiracist is their behavior. Hill then poses the following question to the viewers:

"This raises the question whether those who are against civil rights are really saying they care a great deal about their own freedom but really don't care that much about other people's freedom."

All told, the equality-freedom segment, designed to persuade viewers to increase their commitment to these two values, is six minutes long.

Next comes the pro-environment segment, designed to increase the value people place on a world of beauty. Four and a half minutes long, it is again designed to arouse in viewers feelings of either satisfaction or dissatisfaction, depending upon their own environmental values. The following comment by Hill illustrates the "needling" process: "Young people start out with a natural appreciation of beauty. But in the process of growing up appreciation is knocked out of them. Eleven-year-olds rank a world of beauty seventh in importance. Fifteen-year-olds rank it 14th. And by the time they reach adulthood, a world of beauty has plummeted to 17th down the list of importance . . . and there it remains for most adult Americans. (A full-screen graphic of these statistics is shown.) Perhaps that explains why so many Americans are willing to live with pollution and ugliness."

A world of beauty is a socially desirable value but, as Hill and Asner go on to discuss, it often conflicts with the desire for material comfort. They note that while environmentalists rank a world of beauty sixth, on the average, and a comfortable life 17th, people who are unconcerned with the environment rank comfort higher. Asner then concludes the program with these remarks: "Also, people who prefer products that can be recycled place a higher value on a world of beauty. So do people who favor laws to ban throwaway beverage containers."

The Great American Values Test was shown at 7:30 on the evening of February 27, 1979, but it aired under very unusual circumstances. In the Tri-Cities area of eastern Washington—our experimental site, which encompasses Richland, Pasco and Kennewick—all three commercial channels carried the program, drastically limiting the residents' viewing options (and, of course, increasing the odds that they would tune in). In Yakima, a city with a very similar population 80 miles away, the show was blacked out; Yakima was our control city.

We chose for study a random sample of adults in the Tri-Cities area selected from a telephone directory. Unlike participants in the classic laboratory experiment, however, our research subjects were not recruited or contacted in advance. Since they didn't know they were being studied, they were altogether free to watch or ignore our TV program in the privacy of their own homes, just as they might treat any other program. By creating such a natural experiment we also created a number of research problems that we had to overcome.

First, we had to find ways to maximize the probability that our preselected participants would be sufficiently interested in *The Great American Values Test* to watch it voluntarily when it aired. That is one reason we recruited the popular Ed Asner and Sandy Hill to be our cohosts. We also persuaded the station managers of the local ABC, CBS and NBC affiliates to show our program simultaneously as a public-service program; we promoted the show in *TV Guide,* the local newspaper and on radio and TV; and we aired the program as close to prime time as possible and gave it a title that we thought would have wide appeal.

Our next challenge was to find out whether our preselected participants did in fact watch our program and, if so, whether they watched without interruption. To do this we and the Washington State University TV station hired 30 telephone operators, who called the 1,699 respondents in the Tri-Cities area immediately after the program. In phone calls lasting about a minute and a half they obtained information about whether the preselected participant or anyone else in the household had watched the TV program, how much of the program had been seen and with what level of attention, whether the viewer had been interrupted and, if so, the reason for the interruption. We also collected basic demographic information (age, sex, education and ethnicity).

In addition we had to find out if our viewers had actually had their basic values, related social attitudes and, most important, political behavior changed. All participants in both the experimental and control cities received an opinion survey from Washington State University, which asked for a ranking, in order of importance, for the 18 values studied in the national survey—including equality, freedom and a world of beauty and others such as wisdom, salvation and mature love (see box at right). The survey also measured related attitudes, specifically toward racism, sexism and environmental conservatism. We also measured the extent to which each participant depended on television for information leading to self-understanding and understanding of the world. We hypothesized that people who scored high on these measures of dependency on TV would be more likely to watch our program and, moreover, would be more likely to be affected by it.

Half of the participants in both Tri-Cities and Yakima received this survey seven weeks before our TV program aired, and the remaining half received it four weeks afterwards. Although we could not get a record of any individual viewer's values both before and after the program, we had a sufficiently large sample of randomly selected subjects that any significant change in collective values or attitudes was most likely caused by having watched our program.

Finally, we had to determine whether our TV program had also influenced the viewers' political behavior. To find out, we mailed three solicitations for money to every one of our preselected participants in the experimental and control cities 8, 10 and 13 weeks after our TV program had aired. Two of these solicitations were designed to assess the long-term behavioral effects of the freedom-equality segment; the third was designed to assess the effects of the pro-environmental segment.

All three solicitations were mailed out from (and with the cooperation of) actual organizations, headquartered (and thus postmarked) in different cities in the state of Washington. One came from the Afro-American Players in Yakima, a cultural organization devoted to providing opportunities for black children to participate in music, drama and dance. The second came from the Women's Intercollegiate Athletics Program at Washington State University in Pullman. The third was mailed out from the Committee for Initiative 61 in Seattle, an organization formed to secure passage of an anti-pollution measure requiring mandatory deposits on beer and soft-drink bottles; it was to appear on the ballot in the November 1979 elections in the state of Washington.

Thus, even though we had no direct contact with our participants before *The Great American Values Test* had aired, we were able to find out whether they watched the show, whether they watched it with or without interruption, whether their basic political values and attitudes had undergone change and, most important, whether their political behavior—namely, donating money to political causes—had been affected.

Our findings exceeded our wildest expectations. We estimate that our "Nielsen rating" was a whopping 65 percent; that is, 65 percent of all Tri-Cities participants who watched TV at 7:30 p.m. on February 27, 1979, watched our program. Nonetheless, roughly 74 percent of our participants did not watch television at all because they were doing other things: eating, cleaning up in the kitchen, attending to the children, working, shopping and so on. Thus, we estimate that only about 26 percent actually watched, and that only about half of those watched without any interruption.

Notwithstanding this low proportion of uninterrupted viewers, about one in eight, our data on the responses to the three solicitations mailed out two to three months after the program aired usually showed significant differences between our experimental sample and our controls. There were significantly more responses, in the form of donations from Tri-Cities residents. And there were also significantly fewer negative responses. Some people could not resist the temptation to mail back the return envelope with such negative remarks as: "Teach the blacks to work. If that doesn't work, shoot them"; "I am strictly opposed to this program. I think God made women for home and family and I am very much against women's lib"; and "I would like to help with the expenses of getting Initiative 61 to fail by making a contribution against it." Significantly fewer of such negative responses came from the Tri-Cities area. We refer to this as the "Asner effect." Both Hill and Asner volunteered to help in this research, and Asner told us he had decided to participate not so much because he expected positive changes but because he hoped the show "would at least shut up the bigots." It did not completely achieve Asner's goal, but our results suggest that it shut up significantly more bigots in the experimental cities than in the control.

Even more dramatic were the results obtained when we compared the uninterrupted viewers with interrupted viewers and nonviewers. The interrupted viewers were those who intended to watch our program but were interrupted by circumstances beyond their control, such as the telephone ringing, a fight between the children or a knock at the door. They offer an important comparison because, while they were presumably as highly motivated as the uninterrupted viewers to tune in, they did not receive full exposure to the program.

Interestingly, we discovered that these viewers did not differ from the nonviewers in experimental and control cities in basic political values, or in attitudes toward racism, sexism and the environment, either before or after the TV show had aired. In essence, they were unchanged.

By contrast, those who watched the entire show did change significantly. Before the show their political behavior, values and social attitudes were like the others, but weeks and months later they were more egalitarian and more pro-environment.

Surely the most impressive of our findings have to do with the money collected. As a group, viewers who watched *The Great American Values Test* without a break contributed on the average about

four to six times as much money as did the nonviewers in both the Tri-Cities area and in Yakima, and about nine times as much as did the interrupted viewers. Moreover, the uninterrupted viewers contributed more money on the average to each of the three solicitations—pro-environment, antiracism and antisexism—than did any of the remaining three groups. Furthermore the average per-capita contribution was generally greater.

Beyond these behavioral differences, our findings show that the three values targeted in our TV program also underwent the expected changes. Uninterrupted viewers significantly increased their ranking of two target values, freedom and equality, and less dramatically increased their ranking of the third, a world of beauty. In contrast, the remaining three groups showed not a single significant change.

The three social attitudes that are related to these three basic values were also affected. Two of these three attitudes, attitude toward the environment and attitude toward blacks, changed significantly, with viewers (and only viewers) becoming more pro-environment and more antiracist. Considering that the Tri-Cities is home to Washington's Hanford nuclear power plant and that its people, for understandable economic reasons, have been traditionally pro-nuclear and resistant to environmentalist activism, the shift toward a pro-environment position is particularly interesting. Viewers' attitudes toward women also became more favorable, though the change was not so striking.

Finally, participants' dependency on TV also played an important role. Those who were highly dependent on TV for understanding themselves and society were more apt to watch in the first place. And when they watched, they subsequently contributed more money, rearranged their fundamental values more noticeably and improved their attitudes toward racism, sexism and the environment more than did those who were less dependent on TV.

While alternative interpretations of such findings are always possible, we believe that the most plausible explanation is that *The Great American Values Test* caused the changes we see. We think it led some of the viewers to become dissatisfied with their values, thus prompting a change in values and related attitudes and behavior in a direction that would make them feel better about themselves. Alternatively, our program could have made those who already valued freedom, equality and beauty highly feel good about themselves, thus making these values more salient and more likely to be acted upon when solicitations came from organizations specializing in implementing these values. In a separate, smaller study we actually used the same TV program to arouse the predicted feelings of satisfaction and dissatisfaction, and we believe as a result that viewers' concepts of themselves as competent or moral citizens play an important role in the behavioral changes we saw.

Questions and Answers On Ethics

An experiment like *The Great American Values Test* raises difficult ethical questions, which we have considered at length. Here is a summary of our thoughts on two important ethical issues.

First, did we manipulate or brainwash our viewers? The main elements of manipulation and brainwashing are deception, group pressure and coerciveness. None of those techniques was used in our research. Our television program provided only truthful information drawn from empirical research on Americans' value priorities.

Participants were selected at random from telephone directories; they responded voluntarily to mail surveys, telephone calls and mail solicitations for money. Participants were not contacted in advance or in any way induced to watch our program. They were free to turn it on, watch with whatever level of attention they chose, turn it off, switch channels or interrupt their watching—all in the privacy of their homes. Thus, we systematically eliminated all forms of coercion, even the mild coercion that might be involved in recruiting participants for an experiment.

Our approach was aimed at education rather than persuasion. We shunned arbitrary conditioning and foot-in-the-door techniques. This educational approach, designed to make people aware of internal contradictions, was thus in the tradition of John Dewey, who said, "Thinking begins with a felt difficulty"; it is also consistent with Benjamin Franklin's aphorism: "The things which hurt, instruct."

Second, could our theories and procedures be used to influence viewers' values in an undesirable way? If we succeeded in altering TV viewers' values, attitudes and behaviors in a pro-egalitarian and pro-environmental direction, could we just as easily have made those same viewers anti-egalitarian and anti-environment? Earlier findings from experimental studies suggest that the answer is no. A person is receptive to being influenced in only one direction—the direction that maintains or enhances self-esteem—but not in the opposite direction. That does not mean, however, that politicians and advertisers aren't able to take advantage of our findings. Even though a person's values may be changed in only one direction, our theories and methods might also serve ignoble purposes. Such attempts at influence would work with people who already hold certain values—who are hedonistic or anti-egalitarian, for example. By arousing a feeling of satisfaction about holding such values, advertisers and politicians could then appeal for behavior that is consistent with those values—buying fast cars, for example, or voting for a racist candidate. Or, by showing hedonism or personal power as admirable values, they could arouse the feelings of dissatisfaction necessary for value change. We remain uneasy about the possibility that our work might be used for evil, antidemocratic or self-serving purposes.

The findings and conclusions stemming from our work with *The Great American Values Test* force us to a conclusion that many will consider to be very strong: A single 30-minute exposure to TV can significantly alter basic beliefs, related attitudes and behavior of large numbers of people for at least several months. For us this seems to have important implications — scientific, political and ethical.

In a recent essay, syndicated columnist David Broder wrote: "Words are important symbols, and for 200 years, the words 'freedom' and 'equality' have defined the twin guideposts of American democracy." Broder did an analysis of the language in President Reagan's recent speeches and found, according to his report, that while Reagan used forms of "freedom" and "liberty" 44 times, he used the word "equality" only once. (He did use the term "equal rights" on another occasion.) "The words 'equality' and 'equal,' " Broder concluded, "are not words Reagan likes to throw around."

Broder's small study is interesting to us, because it corroborates what we have been finding in our empirical research for years: The political spectrum is defined in large part by the relative importance placed on freedom and equality. An analysis of political texts, for example, shows that socialists rank both freedom and equality very high; fascists rank both very low. Communists rank equality very high, but freedom very low; conservatives place a high value on freedom and a very low value on equality.

These values define American politics as well. In 1968, we asked campaign workers for various candidates to rank the 18 values used in our national survey. The majority of them ranked freedom very high: Reagan supporters ranked it first, as did supporters of George Wallace; supporters of Richard Nixon, Nelson Rockefeller and Eugene McCarthy ranked freedom second; Hubert Humphrey activists ranked freedom fourth. But where supporters of Humphrey and McCarthy ranked equality second and third respectively, Nixon and Rockefeller supporters ranked it ninth, Reagan supporters ranked it 17th and Wallace supporters ranked it 18th, at the very bottom of the list. The data are clear. And the findings we have now gotten from *The Great American Values Test* suggest that some adult Americans with such a value orientation can be influenced to rethink their basic values, and presumably their behavior at the ballot box, to bring freedom and equality into better balance.

George Orwell's *1984* presaged the use of television for thought control and stifling of such values as liberty, equality and beauty. But we believe we have found a way to use television to actually enhance liberty, equality and beauty and to encourage political behavior consistent with such values. We did this by providing viewers with an opportunity to contemplate in privacy, stimulated by their television sets, possible inconsistencies between their own values and their ideal conceptions of themselves as citizens of a democratic society.

However, our sanguine view notwithstanding, we are still forced to close on an uneasy Orwellian note. Our theories and our techniques do have the potential for destructive as well as constructive use, a potential demanding vigilance and sensitivity as we move beyond 1984.

CRITICAL THINKING QUESTIONS

1. How would you set up a laboratory study to investigate the topic of this article? What would be the relative advantages and disadvantages of such a laboratory study over the methodology employed in "The Great American Values Test."

2. Half of the randomly selected subjects in the study were contacted before the televised program and asked questions about the values being investigated; they did not watch the program. This comprised the control group. The experimental group was asked the same questions after viewing the program. Furthermore,

these two groups were from different but nearby cities. Is this methodologically sound? Would it have been better to ask the same people the same questions in a before-after format? Is there anything else that might account for the differences in attitudes between these two groups, other than exposure to the program?

3. One of the dependent measures used was change in political behavior as measured by contributions of money to various organizations. Would the group making the solicitation have an effect on levels of contributions? Could differences in contributions be attributed to factors other than exposure to the program?

4. The article included a box on ethics. Do you agree or disagree with the authors' comments on the ethical issues of the study? Why?

5. Were there any differences between the values of those who watched the program and those who chose not to watch? How do you know that the nonviewers somehow were different than the viewers in an important respect, such as susceptibility to persuasion? If that were the case, how would it affect the generalizability of this study?

ARTICLE 11 _____

Attitudes are commonly viewed as having three components: cognitive, affective, and behavioral. The *cognitive* (or belief) component of an attitude consists of what the person believes to be true. If you believe that smoking does not cause lung cancer, that is a cognitive component of an attitude; whether or not it is actually true is beside the point. The *affective* (or emotional) component consists of the feelings we attach to a particular attitude. For example, prejudice is an attitude that is usually high in affect. You may have a strong dislike for a certain group of people, sometimes without even knowing why you feel that way; you just don't like them, period. Finally, the *behavioral* component suggests that if you hold a certain attitude, you will be inclined to act in certain ways. With regard to prejudice, if you have negative beliefs about a group of people and have strong negative emotional feelings toward them, then it stands to reason that you will act in negative ways toward them.

Or does it? Are we always consistent in our attitudes and behaviors? Sometimes there is a strong consistency between what people say about their beliefs and how they act. For example, surveys are usually accurate in predicting outcomes of elections based upon asking people about their attitudes toward the candidates. In other cases, such consistency simply does not exist.

"Social Forces: Attitudes vs. Actions" is a classic work in the field that addresses the issue of attitude-behavior consistency. Before LaPiere's publication of this study in 1934, attitude research on prejudice involved asking respondents to give hypothetical responses to hypothetical situations (e.g., Would you serve a person of a given race at your restaurant?). LaPiere measured the number of times that a Chinese couple was actually refused lodging or food and then followed up with a questionnaire to the same establishments six months later, asking if they would serve Chinese persons in their establishments. In doing so, LaPiere claimed to demonstrate the lack of consistency between what people said and what they actually did. Even though the study does have some methodological flaws, it is a good example of pioneering research in the field. It also provides an interesting microcosm of prejudice and discrimination issues that existed in the United States over a half-century ago.

Social Forces
Attitudes vs. Actions

■ Richard T. LaPiere

By definition, a social attitude is a behaviour pattern, anticipatory set or tendency, predisposition to specific adjustment to designated social situations, or, more simply, a conditioned response to social stimuli.[1] Terminological usage differs, but students who have concerned themselves with attitudes apparently agree that they are acquired out of social experience and provide the individ-

Reprinted from *Social Forces,* Vol. 13, 1934. "Attitudes vs. Actions" by Richard T. LaPiere. Copyright © The University of North Carolina Press. Some of the language used and views presented are indicative of the time in which the article was written. The reader should consider the article in that context.

ual organism with some degree of preparation to adjust, in a well-defined way, to certain types of social situations if and when these situations arise. It would seem, therefore, that the totality of the social attitudes of a single individual would include all his socially acquired personality which is involved in the making of adjustments to other human beings.

But by derivation social attitudes are seldom more than a verbal response to a symbolic situation. For the conventional method of measuring social attitudes is to ask questions (usually in writing) which demand a verbal adjustment to an entirely symbolic situation. Because it is easy, cheap, and mechanical, the attitudinal questionnaire is rapidly becoming a major method of sociological and socio-psychological investigation. The technique is simple. Thus from a hundred or a thousand responses to the question "Would you get up to give an Armenian woman your seat in a street car?" the investigator derives the "attitude" of non-Armenian males toward Armenian females. Now the question may be constructed with elaborate skill and hidden with consummate cunning in a maze of supplementary or even irrelevant questions yet all that has been obtained is a symbolic response to a symbolic situation. The words "Armenian woman" do not constitute an Armenian woman of flesh and blood, who might be tall or squat, fat or thin, old or young, well or poorly dressed—who might, in fact, be a goddess or just another old and dirty hag. And the questionnaire response, whether it be "yes" or "no," is but a verbal reaction and this does not involve rising from the seat or stolidly avoiding the hurt eyes of the hypothetical woman and the derogatory states of other street-car occupants. Yet, ignoring these limitations, the diligent investigator will jump briskly from his factual evidence to the unwarranted conclusion that he has measured the "anticipatory behavior patterns" of non-Armenian males toward Armenian females encountered on street cars. Usually he does not stop here, but proceeds to deduce certain general conclusions regarding the social relationships between Armenians and non-Armenians. Most of us have applied the questionnaire technique with greater

caution, but not I fear with any greater certainty of success.

Some years ago I endeavored to obtain comparative data on the degree of French and English antipathy towards dark-skinned peoples.[2] The informal questionnaire technique was used, but, although the responses so obtained were exceedingly consistent, I supplemented them with what I then considered an index to overt behavior. The hypothesis as then stated *seemed* entirely logical. "Whatever our attitude on the validity of 'verbalization' may be, it must be recognized that any study of attitudes through direct questioning is open to serious objection, both because of the limitations of the sampling method and because in classifying attitudes the inaccuracy of human judgment is an inevitable variable. In this study, however, there is corroborating evidence on these attitudes in the policies adopted by hotel proprietors. Nothing could be used as a more accurate index of color prejudice than the admission or non-admission of colored people to hotels. For the proprietor must reflect the group attitude in his policy regardless of his own feelings in the matter. Since he determines what the group attitude is towards Negroes through the expression of that attitude in overt behavior and over a long period of actual experience, the results will be exceptionally free from those disturbing factors which inevitably affect the effort to study attitudes by direct questioning."

But at that time I overlooked the fact that what I was obtaining from the hotel proprietors was still a "verbalized" reaction to a symbolic situation. The response to a Negro's request for lodgings might have been an excellent index of the attitude of hotel patrons towards living in the same hotel as a Negro. Yet to ask the proprietor "Do you permit members of the Negro race to stay here?" does not, it appears, measure his potential response to an actual Negro.

All measurement of attitudes by the questionnaire technique proceeds on the assumption that there is a mechanical relationship between symbolic and non-symbolic behavior. It is simple enough to prove that there is no *necessary* correlation between speech and action, between response to words and to the realities they symbolize. A parrot can be taught to swear, a child to sing "Frankie and Johnny" in the Mae West manner. The words will have no meaning to either child or parrot. But to prove that there is no *necessary* relationship does not prove that such a relationship may not exist. There need be no relationship between what the hotel proprietor says he will do and what he actually does when confronted with a colored patron. Yet there may be. Certainly we are justified in assuming that the verbal response of the hotel proprietor would be more likely to indicate what he would actually do than would the verbal response of people whose personal feelings are less subordinated to economic expediency. However, the following study indicates that the reliability of even such responses is very small indeed.

Beginning in 1930 and continuing for two years thereafter, I had the good fortune to travel rather extensively with a young Chinese student and his wife.[3] Both were personable, charming, and quick to win the admiration and respect of those they had the opportunity to become intimate with. But they were foreign-born Chinese, a fact that could not be disguised. Knowing the general "attitude" of Americans towards the Chinese as indicated by the "social distance" studies which have been made, it was with considerable trepidation that I first approached a hotel clerk in their company. Perhaps the clerk's eyebrows lifted slightly, but he accommodated us without a show of hesitation. And this in the "best" hotel in a small town noted for its narrow and bigoted "attitude" towards Orientals. Two months later I passed that way again, phoned the hotel and asked if they would accommodate "an important Chinese gentleman." The reply was an unequivocal "No." That aroused my curiosity and led to this study.

In something like ten thousand miles of motor travel, twice across the United States, up and down the Pacific Coast, we met definite rejection from those asked to serve us just once. We were received at 66 hotels, auto camps, and "Tourist Homes," refused at one. We were served in 184 restaurants and cafes scattered throughout the

country and treated with what I judged to be more than ordinary consideration in 72 of them. Accurate and detailed records were kept of all these instances. An effort, necessarily subjective, was made to evaluate the overt response of hotel clerks, bell boys, elevator operators, and waitresses to the presence of my Chinese friends. The factors entering into the situations were varied as far and as often as possible. Control was not, of course, as exacting as that required by laboratory experimentation. But it was as rigid as is humanly possible in human situations. For example, I did not take the "test" subjects into my confidence fearing that their behavior might become self-conscious and thus abnormally affect the response of others towards them. Whenever possible I let my Chinese friend negotiate for accommodations (while I concerned myself with the car or luggage) or sent them into a restaurant ahead of me. In this way I attempted to "factor" myself out. We sometimes patronized high-class establishments after a hard and dusty day on the road and stopped at inferior auto camps when in our most presentable condition.

In the end I was forced to conclude that those factors which most influenced the behavior of others towards the Chinese had nothing at all to do with race. Quality and condition of clothing, appearance of baggage (by which, it seems, hotel clerks are prone to base their quick evaluations), cleanliness and neatness were far more significant for person to person reaction in the situations I was studying than skin pigmentation, straight black hair, slanting eyes, and flat noses. And yet an air of self-confidence might entirely offset the "unfavorable" impression made by dusty clothes and the usual disorder to appearance consequent upon some hundred miles of motor travel. A supercilious desk clerk in a hotel of noble aspirations could not refuse his master's hospitality to people who appeared to take their request as a perfectly normal and conventional thing, though they might look like tin-can tourists and two of them belong to the racial category "Oriental." On the other hand, I became rather adept at approaching hotel clerks with that peculiar crab-wise manner which is so effective in provoking a somewhat scornful disregard. And then a bland smile would serve to reverse the entire situation. Indeed, it appeared that a genial smile was the most effective password to acceptance. My Chinese friends were skillful smilers, which may account, in part, for the fact that we received but one rebuff in all our experience. Finally, I was impressed with the fact that even where some tension developed due to the strangeness for the Chinese it would evaporate immediately when they spoke in unaccented English.

The one instance in which we were refused accommodations is worth recording here. The place was a small California town, a rather inferior auto-camp into which we drove in a very dilapidated car piled with camp equipment. It was early evening, the light so dim that the proprietor found it somewhat difficult to decide the genus *voyageur* to which we belonged. I left the car and spoke to him. He hesitated, wavered, said he was not sure that he had two cabins, meanwhile edging towards our car. The realization that the two occupants were Orientals turned the balance or, more likely, gave him the excuse he was looking for. "No," he said, "I don't take Japs!" In a more pretentious establishment we secured accommodations, and with an extra flourish of hospitality.

To offset this one flat refusal were the many instances in which the physical peculiarities of the Chinese served to heighten curiosity. With few exceptions this curiosity was considerately hidden behind an exceptional interest in serving us. Of course, outside of the Pacific Coast region, New York, and Chicago, the Chinese physiognomy attracts attention. It is different, hence noticeable. But the principal effect this curiosity has upon the behavior of those who cater to the traveler's needs is to make them more attentive, more responsive, more reliable. A Chinese companion is to be recommended to the white traveling in his native land. Strange features when combined with "human" speech and action seems, at times, to heighten sympathetic response, perhaps on the same principle that makes us uncommonly sympathetic toward the dog that has a "human" expression in his face.

What I am trying to say is that in only one out of 251 instances in which we purchased goods or services necessitating intimate human relationships did the fact that my companions were Chinese adversely affect us. Factors entirely unassociated with race were, in the main, the determinant of significant variations in our reception. It would appear reasonable to conclude that the "attitude" of the American people, as reflected in the behavior of those who are for pecuniary reasons presumably most sensitive to the antipathies of their white clientele, is anything but negative towards the Chinese. In terms of "social distance" we might conclude that native Caucasians are not averse to residing in the same hotels, auto-camps, and "Tourist Homes" as Chinese and will with complacency accept the presence of Chinese at an adjoining table in restaurant or cafe. It does not follow that there is revealed a distinctly "positive" attitude towards the Chinese, that whites prefer the Chinese to other whites. But the facts as gathered certainly preclude the conclusion that there is an intense prejudice towards the Chinese.

Yet the existence of this prejudice, very intense, is proven by a conventional "attitude" study. To provide a comparison of symbolic reaction to symbolic social situations with actual reaction to real social situations, I "questionnaired" the establishments which we patronized during the two year period. Six months were permitted to lapse between the time I obtained the overt reaction and the symbolic. It was hoped that the effects of the actual experience with Chinese guests, adverse or otherwise, would have faded during the intervening time. To the hotel or restaurant a questionnaire was mailed with an accompanying letter purporting to be a special and personal plea for response. The questionnaires all asked the same question, "Will you accept members of the Chinese race as guests in your establishment?" Two types of questionnaire were used. In one this question was inserted among similar queries concerning Germans, French, Japanese, Russians, Armenians, Jews, Negroes, Italians, and Indians. In the other the pertinent question was unencumbered. With persistence, completed replies were obtained from 128 of the establishments we had visited; 81 restaurants and cafes and 47 hotels, auto-camps, and "Tourist Homes." In response to the relevant question 92 per cent of the former and 91 per cent of the latter replied "No." The remainder replied "Uncertain; depend upon circumstances." From the woman proprietor of a small auto-camp I received the only "Yes," accompanied by a chatty letter describing the nice visit she had had with a Chinese gentleman and his sweet wife during the previous summer.

A rather unflattering interpretation might be put upon the fact that those establishments who had provided for our needs so graciously were, some months later, verbally antagonistic towards hypothetical Chinese. To factor this experience out responses were secured from 32 hotels and 96 restaurants located in approximately the same regions, but uninfluenced by this particular experience with Oriental clients. In this, as in the former case, both types of questionnaires were used. The results indicate that neither the type of questionnaire nor the fact of previous experience had important bearing upon the symbolic response to symbolic social situations.

It is impossible to make direct comparison between the reactions secured through questionnaires and from actual experience. On the basis of the above data it would appear foolhardy for a Chinese to attempt to travel in the United States. And yet, as I have shown, actual experience indicates that the American people, as represented by

the personnel of hotels, restaurants, etc., are not at all averse to fraternizing with Chinese within the limitations which apply to social relationships between Americans themselves. The evaluations which follow are undoubtedly subject to the criticism which any human judgment must withstand. But the fact is that, although they began their travels in this country with considerable trepidations, my Chinese friends soon lost all fear that they might receive a rebuff. At first somewhat timid and considerably dependent upon me for guidance and support, they came in time to feel fully self-reliant and would approach new social situations without the slightest hesitation.

The conventional questionnaire undoubtedly has significant value for the measurement of "political attitudes." The presidential polls conducted by the *Literary Digest* have proven that. But a "political attitude" is exactly what the questionnaire can be justly held to measure; a verbal response to a symbolic situation. Few citizens are ever faced with the necessity of adjusting themselves to the presence of the political leaders whom, periodically, they must vote for — or against. Especially is this true with regard to the president, and it is in relation to political attitudes towards presidential candidates that we have our best evidence. But while the questionnaire may indicate what the voter will do when he goes to vote, it does not and cannot reveal what

TABLE 1 / Distribution of Results from Questionnaire Study of Establishment "Policy" Regarding Acceptance of Chinese as Guests

Replies are to the question: "Will you accept members of the Chinese race as guests in your establishment?"

	Hotels, Etc. Visited		Hotels, Etc. Not Visited		Restaurants, Etc. Visited		Restaurants, Etc. Not Visited	
Total	47		32		81		96	
	1*	2*	1	2	1	2	1	2
Number replying	22	25	20	12	43	38	51	45
No	20	23	19	11	40	35	37	41
Undecided: depend upon circumstances	1	2	1	1	3	3	4	3
Yes	1	0	0	0	0	0	0	1

*Column (1) indicates in each case those responses to questionnaires which concerned Chinese only. The figures in column (2) are from the questionnaires in which the above was inserted among questions regarding Germans, French, Japanese, etc.

TABLE 2 / Distribution of Results Obtained from Actual Experience in the Situation Symbolized in the Questionnaire Study

Conditions	Hotels, Etc.		Restaurants, Etc.	
	Accompanied by investigator	Chinese not so accompanied at inception of situation*	Accompanied by investigator	Chinese not so accompanied at inception of situation
Total	55	12	165	19
Reception very much better than investigator would expect to have received had he been alone, but under otherwise similar circumstances	6	19	63	9
Reception different only to extent of heightened curiosity, such as investigator might have incurred were he alone but dressed in manner unconventional to region yet not incongruous	3	22	76	6
Reception "normal"	2	9	21	3
Reception perceptibly hesitant and not to be explained on other than "racial" grounds	1	3	4	1
Reception definitely, though temporarily, embarrassing	0	1	1	0
Not accepted	0	1	0	0

*When the investigator was not present at the inception of the situation the judgments were based upon what transpired after he joined the Chinese. Since intimately acquainted with them it is probable that errors in judgment were no more frequent under these conditions than when he was able to witness the inception as well as results of the situation.

he will do when he meets Candidate Jones on the street, in his office, at his club, on the golf course, or wherever two men may meet and adjust in some way one to the other.

The questionnaire is probably our only means of determining "religious attitudes." An honest answer to the question "Do you believe in God?" reveals all there is to be measured. "God" is a symbol; "belief" a verbal expression. So here, too, the questionnaire is efficacious. But if we would know the emotional responsiveness of a person to the spoken or written word "God" some other method of investigation must be used. And if we would know the extent to which that responsiveness restrains his behavior it is to his behavior that we must look, not to his questionnaire response. Ethical precepts are, I judge, something more

than verbal professions. There would seem little to be gained from asking a man if his religious faith prevents him from committing sin. Of course it does—on paper. But "moral attitudes" must have a significance in the adjustment to actual situations or they are not worth the studying. Sitting at my desk in California I can predict with a high degree of certainty what an "average" business man in an average Mid-Western city will reply to the question "Would you engage in sexual intercourse with a prostitute in a Paris brothel?" Yet no one, least of all the man himself, can predict what he would actually do should he by some misfortune find himself face to face with the situation in question. His moral "attitudes" are no doubt already stamped into his personality. But just what those habits are which will be invoked to provide him with some sort of adjustment to this situation is quite indeterminate.

It is highly probable that when the "Southern Gentleman" says he will not permit Negroes to reside in his neighborhood we have a verbal response to a symbolic situation which reflects the "attitudes" which would become operative in an actual situation. But there is no need to ask such a question of the true "Southern Gentleman." We knew it all the time. I am inclined to think that in most instances where the questionnaire does reveal non-symbolic attitudes the case is much the same. It is only when we cannot easily observe what people do in certain types of situations that the questionnaire is resorted to. But it is just here that the danger in the questionnaire technique arises. If Mr. A adjusts himself to Mr. B in a specified way we can deduce from his behavior that he has a certain "attitude" towards Mr. B and, perhaps, all of Mr. B's class. But if no such overt adjustment is made it is impossible to discover what A's adjustment would be should the situation arise. A questionnaire will reveal what Mr. A writes or says when confronted with a certain combination of words. But not what he will do when he meets Mr. B. Mr. B is a great deal more than a series of words. He is a man and he acts. His action is not necessarily what Mr. A "imagines" it will be when he reacts verbally to the symbol "Mr. B."

No doubt a considerable part of the data which the social scientist deals with can be obtained by the questionnaire method. The census reports are based upon verbal questionnaires and I do not doubt their basic integrity. If we wish to know how many children a man has, his income, the size of his home, his age, and the condition of his parents, we can reasonably ask him. These things he has frequently and conventionally converted into verbal responses. He is competent to report upon them, and will do so accurately, unless indeed he wishes to do otherwise. A careful investigator could no doubt even find out by verbal means whether the man fights with his wife (frequently, infrequently, or not at all), though the

neighbors would be a more reliable source. But we should not expect to obtain by the questionnaire method his "anticipatory set or tendency" to action should his wife pack up and go home to Mother, should Elder Son get into trouble with the neighbor's daughter, the President assume the status of a dictator, the Japanese take over the rest of China, or a Chinese gentleman come to pay a social call.

Only a verbal reaction to an entirely symbolic situation can be secured by the questionnaire. It may indicate what the responder would actually do when confronted with the situation symbolized in the question, but there is no assurance that it will. And so to call the response a reflection of a "social attitude" is to entirely disregard the definition commonly given for the phrase "attitude." If social attitudes are to be conceptualized as partially integrated habit sets which will become operative under specific circumstances and lead to a particular pattern of adjustment they must, in the main, be derived from a study of humans behaving in actual social situations. They must not be imputed on the basis of questionnaire data.

The questionnaire is cheap, easy, and mechanical. The study of human behavior is time consuming, intellectually fatiguing, and depends for its success upon the ability of the investigator. The former method gives quantitative results, the latter mainly qualitative. Quantitative measurements are quantitatively accurate; qualitative evaluations are always subject to the errors of human judgment. Yet it would seem far more worth while to make a shrewd guess regarding that which is essential than to accurately measure that which is likely to prove quite irrelevant.

NOTES

1. See Daniel D. Droba, "Topical Summaries of Current Literature," *The American Journal of Sociology*, 1934, p. 513.
2. "Race Prejudice: France and England," *Social Forces*, September 1928, pp. 102–111.
3. The results of this study have been withheld until the present time out of consideration for their feelings.

CRITICAL THINKING QUESTIONS

1. A central thesis of the LaPiere article was that the method of directly asking people about their attitudes has certain limitations in terms of accuracy and consistency. What are these limitations? Are there ways to overcome them other than those suggested by the author?

2. LaPiere maintained that there is little consistency between responses to attitude surveys and actual behavior. If that is the case, then what is the value (if any) of the multitude of attitude surveys that are regularly administered in the United States?

3. Did the study involve any ethical issues? For example, what do you think about the fact that the author did not tell his Chinese friends that they were part of a study he was conducting? Are there any other ethical considerations?

4. The article ended by making a distinction between *quantitative results,* such as those obtained by questionnaires, and *qualitative results,* such as those obtained by the author in his visits to the establishments. LaPiere obviously favors qualitative methods, arguing that although they are prone to errors of human judgment, such methods are preferred because it is better to "make a shrewd guess regarding what is essential than to accurately measure that which is likely quite irrelevant." Do you feel that the results of attitude questionnaires are "likely quite irrelevant"?

5. If you were to conduct the study, what methodological improvements would you make to reduce the subjectivity of the measures?

6. A major conclusion of the study was that responses to hypothetical questions do not necessarily predict actual behavior. Is this evidence for a lack of consistency between attitudes and behavior? In answering this, think of the specific methodology that was employed. Was there anything wrong with it, given the conclusions that were drawn? What methodology could be used to more directly assess the consistency between attitudes and behavior?

7. LaPiere made the observation that factors such as clothing, cleanliness, and smiles were more important in determining whether the couple was served than was skin color. How would you design a study to experimentally test this observation?

ADDITIONAL RELATED READINGS

Ajzen, I., & Fishbein, M. (1980). *Understanding attitudes and predicting social behavior.* Englewood Cliffs, NJ: Prentice-Hall.

Fazio, R. H. (1986). How do attitudes guide behavior? In R. M. Sorrentino & E. T. Higgins (eds.), *The handbook of motivation and cognition.* New York: Guilford Press.

Fazio, R. H., Powell, M. C., & Herr, P. M. (1983). Toward a process model of the attitude-behavior relation: Accessing one's attitude upon mere observation of the attitude objects. *Journal of Personality and Social Psychology, 44,* 723–735.

Wicker, A. W. (1969). Attitudes versus actions: The relationship of verbal and overt behavioral responses to attitude object. *Journal of Social Issues, 25,* 41–78.

ARTICLE 12 _____

The final study included in Chapter 4 is about cognitive dissonance. Cognitive dissonance theory says that people feel tension when they are aware of an inconsistency either between two attitudes or between an attitude and a behavior. Moreover, the theory asserts that such tension produces some type of change to reduce the state of dissonance. The exact conditions under which cognitive dissonance operates and how it is reduced have been investigated in many experiments over the years.

"Cognitive Dissonance and Energy Conservation," by Kantola, Syme, and Campbell, is an application of dissonance theory to a real-world issue. The study examines actual and self-reported changes in electricity consumption due to feedback on energy usage, tips about how to conserve energy, information on the inconsistency between previously stated attitudes about conservation and current consumption of electricity, or some combination of these variables. The study reports some interesting findings, including that arousing dissonance may be an effective way to increase energy conservation. The article also deals with a theme that was mentioned in the preceding study, namely, the consistency (or lack of consistency) between what people say and what they actually do.

Cognitive Dissonance and Energy Conservation

■ S. J. Kantola, G. J. Syme, and N. A. Campbell

A study was conducted to establish whether high consumers of electricity placed in a cognitively dissonant situation would conserve electricity over a 4-week period. Households in Perth, Western Australia owning ducted air conditioning and consuming above average amounts of electricity were included in the study. Four experimental groups were compared. The four groups were as follows: (a) the dissonance plus tips plus feedback group, who were informed of an inconsistency between their previously measured attitudes toward conservation and actual high consumption of electricity; (b) the feedback plus tips group, who were notified that they were high consumers of electricity; (c) the tips-only group, who were sent information on ways to conserve electricity (also sent to Groups 1 and 2); and (d) the control group, who were sent a thank-you letter for participating in the study. It was found, in keeping with bolstering behavior predictions of cognitive dissonance theory, that the dissonance group conserved more electricity than all other groups in the first 2-week measurement period. For the second 2-week measurement period, the dissonance group differed only from the control group. The study also found that self-reported behavior change and number of requests for additional conservation materials are not reliable indicators of actual conservation behavior.

In recent years, psychologists have become increasingly interested in finding ways to promote

Reprinted from the *Journal of Applied Psychology*, 1984, *69*, 416–421. Copyright 1984 by the American Psychological Association. Reprinted by permission.

energy conservation in households. Studies have concentrated on the effectiveness, either alone or in combination, of three approaches: (a) monetary rebates, (b) feedback about consumption, and (c) information about conservation.

Reviews have shown that information in the form of educational material alone has little, if any, effect on energy consumption. Providing feedback on consumption levels sometimes decreases consumption, and monetary rebates appear to be the most effective method of promoting conservation (see Cone & Hayes, 1977; Katzev, Cooper, & Fisher, 1980–81).

But before the use of information to promote conservation is dismissed, there is a need to distinguish between information that presents tips on how to save energy and information that attempts to motivate householders to act on these tips; these two aspects have often been confounded in past studies. Very few studies have evaluated the effectiveness of the motivational content of the message (see Hass, Bagley, & Rogers, 1975, for an exception).

Additionally, although feedback and rebates have shown most promise for promoting conservation, it is inappropriate to view them as competing with the informational/motivational approach. If applications of feedback and/or rebate systems are shown to be effective (see, for reviews, Cook & Berrenberg, 1981; Shippee, 1980), then the need for the informational approach with a motivational content will be enhanced because of the need to sustain interest in any feedback or rebate programs.

The study reported here is based on cognitive dissonance theory (see Festinger, 1957). The central premise of this theory is that when a person has two beliefs or items of knowledge that are not consistent with each other, then there is a tendency to reduce this dissonant state.

Sherman and Ghorkin (1980) discuss the likely ways of resolving dissonance when a behavior performed without coercion is inconsistent with an attitude. The usual method of dissonance reduction is an attitude change in the direction of the discrepant behavior. This is particularly the case when the attitude is not highly central, when there is no external justification for the behavior, when there is a sense of responsibility for adopting the behavior, and when negative consequences due to the behavior are foreseen or forseeable (see also Cialdini, Petty, & Cacioppo, 1981; Wicklund & Brehm, 1976).

However, if a central attitude is involved that is resistant to change and the behavior cannot be discounted, then there is a likelihood that bolstering (reaffirmation) of the initial central attitude will occur (see Abelson, 1959; Sherman & Ghorkin, 1980). In a demonstration of this phenomenon, Sherman and Ghorkin (1980) showed that a freely adopted behavior (failure of a sex role logic problem) discrepant with a central attitude (women's rights) resulted in a reaffirmation of this attitude in subsequent behaviors (response to affirmative hiring measures).

In the present study, subjects in a dissonance condition were informed that their attitude toward energy conservation was inconsistent with the level of their household electricity consumption and were given tips about how to conserve energy. Subsequently electricity consumption was taken as the response variable to assess bolstering behavior. Self-reported electricity conservation and requests for conservation information were used as alternate response variables. This study tests the hypothesis that the dissonance-aroused group with feedback and tips will conserve more electricity than either a feedback plus tips group, or a tips-only group, or a control group (i.e., no dissonance arousal, no feedback, no tips). It was also predicted that self-reported electricity conservation and requests for conservation information would be greatest for the dissonance group. Because of the increased level of intervention, it was hypothesized that the feedback group would conserve more electricity than the tips group. It was assumed that the control group would conserve least. Because dissonance reduction was predicted to be accomplished through bolstering behavior, the dissonance group was expected to be similar to all the other groups on attitudinal measures of duty to conserve energy, importance of energy, and derogation of the source of the dissonance information.

METHOD

Subjects

Subjects were selected from warranty lists of houses having ducted refrigerated air conditioning units. Several suburbs in the middle to upper socioeconomic range in Perth, Western Australia were included in the sample. The adult spending most time in the home was selected as the respondent for each household.

Procedure and Stimulus Materials

The experiment was conducted in the hot part of the year but outside the peak holiday period. A personal questionnaire measuring attitudes toward energy conservation and demographic characteristics of the household was first administered to a sample of 272 subjects. This sample came from a list of 439 addresses supplied by air conditioning companies. There were 18 refusals, 91 noncontacts with two callbacks, 49 incorrect or business addresses, and 9 incomplete questionnaires due to language difficulties.

The first question from this questionnaire was "Would you please indicate how important the following issues are to you?" This was followed by a list of six social issues, one of which was household energy conservation. A 5-point unipolar scale ranging from *extremely* (+ 5) to *not* (+ 1) followed each issue. These responses were recorded before the subject was aware that the survey was related to energy.

The statement measuring personal duty was "It is your personal duty as a responsible citizen to save as much electricity as possible." This was followed by a bipolar scale with responses ranging from *strongly agree* (+ 3) to *strongly disagree* (− 3). Subjects were also asked whether they had ducted air conditioning or a dishwasher.

Family size and income, age, and sex of family members were also recorded. Subjects were also asked if there were going to be any absences or visitors during the following two months. Finally,

subjects were asked for permission to read their electricity meters in the next 2 months and to obtain annual gas and electricity consumption figures from the State Energy Commission.

From this initial sample, subjects were selected for the experiment (a) if they agreed or strongly agreed that it was their personal duty as citizens to conserve electricity (97% of respondents were in these two categories); (b) if there were only minor visitors or absences (less than 3 days visit or absence) expected during the experiment; and (c) if they gave permission to have their consumption monitored. Also, subjects in this initial sample were checked to see if they were high yearly consumers of electricity and gas. High consumption was defined as being greater than the average consumption for a household in the Perth metropolitan area with the same number of occupants.

The 203 subjects who met the above criteria then had their electricity consumption measured for a 2-week baseline period. All consumption readings were made unobtrusively, without the subject observing the reading. However, because permission was given to have their electricity monitored, the subjects were aware that meter readings might be taking place. On the day of final reading for this baseline period, one of four different letters was dropped in the subject's mail box. Groups were matched for income, electricity consumption, perceived duty to save electricity, and dishwasher ownership. Specifically, the subjects were stratified by dishwasher ownership or lack of it, their response to the question measuring personal duty (only two responses—*strongly agree* and *agree*—were used by the respondents) and their income (in 6 categories). Within each of the resulting classes, subjects were ranked by electricity and gas consumption during the previous 12 months. The first four subjects from this ranked list in each of the classes were then allocated at random to one of the four experimental groups, then the next four subjects, and so on. An allocation decision based on consumption was used when the number of subjects in a class was not a multiple of four.

The four letters represented the four different experimental conditions used in this study. All four versions of the letter thanked people for answering the initial questionnaire. Also, a postage-paid postcard was included, which the subjects could return if they wanted information about ways to conserve electricity. The variations in the letters were as follows.

1. *Dissonance plus feedback group plus tips (dissonance group).* Subjects in this group were informed that they were high consumers of electricity and that they had said in the earlier survey that they felt it was their duty to save electricity. They also received a pamphlet and card listing ways to reduce the electricity consumed by air conditioners, together with a note informing them that dishwashers also use a lot of electricity.
2. *Feedback plus tips group (feedback group).* Subjects in this group were notified that they were high consumers of electricity; they also received a pamphlet and card listing ways to reduce electricity consumption. No mention of "duty to save" was included in this letter.
3. *Tips-only group (tips group).* Subjects in this group received only the pamphlet and card listing ways to reduce electricity consumption.
4. *Control group.* Subjects in this group received only the thank-you letter and the postage-paid postcard requesting further conservation information that was sent to all groups.

Following the presentation of the letter, electricity consumption over two consecutive 2-week periods was recorded. The average maximum temperature during the first 2-week experimental period was 26.5°C (79.7°F); for the second 2-week period the average was 30.1°C (86.2°F).

Approximately 1 week after the final reading of electricity consumption was taken, the second questionnaire was administered. This was again a personal interview with the same subject who responded to the first survey.

This second questionnaire included questions on the following: (a) any absences or visitors during the experimental period; (b) a retest of the perceived importance of energy conservation; (c) a retest of the respondent's perception of their duty to save electricity; (d) the respondent's self-report of whether energy conservation was attempted over the study period; (e) which electricity-

conserving behaviors were adopted (i.e., dishwasher, air conditioner usage); (f) open-ended comments on any phase of the study, subsequently coded as *no comment, positive, neutral,* and *negative;* and (g) whether the respondent was interested in participating in future studies, with response choices of *definitely, possibly* and *not interested.*

For this study, the four response variables that assessed the effect of experimental manipulations on behavior or reported behavior were as follows: (a) whether the person returned the postcard requesting more information on conservation; (b) whether the person reported that an attempt was made to conserve electricity; (c) the electricity consumption during the first 2-week experimental period; and (d) the electricity consumption during the second 2-week experimental period.

The four measures of the effects of the experimental manipulations on attitudes were as follows: (a) attitude with respect to the personal duty of the respondent to conserve energy; (b) attitude with respect to the importance of energy conservation; (c) derogation of the source of the dissonant information (reflected in a negative comment about the study or lack of willingness to participate in further studies); and (d) intentions to conserve energy.

The final sample size was 118, obtained after removing households with significant absences or visitors (i.e., more than 3 days visit or absence) and noncontacts. Numbers in the experimental groups were as follows: dissonance, 31; feedback, 32; tips, 30; and control, 25. Analysis of covariance was used to adjust for any resulting differences in the composition of the groups with respect to the factors used for stratification (see below).

RESULTS

Questionnaire Responses (Attitude and Self-Reported Change)

The response of an individual to any one of the questions in the questionnaire is qualitative, with two or more categories of response. For each individual in a particular treatment group, we may assume that the response is multinomial (or binomial when the response is binary).

Our interest is in examining whether the proportions for the underlying multinomial distributions are the same for the four experimental groups or for subsets of the groups (e.g., for the contrast between the dissonance group and the feedback group). Maximum likelihood estimates for the parameters for the various multinomials can be computed using log-linear model methodology, with terms included in the model to ensure that appropriate margins are fixed (in the case of two groups logistic linear regression methodology can be used). A description of the approach is given in Nelder (1974, Section 3). Comparisons of the different (subsets of) groups can be evaluated using chi-squared statistics based on the ratios of likelihoods under the assumption of different multinomial probabilities for the (subset of) groups and common multinomial probabilities for the (subset of) groups.

For a binary response, the stratification adopted to allocate subjects to the four experimental groups was incorporated into the analysis by adopting logistic linear regression methodology, with the stratification factors as covariates. Because of the simplicity of this approach, we also chose to examine the effects of the stratification factors on the multinomial responses by treating the latter as a series of binary responses (e.g., for a response with levels *strongly agree, agree,* and *neutral,* we analyzed *strongly agree* versus [*agree, neutral,*] and [*strongly agree, agree*] versus *neutral* as two alternative binary responses). For only a few of the responses was one or more of the covariates significant, and in none of these cases did the significance or otherwise of the differences between the experimental groups (or of contrasts between the groups) change.

In general, we chose to examine contrasts among the intervention groups in the same order as the degree of intervention. For example, tips would be compared with feedback, and if there was no difference these groups would be combined and compared with the dissonance condition. That is, we combined responses for "adjacent" treatments when they did not differ significantly and compared the combined response with

adjacent remaining groups. The control group is then compared with tips and those groups similar to tips. An exception was made for the consumption variable where means obviously did not follow the linear pattern assumed by our general approach.

Evidence of dissonance reduction by means of verbal report from the follow-up questionnaire is now examined.

Duty to Save   There was a trend (p = .07) for fewer in the dissonant group to *strongly agree* that it is their personal duty to save electricity than in the remaining groups. The proportions were as follows: dissonance (.61); feedback (.87); tips (.83); and control (.76).

Importance of Energy Conservation   There was no significant difference between the groups in the rating of the importance of energy conservation. Overall proportions were as follows: extremely, .27; very, .59; and moderately, .14.

Comments on Study   There was no difference between groups in the rated favorability of the comments. Overall proportions were as follows: no comment, .48; positive comment, .22; neutral comment, 18; and negative comment, .12.

Willingness to Participate in Further Studies   There was no difference between the groups in the willingness to participate in further studies. The overall proportions were as follows: definitely, .49; possibly, .33; and not interested, .18.

Self-Reported Attempts to Reduce Use of Electricity   Significantly fewer in the tips and control groups reported that they attempted to reduce their usage of electricity than in the dissonance and feedback groups (p < .05). The proportions were as follows: dissonance, 0.69; feedback, 0.65; tips, 0.39; and control, 0.48.

Cut Down on Use of Dishwashers   Of the 44 subjects owning dishwashers, significantly fewer in the control group stated that they reduced their use of dishwashers than in the remaining groups.

The proportions were as follows: dissonance, .36 (*n* = 11); feedback, .10 (*n* = 10); tips, .30 (*n* = 10); and control, .00 (*n* = 13).

Cut Down on Use of Air Conditioner   Significantly fewer in the control group stated that they cut down on the use of air conditioners than in the remaining groups (*p* < .05). The proportions were as follows: dissonance, .43; feedback, .46; tips, .54; and control, .24.

Changed Air Conditioning Setting   There was no difference between the groups in the proportion that reported that they changed the thermostat setting on their air conditioner. The overall proportion was .17.

Postcard Returns

This analysis was restricted to the experimental groups that received tips initially. Significantly fewer in the dissonance group returned postcards than in the feedback group (*p* < .05). The proportions were as follows: dissonance, .00; feedback, .23; and tips, .14.

Electricity Consumption

Household electricity consumption during the two 2-week measurement periods and during the total 4-week period was analyzed. Electricity consumption figures for the 2-week prestudy baseline period and for the previous 12 months were considered as covariates. There was a highly significant adjustment for the consumption for the previous 12 months (*p* < .001), and this was similar for all four experimental groups. The mean consumption figures (in kilowatt hours) adjusted for yearly electricity consumption are shown in Table 1.

The consumption for the dissonance group was significantly lower than that in the control group for the total 4-week experimental period (*p* < .05) and for the first 2-week experimental period (*p* < .05); factors for the covariates and the treatment groups explained approximately 70% of the variation in the response for the 4-week period.

TABLE 1 / Electricity Consumption of the Four Groups (Kilowatt Hours Adjusted for Yearly Electricity Consumption)

Group	Time after intervention		
	First 2 weeks	Second 2 weeks	4 weeks
Dissonance	256	383	640
Feedback	289	416	705
Tips	285	382	667
Control	297	432	729
Standard error (approx.)	13	19	29

DISCUSSION

As hypothesized, the results indicate that there was some effect of dissonance on consumption but none on attitudes. The dissonance group for a 2-week period consumed less electricity than the other three groups. This effect did not persist in the second 2-week measurement period. Although the observed effects were limited to the first fortnight, the findings are promising when the level of intervention (a single resident in a multiple resident dwelling) and the minimal treatment difference between groups (all manipulated within a few lines of a standardized letter) are considered. The diminution of our effect is also similar to that often observed when financial incentives such as rebates or fines are used to encourage conservation behavior (Cook & Berrenberg 1981).

Although dissonance effects were demonstrated at a behavioral level, this was not the case for the alternative measures: reported behavior change and postcard returns. In the first case more subjects in the dissonance and feedback groups reported that they attempted to reduce electricity consumption than in the tips and control groups. Although the feedback group had greater proportions of individuals reporting that they attempted to reduce electricity consumption than the tips or control groups, this group did not actually consume significantly less electricity than these groups. This may have been because this group were motivated only enough to say they made some attempts to conserve or that the attempts they did make were not as diligent as the dissonance group.

When the reported changes in specific conservation behaviors (i.e., dishwasher and air conditioner usage) and postcard returns are considered, the importance of a valid response variable (i.e., actual electricity figures) becomes even more obvious. From the reported reductions in dishwasher and air conditioner usage it is only possible to conclude that the control group probably conserved less than the other three groups. This is not totally inconsistent with the consumption data, but it does not indicate the superior conservation behavior of the dissonance group. Thus, the importance of gaining consumption data in addition to self-report measures is emphasized.

The second behavioral measure, that of postcard returns, showed opposite results to that of consumption. Lowest returns occurred in the dissonance group. The use of data from postcard returns as an indicator of motivation to conserve electricity may, therefore, lead to erroneous conclusions. The failure of the dissonance group to return any postcards could lead to the assumption that these people are not motivated to conserve or had even shown reactance (Brehm, 1966) to the dissonance manipulation. This is not consistent with the findings from the analysis of the actual electricity consumption figures nor with the attitudes of the respondents in the final survey. It is also incompatible with the study of Craig and McCann (1978) on the effects of credibility and repetition of a message on electricity consumption, which found similar responses for consumption and postcard returns.

Because of subject availability, a number of control groups that would have aided interpretation had to be omitted. In interpreting the superior conservation of the dissonance group, it should be recognized that the design of the study omitted a condition of reminding people of their values without informing them of their high consumption. It could be assumed that if such a group conserved as much as the dissonance condition then subjects were responding to a reminder

of their values rather than to dissonance per se. In practice some "value reminder" influence was present to a significant degree throughout the three non-dissonance groups. When they received their letter, they were inevitably reminded of a highly conservation-oriented interview, especially in the feedback condition. Thus, the dissonance effect had to be measured above three implicitly value-influenced control conditions. A design incorporating both a no-letter group and a values reminder only would, therefore, be desirable.

A further design issue is that of assessing the relative effects of information and feedback or dissonance when they are used in combination. Groups receiving either dissonance inducton or feedback *without* information could also have been incorporated in the design to give an indication of possible interaction between both dissonance and feedback and information. In this study, as in many in behavior modification (Cook & Berrenberg 1981), we have assessed the effects of each variable in an additive sense, with the effects of information being considered as being "controlled for" in comparisons between feedback and dissonance. For this reason our analysis makes statistical comparisons sequentially. It was, of course, impossible to have a dissonance group without feedback.

Finally, this study, although mainly addressing itself to motivational issues in relation to information, also suggests a different direction for attitudinal research. Many studies (see Olsen, 1981) have found a poor correlation between attitudes toward conservation and actual patterns of consumption. However this study suggests that if consumers are made aware of a discrepancy between their attitudes and behavior then more consistency might be observed.

REFERENCES

Abelson, R. P. (1959). Models of resolution of belief dilemmas. *Journal of Conflict Resolution, 3,* 343–352.

Brehm, J. W. (1966). *A theory of psychological reactance.* New York: Academic Press.

Cialdini, R. B., Petty, R. E., & Cacioppo, J. T. (1981). Attitude and attitude change. *Annual Review of Psychology, 32,* 357–404.

Cone, J. D., & Hayes, S. C. (1977). Applied behavior analysis and the solution of environmental problems. In Altman, I., & Wohwill, J. F. (Eds.), *Human behavior and environment* (Vol. 2; pp. 129–176). New York: Plenum Press.

Cook, S. W., & Berrenberg, J. L. (1981). Approaches to encouraging conservation behavior: A review and conceptual framework. *Journal of Social Issues, 37,* 73–107.

Craig, C. S., & McCannn, J. M. (1978). Assessing communication effects on energy conservation. *Journal of Consumer Research, 5,* 82–88.

Festinger, L. (1957). *A theory of cognitive dissonance.* Stanford CA: Stanford University Press.

Hass, J W., Bagley, G. S., & Rogers, R. W. (1975). Coping with the energy crisis: Effects of fear appeals upon attitudes toward energy consumption. *Journal of Applied Psychology, 60,* 754–756.

Katzev, R., Cooper, L., & Fisher, P. (1980–81). The effect of feedback and social reinforcement on residential electricity consumption. *Journal of Environmental Systems, 10*(3), 215–227.

Nelder, J. A. (1974). Log linear models for contingency tables: A generalization of classical least squares. *Applied Statistics, 23,* 323–329.

Olsen, M. E. (1981). Consumers' attitudes toward energy conservation. *Journal of Social Issues, 37,* 108–131.

Sherman, S. J., & Gorkin, L. (1980). Attitude bolstering when behavior is inconsistent with central attitudes. *Journal of Experimental Social Psychology, 16,* 388–403.

Shippee, G. (1980). Energy consumption and conservation psychology: A review and conceptual analysis. *Environmental Management, 4,* 297–314.

Wicklund, R. A., & Brehm, J. W. (1976). *Perspectives on cognitive dissonance.* Hillsdale, NJ: Erlbaum.

The authors would like to thank the Perth office of the Australian Bureau of Statistics for their assistance with the data collection and Philip Fry for his substantial contribution to the design and conduct of this study.

CRITICAL THINKING QUESTIONS

1. A major finding of the study was that subjects in the dissonance group conserved more electricity than all other groups during the first two-week measurement period. However, during the next two weeks, the dissonance group differed only from the control group. Although the study produced a good effect initially, from a practical standpoint, it would be better if the increased energy conservation effect could be maintained over an even longer time period. Given the methodology and findings of the study, suggest some techniques to maintain the energy conservation levels of the dissonance group for a longer period of time.

2. As mentioned in the study, the design did not include two conditions: a "no-letter" group and a "values-reminder-only" group. Predict the outcomes of these two conditions on energy conservation.

3. How would you adapt/modify the methodology of this study to other conservation issues? For example, could you design a program to reduce littering using the principles of cognitive dissonance?

4. This study used several dependent measures of energy conservation: actual electricity usage, self-report measures of conservation, and requests for more information about conservation. These dependent measures did not respond the same way for given experimental conditions (e.g., the dissonance group showed decreases in actual electricity usage but not in requests for more information). What does this finding imply for studies in general that employ only a single dependent variable?

5. Do you think the implications of the study can be generalized to behaviors other than conservation issues? For example, AIDS-education programs have been developed to promote so-called "safe-sex" practices. Do you think that there is necessarily a connection between attitudes about safe sex and actually practicing safe sex? Is there any way that a program could be developed to actually change sexual behavior, rather than just attitudes towards AIDS and safe sex?

Chapter Five

PREJUDICE AND DISCRIMINATION

PREJUDICE. THINK OF the implications of that word. It is so negative that even people who are highly prejudiced often are reluctant to use that term to describe themselves. Instead, prejudiced people may say that their opinions about members of certain groups are accurate and well founded, perhaps even that these groups deserve disdain.

Although the words *prejudice* and *discrimination* are often used interchangeably, they actually refer to two different things. Prejudice is an attitude, a set of beliefs about a member of a group based just on membership in that group. Discrimination, on the other hand, is a behavior, the differential treatment of a person based on membership in a particular group. You don't need to look far for the results of prejudiced attitudes and discriminatory behaviors: History is full of suffering inflicted on people due solely to their membership in particular groups.

Psychological research on prejudice has studied three topics: (1) the causes of prejudice; (2) the consequences of prejudice and discrimination; and (3) ways that prejudice can be reduced. Most studies have focused on the most overt forms of prejudice—racial, religious, and sexual. Article 13, "The Wheelchair Rebellion," addresses another very common form of prejudice, and perhaps one that works in a more subtle fashion: attitudes toward and treatment of the disabled.

Article 14, "Experiments in Group Conflict," on the other hand, demonstrates the development as well as the eventual elimination of prejudice in a group of boys. The article clearly addresses some of the factors that may contribute to the development of prejudice and demonstrates at least one way that such prejudices may be reduced.

Article 15, "Stereotypes and Prejudice," considers the cognitive mechanisms underlying prejudice: What role do stereotypes play in prejudice? Can negative stereotypes be overcome, or do they automatically lead to prejudiced attitudes? There is sort of a "good news, bad news" tone to the results of the three studies presented in the article. The "bad news" is that even people with low prejudice have the same negative cultural stereotypes as people with high prejudice. The "good news" is that this doesn't mean that they will always use these stereotypes in making judgments about groups. The conditions under which this happens are explored in the reading.

ARTICLE 13 _____

When you think of prejudice and discrimination, what comes to mind? Most likely, you think of unfair treatment of people based upon their race, ethnic background, sex, or religion. Historically, groups that have differed from the majority on the basis of some distinguishing feature, such as skin color or religious beliefs, have been discriminated against in everything from education to employment opportunities. But they are not the only victims of such unjust treatment.

In "The Wheelchair Rebellion," Gliedman not only strongly demonstrates that people have negative stereotypes of those with disabilities but also that these beliefs are related to discriminatory patterns of behavior, such as employment opportunities. Moreover, Gliedman argues that members of the helping professions, those individuals who are dedicated to working with the disabled, are often the worst offenders. The nature of this prejudice and discrimination and the underlying mental processes that may account for these beliefs and behaviors are discussed in the article.

The Wheelchair Rebellion

■ John Gliedman

By the early 1970s, many of the nation's black leaders, political activists, and liberal reformers had been exhausted by a decade of confrontation and violence. Undaunted, or perhaps too desperate to care, people with various kinds of handicaps nevertheless began to organize a civil rights movement of their own. A new generation of groups for the disabled was born, such as the American Coalition of Citizens with Disabilities and Mainstream, Inc. Like older and more established groups, they lobbied for better social services and protested the endless Catch-22 provisions in the welfare laws that hurt the severely disabled. But they also demanded something more: they called for significant structural changes in housing, public buildings, and transportation that have long posed barriers to their mobility; and they began working for an end to the prejudice and job discrimination that had proved far more obstructive to an active life than such handicaps as blindness, deafness, or paraplegia.

For all its achievements in the rehabilitation

and education laws of the 1970s, what many have called the "Quiet Revolution" in disability was an incomplete and one-sided revolution. It was one-sided because the new image of the handicapped as an oppressed minority group was held only by some of the disabled themselves, their relatives, and many professionals who cared for them. The legislative reforms that the organizers succeeded in winning in the 70s were not the result of massive grass-roots pressure from millions of handicapped people and their able-bodied allies. Moreover, key provisions in the laws are in jeopardy because of the recent Supreme Court ruling that held that a college is not required to admit a deaf person who cannot benefit from the program without substantial modification of its standards.

Even today, the civil rights movement for the disabled is relatively small. The impetus for change comes from the top. A sympathetic Congress (many of whose members themselves have disabled relatives), the efforts of diligent lobbyists, the initiative of legal advocates, and a federal

Reprinted from *Psychology Today*, 1979 (August), *13*, 59–101. Reprinted with permission from *Psychology Today Magazine*. Copyright © 1979 (PT Partners, L.P.).

bureaucracy receptive, at least in principle, to the idea of treating the disabled as another disadvantaged minority group—all contributed to the relatively unpublicized passage of landmark legislation in the 1970s. Nevertheless, Frank Bowe, director of the American Coalition, sized up the status of the movement this way: "It is possible to legislate rights, and this has been done. But rights become reality only after political struggle."

Bowe says more than half of all working-age disabled adults who could work are jobless. There is systematic discrimination against those who do work, according to Bowe and others, which keeps them in menial or futureless jobs; across the United States, a network of "sheltered workshops" employs 200,000 handicapped people whose wages average under $1 an hour—far less than the minimum wage. Little energy goes to inventing, producing, or marketing products specially designed for the disabled, and what is marketed generally goes through the medical or social-service system as mediator. Thus are the handicapped barred from behaving as independent producers, consumers, and citizens in the economy.

Along with those tangible disadvantages, the disabled must also cope with a kind of paternalism from their able-bodied allies that has long been discredited in race relations. Even today, many unprejudiced Americans accept traditional stereotypes about different kinds of handicaps. However, instead of reacting cruelly because of the fears and anxieties aroused by those disabilities, we take a more humane approach. We extend to handicapped people what seems to be an enlightened model of medical tolerance. Rather than blame them for their pitiful condition, we say that their social and mental incompetence is produced by a disease or a disease-like condition beyond their control to alter. We believe that, in a social sense, they are chronic patients; and that we owe them the same struggle with our fears and prejudices, the same understanding and tolerance, that we owe victims of any serious disease or injury.

The problem with this analysis, from the dis-

abled person's point of view, is that it allows him or her no scope whatsoever for leading an adult social life. As Talcott Parsons first noted, the role of a patient in middle-class society is functionally very similar to that of a child. We expect the patient to be cheerful and accepting, to obey doctors' orders, and, in general, to devote all his energies to getting well. When an able-bodied person falls sick, he ceases to be judged as an adult; in return, he is expected to work actively to get well. The area defined as his to control shifts to the sickbed. But in America a person labeled handicapped is assigned a specially destructive variant of the sick role. Not merely powerless because he is sick, he is defined as doubly powerless because he cannot master the job of "getting well." Unable to fill that role obligation, he is seen as socially powerless, deprived of a political identity—until he chooses to assert one.

Many members of the civil rights movement for the disabled have told me that the annual cerebral palsy telethon symbolizes for them the deeply humiliating paternalism of society's medical tolerance toward handicapped people. Michael Poachovis, a political organizer on the West Coast, said, "It's absolutely degrading. Watching those telethons you might think that all palsied adults are mentally retarded, pathetically trusting, asexual children." Others find little comfort in the usual image of disabled people presented in the media. Ron Whyte, a writer in New York City, summed up his feelings this way: "You don't learn about Harlem by listening to 'Amos 'n' Andy.'" Only rarely are we forced to confront the paternalism that lurks behind our attempts to deal fairly with the handicapped. Witness the discomfort of audiences watching Jon Voight as a demanding, rebellious, and unabashedly erotic crippled veteran in the recent film *Coming Home*.

Over the past five years, I have studied the problems of disability while on the research staff of the Carnegie Council on Children. Handicapped children were the point of departure for my work. But, along with my colleague William Roth, I eventually devoted as much time to adults as to children, since the problems of the different age groups tend to be closely related.

In the 1960s and 1970s, about 20 million people of working age described themselves as disabled. Those estimates might easily be 50 percent too high or too low. They might be too low because they do not include most people whom a psychologist would classify as mildly retarded; most people who have experienced a major mental illness; or those with speech or learning disabilities. The figures might be too high because they are based upon answers to the question, "Do you have any medical condition or other impairment lasting three months or longer that limits the kind or amount of work that you can do?" Answers given to this kind of question are highly unreliable. On the other hand, it is perfectly possible that these contradictory factors cancel out, and that the figure of 20 million is not too far off after all.

Accepting this estimate provisionally, it seems reasonable to assume that disabled people comprise between 5 and 10 percent of the total working-age population. This is a huge number, at least as large as the number of able-bodies Hispanics in this age range and quite possibly as large as the number of able-bodied blacks.

Disabilities are, of course, much more common among the elderly. The best guess is that between one-third and one-fourth of all people 65 years or older are currently disabled. But the sociological relationships between disability and old age require further study; it is quite possible that the social experiences of most elderly people in possession of their mental faculties can also be described by the minority-group model of disability, which views the social stigma as attached to the condition of being aged rather than a result of any actual disability.

It is even more difficult to assess the number of children with real disabilities. Many kinds of handicaps that pass unnoticed among adults may be blown up out of proportion by parents, teachers, and a child's peers. A host of clinical findings also suggests that perceptions of the severity of a handicap are exquisitely sensitive to social milieu. What some people in one social stratum treat as a mild or negligible disability may be considered severely disabling in another. For the present, one can only guess that the total number of disabled children and youths lies somewhere between five and 10 million.

Members of an oppressed social group have little in common apart from the fact that society singles them out for systematic oppression. Examples abound: European Jews in the 1920s and 1930s, many of whom did not consider themselves primarily Jewish; and, closer to home, women, homosexuals, the elderly. Similarly, handicapped people are beginning to see themselves as an oppressed minority because society exposes most of them to a common set of pressures that violate their civil rights. Long ago, the social psychologist Kurt Lewin called the defining characteristics of a minority group an "interdependence of fate." Discrimination—much of it in the economic marketplace—constitutes the sociological fate of the disabled. This discrimination imposes a minority-group identity upon a collection of adults and children, each of whom has, in most other respects, as much in common with able-bodied people as with one another.

Two or three decades ago, sociologists often studied the phenomenon of "passing"—the attempt of light-skinned blacks to pass as whites, of Jews to pass as gentiles. That phenomenon helps to clarify the relevance of a minority-group analysis to disabled people. The first group of disabled people who fit the minority-group model are those who can rarely pass as able-bodied. They include the deaf, the blind, the physically disabled, the cosmetically disfigured, the very short, and individuals with chronic diseases whose symptoms are unpleasant and obtrusive. Another group of disabled people encounters many of the same problems as the black who passed as white in the 1930s or 1940s. They can usually come off as able-bodied, but they often pay a high psychological price for their successful strategies of concealment. The passers include many people once institutionalized in mental hospitals or custodial institutions for the mildly retarded; many epileptics; many people with severe reading disabilities;

many with concealable but socially stigmatizing medical conditions or chronic diseases.

For most people with cancer, heart disease, diabetes, and back ailments, the minority-group analysis is probably of secondary importance. Still, even those with such disabilities would benefit greatly from an end to job discrimination against disabled persons, improvement in the quality of the nation's social and health services, and, in many instances, elimination of architectural and transportation barriers to mobility. One other group of disabled adults requires mention — those who are so incapacitated by their mental or emotional limitations that they could not lead normal lives even if society's considerable prejudice against them were to melt away. That group includes the severely (and intractably) psychotic, and somewhere between one-tenth and one-fourth of all mentally retarded people.

Measured against two centuries of neglect, stigma, and degradation, the gains registered by disabled people in the 1970s were impressive indeed. Even as the Equal Rights Amendment for women was stalled, Congress overrode two Nixon vetoes of the first legislation that specifically prohibited discrimination against disabled workers. The legislation, the Rehabilitation Act of 1973, required affirmative-action or nondiscriminatory hiring programs to be instituted in all federal agencies for all federal contractors doing more than $2,500-a-year worth of work for the government, as well as in any public or private organization that receives federal funds.

The section of the Rehabilitation Act dealing with discrimination against the disabled has been regularly challenged and regularly reaffirmed in the courts. But in June, the Supreme Court established limits on its scope when it ruled that Southeastern Community College in North Carolina was within its rights in refusing admission of Frances B. Davis, a hearing-impaired woman, to its nursing program. Mrs. Davis, who relies largely on lip-reading to understand others, is a practical nurse who sought admission to the clinical part of the registered-nurse curriculum that would have brought her into contact with pa-

tients. Reversing an appeals court ruling, the justices held that the law does not require a college to compromise its admission standards or make "extensive modifications" of its program to accommodate all handicapped persons; it prohibits only discrimination against those who are "otherwise qualified" in spite of their handicaps.

Leaders of handicapped people's organizations believe that while the decision establishes a potentially harmful precedent, it may apply to only a small number of cases. "It's the kind of case I call a "blind busdriver' claim," said Leslie Milk, executive director of Mainstream, Inc., implying that it is not unreasonable for an employer to refuse to let a blind man drive a bus. "The court ruled very narrowly, apparently to limit the implications of the decision, and left it to HEW to go on clarifying the situation as it makes regulations. It's a limitation on the law, but one we can live with."

Frank Bowe of the American Coalition also thinks the court's decision makes some sense. Bowe, who is himself deaf, said that most people would agree that a hearing impairment could prevent a nurse from responding effectively to a patient in all critical situations. "But most disabled people are like me," Bowe said. "They want to enter fields where their disability doesn't interfere with the job." But both Milk and Bowe fear that the ruling will have a deterrent effect: that it may discourage some handicapped people from applying to professional schools, or encourage some schools to believe that they can avoid compliance with the law in the future.

The ruling does not curtail the great progress made in primary and secondary education. While public interest in the desperate plight of the inner-city school ebbed, a series of class-action suits on behalf of mentally retarded children established the right of every handicapped child to a free and appropriately designed public education. Responding to these legal decisions, Congress passed a law that attempts to end the traditional pattern of segregated public education for handicapped children: it stipulates that every child should be educated in the least-segregated educational setting that does justice to his academic and emotional needs. The law's insistence upon the school's accountability to the child's parents and its requirement that the school provide an individualized program of education to every child represent an even more far-reaching departure from traditional practice in public education.

In making its case to the able-bodied mainstream, the central obstacle confronted by the movement is the widespread acceptance of the medical model. Even when it is invoked out of a genuine desire to help the disadvantaged—for instance, as when homosexuality is defined as a disease—this set of assumptions can be damaging. Regardless of whether the economy is growing or contracting, the disabled have a right to their fair share of jobs, goods, and services. But the moment any group is defined as a collection of ill or defective people, social priorities insensibly change. Questions of stigma and systemic discrimination fade into the background: the first priority goes to *treating* the putative inferiority.

As in the case of other disadvantaged groups, the professionals who work with the disabled are often among the worse offenders. Most workers in the human services still acquire in their training a basically medical view of social problems, what the historian Christopher Lasch has recently called the social-pathology model. The disease metaphor is far more pervasive in care of the disabled than in most other areas. It influences not only the policymakers and the care-givers, but also the social scientists who are doing the very research that could bring about changes in attitudes.

Most often, such researchers will postulate the presence of a single diseaselike entity that colors the attitudes of the majority of able-bodied people—a maladjustment in relating to disabled people—and then proceed to measure the prevalence of the disease among the groups studied. Even the best of this work suffers from the failing of so much social science: the discovery of striking facts whose exact significance is unclear because the underlying social phenomenon is far more complex than the experimenters' theories admit. Studies of the attitudes of able-bodied people toward the handicapped usually report what they

say about the disabled, not how they act toward them. Virtually none of the research sorts out the relative roles of fear, ignorance, inexperience, or prejudice.

Jerome Siller, professor of educational psychology at New York University, has done extensive studies on able-bodied people's expressed attitudes toward different disability groups. Siller asked his subjects what characteristics they attribute to different sorts of disability (for instance, amputees may be seen as more intelligent, aggressive, or kind than people with other handicaps).

He uncovered a hierarchy of acceptability. The most acceptable disabilities were the relatively minor ones, like partial vision or hearing loss, a speech impediment or a heart condition. Amputees were a rung lower on the acceptability hierarchy. The deaf and the blind ranked somewhere in the middle, then came the mentally ill; below them stood people with epilepsy, cerebral palsy, or total paralysis.

When ranking included blacks, they usually ended up in the middle of the hierarchy, near the deaf and the blind. In some studies, such as one of employer attitudes made in the early 1970s by clinical psychologist James A. Colbert and his associates, blacks were preferred above all disability groups. Here, too, the sociological implications of these results are unclear. For instance, many investigators have found that the most negative attitudes of all expressed are about obese people. Yet it is hard to believe that we actually equate the stigma attached to being fat, crushing as it may be, with the kinds of stigma experienced by inner-city blacks, epileptics, or people with cerebral palsy. Some important distinctions among those stigmata are being missed by the research design.

Similar ambiguities cloud the interpretation of what is still the most important finding in the field: Stephen A. Richardson of Albert Einstein College of Medicine discovered that as children age, there are significant changes in their expressed attitude toward physical disabilities. Richardson found that a stable preference ladder first appeared around age six. Asked their feelings about six pictures of children—all but one of them disabled—six-year-olds tended to rank slight facial disfigurement as most acceptable, second only to normalcy. Eight- to 10-year-olds ranked those with crutches and leg braces as most acceptable after the able-bodied child, followed by a child in a wheelchair, one with an amputated forearm, one with facial disfigurement, and finally, an obese child. By senior year, girls set facial disfigurement as least acceptable while boys ranked it fourth out of six in acceptability. (Male and female adults tend to follow the same pattern.) Again, there was the paradoxical finding that race was less stigmatizing than disability, and obesity often more stigmatizing.

Basic research into the psychology of disabled people themselves suffers from a similar medical bias. Because of the stigmata of disability, for example, handicapped people often move through a different social world from the one the rest of us inhabit; many of them do so in bodies that place important constraints on the way they obtain information about the world around them. Researchers frequently appear to assume that the developmental theories proposed by Piaget and others, elaborated from observations of able-bodied children, will work for the handicapped. But it may be that the cognitive and emotional growth of handicapped children follows its own healthy logic. A disabled child who is physically dependent may be putting his most sophisticated cognitive skills into learning how to charm, manipulate, or otherwise enlist the help of others; to keep safe from harm; to deal with the split between his social worlds: the home, where he is loved and respected, and the street, where he is viewed as a biological fact. The able-bodied child of the same age may be spending the same energy on working free of his dependence on parents and building his sense of competence by developing skills.

Here and there, voices have called for a reexamination of traditional assumptions about the development of disabled people. During the 1960s, Thérèse Gouin-Décarie, professor of psychology at the University of Montreal, studied Canadian children who were born with deformities because their mothers had taken the drug thalidomide

during pregnancy. She was struck by the failure of conventional psychological theories to shed light on the children's development, and proposed instead "the methods of analysis . . . used to treat the problems of minorities." André Lussier came to similar conclusions in his case history of an English child born with severe limb deformities. Lussier, a psychoanalyst, reported that he was consistently played false by his theoretical framework. Behavior that he first interpreted as pathological and harmful to the child's development frequently turned out to be an essential ingredient in the child's conquests of his physical limitations. For example, when the child boasted that he could learn to play the trumpet, Lussier interpreted it as unrealistic fantasy—until the boy actually succeeded in doing it. All manner of actions that seemed pathological when assessed by the norms of standard psychoanalytic theory turned out to have a different functional meaning in the disabled child's life. Lussier concluded, "We must look beyond pathological mechanisms for a comprehensive explanation." Twenty years after the appearance of Lussier's report, that attempt has still not been made.

Very similar kinds of medical biases compromise the value of much present-day theory and research in education for the handicapped. A generation ago, educators assessed the academic needs of black children and handicapped children in the same way, by measuring the disadvantaged child's academic behavior against what was assumed to be normal for a white, middle-class, able-bodied child. After determining the ways in which the child deviated from these presumably universal norms, the educator devised special compensatory programs to cure or to lessen the child's academic deviance.

Increasingly, this conception of minority education has come under sharp attack as Frank Riessman, professor of education at Queens College, notes, "If one analyzes the approaches that have been successful in improving the educational performance of inner-city children, one realizes that they are rooted in the strengths and the cognitive styles of the children rather than in a compensatory emphasis on deficiencies." Sadly, the deviance approach so common in minority education in the 1960s continues to go unchallenged in special education.

By far the greatest abuses of the medical model of disability occur in the technical literature that discusses the economic needs of disabled people. Most of this literature simply assumes that the employment problems of disabled people are caused by their physical limitations, rather than by the interaction of their limitation with job discrimination, environmental obstacles to mobility, and other forms of discrimination. The assumption has the unhappy ring of arguments that the economic problems of black Americans are caused by inherited genes that make them biologically inferior.

For society at large, the "therapeutic state" (to recall Nicholas N. Kittrie's term) is a threat, not a reality. But millions of disabled Americans already live within the invisible walls of a therapeutic society. In this society of the "sick," there is no place for the ordinary hallmarks of a present or future adult identity, no place for choice between competing moralities, no place for politics, no place for work, and no place for sexuality. All political, legal, and ethical issues are transformed into questions of disease and health, deviance and normal adjustment, proper and improper "management" of the disability. To recall political scientist Sheldon S. Wolin's fine phrase, the "sublimation of politics" has proceeded furthest of all with handicapped people. Of all America's oppressed groups, only the handicapped have been so fully disenfranchised in the name of health.

CRITICAL THINKING QUESTIONS

1. How can prejudiced attitudes and behaviors be changed? For example, if you wanted to reduce the negative images people hold of the disabled and stop discrimination against them, how would you do it? Would educating people about the disabled be sufficient? Would laws that forbid discrimination be sufficient? What might be best?

2. This article is over a decade old. Do you think that attitudes about and treatment of the disabled have changed significantly over the years? How so?

3. Studies cited in the article seem to find that disability is more stigmatizing than race and that obesity is even more stigmatizing than disability. How can you account for this pattern?

4. Do you think that disabled people might be viewed and treated differently depending on the type of disability they have as well as the perceived amount of self-responsibility for the disability? For example, suppose that a person who had a long history of untreated high blood pressure had a stroke that left him paralyzed. Would people view and treat him differently from someone who could not be held responsible for his actions, such as a person who was paralyzed after being struck by an automobile? What types of disorders might involve some sort of blaming the victims?

ARTICLE 14 _____

In social psychology, the majority of research on prejudice and discrimination has focused on the patterns of attitudes that people have, the way they treat people differently depending on those attitudes, and the methods for trying to reduce or eliminate prejudiced attitudes and discriminatory behaviors. Not nearly as much effort has been directed to examining how prejudices are acquired in the first place.

The search for the origins of prejudice has taken many different routes. Some efforts have examined the historical origins of prejudice, considering factors such as the conditions of contact between the groups. Other approaches have looked at sociocultural and situational causes, such as conflict between groups and the socialization of children. Yet another factor that may cause prejudice is personality. Whether or not particular patterns of personality are more likely to be associated with prejudice is something that has been extensively examined.

The classic study that follows by Muzafer Sherif is an attempt to demonstrate the creation of prejudice in groups of boys. The article is of interest for several reasons. Namely, it includes the manipulation of a situation that led to creating prejudice in boys where no prejudice had existed before; it also examines a method for eliminating the prejudice that had been created. Another interesting feature of the study is the naturalistic setting in which it was conducted.

Experiments in Group Conflict
■ Muzafer Sherif

Conflict between groups—whether between boys' gangs, social classes, "races" or nations—has no simple cause, nor is mankind yet in sight of a cure. It is often rooted deep in personal, social, economic, religious and historical forces. Nevertheless, it is possible to identify certain general factors which have a crucial influence on the attitude of any group toward others. Social scientists have long sought to bring these factors to light by studying what might be called the "natural history" of groups and group relations. Intergroup conflict and harmony is not a subject that lends itself easily to laboratory experiments. But in recent years there has been a beginning of attempts to investigate the problem under controlled yet life-like conditions, and I shall report here the results of a program of experimental studies of groups which I started in 1948. Among the persons working with me were Marvin B. Sussman, Robert Huntington, O. J. Harvey, B. Jack White, William R. Hood and Carolyn W. Sherif. The experiments were conducted in 1949, 1953 and 1954; this article gives a composite of the findings.

We wanted to conduct our study with groups of the informal type, where group organization and attitudes would evolve naturally and spontaneously, without formal direction or external pressures. For this purpose we conceived that an isolated summer camp would make a good experimental setting, and that decision led us to choose as subjects boys about eleven or twelve years old, who would find camping natural and fascinating. Since our aim was to study the development of group relations among these boys under carefully controlled conditions, with as little interference as

Reprinted with permission. Coypright © 1956 by *Scientific American*, Inc. All rights reserved.

possible from personal neuroses, background influences or prior experiences, we selected normal boys of homogeneous background who did not know one another before they came to the camp.

They were picked by a long and thorough procedure. We interviewed each boy's family, teachers and school officials, studied his school and medical records, obtained his scores on personality tests and observed him in his classes and at play with his schoolmates. With all this information we were able to assure ourselves that the boys chosen were of like kind and background: all were healthy, socially well-adjusted, somewhat above average in intelligence and from stable, white, Protestant, middle-class homes.

None of the boys was aware that he was part of an experiment on group relations. The investigators appeared as a regular camp staff—camp directors, counselors and so on. The boys met one another for the first time in buses that took them to the camp, and so far as they knew it was a normal summer of camping. To keep the situation as lifelike as possible, we conducted all our experiments within the framework of regular camp activities and games. We set up projects which were so interesting and attractive that the boys plunged into them enthusiastically without suspecting that they might be test situations. Unobtrusively we made records of their behavior, even using "candid" cameras and microphones when feasible.

We began by observing how the boys became a coherent group. The first of our camps was conducted in the hills of northern Connecticut in the summer of 1949. When the boys arrived, they were all housed at first in one large bunkhouse. As was to be expected, they quickly formed particular friendships and chose buddies. We had deliberately put all the boys together in this expectation, because we wanted to see what would happen later after the boys were separated into different groups. Our object was to reduce the factor of personal attraction in the formation of groups. In a few days we divided the boys into two groups and put them in different cabins. Before doing so, we asked each boy informally who his best friends were, and then took pains to place the "best friends" in different groups as far as possible. (The pain of separation was assuaged by allowing each group to go at once on a hike and campout.)

As everyone knows, a group of strangers brought together in some common activity soon acquires an informal and spontaneous kind of organization. It comes to look upon some members as leaders, divides up duties, adopts unwritten norms of behavior, develops an *esprit de corps*. Our boys followed this pattern as they shared a series of experiences. In each group the boys pooled their efforts, organized duties and divided up tasks in work and play. Different individuals assumed different responsibilities. One boy excelled in cooking. Another led in athletics. Others, though not outstanding in any one skill, could be counted on to pitch in and do their level best in anything the group attempted. One or two seemed to disrupt activities, to start teasing at the wrong moment or offer useless suggestions. A few boys consistently had good suggestions and showed ability to coordinate the efforts of others in carrying them through. Within a few days one person had proved himself more resourceful and skillful than the rest. Thus, rather quickly, a leader and lieutenants emerged. Some boys sifted toward the bottom of the heap, while others jockeyed for higher positions.

We watched these developments closely and rated the boys' relative positions in the group, not only on the basis of our own observations but also by informal sounding of the boys' opinions as to who got things started, who got things done, who could be counted on to support group activities.

As the group became an organization, the boys coined nicknames. The big, blond, hardy leader of one group was dubbed "Baby Face" by his admiring followers. A boy with a rather long head became "Lemon Head." Each group developed its own jargon, special jokes, secrets and special ways of performing tasks. One group, after killing a snake near a place where it had gone to swim, named the place "Moccasin Creek" and thereafter preferred this swimming hole to any other, though there were better ones nearby.

Wayward members who failed to do things "right" or who did not contribute their bit to the common effort found themselves receiving the "silent treatment," ridicule or even threats. Each group selected symbols and a name, and they had these put on their caps and T-shirts. The 1954 camp was conducted in Oklahoma, near a famous hideaway of Jesse James called Robber's Cave. The two groups of boys at this camp named themselves the Rattlers and the Eagles.

Our conclusions on every phase of the study were based on a variety of observations, rather than on any single method. For example, we devised a game to test the boys' evaluations of one another. Before an important baseball game, we set up a target board for the boys to throw at, on the pretense of making practice for the game more interesting. There were no marks on the front of the board for the boys to judge objectively how close the ball came to a bull's-eye, but, unknown to them, the board was wired to flashing lights behind so that an observer could see exactly where the balls hit. We found that the boys consistently overestimated the performances by the most highly regarded members of their group and underestimated the scores of those of low social standing.

The attitudes of group members were even more dramatically illustrated during a cook-out in the woods. The staff supplied the boys with unprepared food and let them cook it themselves. One boy promptly started to build a fire, asking for help in getting wood. Another attacked the raw hamburger to make patties. Others prepared a place to put buns, relishes and the like. Two mixed soft drinks from flavoring and sugar. One boy who stood around without helping was told by others to "get to it." Shortly the fire was blazing and the cook had hamburgers sizzling. Two boys distributed them as rapidly as they became edible. Soon it was time for the watermelon. A low-ranking member of the group took a knife and started toward the melon. Some of the boys protested. The most highly regarded boy in the group took over the knife, saying, "You guys who yell the loudest get yours last."

When the two groups in the camp had developed group organization and spirit, we proceeded to the experimental studies of intergroup rela-

tions. The groups had had no previous encounters; indeed, in the 1954 camp at Robber's Cave the two groups came in separate buses and were kept apart while each acquired a group feeling.

Our working hypothesis was that when two groups have conflicting aims—i.e., when one can achieve its ends only at the expense of the other— their members will become hostile to each other even though the groups are composed of normal well-adjusted individuals. There is a corollary to this assumption which we shall consider later. To produce friction between the groups of boys we arranged a tournament of games: baseball, touch football, a tug-of-war, a treasure hunt and so on. The tournament started in a spirit of good sportsmanship. But as it progressed good feeling soon evaporated. The members of each group began to call their rivals "stinkers," "sneaks" and "cheaters." They refused to have anything more to do with individuals in the opposing group. The boys in the 1949 camp turned against buddies whom they had chosen as "best friends" when they first arrived at the camp. A large proportion of the boys

FIGURE 1 / Friendship choices of campers for others in their own cabin are shown for Red Devils (*white*) and Bulldogs (*black*). At first a low percentage of friendships were in the cabin group (*left*). After five days, most friendship choices were within the group (*right*).

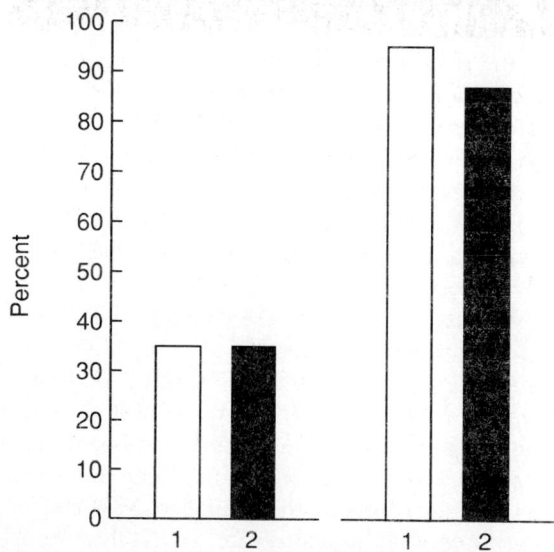

in each group gave negative ratings to all the boys in the other. The rival groups made threatening posters and planned raids, collecting secret hoards of green apples for ammunition. In the Robber's Cave camp the Eagles, after a defeat in a tournament game, burned a banner left behind by the Rattlers; the next morning the Rattlers seized the Eagles' flag when they arrived on the athletic field. From that time on name-calling scuffles and raids were the rule of the day.

Within each group, of course, solidarity increased. There were changes: one group deposed its leader because he could not "take it" in the contests with the adversary; another group overnight made something of a hero of a big boy who had previously been regarded as a bully. But morale and cooperativeness within the group became stronger. It is noteworthy that this heightening of cooperativeness and generally democratic behavior did not carry over to the group's relations with other groups.

We now turned to the other side of the problem. How can two groups in conflict be brought into harmony? We first undertook to test the theory that pleasant social contacts between members of conflicting groups will reduce friction between them. In the 1954 camp we brought the hostile Rattlers and Eagles together for social events: going to the movies, eating in the same dining room and so on. But far from reducing conflict, these situations only served as opportunities for the rival groups to berate and attack each other. In the dining-hall line they shoved each other aside, and the group that lost the contest for the head of the line shouted "Ladies first!" at the winner. They threw paper, food and vile names at each other at the tables. An Eagle bumped by a Rattler was admonished by his fellow Eagles to brush "the dirt" off his clothes.

We then returned to the corollary of our assumption about the creation of conflict. Just as competition generates friction, working in a common endeavor should promote harmony. It seemed to us, considering group relations in the everyday world, that where harmony between groups is established, the most decisive factor is the existence of "superordinate" goals which have

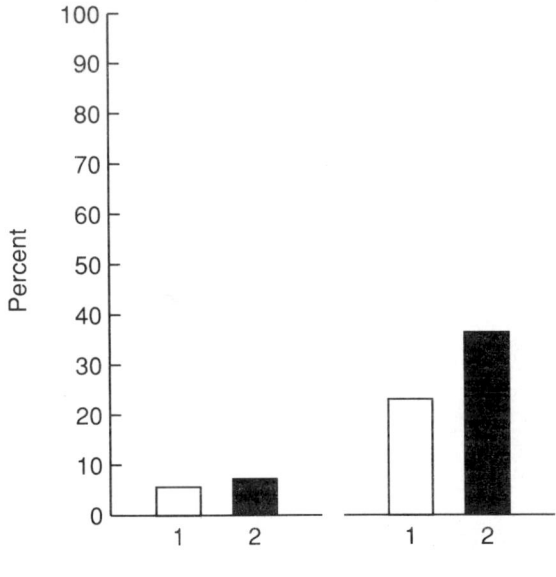

FIGURE 2 / **During conflict between the two groups in the Robber's Cave experiment there were few friendships between cabins (*left*). After cooperation toward common goals had restored good feelings, the number of friendships between groups rose significantly (*right*).**

a compelling appeal for both but which neither could achieve without the other. To test this hypothesis experimentally, we created a series of urgent, and natural, situations which challenged our boys.

One was a breakdown in the water supply. Water came to our camp in pipes from a tank about a mile away. We arranged to interrupt it and then called the boys together to inform them of the crisis. Both groups promptly volunteered to search the water line for the trouble. They worked together harmoniously, and before the end of the afternoon they had located and corrected the difficulty.

A similar opportunity offered itself when the boys requested a movie. We told them that the camp could not afford to rent one. The two groups then got together, figured out how much each group would have to contribute, chose the film by a vote and enjoyed the showing together.

One day the two groups went on an outing at a lake some distance away. A large truck was to go to town for food. But when everyone was hungry and ready to eat, it developed that the truck would not start (we had taken care of that). The boys got a rope — the same rope they had used in their acrimonious tug-of-war — and all pulled together to start the truck.

These joint efforts did not immediately dispel hostility. At first the groups returned to the old bickering and name-calling as soon as the job in hand was finished. But gradually the series of cooperative acts reduced friction and conflict. The members of the two groups began to feel more friendly to each other. For example, a Rattler whom the Eagles disliked for his sharp tongue and skill in defeating them became a "good egg." The boys stopped shoving in the meal line. They no longer called each other names, and sat together at the table. New friendships developed between individuals in the two groups.

In the end the groups were actively seeking opportunities to mingle, to entertain and "treat" each other. They decided to hold a joint campfire. They took turns presenting skits and songs. Members of both groups requested that they go home together on the same bus, rather than on the separate buses in which they had come. On the way the bus stopped for refreshments. One group still had five dollars which they had won as a prize in a contest. They decided to spend this sum on refreshments. On their own initiative they invited their former rivals to be their guests for malted milks.

Our interviews with the boys confirmed this change. From choosing their "best friends" almost exclusively in their own group, many of them shifted to listing boys in the other group as best friends (see Fig. 2). They were glad to have a second chance to rate boys in the other group, some of them remarking that they had changed their minds since the first rating made after the tournament. Indeed they had. The new ratings were largely favorable (see Fig. 4).

FIGURE 3 / Sociograms represent patterns of friendship choice within the fully developed groups. One-way friendships are indicated by broken arrows; reciprocated friendships, by solid lines. Leaders were among those highest in the popularity scale. Bulldogs (*left*) had a close-knit organization with good group spirit. Low-ranking members participated less in the life of the group but were not rejected. Red Devils (*right*) lost the tournament of games between the groups. They had less group unity and were sharply stratified.

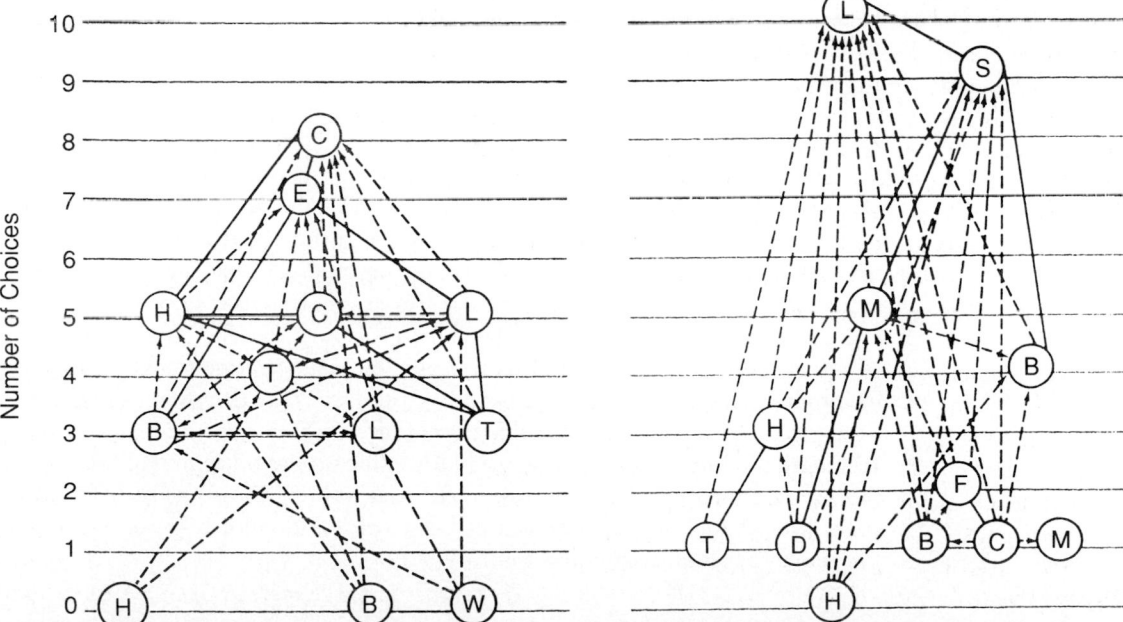

FIGURE 4 / Negative ratings of each group by the other were common during the period of conflict (*left*) but decreased when harmony was restored (*right*). The graphs show percent who thought that *all* (rather than *some* or *none*) of the other group were cheaters, sneaks, etc.

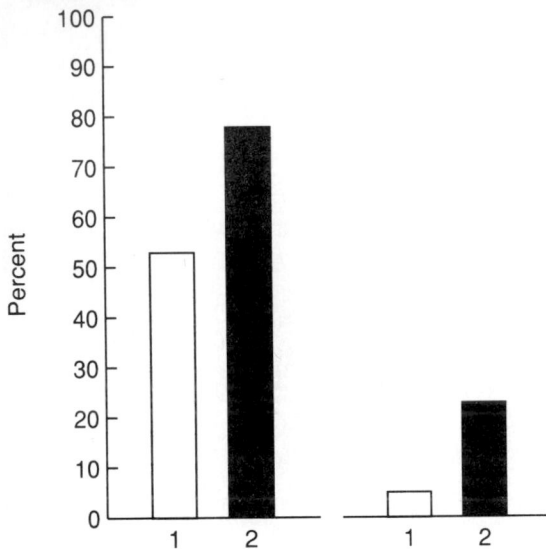

together socially, to communicating accurate and favorable information about one group to the other, and to bringing the leaders of groups together to enlist their influence. But as everyone knows, such measures sometimes reduce intergroup tensions and sometimes do not. Social contacts, as our experiments demonstrated, may only serve as occasions for intensifying conflict. Favorable information about a disliked group may be ignored or reinterpreted to fit stereotyped notions about the group. Leaders cannot act without regard for the prevailing temper in their own groups.

What our limited experiments have shown is that the possibilities for achieving harmony are greatly enhanced when groups are brought together to work toward common ends. Then favorable information about a disliked group is seen in a new light, and leaders are in a position to take bolder steps toward cooperation. In short, hostility gives way when groups pull together to achieve overriding goals which are real and compelling to all concerned.

Efforts to reduce friction and prejudice between groups in our society have usually followed rather different methods. Much attention has been given to bringing members of hostile groups

REFERENCES

Sherif, M. & Sherif, C. W. (1953). *Groups in harmony and tension*. New York: Harper & Brothers.

CRITICAL THINKING QUESTIONS

1. Design a laboratory experiment that would examine the development of prejudice in a more controlled fashion than was possible in the Sherif study. What are the pros and cons of the methodology used in this study as compared to a standard laboratory experiment that could be used to examine the same topic?

2. From your reading of the article, how fair (unbiased) were the observations made by the experimenters? Do you think it is possible that the experimenters may have unintentionally and subtly influenced the processes that they were observing, or were precautions taken to avoid this potential pitfall?

3. What are the implications of this study for reducing prejudice in real life? Would the method used in the study work in the real world? Would the strength of the prejudice, as well as how long it has been held, influence how successful such prejudice reduction techniques would be?

ADDITIONAL RELATED READINGS

Aronson, E., & Bridgeman, D. (1979). Jigsaw groups and the desegregated classroom: In pursuit of common goals. *Personality and Social Psychology Bulletin, 5,* 438–446.

Novvell, N., & Worchel, S. (1981). A reexamination of the relation between equal status contact and intergroup attraction. *Journal of Personality and Social Psychology, 41,* 902–908.

Tajfel, H. (1982). Social psychology of intergroup relations. *Annual Review of Psychology, 33,* 1–41.

ARTICLE 15 _____

Stereotypes are an everyday fact of life. Although we may hope that we judge every person as an individual, the cognitive strategies we use to make sense of our world, as discussed in Chapter 3, suggest otherwise. In particular, when confronted with a member of an identifiable group, we may rely on stereotypes: generalized beliefs as to what members of that group are like. Right or wrong, these stereotypes may influence how we feel about individuals in those groups and how we treat them. As such, stereotypes frequently underlie prejudiced attitudes and discriminatory behaviors.

In a series of three studies, Devine examines the relationship between stereotypes and prejudice. Specifically, she looks at the conditions under which stereotypes may influence prejudice and also those under which stereotypes may be ignored and nonprejudiced attitudes prevail.

Stereotypes and Prejudice
Their Automatic and Controlled Components
■ Patricia G. Devine

Three studies tested basic assumptions derived from a theoretical model based on the dissociation of automatic and controlled processes involved in prejudice. Study 1 supported the model's assumption that high- and low-prejudice persons are equally knowledgeable of the cultural stereotype. The model suggests that the stereotype is automatically activated in the presence of a member (or some symbolic equivalent) of the stereotyped group and that low-prejudice responses require controlled inhibition of the automatically activated stereotype. Study 2, which examined the effects of automatic stereotype activation on the evaluation of ambiguous stereotype-relevant behaviors performed by a race-unspecified person, suggested that when subjects' ability to consciously monitor stereotype activation is precluded, both high- and low-prejudice subjects produce stereotype-congruent evaluations of ambiguous behaviors. Study 3 examined high- and low-prejudice subjects' responses in a consciously directed thought-listing task.

Consistent with the model, only low-prejudice subjects inhibited the automatically activated stereotype-congruent thoughts and replaced them with thoughts reflecting equality and negations of the stereotype. The relation between stereotypes and prejudice and implications for prejudice reduction are discussed.

Social psychologists have long been interested in stereotypes and prejudice, concepts that are typically viewed as being very much interrelated. For example, those who subscribe to the tripartite model of attitudes hold that a stereotype is the cognitive component of prejudiced attitudes (Harding, Proshansky, Kutner, & Chein, 1969; Secord & Backman, 1974). Other theorists suggest that stereotypes are functional for the individual, allowing rationalization of his or her prejudice against a group (Allport, 1954; LaViolette & Silvert, 1951; Saenger, 1953; Simpson & Yinger, 1965).

In fact, many classic and contemporary theorists have suggested that prejudice is an

Reprinted from the *Journal of Personality and Social Psychology*, 1989, *56*, 5–18. Copyright 1989 by the American Psychological Association. Reprinted by permission.

inevitable consequence of ordinary categorization (stereotyping) processes (Allport, 1954; Billig, 1985; Ehrlich, 1973; Hamilton, 1981; Tajfel, 1981). The basic argument of the *inevitability of prejudice* perspective is that as long as stereotypes exist, prejudice will follow. This approach suggests that stereotypes are automatically (or heuristically) applied to members of the stereotyped group. In essence, knowledge of a stereotype is equated with prejudice toward the group. This perspective has serious implications because, as Ehrlich (1973) argued, ethnic attitudes and stereotypes are part of the social heritage of a society and no one can escape learning the prevailing attitudes and stereotypes assigned to the major ethnic groups.

The inevitability of prejudice approach, however, overlooks an important distinction between knowledge of a cultural stereotype and acceptance or endorsement of the stereotype (Ashmore & Del Boca, 1981; Billig, 1985). That is, although one may have *knowledge of a stereotype,* his or her *personal beliefs* may or may not be congruent with the stereotype. Moreover, there is no good evidence that knowledge of a stereotype of a group implies prejudice toward that group. For example, in an in-depth interview study of prejudice in war veterans, Bettelheim and Janowitz (1964) found no significant relation between stereotypes reported about Blacks and Jews and the degree of prejudice the veterans displayed toward these groups (see also Brigham, 1972; Devine, 1988; Karlins, Coffman, & Walters, 1969).

Although they may have some overlapping features, it is argued that stereotypes and personal beliefs are conceptually distinct cognitive structures. Each structure represents part of one's entire knowledge base of a particular group (see Pratkanis, in press, for a supporting argument in the attitude domain). Beliefs are propositions that are endorsed and accepted as being true. Beliefs can differ from one's knowledge about an object or group of one's affective reaction toward the object or group (Pratkanis, in press). To the extent that stereotypes and personal beliefs represent different and only potentially overlapping subsets

of information about ethnic or racial groups, they may have different implications for evaluation of and behavior toward members of the ethnic and racial groups. Previous theorists have not adequately captured this distinction and explored its implications for responding to stereotyped group members. The primary goal of the three studies reported here was to examine how stereotypes and personal beliefs are involved in responses toward stereotyped groups.

This work challenges the inevitability of prejudice framework and offers a model of responses to members of stereotyped groups that is derived largely from work in information processing that distinguishes between automatic (mostly involuntary) and controlled (mostly voluntary) processes (e.g., Posner & Snyder, 1975; Schneider & Shiffrin, 1977; Shiffrin & Schneider, 1977). Automatic processes involve the unintentional or spontaneous activation of some well-learned set of associations or responses that have been developed through repeated activation in memory. They do not require conscious effort and appear to be initiated by the presence of stimulus cues in the environment (Shiffrin & Dumais, 1981). A crucial component of automatic processes is their inescapability; they occur despite deliberate attempts to bypass or ignore them (Neely, 1977; Shiffrin & Dumais, 1981). In contrast, controlled processes are intentional and require the active attention of the individual. Controlled processes, although limited by capacity, are more flexible than automatic processes. Their intentionality and flexibility makes them particularly useful for decision making, problem solving, and the initiation of new behaviors.

Previous theoretical and empirical work on automatic and controlled processes suggests that they can operate independently of each other (Logan, 1980; Logan & Cowan, 1984; Neely, 1977; Posner & Snyder, 1975). For example, by using a semantic priming task, Neely demonstrated that when automatic processing would produce a response that conflicted with conscious expectancies (induced through experimenter instructions), subjects inhibited the automatic response and intentionally replaced it with one consistent with their conscious expectancy.

For example, Neely (1977) examined the influence of a single-word prime on the processing of a single-word target in a lexical decision task (i.e., whether the target was a word). The prime was either semantically related to the target (e.g., *body*-arm) or related to the target through experimenter instructions (e.g., subjects were told that *body* would be followed by a bird name such as sparrow). In this latter condition, subjects had a conscious expectancy for a bird name when they saw the *body* prime, but *body* should also have automatically primed its semantic category of body parts.

Neely (1977) found that with brief intervals between the prime and target (i.e., 250 ms), the prime facilitated decisions for semantically related targets regardless of experimenter instructions. Neely argued that this facilitation was a function of automatic processes. At longer delays (i.e., 2,000 ms), however, experimenter-induced expectancies produced both facilitation for expected targets and inhibition for unexpected targets regardless of their semantic relation to the prime. Before such inhibition of automatically activated responses can occur, there has to be enough *time* and *cognitive capacity* available for the conscious expectancy to develop and inhibit the automatic processes.

AUTOMATIC AND CONTROLLED PROCESSES: IMPLICATIONS FOR ACTIVATION OF STEREOTYPES AND PERSONAL BELIEFS

The dissociation of automatic and controlled processes may provide some theoretical leverage for understanding the role of stereotypes and personal beliefs in responses to members of racial or ethnic groups. In the model proposed, interest centers on the conditions under which stereotypes and personal beliefs are activated and the likelihood that personal beliefs overlap with the cultural stereotype. There is strong evidence that stereotypes are well established in children's

memories before children develop the cognitive ability and flexibility to question or critically evaluate the stereotype's validity or acceptability (Allport, 1954; P. Katz, 1976; Porter, 1971; Proshansky, 1966). As a result, personal beliefs (i.e., decisions about the appropriateness of stereotypic ascriptions) are necessarily newer cognitive structures (Higgins & King, 1981). An additional consequence of this developmental sequence is that stereotypes have a longer history of activation and are therefore likely to be more accessible than are personal beliefs. To the extent that an individual rejects the stereotype, he or she experiences a fundamental conflict between the already established stereotype and the more recently established personal beliefs.

The present model assumes that primarily because of common socialization experiences (Brigham, 1972; Ehrlich, 1973; P. Katz, 1976; Proshansky, 1966), high- and low-prejudice persons are equally knowledgeable of the cultural stereotype of Blacks. In addition, because the stereotype has been frequently activated in the past, it is a well-learned set of associations (Dovidio, Evans, & Tyler, 1986) that is *automatically* activated in the presence of a member (or symbolic equivalent) of the target group (Smith & Branscombe, 1985). The model holds that this unintentional activation of the stereotype is equally strong and equally inescapable for high- and low-prejudice persons.

A major assumption of the model is that high- and low-prejudice persons differ with respect to their personal beliefs about Blacks (Greeley & Sheatsley, 1971; Taylor, Sheatsley, & Greeley, 1978). Whereas high-prejudice persons are likely to have personal beliefs that overlap substantially with the cultural stereotype, low-prejudice persons have *decided* that the stereotype is an inappropriate basis for behavior or evaluation and experience a conflict between the automatically activated stereotype and their personal beliefs. The stereotype conflicts with their nonprejudiced, egalitarian values. The model assumes that the low-prejudice person must create a cognitive structure that represents his or her newer beliefs (e.g., belief in equality between the races, rejection of the stereotype, etc.). Because the stereotype has a longer history of activation (and thus greater frequency of activation) than the newly acquired personal beliefs, overt nonprejudiced responses require intentional inhibition of the automatically activated stereotype and activation of the newer personal belief structure. Such inhibition and initiation of new responses involves controlled processes.

This analysis suggests that whereas stereotypes are automatically activated, activation of personal beliefs require conscious attention. In addition, nonprejudiced responses require both the inhibition of the automatically activated stereotype and the intentional activation of nonprejudiced beliefs (see also Higgins & King, 1981). This should not be surprising because an individual must overcome a lifetime of socialization experiences. The present model, which suggests that automatic and controlled processes involved in stereotypes and prejudice can be dissociated, posits that the inevitability of prejudice arguments follow from tasks that are likely to engage automatic processes on which those high and low in prejudice are presumed not to differ (i.e., activation of a negative stereotype in the absence of controlled stereotype-inhibiting processes). Interestingly, the model implies that if a stereotype is automatically activated in the presence of a member of the target group and those who reject the cultural stereotype do not (or perhaps cannot) monitor consciously this activation, information activated in the stereotype could influence subsequent information processing. A particular strength of the model, then, is that it suggests how knowledge of a stereotype can influence responses even for those who do not endorse the stereotype or have changed their beliefs about the stereotyped group.

Higgins and King (1981) presented a similar analysis with respect to the effect of gender stereotypes on memory. They demonstrated that when gender was not salient, subjects' descriptions of self and others reflected traditional views of gender-linked attributes. They suggested that under such conditions traditional gender stereotypes, with their longer history (i.e., greater frequency) of activation, are passively (automatically) activated and influence recall. When gender was made salient, however, subjects apparently inhibited the traditional stereotype and descriptions were more consistent with their more recently developed, modern views of gender-linked attributes.

In summary, the present model suggests that a target's group membership activates, or primes, the stereotype in the perceiver's memory (Smith, 1984; Wyer & Srull, 1981), making other traits or attributes associated with the stereotype highly accessible for future processing (Dovidio et al., 1986; Gaertner & McLaughlin, 1983; Smith & Branscombe, 1985). The implications of this automatic stereotype activation may be serious, particularly when the content of the stereotype is predominately negative, as is the case with racial stereotypes. For example, Duncan (1976) found that Whites interpreted the same ambiguous shove as hostile or violent when the actor was Black and as playing around or dramatizing when the actor was White. Duncan assumed that the presence of the Black actor automatically primed the stereotype of Blacks and because the stereotype associates Blacks with violence, the violent behavior category was more accessible when viewing a Black compared with a White actor. Sager and Schofield (1980) replicated these findings with schoolchildren. Both Black and White children rated ambiguously aggressive behaviors (e.g., bumping in the hallway) of Black actors as being more mean or threatening than the same behaviors of White actors.

In only one of these studies (Gaertner & McLaughlin, 1983) was prejudice assessed and responses of high- and low-prejudice subjects compared. Thus the extent to which high- and low-prejudice persons differ or are similar in their automatic and controlled responses to target group members remains unclear. The present studies were designed to test implications of the dissociation of automatic and controlled processes in prejudice. Study 1 examined the validity of the assumption that high- and low-prejudice subjects are equally knowledgeable of the cultural stereotype. Study 2 explored the implications of automatic racial stereotype priming on the evaluation of ambiguous stereotype-relevant behaviors. This task permitted examination of the effects of automatic stereotype activation independently of controlled processes relevant to the stereotype. Finally, Study 3 examined the likelihood that high- and low-prejudice subjects will engage in controlled processes to inhibit prejudiced responses in a consciously directed thought-listing task.

STUDY 1: STEREOTYPE CONTENT AND PREJUDICE LEVEL

Historically, little attention has focused on individual differences in prejudice when assessing the content of stereotypes. Although implicit in the stereotype assessment literature (Brigham, 1971), the assumption that high- and low-prejudice subjects are equally knowledgeable of the cultural stereotype has not been documented. The first step in validating the present model was to examine directly high- and low-prejudice subjects' knowledge of the content of the cultural stereotype of Blacks.

In contrast to the typical adjective checklist assessment of stereotype content (Gilbert, 1951; Karlins et al., 1969; D. Katz & Braly, 1933), a free response task was used in the present study. This task provides a more sensitive test of subjects' knowledge of the stereotype because no cues (e.g., a list of possible characteristics) regarding possible content are provided. Thus, high- and low-prejudice subjects were asked to list the content of the cultural stereotype of Blacks regardless of their personal beliefs.

Method

Subjects and Procedure   Forty White introductory psychology students participated in groups of 4–6 for course credit. To ensure anonymity, subjects were isolated from each other and the experimenter left the room after giving general instructions. Written instructions told subjects that the questionnaire was designed to help researchers better understand social stereotypes and

that interest centered on the cultural stereotype of Blacks. The experimenter informed them that she was not interested in their personal beliefs but in their knowledge of the content of the cultural stereotype. Subjects were provided with a page with several blank lines on which to list the components of the stereotype and were asked not to write any identifying marks on the booklet.

After listing the components of the stereotype, subjects completed the seven-item Modern Racism Scale (McConahay, Hardee, & Batts, 1981). The Modern Racism Scale is designed to measure subjects' anti-Black attitudes in a nonreactive fashion. The Modern Racism Scale has proven to be useful in predicting a variety of behaviors including voting patterns and reactions to busing (Kinder & Sears, 1981; Sears & Kinder, 1971; Sears & McConahay, 1973). Subjects indicated their agreement with each of the items on the 5-point rating scale that ranged from – 2 (*disagree strongly*) to + 2 (*agree strongly*). Subjects put the completed booklet into an unmarked envelope and dropped it into a large box containing several envelopes. Finally, subjects were debriefed and thanked for their participation. The Modern Racism Scale ranges from – 14 (*low prejudice*) to + 14 (*high prejudice*). The scale had good reliability (Cronbach's alpha = .83). Subjects were assigned to a high-prejudice (N = 21) or a low-prejudice (N = 19) group on the basis of a median split of scores on the scale.

Results and Discussion

The coding scheme, based primarily on the previous stereotype assessment literature, included traits such as lazy, poor, athletic, rhythmic, ostentatious, and so on. In addition, a category was included for themes related to hostility, violence, or aggressiveness. Although these terms have not been included in the traditional assessment literature, the assumption that Blacks are hostile or aggressive has guided much of the research on the effect of racial stereotypes on perception and behavior (Donnerstein & Donnerstein, 1972; Donnerstein, Donnerstein, Simon, & Ditrichs, 1972; Duncan, 1976; Sager & Schofield, 1980). Trait listings, however, do not completely capture the components of cultural stereotypes. For example, subjects also listed descriptive features (e.g., afro, brown eyes) and family characteristics (e.g., many children, single-parent homes). Coding categories for these components and a miscellaneous category for components listed that did not clearly fit into the existing categories were included. In all, there were 16 coding categories (see Table 1).

Two judges, blind to subjects' prejudice level, were provided with the coding instructions and the 40 protocols in different random orders. Each characteristic listed received one classification by each judge; the judges agreed on 88% of their classifications.

Table 1 shows coding categories and the proportion of high- and low-prejudice subjects who used the coding category in describing the stereotype. There are several noteworthy aspects of these data. First, the most striking aspect of these data is that the most common theme in subjects' protocols was that Blacks are aggressive, hostile, or criminal-like (see Table 1). All subjects listed either the aggressive or criminal categories and many listed both categories. This finding is important because, as was suggested earlier, much of

the intergroup perception literature has been predicated on the assumption that Blacks are hostile and aggressive. Second, consistent with the stereotype assessment literature, the protocols were dominated by trait listings and were predominately negative. Third, there appeared to be few differences in the content reported by high- and low-prejudice subjects.

The prediction of no difference between the high- and low-prejudice subjects' knowledge of the cultural stereotype was tested in two different ways. First, none of the differences in Table 1 was statistically reliable. Second, two separate judges were given subjects' protocols and were instructed to read the content listed and to separate the protocols into high- and low-prejudice groups. The judges could not reliably predict the subjects' prejudice level from the content of their protocols. These data validate Ehrlich's (1973) assumption as well as the first assumption of the present model: High- and low-prejudice persons are indeed equally knowledgeable of the cultural stereotype.

STUDY 2: AUTOMATIC PRIMING, PREJUDICE LEVEL, AND SOCIAL JUDGMENT

Study 1 showed that prejudice has little effect on direct reports of stereotype content. However, the free response task directly involved controlled processes. Subjects were explicitly instructed to be bias-free when making these reports. These data, then, are not necessarily informative regarding the implicit cognitive structures that are accessed during automatic processing. What is needed is a task in which the controlled processes do not provide an alternative explanation for the automatic processes. Thus, the goal of the Study 2 was to examine automatic stereotype priming effects for both high- and low-prejudice subjects.

Several studies have demonstrated that increasing the temporary accessibility of trait categories available in memory influences subsequent evaluations of a target person who performs ambiguous trait-relevant behaviors. These findings have been produced with conscious processing of the primes (Carver, Ganellin, Froming, & Chambers, 1983;

TABLE 1 / Proportion of Thoughts Listed in Each of the Coding Categories as a Function of Prejudice Level

Category	High prejudice	Low prejudice
Poor	.80	.75
Aggressive/tough	.60	.60
Criminal	.65	.80
Low intelligence	.50	.65
Uneducated	.50	.50
Lazy	.55	.75
Sexually perverse	.50	.70
Athletic	.75	.50
Rhythmic	.50	.40
Ostentatious	.50	.40
Inferior	.20	.30
Food preferences	.25	.35
Family characteristic	.25	.30
Dirty/smelly	.20	.30
Descriptive terms	.55	.50

Note. None of these differences is significant.

Srull & Wyer, 1979, 1980) and with priming that is reported to be nonconscious (Bargh, Bond, Lombardi, & Tota, 1986; Bargh & Pietromonaco, 1982). That is, Bargh and Pietromonaco (1982) demonstrated that even when subjects were unaware of the content of the primes, priming increased the likelihood that the primed category was used to interpret subsequently presented ambiguous category-related information.

Nonconscious priming was of particular interest in this research because it is this type of processing that would allow the clearest dissociation of automatic and controlled processes involved in responses to members of a stereotyped group. Thus, the priming technique developed by Bargh and Pietromonaco (1982) was used in this study to automatically or passively prime the racial stereotype. Because the priming task activates the stereotype without conscious identification of the primes, the effects of stereotype activation can be studied independently of controlled stereotype-related processes. Specifically, interest centered on the effect of automatic racial stereotype activation on the interpretation of ambiguous stereotype-related behaviors performed by a race-unspecified target person.

In this study, evaluation of ambiguously hostile behaviors was examined because the assumption that Blacks are hostile is part of the racial stereotype (Brigham, 1971; Study 1) and because it has guided research in intergroup perception (Duncan, 1976; Sager & Schofield, 1980; Stephan, 1985). Because interest centered on the effects of activation of the stereotype on the ratings of a target person's hostility, no words directly related to hostility were used in the priming task. This study explicitly examined Duncan's (1976) hypothesis that the activation of the racial stereotype, which presumably activates a link between Blacks and hostility, explains why ambiguously aggressive behaviors were judged as being more aggressive when performed by a Black than a White actor.

According to the assumptions of the present model, priming will automatically activate the cultural stereotype for both those high and low in prejudice. Because hostility is part of the racial stereotype, increased priming should lead to more

extreme ratings on the hostility-related scales for both high- and low-prejudice subjects.

Thus, following Bargh and Pietromonaco (1982), during an initial perceptual vigilance task, subjects were asked to identify the location of stimuli, which were actually words, presented rapidly in subjects' parafoveal visual field. These strategies were used to prevent subjects from consciously identifying the content of the primes. During the vigilance task either 20% or 80% of the words presented were related to the racial stereotype. Then, during an ostensibly unrelated impression-formation task, subjects read a paragraph describing a race-unspecified target person's ambiguously hostile behaviors and rated the target person on several trait scales. Half of the trait scales were related to hostility and thus allowed a test of the effect of stereotype activation on ratings of the target person's hostility. The remaining trait scales were not related to hostility and provided the opportunity to examine the possibility that stereotype activation led to a global negative evaluation that generalized beyond hostility ratings.

The data from this study could have important theoretical implications regarding the role of controlled processes and automatic processes involved in prejudice. However, the criteria required to establish automatic activation have been debated (see Holender, 1986, and Marcel, 1983b, for reviews). Greenwald, Klinger, and Liu (in press) recently suggested that automatic activation can be achieved through either *detectionless processing* or *attentionless processing,* both of which have been shown to produce reliable priming effects. Detectionless processing involves presenting stimuli below subjects' threshold level for reliable detection (Bolota, 1983; Fowler, Wolford, Slade, & Tassinary, 1981; Greenwald et al., in press; Marcel, 1983a). Attentionless processing involves processing stimuli that, although detectable, cannot be recalled or recognized (Klatzky, 1984).

In this study attentionless processing was accomplished by presenting the primes parafoveally (Bargh & Pietromonaco, 1982) followed immediately with a pattern mask. With phenomenal awareness of the semantic content of the primes as the criterion for conscious processing (Marcel, 1983a, 1983b), any effects of priming in this study without immediate conscious identification of the primes or recognition for them will be taken as evidence of attentionless automatic processing effects.

Method

Subjects and Selection Criteria Data were collected over two academic quarters. Introductory psychology students were pretested on the seven-item Modern Racism Scale embedded in a number of political, gender, and racial items. This was done to minimize the likelihood that subjects would identify the scale as a measure of prejudice. The experimenter told subjects that completion of the questionnaire was voluntary and that responses would be kept confidential. Subjects were also provided with a form concerning participation in subsequent experiments and provided their names and phone numbers if they were willing to be contacted for a second study for which they could earn extra credit.

Over the two quarters a total of 483 students filled out the Modern Racism Scale. Participants from the upper and lower third of the distribution of scores were identified as potential subjects ($N = 323$). When contacted by phone, potential subjects were asked about their vision, and only subjects with perfect vision or corrected perfect vision were considered eligible. High-prejudice subjects' scores on the Modern Racism Scale fell within the upper third of scores (between $+ 2$ and $+ 14$), and low-prejudice subjects' scores fell within the lower third of scores (between $- 9$ and $- 14$). The scale had good reliability (Cronbach's alpha $= .81$). From this sample of 323 subjects, 129 who agreed and had good vision participated in the experiment. After replacing 3 Black subjects, 1 subject who reported having dyslexia following the vigilance task, and 3 subjects who failed to follow instructions, the sample consisted of 78 White subjects in the judgment condition, 32 White subjects in the recognition condition, and 12 White subjects in the guess condition.

The experimenter remained blind to subjects' prejudice level, priming condition, and stimulus replication condition. Subjects were telephoned by one experimenter, who prepared the materials (with no treatment information) for the second experimenter, who conducted the experiment.

The method and procedure for this study were modeled after Bargh and Pietromonaco (1982). The only difference between their procedure and the one in this study was that in this study, stimuli were presented tachistoscopically rather than on a computer monitor. The experimental room contained a Scientific Prototype two-channel tachistoscope connected to an experimenter-controlled panel for presenting stimuli. Subjects placed their heads against the eyepiece such that the distance from subjects' eyes to the central fixation point was constant. The presentation of a stimulus activated a Hunter Model 120 Klockounter on which the interval between stimulus onset and the response was recorded to the nearest millisecond. Subjects indicated their responses by pushing one of two buttons (labeled *left* or *right*) on a response box. The experimenter recorded each response and its latency.

The stimuli were black and presented on a white background. Each stimulus was presented for 80 ms and was immediately followed by a mask (a jumbled series of letters). In addition, following Bargh and Pietromonaco (1982), the interstimulus interval was 2–7 s. The stimuli (words) were centered in each quadrant, with the center of each word being approximately 2.3 in. (0.06 m) from the central fixation point. The eye-to-dot distance was 31 in. (0.79 m) for the Scientific Prototype tachistoscope. As a result to keep the stimulus within the parofoveal visual field (from 2° to 6° of visual angle), words could not be presented closer than 1.08 in. (0.03 m) or farther than 3.25 in. (0.08 m) from the fixation point. Twenty-five of the 100 trials within each replication were randomly assigned to each quadrant.

Stimulus Materials Words that are labels for the social category *Blacks* (e.g., Blacks, Negroes, niggers) or are stereotypic associates (e.g., poor, lazy, athletic) were the priming stimuli. Twenty-four primes were used to generate two stimulus replications. Efforts were made to produce roughly equivalent content in the two replications. Replication 1 primes included the following: nigger, poor, afro, jazz, slavery, musical, Harlem, busing, minority, oppressed, athletic, and prejudice. Replication 2 primes included the following: Negroes, lazy, Blacks, blues, rhythm, Africa, stereotype, ghetto, welfare, basketball, unemployed, and plantation. Twelve neutral words (unrelated to the stereotype) were included in each replication. All neutral words were high-frequency words (Carrol, Davies, & Richman, 1971) and were matched in length to the stereotype-related words. Neutral words for Replication 1 included the following: number, considered, what, that, however, remember, example, called, said, animal, sentences, and important. Replication 2 neutral words included the following: water, then, would, about, things, completely, people, difference, television, experience, something, and thought. Ten additional neutral words were selected and used during practice trials.

Within each stimulus replication, the stereotype-related and neutral words were used to generate two separate 100-word lists. One list contained 80 stereotype-related words (the rest were neutral words) and the other contained 20 stereotype-related words (the rest were neutral words). The lists were organized into blocks of 20 words. In the 80% stereotype-priming condition, each block contained 16 stereotype-related words and 4 neutral words. Within each block, to make 16 stereotype-related words, 4 of the 12 stereotype-related words were randomly selected and presented twice.

For both stimulus replications, the words within each block were randomly ordered with the restriction that the first stereotype-related word was a label for the group (e.g., Negro or nigger). The positions of the minority items (stereotype-related words in the 20% priming list and neutral words in the 80% priming list) were the same for the 20% and 80% priming lists. Each of the 12 stereotype-related and the 12 con-

trol words appeared approximately the same number of times as the other stereotype-related and neutral words, respectively.

Judgment Condition   The experimenter told subjects that they would participate in two separate tasks. First, they were seated at the tachistoscope and then provided with a description of the vigilance task. The experimenter told subjects that the vigilance task involved identifying the location of stimuli presented for brief intervals. Subjects also learned that stimuli could appear in one of the four quadrants around the dot in the center of the screen. They were to identify as quickly and as accurately as possible whether the stimulus was presented to the left or the right of the central dot. Subjects indicated their responses by pressing the button labeled *left* or *right* on the response panel. The experimenter informed subjects that the timing and the location of the stimuli were unpredictable. Because both speed and accuracy were emphasized, subjects were encouraged to concentrate on the dot, as this strategy would facilitate detection performance. All subjects first completed 10 practice trials and then 100 experimental trials. Overall, the vigilance task took 11–13 min to complete.

Following the vigilance task, the second task was introduced. Subjects were told that the experimenter was interested in how people form impressions of others. They were asked to read a paragraph describing the events in the day of the person about whom they were to form an impression. This paragraph is the now familiar "Donald" paragraph developed by Srull and Wyer (1979, 1980; see also Bargh & Pietromonaco, 1982, and Carver et al., 1983). This 12-sentence paragraph portrays Donald engaging in a series of empirically established ambiguously hostile behaviors. For example, Donald demands his money back from a store clerk immediately after a purchase and refuses to pay his rent until his apartment is repainted.

After reading the paragraph, subjects were asked to make a series of evaluative judgments about Donald. Subjects rated Donald on each of 12 randomly ordered trait scales that ranged from

0 (*not at all*) to 10 (*extremely*). Six of the scales were descriptively related to hostility; 3 of these scales were evaluatively negative (hostile, dislikeable, and unfriendly) and 3 were evaluatively positive (thoughtful, kind, and considerate). The remaining 6 scales were not related to hostility; 3 of these scales were evaluatively negative (boring, narrow-minded, and conceited) and 3 were evaluatively positive (intelligent, dependable, and interesting).

After completing the rating scales, the experimenter questioned subjects about whether they believed that the vigilance task and the impression-formation task were related. No subject reported thinking the tasks were related or indicated any knowledge of why the vigilance task would have affected impression ratings. The experimenter then explained the nature of priming effects to the subjects. During this debriefing, however, the fact that subjects had been selected for participation on the basis of their Modern Racism Scale scores was not revealed. Subjects were then thanked for their participation.

Recognition Test Condition   Up through completion of the vigilance task, recognition test subjects were treated exactly the same as the judgment subjects. Subjects in this condition were exposed to either the 80% or 20% priming lists of Replication 1 or Replication 2. Following the vigilance task, however, the experimenter explained that the stimuli were actually words and that subjects would be asked to try to recognize the words previously presented. The recognition test was distributed and subjects were instructed to check off the items that they believed had been presented. The experimenter told them that only half of the words on the list had been presented during the vigilance task.

The 48 items of this test consisted of the 24 words in Replication 1 (12 stereotype-related and 12 neutral words) and the 24 words in Replication 2 (12 stereotype-related and 12 neutral words). Words in Replication 2 served as distractors (words not presented) for Replication 1 targets (words actually presented), and Replication 1 words were used as distractors for Replication 2 targets during

the recognition test. The recognition test items were randomly ordered.

Guess Condition   The experimenter told subjects in this condition that the words would be presented quickly in one of four locations around the central fixation point. Their task was to guess each word immediately following its presentation. The experimenter instructed subjects to maintain their gaze on the fixation point, as this was the best strategy for guessing words given their unpredictable location and timing. Subjects saw either the 80% list of Replication 1 or the 80% list of Replication 2. Subjects were to make a guess for each word presented, even making blind guesses if necessary, and were prompted to guess if they failed to do so spontaneously. This requirement was introduced to lower subjects' guessing criterion so as to provide a fair test of their immediate awareness of the stimuli (Bargh & Pietromonaco, 1982).

Results

Several checks on subjects' awareness of the content of primes were included in this study. Attentionless processing should allow detection but not immediate or delayed recognition of the stimuli.

Guess Condition: A Check on Immediate Awareness: Six high- and 6 low-prejudice subjects were run in this condition. Half of each group were presented with the 80% list of Replication 1 and half with the 80% list of Replication 2. If word content were truly not available to consciousness under the viewing conditions of this study, then subjects should not have been able to guess the content of the stereotype-related or neutral words. Subjects reported that this was a difficult task and that they had no idea of the content of the stimuli. Overall, they made few accurate guesses.

Of the 1,200 guesses, subjects guessed 20 words accurately, a hit rate of 1.67%. Overall, subjects guessed 1.4% of the stereotype-related words and 3.33% of the neutral words. Replicating Bargh and Pietromonaco (1982), the neutral word hit rate was appreciably higher than that for stereotype-related words. The neutral words were high-frequency words and thus would presumably be more easily detectable under the viewing conditions in this study.

Incorrect guesses were examined for their relatedness to the racial stereotype. Only three of the incorrect guesses could be interpreted as being related to the stereotype. Twice *Black* appeared as a guess, once from a high-prejudice subject and once from a low-prejudice subject. These data suggest that neither high- nor low-prejudice subjects were able to identify the content of the priming words at the point of encoding, thus satisfying one criterion for attentionless processing.

Recognition Condition: A Check on Memory for Primes Although subjects could not guess the content of the words at the point of stimulus presentation, it is possible that a recognition test would provide a more sensitive test of subjects' awareness of the content primes. On the basis of their performance on the recognition test, subjects were assigned a hit (correct recognition of presented items) and a false alarm (incorrect recognition of new items) score for both stereotype-related and neutral words.

The hits and false alarms were used to generate d' scores for both stereotype-related and neutral words, which corresponded to subjects' ability to correctly identify previously presented information. Green and Swets (1966) have tabled d' scores for all possible combinations of hits and false alarms. The primary analysis concerned whether subjects performed the recognition task better than would be expected by chance. Over all subjects, neither d' for stereotype-related words (M = .01) nor for neutral words (M = .07) differed significantly from zero (ps > .42). These same comparisons were also done separately for high- and low-prejudice subjects. These analyses, like the overall analysis, suggest that subjects could not reliably recognize the primes. High-prejudice subjects' mean d' scores for stereotype-related and neutral words were .02 and .12, respectively (ps >

.40). Low-prejudice subjects' mean d' scores for stereotype-related and neutral words were .01 and .02, respectively (ps > .84).

In addition, the d' scores were submitted to a four-way mixed-model analysis of variance (ANOVA)—Prejudice Level × Priming × Replication × Word Type—with word type (stereotype-related vs. neutral) as a repeated measure.[1] Interest centered on whether (a) high- and low-prejudice subjects were differentially sensitive to stereotype-related and neutral words on the recognition test and (b) priming affected recognition performance. The analysis revealed that prejudice level did not affect subjects' overall performance, $F(1, 24) = 0.07, p = .78$, and that it did not interact with word type, $F(1, 24) = 0.04, p = .84$.

The second crucial test concerned whether increasing the number of primes interacted with recognition of the word type or subjects' prejudice level to affect performance on the recognition test. None of these tests was significant. Priming did not interact with word type, $F(1, 24) = 0.47, p = .50$, or affect the Prejudice × Word Type interaction, $F(1, 24) = 0.32, p < .56$. The analysis revealed no other significant main effects or interactions. Subjects were not able to reliably recognize either stereotype-related or neutral words, suggesting that subjects did not have conscious access to the content of the primes, thus establishing the second criterion for attentionless processing.

Automatic Stereotype Activation and Hostility Ratings The major issue concerned the effect of automatic stereotype activation on the interpretation of ambiguous stereotype-congruent (i.e., hostile) behaviors performed by a race-unspecified target person. Following Srull and Wyer (1979) and Bargh and Pietromonaco (1982), two subscores were computed for each subject. A hostility-related subscore was computed by taking the mean of the six traits denotatively related to hostility (hostile, dislikeable, unfriendly, kind, thoughtful, and considerate). The positively valenced scales (thoughtful, considerate, and kind) were reverse scored so that higher mean ratings indicated higher levels of hostility. Similarly, an overall hostility-unrelated subscore was computed by taking the mean of the six hostility-unrelated scales. Again, the positive scales were reverse scored.

The mean ratings were submitted to a mixed-model ANOVA, with prejudice level (high vs. low), priming (20% vs. 80%), and replication (1 vs. 2) as between-subjects variables and scale (hostility related vs. hostility unrelated) as a within-subjects variable. The analysis revealed that the Priming × Scale interaction was significant, $F(1, 70) = 5.04$, $p < .03$. Ratings on the hostility-related scales were more extreme in the 80% ($M = 7.52$) than in the 20% ($M = 6.87$) priming condition.[2] The hostility-unrelated scales, however, were unaffected by priming ($Ms = 5.89$ and 6.00 for the 20% and 80% priming conditions, respectively). Moreover, the three-way Prejudice Level × Priming × Scale interaction was not significant, $F(1, 70) = 1.19, p = .27$. These results were consistent with the present model and suggest that the effects of automatic stereotype priming were equally strong for high- and low-prejudice subjects. Activating the stereotype did not, however, produce a global negative evaluation of the stimulus person, as only trait scales related to the behaviors in the ambiguous passage were affected by priming.

These analyses suggest that the automatic activation of the racial stereotype affects the encoding and interpretation of ambiguously hostile behaviors for both high- and low-prejudice subjects. To examine this more closely, separate tests on the hostility-related and hostility-unrelated scales were conducted. If high- and low-prejudice subjects are equally affected by the priming manipulation, then prejudice level should not interact with priming in either analysis. The analysis on hostility-related scales revealed only a significant priming main effect, $F(1, 70) = 7.59, p < .008$. The Prejudice Level × Priming interaction was nonsignificant, $F(1, 70) = 1.19, p = .28$. None of the other main effects or interactions was significant. In the analysis of the hostility-unrelated scales, neither the priming main effect, $F(1, 70)$

= 0.23, p = .63, nor the Prejudice Level × Priming interaction, $F(1, 70) = 0.02, p = .88$, reached significance.

Subjects' prejudice level did enter into several higher order interactions. The Prejudice Level × Priming × Replication interaction, $F(1, 70) = 4.69, p < .03$, indicated that the priming effect was slightly reversed for low-prejudice subjects exposed to Replication 1. A Prejudice Level × Scale Relatedness × Replication interaction, $F(1, 70) = 4.42, p < .04$, suggested that the difference between scores on hostility-related and hostility-unrelated scales was greater for low-prejudice subjects in Replication 1 and high-prejudice subjects in Replication 2.

Discussion

Study 2 examined the effects of prejudice and automatic stereotype priming on subjects' evaluations of ambiguous stereotype-related behaviors performed by a race-unspecified target person under conditions that precluded the possibility that controlled processes could explain the priming effect. The judgment data of this study suggest that when subjects' ability to consciously monitor stereotype activation is precluded, both high- and low-prejudiced subjects produce stereotype-congruent or prejudice-like responses (i.e., stereotype-congruent evaluations of ambiguous behaviors).

These findings extend those of Srull and Wyer (1979, 1980), Bargh and Pietromonaco (1982), Bargh et al. (1986), and Carver et al. (1983) in demonstrating that in addition to trait categories, stereotypes can be primed and can affect the interpretation of subsequently encoded social information. Moreover, it appears that stereotypes can be primed automatically by using procedures that produce attentionless processing of primes (Bargh & Pietromonaco, 1982). The effects of stereotype priming on subjects' evaluation of the target person's hostility are especially interesting because no hostility-related traits were used as primes. The data are consistent with Duncan's (1976) hypothesis that priming the racial stereotype activates a link between Blacks and hostility. Unlike Duncan's research, however, stereotype activation was achieved through attentionless priming with stereotype-related words and not by the race of the target person.

In summary, the data from Studies 1 and 2 suggest that both those high and low in prejudice have cognitive structures (i.e., stereotypes) that can support prejudiced responses. These data, however, should not be interpreted as suggesting that all people are prejudiced. It could be argued that neither task allowed for the possibility of nonprejudiced responses. Study 1 encouraged subjects not to inhibit prejudiced responses. Study 2 suggested that when the racial category is activated and subjects' ability to consciously monitor this activation is bypassed, their responses reflect the activation of cognitive structures with a longer history (i.e., greater frequency) of activation. As previously indicated, it appears that these structures are the culturally defined stereotypes (Higgins & King, 1981), which are part of people's social heritage, rather than necessarily part of subjects' personal beliefs.

This analysis suggests that the effect of automatic stereotype activation may be an inappropriate criterion for prejudice because to use it as such equates knowledge of stereotype with prejudice. People have knowledge of a lot of information they may not endorse. Feminists, for example, may be knowledgeable of the stereotype of women. Blacks and Jews may have knowledge of the Black or Jewish stereotype.[3] In none of these cases does knowledge of the stereotype imply acceptance of it (see also Bettelheim & Janowitz, 1964). In fact, members of these groups are likely to be motivated to reject the stereotype corresponding to their own group. In each of these cases, however, the stereotypes can likely be intentionally or automatically accessed from memory.

The present data suggest that when automatically accessed the stereotype may have effects that are inaccessible to the subject (Nisbett & Wilson, 1977). Thus, even for subjects who honestly report having no negative prejudices against Blacks, activation of stereotypes can have automatic effects that if not consciously monitored produce effects that resemble prejudiced responses. Study 3 examined the responses of high- and low-prejudice subjects to a task designed to focus attention on and thus activate subjects' personal beliefs about Blacks (in addition to the automatically activated stereotype).

STUDY 3: CONTROLLED PROCESSES AND PREJUDICE LEVEL

The present model suggests that one feature that differentiates low- from high-prejudice persons is the effort that they will put into stereotype-inhibition processes. When their nonprejudiced identity is threatened, low-prejudice persons are motivated to reaffirm their nonprejudiced self-concepts (Dutton, 1976; Dutton & Lake, 1973). Thus, when the conflict between their nonprejudiced personal beliefs and the stereotype of Blacks is made salient, low-prejudiced persons are likely to resolve the conflict by denouncing the stereotype and expressing their nonprejudiced beliefs. To express stereotype-congruent ideas would be inconsistent with and perhaps threaten their nonprejudiced identities.

Study 3 tested this hypothesis by asking high- and low-prejudice subjects to list their thoughts about the racial group *Blacks* under anonymous conditions. This type of task is likely to make the stereotype–personal belief conflict salient for low-prejudice subjects. The model suggests that under these conditions, high- and low-prejudice subjects will write different thoughts about Blacks. High-prejudice subjects, because their beliefs overlap with the stereotype, are expected to list stereotype-congruent thoughts. Low-prejudice subjects, it is argued, will take this opportunity to demonstrate that they do not endorse the cultural stereotype; they are likely to inhibit stereotype-congruent thoughts and intentionally replace them with thoughts consistent with their nonprejudiced personal beliefs. According to the model, resolution of the conflict between personal beliefs and the cultural stereotype in the form of nonprejudiced responses requires controlled inhibition (Logan & Cowan, 1984; Neely, 1977) of the automatically activated stereotype.

Method

Subjects   Subjects were 67 White introductory psychology students who participated for course credit.[4] Subjects were run in groups of 3–6 and were seated at partitioned tables so that subjects were isolated from each other. These procedures were used to enhance anonymity so that subjects would not feel inhibited and would write whatever came to mind.

An additional precaution was taken to ensure anonymity. Before subjects were given instructions regarding the thought-listing task, their experimental participation cards were collected, signed, and left in a pile in the front of the room for subjects to pick up after the study. The experimenter asked subjects not to put any identifying information on their booklets. These procedures were followed so that it would be clear that subjects' names could not be associated with their booklets and that they would receive credit regardless of whether they completed the booklet. No subject refused to complete the measures.

Procedure   After subjects' cards were signed the experimenter asked them to turn over and read the general instructions on the first page of the booklet. Subjects' first task was to list as many alternate labels as they were aware of for the social group *Black Americans*. They were told that the experimenter was interested in how people think about and talk informally about social groups. As such, the experimenter told them that slang or other unconventional group labels were acceptable. Subjects were allowed 1 min to complete this task. The purpose of this task was to encourage activation of subjects' cognitive representation of Blacks. If, for example, high- and low-prejudice persons refer to the social group with different labels (i.e., pejorative vs. nonpejorative) and the labels have different associates, this could provide a basis for explaining any potential differences in content between high- and low-prejudice subjects.

Following the label-generation task, subjects read the thought-listing instructions that asked them to list all of their thoughts in response to the social group *Black Americans* and to the alternate labels they generated. The experimenter told them that any and all of their thoughts (e.g., beliefs, feelings, expectations), flattering or unflattering, were acceptable. Subjects were encouraged to be honest and forthright. The experimenter provided them with two pages of 10 thought-listing boxes in which to record their thoughts and asked them to put only one thought in each box. They were allowed 10 min to complete the task. Finally, subjects completed the seven-item Modern Racism Scale and read through a debriefing document that described the goals of the research and thanked them for their participation.

Results

Coding Scheme   On the basis of a pilot study[5] a scheme for coding the types of thoughts generated was developed. Two judges, blind to subjects' prejudice level, were provided with the coding scheme instructions. A statement or set of statements listed in a box was considered one thought and was assigned one classification by each judge. Each judge rated the 67 protocols in different random orders. The judges agreed on 92% of their classifications. A third judge resolved discrepancies in scoring.

The major interest in this study was in whether the content of thoughts generated would differ as a function of prejudice level.[6] Before examining those data, however, the alternate labels subjects generated for Black Americans were examined. If high-prejudice subjects generate more negative labels (e.g., nigger, jigaboo, etc.) than low-prejudice subjects and pejorative labels are more strongly associated with stereotype-congruent information, this could explain possible differences between high- and low-prejudice subjects. Subjects were divided into high-prejudice ($N = 34$) and low-prejudice ($N = 33$) groups on the basis of a median split of scores on the Modern Racism Scale.

The proportion of pejorative and nonpejorative labels generated was calculated for each subject. Pejorative labels included terms such as the following: niggers, coons, spades, spear-chuckers, jungle bunnies, and jigs. Nonpejorative labels included the following: Blacks, Afro Americans, Brothers, and colored people. One high-prejudice subject was eliminated from this comparison because she failed to generate any alternate labels. The comparison indicated that the proportion of pejorative alternate labels did not differ between high-prejudice (M = .53) and low-prejudice (M = .44) subjects, $t(64)$ = .68, p > .10. It appears, then, that high- and low-prejudice subjects were aware of the various pejorative labels.

Examination of the thought-listing protocols, however, revealed important differences between high- and low-prejudice subjects. The important differences appeared to be associated with the belief and trait categories.[7] Negative beliefs included thoughts such as "Blacks are free loaders"; "Blacks cause problems (e.g., mugging, fights)"; "Affirmative action sucks"; and so on. Positive-belief thoughts included "Blacks and Whites are equal"; "Affirmative action will restore historical inequities"; "My father says all Blacks are lazy, I think he is wrong" (e.g., negation of the cultural stereotype); "It's unfair to judge people by their color — they are individuals"; and so on. The positive and negative traits were typically listed as single words rather than being written in complete sentences. Negative traits included hostile, lazy, stupid, poor, dirty, and so on. The positive traits included musical, friendly, athletic, and so on.

The frequency of these positive-belief, negative-belief, and trait thoughts listed in subjects' protocols were submitted to a Prejudice Level (high vs. low) × Valence (positive vs. negative) × Thought Type (trait vs. belief) mixed-model ANOVA. Prejudice level was a between-subjects variable, and valence and thought type were within-subjects variables. The analysis revealed the expected Prejudice Level × Valence interaction, $F(1, 65)$ = 28.82, p < .0001. High-prejudice subjects listed more negative (M = 2.06) than positive (M = 1.48) thoughts, and low-prejudice subjects listed more positive (M = 2.28) than negative (M = 1.10) thoughts. In addition, there was a Prejudice Level × Type interaction, $F(1, 65)$ = 18.04, p < .0001. This interaction suggested that high-prejudice

subjects were more likely to list trait (M = 2.56) than belief (M = 1.52) thoughts. In contrast, low-prejudice subjects were more likely to list belief (M = 2.86) than trait (M = 1.12) thoughts. These interactions are important because the Black stereotype traditionally has been largely negative and composed of traits (Brigham, 1971). Ascription of negative components of the stereotype was verified in these data only for high-prejudice subjects.

These two-way interactions were qualified, however, by a significant Prejudice Level × Valence × Thought Type interaction, $F(1, 65)$ = 4.88, p < .03. High-prejudice subjects most often listed negative traits (M = 3.32). A post hoc Duncan test (p = .05) revealed that for high-prejudice subjects, the frequency of negative trait thoughts differed significantly from each of the other three thought types but that the frequency of positive-belief (M = 1.17), negative-belief (M = 1.18) and positive trait (M = 1.79) thoughts did not differ from each other. In contrast, low-prejudice subjects most frequently listed positive-belief thoughts (M = 4.52). This mean differed significantly (Duncan test, p = .05) from the negative-belief (M = 1.21), positive trait (M = 1.24), and negative trait (M = 1.00) means, but the latter three means did not differ from each other.

It was argued earlier that this type of task would encourage subjects to intentionally access and report thoughts consistent with their personal beliefs. Trait ascriptions are part of high-prejudice, but not low-prejudice, subjects' beliefs according to the present model. It appears that in this task, both high- and low-prejudice subjects' thoughts reflected their beliefs. High-prejudice subjects reported primarily traits and low-prejudice subjects reported beliefs that contradicted the cultural stereotype and emphasized equality between the races.

To follow up implications from the previous studies, subjects' protocols were examined to determine whether the themes of hostility, aggressiveness, or violence were present. Statements such as "They are hostile," "Blacks are violent," "Blacks are aggressive," and so on were considered to reflect this theme. Non-trait-based thoughts such as "They rape women" or "I'm scared of them" were less frequent but were also considered to reflect the general theme. Sixty percent of the high-prejudice subjects directly included such themes in their thought listing protocols. In contrast, only 9% of the subjects scoring low in prejudice included hostility themes in their protocols. A z test on proportions indicated that this difference was reliable ($z = 4.41, p < .01$).

Discussion

Taken together, these sets of analyses indicate that high- and low-prejudice subjects were willing to report different thoughts about Blacks. In addition, these analyses suggested that there were sufficient levels of variability of prejudice levels among the subjects to detect the effects of prejudice in the previous studies should those effects exist. The thought-listing task was one in which subjects were likely to think carefully about what their responses implied about their prejudice-relevant self-concepts. For those who valued a nonprejudiced identity, writing stereotype-congruent thoughts would have been inconsistent with and perhaps would have threatened their nonprejudiced identity.

Thus, even under anonymous conditions, low-prejudice subjects apparently censored and inhibited (Neely, 1977) the automatically activated negative stereotype-congruent information and consciously replaced it with thoughts that expressed their nonprejudiced values. Low-prejudice subjects wrote few pejorative thoughts. Their thoughts were more likely to have reflected the importance of equality or the negation of the cultural stereotype. Moreover, low-prejudice subjects appeared reluctant to ascribe traits to the group as a whole. In contrast, the protocols of high-prejudice subjects seemed much more consistent with the cultural stereotype of Blacks. Their thoughts were primarily negative, and they seemed willing to ascribe traits to the group (especially negative traits).

A most important comparison for the present three studies, and for the intergroup perception literature more generally, concerns the likelihood of subjects reporting thoughts reflecting the theme of hostility. Much of the intergroup perception literature has assumed that the hostility component of the stereotype influences perceptions of Blacks (Donnerstein et al., 1972; Duncan, 1976; Sager & Schofield, 1980), and Studies 1 and 2 suggested that hostility is strongly associated with Blacks for both high- and low-prejudice subjects. Study 2 in particular suggested that hostility is automatically activated when the category label and associates are presented. The present data, however, suggest that high- and low-prejudice subjects differ in their willingness to attribute this characteristic to the entire group. High-prejudice subjects included thoughts suggesting that Blacks are hostile and aggressive much more frequently than did low-prejudice subjects. The present framework suggests that this difference likely reflects low-prejudice subjects engaging in controlled, stereotype-inhibiting processes. Low-prejudice subjects apparently censored negative, what they considered inappropriate, thoughts that came to mind.

GENERAL DISCUSSION

The model examined in these studies makes a clear distinction between knowledge of the racial stereotype, which Study 1 suggested both high- and low-prejudice persons possess, and personal beliefs about the stereotyped group. Study 2 suggested that automatic stereotype activation is equally strong and equally inescapable for high- and low-prejudice subjects. In the absence of controlled stereotype-related processes, automatic stereotype activation leads to stereotype-congruent or prejudice-like responses for both those high and low in prejudice. Study 3, however, provided evidence that controlled processes can inhibit the effects of automatic processing when the implications of such processing compete with goals to establish or maintain a nonprejudiced identity.

The present model suggests that a change in one's beliefs or attitude toward a stereotyped group may or may not be reflected in a change in the corresponding evaluations of or behaviors toward members of that group. Consider the following quote by Pettigrew (1987):

> *Many southerners have confessed to me, for instance, that even though in their minds they no longer feel prejudice toward blacks, they still feel squeamish when they shake hands with a black. These feelings are left over from what they learned in their families as children. (p. 20)*

It would appear that the automatically activated stereotype-congruent or prejudice-like responses have become independent of one's current attitudes or beliefs. Crosby, Bromley, and Saxe (1980) argued that the inconsistency sometimes observed between expressed attitudes and behaviors that are less consciously mediated is evidence that (all) White Americans are prejudiced against Blacks and that nonprejudiced responses are attempts at impression management (i.e., efforts to cover up truly believed but socially undesirable attitudes). (See also Baxter, 1973; Gaertner, 1976; Gaertner & Dovidio, 1977; Linn, 1965; Weitz, 1972). Crosby et al. argued that nonconsciously monitored responses are more trustworthy than are consciously mediated responses.

In the context of the present model in which automatic processes and controlled processes can be dissociated, I disagree fundamentally with this premise. Such an argument denies the possibility for change in one's attitudes and beliefs, and I view this as a severe limitation of the Crosby et al. (1980) analysis. Crosby and her colleagues seem to identify the flexibility of controlled processes as a limitation. In contrast, the present framework considers such processes as the key to escaping prejudice. This statement does not imply that change is likely to be easy or speedy (and it is certainly not all or nothing). Nonprejudiced responses are, according to the dissociation model, a function of intentional, controlled processes and require a conscious decision to behave in a nonprejudiced fashion. In addition, new responses must be learned and well practiced before they can serve as competitive responses to the automatically activated stereotype-congruent responses.

What is needed now is a fully articulated model of controlled processes that delineates the cognitive mechanisms involved in inhibition. Logan and Cowan (1984; see also Bargh, 1984) have developed a model of controlled processes that may provide valuable insights into the inhibition process.

Thus, in contrast to the pessimistic analysis by Crosby et al. (1980), the present framework suggests that rather than all people being prejudiced, all are victims of being limited capacity processors. Perceivers cannot attend to all aspects of a situation or their behavior. In situations in which controlled processes are precluded or interfered with, automatic processing effects may exert the greatest influence on responses. In the context of racial stereotypes and attitudes, automatic processing effects appear to have negative implications.

Inhibiting stereotype-congruent or prejudice-like responses and intentionally replacing them with nonprejudiced responses can be likened to the breaking of a bad habit. That is, automatic stereotype activation functions in much the same way as a bad habit. Its consequences are spontaneous and undesirable, at least for the low-prejudice person. For those who have integrated egalitarian ideals into their value system, a conflict would exist between these ideals and expressions of racial prejudice. The conflict experienced is likely to be involved in the initiation of controlled stereotype-inhibiting processes that are required to eliminate the habitual response (activation). Ronis, Yates, and Kirscht (in press) argued that elimination of a bad habit requires essentially the same steps as the formation of a habit. The individual must (a) initially decide to stop the old behavior, (b) remember the resolution, and (c) try repeatedly and decide repeatedly to eliminate the habit before the habit can be eliminated. In addition, the individual must develop a new cognitive (attitudinal and belief) structure that is consistent with the newly determined pattern of responses.

An important assumption to keep in mind in the change process, however, is that neither the formation of an attitude from beliefs nor the formation of a decision from attitudes or beliefs entails the elimination of earlier established attitudinal or stereotype representations. The dissociation model holds that although low-prejudiced persons have changed their beliefs concerning stereotyped group members, the stereotype has not been eliminated from the memory system. In fact, it remains a well-organized, frequently activated knowledge structure. During the change process the new pattern of ideas and behaviors must be consciously activated and serve as the basis for responses or the individual is likely to fall into old habits (e.g., stereotype-congruent or prejudice-like responses).

The model suggests that the change process involves developing associations between the stereotype structure and the personal belief structure. For change to be successful, each time the stereotype is activated the person must activate and think about his or her personal beliefs. That is, the individual must increase the frequency with which the personal belief structure is activated when responding to members of the stereotyped group. To the extent that the personal belief structure becomes increasingly accessible, it will better provide a rival response to the responses that would likely follow from automatic stereotype activation. In cognitive terms, before the newer beliefs and attitudes can serve as a rival, the strong association between the previously learned negative attitude and Blacks will have to be weakened and the association of Blacks to the new nonprejudiced attitudes and beliefs will have to be made stronger and conscious.

In summary, at minimum, the attitude and belief change process requires intention, attention, and time. During the change process an individual must not only inhibit automatically activated information but also intentionally replace such activation with nonprejudiced ideas and responses. It is likely that these variables contribute to the difficulty of changing one's responses to members of stereotyped groups. In addition, these variables probably contribute to the often observed inconsistency between expressed attitudes and behavior. The nonprejudiced responses take time, attention, and effort. To the extent that any (or all) of these are limited,

the outcome is likely to be stereotype-congruent or prejudice-like responses.

In conclusion, it is argued that prejudice need not be the consequence or ordinary thought processes. Although stereotypes still exist and can influence the responses of both high- and low-prejudice subjects, particularly when those responses are not subject to close conscious scrutiny, there are individuals who actively reject the negative stereotype and make efforts to respond in nonprejudiced ways. At least in situations involving consciously controlled stereotype-related processes, those who score low in prejudice on an attitude scale are attempting to inhibit stereotypic responses (e.g., Study 3; Greeley & Sheatsley, 1971; Taylor et al., 1978; see also Higgins & King, 1981). The present framework, because of its emphasis on the possible dissociation of automatic and controlled processes, *allows for the possibility* that those who report being nonprejudiced are in reality low in prejudice.

This analysis is not meant to imply that prejudice has disappeared or to give people an excuse for their prejudices. In addition, it does not imply that only low-prejudice persons are capable of controlled stereotype inhibition. High-prejudice persons could also consciously censor their responses to present a non-prejudiced identity (probably for different reasons than low-prejudice persons, however). What this analysis requires is that theoreticians be more precise on the criteria established for labeling behavior as prejudiced or nonprejudiced. The present model and set of empirical studies certainly does not resolve this issue. However, the present framework highlights the potential for nonprejudiced behaviors when social desirability concerns are minimal (Study 3) and invites researchers to explore the variables that are likely to engage controlled stereotype-inhibiting processes in intergroup settings. At present, it seems productive to entertain and systematically explore the possibility that being low in prejudice reflects more than impression-management efforts and to explore the conditions under which controlled stereotype-inhibition processes are engaged.

REFERENCES

Allport, G. W. (1954). *The nature of prejudice*. Reading, MA: Addison-Wesley.

Ashmore, R. D., & Del Boca, F. K. (1981). Conceptual approaches to stereotypes and stereotyping. In D. L. Hamilton (Ed.), *Cognitive processes in stereotyping and intergroup behavior* (pp. 1–35). Hillsdale, NJ: Erlbaum.

Bargh, J. A. (1984). Automatic and conscious processing of social information. In R. S. Wyer Jr., & T. K. Srull (Eds.), *The handbook of social cognition* (Vol. 3, pp. 1–43). Hillsdale, NJ: Erlbaum.

Bargh, J. A., Bond, R. N., Lombardi, W. J., & Tota, M. E. (1986). The additive nature of chronic and temporary sources of construct accessibility. *Journal of Personality and Social Psychology, 50,* 869–878.

Bargh, J. A., & Pietromonaco, P. (1982). Automatic information processing and social perception: The influence of trait information presented outside of conscious awareness on impression formation. *Journal of Personality and Social Psychology, 43,* 437–449.

Baxter, G. W. (1973). Prejudiced liberals? Race and information effects in a two person game. *Journal of Conflict Resolution, 17,* 131–161.

Bettelheim, B., & Janowitz, M. (1964). *Social change and prejudice*. New York: Free Press of Glencoe.

Bolota, D. A. (1983). Automatic semantic activation and episodic memory encoding. *Journal of Verbal Learning and Verbal Behavior, 22,* 88–104.

Billig, M. (1985). Prejudice, categorization, and particularization: From a perceptual to a rhetorical approach. *European Journal of Social Psychology, 15,* 79–103.

Brigham, J. C. (1971). Ethnic stereotypes. *Psychological Bulletin, 76,* 15–33.

Brigham, J. C. (1972). Racial stereotypes: Measurement variables and the stereotype-attitude relationship. *Journal of Applied Social Psychology, 2,* 63–76.

Carrol, J. B. Davies, P., & Richman, B. (1971). *The American Heritage word frequency book*. New York: Houghton Mifflin.

Carver, C. S., Ganellin, R. J., Froming, W. J., & Chambers, W. (1983). Modeling: An analysis in terms of category accessibility. *Journal of Experimental Social Psychology, 19,* 403–421.

Collins, A. M., & Quillian, M. R. (1969). Retrieval time from semantic memory. *Journal of Verbal Learning and Verbal Behavior, 8,* 240–247.

Crosby, F., Bromley, S., & Saxe, L. (1980). Recent unobtrusive studies of black and white discrimination and prejudice: A literature review. *Psychological Bulletin, 87,* 546–563.

Devine, P. G. (1988). *Stereotype assessment: Theoretical and methodological issues*. Unpublished manuscript, University of Wisconsin—Madison.

Donnerstein, E., & Donnerstein, M. (1972). White rewarding behavior as a function of the potential for black retaliation. *Journal of Personality and Social Psychology, 24,* 327–333.

Donnerstein, E., Donnerstein, M., Simon S., & Ditrichs, R. (1972). Variables in interracial aggression: Anonymity, expected retaliation, and a riot. *Journal of Personality and Social Psychology, 22,* 236–245.

Dovidio, J. F., Evans, N. E., & Tyler, R. B. (1986). Racial stereotypes: The contents of their cognitive representations. *Journal of Experimental Social Psychology, 22,* 22–37.

Duncan, B. L. (1976). Differential social perception and attribution of intergroup violence: Testing the lower limits of stereotyping of blacks. *Journal of Personality and Social Psychology, 34,* 590–598.

Dutton, D. G. (1976). Tokenism, reverse discrimination, and egalitarianism in interracial behavior. *Journal of Social Issues, 32,* 93–107.

Dutton, D. G., & Lake, R. A. (1973). Threat of own prejudice and reverse discrimination in interracial situations. *Journal of Personality and Social Psychology, 28,* 94–100.

Ehrlich, H. J. (1973). *The social psychology of prejudice*. New York: Wiley.

Fowler, C. A., Wolford, G., Slade, R., & Tassinary, L. (1981). Lexical access with and without awareness. *Journal of Experimental Psychology: General, 110,* 341–362.

Gaertner, S. L. (1976). Nonreactive measures in racial attitude research: A focus on "liberals." In P. A. Katz (Ed.), *Towards the elimination of racism* (pp. 183–211). New York: Pergamon Press.

Gaertner, S. L., & Dovidio, J. F. (1977). The subtlety of white racism, arousal, and helping. *Journal of Personality and Social Psychology, 35,* 691–707.

Gaertner, S. L., & McLaughlin, J. P. (1983). Racial stereotypes: Associations and ascriptions of positive and negative characteristics. *Social Psychology Quarterly, 46,* 23–30.

Gilbert, G. M. (1951). Stereotype persistence and change among college students. *Journal of Abnormal and Social Psychology, 46,* 245–254.

Greeley, A., & Sheatsley, P. (1971). Attitudes toward racial integration. *Scientific American, 222,* 13–19.

Green, D. M., & Swets, J. A. (1966). *Signal detection theory and psychophysics.* New York: Wiley.

Greenwald, A. G., Klinger, M., & Liu, T. J. (in press). Unconscious processing of word meaning. *Memory & Cognition.*

Hamilton, D. L. (1981). Stereotyping and intergroup behavior: Some thoughts on the cognitive approach. In D. L. Hamilton (Ed.), *Cognitive processes in stereotyping and intergroup behavior* (pp. 333–353). Hillsdale, NJ: Erlbaum.

Harding, J., Proshansky, H., Kutner, B., & Chein, I. (1969). Prejudice and ethnic relations. In G. Lindzey (Ed.), *Handbook of social psychology* (Vol. 5). Reading, MA: Addison-Wesley.

Higgins, E. T., & King, G. (1981). Accessibility of social constructs: Information-processing consequences of individual and contextual variability. In N. Cantor & J. F. Kihlstrom (Eds.), *Personality and social interaction* (pp. 69–121). Hillsdale, NJ: Erlbaum.

Holender, D. (1986). Semantic activation without conscious identification in dichotic listening, parafoveal vision, and visual masking: A survey and appraisal. *Behavioral and Brain Sciences, 9,* 1–66.

Karlins, M., Coffman, T. L., & Walters, G. (1969). On the fading of social stereotypes: Studies in three generations of college students. *Journal of Personality and Social Psychology, 13,* 1–16.

Katz, D., & Braly, K. (1933). Racial stereotypes in one hundred college students. *Journal of Abnormal and Social Psychology, 28,* 280–290.

Katz, P. A. (1976). The acquisition of racial attitudes in children. In P. A. Katz (Ed.), *Towards the elimination of racism* (pp. 125–154). New York: Pergamon Press.

Kinder, D. R., & Sears, D. O. (1981). Prejudice and politics: Symbolic racism versus racial threats to the good life. *Journal of Personality and Social Psychology, 40,* 414–431.

Klatzky, R. L. (1984). *Memory and awareness.* San Francisco: Freeman.

LaViolette, F., & Silvert, K. H. (1951). A theory of stereotypes. *Social Forces, 29,* 237–257.

Linn, L. S. (1965). Verbal attitudes and overt behavior: A study of racial discrimination. *Social Forces, 43,* 353–364.

Logan, G. D. (1980). Attention and automaticity in Stroop and priming tasks: Theory and data. *Cognitive Psychology, 12,* 523–553.

Logan, G. D., & Cowan, W. G. (1984). On the ability to inhibit thought and action: A theory of act control. *Psychological Review, 91,* 295–327.

Marcel, A. J. (1983a). Conscious and unconscious perception: Experiments on visual masking and word recognition. *Cognitive Psychology, 15,* 197–237.

Marcel, A. J. (1983b). Conscious and unconcious perception: An approach to the relations between phenomenal experience and perceptual processes. *Cognitive Psychology, 15,* 238–300.

McConahay, J. B., Hardee, B. B., & Batts, V. (1981). Has racism declined? It depends upon who's asking and what is asked. *Journal of Conflict Resolution, 25,* 536–579.

Neely, J. H. (1977). Semantic priming and retrieval from lexical memory: Roles of inhibitionless spreading activation and limited-capacity attention. *Journal of Experimental Psychology, 106,* 226–254.

Nisbett, R. E., & Wilson, T. D. (1977). Telling more than we can know: Verbal reports on mental processes. *Psychological Review, 84,* 231–259.

Pettigrew, T. (1987, May 12). "Useful" modes of thought contribute to prejudice. *New York Times,* pp. 17, 20.

Porter, J. D. R. (1971). *Black child, white child: The development of racial attitudes.* Cambridge, MA: Harvard University Press.

Posner, M. I., & Snyder, C. R. R. (1975). Attention and cognitive control. In R. L. Solso (Ed.), *Information processing and cognition: The Loyola Symposium.* Hillsdale, NJ: Erlbaum.

Pratkanis, A. R. (in press). The cognitive representation of attitudes. In A. R. Pratkanis, S. J. Breckler, & A. G. Greenwald (Eds.), *Attitude structure and function.* Hillsdale, NJ: Erlbaum.

Proshansky, H. M. (1966). The development of intergroup attitudes. In L. W. Hoffman & M. L. Hoffman (Eds.), *Review of child development research* (Vol. 2, pp. 311–371). New York: Russell Sage Foundation.

Rips, L. J., Shoben, E. J., & Smith, E. E. (1973). Semantic distance and the verification of semantic relations. *Journal of Verbal Learning and Verbal Behavior, 12,* 1–20.

Ronis, D. L., Yates, J. F., & Kirscht, J. P. (in press). Attitudes, decisions, and habits as determinants of repeated behavior. In A. R. Pratkanis, S. J. Breckler, & A. G. Greenwald (Eds.), *Attitude structure and function.* Hillsdale, NJ: Erlbaum.

Rosch, E. (1978). Principles of categorization. In E. Rosch and B. B. Lloyd (Eds.), *Cognition and categorization* (pp. 28–48). Hillsdale, NJ: Erlbaum.

Saenger, G. (1953). *The social psychology of prejudice.* New York: Harper.

Sager, H. A., & Schofield, J. W. (1980). Racial and behavioral cues in black and white children's perceptions of ambiguously aggressive acts. *Journal of Personality and Social Psychology, 39,* 590–598.

Schneider, W., & Shiffrin, R. M. (1977). Controlled and automatic human information processing: I. Detection, search, and attention. *Psychological Review, 84,* 1–66,

Sears, D. O., & Kinder, D. R. (1971). Racial tensions and voting in Los Angeles. In W. Z. Hirsch (Ed.), *Los Angeles: Viability and prospects for metropolitan leadership* (pp. 51–88). New York: Praeger.

Sears, D. O., & McConahay, J. B. (1973). *The politics of violence: The new urban blacks and the Watts riot.* Boston: Houghton Mifflin.

Secord, P. F., & Backman, C. W. (1974). *Social psychology.* New York: McGraw-Hill.

Shiffrin, R. M., & Dumais, S. T. (1981). The development of automatism. In J. R. Anderson (Ed.), *Cognitive skills and their acquisition* (pp. 111–140). Hillsdale, NJ: Erlbaum.

Shiffrin, R. M., & Schneider, W. (1977). Controlled and automatic human information processing: II. Perceptual learning, automatic attending, and a general theory. *Psychological Review, 84,* 127–190.

Simpson, G. E., & Yinger, J. M. (1965). *Racial and cultural minorities* (rev. ed.) New York: Harper & Row.

Smith, E. R. (1984). Model of social inference processes. *Psychological Review, 91,* 392–413.

Smith, E. R., & Branscombe, N. R. (1985). *Stereotype traits can be processed automatically.* Unpublished manuscript, Purdue University, West Lafayette, IN.

Srull, T. K., & Wyer, R. S., Jr. (1979). The role of category accessibility in the interpretation of information about persons: Some determinants and implications. *Journal of Personality and Social Psychology, 37,* 1660–1672.

Srull, T. K., & Wyer, R. S., Jr. (1980). Category accessibility and social perception: Some implications for the study of person memory and interpersonal judgments. *Journal of Personality and Social Psychology, 38,* 841–856.

Stephan, W. G. (1985). Intergroup relations. In G. Lindzey & E. Aronson (Eds.), *The handbook of social psychology* (3rd ed., Vol. 2, pp.559–658). Hillsdale, NJ: Erlbaum.

Tajfel, H. (1981). *Human groups and social categories: Studies in social psychology.* Cambridge, England: Cambridge University Press.

Taylor, D. G., Sheatsley, P. B., & Greeley, A. M. (1978). Attitudes toward racial integration. *Scientific American, 238,* 42–49.

Weitz, S. (1972). Attitude, voice, and behavior: A repressed affect model of interracial interaction. *Journal of Personality and Social Psychology, 24,* 14–21.

Wyer, R. S., Jr., & Srull, T. K. (1981). Category accessibility: Some theoretical and empirical issues concerning the processing of social stimulus information. In E. T. Higgins, C. P. Herman, & M. P. Zanna (Eds.), *Social cognition: The Ontario Symposium* (Vol. 1, pp. 161–197). Hillsdale, NJ: Erlbaum.

NOTES

1. The overall hit and false alarm rates for stereotype-related and neutral words were also examined as a function of prejudice level, priming, and replication. These data were submitted to a five-way mixed-model analysis of variance. Prejudice level, priming, and replication were between-subjects variables; word type (stereotype-related vs. neutral) and response type (hits vs. false alarms) were within-subject variables. This analysis, like the d' analysis, revealed no significant main effects or interactions.

2. The primary analysis was repeated for high- and low-prejudice subjects separately. The two-way Priming × Scale Related interaction was obtained for both high- and low-prejudice subjects (both $ps < .05$), thus supporting the primary analysis.

3. Data from 4 Black subjects who participated in Study 1, but who were not included in the analyses, suggest that Blacks are at least knowledgeable of the cultural stereotype. That is, there was considerable overlap between the content reported by the Black and White subjects. Two independent raters could not reliably predict the race of subjects from the protocols. In addition, Sager and Schofield (1980) found that Black and White children interpreted the same ambiguously hostile behaviors as being more aggressive or hostile when performed by a Black than a White actor. Sager and Schofield argued that subjects were making stereotype-congruent judgments of the Black actor.

4. Four Black students signed up to participate. These students did not fill out the thought-listing or Modern Racism measure but were given credit for showing up to participate. The nature of the study was described to them, and they were told why interest centered on the responses of White subjects.

5. The coding scheme was developed and pretested in a pilot study, the goal of which was to demonstrate that subjects' cognitive representations of social groups are richer and more complex than simple trait-based structures. The coding scheme was developed on the basis of considerations of the stereotype assessment, prejudice, attitude, and cognitive organization literature. The stereotype literature, for example, led

to an examination of the types of traits (i.e., positive or negative) listed in response to the category label. The prejudice and attitude measurement literature, however, led to examination of whether positive (e.g., statements of equality, recognition of Blacks' plight historically, etc.) or negative (resentment of affirmative action, avoid interactions with Blacks) belief thoughts would be elicited by the label.

The cognitive organization literature (Collins & Quillian, 1969; Rips, Shoben, & Smith, 1973) suggested that both criterial (e.g., physical descriptors) as well as noncriterial (e.g., associated terms) should be examined. On the basis of Rosch's (1978) categorization model, the coding scheme included a category for basic (e.g., athletes) and subordinate (e.g., Richard Pryor) level exemplars of the social category. Superordinate labels were not included because subjects had been asked to generate alternate labels prior to the thought-listing task. Strong support for the coding scheme was found in the pilot study. The pilot study did not examine the complexity of thought listings as a function of subjects' prejudice level. That was the goal of this study.

6. As a prerequisite to examining the content of the protocols, an analysis on the number of thoughts and the number of alternate labels generated by high- and low-prejudice subjects was performed to examine whether prejudice level affected these tasks. Although it was expected that subjects would generate more thoughts than alternate labels, the key tests of interest were provided by the prejudice-level main effect (whether one group listed more items than the other) and the Prejudice Level × Task interaction (whether prejudice level differentially affected the tasks). These data were submitted to a Prejudice Level (high vs. low) × Task (label generation vs. thought generation) mixed-model analysis of variance. The analysis revealed that subjects generated a greater number of thoughts ($M = 12.67$) than labels ($M = 4.72$), $F(1, 65) = 150.85, p < .0001$. However, neither the prejudice main effect, $F(1, 65) = 0.66, p < .42$, nor the Prejudice Level × Task interaction, $F(1, 65) = 0.01, p < .94$, was significant.

7. A canonical discriminant function analysis in which subjects' prejudice level was predicted as a function of the best linear combination of the 10 coding categories revealed a single canonical variable (Wilks's lambda = 0.63), $F(10, 56) = 3.25, p < .002$. The canonical squared multiple correlation was 0.37. Positive-belief thoughts were located at one extreme of the canonical structure (-0.88) and negative trait thoughts at the other (0.78). None of the other categories discriminated significantly between high- and low-prejudice groups.

This article is based on a dissertation submitted by Patricia G. Devine to the Ohio State University Graduate School in partial fulfillment of the requirement for the doctoral degree. This research was supported by a Presidential Fellowship and by a Graduate Student Alumni Research Award both awarded by the Ohio State University Graduate School.

Thanks are extended to Thomas M. Ostrom, chair of the dissertation committee, and to the other members of the committee, Anthony G. Greenwald and Gifford Weary.

CRITICAL THINKING QUESTIONS

1. In study 3, subjects responded anonymously. What if the responses were not anonymous? Would the high- and low-prejudice subjects respond differently? Specifically, do you think the high-prejudice subjects could control (inhibit) the activation of their prejudiced stereotypes? If they could, would it be for the same reason as the low-prejudice subjects?

2. Using the findings and implications of these studies, design a program to teach children to overcome their reliance on stereotypes in making judgments about people.

3. Many studies on prejudice involve asking subjects about their attitudes toward particular groups. What are the implications of the findings of this article regarding such techniques? Which is more likely to be activated in such research settings, automatic or controlled processes?

4. Study 3 found that low- and high-prejudice subjects relied on different processes in making their judgments. How could the prejudice levels of the high-prejudice subjects be reduced, or are these individuals doomed to automatically continue using stereotypes?

Chapter Six

INTERPERSONAL ATTRACTION

THE TOPIC OF interpersonal attraction is one to which most people can directly relate: Who do we come to like and why? The research on factors affecting attraction has gone in several directions. One major thrust has been to identify the conditions that are important in determining if two people will like one another. Many factors have been identified, but two very important ones are physical attractiveness and attitude similarity.

"The Eye of the Beholder," Article 16, summarizes the large impact that physical attractiveness has on our judgments of other people. Most of us would feel somewhat reluctant to admit that such factors play an important role. After all, we shouldn't judge people by superficial characteristics, such as how they look. Nonetheless, a large body of research suggests that we do exactly that. Given the pervasiveness of this phenomenon, the practical implications for how we deal with and judge others in our daily lives are indeed important.

Article 17, "Interpersonal Attraction and Attitude Similarity," is an early study that examined the relationship between attraction and perceived similarity. Studies done prior to the Byrne article had indicated that friends were more likely to have similar attitudes than were nonfriends. However, such studies were not able to determine which came first: attitude similarity (which then led to attraction) or attraction (which then led to increased contact and convergence of attitudes). This study represents one of the first experimental demonstrations that attitude similarity leads to increased attraction.

The final article in this section, Article 18, also addresses the question of attitude similarity and attraction. "The Repulsion Hypothesis Revisited" was written nearly three decades after the publication of the previous classic article, and it is co-authored by Donn Byrne, the author of the classic piece. This recent study is a good example of how research evolves over time, exploring the more precise conditions under which a given event operates. It also illustrates the testing of rival hypotheses that both claim to explain the mechanisms underlying attitude similarity and interpersonal attraction.

ARTICLE 16 _____

Physical attractiveness is perhaps the most widely researched topic in the area of interpersonal attraction. Part of this interest may be due to the importance of physical appearance in interpersonal interactions. When we meet a new person, physical appearance is the first thing we notice. Although perceptions of attractiveness are to some extent a matter of individual taste, some cultural stereotypes also define what constitutes attractiveness. Thus, another reason that attractiveness is so heavily investigated may be that it is relatively easy to get subjects to agree on what it means. Beauty is not just in the eye of the beholder, in other words.

Although attractiveness is something that can be readily observed about a person, most people would agree that it should not be used to make judgments about him or her. Indeed, most people would strongly protest the suggestion that how they see a person's values, skills, personality, or attributes may be influenced by what that person looks like. Yet a large body of literature developed over the years suggests that this indeed is the case. For example, research suggests that attractive people are rated more highly on a number of valued attributes; this is perhaps best summarized as the "what-is-beautiful-is-good" stereotype. Other studies have demonstrated that attractiveness may influence outcomes in serious situations. For example, attractive defendants are generally less likely to be convicted, and when they are convicted, they are more likely to receive lighter sentences than their less attractive counterparts.

The following article by Cash and Janda summarizes a number of studies concerning the impact of physical attractiveness in the work setting. In particular, the article reports that attractiveness may have a significant effect on how a person is viewed at work; the phenomenon is complex, being determined by the sex of the person as well as the type of employment being considered. The article suggests that a form of discrimination called *beautyism* may operate in the workplace.

The Eye of the Beholder

■ Thomas F. Cash and Louis H. Janda

Ask most people to list what makes them like someone on first meeting and they'll tell you personality, intelligence, sense of humor. But they're probably deceiving themselves. The characteristic that impresses people the most, when meeting anyone from a job applicant to a blind date, is appearance. And unfair and unenlightened as it may seem, attractive people are frequently preferred over their less attractive peers.

Research begun in the early 1970s has shown that not only do good looks influence such things as choice of friends, lovers and mates, but that they can also affect school grades, selection for jobs and even the outcome of a trial. Psychologist Ellen Berscheid of the University of Minnesota and psychologist Elaine Walster, then at the University of Wisconsin, were among the first researchers to deal with the topic of attractiveness. Their seminal 1974 paper on the subject showed that the more attractive a person, the more desir-

Reprinted from *Psychology Today*, 1984 (December), *18*, 46–52. Reprinted with permission from *Psychology Today Magazine*. Copyright © 1984 (PT Partners, L.P.).

able characteristics others will attribute to him or her. Attractive people are viewed as being happier, more sensitive, more interesting, warmer, more poised, more sociable and as having better character than their less attractive counterparts. Psychologist Karen Dion of the University of Toronto has dubbed this stereotypical view as: "What is beautiful is good."

Our current work at Old Dominion University in Norfolk, Virginia, with colleagues and students, focuses on the role that appearance plays in judgments made about people. Our studies have been done in a variety of settings: basic research laboratories, beauty and cosmetics industry labs, plastic and reconstructive surgery practices, psychiatric hospitals and psychotherapeutic consulting rooms.

One topic that has led to many avenues of research is how attractiveness influences sextyping—the tendency of people to attribute certain stereotypical qualities to each sex. Besides being perceived as sensitive, kind, interesting and generally happy, attractive people tend to fit easily into sexual stereotypes, according to a study done by Barry Gillen, a social psychologist in our department.

Gillen speculated that attractive people possess two types of "goodness," one related to and the other unrelated to their sex. To test this hypothesis he showed a group of students photographs of both men and women of high, moderate and low attractiveness, as determined by the previous rankings of students according to a seven-point scale (contrary to popular belief, researchers usually don't use the Bo Derek scale of 10). The judges were asked to rate the subjects according to the masculinity, femininity and social desirability scales of the Bem Sex Role Inventory. Gillen's study found that attractive women were perceived as being more feminine, and that attractive men were viewed as being more masculine than their less attractive counterparts. This suggests a second stereotype: "What is beautiful is sex-typed."

One implication of Gillen's work that we wanted to test was whether good looks are a disadvantage for some people, especially women, in work situations that conflict with sexual stereo-

types. By the late 1970s, there was already a sizable body of literature documenting the problems women face because of sex-role stereotypes. We speculated that attractive women might be at a real disadvantage when they aspire to occupations in which stereotypically masculine traits—such as being strong, independent and decisive—are thought to be required for success.

To test that possibility we did a study with Gillen and Steve Burns, a student in our department, in which professional personnel consultants were hired to rate a "job applicant's" suitability for six positions. We matched the positions for the skill required, the prestige offered and the degree of supervisory independence allowed. Two jobs were stereotypically masculine (automobile salesperson and wholesale hardware shipping and receiving clerk), two feminine (telephone operator and office receptionist) and two were sex-neutral (motel desk clerk and photographic darkroom assistant).

Each of the 72 personnel consultants who participated received a résumé package for an individual that contained the typical kinds of information that a job applicant might submit: academic standing, a list of hobbies and interests, specific skills and recommendations from teachers and counselors. All of the résumés were identical with the exception of the name ("John" vs. "Janet" Williams) and the inclusion of a photograph of the applicant. Photographs showed either an extremely attractive applicant or an unattractive one, previously judged on an attractiveness scale.

The results documented the existence of both sexism and "beautyism." On the sexism front, men were given stronger endorsements by the personnel consultants for the traditionally masculine jobs, while women were rated higher for the traditionally feminine jobs. Men were also judged to have just as much chance of success on the neutral jobs as on the masculine ones, while women were perceived to be less likely to succeed on the neutral jobs than on the feminine ones.

"Beautyism" had several facets: Attractive men were favored over their less attractive male competitors for all three types of jobs. Similarly, attractiveness gave women a competitive edge against other women, but only for traditionally female or neutral jobs. When it came to jobs inappropriate to society's traditional sex roles, the attractive women were rated lower than their less attractive female competitors.

These findings gain support from a subsequent study by Madeline Heilman and Lois Saruwatari, psychologists at Yale University. They examined the effects of appearance and gender on selection for both managerial and nonmanagerial jobs. Male and female students in a business administration class received résumé packages for equally qualified candidates. Each résumé included a photograph of either an attractive or unattractive man or woman. Being attractive was always an advantage for men. Attractive men received stronger recommendations for hiring, were judged to have better qualifications and were given higher suggested starting salaries than unattractive men for both the managerial and the nonmanagerial positions.

Among woman, however, those who were less attractive actually had a significant edge over their more attractive peers when seeking a place in management, a traditionally masculine occupation. Good looks were an advantage only when women were applying for the nonmanagerial positions. Attractiveness resulted in lower salary recommendations when the women were viewed as stepping into an out-of-sex-role position.

Heilman says that her findings "imply that women should strive to appear as unattractive and masculine as possible if they are to succeed in advancing their careers by moving into powerful organizational positions."

So, beauty—at least in a woman—doesn't always pay in the workplace, nor does it guarantee higher marks in the classroom. Recently, we tested the notion that attractiveness can work against women attempting to cross sex-role boundaries in academic as well as work settings. We constructed a series of essays, purportedly written by college freshmen, that were equivalent in quality, but which varied in the "masculinity" or "femininity" of the topic. The essays were accompanied by photographs of attractive and unattractive "authors."

The masculine topics were "How to Hunt Safely" and "How to Buy a Used Motorcycle," and the feminine topics were "How to Make a Quilt" and "How to Give a Manicure." The essays were read and judged by 216 female college students.

Once again, attractiveness proved to be an advantage for the men, regardless of the sex-typing of the essay topic. For the women, however, beauty was an advantage only when they stuck to a feminine topic. When they were presented as authors of the masculine essays, the attractive women were given a lower score relative to their less attractive peers.

It is clear that beauty can be a double-edged sword for women. Attractive women are viewed as having a host of desirable personality characteristics, except the ones needed to step out of prescribed sex roles.

What are the specific cues for gender role stereotyping? Grooming—the way people dress, use cosmetics and style their hair—appears to be a factor. The differing ideal physiques—thin for women, more muscular for men—also influence gender stereotyping, according to recent experiments by Purdue psychologists Kay Deaux and Laurie Lewis. People who are tall, strong, sturdy and broad-shouldered—regardless of gender—are viewed as more likely to have masculine personality traits, to fit the assertive, bread-winner role and to hold a traditionally masculine occupation. Meanwhile, people who are dainty, graceful and soft in voice and appearance are expected to have typically feminine traits, roles and occupations.

How does grooming affect sex-typing of attractive women, especially as it relates to their employability? This question was partially answered by a series of studies in which we asked male and female corporate personnel consultants to judge how qualified various attractive women, shown in photographs, were for jobs in corporate management. In the first study, we showed 16 personnel managers photographs of women wearing various types of clothing, jewelry, hairstyles and cosmetics. The results showed that the more sex-typed, or "feminized," the grooming styles, the less likely were personnel consultants to judge the women to be potential managers.

In a second study, personnel consultants judged businesswomen photographed under two different grooming conditions: one very feminine and made up, the other plainer and less sex-typed. The more feminine style included longer hair or hairstyles that concealed the face; soft sweaters, low necklines or ruffled blouses; dangling jewelry; and heavy make-up. In the other condition "candidates" wore tailored clothes with a jacket, subtle make-up and either short hair or hair swept away from the face. These criteria were chosen on the basis of descriptions given by judges in the previous study.

Once again the corporate personnel consultants made choices suggesting that the less feminine the appearance, the more competent the woman, even though the candidates had been perceived by the consultants as equally attractive under both conditions. Specifically, candidates groomed in a more feminine style were perceived to be less managerial; less intrinsically interested in work; less likely to be taken seriously by others; more illogical and overemotional in critical decision-making; less financially responsible; more helpless and dependent on the influences of others; sexier and more flirtatious in social relations; and less assertive, independent and self-confident than those groomed in a less sex-typed style.

In the third phase of this project, male and female executives and managers from more than 200 corporations in major cities nationwide were shown applications containing photographs of attractive businesswomen in various grooming styles and asked how they thought they would fare in the corporate world. Once again, candidates groomed in a less sex-typed style were expected to have a better chance at reaching the management levels of the corporate structure, to be offered higher salaries and to be afforded greater social acceptance and credibility on the job than when they were groomed in a more traditionally feminine manner. These effects were especially prominent when the judges were men, often the gatekeepers of corporate management.

These studies, taken together, suggest that grooming style has a definite effect on whether women are sex-typed, and thus whether they are viewed as having good management potential. To some extent, our research has confirmed what many people always suspected: If a woman wants to succeed in a man's world, she had better not look too feminine. Several "dress for success" books have made it to the best-seller list by advising women to get ahead in business by wearing their hair short, using cosmetics sparingly and wearing conservative suits. Our research suggests, sadly, that the advice is sound.

It is interesting how deeply ingrained these attitudes are. Many people, both men and women, who are seriously concerned and offended by the sexism in our society never question this dress-for-success formula, which has different standards for men than it does for women. Men must follow certain clothing norms in the office in regard to neatness and formality, but not masculinity. No one would suggest to a man that he try not to look too masculine when he shows up at the office or expect him to comb his hair one way for the office and another way when he goes out to dinner. It is doubtful that any man has ever been advised not to look too good if he wants to be taken seriously at the next board meeting. But rules of dress for women are far more complex.

Prejudices are slow to fade away. It will be interesting to see if grooming styles for women become more flexible as they move up the corporate ladder in greater numbers and become more powerful.

Attractive women can face problems outside the boardroom as well. Everyone wants to be thought of as desirable and attractive, but a woman's beauty can invite unwanted advances and treatment as a sex object. Perhaps, then, it should come as no surprise that social psychologist Harry Reis of the University of Rochester found attractive women to be more distrustful of men than were their plainer counterparts.

Our research has also confirmed that a third stereotype exists: "What is beautiful is self-centered." We've found that many people assume that attractive people are vain and egotistical. After all, if what is beautiful is good, then the beautiful people must know how wonderful they are. Further, people of low and average attractiveness are often reluctant to choose extremely attractive mates for fear of losing them. In fact, breakups are more common among couples who are mismatched on attractiveness. So once again, thorns appear on the rose of beauty.

We have been discussing how people judge and react to the attractiveness of others. What about people's perceptions of themselves? Currently, in collaboration with Barbara Winstead, a psychologist at Old Dominion, we are examining how body images—the feelings people have about their own appearance—influence their lives. Surprisingly, how people view their own level of attractiveness has almost nothing to do with how others view them. People whom others consider beautiful may not like their looks at all. Conversely, people whom others might judge as

downright unattractive or even ugly feel completely comfortable with their appearance.

Using our newly developed Winstead-Cash Body Self-Relations Questionnaire, we are beginning to accumulate evidence that body image may have as much impact on one's life as external evaluations of beauty. In a study with Steve Noles, a graduate student in the Virginia Consortium for Professional Psychology, for example, we have found a greater vulnerability to depression among people who place importance on being good-looking yet see themselves as less attractive than they really are.

Aristotle once maintained that "beauty is a greater recommendation than any letter of introduction." In many respects he was right. But then again, may he should have collected more data.

CRITICAL THINKING QUESTIONS

1. Several of the studies reported did not mention if the raters were female or male. Do you think this would make a difference? If so, what would you hypothesize the difference to be?
2. In one study, female college students rated essays purportedly written by college freshmen but that varied in the supposed masculinity or femininity of the topic. Do you think that college professors are influenced by attractiveness of students? Do you think that the specific course or major might be a mediating factor? How would you design an experiment to test this? Could you test this hypothesis other than by using a laboratory experiment?
3. Do you think that the attractiveness of the rater has an impact on how a particular candidate is rated? For example, would an attractive female working in a traditionally male-dominated profession be influenced by the attractiveness of an applicant in the same way as a less attractive female working in the same field? Could this be tested in some way?
4. Based on your own experience, have you seen any evidence for beautyism? Do you feel the effect of attractiveness is really as pervasive as seems to be suggested by the article? If it is, how could this form of prejudice be reduced or eliminated?

ARTICLE 17 _____

As indicated in Article 16, physical attractiveness plays an important role in interpersonal attraction. But what other factors are important? One factor is similarity. Common sense suggests that we should like those who are similar to ourselves. Early research, as well as everyday observation, seems to indicate that spouses and friends often hold similar attitudes.

But how and why does this happen? Do we seek out people who have attitudes similar to our own and then become friends with them (or marry them)? Or after we become friends (or marry), do our attitudes gradually tend to become more similar?

The article that follows was an early attempt at determining if attitude similarity caused interpersonal attraction, rather than resulted from it. Donn Byrne examined the process in a laboratory setting and tested some reasons for why this effect may occur.

Interpersonal Attraction and Attitude Similarity[1]

■ Donn Byrne[2]

In investigating the direction and the strength of the affect engendered between the two participants in a dyad, we may arrange the expressed feelings of each individual along a continuum ranging from strongly positive to strongly negative. The accurate prediction of interpersonal attraction and repulsion in such relationships will undoubtedly require that we secure knowledge about several classes of independent variables.

Probably the most obvious and also best documented variable is that of propinquity. Studies in a wide variety of settings have shown that physical and functional distance influence interaction and interpersonal attraction (Byrne, in press). Once the environmental situation permits or encourages interaction, affiliation need should be helpful in predicting individual differences in interpersonal behavior (Atkinson, Heyns, & Veroff, 1954; Schachter, 1959). A third class of variables consists of the overt stimulus properties of each individual to which other individuals would be expected to respond on the basis of

generalization from previous interpersonal interactions.

Once interaction has begun, reciprocal reward and punishment is proposed as the crucial determining factor. It has been suggested (Newcomb, 1956) that attraction between persons is a function of the extent to which reciprocal rewards are present in their interaction; perhaps dislike is a function of reciprocal punishments. A special subclass of this variable would be perceived similarity and dissimilarity of the attitudes of two individuals. It can be assumed that persons in our culture have well established learned drives to be logical and to make a correct report of the environment. Those who seem deficient in this respect are generally categorized as being uninformed, of low intelligence, immoral, and/or as being out of contact with reality. It is primarily through consensual validation that we determine whether we or anyone else is logical or correct in interpreting environmental events. Hence, any time that another person offers us validation by

Reprinted from the *Journal of Abnormal and Social Psychology*, 1961, 62, 713–715.

indicating that his percepts and concepts are congruent with ours, it constitutes a rewarding interaction, and, hence, one element in forming a positive relationship. Any time that another person indicates dissimilarity between our two notions, it constitutes a punishing interaction and thus one element in forming a negative relationship. Disagreement raises the unpleasant possibility that we are to some degree stupid, uninformed, immoral, or insane. An alternative possibility is that it is the other person who is deficient in one or more of these characteristics. Probably other variables, such as the importance of the issue to each individual, contribute to the effect.

A number of studies have found greater similarity among friends than among nonfriends with respect to a variety of issues (Bonney, 1946; Loomis, 1946; Newcomb, 1956; Precker, 1952; Richardson, 1940; Winslow, 1937). A few studies of a more experimental nature also support the notion of a relationship between attitude similarity and interpersonal attraction (Jones & Daugherty, 1959; Smith, 1957).

In order to test the proposition that the effect of attitude similarity is a causative one and to test some implications arising from the preceding speculations about the reason for the effect, it was hypothesized that (a) a stranger who is known to have attitudes similar to those of the subject is better liked than a stranger with attitudes dissimilar to those of the subject, (b) a stranger who is known to have attitudes similar to those of the subject is judged to be more intelligent, better informed, more moral, and better adjusted than a stranger with attitudes dissimilar to those of the subject, and (c) a stranger who is known to have similar attitudes on issues important to the subject and dissimilar attitudes on unimportant issues is better liked and is evaluated more positively on the other four variables than a stranger for whom the reverse is true.

METHOD

Attitude Measure[3]   On the basis of a pilot study, 26 issues were selected for inclusion in an attitude and opinion scale. Each issue was presented in a seven-point scale. The issues ranged from those thought to be extremely important by the pilot subjects (e.g., integration, God, premarital sex relations) to those considered to be of minor importance (e.g., western movies and television programs, classical music, politics).

Procedure   The attitude scale was administered to 64 students (36 male, 28 female) enrolled in an introductory psychology course at the University of Texas. Response heterogeneity differed from item to item, but there was moderately wide diversity of opinion among the 64 subjects. After filling out the attitude scale, the subjects were asked to indicate which they believed to be the 13 most important and 13 least important issues.

Two weeks later they were falsely informed that the attitude scale had been given as part of a study in interpersonal prediction. They were told that individuals in another class had been given the same scale that they took, students in the two classes were matched on the basis of sex, and they were to be given each other's tests (name removed) in order to determine how much they could learn about one another from this information alone.

Actually the questionnaire they received at this time was a fake one made up by the experimenter. The subjects had been randomly divided into four groups; one group received attitude scales filled out exactly the same as theirs had been, one received scales with exactly opposite views expressed, one received scales with similar opinions on the most important issues and dissimilar on the least important, and the fourth received scales with similar opinions on the least important issues and dissimilar opinions on the most important. The four groups of subjects did not differ significantly in their initial responses to any of the 26 issues.

Interpersonal Attraction and Evaluation   A rating scale was used as the measure of interpersonal attraction and evaluation with each dependent variable represented in a seven-point scale. As a measure of interpersonal attraction, subjects were asked to indicate how well they felt they would like this person and whether they believed they would enjoy working with him (or her) as a partner in an experiment. Four scales dealt with evaluation; the subjects were asked for their judgments as to the other student's intelligence, knowledge of current events, morality, and adjustment.

RESULTS

First Hypothesis Table 1 shows the comparisons of the two groups on each of the dependent variables. The first hypothesis was overwhelmingly confirmed for each of the two attraction scales. The group with attitude scales filled out the same as their own (SA) indicated significantly more positive feelings toward the "stranger" than did the group which received scales indicating dissimilar attitudes (DA). Each difference was significant at less than the .001 level.

Second Hypothesis As is indicated in Table 1, the second hypothesis was also confirmed. The SA group rated the "stranger" significantly higher than did the DA group on intelligence, knowledge of current events, morality, and adjustment. Again, each difference reached a level of significance beyond the .001 level.

Third Hypothesis The third hypothesis, concerning the influence of important vs. unimportant issues, was only partially confirmed. As is shown in Table 2, the Similar on Important Attitudes Group (SIA) rated the "stranger" significantly more positively than did the Similar on Unimportant Attitudes Group (SUA) with respect to their personal feelings about him, his morality, and his adjustment. On the other three variables, the two groups did not differ.

TABLE 1 / Comparison of the Similar Attitude (SA) and Dissimilar Attitude (DA) Groups on Interpersonal Attraction and Evaluation

	SA (N = 17)		DA (N = 17)		D	t	df	p
	M	SD	M	SD				
Personal Feelings	6.53	.50	1.76	.73	4.77	21.46	32	<.001
Desirability as Work Partner	6.47	.50	2.65	1.88	3.82	7.88	32	<.001
Intelligence	5.65	.68	3.06	.87	2.59	9.37	32	<.001
Knowledge of Current Events	4.65	1.14	2.65	.91	2.00	5.51	32	<.001
Morality	5.76	.73	3.47	2.09	2.29	4.14	32	<.001
Adjustment	6.00	.84	2.71	1.13	3.29	9.36	32	<.001

TABLE 2 / Comparison of the Similar on Important Attitudes (SIA) and Similar on Unimportant Attitudes (SUA) Groups on Interpersonal Attraction and Evaluation

	SIA (N = 15)		SUA (N = 15)		D	t	df	p
	M	SD	M	SD				
Personal Feelings	4.20	1.51	2.60	1.20	1.60	3.10	28	<.01
Desirability as Work Partner	4.27	1.44	3.33	1.40	.94	1.76	28	ns
Intelligence	4.13	.62	3.73	1.34	.40	1.01	28	ns
Knowledge of Current Events	3.60	.95	3.53	.96	.07	.19	28	ns
Morality	5.33	1.25	3.33	1.66	2.00	3.60	28	<.01
Adjustment	4.07	1.57	2.93	1.18	1.14	2.17	28	<.05

DISCUSSION

The experimental confirmation of the first two hypotheses is very encouraging for further research designed to investigate other aspects of the relationship between interpersonal attraction and attitude similarity. It should be possible now to study the effect of attitude differences less extreme than those in the present study and to combine this variable with the others that influence interpersonal attraction in order to determine interaction effects.

Because of the fact that this group of subjects showed a degree of homogeneity of opinion on some of the attitude items, a possible alternative interpretation is that they were responding negatively to unusual and deviant beliefs rather than to disagreement per se. On 19 of the 26 issues it was possible for a subject to fall in the deviant one fourth of the group by expressing a positive or a negative opinion. The range among the subjects was from no deviant attitudes to nine; they were divided into high and low subgroups on the basis of this score. Since these "conforming" and "deviant" subgroups did not differ from one another in responding to strangers with similar vs. different attitudes, there is no evidence to support this other interpretation of the results.

The partial failure of the third hypothesis led to a comparison of all four groups on each of the dependent variables. The results suggest that the Personal Feelings scale is the most sensitive measure of interpersonal attraction. With the other five interpersonal judgment scales, additional factors apparently contribute to the variance.

REFERENCES

Atkinson, J. W., Heyns, R. W., & Veroff, J. The effect of experimental arousal of the affiliation motive on thematic apperception. *J. abnorm. soc. Psychol.*, 1954, 49, 405–410.

Bonney, M. E. A sociometric study of the relationship of some factors to mutual friendships on the elementary, secondary, and college levels. *Sociometry*, 1946, 9, 21–47.

Byrne, D. The influence of propinquity and opportunities for interaction on classroom relationships. *Hum. Relat.*, in press.

Jones, E. E., & Daugherty, B. N. Political orientation and the perceptual effects of an anticipated interaction. *J. abnorm. soc. Psychol.*, 1959, 59, 340–349.

Loomis, C. P. Political and occupational cleavages in a Hanoverian village, Germany: A sociometric study. *Sociometry*, 1946, 9, 316–333.

Newcomb, T. M. The prediction of interpersonal attraction. *Amer. Psychologist*, 1956, 11, 575–586.

Precker, J. A. Similarity of valuings as a factor in selection. *J. abnorm. soc. Psychol.*, 1952, 47, 406–414.

Richardson, Helen M. Community of values as a factor in friendships of college and adult women. *J. soc. Psychol.*, 1940, 11, 303–312.

Schachter, S. *The psychology of affiliation.* Stanford: Stanford Univer. Press, 1959.

Smith, A. J. Similarity of values and its relation to acceptance and the projection of similarity. *J. Psychol.*, 1957, 43, 251–260.

Winslow, C. N. A study of the extent of agreement between friends' opinions and their ability to estimate the opinions of each other. *J. soc. Psychol.*, 1937, 8, 433–442.

NOTES

1. A portion of this paper was read at the meetings of the Southwestern Psychological Association, Galveston, 1960.
   This investigation was supported in part by a research grant (EF-140) from the University of Texas Research Institute.
2. From the Laboratory for Personality Research.
3. The attitude measure, response frequencies, and the rating scales for interpersonal attraction and evaluation have been deposited with the American Documentation Institute.

CRITICAL THINKING QUESTIONS

1. How could you study the same phenomena as Byrne did but in a field (nonlaboratory) setting?
2. This study employed a paper-and-pencil manipulation of perceived attitude similarity; the subject never actually met another person. In a more natural setting,

physical attraction

where one person is interacting face to face with another, how important is attitude similarity? What other factors might be more important? How could you study the relative importance of these factors?

3. Consider your choice of friends. How similar are your attitudes? Are there exceptions? Do any of your friends have attitudes that are very different than your own? How do you account for these exceptions?

ADDITIONAL RELATED READINGS

Berscheid, E. (1985). Interpersonal attraction. In G. Lindzey and E. Aronson (Eds.), *Handbook of Social Psychology,* vol. 2. New York: Random House.

Byrne, D., Clore, G. L., & Smeaton, G. (1986). The attraction hypothesis: Do similar attitudes affect anything? *Journal of Personality and Social Psychology, 51,* 1167–1170.

Kelley, H. H., Berscheid, E., Christensen, A., Harvey, J. H., Huston, T. L., Levinger, G., McClintock, E., Peplan, L. A., & Peterson, D. (1985). *The Psychology of Close Relationships.* New York: Plenum.

ARTICLE 18 ————————————

The previous classic article by Byrne demonstrated that attitude similarity caused increased interpersonal attraction. In the years since the publication of this article, many other studies have been conducted, investigating the relationship of attitude similarity and attraction. Some of these studies have focused on identifying the conditions under which attitude similarity does or does not lead to attraction. Other studies have addressed the underlying theoretical reasons for why this relationship occurs.

The next article by Smeaton, Byrne, and Murnen examines some of the conditions under which attitude similarity affects attraction; moreover, it further tests two alternate hypotheses for how the whole process operates. The article is a good example of what happens to research in social psychology with the passage of time. Early studies often identify a variable, such as attitude similarity, as being important. Subsequent research often involves exploration of the parameters surrounding the variable: Does it always happen? If not, under what conditions does it operate? What mechanism underlies the observed behavior (in other words, what is the theory as to why it happens)? By comparing this article with the previous one by Byrne (Article 17), you can understand the evolution of theory and research on a selected topic.

The Repulsion Hypothesis Revisited
Similarity Irrelevance or Dissimilarity Bias?

■ George Smeaton, Donn Byrne, and Sarah K. Murnen

Rosenbaum (1986b) proposed a reinterpretation of attraction research and theory in which similar attitudes constitute irrelevant stimuli; only dissimilar attitudes affect either attraction or performance in a learning task. He presented data seemingly consistent with these propositions, but Byrne, Clore, and Smeaton (1986) criticized the adequacy of his designs and suggested appropriate empirical tests of the competing hypotheses. This article reports two experiments in which the results are clearly inconsistent with the repulsion hypothesis. With number of dissimilar attitudes held constant, attraction toward a stranger increased as the number of similar attitudes increased. In a discrimination learning task, response acquisition occurred when correct responses were followed by similar attitude statements and incorrect responses by nonsense syllables, or when correct responses were followed by nonsense syllables and incorrect responses by dissimilar attitude statements. Despite the inadequacy of the repulsion hypothesis, Rosenbaum's analysis has raised several new and interesting possibilities for attraction research.

In a recent article, Rosenbaum (1986b) reported the results of three studies that were conducted to compare the validity of the familiar contention that attitude similarity exerts a positive effect on interpersonal attraction with his recent, contrasting repulsion hypothesis. Briefly, the repulsion hypothesis states that attitude similarity has no ef-

Reprinted from the *Journal of Personality and Social Psychology*, 1989, *56*, 54–59. Copyright 1989 by the American Psychological Association. Reprinted by permission.

fect on interpersonal attraction, although attitude dissimilarity elicits repulsion. Rosenbaum suggested that the effect or lack of effect of similar attitudes could be assessed by comparing a similar-attitude condition with a no-attitude control condition.

In Rosenbaum's (1986b) first investigation, subjects were presented with college yearbook photos that were paired with similar-attitude statements, dissimilar-attitude statements, or no attitudinal information. Consistent with the repulsion hypothesis, attraction responses as assessed by the Interpersonal Judgment Scale (IJS) obtained in the similar- and no-attitude conditions did not differ, but attraction in the dissimilar-attitude condition was significantly lower than in the other two conditions. Analogous findings were obtained in Rosenbaum's second study, in which participants in the Iowa Democratic presidential caucuses did not differ in attraction toward strangers described as Iowans and those described as Democrats; strangers described as Republicans were given significantly lower ratings.

The validity of Rosenbaum's (1986b) interpretation of these findings hinges on the assumption that no attitudinal information was either available or operative in the no-attitude control conditions. If this requirement is not met, there is no adequate control group with which to compare the independent effects of similarity and dissimilarity. Rosenbaum's information-free assumption appears to be unrealistic, however, as the college yearbook photographs revealed to the subjects the stimulus person's sex, race, and age group, plus considerable additional information such as physical attractiveness, clothing style, and so forth. As a result, it is quite likely that the subjects assumed that this fellow college student shared many of their beliefs. In the second study, after being surrounded by individuals of the same party affiliation for an extended period of time, the caucus participants were likely to assume that the "Iowan" was a fellow Democrat. Given such assumptions of similar attitudes and party affiliation, one would not expect information that is consistent with these beliefs to have as great an impact on

attraction as information that contradicts these beliefs. From this perspective, instead of examining the independent effects of attitude similarity, Rosenbaum was simply demonstrating that redundant information failed to influence attraction.

As support for the significance of assumed similarity in evaluating a stranger, Byrne, Clore, and Smeaton (1986) cited a study by Byrne and Wong (1962) that found that even highly prejudiced White subjects assumed a Black stranger would agree with them on 62% of the attitudes appearing on a survey. The same study found that both high and low prejudiced subjects assumed a White stranger responded as they did on 73% of the attitude items. When Byrne et al. entered this percentage of attitude similarity into the Byrne-Nelson (1965) formula, they were able to generate predicted values of the mean IJS scores that did not differ significantly from those obtained by Rosenbaum (1986b) in his first experiment. The general point is that a no-attitude control group is not in fact a no-attitude control group, because subjects spontaneously make attitudinal assumptions and attributions.

In summary, when assumed similarity is taken into consideration, the findings obtained from Rosenbaum's (1986b) first 2 experiments are as consistent with the Byrne-Nelson (1965) attraction formula as with the repulsion hypothesis. As a result, a conclusive empirical test of the validity of the two opposing formulations of attitudinal effects is still needed. When one considers the basic assumptions of the two theories, such a test becomes apparent. According to the repulsion hypothesis, similar attitudes have no effect on attraction, but according to the Byrne-Nelson formula, similarity and dissimilarity both affect attraction. Therefore, the repulsion hypothesis would predict that as long as one keeps the number of dissimilar attitudes constant, the presence of varying numbers of similar attitudes has no effect on the level of attraction (or repulsion). On the other hand, the Byrne-Nelson formula would predict that with dissimilarity held constant, the presence of increasing numbers of similar attitudes leads to higher levels of attraction. Such a test was carried out in Experiment 1 of this study.

EXPERIMENT 1

Method

Subjects and Design Subjects were 59 undergraduate men and women enrolled in introductory psychology at the University at Albany, State University of New York. All participated to fulfill a course requirement. We used a one-way design based on three levels of the total number of similar attitudes (0, 28, and 62).

Materials Attitudes were operationalized as responses to a 70-item attitude scale. Most of the items were taken from the 56-item attitude scale developed by Byrne (1971), and the remainder were created on the basis of the responses of a recent sample of undergraduates to a survey requesting them to list any issues they had recently discussed with friends. The resulting topics included draft registration for women, comedians who use profanity, welfare spending, and soft-core pornography. On the final scale, each item dealt with one issue, and each subject was requested to indicate his or her position on that issue by choosing one of six attitudinal statements. These consisted of varying levels of conviction toward one of two opposing positions on the issue (three statements favoring one position and three favoring the opposite). Interpersonal attraction was assessed with the two 7-point attraction items of the IJS, which yields a response measure ranging from 2 (*most negative*) to 14 (*most positive*) as described in Byrne (1971).

Procedure Two weeks prior to the experimental session, all subjects were administered the 70-item attitude survey during class. The subjects were then randomly assigned to one of three groups. A bogus completed survey was prepared for each subject. These surveys varied in length (number of attitudes) and in the number of similar versus dissimilar responses purportedly made by a stranger. For the subjects in Group 1, this survey contained 8 items with dissimilar responses and none with similar responses. Subjects in Group 2 each received a survey containing 8 dis-

similar responses and 28 similar responses. The Group 3 surveys contained 8 dissimilar responses and 62 similar responses. All dissimilar responses were the mirror image of the subjects' responses (e.g., 1 = 6, 2 = 5, etc.), and all similar responses were identical (no response discrepancy) to the subjects' responses. The specific items used to convey similarity or dissimilarity were varied randomly across subjects.

During the experimental session, we informed the subjects that the purpose of the experiment was to determine how much information was needed to form opinions about other people. For this reason, they were told, attitude surveys of varying lengths completed by individuals from other psychology classes would be distributed among the class members. We then instructed them to read the survey responses and to evaluate the person on the scales provided. When all of the subjects had completed this task, they were completely debriefed. Discussion with the subjects following the debriefing revealed that none expressed awareness of the relation between his or her own survey responses and those of the stranger. Also, no one indicated awareness of the fictitious nature of the strangers they were to evaluate or the actual purpose of the experiment.

Results

The mean attraction scores of each of the three groups are presented in Table 1. A one-way analysis of variance (ANOVA) revealed that the group means differed significantly, $F(2, 56) = 4.73$, $p < .05$, and as can be seen in the table, a Schefflé post hoc test indicated that only Groups 1 and 3 were significantly different ($p < .05$). Nevertheless, despite the absence of significant differences between Group 2 and the other two groups, a highly significant linear trend was obtained across the three groups, $F(1, 56) = 9.26$, $p < .01$.

Discussion

As predicted by the Byrne-Nelson (1965) formula, similarity independently affected interpersonal attraction with dissimilarity held constant.

TABLE 1 / Mean Attraction Responses in Each Attitudinal Group

Group and condition	Mean attraction
1 (8 dissimilar, 0 similar)	7.35_a
2 (8 dissimilar, 28 similar)	9.17_{ab}
3 (8 dissimilar, 62 similar)	10.22_b

Note: Means with different subscripts differ at $p < .05$.

In the strictest sense, the repulsion hypothesis is disconfirmed. It must be noted, however, that Rosenbaum (1986b) did not state that it was *impossible* for attitude similarity to exert a positive effect on attraction. To the contrary, he proposed that similarity could affect attraction if (a) the presence of a similar other in a group of very dissimilar individuals elicits a contrast effect or (b) the attitude is newly formed and important. Neither of these two requirements, however, was met in this study. Because the subjects were exposed to only one bogus attitude survey, contrast effects were precluded. With respect to the content of the attitudes, most items dealt with long-standing societal and personal issues for which, according to Rosenbaum, individuals have little need for consensual validation. Examples of these include marijuana legalization, belief in God, draft registration, busing to achieve racial integration, casual sex, and the value of strict parental discipline. Thus, even in its broadest sense, the repulsion hypothesis was not validated.

One could argue, however, that the results obtained in this experiment might be attributed to the failure of subjects in Group 3 to observe or recall all eight dissimilar responses. This possibility could be tested in future research, but note that the presence of a small number of dissimilar responses in the context of a large field of similar responses should yield a contrast effect analogous to the one proposed by Rosenbaum (1986b). Furthermore, with or without a contrast effect, if similar attitudes have no informational value, Rosenbaum should have predicted that subjects would ignore the similar responses and concentrate only on the dissimilar ones. If the presence of a large number of "irrelevant" similar attitudes somehow induces subjects to disregard the presence of relevant dissimilar attitudes or to become amnesic about them, a new and potentially interesting phenomenon must be operating. More parsimoniously, one might conclude that individuals express attraction toward the stranger on the basis of the proportion of similar attitudes, as predicted by the Byrne-Nelson (1965) formula.

IMPACT OF THE REPULSION HYPOTHESIS ON THE REINFORCEMENT-AFFECT MODEL

On the basis of the findings obtained in his first 2 experiments, Rosenbaum (1986b) concluded that, contrary to the reinforcement-affect model (Byrne & Clore, 1970), similar attitudes are not only irrelevant with respect to attraction but also have no reinforcement value. We have shown that Rosenbaum's attraction proposal is inconsistent with the data in Experiment 1, but what can be said about reinforcement effects? In support of his contention, Rosenbaum cited a study by Byrne, Young, and Griffitt (1966) that found that individuals could not learn to respond correctly to a two-choice discrimination task when correct responses were paired with similar attitude statements and incorrect statements were paired with neutral statements of fact. Subjects in the same experiment could, however, learn the discrimination when correct responses were paired with neutral statements of fact and incorrect responses were paired with dissimilar attitude statements.

Although Byrne et al. (1966) had considered the possibility that these findings indicate that similar attitudes are irrelevant, they hypothesized that the discrimination could not be learned in the similar-neutral condition because the statements of fact were also reinforcing. Supportive of this interpretation was the authors' subsequent finding that the discrimination was learned when statements of fact were contrasted with blank cards. That is, correct responses were followed by factual statements, whereas incorrect responses were followed by blank cards. The same performance changes were obtained with similar attitude statements versus blank cards. In a third condition, dissimilar attitude statements followed incorrect responses and blank cards followed correct responses; once again the discrimination was learned.

Rosenbaum (1986b) conducted a similar experiment, however, and found that subjects can learn the discrimination when nonsense syllables are paired with correct responses and blank cards are paired with incorrect responses. The implication, Rosenbaum argued, is that statements of fact and similar attitudes have no more incentive value than nonsense syllables.

Byrne et al. (1986) challenged this interpretation of Rosenbaum's (1986b) third experiment on the grounds that "subjects tend to assume that *something* is a more positive indicator than *nothing*" (p. 1169). If so, a convincing empirical test of the opposing hypotheses is required.

To compare the validity of the two proposals, Byrne et al. (1986) suggested that the learning experiment be replicated using similar attitudes to denote correct responses and nonsense syllables to denote incorrect responses. Given this stimulus pairing, the repulsion hypothesis would predict that although the stimuli are readily discriminable, subjects could not learn the discrimination because the two types of stimuli have equal incentive value. On the other hand, because the reinforcement-affect model assumes that similar attitudes do, in fact, possess more incentive value than nonsense syllables, it would predict that such a stimulus pairing would result in the learning of the discrimination.

This crucial test was carried out in our second experiment. In addition, we also used two other stimulus pairings. First, for comparison purposes we included a condition in which nonsense syllables were used to denote *correct* responses and dissimilar attitude statements were used to denote incorrect responses. Second, because Rosenbaum (1986a) suggested that the learning of the discrimination in the similar-nonsense syllable condition may indicate only that subjects prefer something meaningful over something nonsensical, we included a third condition in which a mixture of similar and dissimilar attitude statements were paired with correct responses and nonsense syllables were paired with incorrect responses.

EXPERIMENT 2

Method

Subjects and Design Subjects were 90 male and female undergraduates enrolled in introductory psychology at the University at Albany, State University of New York. All participated to obtain experimental credit.

We used a two-way mixed design based on three types of stimulus pairings (similar attitudes-nonsense syllables, nonsense syllables-dissimilar attitudes, and similar and dissimilar attitudes combined-nonsense syllables) and six blocks of 16 trials each. The number of possible correct responses per trial was 16.

Stimuli We prepared eight stimulus cards that contained a circle and a square printed side by side. One member of each pair of figures was black and the other white, one figure was always larger than the other, and either figure could appear on the left or the right. We also prepared cards that contained 1 of 80 nonsense syllables. The similar and dissimilar attitude statements were based on the subjects' responses to the same survey administered in Experiment 1.

Procedure Subjects were seated facing a large wooden screen with two openings through which the cards could be inserted. We instructed subjects that when a stimulus card appeared in one of the openings, they were to respond by saying either *circle* or *square*. They were then asked to read aloud whatever appeared in the second window. For half of the subjects, the correct response was the larger of the two figures; for the other half, the correct response was the smaller of the two figures. For one third of the subjects, correct responses were followed by the presentation of similar attitude statements and incorrect responses by the presentation of one of the nonsense syllables. For another third, the presentation of nonsense syllables followed correct responses and dissimilar attitude statements followed incorrect responses. For the remaining subjects, correct responses were followed by a mixture of similar and dissimilar attitudes (50% of each) and incorrect responses were followed by the presentation of nonsense syllables.

Results

We obtained significant main effects for conditions, $F(2, 100) = 4.61$, $p < .025$, and trials, $F(5, 500) = 25.99$, $p < .0001$. No significant interactions were obtained. The acquisition curves for the three groups are presented in Figure 1.

We found significant linear trends for the similar-nonsense, $F(1, 41) = 30.73$, $p < .0001$, nonsense-dissimilar, $F(1, 33) = 11.64$, $p < .01$, and mixed-nonsense, $F(1, 26) = 13.98$, $p <$

FIGURE 1 / Mean number of correct responses per trial in each block of 16 trials as a function of reinforcement condition. (Response acquisition was demonstrated in each condition with a higher level of correct responses in the similar attitudes-nonsense syllables condition than in either the nonsense syllables-dissimilar attitudes or mixed similar and dissimilar attitudes-nonsense syllables condition.)

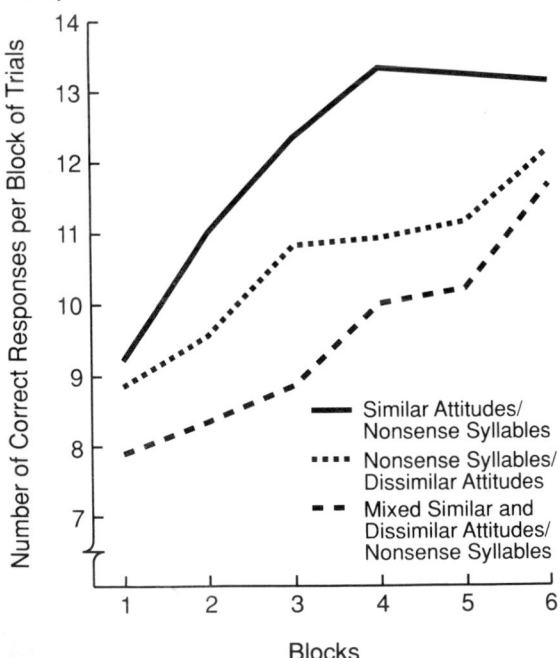

.001, conditions. Tukey post hoc tests of the group effects indicated that, in every block of trials, significantly more correct responses were made by individuals in the similar-nonsense condition than by those in the mixed similar/dissimilar-nonsense condition. We obtained no significant differences between the nonsense-dissimilar condition and either of the other two conditions. In this experiment, then, response acquisition was demonstrated in each condition, and performance was best in the condition predicted to have the *least* effect on the basis of the repulsion hypothesis.

Using the Statistical Package for the Social Sciences repeated measures multivariate analysis of variance program, we assigned polynomial coefficients to means in each of the three conditions. Again, we found an effect for condition, $F(2, 100) = 4.61$, $p < .02$, but there was not a significant Condition × Trend effect across trials in the multivariate test. None of the univariate tests was significant. In other words, a linear trend did not differentially describe data in the three conditions, and neither did any of the other trends. We found a significant linear trend across trials, $F(1, 100) = 61.39$, $p < .001$. Within each condition a linear trend also described the data, as would be expected, because there was no Condition × Trend interaction.

Discussion

Consistent with the reinforcement-affect model, similar attitude statements acted as reinforcers in a visual discrimination task. Although the significant linear trend obtained in the mixed-nonsense group suggests that Rosenbaum (1986a) was correct in predicting that subjects would prefer something meaningful over something nonsensical, the consistently higher response accuracy of the similar-nonsense group indicates that the reinforcement value of the similar statements cannot be attributed solely to their meaningfulness relative to nonsense syllables. Thus, Rosenbaum's (1986b) contention that similar attitudes have no reinforcement value is clearly untenable.

GENERAL DISCUSSION

Although nothing in science can be unequivocally proven or falsified, it is difficult to conceive of any way that the repulsion hypothesis could account for the findings obtained in the two experiments here. In addition to accounting for the present findings, the Byrne-Nelson (1965) formula can, as demonstrated by Byrne et al. (1986), readily account for Rosenbaum's (1986b) findings. Altogether, the original Byrne-Clore (1970) formulation postulating the effects of similar and dissimilar attitudes has greater explanatory power and predictive validity than the recently formulated repulsion hypothesis.

In view of the findings of this study, Rosenbaum's (1986b) findings can be more plausibly interpreted as indicating that interpersonal attraction often is more heavily influenced by dissimilar attitudes than by similar attitudes. This dissimilarity bias appears to be another example of the overall negativity bias that has frequently been reported in the impression formation literature (Amabile & Glazebrook, 1981; Bolster & Springbett, 1961; Fiske, 1980; Hamilton & Huffman, 1971). This negativity bias has been attributed to the fact that favorable information is relatively commonplace, whereas unfavorable information is quite unusual (Fiske, 1980). Thus, consistent with the Byrne et al. (1986) assumed-similarity interpretation of dissimilarity bias (i.e., positive qualities are assumed to be present), the confirmation of that assumption has little impact on impression formation. In contrast, negative information, like dissimilar attitudes, disconfirms one's initial assumptions and as a result strongly affects the impressions one forms. It is assumed in the reinforcement-affect model that attraction toward X is a function of the positive versus negative affect associated with X, as well as the relative intensity of such affect (K. Kelley, 1982; Singh, 1973). Thus, when impressions are formed, it is hypothesized that the negative affect elicited by unfavorable information is more intense than the positive affect elicited by favorable information.

The ubiquity of the dissimilarity-negativity bias suggests several directions for further investigation in the areas of interpersonal attraction and relationship formation. First, as suggested by Byrne et al. (1986), relationship formation may be a two-stage process. In the first stage, dissimilar attitudes and other negative information may be used to exclude undesirable others from the pool of potential friendship and dating partners. In the second stage, individuals turn to attitude similarity and other positive information to select candidates for interpersonal closeness from the small pool of individuals who possess relatively few negative qualities. If so, one would predict that comparable levels of dissimilarity should be present in one's closest friends and one's casual acquaintances, but a greater level of similarity should be present in the former group. Moreover, when evaluating strangers, individuals should pay closer attention to dissimilar attitudes than to similar attitudes, but when evaluating acquaintances the opposite should be true. The latter prediction is particularly noteworthy because, if valid, it would indicate that the negativity bias applies only to the evaluation of strangers. Among close friends, a positivity bias would be present. At the closest relationship level, the presence of such a bias is expressed in the belief that "love is blind." Here, the negative affect elicited by unfavorable information should be *less* intense than the positive affect elicited by favorable information. For the moment, obviously, these predictions remain highly speculative.

Second, the basis of the assumed-similarity phenomenon merits additional research. It is possible that because people tend to seek out and associate with similar others, their assumption of similarity on the part of strangers is simply a generalization or extrapolation of their everyday experiences with the people they know. It is also possible that assumed similarity is not based on actual experience and is instead an example of the false-consensus effect. Research examining false consensus has consistently shown that people tend to overestimate the degree to which other people share their opinions (Goethals, 1986; Marks, 1984; Mullen et al., 1985), possibly motivated by the need to validate one's own views (Byrne & Clore, 1967; Festinger, 1950; Heider, 1958; Newcomb, 1961). Assumed similarity may, in fact, be based both on experience with similar others and on distortions that serve self-validation needs.

To the extent that experience leads to assumed similarity, an interesting possibility is raised. One would predict that those who espouse extremely rare positions on certain issues would assume (correctly) that most others disagree with them on these specific topics. If so, this suggests a context in which the dissimilarity bias would be reversed: Attitude similarity on these special issues should carry more weight than dissimilarity. Clearly, such predictions go well beyond the data of the present experiments, but they suggest ways to elucidate the interrelations among assumed similarity, relative weighting of similar versus dissimilar views, and attraction.

Finally, it may be advisable to include expected reinforcement (assumed similarity, etc.) in the Byrne-Nelson (1965) formula. This inclusion would be consistent with Byrne and Kelley's (1983) Behavior Sequence, as well as with social exchange theory (Levinger, 1982; Lewis & Spanier, 1982; Nye, 1979) and interdependence theory (H. Kelley & Thibaut, 1978).

Although the findings of this study cast doubt on Rosenbaum's (1986a, 1986b) conclusions, his work suggests new lines of research on the effects of attitudes on attraction and has identified numerous questions that remain to be answered. Because the relative importance of similar and dissimilar attitudes has not previously been examined and because this comparison may be specific to the developmental stage of a relationship follow-up research may yield findings with interesting implications for impression formation, attraction, friendship, and love.

REFERENCES

Amabile, T. M., & Glazebrook, A. H. (1981). A negativity bias in interpersonal evaluation. *Journal of Experimental Social Psychology, 18,* 1–22.

Bolster, B. I., & Springbett, B. M. (1961). The reaction of interviewers to favorable and unfavorable information. *Journal of Applied Psychology, 45,* 97–103.

Byrne, D. (1971). *The attraction paradigm.* New York: Academic Press.

Byrne, D., & Clore, G. L. (1967). Effectance arousal and attraction. *Journal of Personality and Social Psychology, 6* (4, Whole No. 638).

Byrne, D., & Clore, G. L. (1970). A reinforcement model of evaluative responses. *Personality: An International Journal, 1,* 103–128.

Byrne, D., Clore, G. L., & Smeaton, G. (1986). The attraction hypothesis: Do similar attitudes affect anything? *Journal of Personality and Social Psychology, 51,* 1167–1170.

Byrne, D., & Kelley, K. (1983). *An introduction to personality.* Englewood Cliffs, NJ: Prentice-Hall.

Byrne, D., & Nelson, D. (1965). Attraction as a linear function of proportion of positive reinforcements. *Journal of Personality and Social Psychology, 1,* 659–663.

Byrne, D., & Wong, T. J. (1962). Racial prejudice, interpersonal attraction, and assumed dissimilarity of attitudes. *Journal of Abnormal and Social Psychology, 65,* 246–253.

Byrne, D., Young, R. K., & Griffitt, W. (1966). The reinforcement properties of attitude statements. *Journal of Experimental Research in Personality, 1,* 266–276.

Festinger, L. (1950). Informal social communication. *Psychological Review, 57,* 271–282.

Fiske, S. T. (1980). Attention and weight in person perception: The impact of negative and extreme behavior. *Journal of Personality and Social Psychology, 38,* 859–906.

Goethals, G. (1986). Fabricating and ignoring social reality: Self-serving estimates of consensus. In J. M. Olson, C. P. Herman, & M. P. Zanna (Eds.), *Relative deprivation and social comparison: The Ontario Symposium* (Vol. 4, pp. 135–157). Hillsdale, NJ: Erlbaum.

Hamilton, D. L., & Huffman, L. J. (1971). Generality of impression formation processes for evaluative and nonevaluative judgments. *Journal of Personality and Social Psychology, 20,* 200–207.

Heider, F. (1958). *The psychology of interpersonal relations.* New York: Wiley.

Kelley, H., & Thibaut, J. (1978). *Interpersonal relations: A theory of interdependence.* New York: Wiley.

Kelley, K. (1982). Predicting attraction to the novel

stimulus person: Affect and concern. *Journal of Research in Personality, 16,* 32–40.

Levinger, G. (1982). A social exchange view on the dissolution of pair relationships. In F. I. Nye (Ed.), *Family relationships, rewards and costs* (pp. 97–122). Beverly Hills, CA: Sage.

Lewis, R. A., & Spanier, G. B. (1982). Marital quality, marital stability, and social exchange. In F. I. Nye (Ed.), *Family relationships, rewards and costs* (pp. 49–65). Beverly Hills, CA: Sage.

Marks, G. (1984). Thinking one's abilities are unique and one's opinions are common. *Personality and Social Psychology Bulletin, 10,* 203–208.

Mullen, B., Atkins, J. L., Champion, D. S., Edwards, C., Hardy, D., Story, J. E., & Vanderklok, M. (1985). The false consensus effect: A meta-analysis of 115 hypothesis tests. *Journal of Experimental Social Psychology, 21,* 262–283.

Newcomb, T. M. (1961). *The acquaintance process.* New York: Holt, Rinehart & Winston.

Nye, F. I. (1979). Choice, exchange and the family. In W. R. Burr, R. Hill, F. I. Nye, & I. L. Reiss (Eds.), *Contemporary theories about the family* (Vol. 2, pp. 1–41). New York: Free Press.

Rosenbaum, M. E. (1986a). Comment on a proposed two-stage theory of relationship formation: First, repulsion; then attraction. *Journal of Personality and Social Psychology, 51,* 1171–1172.

Rosenbaum, M. E. (1986b). The repulsion hypothesis: On the nondevelopment of relationships. *Journal of Personality and Social Psychology, 51,* 1156–1166.

Singh, R. (1973). *Affective implications of the weighting coefficient in attraction research.* Unpublished doctoral dissertation, Purdue University, West Lafayette, IN.

CRITICAL THINKING QUESTIONS

1. The article concluded with some predictions that can be tested with further research. One such prediction was that we may pay more attention to *dissimilar* attitudes when evaluating strangers but more attention to *similar* attitudes when evaluating friends. Design a study to test these possibilities.

2. The first study described in the article used laboratory, paper-and-pencil tests. How could you test the same concepts using real people instead of hypothetical stimulus situations? What about a field (nonlaboratory) study?

3. Do we always tend to dislike and reject people with attitudes dissimilar to our own? Under what conditions do you think we might actually like people we know are dissimilar to us?

Chapter Seven

RELATIONSHIP ISSUES

OF ALL OF the interactions that occur between human beings, perhaps none is more capable of producing such intense feelings as love. If we look at how often love is portrayed in the popular media, we get the definite impression that it is a major concern, almost a preoccupation, of modern Americans. However, if we look at the literature in social psychology, we might get a very different impression. Until recently, the topic of love was largely ignored in the research literature.

Some of the reluctance to study this common human experience may be due to the difficulty of the subject matter. What is love? How do you measure it? However, there also may have been some bias in not considering love to be an appropriate research topic. Whatever the reason, it was not until the publication of Rubin's classic work (Article 20) that researchers began to give serious attention to this emotion and experience.

Love is usually thought of in a positive way, as something good that most people enjoy experiencing. However, love sometimes has a darker side. Jealousy very often accompanies feelings of love. Is jealousy the natural byproduct of love? Why are some people more jealous than others? What types of situations are most likely to provoke jealousy? Article 19, "Getting at the Heart of Jealous Love," gives a good summary of a number of articles that try to explain and understand love and jealousy.

In looking at intimate relationships, it is necessary to focus not only on experiences such as love and jealousy but also on why relationships fail. Given the high divorce rate in the United States, understanding what factors contribute to divorce is of obvious importance. Article 21, "Divorce, Disputation, and Discussion," examines communication style, one factor that may affect marital success, and how such stylistic differences between separated spouses influences adjustment to divorce. The implications of the study are not only for counselors working with divorced clients but also for people who may be undergoing divorce themselves.

ARTICLE 19 _____

When you are involved in a romantic relationship with another person, is it natural to feel jealousy when you fear the loss of his or her attention or affection to someone else? Jealousy is an almost universal emotion, something most people experience at different points in their lives. Is jealousy an integral part of human nature? Or is it the sign of an insecure individual?

Research on intimate relationships such as love has only recently been initiated. Research on the nature of jealousy is even more recent. The factors that predict jealousy, show how it affects behavior, and show how people react to it have obvious practical implications for the success of intimate relationships; thus, these factors have some bearing on when and why such relationships may come to an end.

In the following article, Adams summarizes several studies on jealousy drawn from psychology, sociology, and anthropology. As Adams points out, common findings emerge from the studies about this human experience. However, the topic is complex, one about which simple statements and generalizations are hard to make.

Getting at the Heart of Jealous Love

■ Virginia Adams

Their names are Way, Azo, Laf, Lil, Tip Tye, Geo Logical, Brother Jud, and Even Eve. Calling themselves a Best Friend Identity Cluster (B-FIC), or the Purple Submarine, the five women and three men live together in two old Victorian houses in the Haight-Ashbury section of San Francisco. Nonmonogamous in their relationships, they pair off nightly according to a fixed sleeping schedule they describe as "nonpreferential" and "rotational." Members of the Purple Submarine—all heterosexual—are sexually faithful to one another, and they believe that through their experiment in group living, they have eliminated, or at least transcended, the age-old problem of sexual jealousy.

If so, their achievement is remarkable, for sexual jealousy was the undoing of numerous failed Utopias in the past and is assumed by many to be an all-but-universal emotion. "It is a tragic characteristic of all people, to be unable to share," the Viennese psychoanalyst Wilhelm Stekel once

wrote. Or, as Jeff B. Bryson, a social psychologist at San Diego State University in California, says, "Jealousy is at least as common as chicken pox."

The Purple Submarine is one of two such groups that together form Kerista Village in San Francisco. An organization, not a place, Kerista Village is held together by the ideal of "polyfidelity," a word the Keristans coined to express their goal of loyalty to the group rather than to any one person [see box at the end of this article]. Behavioral science has begun to take an interest in the nine-year-old Keristan venture, but knowledge about sexual jealousy is as yet too limited to explain how the crew of the Purple Submarine has routed jealousy—if, indeed, they have really done so.

Theories about jealousy abound. Most were derived from on-the-spot observations by anthropologists, armchair speculation by sociologists, or conclusions reached by psychoanalysts treating emotionally disturbed patients. "Unfortunately,"

Reprinted from *Psychology Today*, 1980 (May), *14*, 38–50. Reprinted with permission from *Psychology Today Magazine.* Copyright © 1980 (PT Partners, L.P.).

a University of Maryland social psychologist named Gregory L. White wrote not long ago, "this theoretical fire has not produced much research heat." In fact, Bryson told the American Psychological Association a couple of years ago, "Some future historian, reviewing our scientific literature, would feel justified in presuming that jealousy was either nonexistent in our society or, at most, experienced by an isolated subset of pathological individuals."

Finally, in the late 1970s, Bryson, White, Robert G. Bringle of Indiana-Purdue University at Indianapolis, and a few other social psychologists brought the rigor of the laboratory to bear on the study of sexual, or romantic, jealousy. They began by trying to define it, and soon found that there were almost as many definitions of jealousy as there were writers about it. It has been described, somewhat pretentiously, as "a cry of pain," "the fear of annihilation," and "the shadow of love." Almost certainly, it is not one emotion but many; definitions mention anger and anxiety; hatred and humiliation; shame, sorrow, and suspicion. Rather like love, Bryson suggests, jealousy is whatever a person chooses to label jealousy.

For research purposes, that is not very useful. Today, most social psychologists accept as basic the distinction psychoanalysts and sociologists have long made between envy, felt when a person covets what someone else has but claims no right to it, and jealousy, distinguished by fear of losing to someone else what rightfully belongs to the jealous person. Most psychologists also believe that jealousy entails a threat to self-esteem as well as to a valued relationship. It is agreed, too, that the threat may be actual, potential, or entirely imaginary.

What the pioneers of jealousy research wanted to know was what kinds of people are most vulnerable to sexual jealousy; what circumstances are most likely to provoke it; what jealousy actually feels like; and what specific behavior stems from it. Several studies confirm the link between romantic jealousy and self-esteem. Others reveal marked sex differences. Women, for instance, are more likely than men are to try to make their partners jealous. And when an interloper threatens an intimate relationship, women generally react by trying to save the relationship, while men more often concentrate on saving face.

WHO GETS JEALOUS? A NEW STUDY

The newest findings about sexual jealousy are just now being reported by the social psychologists Elliot Aronson of the University of California at Santa Cruz and Ayala Pines of the University of California at Berkeley. Their work relies chiefly on a "Sexual Jealousy Inventory," a compilation of more than 200 questions chosen by the researchers to elicit data on almost every conceivable aspect of jealousy and its presumed or possible antecedents and effects. The inventory includes numerous yes-or-no queries, such as, "Would you experience jealousy if you are at a party and don't know where your mate is?" Most questions, however, are answered by circling the number, on a scale of 1 to 7, that most nearly corresponds to the subject's attitude or experience.

So far, about 100 men and women ranging in age from their late 20s to their early 50s have filled out the inventory. Many were students; others were participants in a two-day discussion of romantic jealousy conducted by the researchers last year.

Statistical analysis of one sample of 53 subjects has yielded "correlations" between jealousy and certain personal characteristics, circumstances, and events. A correlation between two factors means that they occur together frequently; it does not prove that one causes the other. Aronson and Pines say the correlations are "highly significant," meaning they are probably not due to chance.

To begin with, the study supports the impression of other investigators (Bringle among them) that jealousy goes with feelings of insecurity and an unflattering self-image. The study also shows that the less education people have, the more often they feel jealous, conceivably because educational deficiencies may lower self-esteem.

If the Aronson and Pines findings are to be believed, people who feel jealous because of a mate's real or imagined infidelity may themselves be faithless. Subjects who admitted that they had betrayed their current sexual partner were very likely not only to feel insecure about their relationship but also to suffer often from jealousy. A possible explanation is that a person's own tendency to stray may lead to a suspicion that the partner is capable of yielding to similar tendencies.

Jealous people seem to be unhappy people. The men and women who reported the greatest overall dissatisfaction with their lives were those who felt jealous most often. People who said they were not happy with their partners were nevertheless very often jealous. That correlation struck Aronson and Pines as ironic, because a person in an unhappy relationship might be expected to feel indifferent toward a mate's dalliance. On the other hand, the causal sequence—if there is *any* causal connection between the two factors—may go in the other direction: perhaps jealousy makes a relationship unhappy, not the reverse.

Happy or not, jealous people apparently feel bound to their mates, no matter what alternatives might be open to them. According to Aronson and Pines, jealousy was most frequently experienced by the men and women who gave the most emphatic no's when asked, "If you found another person you could be intimate with, would you leave your present sexual partner?" A response of 1 stood for "definitely not," while 4 was labeled "perhaps," and 7 denoted "definitely." The ratings chosen by the most jealous subjects clustered at the low end of the scale.

Staying in a relationship a long time was strongly linked to an absence of jealous feelings. Subjects who rated themselves as very jealous people had been with their present partner an average of 58 months, while those who did not think of themselves as jealous had been with the same mate for 110 months. Like Bringle, Aronson and Pines found that a partner's own chronological age was important; younger people reported jealousy more often than did older ones.

Notably, it doesn't take much to stir up jealousy in a jealous person. The men and women who reported feeling jealous most often were those who replied yes to the question, "Would you experience jealousy when you call your mate

and the phone is busy?" The often-jealous were also likely to admit that they felt pangs of jealousy when their telephone rang and the person on the other end either hung up without a word or else said, "Sorry, wrong number."

Yet another finding that may give jealous people pause: It is very difficult to conceal jealousy. Men and women who conceded that they were often jealous also reported that they knew their friends considered them so.

Gregory White has been studying jealousy since 1976, longer than Aronson and Pines. He is a highly prolific researcher who has written some half-dozen papers based on different aspects of one of the widest-ranging studies of jealousy ever made.

White devised a 35-page "Relationships Questionnaire" that asks subjects to rate themselves on 9-point scales measuring jealousy and a host of personality traits, attitudes, and actions that could be correlated with it. Jealousy itself was assessed by posing six queries: "How jealous do you get of your partner's relationship with members of the opposite sex?" "In general, how jealous a person do you think you are?" "Have you ever seriously thought about breaking up with your partner because of his/her attraction to someone else of the opposite sex?" "My relationship with my partner has made me (much more to much less) jealous than I usually am." "How often do you get jealous of your partner's relationship with members of the opposite sex?" "How much is your jealousy of your partner a problem in your relationship?"

White recruited 150 couples for what he described as a study of "heterosexual romantic relationships" through newspaper advertisements, posters, and announcements to college classes. Most of the subjects—84 percent, to be exact— were white, their average age was just under 22, and 91 percent were students at the University of California in Los Angeles. Of the total, 21 percent considered themselves casual daters; at least one partner in a relationship went out with other people. Of the rest, 50 percent rated themselves serious daters who did not see others; 13 percent were living together; and 16 percent were either engaged or married. The unmarried couples had been together an average of nearly a year.

Since the Aronson-Pines and the White questionnaires are not identical, conclusions drawn from them are not precisely comparable. Nevertheless, White's findings support the Aronson-Pines impression that jealousy goes along with both a sense of dependence on a relationship and with a person's feeling that he or she is in some way lacking.

On one point, White's results did seem to contradict those of the California researchers. He found that chronic low self-esteem *as such* correlated with jealousy only for men, not for women. (White measured self-esteem with self-ratings on items such as, "I take a positive attitude toward myself" and "I feel useless.")

But on items measuring other aspects of self-esteem, White found a correlation with jealousy for both sexes. People who reported that their self-esteem depended heavily on what their partners thought of them usually scored high on the jealousy items. Thus the most jealous people ranked themselves toward the upper end of the scale on items such as, "I would feel terrible about myself if my partner didn't respect me." Not-so-jealous people responded with a high rating on items like this one: "I find that I am pretty happy with myself regardless of what my partner thinks of me."

In a related finding, White noted that jealous people were apt to consider themselves inadequate as mates, as measured by responses to such questions as, "Would you agree that you are the type of person your partner is looking for?" The most jealous men and women rated themselves more deeply involved in their relationship than their partners were. Going beyond the usual techniques for figuring out correlations, White analyzed "perceived inadequacy" and "relative involvement" and concluded that these two characteristics not only occur in jealous people but actually *cause* jealousy. His explanation is that both qualities make people consider their relationship fragile, in part because a person who thinks himself or herself inadequate is acutely aware of "a

greater potential for attraction between partner and a rival who may or may not yet exist."

MEN VERSUS WOMEN: WHO'S MORE JEALOUS?

On the always controversial question of sex differences, Aronson and Pines have much to contribute. Nobody will be surprised to learn that results are inconclusive when it comes to the question of which sex has the greater propensity to jealousy—that is, which has more of a personality trait that Bringle calls "dispositional jealousy." But men and women *feel* differently when they are jealous, and on some occasions they *act* differently.

Popular wisdom holds that women are more jealous than men, and in March, newspaper reporters speculated that the woman suspected of shooting diet doctor Herman Tarnower had acted out of jealousy. But a 1976 survey of 143 murders committed in jealous rage found only 20 of the perpetrators to be women. Of course, jealous rage, especially when it ends in murder, is not typical of what most people experience, and researchers have generally discovered no significant sex differences in disposition to jealousy.

Aronson and Pines asked 54 adults, "Who are more jealous—men or women?" and instructed their subjects to pick a number from 1 ("men much more jealous") to 7 ("women much more jealous"), with 4 standing for "equally jealous." The average verdict was 4.4. Thus the consensus was that women are more jealous. But when the researchers assessed the self-reports of actual jealousy (not opinions about other people's jealousy) in the men and women who completed their questionnaire, they found no significant sex differences.

Bringle did find such differences, but only in one group of subjects. He constructed a "Self-Report Jealousy Scale" to appraise jealousy in social, family, and work situations. The scale includes just 20 items, each describing a situation that would make some people jealous. An example or two shows what it is like: "You are stood up and then learn that your date was out with another person," and "Your spouse or steady looks at another." The idea is for subjects to rate their emotional reaction to such a situation on a 9-point scale, from "not very jealous" at one end to "very jealous" at the other. Bringle has administered his test to several groups of people and has generally found that the sexes rack up similar scores. On one occasion, however, when his subjects were 131 married couples between the ages of 20 and 40, women did report more intense jealous reactions. Bringle himself suggests that the finding could be "just an accident of the sample."

Turning to the way it feels to be jealous and to the behavior evoked by jealousy, Aronson and Pines found several statistically significant sex differences. Women scored higher than men when asked how jealous they would feel in the face of a mate's infidelity. (It could be argued that these higher scores show women to be the jealous sex, but Aronson does not interpret them that way, believing that the scores measure particular experiences of jealousy rather than jealousy as a personality trait.) One question took this form: "Would you experience jealousy if you discovered that your mate was having a love affair, but your mate is very discreet, no one else knows about it, and your mate doesn't know that you know?" With 7 indicating extreme jealousy on the scale, women averaged 6.1, and men, 5.

The result was a bit different when subjects were asked if they would feel jealous about an affair when "everybody but you has known about it for a long time." In that case, the average woman's score was 6.4, in contrast to 5.5 for men.

Other findings suggest that jealousy causes women greater suffering than it does men. All subjects were asked to remember "the situation which produced your most extreme experience of jealousy," and to rate the degree to which they had had each of 20 possible physical reactions, such as nausea or headaches. For women, the average score was 2.1, compared with 1.5 for men. On 30 possible emotional reactions, such as humiliation and confusion, the women rated themselves at 2.5, as against 2 for men.

Scores for both sexes were higher when the

questions were theoretical rather than personal—that is, when subjects were asked, in effect, "What does jealousy do to people in general?" rather than, "What does it do to you?" Women then rated physical distress at 6.2 and emotional suffering at 6.3. For men, the comparable figures were 4.8 and 5.4.

Given the intensity of the women's physical and psychological response to betrayal, it is surprising that they did not often translate their response into action. Here the important question was, "Have any of your intimate relationships ended because of your jealousy?" A rating of 1 on the answer scale meant never, while 7 indicated that all relationships had ended for that reason. Women's average response was 1.3; men's was 2.2. Men, in short, were more likely to get out of an alliance that made them jealous.

WHEN AN OLD FLAME SHOWS UP

That finding seems consistent with studies by Jeff Bryson and his colleagues at San Diego State. Bryson's group have found that men try to repair their damaged self-esteem, while women, perhaps swallowing their pride, concentrate on repairing the damaged relationship.

One thing the Bryson group wondered about was whether or not an interloper's attractiveness has any bearing on the way the injured partner reacts. The key research tool was a set of four specially made videotapes depicting a hackneyed but undeniably jealousy-inducing situation: an old rival breaks in on a current relationship.

This is the scenario the research team dreamed up, as outlined by Bryson: "The scene opened with a scan of a party, stopping on a couple sitting on a couch. After a 45-second segment during which the couple cuddled, kissed, and toasted each other, one member of the couple got up and left the room, apparently to refill the wine glasses. Approximately 15 seconds after this, the interloper, the old boyfriend or girlfriend of the partner remaining on the couch, entered the picture. The partner jumped up, hugged the interloper briefly, and the two of them sat down on the couch. During the next 60 seconds, they performed progressively more intimate actions, including touching each other and exchanging one brief kiss. Shortly after the kiss, the absent partner returned, looking down at the two people on the couch." On that dramatic high note, the tape ended.

The scene came in one of four versions. In two tapes, the female partner left for more wine, and the interloper was female (attractive in one tape and unattractive in the other). In the second pair of tapes, the male partner left the room and returned to confront the woman and her "old boyfriend," who was in one case appealing, in the other, decidedly otherwise.

Forty female subjects were randomly assigned to watch either the attractive or the unattractive "old girlfriend" do her interloping best. An equal number of male subjects viewed one or the other of the "old boyfriend" films. After the screening, the subjects rated the likelihood that each of 36 described feelings or actions would correspond to their own behavior.

Analysis of the ratings showed that men were much more likely than women to say they would begin going out with others or become "more sexually aggressive with others." Women were more apt to say they would put on a show of indifference, or try to make themselves more attractive to their partners. The sex differences were particularly marked when the old flame was attractive. "If we assume that an attractive interloper is seen as more threatening to the relationship," the researchers said, "then males become more likely to bolster their egos by pursuing alternative relationships. Females, on the other hand, become less likely to engage in behaviors that might accent the threat to the existing relationship." What may account for the sex difference is the fact that actively seeking new relationships is still socially more acceptable for men than it is for women.

The Bryson males, so ready to abandon a jealousy-provoking relationship, may be compared with men Kinsey studied years ago. Of Kinsey's divorced male subjects, 51 percent gave the wife's infidelity as a major reason for the breakup, in contrast to 27 percent of his divorced female

subjects. The Bryson females, who hoped to patch things up, are like the Aronson-Pines women, of whom so few had ever ended a relationship because they were jealous. Bryson's women also recall Theodor Reik's idea of the female sex. Women, the noted psychoanalyst said, characteristically fight to win back a lost lover instead of giving up the relationship as a lost cause.

INADEQUACY IN ROMANCE

Gregory White has also found some interesting sex differences in jealousy-related behavior. In one phase of his many-faceted study, he gave a new twist to research on the low self-esteem/jealousy connection. His interest was in a particular kind of diminished self-esteem, a person's belief that he or she is inadequate as a romantic partner. What White had in mind was a chicken-and-egg sort of question: which comes first, the experience of jealousy or the self-perception of inadequacy? As it turns out, there are two right answers, one for men and one for women.

White's findings are based on his original questionnaire and on a retest of as many of his original subjects as possible (126, as it turned out) after a nine-month lag to be sure that the connection between jealousy and inadequacy was really there and not just an artifact of a single test situation.

This time the relevant parts of the questionnaire were the six queries about feelings of jealousy, along with several questions probing the subjects' ideas about themselves as romantic partners. On that theme, a typical question read, "Have there ever been times when you felt no matter how hard you tried, you couldn't make your partner happy?"

On the basis of complicated statistical procedures, White concluded that in the women, feelings of inadequacy appeared first and lead to jealousy, while in men, the reverse was true. *After* the men felt they had reason to be jealous, they then began to worry that something was wrong with them.

To explain this sex difference, White cited previous research showing that women, perhaps because of the way they are brought up, are more likely than men to "monitor" their relationships—that is, to pay attention to the details of them and to be conscious of the impact of their personalities on their partners. Long before a rival appears, women may look for things in themselves that might disappoint their partners. Men, presumably preoccupied with the outside world, may pay little attention to a relationship, or to qualities in themselves that might disturb it, until things have actually gone wrong.

TESTING THE RELATIONSHIP

In another phase of his project, White studied a phenomenon that Jessie Bernard, a sociologist, had described in 1971: the deliberate provocation of jealousy. "The husband," Bernard wrote, "pretends to be interested in other women in public—makes passes at every pretty girl, leers at other women, pretends excitement at the touch of the hostess—all in an ostentatious manner that calls attention to him, but only when the wife is there to observe and suffer. Or the wife flirts with other men in an equally open and provocative way. The idea is to publicly humiliate the spouse."

Women, White learned, behave that way more often than men do. He also discovered that the motives of the jealousy-inducers, and the techniques they employed, were more various than Bernard had suggested.

Again, White's data came from his Relationships Questionnaire. Now the significant questions were these: "Have you ever tried to get your partner jealous over your relationship with someone else on purpose? If yes, please outline your reasons. If yes, how did you try to make your partner jealous?" And then: "Who would you say is more involved in your relationship, you or your partner? Rate yourself as much more, more, equally, less, or much less involved."

Analysis of the responses revealed five jealousy-inducing techniques. The commonest, reported by more than half the 300 subjects, was to discuss or exaggerate the appeal of some third person. The next most popular method was flirting (cited by 28 percent), dating others (24 percent), fabri-

cating another attachment (14 percent), and talking about a previous partner (11 percent).

Reasons given broke down into five groups. When subjects said things like, "I wanted him to spend more time with me," White labeled their motive *Increase Rewards.* The other categories were *Bolster Self-Esteem* ("I was feeling low and needed to remind him that I'm special to him"); *Test Relationship* ("To see if he still cared"); *Revenge* ("Out of anger because he was going out"); and *Punishment* ("We were having a fight").

More than 38 percent of White's female subjects were motivated by the desire for a reward, compared with 15 percent of the men. In the group as a whole, the attempt to get a reward of some sort motivated 30 percent of the subjects. The commonest motive, though, was to test the relationship; it appeared in almost 40 percent of all cases.

Degree of involvement in the relationship did not seem to have anything to do with whether or not men tried to provoke jealousy, but it was an important factor among the women. Female subjects who considered themselves more involved than their partners were almost twice as likely to report inducement as were the rest of the women. Overall, 73 subjects said they had deliberately induced jealousy. Of these, 31 percent were women; only 17 percent were men.

Why that great dissimilarity? White thinks it reflects not any immutable personality difference between men and women, but the imbalance in power that seems to mark the entire relationship of the sexes, not just romantic or sexual aspects. For women, especially for those who feel more involved than their mates, provoking jealousy may be a way of trying to gain control and of redressing the balance of power. It is as if a woman delivered an ultimatum: "You'd better care as much as I do, or I'll leave you."

HIGH-JEALOUSY CULTURES

As interesting as sex differences in jealousy are cross-cultural variations. Ralph B. Hupka, a social psychologist at California State University in Long Beach, recently surveyed two centuries of anthropological reports and found great differences both in the prevalence of jealousy and in the way it was expressed. So consistent were the quantitative distinctions that Hupka found he could characterize particular societies as either "low-jealousy cultures," like the Todas of Southern India, or "high-jealousy cultures," like the Apache Indians of North America.

According to Hupka, jealousy was rare among the Todas because their culture did not encourage possessiveness toward either things or people, placed few restrictions on sexual gratification, and did not make marriage or progeny a condition for social recognition. In short, there was not much to be jealous about. It was otherwise with the Apache. "Sexual pleasure was something to be earned after a long period of deprivation and to be jealously guarded thereafter against intruders," Hupka said. To the Apache man, an "unsullied" wife, and children he knew to be his, were so important for status reasons that when he planned to be away from home he had a close relative keep secret watch over his wife and report on her behavior when he returned.

Remarking that "there is no one universal way of being jealous," Hupka assembled some illustrations. A jealous Samoan woman used to bite her rival in the nose, while a Zuñi wife in New Mexico got back at her straying husband by refusing to wash his clothes. Among the Plateau tribes of Northern Rhodesia, the whole community avenged a jealous husband by impaling his wife and her lover on stakes. A Hidatsa Indian in North America had a right to kill his faithless wife if he felt like it, but the most admired course he could take was to present the wife formally to her new lover. If a husband wanted to show how glad he was to be rid of her, he might throw in a horse or other valuable gift.

As for the origins of jealousy, Hupka says it "is not inborn; it is intrinsic to the process of socialization; i.e., learning what is valued in our society and protecting it against a rival." Kinsey and other biologically oriented scientists disagree, pointing to evidence of jealousy in mammals as proof that the emotion is inherited. Freud was convinced that adult jealousy stems from the Oedipal pe-

riod; developmental psychologists look for the beginnings of jealousy in rivalry between brothers and sisters; sociologists often blame monogamy. That institution, the sociologist Kingsley Davis has suggested, in what was surely one of the understatements of all time, perhaps "causes adultery to be resented and therefore creates jealousy."

The reasons for so much uncertainty about the roots and characteristics of jealousy lie partly in the complexity of the emotion itself—and partly in research difficulties. Aronson and Pines point out that "experimental social psychologists are undoubtedly discouraged by the fact that 'real' jealousy is almost impossible to observe systematically," yet to induce it in the laboratory is usually considered unethical. (However, Aronson and Pines are planning a "research-encounter" project in which couples troubled by jealousy will try to learn something about the emotion by provoking it in their partners during a workshop. The researchers hope to learn something, too, and they believe they can protect participants by warning them of risks in advance and by gaining fully informed consent.)

The safest research approach, Aronson and Pines observe, "is to ask a wide range of people about their experiences of jealousy in much the same way that Kinsey asked people about their sexual experiences." The trouble with that is the unreliability of "self-report." With jealousy often labeled immature and unattractive, some subjects may just plain lie about it. Some may deny it honestly, in the sincere belief that they are really free of it—but they may be the most jealous people of all. And what about the people who readily tell a researcher that, yes, they often feel jealous? Those people, some scientists suggest, may really be far less jealous than men and women who cannot bring themselves to such an admission.

At least until the experimenters find some way around these difficulties, the writings of the psychoanalysts, who were among the first of the behavioral scientists to pay attention to jealousy, are still among the best sources of information about the origins and characteristics of jealousy.

Beginning with Freud, analysts have stressed

that the difference between normal and pathological jealousy is one of degree, and that even normal jealousy is not entirely rational — an observation about the basic nature of jealousy that few contemporary investigators would deny. No less instructive is the assertion of Theodore Isaac Rubin, a neo-Freudian psychoanalyst in New York, that "Jealousy is born of feeling that we have so little to give compared to someone else." An equally provocative hint that the jealous person might do well to look into his or her own psychic state is Otto Fenichel's suggestion that the basis of jealousy is often "an unconscious tendency toward infidelity which is projected onto the partner." The jealous person, that is, may concentrate on a partner's real or imagined faithlessness in order not to worry about his or her own.

As for descriptions of jealousy, some of the best are to be found in the psychoanalytic literature. Take this sketch of the "eye of jealousy" by psychoanalyst William Evans: "It is furtive because it is frightened. It is covert rather than overt. From its hiding place, it sees innumerable facts but never gets its facts right. It can, at its most flagrant, build up a case on insufficient evidence, so that 'trifles light as air become confirmations strong as proofs of holy writ.' More generally, the jealous man cuts a ridiculous figure. . . . He observes minutely and misses the mark monumentally."

Still, the psychoanalysts leave unanswered the question of whether jealousy can be abolished, as the inhabitants of Kerista Village believe it can. In American society as a whole, Jessie Bernard maintains, "Marital jealousy is declining as our conception of the nature of the marital bond itself is changing. . . . If monogamic marriage is changing, there may be less and less need for jealousy to buttress it, and less socialization of human beings to experience jealousy."

Aronson and Pines are not optimistic about the prospects for doing away with jealousy in the United States. "America is a paired, family-oriented society," they say. "It is a society that emphasizes ownership and private property. It is characterized by competition and by a strong desire to have a perfect relationship. All these aspects of contemporary American society tend to aggravate the feeling and expression of jealousy."

The inevitability of jealousy — to Aronson and Pines, it *is* inevitable — goes deeper than that, to the very nature of love and intimacy. "It may be," the two California researchers say, "that precisely what we most value about certain relationships is what also makes them essentially nonreplicable and nonshareable, and hence leaves a place for jealousy."

Polyfidelity: The Kerista Village Ideal

Don't bother looking up "polyfidelity" in the dictionary; it's not there. Ask Even Eve, one of the founders of Kerista Village, an egalitarian, Utopian community in San Francisco.

Even Eve is a native of Vermont, a writer, an artist, and the editor of two Kerista periodicals, *Utopian Eyes,* a magazine, and *Storefront Classroom,* a newspaper. She will explain that the coined word polyfidelity "describes a group of best friends, highly compatible, who live together as a family unit, with sexual intimacy occurring equally between all members of the opposite sex, no sexual involvement outside the group, an intention of lifetime involvement, and the intention to raise children together with multiple parenting."

Geo Logical, a former psychiatric nurse from Georgia, outlines the most sensational-sounding feature of Keristan life, the "balanced rotational sleeping pattern." All members of B-FICs, the Best Friend Identity Clusters that make up Kerista Village, follow such a cycle.

"It's simply a *sleeping* pattern, *not* a sex

schedule," Geo says. "Having sexual intercourse or not having it is a private decision made by two individuals who are spending their night's horizontal time together. Such a decision is based on many variable factors—level of tiredness, wellness or illness, whether or not people have decided they will or will not have sexual intercourse during a woman's menstrual period."

"Polyfidelity: Beyond Jealousy and Possessiveness," reads the headline for an article in *Utopian Eyes*. The piece conveys the belief of the Keristans that their experiment in group living is successful.

"When we announce to people that we have lived for years without jealousy or possessiveness, most people think we must surely be exaggerating," Eve told *Psychology Today*. "Yet it is true. This is not to say we don't deal with problems of a psychological or interpersonal nature from time to time. . . . We do, but jealousy has not been one of them."

There are no twosomes in Kerista Village. "We feel it is humanly possible to have many primary relationships running simultaneously," Eve says. "To me, the erotic fantasy of sleeping with a variety of delightful men—all of whom I love—and living with a number of other marvelous female partners who are sleeping with the same people is extremely exciting. It is also very 'homey'; it is a family unit involving trust, fidelity, raising children." (So far, Kerista Village has one child, Eve's, with the biological father's identity presumably uncertain and all members of Eve's B-FIC acting as psychological parents. Another child was due this spring.)

Trying to make outsiders understand their multiple, "nonpreferential, rotational" relationships, Keristans like to draw analogies and to ask Socratic questions: "What if someone said to you that out of all the fruits that exist—bananas, pears, oranges, apples, strawberries, papaya, mangoes—you must choose *one* to eat to the exclusion of all others for the rest of your life. Which *one* would you choose?" And then: "You don't believe that

nature's rotational fruit-production cycle interferes with your spontaneity?"

The Keristans range in age from 20 to 57, with most about 30. About half finished college, but few (apart from the nurse, an elementary school teacher, and an auditor) have ever pursued conventional careers.

The villagers have won few converts. Their maximum strength was 20, and now there are only 15 of them. Two have been with the organization since it was formed nine years ago; others have belonged for periods of six months to seven years.

What the Keristans call their "social laboratory" or "live-in test-tube" brings to mind nonmonogamous Utopias of the past that foundered after a few months or a few years: Oneida in the 19th century, which lasted for some 30 years, and some of the hippie communes of the 1960s. Why should Kerista Village succeed where they failed?

The new collectivists say the important factors are their devotion to Utopian ideals, their sharing of living space, their efforts to break with the past, and, above all, their avoidance of romantic love.

Their ideals of sharing and equality reach beyond the sexual, and Keristans try to express them in a multiplicity of activities. They work at regular jobs or in Village-owned enterprises such as publishing, carpentry, gardening, home services, and repairs. They write and produce plays, make speeches, conduct seminars. They swim and prepare gourmet meals for themselves. In addition, Geo writes: "We keep our dishes washed and our laundry done." What they consider to be their uniqueness derives partly from the fact that, as the Kerista Village Handbook asserts, "judgment, morality, evaluation, and intellectuality are not dirty words in Kerista Village." Many similar-sounding but failed communes were "more into hedonism," Eve says.

The Best Friends are "not angry revolutionaries," do not feel alienated, and are by no means ascetics. "One of our mottoes, and the name of one of our oldest songs," the handbook says, "is 'If it ain't fun, it won't git done.' " Summing up, the handbook affirms that "we love our ideals above all else, and this is what makes all of our different love relationships, sex, and home lives so cozy, so indescribably delicious."

Eve also stresses the importance of the new beginning the Keristans believe they have made: "Ours is an alternative approach involving a complete restructuring of sexual attitudes, not to speak of attitudes toward many other things, and works best for people who are making a fresh, clean start in lifestyle. You begin a process of psychological transformation and preparation *before* entering into sexual relationships."

Still, the past can get in the way of the present; but the Keristans have found a remedy. Eve speaking again: "We do a lot of Gestalt work among ourselves (we use our own term for it, Gestalt-O-Rama), some of which is aimed at learning more about past conditioning, so that we can become conscious of what's going on inside ourselves, and, eventually, overcome the pull of those parts of it that we don't like. In this process we've found that jealousy is inextricably interwoven with romantic love."

She goes on to explain why the group is opposed to romantic love and what they mean when they use the term. "I'm referring to the exclusive 'zap' sort of relationship so often depicted on film or TV. Those relationships are personality-centered rather than based on shared ideals and interests, and the pattern is that there can only be one primary involvement of this sort happening at a time. Since everyone believes this, people are naturally going to get worried when a partner strikes up a relationship with anyone else, since this implies that one person or the other is going to be in first place, and the original person might be replaced. Jealousy and possessiveness are thus obvious outcomes."

Elliot Aronson, a social psychologist who has met with members of Kerista, likes them, respects their sincerity ("They're not kooks"), and hopes to study the group to further his understanding of jealousy. But he does not think they have gone "beyond" jealousy and possessiveness. "I believe that preferentiality is part of the human condition," he says.

Skeptics, of course, might add that among human beings, romantic love is inevitable. On one occasion, the Keristans were trying to explain polyfidelity to a group of Russians: "But what about falling in love?" one of the visitors asked. "Isn't that just a natural, irrational happening between two people? How do you deal with this?"

The Keristans were doing their best to get their ideas across, and they were failing. But they weren't about to give up. "Falling in love," they said, "is the opiate of the people."

CRITICAL THINKING QUESTIONS

1. The majority of studies cited in the article involved self-reports of how people felt when they were jealous, what types of situations provoked jealousy, and so on. How reliable are such self-report measures? Are people generally accurate and/or honest when it comes to reporting on themselves? What other method of data gathering would address the same issues without relying solely on what people say?

2. The article reported considerable variation not only between people but also between cultures as to how much jealousy is experienced and how it is expressed. Is it possible to truly love someone and not feel any jealousy if a real or imagined loss of that person is apparent? Or could it be that jealousy is tied to how much the person cares about the other individual?

3. The divorce rate in the United States has risen dramatically over the years; it has been especially high in the last two decades. How does the information presented in the article relate to divorce? Specifically, what role does jealousy play in divorce? How can relationships be studied?

4. One line of research presented in the article seems to suggest that cultural differences may be related to possessiveness in general toward things and people. Do you think that jealousy over relationships is related to possessiveness in general? (For example, are people who are unwilling to lend valued possessions also jealous over individuals?) How could you test this possibility?

ARTICLE 20

Think of the number of popular songs that have been written about love. Likewise, the number of books, articles, and movies that have love themes is large indeed. Subjectively, the experience of falling or being in love is one of the most cherished human experiences. Yet in spite of all this, many psychologists chose not to investigate the topic of love prior to the publication of the following article by Zick Rubin.

Before reading the article, try to put yourself in Rubin's shoes: If you wanted to somehow measure love, how would you go about doing it? How would you define *love*? Are there different types of love? If so, how do they differ?

The following classic article is of significance for several reasons. It very nicely illustrates a systematic program for investigating romantic love, beginning with the development of a paper-and-pencil love scale, followed by verification of the scale by administration to couples in varying stages of love, and concluding with a study relating scores on the love scale with observed differences in behavior. However, the larger value of the study is that it opened up the area of love to systematic inquiry. Many studies of love have been conducted over the last two decades, after Rubin first attempted it.

Measurement of Romantic Love[1]

■ Zick Rubin

This study reports the initial results of an attempt to introduce and validate a social-psychological construct of romantic love. Starting with the assumption that love is an interpersonal attitude, an internally consistent paper-and-pencil love scale was developed. The conception of romantic love included three components: affiliative and dependent need, a predisposition to help, and an orientation of exclusiveness and absorption. Love-scale scores were only moderately correlated with scores on a parallel scale of "liking," which reflected a more traditional conception of interpersonal attraction. The validity of the love scale was assessed in a questionnaire study and a laboratory experiment. On the basis of the emerging conception of love, it was predicted that college dating couples who loved each other a great deal (as categorized by their love-scale scores) would spend more time gazing into one another's eyes than would couples who loved each other to a lesser degree. The prediction was confirmed.

Love is generally regarded to be the deepest and most meaningful of sentiments. It has occupied a preeminent position in the art and literature of every age, and it is presumably experienced, at least occasionally, by the vast majority of people. In Western culture, moreover, the association between love and marriage gives it a unique status as a link between the individual and the structure of society.

In view of these considerations, it is surprising to discover that social psychologists have devoted virtually no attention to love. Although interpersonal attraction has been a major focus of social-psychological theory and research, workers in this area have not attempted to conceptualize love as an independent entity. For Heider (1958), for ex-

Reprinted from the *Journal of Personality and Social Psychology*, 1970, *16*, 265–273. Copyright 1970 by the American Psychological Association. Reprinted by permission.

ample, "loving" is merely intense liking—there is no discussion of possible qualitative differences between the two. Newcomb (1960) does not include love on his list of the "varieties of interpersonal attraction." Even in experiments directed specifically at "romantic" attraction (e.g., Walster, 1965), the dependent measure is simply a verbal report of "liking."

The present research was predicated on the assumption that love may be independently conceptualized and measured. In keeping with a strategy of construct validation (cf. Cronbach & Meehl, 1955), the attempts to define love, to measure it, and to assess its relationships to other variables are all seen as parts of a single endeavor. An initial assumption in this enterprise is that love is an *attitude* held by a person toward a particular other person, involving predispositions to think, feel, and behave in certain ways toward that other person. This assumption places love in the mainstream of social-psychological approaches to interpersonal attraction, alongside such other varieties of attraction as liking, admiration, and respect (cf. Newcomb, 1960).

The view of love as a multifaceted attitude implies a broader perspective than that held by those theorists who view love as an "emotion," a "need," or a set of behaviors. On the other hand, its linkage to a particular target implies a more restricted view than that held by those who regard love as an aspect of the individual's personality or experience which transcends particular persons and situations (e.g., Fromm, 1956). As Orlinsky (1970) has suggested, there may well be important common elements among different varieties of "love" (e.g., filial love, marital love, love of God). The focus of the present research, however, was restricted to *romantic love,* which may be defined simply as love between unmarried opposite-sex peers, of the sort which could possibly lead to marriage.

The research had three major phases. First, a paper-and-pencil love scale was developed. Second, the love scale was employed in a questionnaire study of student dating couples. Third, the predictive validity of the love scale was assessed in a laboratory experiment.

DEVELOPING A LOVE SCALE

The development of a love scale was guided by several considerations:

1. Inasmuch as the content of the scale would constitute the initial conceptual definition of romantic love, its items must be grounded in existing theoretical and popular conceptions of love.
2. Responses to these items, if they are tapping a single underlying attitude, must be highly intercorrelated.
3. In order to establish the discriminant validity (cf. Campbell, 1960) of the love scale, it was constructed in conjunction with a parallel scale of liking. The goal was to develop internally consistent scales of love and of liking which would be conceptually distinct from one another and which would, in practice, be only moderately intercorrelated.

The first step in this procedure was the assembling of a large pool of questionnaire items referring to a respondent's attitude toward a particular other person (the "target person"). Half of these items were suggested by a wide range of speculations about the nature of love (e.g., de Rougemont, 1940; Freud, 1955; Fromm, 1956; Goode, 1959; Slater, 1963). These items referred to physical attraction, idealization, a predisposition to help, the desire to share emotions and experiences, feelings of exclusiveness and absorption, felt affiliative and dependent needs, the holding of ambivalent feelings, and the relative unimportance of universalistic norms in the relationship. The other half of the items were suggested by the existing theoretical and empirical literature on interpersonal attraction (or liking; cf. Lindzey & Byrne, 1968). They included references to the desire to affiliate with the target in various settings, evaluation of the target on several dimensions, the salience of norms of responsibility and equity, feelings of respect and trust, and the perception that the target is similar to oneself.

To provide some degree of consensual validation for this initial categorization of items, two successive panels of student and faculty judges sorted the items into love and liking categories, relying simply on their personal understanding of the connotations of the two labels. Following this screening procedure, a revised set of 70 items was administered to 198 introductory psychology students during their regular class sessions. Each respondent completed the items with reference to his girlfriend or boyfriend (if he had one), and also with reference to a nonromantically viewed "platonic friend" of the opposite sex. The scales of love and of liking which were employed in the subsequent phases of the research were arrived at through factor analyses of these responses. Two separate factor analyses were performed—one for responses with reference to boyfriends and girlfriends (or "lovers") and one for responses with reference to platonic friends. In each case, there was a general factor accounting for a large proportion of the total variance. The items loading highest on this general factor, particularly for lovers, were almost exclusively those which had previously been categorized as love items. These high-loading items defined the more circumscribed conception of love adopted. The items forming the liking scale were based on those which loaded highly on the second factor with respect to platonic friends. Details of the scale development procedure are reported in Rubin (1969, Ch. 2).

The items forming the love and liking scales are listed in Table 1. Although it was constructed in such a way as to be factorially unitary, the content of the love scale points to three major components of romantic love:

1. Affiliative and dependent need—for example, "If I could never be with _____, I would feel miserable"; "It would be hard for me to get along without _____."
2. Predisposition to help—for example, "If _____ were feeling badly, my first duty would be to cheer him (her) up"; "I would do almost anything for _____."
3. Exclusiveness and absorption—for example, "I feel very possessive toward _____"; "I feel that

I can confide in _____ about virtually everything."

The emerging conception of romantic love, as defined by the content of the scale, has an eclectic flavor. The affiliative and dependent need component evokes both Freud's (1955) view of love as sublimated sexuality and Harlow's (1958) equation of love with attachment behavior. The predisposition to help is congruent with Fromm's (1956) analysis of the components of love, which he identifies as care, responsibility, respect, and knowledge. Absorption in a single other person is the aspect of love which is pointed to most directly by Slater's (1963) analysis of the social-structural implications of dyadic intimacy. The conception of liking, as defined by the liking-scale items, includes components of favorable evaluation and respect for the target person, as well as the perception that the target is similar to oneself. It is in reasonably close accord with measures of "attraction" employed in previous research (cf. Lindzey & Byrne, 1968).

QUESTIONNAIRE STUDY

The 13-item love and liking scales, with their component items interspersed, were included in a questionnaire administered in October 1968 to 158 dating (but non-engaged) couples at the University of Michigan, recruited by means of posters and newspaper ads. In addition to the love and liking scales, completed first with respect to one's dating partner and later with respect to a close, same-sex friend, the questionnaire contained several personality scales and requests for background information about the dating relationship. Each partner completed the questionnaire individually and was paid $1 for taking part. The modal couple consisted of a junior man and a sophomore or junior woman who had been dating for about 1 year.

Each item on the love and liking scales was responded to on a continuum ranging from "Not at all true; disagree completely" (scored as 1) to "Definitely true; agree completely" (scored as 9),

TABLE 1 / Means, Standard Deviations, and Correlations with Total Scale Scores of Love-Scale and Liking-Scale Items

Love-scale items	Women				Men			
	$\overline{X}$	SD	r^a Love	r Like	$\overline{X}$	SD	r^a Love	r Like
1. If ___ were feeling badly, my first duty would be to cheer him (her) up.	7.56	1.79	.393	.335	7.28	1.67	.432	.304
2. I feel that I can confide in ___ about virtually everything.	7.77	1.73	.524	.274	7.80	1.65	.425	.408
3. I find it easy to ignore ___'s faults.	5.83	1.90	.184	.436	5.61	2.13	.248	.428
4. I would do almost anything for ___.	7.15	2.03	.630	.341	7.35	1.83	.724	.530
5. I feel very possessive toward ___.	6.26	2.36	.438	−.005	6.24	2.33	.481	.342
6. If I could never be with ___, I would feel miserable.	6.52	2.43	.633	.276	6.58	2.26	.699	.422
7. If I were lonely, my first thought would be to seek ___ out.	7.90	1.72	.555	.204	7.75	1.54	.546	.328
8. One of my primary concerns is ___'s welfare.	7.47	1.62	.606	.218	7.59	1.56	.683	.290
9. I would forgive ___ for practically anything.	6.77	2.03	.551	.185	6.54	2.05	.394	.237
10. I feel responsible for ___'s well-being.	6.35	2.25	.582	.178	6.67	1.88	.548	.307
11. When I am with ___, I spend a good deal of time just looking at him (her).	5.42	2.36	.271	.137	5.94	2.18	.491	.318
12. I would greatly enjoy being confided in by ___.	8.35	1.14	.498	.292	7.88	1.47	.513	.383
13. It would be hard for me to get along without ___.	6.27	2.54	.676	.254	6.19	2.16	.663	.464

Liking-scale items	Women				Men			
	$\overline{X}$	SD	r Love	r^b Like	$\overline{X}$	SD	r Love	r^b Like
1. When I am with ___, we are almost always in the same mood.	5.51	1.72	1.63	.270	5.30	1.77	.235	.294
2. I think that ___ is unusually well-adjusted.	6.36	2.07	.093	.452	6.04	1.98	.339	.610
3. I would highly recommend ___ for a responsible job.	7.87	1.77	.199	.370	7.90	1.55	.281	.422
4. In my opinion, ___ is an exceptionally mature person.	6.72	1.93	.190	.559	6.40	2.00	.372	.609
5. I have great confidence in ___'s good judgment.	7.37	1.59	.310	.538	6.68	1.80	.381	.562

TABLE 1 (Continued)

6. Most people would react very favorably to ___ after a brief acquaintance.	7.08	2.00	.167	.366	7.32	1.73	.202	.287
7. I think that ___ and I are quite similar to each other.	6.12	2.24	.292	.410	5.94	2.14	.407	.417
8. I would vote for ___ in a class or group election.	7.29	2.00	.057	.381	6.28	2.36	.299	.297
9. I think that ___ is one of those people who quickly wins respect.	7.11	1.67	.182	.588	6.71	1.69	.370	.669
10. I feel that ___ is an extremely intelligent person.	8.04	1.42	.193	.155	7.48	1.50	.377	.415
11. ___ is one of the most likable people I know.	6.99	1.98	.346	.402	7.33	1.63	.438	.514
12. ___ is the sort of person whom I myself would like to be.	5.50	2.00	.253	.340	4.71	2.26	.417	.552
13. It seems to me that it is very easy for ___ to gain admiration.	6.71	1.87	.176	.528	6.53	1.64	.345	.519

Note.—Based on responses of 158 couples. Scores on individual items can range from 1 to 9, with 9 always indicating the positive end of the continuum.
[a]Correlation between item and love scale total minus that item.
[b]Correlation between item and liking scale total minus that item.

and total scale scores were computed by summing scores on individual items. Table 1 presents the mean scores and standard deviations for the items, together with the correlations between individual items and total scale scores. In several cases an inappropriate pattern of correlations was obtained, such as a love item correlating more highly with the total liking score than with the total love score (minus that item). These inappropriate patterns suggest specific revisions for future versions of the scales. On the whole, however, the pattern of correlations was appropriate. The love scale had high internal consistency (coefficient alpha was .84 for women and .86 for men)[2] and, as desired, was only moderately correlated with the liking scale (r = .39 for women and .60 for men). The finding that love and liking were more highly correlated among men than among women (z = 2.48, $p < .02$) was unexpected. It provides at least suggestive support for the notion that women discriminate more sharply between the two sentiments than men do (cf. Banta & Hetherington, 1963).

Table 2 reveals that the love scores of men (for their girlfriends) and women (for their boyfriends)

were almost identical. Women liked their boyfriends somewhat more than they were liked in return, however (t = 2.95, df = 157, $p < .01$). Inspection of the item means in Table 1 indicates that this sex difference may be attributed to the higher ratings given by women to their boyfriends on such "task-related" dimensions as intelligence, good judgment, and leadership potential. To the extent that these items accurately represent the construct of liking, men may indeed tend to be

TABLE 2 / Love and Liking for Dating Partners and Same-Sex Friends

Index	Women		Men	
	$\overline{X}$	SD	$\overline{X}$	SD
Love for partner	89.46	15.54	89.37	15.16
Liking for partner	88.48	13.40	84.65	13.81
Love for friend	65.27	17.84	55.07	16.08
Liking for friend	80.47	16.47	79.10	18.07

Note—Based on responses of 158 couples.

more "likeable" (but not more "lovable") than women. Table 2 also reveals, however, that there was no such sex difference with respect to the respondents' liking for their same-sex friends. The mean liking-for-friend scores for the two sexes were virtually identical. Thus, the data do not support the conclusion that men are generally more likable than women, but only that they are liked more in the context of the dating relationship.

Table 2 also indicates that women tended to *love* their same-sex friends more than men did ($t = 5.33$, $df = 314$, $p < .01$). This result is in accord with cultural stereotypes concerning male and female friendships. It is more socially acceptable for female than for male friends to speak of themselves as "loving" one another, and it has been reported that women tend to confide in same-sex friends more than men do (Jourard & Lasakow, 1958). Finally, the means presented in Table 2 show that whereas both women and men *liked* their dating partners only slightly more than they liked their same-sex friends, they *loved* their dating partners much more than their friends.

Further insight into the conceptual distinction between love and liking may be derived from the correlational results presented in Table 3. As expected, love scores were highly correlated both with respondents' reports of whether or not they were "in love" and with their estimates of the likelihood that they would marry their current dating partners. Liking scores were only moderately correlated with these indexes.

Although love scores were highly related to perceived marriage probability, these variables may be distinguished from one another on empirical as well as conceptual grounds. As Table 3 indicates, the length of time that the couple had been dating was unrelated to love scores among men, and only slightly related among women. In contrast, the respondents' perceptions of their closeness to marriage were significantly correlated with length of dating among both men and women. These results are in keeping with the common observations that although love may develop rather quickly, progress toward marriage typically occurs only over a longer period of time.

The construct validity of the love scale was fur-

TABLE 3 / Intercorrelations among Indexes of Attraction

Index	1	2	3	4
Women				
1. Love for partner				
2. Liking for partner	.39			
3. "In love"[a]	.59	.28		
4. Marriage probability[b]	.59	.32	.65	
5. Dating length[c]	.16	.01	.27	.46
Men				
1. Love for partner				
2. Liking for partner	.60			
3. "In love"[a]	.52	.35		
4. Marriage probability[b]	.59	.35	.62	
5. Dating length[c]	.04	−.03	.22	.38

Note — Based on responses of 158 couples. With an *N* of 158, a correlation of .16 is significant at the .05 level and a correlation of .21 is significant at the .01 level (two-tailed values).
[a]Responses to question, "Would you say that you and ___ are in love?" scored on a 3-point scale ("No" = 0, "Uncertain" = 1, "Yes" = 2).
[b]Responses to question, "What is your best estimate of the likelihood that you and ___ will marry one another?" Scale ranges from 0 (0%–10% probability) to 9 (91%–100% probability).
[c]The correlation across couples between the two partners' reports of the length of time they had been dating (in months) was .967. In this table, "dating length" was arbitrarily equated with the woman's estimates.

ther attested to by the findings that love for one's dating partner was only slightly correlated with love for one's same-sex friend ($r = .18$ for women, and $r = .15$ for men) and was uncorrelated with scores on the Marlowe-Crowne Social Desirability Scale ($r = .01$ for both women and men). These findings are consistent with the assumption that the love scale was tapping an attitude toward a specific other person, rather than more general interpersonal orientations or response tendencies. Finally, the love scores of the two partners tended to be moderately symmetrical. The correlation across couples between the woman's and the man's love was .42. The corresponding intra-couple correlation with respect to liking was somewhat lower ($r = .28$). With respect to the partners' estimates of the probability of marriage, on the other hand, the intracouple correlation was considerably higher ($r = .68$).

LABORATORY EXPERIMENT: LOVE AND GAZING

Although the questionnaire results provided evidence for the construct validity of the emerging conception of romantic love, it remained to be determined whether love-scale scores could be used to predict behavior outside the realm of questionnaire responses. The notion that romantic love includes a component of exclusiveness and absorption led to the prediction that in an unstructured laboratory situation, dating partners who loved each other a great deal would gaze into one another's eyes more than would partners who loved each other to a lesser degree.

The test of the prediction involved a comparison between "strong-love" and "weak-love" couples, as categorized by their scores on the love scale. To control for the possibility that "strong" and "weak" lovers differ from one another in their more general interpersonal orientations, additional groups were included in which subjects were paired with opposite-sex strangers. The love scores of subjects in these "apart" groups were equated with those of the subjects who were paired with their own dating partners (the "together" groups). In contrast to the prediction for the together groups, no difference in the amount of eye contact engaged in by the strong-apart and weak-apart groups was expected.

METHOD

Subjects

Two pools of subjects were established from among the couples who completed the questionnaire. Those couples in which both partners scored above the median on the love scale (92 or higher) were designated strong-love couples, and those in which both partners scored below the median were designated weak-love couples. Couples in which one partner scored above and the other below the median were not included in the experiment. Within each of the two pools, the couples were divided into two subgroups with approximately equal love scores. One subgroup in each pool was randomly designated as a together group, the other as an apart group. Subjects in the together group were invited to take part in the experiment together with their boyfriends or girlfriends. Subjects in the apart groups were requested to appear at the experimental session individually, where they would be paired with other people's boyfriends or girlfriends. Pairings in the apart conditions were made on the basis of scheduling convenience, with the additional guideline that women should not be paired with men who were younger than themselves. In this way, four experimental groups were created: strong together (19 pairs), weak together (19 pairs), strong apart (21 pairs), and weak apart (20 pairs). Only 5 of the couples contacted (not included in the above cell sizes) refused to participate — 2 who had been preassigned to the strong together group, 2 to the weak together group, and 1 to the strong apart group. No changes in the preassignment of subjects to groups were requested or permitted. As desired, none of the pairs of subjects created in the apart groups were previously acquainted. Each subject was paid $1.25 for his participation.

Sessions

When both members of a scheduled pair had arrived at the laboratory, they were seated across a 52-inch table from one another in an observation room. The experimenter, a male graduate student, explained that the experiment was part of a study of communication among dating and unacquainted couples. The subjects were then asked to read a paragraph about "a couple contemplating marriage" (one of the "choice situations" developed by Wallach & Kogan, 1959). They were told that they would subsequently discuss the case, and that their discussion would be tape recorded. The experimenter told the pair that it would take a few minutes for him to set up the tape recorder, and that meanwhile they could talk about anything except the case to be discussed. He then left the room. After 1 minute had elapsed (to allow the subjects to adapt themselves to the situation), their visual behavior was observed for a 3-minute period.[3]

Measurement

The subjects' visual behavior was recorded by two observers stationed behind a one-way mirror, one facing each subject. Each observer pressed a button, which was connected to a cumulative clock, whenever the subject he was watching was looking across the table at his partner's face. The readings on these clocks provided measures of *individual gazing*. In addition, a third clock was activated whenever the two observers were pressing their buttons simultaneously. The reading on this clock provided a measure of *mutual gazing*. The mean percentage of agreement between pairs of observers in 12 reliability trials, interspersed among the experimental sessions, was 92.8. The observers never knew whether a pair of subjects was in a strong-love or weak-love group. They were sometimes able to infer whether the pair was in the together or the apart condition, however. Each observer's assignment alternated between watching the woman and watching the man in successive sessions.

RESULTS

Table 4 reveals that as predicted, there was a tendency for strong-together couples to engage in more mutual gazing (or "eye contact") than weak-together couples ($t = 1.52, p < .07$, one-tailed). Although there was also a tendency for strong-apart couples to make more eye contact than weak-apart couples, it was not a reliable one ($t = .92$).

Another approach toward assessing the couples' visual behavior is to consider the percentage of "total gazing" time (i.e., the amount of time during which at least one of the partners was looking at the other) which was occupied by mutual gazing. This measure, to be referred to as *mutual focus,* differs from mutual gazing in that it specifically takes into account the individual

TABLE 4 / Mutual Gazing (In Seconds)

Group	n	$\overline{X}$	SD
Strong together	19	56.2	17.1
Weak together	18[a]	44.7	25.0
Strong apart	21	46.7	29.6
Weak apart	20	40.0	17.5

[a]Because of an equipment failure, the mutual-gazing measure was not obtained for one couple in the weak-together group.

gazing tendencies of the two partners. It is possible, for example, that neither member of a particular pair gazed very much at his partner, but that when they did gaze, they did so simultaneously. Such a pair would have a low mutual gazing score, but a high mutual focus score. Within certain limits, the converse of this situation is also possible. Using this measure (see Table 5), the difference between the strong-together and the weak-together groups was more striking than it was in the case of mutual gazing ($t = 2.31, p < .02$, one-tailed). The difference between the strong-apart and weak-apart groups was clearly not significant ($t = .72$).

Finally, the individual gazing scores of subjects in the four experimental groups are presented in Table 6. The only significant finding was that in all groups, the women spent much more time looking at the men than the men spent looking at the women ($F = 15.38, df = 1/150, p < .01$). Although there was a tendency for strong-together subjects of both sexes to look at their

TABLE 5 / Mutual Focus

Group	n	$\overline{X}$	SD
Strong together	19	44.0	9.8
Weak together	18	34.7	14.0
Strong apart	21	35.3	14.6
Weak apart	20	32.5	9.4

Note—
Mutual focus = 100 × $\dfrac{\text{mutual gazing}}{\text{woman's nonmutual gazing} + \text{man's nonmutual gazing} + \text{mutual gazing}}$

TABLE 6 / Individual Gazing (in seconds)

Group	Women			Men		
	n	X̄	SD	n	X̄	SD
Strong together	19	98.7	23.2	19	83.7	20.2
Weak together	19	87.4	30.4	19	77.7	33.1
Strong apart	21	94.5	39.7	21	75.0	39.3
Weak apart	20	96.8	27.8	20	64.0	25.2

partners more than weak-together subjects, these comparisons did not approach significance.

DISCUSSION

The main prediction of the experiment was confirmed. Couples who were strongly in love, as categorized by their scores on the love scale, spent more time gazing into one another's eyes than did couples who were only weakly in love. With respect to the measure of individual gazing, however, the tendency for strong-together subjects to devote more time than the weak-together subjects to looking at their partners was not substantial for either women or men. This finding suggests that the obtained difference in mutual gazing between these two groups must be attributed to differences in the *simultaneousness*, rather than in the sheer quantity, of gazing. This conclusion is bolstered by the fact that the clearest difference between the strong-together and weak-together groups emerged on the percentage measure of mutual focus.

This pattern of results is in accord with the assumption that gazing is a manifestation of the exclusive and absorptive component of romantic love. Freud (1955) maintained that "The more [two people] are in love, the more completely they suffice for each other [p. 140]." More recently, Slater (1963) has linked Freud's theory of love to the popular concept of "the oblivious lovers, who are 'all wrapped up in each other,' and somewhat careless of their social obligations [p. 349]." One way in which this oblivious absorption may be

manifested is through eye contact. As the popular song has it, "Millions of people go by, but they all disappear from view—'cause I only have eyes for you."

Another possible explanation for the findings is that people who are in love (or who complete attitude scales in such a way as to indicate that they are in love) are also the sort of people who are most predisposed to make eye contact with others, regardless of whether or not those others are the people they are in love with. The inclusion of the apart groups helped to rule out this possibility, however. Although there was a slight tendency for strong-apart couples to engage in more eye contact than weak-apart couples (see Table 5), it fell far short of significance. Moreover, when the percentage measure of mutual focus was employed (see Table 6), this difference virtually disappeared. It should be noted that no predictions were made concerning the comparisons between strong-together and strong-apart couples or between weak-together and weak-apart couples. It seemed plausible that unacquainted couples might make use of a relatively large amount of eye contact as a means of getting acquainted. The results indicate, in fact, that subjects in the apart groups typically engaged in as much eye contact as those in the weak-together group, with the strong-together subjects outgazing the other three groups. Future studies which systematically vary the extent to which partners are acquainted would be useful in specifying the acquaintance-seeking functions of eye contact.

The finding that in all experimental groups, women spent more time looking at men than vice versa may reflect the frequently reported tendency of women to specialize in the "social-emotional" aspects of interaction (e.g., Strodtbeck & Mann, 1956). Gazing may serve as a vehicle of emotional expression for women and, in addition, may allow women to obtain cues from their male partners concerning the appropriateness of their behavior. The present result is in accord with earlier findings that women tend to make more eye contact than men in same-sex groups (Exline, 1963) and in an interview situation, regardless of the sex of the interviewer (Exline, Gray, & Schuette, 1965).

CONCLUSION

"So far as love or affection is concerned," Harlow wrote in 1958, "psychologists have failed in their mission. The little we know about love does not transcend simple observation, and the little we write about it has been written better by poets and novelists [p. 673]." The research reported in this paper represents an attempt to improve this situation by introducing and validating a preliminary social-psychological conception of romantic love. A distinction was drawn between love and liking, and its reasonableness was attested to by the results of the questionnaire study. It was found, for example, that respondents' estimates of the likelihood that they would marry their partners were more highly related to their love than to their liking for their partners. In light of the culturally prescribed association between love and marriage (but not necessarily between liking and marriage), this pattern of correlations seems appropriate. Other findings of the questionnaire study, to be reported elsewhere, point to the value of a measurable construct of romantic love as a link between the individual and social-structural levels of analysis of social behavior.

Although the present investigation was aimed at developing a unitary conception of romantic love, a promising direction for future research is the attempt to distinguish among patterns of romantic love relationships. One theoretical basis for such distinctions is the nature of the interpersonal rewards exchanged between partners (cf. Wright, 1969). The attitudes and behaviors of romantic love may differ, for example, depending on whether the most salient rewards exchanged are those of security or those of stimulation (cf. Maslow's discussion of "Deficiency Love" and "Being Love," 1955). Some of the behavioral variables which might be focused on in the attempt to distinguish among such patterns are in the areas of sexual behavior, helping, and self-disclosure.

REFERENCES

Banta, T J., & Hetherington, M. Relations between needs of friends and fiancees. *Journal of Abnormal and Social Psychology*, 1963, 66, 401–404.

Campbell, D. T. Recommendations for APA test standards regarding construct, trait, and discriminant validity. *American Psychologist*, 1960, 15, 546–553.

Cronbach, L. J., & Meehl, P. E. Construct validity in psychological tests. *Psychological Bulletin*, 1955, 52, 281–302.

De Rougemont, D. *Love in the western world*. New York: Harcourt, Brace, 1940.

Exline, R. V. Explorations in the process of person perception: Visual interaction in relation to competition, sex, and need for affiliation. *Journal of Personality*, 1963, 31, 1–20.

Exline, R., Gray, D., & Schuette, D. Visual behavior in a dyad as affected by interview content and sex of respondent. *Journal of Personality and Social Psychology*, 1965, 1, 201–209.

Freud, S. Group psychology and the analysis of the ego. In *The standard edition of the complete psychological works of Sigmund Freud*. Vol. 18. London: Hogarth, 1955.

Fromm, E. *The art of loving*. New York: Harper, 1956.

Goode, W. J. The theoretical importance of love. *American Sociological Review*, 1959, 24, 38–47.

Harlow, H. F. The nature of love. *American Psychologist*, 1958, 13, 673–685.

Heider, F. *The psychology of interpersonal relations*. New York: Wiley, 1958.

Jourard, S. M., & Lasakow, P. Some factors in self-disclosure. *Journal of Abnormal and Social Psychology*, 1958, 56, 91–98.

Lindzey, G., & Byrne, D. Measurement of social choice and interpersonal attractiveness. In G. Lindzey & E. Aronson (Eds.), *Handbook of social psychology*, Vol. 2. (2nd ed.) Reading, Mass.: Addison-Wesley, 1968.

Maslow, A. H. Deficiency motivation and growth motivation. *Nebraska Symposium on Motivation*, 1955, 2.

Newcomb, T. M. The varieties of interpersonal attraction. In D. Cartwright & A. Zander (Eds.), *Group dynamics*. (2nd ed.) Evanston: Row, Peterson, 1960.

Orlinsky, D. E. Love relationships in the life cycle: A developmental interpersonal perspective. Unpublished manuscript, University of Chicago, 1970.

Rubin, Z. *The social psychology of romantic love*. Ann Arbor, Mich.: University Microfilms, 1969, No. 70-4179.

Slater, P. E. On social regression. *American Sociological Review*, 1963, 28, 339–364.

Strodtbeck, F. L., & Mann, R. D. Sex role differentiation in jury deliberations. *Sociometry*, 1956, 19, 3–11.

Wallach, M. A., & Kogan, N. Sex differences and judgment processes. *Journal of Personality,* 1959, *27,* 555–564.

Walster, E. The effect of self-esteem on romantic liking. *Journal of Experimental Social Psychology,* 1965, *1,* 184–197.

Wright, P. H. A model and a technique for studies of friendship. *Journal of Experimental Social Psychology,* 1969, *5,* 295–309.

NOTES

1. This report is based on a doctoral dissertation submitted to the University of Michigan. The research was supported by a predoctoral fellowship from the National Institute of Mental Health and by a grant-in-aid from the Society for the Psychological Study of Social Issues. The author is grateful to Theodore M. Newcomb, chairman of the dissertation committee, for his invaluable guidance and support. Mitchell Baris, Cheryl Eisenman, Linda Muller, Judy Newman, Marlyn Rame, Stuart Katz, Edward Kupersmit, and Phillip Shaver served as observers in the experiment, and Mr. Shaver also helped design and assemble the equipment.
2. Coefficient alpha of the liking scale was .81 for women and .83 for men.
3. Visual behavior was also observed during a subsequent 3-minute discussion period. The results for this period, which differed from those for the prediscussion waiting period, are reported in Rubin (1969, Ch. 5).

CRITICAL THINKING QUESTIONS

1. Is *love* the ultimate of *like?* Or is it qualitatively a different experience? Do you agree with the definition of romantic love used by Rubin?

2. As Rubin pointed out, love is a human experience that until recently had largely been excluded from research. Why do you think that was the case? For example, is the topic inherently more difficult to study than other topics investigated by psychologists? Or might other reasons account for this?

3. After the study was published, Senator William Proxmire presented his Golden Fleece Award to federally funded research on love and attraction, citing it as an example of wasteful expenditures of taxpayers' money. Do you agree with him that love is simply not worthy of study? Is it appropriate to study love? Is there some practical reason that love should be studied? How could information on love, such as presented in the article, be used?

4. Many married couples who have known and loved each other for many years report that the nature of love changes over the years. Feelings and how they are expressed may be different during the first and twentieth years of the relationship, for example. This study employed unmarried couples who knew each other for a relatively short period of time. Would these results apply to couples who have been married for varying numbers of years? How do you think things would change over time? How would you test this?

5. What is the difference between romantic love and infatuation? How could you test the differences (if any) between the two? Would there be any real value in conducting such a study?

ADDITIONAL RELATED READINGS

Hendrick, C., & Hendrick, S. (1986). A theory and method of love. *Journal of Personality and Social Psychology, 50,* 392–402.

Lee, J. A. (1977). A topology of styles of loving. *Personality and Social Psychology Bulletin, 3,* 173–182.

Sternberg, R. J. (1986). A triangular theory of love. *Psychological Reviews, 93,* 119–135.

ARTICLE 21 _____

The high divorce rate in the United State is of social concern to a large number of Americans. Current statistics indicate that nearly half of all marriages will end in divorce; whether the observed rise in divorce over the past 20 years will continue remains to be seen. Nonetheless, the prevalence of divorce is certainly characteristic of contemporary U.S. society.

Divorce is generally viewed negatively, with the focus on the pain and suffering that it usually produces for all parties involved, including any children involved. In fact, most people consider divorce to be one of the most traumatic of life's experiences. But do all divorces take such a negative toll on the partners? Or are some divorces less stressful and traumatic than others?

The article that follows by Isaacs and Leon examines one aspect of the relations between recently separated couples: communication style, as it relates to the experience of the divorce. In addition, the article examines marital factors that may predict eventual outcomes. As you will discover in the article, certain patterns of communication following separation may be better (both psychologically and physically) for the partners than others. The implications of such findings for people such as counselors, who work in the direct helping areas, as well as for people who may be separated or divorced, are discussed.

Divorce, Disputation, and Discussion
Communicational Styles among Recently Separated Spouses

■ Marla B. Isaacs and George Leon

Communicational styles between recently separated spouses are identified among a sample of divorcing women during the first year of separation. Feelings of hostility and friendliness associated with these styles are examined, as are the antecedents of each style in the marriage. The consequences for the woman's adjustment are also examined.

Are hostility and conflict inevitable parts of marital separation, or are alternative communicational styles possible? Do communicational styles following separation have antecedents in the preseparation marital relationship? Are they related to feelings of hostility or friendliness following the separation? Are they related to adjustment?

These questions are important to both researchers and practitioners in the field of divorce. An examination of the communicational styles between recently separated spouses will enhance existing knowledge concerning the postseparation relationship and will aid in the development of therapeutic strategies.

This article presents findings from a study of 124 women during their first year of marital separation. We explore the possibility that the postseparation relationship between former spouses can be characterized by distinct communicational styles that are not necessarily conflictual. We further explore the possibility that these postseparation communicational styles may have antecedents in the marital relationship and may be differentially related to adjustment.

Reprinted from the *Journal of Family Psychology*, 1988, *1*, 298–311. Copyright 1988 by Division 43 of the American Psychological Association. Reprinted by permission of Sage Publications, Inc.

THE LITERATURE

Most research on the postseparation relationship has emphasized hostility between the former spouses on the one hand and long-lasting bonds between them on the other hand. The association between hostility and the intensity of the bonds is not necessarily straightforward.

Goode (1956), for instance, found that although a positive attitude toward the former spouse was generally associated with more frequent contact, a large proportion of women nevertheless had a negative attitude toward the husband yet a high frequency of contact with him. Similarly, Wallerstein and Kelly (1980) report that although the divorced parents in their study often maintained contact with each other, frequent contact did not necessarily indicate friendliness. Those who communicated tended either to hold feelings of comradeship resulting from continued parental responsibilities or to feel no friendship whatsoever. Many remained angry several years after the divorce. In the early separation period they found that the great majority of parents expressed anger and bitterness toward their spouses. The women were more intensely angry than the men, and this anger may have helped in recovering the self-esteem that the women had lost in marriages in which they felt demeaned and belittled. Close to one-fifth of the sample were what Wallerstein and Kelly called "embittered-chaotic" parents, and this rage to some extent helped to ward off depression and to organize them psychologically.

Weiss (1975, 1979) addressed the bonds that persist after separation as well as the anger and ambivalence that are experienced toward the former spouse. He noted that all husbands and wives after separation feel some anger toward their spouses, but the anger of the spouse who did not wish for the separation usually appears more intense. Whereas some postmarital relationships are organized around only one set of feelings— affection on the one hand or distrust on the other—many display a mixture of both positive and negative feelings. Hunt and Hunt (1977) found that for most newly separated individuals, anger toward the ex-spouse is the predominant feeling and that for the great majority, "leftover love and desire" wane quickly during the early months of separation. Isaacs, Montalvo, and Abelsohn (1986) present clinical examples of how hostility and attachment affect family relationships after separation and, particularly, how hostility between the parents can impede the process of divorce and greatly upset the children.

Hostility in the postseparation relationship has been found to hold implications for the mental health of the former spouses. Jacobson (1983) studied both men and women who were in the process of separation and divorce and found self-reported hostility toward the spouse to be ubiquitous. Though hostility tapered off over time, some of the most serious types of hostility persisted among spouses who remained in contact and were associated with greater somatic discomfort and depression. Some studies have focused on the topics of postseparation communication and have identified communicational styles. Hetherington, Cox, and Cox (1978) found that two months after divorce, most of the communication between the spouses was conflictual in nature, concerning finances, support, visitation, child rearing, and intimate relationships with others. She found that both conflict and attachment decreased with time. Goldsmith (1980), on the other hand, highlighted "kin"-type interaction and positive feelings among former spouses, finding caring feelings and friendly interaction to be normative.

Ahrons's (1981) typology of the former spousal relationship incorporated both friendly and hostile kinds of relationships. She identified four interactional styles that she labeled "perfect pals," "cooperative colleagues," "angry associates," and "fiery foes," as well as a fifth group in which the former spouses were no longer in contact with each other. The styles ranged from very friendly to very hostile, and Ahrons argues that the first two styles represent "functional" divorces (Ahrons & Rodgers, 1987). She found slighty over half of her former spouses to have an antagonistic relationship to each other (Ahrons & Wallisch, 1986), in which interactions are rare and are focused on the children. Some are indifferent toward each other, but many are still angry. On the other hand, she found that approximately 40% of her sample had at least a moderate amount of interaction, which included discussing the children but also other issues that had a component of friendship. In summary, most of the existing literature has emphasized both the lasting bonds and the persistent hostility between former spouses. The implications of long-lasting hostility for the adjustment of the former spouses have also been explored. Recent studies have moved toward an examination of specific topics of disputation and have identified communicational styles among former spouses. However, these studies did not examine differences in adjustment among the styles, nor have they explored the possibility of antecedents in the marital relationship.

The present study examines communicational styles between former spouses by analyzing what they talk about and fight about. We shall explore the possibility of distinct communicational styles among recently separated former spouses and look for antecedents in the marital relationship and associations with feelings of hostility and friendliness, as well as with psychological adjustment.

METHOD

Sample

The sample consisted of 124 women who were interviewed shortly after marital separation. The sample included volunteers recruited through advertisements and newspaper articles as well as women who requested counseling for their children in the aftermath of the separation. Our sample and methodology have been described in depth elsewhere (Isaacs & Leon, 1986; Isaacs, Leon, & Donohue, 1986; Isaacs, Montalvo, & Abelsohn, 1986). A total of 87% of the respondents were separated for one year or less, with the median separation period of 6 months. All of the women were mothers of children who ranged in age from 2 to 17. In 113 of the cases, the mothers

had custody, and the remaining 11 were either father- or joint-custody arrangements.

The sample was varied demographically. In all, 94 of the divorcing women were White and 30 were Black, and their educational levels included less than high school (5%), high school graduates (33%), some college (25%), college graduates (20%), and professional training (17%). Thirty-six percent of the women were Catholic, 24% Protestant, 19% Jewish, and the remaining 21% "other" or "none."

The Measures

The interview schedule consisted of structured questions and unstructured in-depth questions concerning various aspects of the divorce experience. In order to ascertain what the divorcing couple fought and talked about, we asked the respondents how frequently they argued with their husbands about financial arrangements, property settlement, child support, visitation, and custody. We also asked whether they discussed their relationship, daily happenings, personal problems, practical problems, and the children. Finally, we asked several questions concerning how they got along with each other before the separation as well as their feelings toward their husbands, about each other, and about the separation. The women's adjustment was ascertained through the Hopkins Symptom Checklist (Derogatis, Lipman, Rickels, Uhlenhuth, & Covi, 1974), a self-report standardized instrument.

Analyses

Because this was an exploratory study, we were most interested in identifying communicational patterns, rather than testing specific hypotheses. In order to identify patterns of disputation and discussion, we performed a factor analysis on 10 items that measured what the couple fought about and talked about. The respondents were asked to answer the following question by selecting, often, sometimes, rarely, or never:

How often is there a dispute between the two of you over:

- financial arrangements
- property settlement
- child support
- visitation
- custody

They were then asked whether or not they discussed any of the following five topics:

When you talk to your former spouse, do you usually discuss:

- your children
- your relationship
- daily happenings
- personal problems
- practical problems

Although these questions were asked of both separated spouses, we used only the wives' responses in this study, because (a) the sample of women was substantially larger than that of husband-wife pairs and (b) our preliminary analyses indicated that the sample of husband-wife pairs was somewhat biased toward the less hostile, compared with the larger sample of all-women's responses. That is, the cases in which the husband did not participate in the study are those separations that tended to be more hostile and less communicative, and those would have been excluded if we restricted the analyses to only those cases for which we had both the husband's and the wife's data.

Although use of the larger sample of wives' responses eliminates the problem of bias toward the less hostile situations, it raises the question of another bias: Do the wives' responses accurately portray the relationship? To answer this question, we compared the husbands' with the wives' responses across each of the 10 disputation and discussion questions for the smaller sample of husband-wife pairs. We also included an item that asked the respondents to rate their current relationship, in an overall sense, as friendly, neutral, or hostile. Following Ahrons and Bowman (1981), we computed t-tests to check for distributional differences between the husbands' and wives' responses and correlation coefficients to measure the consistency of husband-wife responses. The results of those tests are shown in Table 1.

As shown by the results of the t-tests, there were no significant differences between the husbands' and the wives' responses for 9 out of 10 of

TABLE 1 / Distributional Differences between and Correlational Coefficients Measuring Consistency of Husband-Wife Responses

	t	df	Significance	r	Significance
Disputation:					
financial arrangements	− 2.53	64	.014	.46	.000
property settlement	− .51	63	.612	.42	.001
child support	.20	62	.842	.47	.001
visitation	1.40	64	.165	.21	.092
custody	1.33	61	.187	.13	.302
Discussion:					
your children	.38	62	.709	.16	.198
your relationship	− .83	62	.410	.42	.001
daily happenings	.23	60	.821	.37	.003
personal problems	− 1.43	61	.159	.31	.014
practical problems	.00	60	1.000	.39	.002
Relationship scale	.20	55	.842	.56	.000

the communicational items, and for 7 of the 10, the husbands' and wives' responses were positively and significantly correlated. The husbands' and wives' overall ratings of the relationship are also in close agreement.

These results indicate that the wives' responses are an accurate portrayal of the relationship, and we therefore conclude that it is reasonable to use the broader sample in order to overcome biases toward the less hostile cases.

Based on the results of the factor analysis of the 10 communicational items, we constructed additive indices and correlated them with three measures of the preseparation relationship: "Did arguments increase during the last year of marriage?" "During the marriage, was the atmosphere in your house usually: (a) very tense, (b) somewhat tense, (c) not tense?" "Did that tension get worse in the last year of your marriage?"

We also correlated the indices with the overall rating of the relationship as friendly, neutral, or hostile and two other measures of the current rela-

tionship: "How often do you and your children have meals with your husband: (a) often, (b) sometimes, (c) rarely, (d) never?" "How often does your husband talk to you 'like a friend': (a) often, (b) sometimes, (c) rarely, (d) never?"

Finally, we correlated the indices with five subscales and the total score of the woman's Hopkins Symptom Checklist (Derogatis et al., 1974) used as the measure of her adjustment.

RESULTS

The results of the factor analysis on the 10 topics of disputation and discussion are shown in Table 2. Based on these results, three communicational styles can be identified. The first, which we shall call *disputing*, is characterized by arguments in all of the areas under examination. This suggests that couples who fight in one area are likely to be fighting in a variety of areas. In contrast, the other two styles involve discussion of several of the topics. In the second style, which we call *practical* discussing, the parents discuss the children, practical problems, and daily happenings. In the third, which we call *personal* discussing, the topics include personal problems, daily happenings and, to a lesser extent, the couple's relationship.

Did these communicational styles arise from the divorce process itself or can antecedents be found in the latter stages of the marriage? To answer this question, we examined how arguments and tension in the marital household were correlated with the three postseparation communicational styles. The results appear in Table 3.

Disputing was associated with an increase in arguments during the last year of the marriage and with a tense atmosphere in the home. This suggests that chronic, postseparation disputation is a continuation of arguing that existed in the marriage rather than the result of the separation process itself. Neither style of discussing was associated with marital arguments, and each was negatively correlated with one or the other measures of tension in the marital household.

How are the communicational styles related to the wife's feelings toward her husband? Are they reflected in other indicators of how the couple interacts? Table 4 shows the correlations between

TABLE 2 / Factor Analysis of Measures of Discussion and Disputation between Ex-Spouses

		Factor	
	Disputation	Practical Discussion	Personal Discussion
Discuss:			
children	.04	.76	− .04
relationship	.33	.09	.33
daily events	− .14	.65	.49
personal problems	.08	.28	.76
practical problems	− .05	.77	.18
Dispute over:			
financial arrangements	.84	− .02	− .04
property settlement	.71	.19	− .08
child support	.84	− .20	− .03
visitation	.59	− .22	.22
custody	.48	.29	− .54

Note: Principal components factor analysis with varimax rotation was performed; table entries are the rotated factor matrix loadings.

TABLE 3 / Correlations between Discussion and Disputation Indexes and Measures of the Preseparation Relationship

	Disputation	Practical Discussion	Personal Discussion
Arguments increased during last year of marriage	.27*	.05	−.06
	(.00)	(.30)	(.25)
Tense atmosphere in home during marriage	.17*	−.23*	−.06
	(.04)	(.01)	(.26)
Tension increased during last year of marriage	.07	−.10	−.24*
	(.23)	(.24)	(.01)

Note: Table entries are zero-order Pearson correlation coefficients. Significance levels are reported in parentheses.
*significance ≤ .05.

TABLE 4 / Correlations between Discussion and Disputation Indexes and Measures of the Postseparation Relationship

	Disputation	Practical Discussion	Personal Discussion
Relationship scale: friendly, neutral or hostile	.31*	−.46*	−.34*
	(.00)	(.00)	(.00)
Father talks to the mother "like a friend"	−.19*	.53*	.42*
	(.03)	(.00)	(.00)
Father has meals with mother and children together	−.26*	.44*	.43*
	(.00)	(.00)	(.00)

Note: Table entries are zero-order Pearson correlation coefficients. Significance levels are reported in parentheses.
*significance ≤ .05.

the communicational styles and measures of the couple's interactions. We looked at whether the wife describes the relationship as friendly, neutral, or hostile; whether the husband talks to her "like a friend"; and whether he has meals with her and the children. Not surprisingly, disputing is associated with the wife characterizing the current relationship as hostile, one in which the spouses do not talk as friends and the husband is unlikely to have meals with her and the children together.

Both styles of discussing, on the other hand, were associated with a more friendly relationship, with a likelihood of talking to the husband as a "friend," and with the husband having meals on occasion with his wife and the children.

How are the communicational styles related to the woman's mental health? Table 5 shows the correlations among the communicational indices and each of the five dimensions of the mother's

TABLE 5 / Correlations between Discussion and Disputation Indexes and Measures of the Mother's Adjustment

	Disputation	Practical Discussion	Personal Discussion
Somatization	.08	−.20*	−.05
	(.19)	(.02)	(.30)
Obsessive/ Compulsive	.16*	−.12	−.07
	(.05)	(.10)	(.25)
Interpersonal Sensitivity	.01	.02	.06
	(.44)	(.42)	(.27)
Depression	.08	−.08	−.02
	(.20)	(.21)	(.41)
Anxiety	.25*	−.13	−.06*
	(.03)	(.09)	(.28)
Total scale	.12	−.16*	−.09
	(.11)	(.05)	(.19)

Note: Table entries are zero-order Pearson correlation coefficients. Significance levels are reported in parentheses.
*significance ≤ .05.

Hopkins Symptom Checklist score, as well as her total score. Disputation is significantly related to heightened obsessive/compulsive and anxiety scores. Practical discussion, however, is associated with a lower somatization score as well as a lower total score. This style may be beneficial because it is characterized by talking about practical matters rather than personal problems and therefore does not involve getting overly personal with one's former spouse. A kind of effective affective control is implied.

The mother's adjustment was not correlated with personal discussing. A clear pattern therefore emerges. Disputing behavior is associated with poorer adjustment, a practical and less personal kind of discussing is positively associated with adjustment, and personal discussing falls between the two.

DISCUSSION

The communicational styles that we have identified were highlighted in our in-depth interviews as our subjects discussed their relationships. One woman, raging at her husband, described feeling "gripped" on several accounts. Having sacrificed her career for his by working to put him through law school, he now denied that she had sacrificed herself on his behalf. She was furious that he left the marriage suddenly, refusing her urgings to go into therapy. And when they separated, he told her that he never loved her, leaving her feeling worthless. Another woman, who was in a rage for weeks after the separation, saw her husband's car parked in front of his girlfriend's house. The wife unlocked his car, put her 5-year-old daughter in it, and sent one of the older children upstairs to knock on the girlfriend's door. Her intended message was that she knows that he is sleeping with another woman and the children know it too.

Describing on the surface a more "neutral" relationship, one man said the following about his relationship after the separation:

We can talk and discuss things about the boys or Sandy's new job. It's not a friendship. I

don't know what kind of relationship I'd like. At times, I miss being married. It goes from hurt to rage—a whole gamut of emotions— from anger to sympathy.

Similarly, a wife described her thoughts: "We are civil to each other. I still have a lot of left over feelings. I haven't processed everything at a gut level. I need to let go completely." When asked what kind of relationship she would like, she replied "a pleasant business relationship—where I didn't have to personalize things, where I could be more detached." Her husband described their relationship as

a business relationship. I haven't discussed anything of a personal nature and would like to leave it that way. Part of me says, "Maybe it could be better." Another part says, "Why do you want that?" Every time we get past "hello" we get into a conflict area. But I want to have a relationship with her because she has such responsibility raising the kids. I want to be civil so that we're able to talk about issues concerning the kids. Once the kids are on their own, no relationship is needed or wanted.

And finally, a group of people described the friendlier, more personal relationship that we have discussed. One husband said: "I have no animosity toward her at all. I would do anything I could to help her and remain friendly, if not friends." Another man, who was seeing his wife weekly, explained he wanted to spend time with her: "She looks good! and I forget. She remembers only the good too. We never really hated each other and we forget the bitterness." He expressed his hesitation: "Maybe I'm afraid of attachment with her." His wife, talking about their daughter's birthday party in her interview with us said, "Carl is always invited and always comes. People would think we're a family and married and there's absolutely no difference. He calls several times during the week to talk to me and Kim."

Thus, although it is more often expected that people are angry when they divorce—angry at their spouse and angry that so many years have been wasted—this article confirms more recent research on the divorcing process (Ahrons & Rodgers, 1987; Goldsmith, 1980) that points to alternative reactions. How much anger is too much anger and how much friendship is too much friendship becomes the job of the clinician to tease out. Our clinical work (Isaacs, 1981, 1982; Isaacs, et al., 1986) suggests that anger has its place, particularly in the early separation period, in that it can ward off a more immobilizing depression and make available energy to reconstruct one's life. This anger, however, needs to be encapsulated, so that the children are not exposed to it unendingly and are not drawn into the fight between their parents. But anger that persists unabated well into the divorcing process becomes unproductive and destructive—both to the adults themselves and to their children, who are unlikely to be protected when the anger is unduly prolonged. The therapist's job is to diagnose the role that anger is playing for the participants—intrapsychically as well as interpersonally. An anger that is keeping a husband or wife from becoming suicidal needs to be treated very differently from one that is preserving the intensity of the marital relationship and preventing the couple from effectively separating.

On the other extreme from anger is a friendly and very personal relationship after separation. Our findings suggest that this type of friendship, though not detrimental, did not enhance the woman's postseparation adjustment. It is interesting to note that although a sexual relationship in the first year of separation was unusual for our sample as a whole, when it did occur, it was in the context of the "personal" communicational style, highlighting one risk with this group. These may be the people who hang onto their previous relationship as a way of not moving on with their lives. Rather than developing a supportive network exclusive of the spouse, it is the husband or wife who continues to be a key person to rely on. Our clinical work shows us that when the husband or wife finally does decide to break away and begin an involvement with another person, the spouse left behind feels "left" a second time, and must reexperience the rejection, anger, and de-

pression that came with the separation. To reexperience this months after the separation can be confusing to them and their children alike, who, after living with a separation that was not a separation, now have to experience once again a resurgence of anger and hurt.

Whereas the previous type of relationship was one in which the adults did not draw sufficient boundaries, the communicational style characterized by practical as opposed to personal discussion is one in which they did. These were the people who did not have to use anger to ostensibly separate from their spouse, nor were they incapable of separating. They were able to relate to their spouse in a more balanced way and may well be the people who were more psychologically free to pick up the pieces and move on, as well as to get some assistance and sustenance from the familiar source, but within bounds. This more balanced relationship is reflected in the better adjustment of these women. In terms of clinical intervention, our data suggest that a history of the marriage can alert the clinician to the direction in which the couple may be headed. Those couples, for example, who describe a tense atmosphere during the marriage in which arguments increase during the last year of marriage, may be more likely to turn into the warring ex-spouses that we have described elsewhere (Isaacs et al., 1986) than those who do not characterize their marriage in such terms. For such families, the work of the clinician may initially have to be helping the adults encapsulate their fight so that the children receive some modicum of protection. For those couples who continue to relate in an overly personal way, the work of therapy may be to help them to draw more adequate boundaries, so that their long-term adjustment can be facilitated.

SUMMARY AND CONCLUSION

We have identified three broad communicational styles in the first year of the separation and have found that they have antecedents in the marital relationship and are related to other measures of the postseparation relationship as well as the woman's adjustment. Disputing in the first year had negative effects on adjustment, whereas a practical, as opposed to a more personal, discussing between separated spouses was beneficial.

These findings call into question common assumptions concerning the inevitability of disputation in the divorce process. Although some couples seem to be continually embroiled in conflict, others are able to relate to each other on neutral or even friendly terms. Not all divorces follow the same path, and our findings indicate that these paths are a continuation of the marital relationship rather than a by-product of the divorce process per se. Thus different kinds of marriages result in different kinds of divorces, which influence adjustment in different ways.

For clinicians, this implies that one must not assume that all divorces traverse the same path of conflict, nor can they all be treated in the same fashion. A history of the marriage, gathered early in the divorcing process, can alert the clinician to the direction in which the couple may be headed. Couples should be encouraged to discuss practical matters but not overly personal concerns. Intervention early in the divorcing process may be particularly useful in facilitating adjustment for all family members.

REFERENCES

Ahrons, C. (1981). The continuing relationship between divorced spouses. *American Journal of Orthopsychiatry, 51,* 415–428.

Ahrons, C., & Bowman, M. (1981). *Analysis of couple data: Theoretical and methodological issues.* Paper presented at the HCFR Pre-Conference Workshop on Theory Construction and Research Methodology, Milwaukee, WI.

Ahrons, C., & Rodgers, R. (1987). *Divorced families: A multidisciplinary developmental view.* New York: W. W. Norton.

Ahrons, C., & Wallisch, L. (1986). The relationship between former spouses. In S. Duck & D. Perlman (Eds.), *Close relationships: Development, dynamics, and deterioration.* Beverly Hills, CA: Sage.

Derogatis, L., Lipman, R., Rickels, K., Uhlenhuth, E., & Covi, L. (1974). The Hopkins Symptom Checklist (HSCL): A self-report symptom inventory. *Behavioral Science, 19,* 1–15.

Goldsmith, J. (1980). Relationships between former spouses: Descriptive findings. *Journal of Divorce, 2,* 1–20.

Goode, W. (1956). *After divorce.* New York: Free Press.

Hetherington, E., Cox, M., & Cox, R. (1978). The aftermath of divorce. In J. H. Stevens, Jr., & M. Matthews (Eds.), *Mother/child, father/child relationships.* Washington, DC: NAEYC.

Hunt, M., & Hunt, B. (1977). *The divorce experience.* New York: McGraw-Hill.

Isaacs, M. (1981). Treatment for families of divorce: A systems model of prevention. In Stuart, I., & Abt, L. (Eds.), *Children of separation and divorce: Management and treatment.* New York: Van Nostrand Reinhold.

Isaacs, M. (1982). Helping mom fail: A case of stalemated divorcing process. *Family Process, 21,* 225–234.

Isaacs, M., & Leon, G. (1986). Social networks, divorce and adjustment: A tale of three generations. *Journal of Divorce, 9,* 1–16.

Isaacs, M., Leon, G., & Donohue, A. M. (1986). Who are the "normal" children of divorce? On the need to specify populations. *Journal of Divorce, 10,* 107–119.

Isaacs, M., Montalvo, B., & Abelsohn, D. (1986). *The difficult divorce: Therapy for children and families.* New York: Basic Books.

Jacobson, G. (1983). *The multiple crises of marital separation and divorce.* New York: Grune & Stratton.

Wallerstein, J., & Kelly, J. (1980). *Surviving the breakup: How parents and children cope with divorce.* New York: Basic Books.

Weiss, R. (1975). *Marital separation,* New York: Basic Books.

Weiss, R. (1979). The emotional impact of marital separation. In Levinger, G., & Moles, O. (Eds.), *Divorce and separation.* New York: Basic Books.

Funding for this research was provided by a grant from the Pew Memorial Trust and by NIMH Grant 1-RO1-MH37925-02 to the Families of Divorce Project, Philadelphia Child Guidance Clinic.

CRITICAL THINKING QUESTIONS

1. This article examined communication styles in recently separated spouses and what marital factors may have been predictive of divorce. How analogous are the findings reported to those that might be involved in the termination of other types of relationships, such as those of two people who have lived together or who have been in a long-standing dating relationship? Design a study to test these possibilities.

2. The study asked recently separated women to comment on their current relationships with their former spouses, as well as on what their relationships were like in the year preceding the separation. Marriage factors that may predict later communication patterns and adjustment were presented. Is it possible that the women's current situations may have influenced their perceptions of what their marriages were like? In other words, are the women's after-the-fact assessments necessarily accurate?

3. One conclusion of the article was that the practical communication style is best for several reasons. If this is indeed the case, would it be desirable to try to make early interventions in marriages to teach people how to communicate along these lines? Or are such patterns of communication basic to the relationship and not skills that can be taught?

4. Statistics show that most people who divorce will eventually remarry. Do you think that the pattern of communication and adjustment to the breakup of the first marriage have an impact on marital adjustment and satisfaction in later marriages? How could you study such a question?

Chapter Eight

CONFORMITY
AND OBEDIENCE

SOCIAL INFLUENCE IS the process of inducing change in other people. Sometimes social change results from direct orders to do something, such as when an officer gives an order to a subordinate. When this happens, we call it *obedience*. Basic to situations involving obedience is some sort of power, either real or imagined, that the person giving the orders has over the person obeying.

Not all social influence is due to direct orders from people in positions of authority. Instead, we may simply ask that a person do something for us. *Compliance* is when a person does something just because he or she was asked to, not because the requestor had any type of power over him or her.

Finally, social influence also operates in a very subtle way, when people follow norms, or generally expected ways of behaving in certain situations. For example, when you are in an elevator, what do you do? Most likely, you face forward and stare at the numbers. Conformity occurs in many situations where norms exist for proper behavior. In a sense, conformity is the lifeblood of a society, for without conformity to rules, society could not exist.

The articles selected for this chapter primarily deal with obedience and compliance, although issues of conformity also can be found. Article 22, "The Education of a Torturer," gives a chilling account of what types of social influence go into the transformation of a normal human being into someone capable of inflicting the most hideous punishment and pain on someone else. As the article notes, the transformation is not due just to obedience to authority but also to compliance to requests and conformity to the norms of the torturer subculture.

Article 23 is Stanley Milgram's classic work on obedience to authority, which is perhaps one of the most widely known studies in the field of social psychology. "Behavioral Study of Obedience" seeks to demonstrate experimentally that the average person could be induced to harm another person simply by being ordered to do so by someone in a position of authority. The large number of people who fully obeyed surprised many.

Finally, Article 24, "Perceived Symbols of Authority and Their Influence on Compliance," examines how symbols such as clothing worn can influence compliance to requests. This article is included not only to present information on the role of a uniform on inducing compliance but also to show how the process works in a non-life-and-death situation.

ARTICLE 22 _____

When people read about a horrendous act that has been committed, they naturally think that the person who committed it is somehow deranged or inhuman. Sometimes that is indeed the case, as when a psychotic commits an act under orders he has supposedly received during hallucinations. Personal pathology and mental illness are certainly involved in many of the hideous acts that people commit. But are personality or psychological factors always the cause of such behavior? Is it possible that an otherwise normal individual may commit an abnormal, sick act, not because there is something wrong with him or her but because of the situation he or she might be in?

History is full of examples of normal people who have committed abnormal acts. For example, warfare has often induced otherwise normal, nonviolent people not only to kill but also to commit atrocities. Yet the suggestion that somehow anyone placed in the same situation may act the same way is a repugnant thought. It might be a lot more personally comforting to believe that people who do bad things are somehow different from us. We, after all, are good and certainly incapable of being mass murderers. Only other people who are either sick or are somehow overly conforming could do such things. In other words, we tend to attribute others' acts to their disposition—that is, some personality or other enduring trait causes them to act that way.

In this article, Gibson and Haritos-Fatourus present both field and experimental research to suggest that perhaps it is not so much individual characteristics (disposition) that result in performing terrible acts but rather the situation that produces the behavior. The authors review the step-by-step process of taking a normal person who does not enjoy hurting other people and transforming him into a torturer. The similar steps of inducing obedience found in other studies also are presented. If you strongly believe that a torturer is somehow different than other people, this article may make you think again.

The Education of a Torturer

■ Janice T. Gibson and Mika Haritos-Fatouros

Torture—for whatever purpose and in whatever name—requires a torturer, an individual responsible for planning and causing pain to others. "A man's hands are shackled behind him, his eyes blindfolded," wrote Argentine journalist Jacobo Timerman about his torture by Argentine army extremists. "No one says a word. Blows are showered . . . [He is] stripped, doused with water, tied . . . And the application of electric shocks begins. It's impossible to shout—you howl." The governments of at least 90 countries use similar methods to torture people all over the world, Amnesty International reports.

What kind of person can behave so monstrously to another human being? A sadist or a sexual deviant? Someone with an authoritarian upbringing or who was abused by parents? A disturbed personality affected somehow by hereditary characteristics?

On the contrary, the Nazis who tortured and

Reprinted from *Psychology Today*, 1986 (November), *20*, 50–58. Reprinted with permission from *Psychology Today Magazine*. Copyright © 1986 (PT Partners, L.P.).

killed millions during World War II "weren't sadists or killers by nature," Hannah Arendt reported in her book *Eichmann in Jerusalem*. Many studies of Nazi behavior concluded that monstrous acts, despite their horrors, were often simply a matter of faithful bureaucrats slavishly following orders.

In a 1976 study, University of Florida psychologist Molly Harrower asked 15 Rorschach experts to examine ink-blot test reports from Adolph Eichmann, Rudolf Hess, Hermann Goering and five other Nazi war criminals, made just before their trials at Nuremberg. She also sent the specialists Rorschach reports from eight Americans, some with well-adjusted personalities and some who were severely disturbed, without revealing the individuals' identities. The experts were unable to distinguish the Nazis from the Americans and judged an equal number of both to be well-adjusted. The horror that emerges is the likelihood that torturers are not freaks; they are ordinary people.

Obedience to what we call the "authority of violence" often plays an important role in pushing ordinary people to commit cruel, violent and even fatal acts. During wartime, for example, soldiers will follow orders to kill unarmed civilians. Here, we will look at the way obedience and other factors combine to produce willing torturers.

Twenty-five years ago, the late psychologist Stanley Milgram demonstrated convincingly that people unlikely to be cruel in everyday life will administer pain if they are told to by someone in authority. In a famous experiment, Milgram had men wearing laboratory coats direct average American adults to inflict a series of electric shocks on other people. No real shocks were given and the "victims" were acting, but the people didn't know this. They were told that the purpose of the study was to measure the effects of punishment on learning. Obediently, 65 percent of them used what they thought were dangerously high levels of shocks when the experimenter told them to. While they were less likely to administer these supposed shocks as they were moved closer to their victims, almost one-third of them continued to shock when they were close enough to touch.

This readiness to torture is not limited to Americans. Following Milgram's lead, other researchers found that people of all ages, from a wide range of countries, were willing to shock others even when they had nothing to gain by complying with the command or nothing to lose by refusing it. So long as someone else, an authority figure, was responsible for the final outcome of the experiment, almost no one absolutely refused to administer shocks. Each study also found, as Milgram had, that some people would give shocks even when the decision was left up to them.

Milgram proposed that the reasons people obey or disobey authority fall into three categories. The first is personal history: family or school backgrounds that encourage obedience or defiance. The second, which he called "binding," is made up of ongoing experiences that make people feel comfortable when they obey authority. Strain, the third category, consists of bad feelings from unpleasant experiences connected with obedience. Milgram argued that when the binding factors are more powerful than the strain of cooperating, people will do as they are told. When the strain is greater, they are more likely to disobey.

This may explain short-term obedience in the laboratory, but it doesn't explain prolonged patterns of torture during wartime or under some political regimes. Repeatedly, torturers in Argentina and elsewhere performed acts that most of us consider repugnant, and in time this should have placed enough strain on them to prevent their obedience. It didn't. Nor does Milgram's theory explain undirected cruel or violent acts, which occur even when no authority orders them. For this, we have developed a more comprehensive learning model; for torture, we discovered, can be taught (see "Teaching to Torment," this article).

We studied the procedures used to train Greek military police as torturers during that country's military regime from 1967 through 1974. We examined the official testimonies of 21 former soldiers in the ESA (Army Police Corps) given at their 1975 criminal trials in Athens; in addition, Haritos-Fatouros conducted in-depth interviews with 16 of them after their trials. In many cases, these men had been convicted and had completed prison sentences. They were all leading normal lives when interviewed. One was a university graduate, five were graduates of higher technical institutes, nine had completed at least their second year of high school and only one had no more than a primary school education.

All of these men had been drafted, first into regular military service and then into specialized units that required servicemen to torture prisoners. We found no record of delinquent or disturbed behavior before their military service. However, we did find several features of the soldiers' training that helped to turn them into willing and able torturers.

The initial screening for torturers was primarily based on physical strength and "appropriate" political beliefs, which simply meant that the recruits and their families were anticommunists. This ensured that the men had hostile attitudes toward potential victims from the very beginning.

Once they were actually serving as military police, the men were also screened for other attributes. According to former torturer Michaelis Petrou, "The most important criterion was that you had to keep your mouth shut. Second, you had to show aggression. Third, you had to be intelligent and strong. Fourth, you had to be 'their man,' which meant that you would report on the others serving with you, that [the officers] could trust you and that you would follow their orders blindly."

Binding the recruits to the authority of ESA began in basic training, with physically brutal initiation rites. Recruits themselves were cursed, punched, kicked and flogged. They were forced to run until they collapsed and prevented from relieving themselves for long stretches of time. They were required to swear allegiance to a symbol of authority used by the regime (a poster of a soldier superimposed on a large phoenix rising from its own ashes), and they had to promise on their knees to obey their commander-in-chief and the military revolution.

While being harassed and beaten by their officers, servicemen were repeatedly told how fortunate they were to have joined the ESA, the strongest and most important support of the regime. They were told that an ESA serviceman's

action is never questioned: "You can even flog a major." In-group language helped the men to develop elitist attitudes. Servicemen used nicknames for one another and, later, they used them for victims and for the different methods of torture. "Tea party" meant the beating of a prisoner by a group of military police using their fists, and "tea party with toast" meant more severe group beatings using clubs. Gradually, the recruits came to speak of all people who were not in their group, parents and families included, as belonging to the "outside world."

The strain of obedience on the recruits was reduced in several ways. During basic training, they were given daily "national ethical education" lectures that included indoctrination against communism and enemies of the state. During more advanced training, the recruits were constantly reminded that the prisoners were "worms," and that they had to "crush" them. One man reported that when he was torturing prisoners later, he caught himself repeating phrases like "bloody communists!" that he had heard in the lectures.

The military police used a carrot-and-stick method to further diminish the recruits' uneasiness about torture. There were many rewards, such as relaxed military rules after training was completed, and torturers often weren't punished for leaving camp without permission. They were allowed to wear civilian clothes, to keep their hair long and to drive military police cars for their personal use. Torturers were frequently given a leave of absence after they forced a confession from a prisoner. They had many economic benefits as well, including free bus rides and restaurant meals and job placement when military service was over. These were the carrots.

The sticks consisted of the constant harassment, threats and punishment for disobedience. The men were threatened and intimidated, first by their trainers, then later by senior servicemen. "An officer used to tell us that if a warder helps a prisoner, he will take the prisoner's place and the whole platoon will flog him," one man recalled. Soldiers spied on one another, and even the most successful torturers said that they were constantly afraid.

"You will learn to love pain," one officer promised a recruit. Sensitivity to torture was blunted in several steps. First, the men had to endure it themselves, as if torture were a normal act. The beatings and other torments inflicted on them continued and became worse. Next, the servicemen chosen for the Persecution Section, the unit that tortured political prisoners, were brought into contact with the prisoners by carrying food to their cells. The new men watched veteran soldiers torture prisoners, while they stood guard. Occasionally, the veterans would order them to give the prisoners "some blows."

At the next step, the men were required to participate in group beatings. Later, they were told to use a variety of torture methods on the prisoners. The final step, the appointment to prison warder or chief torturer, was announced suddenly by the commander-in-chief, leaving the men no time to reflect on their new duties.

The Greek example illustrates how the ability to torture can be taught. Training that increases binding and reduces strain can cause decent people to commit acts, often over long periods of time, that otherwise would be unthinkable for them. Similar techniques can be found in military training all over the world, when the intent is to teach soldiers to kill or perform some other repellent act. We conducted extensive interviews with soldiers and exsoldiers in the U.S. Marines and the Green Berets, and we found that all the steps in our training model were part and parcel of elite American military training. Soldiers are screened for intellectual and physical ability, achievement and mental health. Binding begins in basic training, with initiation rites that isolate trainees from society, introduce them to new rules and values and leave them little time for clear thinking after exhausting physical exercise and scant sleep. Harassment plays an important role, and soldiers are severely punished for disobedience, with demerits, verbal abuse, hours of calisthenics and loss of eating, sleeping and other privileges.

Military training gradually desensitizes soldiers to violence and reduces the strain normally created by repugnant acts. Their revulsion is diminished by screaming chants and songs about violence and killing during marches and runs. The enemy is given derogatory names and portrayed as less than human; this makes it easier to kill them. Completing the toughest possible training and being rewarded by "making it" in an elite corps bring the soldiers confidence and pride, and those who accomplish this feel they can do anything. "Although I tried to avoid killing, I learned to have confidence in myself and was never afraid," said a former Green Beret who served in Vietnam. "It was part of the job. . . . Anyone who goes through that kind of training could do it."

The effectiveness of these techniques, as several researchers have shown, is not limited to the army. History teacher Ronald Jones started what he called the Third Wave movement as a classroom experiment to show his high school students how people might have become Nazis in World War II. Jones began the Third Wave demonstration by requiring students to stand at attention in a unique new posture and follow strict new rules. He required students to stand beside their desks when asking or answering questions and to begin each statement by saying, "Mr. Jones." The students obeyed. He then required them to shout slogans, "Strength through discipline!" and "Strength through community!" Jones created a salute for class members that he called the Third Wave: the right hand raised to the shoulder with fingers curled. The salute had no meaning, but it served as a symbol of group belonging and a way of isolating members from outsiders.

The organization expanded quickly from 20 original members to 100. The teacher issued membership cards and assigned students to report members who didn't comply with the new rules. Dutifully, 20 students pointed accusing fingers at their classmates.

Then Jones announced that the Third Wave was a "nationwide movement to find students willing to fight for political change," and he organized a rally, which drew a crowd of 200 students. At the rally, after getting students to salute and shout slogans on command, Jones explained the true reasons behind the Third Wave demonstration. Like the Nazis before them, Jones pointed out, "You bargained your freedom for the comfort of discipline."

The students, at an age when group belonging was very important to them, made good candidates for training. Jones didn't teach his students to commit atrocities, and the Third Wave lasted for only five days; in that time, however, Jones created an obedient group that resembled in many ways the Nazi youth groups of World War II (see "The Third Wave: Nazism in a High School," *Psychology Today,* July 1976).

Psychologists Craig Haney, W. Curtis Banks and Philip Zimbardo went even further in a remarkable simulation of prison life done at Stanford University. With no special training and in only six days' time, they changed typical university students into controlling, abusive guards and servile prisoners.

The students who agreed to participate were chosen randomly to be guards or prisoners. The mock guards were given uniforms and nightsticks and told to act as guards. Prisoners were treated as dangerous criminals: Local police rounded them up, finger-printed and booked them and brought them to a simulated cellblock in the basement of the university psychology department. Uniformed guards made them remove their clothing, deloused them, gave them prison uniforms and put them in cells.

The two groups of students, originally found to be very similar in most respects, showed striking changes within one week. Prisoners became passive, dependent and helpless. In contrast, guards expressed feelings of power, status and group belonging. They were aggressive and abusive within the prison, insulting and bullying the prisoners. Some guards reported later that they had enjoyed their power, while others said they had not thought they were capable of behaving as they had. They were surprised and dismayed at what they had done: "It was degrading. . . . To me, those things are sick. But they [the prisoners] did everything I said. They abused each other because I requested them to. No one questioned my authority at all."

The guards' behavior was similar in two important ways to that of the Greek torturers. First, they dehumanized their victims. Second, like the torturers, the guards were abusive only when they were within the prison walls. They could act reasonably outside the prisons because the two prison influences of binding and reduced strain were absent.

All these changes at Stanford occurred with no special training, but the techniques we have outlined were still present. Even without training, the student guards "knew" from television and movies that they were supposed to punish prisoners; they "knew" they were supposed to feel superior; and they "knew" they were supposed to blame their victims. Their own behavior and that of their peers gradually numbed their sensitivity to what they were doing, and they were rewarded by the power they had over their prisoners.

There is no evidence that such short-term experiments produce lasting effects. None were reported from either the Third Wave demonstration or the Stanford University simulation. The Stanford study, however, was cut short when depression, crying and psychosomatic illnesses began to appear among the students. And studies of Vietnam veterans have revealed that committing abhorrent acts, even under the extreme conditions of war, can lead to long-term problems. In one study of 130 Vietnam veterans who came to a therapist for help, almost 30 percent of them were concerned about violent acts they had committed while in the service. The veterans reported feelings of anxiety, guilt, depression and an inability to carry on intimate relationships. In a similar fashion, after the fall of the Greek dictatorship in 1974, former torturers began to report nightmares, irritability and episodes of depression.

"Torturing became a job," said former Greek torturer Petrou. "If the officers ordered you to beat, you beat. If they ordered you to stop, you stopped. You never thought you could do otherwise." His comments bear a disturbing resemblance to the feelings expressed by a Stanford guard: "When I was doing it, I didn't feel regret. . . . I didn't feel guilt. Only afterwards, when I began to reflect . . . did it begin to dawn on me that this was a part of me I hadn't known before."

Teaching to Torment

There are several ways to teach people to do the unthinkable, and we have developed a model to explain how they are used. We have also found that college fraternities, although they are far removed from the grim world of torture and violent combat, use similar methods for initiating new members, to ensure their faithfulness to the fraternity's rules and values. However, this unthinking loyalty can sometimes lead to dangerous actions: Over the past 10 years, there have been countless injuries during fraternity initiations and 39 deaths. These training techniques are designed to instill unquestioning obedience in people, but they can easily be a guide for an intensive course in torture.

1. Screening to find the best prospects: normal, well-adjusted people with the physical, intellectual and, in some cases, political attributes necessary for the task.
2. Techniques to increase binding among these prospects:

■ Initiation rites to isolate people from society and introduce them to a new social order, with different rules and values.
■ Elitist attitudes and "in-group" language, which highlight the differences between the group and the rest of society.
3. Techniques to reduce the strain of obedience:
■ Blaming and dehumanizing the victims, so it is less disturbing to harm them.
■ Harassment, the constant physical and psychological intimidation that prevents logical thinking and promotes the instinctive responses needed for acts of inhuman cruelty.
■ Rewards for obedience and punishments for not cooperating.
■ Social modeling by watching other group members commit violent acts and then receive rewards.
■ Systematic desensitization to repugnant acts by gradual exposure to them, so they appear routine and normal despite conflicts with previous moral standards.

We do not believe that torture came naturally to any of these young men. Haritos-Fatouros found no evidence of sadistic, abusive or authoritarian behaviors in the Greek soldiers' histories prior to their training. This, together with our study of Marine training and the Stanford and Third Wave studies, leads to the conclusion that torturers have normal personalities. Any of us, in a similar situation, might be capable of the same cruelty. One probably cannot train a deranged sadist to be an effective torturer or killer. He must be in complete control of himself while on the job.

CRITICAL THINKING QUESTIONS
1. What are the real implications of the studies summarized in the article? Does it literally mean that anyone, including you, could be induced to do the same things if you were put into the same situations? Does it really mean that personality and perhaps free will have nothing to do with whether you choose to obey the orders? Or is free choice not really possible in such situations?
2. If inhuman behaviors can be induced by the techniques used to get torturers to do their deeds, does that mean that people should not be held responsible for the

things they do? Would a defense of "I was conditioned to do it" absolve an individual of personal responsibility for his or her actions?

3. The article seemed to suggest that it is fairly easy to get people to do some terrible things under the right set of conditions. How could you prevent such effects? For example, would forewarning people about possible recrimination lessen the likelihood that they would be influenced by the process?

ARTICLE 23 ———————————————————————

Stanley Milgram's article "Behavioral Study of Obedience" was one of his first describing a series of studies investigating the conditions that produce obedience to authority. This study, as well as Milgram's subsequent research, is truly classic. In fact, if you asked someone who has had only minimal exposure to the field of social psychology about landmark research, this study would perhaps come to mind.

Part of the widespread interest in Milgram's work is due to the implications it has. Basically, Milgram took a group of male volunteers from various backgrounds and ages and induced them to perform acts that appeared to harm another person. Nearly two-thirds of the subjects were fully obedient, continuing to give shocks even though it was apparent that they were harming the victim. Does that mean that just about anyone could be made to do the same? More importantly, while reading the article, keep in mind the actual situation confronting the subjects: What would have happened to them if they had refused to obey? Would the effect demonstrated by Milgram be greater for real-life situations, where there might be punishments for failing to obey?

Besides the implications of the research, Milgram's work on obedience also has attracted considerable interest over the years because of the ethical issues raised. When reading the article, try to put yourself in the shoes of the subjects: How would you feel if you volunteered for a study on learning and instead walked out of the experiment an hour later with the realization that you were willing to harm someone just because an authority figure told you to do so? Think about the ethical issues involved in the study, including the issue of debriefing subjects following an experiment.

Behavioral Study of Obedience

■ Stanley Milgram

This chapter describes a procedure for the study of destructive obedience in the laboratory. It consists of ordering a naive S to administer increasingly more severe punishment to a victim in the context of a learning experiment. Punishment is administered by means of a shock generator with thirty graded switches ranging from Slight Shock to Danger: Severe Shock. The victim is a confederate of the E. The primary dependent variable is the maximum shock the S is willing to administer before he refuses to continue further. Twenty-six Ss obeyed the experimental commands fully, and administered the highest shock on the generator. Fourteen Ss broke off the experiment at some point after the victim protested and refused to provide further answers. The procedure created extreme levels of nervous tension in some Ss. Profuse sweating, trembling and stuttering were typical expressions of this emotional disturbance. One unexpected sign of tension—yet to be explained—was the regular occurrence of nervous laughter, which in some Ss developed into uncontrollable seizures. The variety of interesting behavioral dynamics observed in the experiment,

Reprinted from the *Journal of Abnormal and Social Psychology*, 1963, 67, 371–378. Copyright 1963 by the American Psychological Association. Reprinted by permission.

the reality of the situation for the S, and the possibility of parametric variation within the framework of the procedure, point to the fruitfulness of further study.

Obedience is as basic an element in the structure of social life as one can point to. Some system of authority is a requirement of all communal living, and it is only the man dwelling in isolation who is not forced to respond, through defiance or submission, to the commands of others. Obedience, as a determinant of behavior, is of particular relevance to our time. It has been reliably established that from 1933–1945 millions of innocent persons were systematically slaughtered on command. Gas chambers were built, death camps were guarded, daily quotas of corpses were produced with the same efficiency as the manufacture of appliances. These inhumane policies may have originated in the mind of a single person, but they could only be carried out on a massive scale if a very large number of persons obeyed orders.

Obedience is the psychological mechanism that links individual action to political purpose. It is the dispositional cement that binds men to systems of authority. Facts of recent history and observation in daily life suggest that for many persons obedience may be a deeply ingrained behavior tendency, indeed, a prepotent impulse overriding training in ethics, sympathy, and moral conduct. C. P. Snow (1961) points to its importance when he writes:

> *When you think of the long and gloomy history of man, you will find more hideous crimes have been committed in the name of obedience than have ever been committed in the name of rebellion. If you doubt that, read William Shirer's "Rise and Fall of the Third Reich." The German Officer Corps were brought up in the most rigorous code of obedience . . . in the name of obedience they were party to, and assisted in, the most wicked large scale actions in the history of the world (p. 24).*

While the particular form of obedience dealt with in the present study has its antecedents in

these episodes, it must not be thought all obedience entails acts of aggression against others. Obedience serves numerous productive functions. Indeed, the very life of society is predicated on its existence. Obedience may be ennobling and educative and refer to acts of charity and kindness, as well as to destruction.

General Procedure

A procedure was devised which seems useful as a tool for studying obedience (Milgram, 1961). It consists of ordering a naive subject to administer electric shock to a victim. A simulated shock generator is used, with 30 clearly marked voltage levels that range from 15 to 450 volts. The instrument bears verbal designations that range from Slight Shock to Danger: Severe Shock. The responses of the victim, who is a trained confederate of the experimenter, are standardized. The orders to administer shocks are given to the naive subject in the context of a "learning experiment" ostensibly set up to study the effects of punishment on memory. As the experiment proceeds the naive subject is commanded to administer increasingly more intense shocks to the victim, even to the point of reaching the level marked Danger: Severe Shock. Internal resistances become stronger, and at a certain point the subject refuses to go on with the experiment. Behavior prior to this rupture is considered "obedience," in that the subject complies with the commands of the experimenter. The point of rupture is the act of disobedience. A quantitative value is assigned to the subject's performance based on the maximum intensity shock he is willing to administer before he refuses to participate further. Thus for any particular subject and for any particular experimental condition the degree of obedience may be specified with a numerical value. The crux of the study is to systematically vary the factors believed to alter the degree of obedience to the experimental commands.

The technique allows important variables to be manipulated at several points in the experiment. One may vary aspects of the source of command, content and form of command, instrumentalities for its execution, target object, general setting, etc. The problem, therefore, is not one of designing increasingly more numerous experimental conditions, but of selecting those that best illuminate the process of obedience from the sociopsychological standpoint.

Related Studies

The inquiry bears an important relation to philosophic analyses of obedience and authority (Arendt, 1958; Friedrich, 1958; Weber, 1947), an early experimental study of obedience by Frank (1944), studies in "authoritarianism" (Adorno, Frenkel-Brunswik, Levinson, and Sanford, 1950; Rokeach, 1961), and a recent series of analytic and empirical studies in social power (Cartwright, 1959). It owes much to the long concern with *suggestion* in social psychology, both in its normal forms (e.g., Binet, 1900) and in its clinical manifestations (Charcot, 1881). But it derives, in the first instance, from direct observation of a social fact; the individual who is commanded by a legitimate authority ordinarily obeys. Obedience comes easily and often. It is a ubiquitous and indispensable feature of social life.

METHOD

Subjects

The subjects were 40 males between the ages of 20 and 50, drawn from New Haven and the surrounding communities. Subjects were obtained by a newspaper advertisement and direct mail solicitation. Those who responded to the appeal believed they were to participate in a study of

memory and learning at Yale University. A wide range of occupations is represented in the sample. Typical subjects were postal clerks, high school teachers, salesmen, engineers, and laborers. Subjects ranged in educational level from one who had not finished elementary school, to those who had doctorate and other professional degrees. They were paid $4.50 for their participation in the experiment. However, subjects were told that payment was simply for coming to the laboratory, and that the money was theirs no matter what happened after they arrived. Table 1 shows the proportion of age and occupational types assigned to the experimental condition.

Personnel and Locale

The experiment was conducted on the grounds of Yale University in the elegant interaction laboratory. (This detail is relevant to the perceived legitimacy of the experiment. In further variations, the experiment was dissociated from the university, with consequences for performance.) The role of experimenter was played by a 31-year-old high school teacher of biology. His manner was impassive, and his appearance somewhat stern throughout the experiment. He was dressed in a gray technician's coat. The victim was played by a 47-year-old accountant, trained for the role; he was of Irish-American stock, whom most observers found mild-mannered and likable.

Procedure

One naive subject and one victim (an accomplice) performed in each experiment. A pretext had to be devised that would justify the administration

TABLE 1 / Distribution of Age and Occupational Types in the Experiment

Occupations	20–29 years *n*	30–39 years *n*	40–50 years *n*	Percentage of total (occupations)
Workers, skilled and unskilled	4	5	6	37.5
Sales, business, and white-collar	3	6	7	40.0
Professional	1	5	3	22.5
Percentage of total (age)	20	40	40	

Note: Total *N* = 40.

of electric shock by the naive subject. This was effectively accomplished by the cover story. After a general introduction on the presumed relation between punishment and learning, subjects were told:

> *But actually, we know very* little *about the effect of punishment on learning, because almost no truly scientific studies have been made of it in human beings.*
>
> *For instance, we don't know how* much *punishment is best for learning—and we don't know how much difference it makes as to who is giving the punishment, whether an adult learns best from a younger or an older person than himself—or many things of that sort.*
>
> *So in this study we are bringing together a number of adults of different occupations and ages. And we're asking some of them to be teachers and some of them to be learners.*
>
> *We want to find out just what effect different people have on each other as teachers and learners, and also what effect* punishment *will have on learning in this situation.*
>
> *Therefore, I'm going to ask one of you to be the teacher here tonight and the other one to be the learner.*
>
> *Does either of you have a preference?*

Subjects then drew slips of paper from a hat to determine who would be the teacher and who would be the learner in the experiment. The drawing was rigged so that the naive subject was always the teacher and the accomplice always the learner. (Both slips contained the word "Teacher.") Immediately after the drawing the teacher and learner were taken to an adjacent room and the learner was strapped into an "electric chair" apparatus.

The experimenter explained that the straps were to prevent excessive movement while the learner was being shocked. The effect was to make it impossible for him to escape from the situation. An electrode was attached to the learner's wrist, and electrode paste was applied "to avoid blisters and burns." Subjects were told that the electrode was attached to the shock generator in the adjoining room.

In order to improve credibility the experimenter declared, in response to a question by the learner: "Although the shocks can be extremely painful, they cause no permanent tissue damage.

Learning Task The lesson administered by the subject was a paired-associate learning task. The subject read a series of word pairs to the learner, and then read the first word of the pair along with four terms. The learner was to indicate which of the four terms had originally been paired with the first word. He communicated his answer by pressing one of four switches in front of him, which in turn lit up one of four numbered quadrants in an answer-box located atop the shock generator.

Shock Generator The instrument panel consists of 30 lever switches set in a horizontal line. Each switch is clearly labeled with a voltage designation that ranges from 15 to 450 volts. There is a 15-volt increment from one switch to the next going from left to right. In addition, the following verbal designations are clearly indicated for groups of four switches going from left to right: Slight Shock, Moderate Shock, Strong Sock, Very Strong Shock, Intense Shock, Extreme Intensity Shock, Danger: Severe Shock. (Two switches after this last designation are simply marked XXX.)

Upon depressing a switch: a pilot light corresponding to each switch is illuminated in bright red; an electric buzzing is heard; an electric blue light, labeled "voltage energizer," flashes; the dial on the voltage meter swings to the right; various relay clicks are sounded.

The upper left-hand corner of the generator is labeled Shock Generator, Type ZLB, Dyson Instrument Company, Waltham, Mass. Output 15 Volts—450 Volts.

Details of the instrument were carefully handled to insure an appearance of authenticity. The panel was engraved by precision industrial engravers, and all components were of high quality. No subject in the experiment suspected that the instrument was merely a simulated shock generator.[1]

Sample Shock Each naive subject is given a sample shock on the shock generator, prior to beginning his run as teacher. This shock is always 45 volts, and is applied by pressing the third switch of the generator. The shock is applied to the wrist of the naive subject, and has its source in a 45-volt battery wired into the generator. This further convinces the subject of the authenticity of the generator.

Shock Instructions The subject is told to administer a shock to the learner each time he gives a wrong response. Moreover—and this is the key command—the subject is instructed to "move one lever higher on the shock generator each time the learner flashes a wrong answer." He is also instructed to announce the voltage level before administering a shock. This serves to continually remind subjects of the increasing intensity of shocks administered to the learner.

Preliminary and Regular Run Pretests revealed that the procedure of reading words and administering shocks requires some practice before it can be handled smoothly. Therefore, immediately preceding the regular run, the teacher is given a preliminary series of 10 words to read to the learner. There are 3 neutral words in the practice series (i.e., words that the learner answers correctly), so that shocks are administered for 7 of the words, with the maximum shock at 105 volts (moderate shock). Almost all subjects master the procedure by the time the preliminary run is over.

Subjects are then presented with a second list, and are told that the procedure is the same as for the first list; the experimenter adds, however:

> *When you get to the bottom of the list, repeat it over again, and continue giving shocks, until the learner has learned all the pairs correctly.*

The experimenter instructs the subject to

> *start from 15 volts and increase the shock level one step each time the learner gives a wrong answer.*

Feedback from the Victim In all conditions the learner gives a predetermined set of responses to the word pair test, based on a schedule of approximately three wrong answers to one correct answer. In the present experimental condition no vocal response or other sign of protest is heard from the learner until Shock Level 300 is reached. When the 300-volt shock is administered, the learner pounds on the wall of the room in which he is bound to the electric chair. The pounding can be heard by the subject. From this point on, the learner's answers no longer appear on the four-way panel.

At this juncture, subjects ordinarily turn to the experimenter for guidance. The experimenter instructs the subject to treat the absence of a response as a wrong answer, and to shock the subject according to the usual schedule. He advises the subjects to allow 5–10 seconds before considering no response as a wrong answer, and to increase the shock level one step each time the learner fails to respond correctly. The learner's pounding is repeated after the 315-volt shock is administered; afterwards he is not heard from, nor do his answers reappear on the four-way signal box.

Experimenter Feedback At various points in the experiment the subject may turn to the experimenter for advice on whether he should continue to administer shocks. Or he may indicate that he does not wish to go on. It was important to standardize the experimenter's responses to these inquiries and reactions.

If the subject indicated his unwillingness to go on, the experimenter responded with a sequence of "prods," using as many as necessary to bring the subject into line.

> *Prod 1: Please continue,* or *Please go on.*
> *Prod 2: The experiment requires that you continue.*
> *Prod 3: It is absolutely essential that you continue.*
> *Prod 4: You have no other choice, you* must *go on.*

The prods were always made in sequence: Only if Prod 1 had been unsuccessful, could Prod 2 be used. If the subject refused to obey the experimenter after Prod 4, the experiment was terminated. The experimenter's tone of voice was at all times firm, but not impolite. The sequence was begun anew on each occasion that the subject balked or showed reluctance to follow orders.

Special prods. If the subject asked if the learner was liable to suffer permanent physical injury, the experimenter said:

Although the shocks may be painful, there is no permanent tissue damage, so please go on. [Followed by Prods 2, 3, and 4 if necessary.]

If the subject said that the learner did not want to go on, the experimenter replied:

Whether the learner likes it or not, you must go on until he has learned all the word pairs correctly. So please go on. [Followed by Prods 2, 3, and 4 if necessary.]

Dependent Measures

The primary dependent measure for any subject is the maximum shock he administers before he refuses to go any further. In principle this may vary from 0 (for a subject who refuses to administer even the first shock) to 30 (for a subject who administers the highest shock on the generator). A subject who breaks off the experiment at any point prior to administering the thirtieth shock level is termed a *defiant* subject. One who complies with experimental commands fully, and proceeds to administer all shock levels commanded, is termed an *obedient* subject.

Further Records   With few exceptions, experimental sessions were recorded on magnetic tape. Occasional photographs were taken through one-way mirrors. Notes were kept on any unusual behavior occurring during the course of the experiments. On occasion, additional observers were directed to write objective descriptions of the subjects' behavior. The latency and duration of shocks were measured by accurate timing devices.

Interview and Dehoax   Following the experiment, subjects were interviewed: open-ended questions, projective measures, and attitude scales were employed. After the interview, procedures were undertaken to assure that the subject would leave the laboratory in a state of well being. A friendly reconciliation was arranged between the subject and the victim, and an effort was made to reduce any tensions that arose as a result of the experiment.

RESULTS

Preliminary Notions

Before giving an account of the experimental results, it is instructive to consider how persons predict others will perform when commanded to administer powerful shocks to another person. Fourteen Yale seniors, all psychology majors, were provided with a detailed description of the experimental situation. They were asked to reflect carefully on it, and to predict the behavior of 100 hypothetical subjects. More specifically, they were instructed to plot the distribution of obedience of "100 Americans of diverse occupations, and ranging in age from 20 to 50 years," who were placed in the experimental situation.

There was considerable agreement among the respondents on the expected behavior of hypothetical subjects. All respondents predicted that only an insignificant minority would go through to the end of the shock series. (The estimates ranged from 0 to 3 percent; i.e., the most "pessimistic" member of the class predicted that of 100 persons, 3 would continue through to the most potent shock available on the shock generator—450 volts.) The class mean was 1.2 percent. The question was also posed informally to colleagues of the author, and the most general feeling was that few if any subjects would go beyond the designation Very Strong Shock.

Result of Experiment I

Subjects Accept Situation With few exceptions subjects were convinced of the reality of the experimental situation, that they were administering shocks to another person, and the most potent shocks were extremely painful. In the post-experimental interview subjects were asked: "How painful to the learner were the last few shocks that you administered to him?" Subjects were instructed to indicate their answers on a printed 14-point scale ranging from "Not at all painful" to "Extremely painful." The modal response was 14 (Extremely painful) with the mean at 13.42.

Signs of Extreme Tension Many subjects showed signs of nervousness in the experimental situation, and especially upon administering the more powerful shocks. In a large number of cases the degree of tension reached extremes that are rarely seen in sociopsychological laboratory studies. Subjects were observed to sweat, tremble, stutter, bite their lips, groan, and dig their fingernails into their flesh. These were characteristic rather than exceptional responses to the experiment.

One sign of tension was the regular occurrence of nervous laughing fits. Fourteen of the 40 subjects showed definite signs of nervous laughter and smiling. The laughter seemed entirely out of place, even bizarre. Full-blown, uncontrollable seizures were observed for 3 subjects. On one occasion we observed a seizure so violently convulsive that it was necessary to call a halt to the experiment. The subject, a 46-year-old encyclopedia salesman, was seriously embarrassed by his untoward and uncontrollable behavior. In the post-experimental interviews subjects took pains to point out that they were not sadistic types, and that the laughter did not mean they enjoyed shocking the victim.

Distribution of Scores It had been conjectured that persons would not, in general, agree to administer shocks beyond the level designated as Very Strong Shock. The distribution of maximum shocks for this experiment is shown in Table 2. The obtained distribution of scores deviates radically from the prediction.

TABLE 2 / Distribution of Breakoff Points

Verbal designation and voltage indication	Number of subjects for whom this was maximum shock
Slight Shock	
15	0
30	0
45	0
60	0
Moderate Shock	
75	0
90	0
105	0
120	0
Strong Shock	
135	0
150	0
165	0
180	0
Very Strong Shock	
195	0
210	0
225	0
240	0
Intense Shock	
255	0
270	0
285	0
300	5
Extreme Intensity Shock	
315	4
330	2
345	1
360	1
Danger: Severe Shock	
375	1
390	0
405	0
420	0
XXX	
435	0
450	26

Upon command of the experimenter, each of the 40 subjects went beyond the expected breakoff point. No subject stopped prior to administering Shock Level 20. (At this level—300 volts—the victim kicks on the wall and no longer provides answers to the teacher's multiple-choice questions.}

Of the 40 subjects, 5 refused to obey the experimental commands beyond the 300-volt level. Four more subjects administered one further shock, and then refused to go on. Two broke off at the 330-volt level, and 1 each at 345, 360, and 375 volts. Thus a total of 14 subjects defied the experimenter. It is instructive to reprint their remarks at the point of defiance, as transcribed from the tape recordings:

> [0124] *I think he's trying to communicate, he's knocking . . . Well it's not fair to shock the guy . . . these are terrific volts. I don't think this is very humane . . . Oh, I can't go on with this; no, this isn't right. It's a hell of an experiment. The guy is suffering in there. No, I don't want to go on. This is crazy. [Subject refused to administer more shocks.]*
>
> [0123] *He's banging in there. I'm gonna chicken out. I'd like to continue, but I can't do that to a man . . . I'm sorry I can't do that to a man. I'll hurt his heart. You take your check . . . No really, I couldn't do it.*

These subjects were frequently in a highly agitated and even angered state. Sometimes, verbal protest was at a minimum, and the subject simply got up from his chair in front of the shock generator, and indicated that he wished to leave the laboratory.

Of the 40 subjects, 26 obeyed the orders of the experimenter to the end, proceeding to punish the victim until they reached the most potent shock available on the shock generator. At that point, the experimenter called a halt to the session. (The maximum shock is labeled 450 volts, and is two steps beyond the designation: Danger: Severe Shock.) Although obedient subjects continued to administer shocks, they often did so under extreme stress. Some expressed reluctance to administer shocks beyond the 300-volt level, and displayed fears similar to those who defied the experimenter; yet they obeyed.

After the maximum shocks had been delivered, and the experimenter called a halt to the proceedings, many obedient subjects heaved sighs of relief, mopped their brows, rubbed their fin-gers over their eyes, or nervously fumbled cigarettes. Some shook their heads, apparently in regret. Some subjects had remained calm throughout the experiment, and displayed only minimal signs of tension from beginning to end.

DISCUSSION

The experiment yielded two findings that were surprising. The first finding concerns the sheer strength of obedient tendencies manifested in this situation. Subjects have learned from childhood that it is a fundamental breach of moral conduct to hurt another person against his will. Yet, 26 subjects abandon this tenet in following the instructions of an authority who has no special powers to enforce his commands. To disobey would bring no material loss to the subject; no punishment would ensue. It is clear from the remarks and outward behavior of many participants that in punishing the victim they are often acting against their own values. Subjects often expressed deep disapproval of shocking a man in the face of his objections, and others denounced it as stupid and senseless. Yet the majority complied with the experimental commands. This outcome was surprising from two perspectives: first, from the standpoint of predictions made in the questionnaire described earlier. (Here, however, it is possible that the remoteness of the respondents from the actual situation, and the difficulty of conveying to them the concrete details of the experiment, could account for the serious underestimation of obedience.)

But the results were also unexpected to persons who observed the experiment in progress, through one-way mirrors. Observers often uttered expressions of disbelief upon seeing a subject administer more powerful shocks to the victim. These persons had a full acquaintance with the details of the situation, and yet systematically underestimated the amount of obedience that subjects would display.

The second unanticipated effect was the extraordinary tension generated by the procedures. One might suppose that a subject would simply break off or continue as his conscience dictated. Yet, this is very far from what happened. There were striking reactions of tension and emotional strain. One observer related:

> *I observed a mature and initially poised businessman enter the laboratory smiling and confident. Within 20 minutes he was reduced to a twitching, stuttering wreck, who was rapidly approaching a point of nervous collapse. He constantly pulled on his earlobe, and twisted his hands. At one point he pushed his fist into his forehead and muttered: "Oh God, let's stop it." And yet he continued to respond to every word of the experimenter, and obeyed to the end.*

Any understanding of the phenomenon of obedience must rest on an analysis of the particular conditions in which it occurs. The following features of the experiment go some distance in explaining the high amount of obedience observed in the situation.

1. The experiment is sponsored by and takes place on the grounds of an institution of unimpeachable reputation, Yale University. It may be reasonably presumed that the personnel are competent and reputable. The importance of this background authority is now being studied by conducting a series of experiments outside of New Haven, and without any visible ties to the university.

2. The experiment is, on the face of it, designed to attain a worthy purpose—advancement of knowledge about learning and memory. Obedience occurs not as an end in itself, but as an instrumental element in a situation that the subject construes as significant, and meaningful. He may not be able to see its full significance, but he may properly assume that the experimenter does.

3. The subject perceives that the victim has voluntarily submitted to the authority system of the experimenter. He is not (at first) an unwilling captive impressed for involuntary service. He has taken the trouble to come to the laboratory presumably to aid the experimental research. That he later becomes an in-

voluntary subject does not alter the fact that, initially, he consented to participate without qualification. Thus he has in some degree incurred an obligation toward the experimenter.

4. The subject, too, has entered the experiment voluntarily, and perceives himself under obligation to aid the experimenter. He has made a commitment, and to disrupt the experiment is a repudiation of this initial promise of aid.

5. Certain features of the procedure strengthen the subject's sense of obligation to the experimenter. For one, he has been paid for coming to the laboratory. In part this is canceled out by the experimenter's statement that:

> *Of course, as in all experiments, the money is yours simply for coming to the laboratory. From this point on, no matter what happens, the money is yours.*[2]

6. From the subject's standpoint, the fact that he is the teacher and the other man the learner is purely a chance consequence (it is determined by drawing lots) and he, the subject, ran the same risk as the other man in being assigned the role of learner. Since the assignment of positions in the experiment was achieved by fair means, the learner is deprived of any basis of complaint on this count. (A similar situation obtains in Army units, in which—in the absence of volunteers—a particularly dangerous mission may be assigned by drawing lots, and the unlucky soldier is expected to bear his misfortune with sportsmanship.)

7. There is, at best, ambiguity with regard to the prerogatives of a psychologist and the corresponding rights of his subject. There is a vagueness of expectation concerning what a psychologist may require of his subject, and when he is overstepping acceptable limits. Moreover, the experiment occurs in a closed setting, and thus provides no opportunity for the subject to remove these ambiguities by

discussion with others. There are few standards that seem directly applicable to the situation, which is a novel one for most subjects.

8. The subjects are assured that the shocks administered to the subject are "painful but not dangerous." Thus they assume that the discomfort caused the victim is momentary, while the scientific gains resulting from the experiment are enduring.

9. Through Shock Level 20 the victim continues to provide answers on the signal box. The subject may construe this as a sign that the victim is still willing to "play the game." It is only after Shock Level 20 that the victim repudiates the rules completely, refusing to answer further.

These features help to explain the high amount of obedience obtained in this experiment. Many of the arguments raised need not remain matters of speculation, but can be reduced to testable propositions to be confirmed or disproved by further experiments.[3]

The following features of the experiment concern the nature of the conflict which the subject faces.

10. The subject is placed in a position in which he must respond to the competing demands of two persons: the experimenter and the victim. The conflict must be resolved by meeting the demands of one or the other; satisfaction of the victim and the experimenter are mutually exclusive. Moreover, the resolution must take the form of a highly visible action, that of continuing to shock the victim or breaking off the experiment. Thus the subject is forced into a public conflict that does not permit any completely satisfactory solution.

11. While the demands of the experimenter carry the weight of scientific authority, the demands of the victim spring from his personal experience of pain and suffering. The two claims need not be regarded as equally pressing and legitimate. The experimenter seeks an abstract scientific datum; the victim cries out for relief from physical suffering caused by the subject's actions.

12. The experiment gives the subject little time for reflection. The conflict comes on rapidly. It is only minutes after the subject has been seated before the shock generator that the victim begins his protests. Moreover, the subject perceives that he has gone through but two-thirds of the shock levels at the time the subject's first protests are heard. Thus he understands that the conflict will have a persistent aspect to it, and may well become more intense as increasingly more powerful shocks are required. The rapidity with which the conflict descends on the subject, and his realization that it is predictably recurrent may well be sources of tension to him.

13. At a more general level, the conflict stems from the opposition of two deeply ingrained behavior dispositions: first, the disposition not to harm other people, and second, the tendency to obey those whom we perceive to be legitimate authorities.

REFERENCES

Adorno, T., Frenkel-Brunswik, Else, Levinson, D. J., and Sanford, R. N. *The authoritarian personality.* New York: Harper, 1950.

Arendt, H. What was authority? In C. J. Friedrich (ed.), *Authority.* Cambridge: Harvard Univer. Press. 1958. Pp. 81–112.

Binet, A. *La suggestibilité.* Paris: Schleicher, 1900.

Buss, A. H. *The psychology of aggression.* New York: Wiley, 1961.

Cartwright, S. (ed.) *Studies in social power.* Ann Arbor: University of Michigan Institute for Social Research, 1959.

Charcot, J. M. *Oeuvres complètes.* Paris: Bureaux du Progrès Médical, 1881.

Frank, J. D. Experimental studies of personal pressure and resistance. *J. gen. Psychol.* 1944, *30,* 23–64.

Freidrich, C. J. (ed.) *Authority.* Cambridge: Harvard Univer. Press, 1958.

Milgram, S. Dynamics of obedience. Washington: National Science Foundation, 25 January 1961. (Mimeo).

Milgram, S. Some conditions of obedience and disobedience to authority. *Hum. Relat.*, 1965, *18*, 57–76.

Rokeach, M. Authority, authoritarianism, and conformity. In I. A. Berg and B. M. Bass (eds.), *Conformity and deviation*. New York: Harper, 1961. Pp. 230–257.

Snow, C. P. Either-or. *Progressive*, 1961 (Feb.) 24.

Weber, M. *The theory of social and economic organization*. Oxford: Oxford Univer. Press 1947.

NOTES

1. A related technique, making use of a shock generator, was reported by Buss (1961) for the study of aggression in the laboratory. Despite the considerable similarity of technical detail in the experimental procedures, each investigator proceeded in ignorance of the other's work. Milgram provided plans and photographs of his shock generator, experimental procedure, and first results in a report to the National Science Foundation in January 1961. This report received only limited circulation. Buss reported his procedure six months later, but to a wider audience. Subsequently, technical information and reports were exchanged. The present article was first received in the editor's office on December 27, 1961; it was resubmitted with deletions on July 27, 1962.

2. Forty-three subjects, undergraduates at Yale University, were run in the experiment without payment. The results are very similar to those obtained with paid subjects.

3. A series of recently completed experiments employing the obedience paradigm is reported in Milgram (1965).

This research was supported by a grant (NSF G-17916) from the National Science Foundation. Exploratory studies conducted in 1960 were supported by a grant from the Higgins Fund at Yale University. The research assistance of Alan E. Elms and Jon Wayland is gratefully acknowledged.

CRITICAL THINKING QUESTIONS

1. What are the ethical implications of this study? In particular, are you satisfied that no lasting harm was done to the participants? Would the debriefing at the end of the experiment be sufficient to eliminate any long-term problems from participation in the study? What about short-term effects? Many of the subjects obviously suffered during the experiment. Was the infliction of this distress on the subjects justified? (Note: For a good discussion of the ethics of the study, see the Baumrind and Milgram articles cited below.)

2. What are the implications of this study for people accused of committing atrocities? Suppose that the results of this study had been known when the Nazi war criminals were put on trial in Nuremburg. Could the information have been used in their defense? Do the results remove some of the personal responsibility that people have for their actions?

3. Subjects were paid a nominal amount for participation in the study. They were told that the money was theirs to keep simply because they showed up, regardless of what happened after they arrived. Do you think that this payment was in some way partly responsible for the findings? Do you think that paying someone, no matter how small the amount, somehow changes the dynamics of the situation?

ADDITIONAL RELATED READINGS

Baumrind, D. (1964). Some thoughts on ethics of research after reading Milgram's "Behavioral study of obedience." *American Psychologist, 19,* 421–423.

Cialdini, R. B. (1988). *Influence: Science and Practice* (2nd ed). Glenview, IL: Scott, Foresman.

Milgram, S. (1964). Issues in the study of obedience: A reply to Baumrind. *American Psychologist, 19,* 848–852.

ARTICLE 24 _____

The two previous articles in this chapter involved rather extreme situations that produced some very significant behaviors. In both cases, authority figures played a role in inducing people to be compliant. But what about obedience to authority under less extreme circumstances? When life or death (or pain and suffering) are not at issue, how do symbols of authority, such as uniforms, affect people's behavior?

Obviously, when a person wearing a police uniform tells you to stop your car and get out, you obey. The perceived symbol of authority — the police uniform — is consistent with the order. Police, after all, are supposed to regulate automobiles. But what if a person wearing a firefighter's uniform, for example, stopped and told you to give money to another person on the street? This order obviously has nothing to do with the legitimate role of people wearing firefighter's uniforms. Do you think that you would be likely to do as you were told, simply because the person was wearing a symbol of authority? The following article by Brad Bushman addresses that question by looking at how clothing influences compliance behavior.

Perceived Symbols of Authority and Their Influence on Compliance[1]

■ Brad J. Bushman

There are many variables that influence compliance. With regard to individuals making requests of others, Bickman (1974) found that the apparel of the person making the request significantly influenced whether another person complied with the request. This study evaluates other factors such as sex, age, and altruism in compliance. Subjects were involved in a replication of Bickman's dime and parking meter study. Results showed that the dress of the perceived authority not only affected the number of subjects who complied but also the type of compliance, the type of noncompliance, and the latency between request and compliance. Also, older subjects complied significantly more often than younger subjects in the role authority condition.

Our initial perceptions of an individual's authority may be largely determined by apparel. This is especially true when an individual is wearing a uniform because uniforms make the wearer's status much more visible (Joseph & Alex, 1972). Uniforms have been found to influence honesty (Bickman, 1971), helping behavior (Emswiller, Deaux, & Willits, 1971; Raymond & Unger, 1971), political behavior (Suedfeld, Bochner, & Matas, 1971; Zimbardo, 1971), aggression (Borden, 1975), and compliance (Bickman, 1974). Bickman (1974) conducted several field studies on the influence of uniforms on compliance. Bickman's studies involved individuals with three levels of perceived authority: a civilian, a milkman, and a guard. Bickman found that when requests were made from an individual who was perceived as an authority, compliance was indeed higher.

Bickman's (1974) study dealt with the variable of perceived symbols of authority. In determining the reasons for compliance one may also wish to

Reprinted with permission from *Journal of Applied Social Psychology*, Vol. *14*, 1984, 501–508. Copyright 1984 by V. H. Winston and Son, Inc.

consider other variables, besides perceived symbols of authority. In this study, age, altruism, and how apparel affected compliance, noncompliance, and the latency to comply were investigated.

METHOD

Subjects

Subjects were 150 adult pedestrians on a major street in downtown Salt Lake City, Utah. The study was done on a warm, clear Saturday in May to increase the likelihood of a representative sample of the population being available. Several pedestrians were present for the duration of the experiment. The subject pool was limited to pedestrians between the ages of 16 and 70. Because of the heterogeneity of subjects at any given time, a quasi-random stratified sampling procedure was used. Selection was based on the demographic characteristics of age, sex, race, and dress.

Between the selection of one subject and the next there was a delay, such that the following subject could not have observed the interaction between the confederate and the previous subject. Overall, 45% of the subjects were female and 55% were male. Seventy-one percent were white, 9% black, and the race of the remainder (20%) could not be determined. Most subjects were judged, by their apparel, as middle-class. Post-experiment analysis of subjects' demographics showed no significant differences between subjects within each of the three conditions (no authority, status authority, and role authority).

Design

This experiment was a field study, functional design with three levels of the independent variable: no authority, status authority, and role authority. In the no authority condition the confederate was dressed as a bum, was unshaven, and wore an old pair of greasy coveralls, an old baseball type hat, and old work shoes. In the status authority condition, the confederate dressed as a business executive, was shaven, wore a conservative two-piece

business suit, white shirt, a conservative tie, and dress shoes. In the role authority condition, the confederate was dressed as a fire fighter, and wore a fire fighter's uniform that included a medium blue shirt, dark blue pants, and a black hat. The shirt had a patch on the sleeve designating the fire department (Ogden City) and a silver fire fighter badge on the pocket. The hat also had a silver badge in the center.

The confederate was male, 47 years old, 5 ft 11 in. tall (1.8 m) and weighed 210 lb (95.45 kg). Bickman's (1974) experiment used four different confederates of similar physique. This experiment used the same confederate for all three conditions to control for variables associated with the person making the request. Bickman's confederates were between the ages of 18 and 20. In this experiment an older confederate was used to increase ecological validity to be consistent with the assumption that authority figures are rarely young.

The person in need of a dime was the experimenter, a 23-year-old college male student, 5 ft 10 in. tall (1.78 m) and 135 lb (61.36 kg), who was dressed in blue jeans and a casual shirt during the data collection.

The dependent variable, compliance, was defined as the subject giving the experimenter a dime (or other change if the subject did not have a dime). The type of compliance was determined by a posttest interview conducted by the experimenter. The behavior of those who complied was divided into four categories: altruism, compliance, unquestioned obedience, or ambiguous.

1. *Altruism.* The subject complied because he or she wanted to help someone in need.
2. *Compliance.* The subject complied because he or she hoped to achieve a favorable reaction from the experimenter, the confederate, or both. The subject's response could have been dual in nature; that is, the subject wanted to comply to the confederate's request and help someone at the same time.
3. *Unquestioned obedience.* The subject complied because "He [the confederate] told me to."
4. *Ambiguous.* The experimenter could not de-

termine why the subject complied because his or her response was vague.

The reasons for noncompliance were divided, by the confederate, into four categories: no change, questioned perceived authority, silent, and hostile.

1. *No change.* The subject said he or she did not have any change.
2. *Questioned perceived authority.* The subject asked the confederate such questions as, "Why don't you give him a dime?"
3. *Silent.* The subject did not reply to the confederate's request.
4. *Hostile.* The subject responded to the confederate's request in a hostile manner (e.g., "Are you kidding? There's no way I'm going to give him any change!")

Procedure

The general procedure used was similar to Bickman's (1974) study. The confederate stopped the chosen subject and pointed to the experimenter who was standing beside a car, parked at an expired parking meter, searching in his pockets for change. After pointing at the experimenter, the confederate said, "This fellow is overparked at the meter but doesn't have any change. Give him a dime!" If the subject did not immediately comply, the confederate added that he had no change either. If the subject did not comply after the explanation, the confederate left.

To ensure an accurate and reliable recording of the data, the confederate recorded specific information about each subject after he or she left the vicinity. This was accomplished by using the checklist in Figure 1.

If the subject did comply, the experimenter debriefed him or her. The debriefing procedure went as follows: The experimenter asked the subject, "Why would you just come over here and give me a dime?" If the subject did not respond clearly, the experimenter attempted to clarify the response. The experimenter then returned the subject's dime and briefly explained the nature of the experiment. After the subject left, the experimenter completed the checklist in Figure 2.

After collecting the data for each condition, the experimenter and the confederate compared descriptions of the subjects in terms of estimated age, race, and status (as indicated by apparel).

FIGURE 1

	Demographic Characteristics			Apparel (Perceived Status)				Type of Noncompliance				Compliance and Description		
Subject Number	Estimated Age	Gender	Race (White—W Black—B Unknown—U)	Work Clothes	Casual Clothes	Semiformal Clothes	Formal Clothes	No Change	Questioned Perceived Authority	Silent	Hostile	Complied	Latency (Fast—F, Medium—M, Slow—S)	Color of Ss Blouse or Shirt
1	68	F	W			✔						✔		White
2	42	M	W	✔					✔					

FIGURE 2

Demographic Characteristics				Apparel (Perceived Status)				Type of Compliance				Description
Subject Number	Estimated Age	Gender	Race (White—W Black—B Unknown—U)	Work Clothes	Casual Clothes	Semiformal Clothes	Formal Clothes	Altruistic	Compliance	Unquestioned Obedience	Ambiguous	Color of Ss Blouse or Shirt
1	68	F	W				✔	✔				White

RESULTS

The results indicate that compliance significantly increased as perceived authority increased, χ^2 (2, $N = 150$) $= 17.10$, $p < .001$. Forty-five percent of the subjects obeyed the bum, 50% the business executive, and 82% the fire fighter.

As judged by the subject's verbal responses, altruistic reasons given for complying were significantly less as perceived authority in increased, χ^2 (6, $N = 88$) $= 26.60$, $p < .001$. although 50% of the reasons given for obeying were altruistic in the no authority condition, 16% were altruistic in the status authority condition, and 10% were altruistic in the role authority condition. Furthermore, 64% of the reasons given for compliance were classified as "unquestioned obedience" in the role authority condition, 48% were classified as unquestioned obedience in the status authority condition, and 23% were classified as unquestioned obedience in the no authority condition.

Noncomplying subjects offered significantly fewer hostile reasons for noncompliance as perceived authority increased, χ^2 (4, $N = 62$) $= 14.66$, $p < .05$. Twenty-nine percent of the subjects gave hostile responses in the no authority condition, whereas 11% gave hostile responses in the role authority condition. Thirty-two percent of the subjects said they would have given the experimenter a dime if they had change in the no authority condition, whereas 89% of the subjects said they would have given the experimenter a dime if they had change in the role authority condition. In addition, not one subject questioned the confederate in the role authority condition.

The latency between request and compliance was significantly affected by the apparel of the perceived authority, χ^2 (4, $N = 150$) $= 44.37$, $p < .05$. In the no authority and status authority conditions, 23%–24% of the subjects complied quickly (under 30 s), whereas in the role authority condition, 85% of the subjects complied quickly. Thirty-six percent complied moderately quickly (30 s to 1 min) in the no authority condition, 64% in the status authority condition, and 15% in the role authority condition. Forty-one percent complied slowly (over 1 min) in the no authority condition, 12% complied slowly in the status authority condition, and not one subject complied slowly in the role authority condition.

TABLE 1 / **Percentage of Subjects Complying in Each Condition**

Condition	Compliance		Noncompliance	
	N	%	*N*	%
No authority	22	44	28	56
Status authority	25	50	25	50
Role authority	41	82	9	18

Older subjects (over 30 years) complied significantly more than younger subjects (16–30 yrs) in the role authority condition. One hundred percent of older subjects and 57% of the younger subjects complied in the role authority condition. Significant age differences were not found in either the status authority or no authority conditions.

There was no significant gender difference with regard to female/male compliance rates. In addition, no significant difference was found between the subject's apparel and the subject's willingness to comply.

DISCUSSION

As did Bickman's (1974) experiment, this experiment showed a significant relation between the apparel the confederate wore and the number of subjects who complied to the confederate's request. In addition, several other interesting differences were noticed between the subjects' responses and the confederate's request. For example, in the role authority condition, the confederate noted that the subjects responded quite differently. The confederate would say, "Give him a dime!" and the majority of subjects would look at his badge and say, "sure."

Altruism, as defined by the subjects' verbal reason given for complying, was also significantly affected by the presence of a perceived authority. It seems that compliance, when requested by an authority, may be less charitable. During the experiment, only one person gave the experimenter a dime without the confederate requesting them to do so (a nun).

The confederate was of the opinion that the nature of noncompliance was also different in the role authority condition. While in the fire fighter's uniform, the confederate felt eight of the nine subjects who did not comply would have complied if they would have had change. For example, one woman said, "I'm really sorry that I can't, but I only have one dime and I need to make an important phone call." The confederate stated that subjects' responses in the role authority condition sounded more sincere. Also, none of the subjects questioned the confederate in the role authority condition, even though fire fighters have nothing to do with parking meter violations.

Perceived authority is apparently an important variable influencing compliance. These findings suggest that those holding authoritative positions have a great responsibility, especially when making requests of others.

REFERENCES

Bickman, L. (1971). The effects of social status on the honesty of others. *Journal of Social Psychology, 85,* 87–92.

Bickman, L. (1974). The social power of a uniform. *Journal of Applied Social Psychology, 4,* 47–61.

Borden, R. J. (1975). Witnessed aggression: Influence of an observer's sex and values on aggressive responding. *Journal of Personality and Social Psychology, 31,* 567–573.

Emswiller, T., Deaux, K., & Willits, J. E. (1971). Similarity, sex, and requests for small favors. *Journal of Applied Social Psychology, 1,* 284–291.

Joseph, N., & Alex, N. (1972). The uniform: A sociological perspective. *American Journal of Sociology, 77,* 719–730.

Raymond, B. J., & Unger, R. K. (1971). Effect of deviant and conventional attire on cooperation [Summary]. *Proceedings of the 79th Annual Convention of the American Psychological Association, 6,* 357–358.

Suedfeld, P., Bochner, S., & Matas, C. (1971). Petitioner's attire and petition signing by peace demonstrators: A field experiment. *Journal of Applied Social Psychology, 1,* 278–283.

Zimbardo, P. (Chair). (1971). *Freaks, hippies, and voters: The effect of deviant dress and appearance on political persuasion process.* Symposium conducted at the meeting of the Eastern Psychological Association, New York City.

NOTE

1. The author would like to thank Merrill May for his helpful comments on earlier drafts of this article and for providing assistance with the statistical analysis of the data.

CRITICAL THINKING QUESTIONS

1. Examine the method by which subjects were selected for the study. Do you find any type of unintentional bias? (Some possibilities are discussed in Article 1 in this book.)

2. Are any ethical issues involved in this study? For example, only people who stopped to help were debriefed. What about the impact of the study on those subjects who did not stop to help?

3. This study involved only a trivial request for help—asking a person for a dime. Would you expect similar findings if the request were more costly, either in terms of time, effort, or money? How could you test this possibility?

4. One interesting finding of the study was that people complied with the orders of a fireman on the street to give money to someone, even though firemen don't typically do such things. Policemen are more likely than firemen to stop people and tell them what to do. Would the uniform effect have been even stronger if the experimenter had been wearing a police uniform instead of a firefighter's uniform? Do the results of the study imply that a uniform, even if not normally connected with the request being made, can increase compliance? Design a study or several studies that could address these issues: Namely, what types of uniforms increase compliance? What types of requests are most likely to produce increased compliance?

Chapter Nine

PROSOCIAL BEHAVIOR

HELP. It is something that we all need at some time in our lives, and it is something that we all hopefully give to others. Dramatic examples of helping or failing to help are not hard to find in the mass media. Consider the various published accounts of people needing help yet receiving none versus those of people who risk their own lives to help strangers.

Why do people help or not help? Is helpfulness a personality trait, so that some people are simply helpful individuals who give assistance in a variety of settings? Or does it have more to do with the specific situation, so that a person who helps in one situation is not necessarily more likely to help in another? Or perhaps these two factors somehow interact with one another, so that people with a certain type of personality in a certain type of situation are more likely to help than others.

The research in this area of social psychology has gone in several directions. Articles 25 and 27 examine some of the situational factors that affect helping behavior. Article 25, "When Will People Help in a Crisis?" presents some of the early work on one factor, *diffusion of responsibility*, as an explanation for helping or not helping. Article 27, "Attributions of Responsibility for Helping and Doing Harm," presents a more recent concept, *confusion of responsibility*, as another possible explanation for why people don't always help. Article 26, "From Jerusalem to Jericho," was selected as a classic example of a study that examines both situational and personality factors that may influence helping behavior.

ARTICLE 25 _____

The following article by John Darley and Bibb Latané presents some of these investigators' early research on the factors influencing when people will help in emergency situations. The article begins with several examples of when people failed to help others in need. Although these examples are more than 20 years old, we need not look far for more contemporary examples of people not helping those in need. Incidents of large numbers of people failing to render help frequently make the news, partly because they are astonishing: How can people be so cruel and heartless that they do not help? In fact, our usual reaction is to explain people's unwillingness to help in terms of their own shortcomings: They didn't care or perhaps have become numb to the needs of others after years of struggling in their urban environments.

Darley and Latané pioneered research suggesting that the decision to help or not to help in an emergency is not due so much to individual characteristics (often referred to as *dispositional attributions*) but rather to the situation confronting the individual. The studies presented in the article help explain why people often fail to help and also give a general model of the processes involved in decision making. The article also makes an interesting and unsettling suggestion: Given the same set of circumstances, perhaps you and I also would be apathetic bystanders, unwilling to provide the help that is needed.

When Will People Help in a Crisis?

■ John M. Darley and Bibb Latané

Kitty Genovese is set upon by a maniac as she returns home from work at 3:00 a.m. Thirty-eight of her neighbors in Kew Gardens come to their windows when she cries out in terror; none come to her assistance even though her stalker takes over half an hour to murder her. No one even so much as calls the police. She dies.

Andrew Mormille is stabbed in the stomach as he rides the A train home to Manhattan. Eleven other riders watch the 17-year-old boy as he bleeds to death; none come to his assistance even though his attackers have left the car. He dies.

An 18-year-old switchboard operator, alone in her office in the Bronx, is raped and beaten. Escaping momentarily, she runs naked and bleeding to the street, screaming for help. A crowd of 40 passersby gathers and watches as, in broad daylight, the rapist tries to drag her back upstairs; no one interferes. Finally two policemen happen by and arrest her assailant.

Eleanor Bradley trips and breaks her leg while shopping on Fifth Avenue. Dazed and in shock, she calls for help, but the hurrying stream of executives and shoppers simply parts and flows past. After 40 minutes a taxi driver helps her to a doctor.

The shocking thing about these cases is that so many people failed to respond. If only one or two

Reprinted from *Psychology Today*, 1968 (December), *2*, 54–58. Reprinted with permission from *Psychology Today Magazine*. Copyright © 1968 (PT Partners, L.P.).

had ignored the victim, we might be able to understand their inaction. But when 38 people, or 11 people, or hundreds of people fail to help, we become disturbed. Actually, this fact that shocks us so much is itself the clue to understanding these cases. Although it seems obvious that the more people who watch a victim in distress, the more likely someone will help, what really happens is exactly the opposite. If each member of a group of bystanders is aware that other people are also present, he will be less likely to notice the emergency, less likely to decide that it is an emergency, and less likely to act even if he thinks there is an emergency.

This is a surprising assertion — what we are saying is that the victim may actually be less likely to get help, the more people who watch his distress and are available to help. We shall discuss in detail the process through which an individual bystander must go in order to intervene, and we shall present the results of some experiments designed to show the effects of the number of onlookers on the likelihood of intervention.

Since we started research on bystander responses to emergencies, we have heard many explanations for the lack of intervention. "I would assign this to the effect of the megapolis in which we live, which makes closeness very difficult and leads to the alienation of the individual from the group," contributed a psychoanalyst. "A disaster syndrome," explained a sociologist, "that shook the sense of safety and sureness of the individuals involved and caused psychological withdrawal from the event by ignoring it." "Apathy," claimed others. "Indifference." "The gratification of unconscious sadistic impulses." "Lack of concern for our fellow men." "The Cold Society." All of these analyses of the person who fails to help share one characteristic: they set the indifferent witness apart from the rest of us as a different kind of person. Certainly not one of us who reads about these incidents in horror is apathetic, alienated or depersonalized. Certainly not one of us enjoys gratifying his sadistic impulses by watching others suffer. These terrifying cases in which people fail to help others certainly have no personal implications for us. That is, we might decide not to ride subways any more, or that New York isn't even "a nice place to visit," or "there ought to be a law" against apathy, but we needn't feel guilty, or re-examine ourselves, or anything like that.

Looking more closely at published descriptions of the behavior of witnesses to these incidents, the people involved begin to look a little less inhuman and a lot more like the rest of us. Although it is unquestionably true that the witnesses in the incidents above did nothing to save the victims, apathy, indifference and unconcern are not entirely accurate descriptions of their reactions. The 38 witnesses of Kitty Genovese's murder did not merely look at the scene once and then ignore it. They continued to stare out of their windows at what was going on. Caught, fascinated, distressed, unwilling to act but unable to turn away, their behavior was neither helpful nor heroic; but it was not indifferent or apathetic.

Actually, it was like crowd behavior in many other emergency situations. Car accidents, drownings, fires and attempted suicides all attract substantial numbers of people who watch the drama in helpless fascination without getting directly involved in the action. Are these people alienated and indifferent? Are the rest of us? Obviously not. Why, then, don't we act?

The bystander to an emergency has to make a series of decisions about what is happening and what he will do about it The consequences of these decisions will determine his actions. There are three things he must do if he is to intervene: *notice* that something is happening, *interpret* that event as an emergency, and decide that he has *personal responsibility* for intervention. If he fails to notice the event, if he decides that it is not an emergency, or if he concludes that he is not personally responsible for acting, he will leave the victim unhelped. This state of affairs is shown graphically as a "decision tree" (see Figure 1). Only one path through this decision tree leads to intervention; all others lead to a failure to help. As we shall show, at each fork of the path in the decision tree, the presence of other bystanders may lead a person down the branch of not helping.

FIGURE 1 / The Decision Tree. In an emergency, a bystander must: 1) notice something is happening; 2) interpret it as an emergency; 3) decide that he has a personal responsibility for intervention.

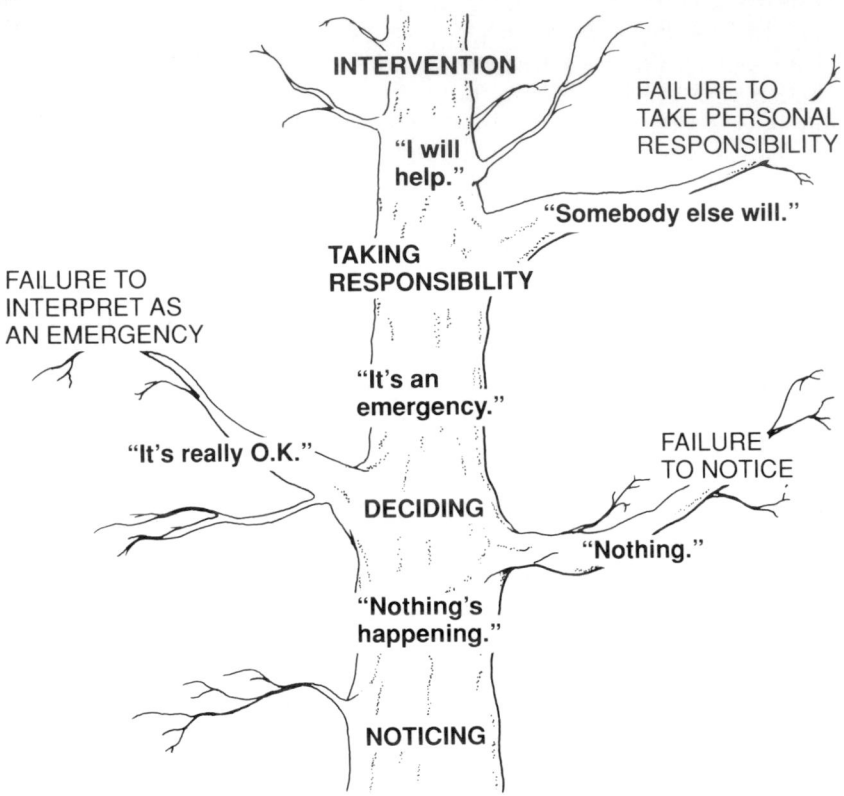

INTERVENTION

FAILURE TO TAKE PERSONAL RESPONSIBILITY

"I will help."

"Somebody else will."

TAKING RESPONSIBILITY

FAILURE TO INTERPRET AS AN EMERGENCY

"It's an emergency."

"It's really O.K."

FAILURE TO NOTICE

DECIDING

"Nothing."

"Nothing's happening."

NOTICING

NOTICING: THE FIRST STEP

Suppose that an emergency is actually taking place; a middle-aged man has a heart attack. He stops short, clutches his chest, and staggers to the nearest building wall, where he slowly slumps to the sidewalk in a sitting position. What is the likelihood that a passerby will come to his assistance? First, the bystander has to *notice* that something is happening. The external event has to break into his thinking and intrude itself on his conscious mind. He must tear himself away from his private thoughts and pay attention to this unusual event.

But Americans consider it bad manners to look too closely at other people in public. We are taught to respect the privacy of others, and when among strangers, we do this by closing our ears and avoiding staring at others — we are embarrassed if caught doing otherwise. In a crowd, then, each person is less likely to notice the first sign of a potential emergency than when alone.

Experimental evidence corroborates this everyday observation. Darley and Latané asked college students to an interview about their reactions to urban living. As the students waited to see the interviewer, either by themselves or with two other students, they filled out a preliminary questionnaire. Solitary students often glanced idly about the room while filling out their questionnaires; those in groups, to avoid seeming rudely inquisitive, kept their eyes on their own papers.

As part of the study, we staged an emergency: smoke was released into the waiting room through a vent. Two-thirds of the subjects who were alone when the smoke appeared noticed it immediately, but only a quarter of the subjects waiting in groups saw it as quickly. Even after the room had completely filled with smoke one subject from a group of three finally looked up and exclaimed, "God! I must be smoking too much!" Although eventually all the subjects did become aware of the smoke, this study indicates that the more people present, the slower an individual may be to perceive that an emergency does exist and the more likely he is not to see it at all.

Once an event is noticed, an onlooker must decide whether or not it is truly an emergency. Emergencies are not always clearly labeled as such; smoke pouring from a building or into a waiting room may be caused by a fire, or it may merely indicate a leak in a steam pipe. Screams in the street may signal an assault or a family quarrel. A man lying in a doorway may be having a coronary or be suffering from diabetic coma—he may simply be sleeping off a drunk. And in any unusual situation, Candid Camera may be watching.

A person trying to decide whether or not a given situation is an emergency often refers to the reactions of those around him; he looks at them to see how he should react himself. If everyone else is calm and indifferent, he will tend to remain calm and indifferent; if everyone else is reacting strongly, he will become aroused. This tendency is not merely slavish conformity; ordinarily we derive much valuable information about new situations from how others around us behave. It's a rare traveler who, in picking a roadside restaurant, chooses to stop at one with no other cars in the parking lot.

But occasionally the reactions of others provide false information. The studied nonchalance of patients in a dentist's waiting room is a poor indication of the pain awaiting them. In general, it is considered embarrassing to look overly concerned, to seem flustered, to "lose your cool" in public. When we are not alone, most of us try to seem less fearful and anxious than we really are.

In a potentially dangerous situation, then, everyone present will appear more unconcerned than they are in fact. Looking at the *apparent* impassivity and lack of reaction of the others, each person is led to believe that nothing really is wrong. Meanwhile the danger may be mounting, to the point where a single person, uninfluenced by the seeming calm of others, would react.

A crowd can thus force inaction on its members by implying, through its passivity and apparent indifference, that an event is not an emergency. Any individual in such a crowd is uncomfortably aware that he'll look like a fool if he behaves as though it were—and in these circumstances, until someone acts, no one acts.

In the smoke-filled-room study, the smoke trickling from the wall constituted an ambiguous but potentially dangerous situation. How did the presence of other people affect a person's response to the situation? Typically, those who were in the waiting room by themselves noticed the smoke at once, gave a slight startle reaction, hesitated, got up and went over to investigate the smoke, hesitated again, and then left the room to find somebody to tell about the smoke. No one showed any signs of panic, but over three-quarters of these people were concerned enough to report the smoke.

Others went through an identical experience but in groups of three strangers. Their behavior was radically different. Typically, once someone noticed the smoke, he would look at the other people, see them doing nothing, shrug his shoulders, and then go back to his questionnaire, casting covert glances first at the smoke and then at the others. From these three-person groups, only three out of 24 people reported the smoke. The inhibiting effect of the group was so strong that the other 21 were willing to sit in a room filled with smoke rather than make themselves conspicuous by reacting with alarm and concern—this despite the fact that after three or four minutes the atmosphere in the waiting room grew most unpleasant. Even though they coughed, rubbed their eyes, tried to wave the smoke away, and opened the window, they apparently were unable to bring themselves to leave.

These dramatic differences between the behavior of people alone and those in a group indicate that the group imposed a definition of the situation upon its members which inhibited action.

"A leak in the air conditioning," said one person when we asked him what he thought caused the smoke. "Must be chemistry labs in the building." "Steam pipes." "Truth gas to make us give true answers on the questionnaire," reported the more imaginative. There were many explanations for the smoke, but they all had one thing in common: they did not mention the word fire. In defining the situation as a nonemergency, people explained to themselves why the other observers did not leave the room; they also removed any reason for action themselves. The other members of the group acted as nonresponsive models for each person—and as an audience for any "inappropriate" action he might consider. In such a situation it is all too easy to do nothing.

The results of this study clearly and strongly support the predictions. But are they general? Would the same effect show up with other emergencies, or is it limited to situations like the smoke study involving danger to the self as well as to others—or to situations in which there's no clearly defined "victim"? It may be that our college-age male subjects played "chicken" with one another to see who would lose face by first fleeing the room. It may be that groups were less likely to respond because no particular person was in danger. To see how generalizable these results are, Latané and Judith Rodin set up a second experiment, in which the emergency would cause no danger for the bystander, and in which a specific person was in trouble.

Subjects were paid $2 to participate in a survey of game and puzzle preferences conducted at Columbia by the Consumer Testing Bureau (CTB). An attractive young woman, the market-research representative, met them at the door and took them to the testing room. On the way, they passed the CTB office and through its open door they could see filing cabinets and a desk and bookcases piled high with papers. They entered the adjacent testing room, which contained a table and chairs and a variety of games, where they were given a preliminary background information and game preference questionnaire to fill out. The representative told subjects that she would be working next door in her office for about 10 minutes while they completed the questionnaires, and left by opening the collapsible curtain which divided the two rooms. She made sure the subjects knew that the curtain was unlocked, easily opened and a means of entry to her office. The representative stayed in her office, shuffling papers, opening drawers, and making enough noise to remind the subjects of her presence. Four minutes after leaving the testing area, she turned on a high fidelity stereophonic tape recorder.

If the subject listened carefully, he heard the representative climb up on a chair to reach for a stack of papers on the bookcase. Even if he were not listening carefully, he heard a loud crash and a scream as the chair collapsed and she fell to the floor. "Oh, my God, my foot . . . I . . . I . . . can't move it. Oh . . . my ankle," the representative moaned. "I . . . can't get this . . . thing . . . off me." She cried and moaned for about a minute longer, but the cries gradually got more subdued and controlled. Finally she muttered something about getting outside, knocked over the chair as she pulled herself up, and thumped to the door, closing it behind her as she left. This drama lasted about two minutes.

Some people were alone in the waiting room when the "accident" occurred. Seventy per cent of them offered to help the victim before she left the room. Many came through the curtain to offer their assistance, others simply called out to offer their help. Others faced the emergency in pairs. Only 20 per cent of this group—eight out of 40— offered to help the victim. The other 32 remained unresponsive to her cries of distress. Again, the presence of other bystanders inhibited action.

And again, the noninterveners seemed to have decided the event was not an emergency. They were unsure what had happened but whatever it was, it was not too serious. "A mild sprain," some said. "I didn't want to embarrass her." In a "real" emergency, they assured us, they would be among the first to help the victim. Perhaps they would be, but in this situation they didn't help, because for them the event was not defined as an emergency.

Again, solitary people exposed to a potential emergency reacted more frequently than those exposed in groups. We found that the action-inhibiting effects of other bystanders works in two different situations, one of which involves risking danger to oneself and the other of which involves helping an injured woman. The result seemed sufficiently general so that we may assume it operates to inhibit helping in real-life emergencies.

DIFFUSED RESPONSIBILITY

Even if a person has noticed an event and defined it as an emergency, the fact that he knows that other bystanders also witnessed it may still make him less likely to intervene. Others may inhibit intervention because they make a person feel that his responsibility is diffused and diluted. Each soldier in a firing squad feels less personally responsible for killing a man than he would if he alone pulled the trigger. Likewise, any person in a crowd of onlookers may feel less responsibility for saving a life than if he alone witnesses the emergency.

If your car breaks down on a busy highway, hundreds of drivers whiz by without anyone's stopping to help; if you are stuck on a nearly deserted country road, whoever passes you first is apt to stop. The personal responsibility that a passerby feels makes the difference. A driver on a lonely road knows that if he doesn't stop to help, the person will not get help; the same individual on the crowded highway feels he personally is no more responsible than any of a hundred other drivers. So even though an event clearly is an emergency, any person in a group who sees an emergency may feel less responsible, simply because any other bystander is equally responsible for helping.

This diffusion of responsibility might have occurred in the famous Kitty Genovese case, in which the observers were walled off from each other in separate apartments. From the silhouettes against windows, all that could be told was that others were also watching.

To test this line of thought, Darley and Latané simulated an emergency in a setting designed to resemble Kitty Genovese's murder. People overheard a victim calling for help. Some knew they were the only one to hear the victim's cries; the rest believed other people were aware of the victim's distress. As with the Genovese witnesses, subjects could not see each other or know what others were doing. The kind of direct group inhibition found in the smoke and fallen-woman studies could not operate.

For the simulation, we recruited male and female students at New York University to participate in a group discussion. Each student was put in an individual room equipped with a set of headphones and a microphone and told to listen for instructions over the headphones. The instructions informed the participant that the discussion was to consider personal problems of the normal college student in a high-pressure urban university. It was explained that, because participants might feel embarrassed about discussing personal problems publicly, several precautions had been taken to insure their anonymity: they would not meet the other people face to face, and the experimenter would not listen to the initial discussion but would only ask for their reactions later. Each person was to talk in turn. The first to talk reported that he had found it difficult to adjust to New York and his studies. Then, very hesitantly and with obvious embarrassment, he mentioned that he was prone to nervous seizures, similar to but not really the same as epilepsy. These occurred particularly when he was under the stresses of studying and being graded.

Other people then discussed their own problems in turn. The number of other people in the discussion varied. But whatever the perceived size of the group—two, three or six people—only the subject was actually present; the others, as well as the instructions and the speeches of the victim-to-be, were present only on a pre-recorded tape.

When it again was the first person's turn to talk, after a few comments he launched into the following performance, getting increasingly louder with increasing speech difficulties:

> *"I can see a lot of er of er how other people's problems are similar to mine because er er I mean er it's er I mean some of the er same er kind of things that I have had and an er I'm sure that every everybody has and er er I mean er they're not er e-easy to handle sometimes and er I er er be upsetting like er er and er I er um I think I I need er if if could er er somebody er er er er er give me give me a little er give me a little help here because er I er I'm er h-h-having a a a a a real problem er right now and I er if somebody could help me out it would it would er er s-s-sure be sure be good be . . . because er there er er a cause I er uh I've got a a one of the er seiz-er er things coming on and and and I c-could really er use er some h-help s-so if somebody would er give me a little h-help us er-er-er-er-er c-could somebody er er help er uh uh uh (choking sounds) . . . I'm gonna die er er I'm . . . gonna . . . die er help er er seizure er er . . ." (chokes, then quiet).*

While this was going on, the experimenter waited outside the student's door to see how soon he would emerge to cope with the emergency. Rather to our surprise, some people sat through the entire fit without helping; a disproportionately large percentage of these nonresponders were from the largest-size group. Eighty-five per cent of the people who believed themselves to be alone with the victim came out of their rooms to help, while 62 per cent of the people who believed there was one other bystander did so. Of those who believed there were four other bystanders, only 31 per cent reported the fit before the tape ended. The responsibility-diluting effect of other people was so strong that single individ-

uals were more than twice as likely to report the emergency as those who thought other people also knew about it.

THE MORAL DILEMMA FELT BY THOSE WHO DO NOT RESPOND

People who failed to report the emergency showed few signs of apathy and indifference thought to characterize "unresponsive bystanders." When the experimenter entered the room to end the situation, the subject often asked if the victim was "all right." Many of these people showed physical signs of nervousness; they often had trembling hands and sweating palms. If anything, they seemed more emotionally aroused than did those who reported the emergency. Their emotional arousal was in sharp contrast to the behavior of the nonresponding subjects in the smoke and fallen-woman studies. Those subjects were calm and unconcerned when their experiments were over. Having interpreted the events as nonemergencies, there was no reason for them to be otherwise. It was only the subjects who did not respond in the face of the clear emergency represented by the fit who felt the moral dilemma.

Why, then, didn't they respond? It is our impression that nonintervening subjects had not decided not to respond. Rather, they were still in a state of indecision and conflict concerning whether to respond or not. The emotional behavior of these nonresponding subjects was a sign of their continuing conflict: a conflict that other people resolved by responding. The distinction seems an academic one for the victim, since he gets no help in either case, but it is an extremely important one for arriving at an understanding of why bystanders fail to help.

The evidence is clear, then, that the presence of other bystanders and the various ways these other bystanders affect our decision processes, make a difference in how likely we are to give help in an emergency. The presence of strangers may keep us from noticing an emergency at all; group behavior may lead us to define the situation as one that does not require action; and when other people are there to share the burden of responsibility, we may feel less obligated to do something when action is required. Therefore, it will often be the case that the *more* people who witness his distress, the *less* likely it is that the victim of an emergency will get help.

Thus, the stereotype of the unconcerned, depersonalized *homo urbanis,* blandly watching the misfortunes of others, proves inaccurate. Instead, we find a bystander to an emergency is an anguished individual in genuine doubt, concerned to do the right thing but compelled to make complex decisions under pressure of stress and fear. His reactions are shaped by the actions of others — and all too frequently by their inaction.

And we are that bystander. Caught up by the apparent indifference of others, we may pass by an emergency without helping or even realizing that help is needed. Aware of the influence of those around us, however, we can resist it. We can choose to see distress and step forward to relieve it.

CRITICAL THINKING QUESTIONS

1. Find an example from the mass media of a real-life emergency situation where a number of bystanders failed to do anything to help. How would you apply the ideas presented in the article to explain this behavior?
2. As in much research, the significant results presented in this study refer to group differences. Thus, when it is reported that individuals who are alone are more likely to help than those who are in groups, this does not mean that 100% of the solitary individuals helped, only that a significantly greater number of them helped than did people in groups. What factors may account for why some of the people in groups *did not help,* while some of the people alone *did help?*
3. All of the studies presented were laboratory studies. Design a field study to test the same hypothesis. What considerations should you take into account before actually conducting such a field study?

ARTICLE 26 ⸻

Many variables can potentially influence whether people help others in need. One such factor, the number of bystanders present, was discussed in the previous article. But what other factors may influence prosocial behavior?

Broadly speaking, two types of determinants can be considered. The first concerns *situational* factors: What circumstances surrounding the specific situation may have an impact on helping behavior? The second variable concerns *dispositions:* To what extent are decisions to help due to relatively permanent personality factors? In other words, are some people more likely to help than others because of their unique personality makeup? Or does the situation, rather than personality, influence helping?

In "From Jerusalem to Jericho," Darley and Batson examine both situational and dispositional variables in an experiment modeled after a biblical parable. Specifically, the study looks at helping as influenced by situational variables—whether the subjects were in a hurry and what they were thinking at the time—and dispositional variables—the religious orientation of the subjects. This classic article is interesting not only because of the methodology used but because of the important implications of the results, as well.

"From Jerusalem to Jericho"
A Study of Situational and Dispositional Variables in Helping Behavior

■ John M. Darley and C. Daniel Batson

The influence of several situational and personality variables on helping behavior was examined in an emergency situation suggested by the parable of the Good Samaritan. People going between two buildings encountered a shabbily dressed person slumped by the side of the road. Subjects in a hurry to reach their destination were more likely to pass by without stopping. Some subjects were going to give a short talk on the parable of the Good Samaritan, others on a nonhelping relevant topic; this made no significant difference in the likelihood of their giving the victim help. Religious personality variables did not predict whether an individual would help the victim or not. However, if a subject did stop to offer help, the character of the helping response was related to his type of religiosity.

Helping other people in distress is, among other things, an ethical act. That is, it is an act governed by ethical norms and precepts taught to children at home, in school, and in church. From Freudian and other personality theories, one would expect individual differences in internalization of these standards that would lead to differences between individuals in the likelihood with which they would help others. But recent research on bystander intervention in emergency situations (Bickman, 1969; Darley & Latané, 1968; Korte, 1969; but see also Schwartz & Clausen, 1970) has had bad luck in finding personality determinants of helping behavior. Although personality variables that one might expect to correlate with helping behavior have been measured (Machiavellianism, authoritarianism, social desirability, ali-

Reprinted from the *Journal of Personality and Social Psychology*, 1973, *27*, 100–108. Copyright 1973 by the American Psychological Association. Reprinted by permission.

enation, and social responsibility), these were not predictive of helping. Nor was this due to a generalized lack of predictability in the helping situation examined, since variations in the experimental situation, such as the availability of other people who might also help, produced marked changes in rates of helping behavior. These findings are reminiscent of Hartshorne and May's (1928) discovery that resistance to temptation, another ethically relevant act, did not seem to be a fixed characteristic of an individual. That is, a person who was likely to be honest in one situation was not particularly likely to be honest in the next (but see also Burton, 1963).

The rather disappointing correlation between the social psychologist's traditional set of personality variables and helping behavior in emergency situations suggests the need for a fresh perspective on possible predictors of helping and possible situations in which to test them. Therefore, for inspiration, we turned to the Bible, to what is perhaps the classical helping story in the Judeo-Christian tradition, the parable of the Good Samaritan. The parable proved of value in suggesting both personality and situational variables relevant to helping.

"And who is my neighbor?" Jesus replied, "A man was going down from Jerusalem to Jericho, and he fell among robbers, who stripped him and beat him, and departed, leaving him half dead. Now by chance a priest was going down the road; and when he saw him he passed by on the other side. So likewise a Levite, when he came to the place and saw him, passed by on the other side. But a Samaritan, as he journeyed, came to where he was; and when he saw him, he had compassion, and went to him and bound his wounds, pouring on oil and wine; then he set him on his own beast and brought him to an inn, and took care of him. And the next day he took out two dennarii and gave them to the innkeeper, saying, "Take care of him; and whatever more you spend, I will repay you when I come back." Which of these three, do you think, proved neighbor to him

who fell among the robbers? He said, "The one who showed mercy on him." And Jesus said to him, "Go and do likewise." [Luke 10: 29–37 RSV]

To psychologists who reflect on the parable, it seems to suggest situational and personality differences between the nonhelpful priest and Levite and the helpful Samaritan. What might each have been thinking and doing when he came upon the robbery victim on that desolate road? What sort of persons were they?

One can speculate on differences in thought. Both the priest and the Levite were religious functionaries who could be expected to have their minds occupied with religious matters. The priest's role in religious activities is obvious. The Levite's role, although less obvious, is equally important: The Levites were necessary participants in temple ceremonies. Much less can be said with any confidence about what the Samaritan might have been thinking, but, in contrast to the others, it was most likely not of a religious nature, for Samaritans were religious outcasts.

Not only was the Samaritan most likely thinking about more mundane matters than the priest and Levite, but, because he was socially less important, it seems likely that he was operating on a quite different time schedule. One can imagine the priest and Levite, prominent public figures, hurrying along with little black books full of meetings and appointments, glancing furtively at their sundials. In contrast, the Samaritan would likely have far fewer and less important people counting on him to be at a particular place at a particular time, and therefore might be expected to be in less of a hurry than the prominent priest or Levite.

In addition to these situational variables, one finds personality factors suggested as well. Central among these, and apparently basic to the point that Jesus was trying to make, is a distinction between types of religiosity. Both the priest and Levite are extremely "religious." But it seems to be precisely their type of religiosity that the parable challenges. At issue is the motivation for one's religion and ethical behavior. Jesus seems to feel that the religious leaders of his time, though certainly respected and upstanding citizens, may be "virtuous" for what it will get them, both in terms of the admiration of their fellowmen and in the eyes of God. New Testament scholar R. W. Funk (1966) noted that the Samaritan is at the other end of the spectrum:

> *The Samaritan does not love with side glances at God. The need of neighbor alone is made self-evident, and the Samaritan responds without other motivation [pp. 218–219].*

That is, the Samaritan is interpreted as responding spontaneously to the situation, not as being preoccupied with the abstract ethical or organizational do's and don'ts of religion as the priest and Levite would seem to be. This is not to say that the Samaritan is portrayed as irreligious. A major intent of the parable would seem to be to present the Samaritan as a religious and ethical example, but at the same time to contrast his type of religiosity with the more common conception of religiosity that the priest and Levite represent.

To summarize the variables suggested as affecting helping behavior by the parable, the situational variables include the content of one's thinking and the amount of hurry in one's journey. The major dispositional variable seems to be differing types of religiosity. Certainly these variables do not exhaust the list that could be elicited from the parable, but they do suggest several research hypotheses.

Hypothesis 1   The parable implies that people who encounter a situation possibly calling for a helping response while thinking religious and ethical thoughts will be no more likely to offer aid than persons thinking about something else. Such a hypothesis seems to run counter to a theory that focuses on norms as determining helping behavior because a normative account would predict that the increased salience of helping norms produced by thinking about religious and ethical examples would increase helping behavior.

Hypothesis 2   Persons encountering a possible helping situation when they are in a hurry will be less likely to offer aid than persons not in a hurry.

Hypothesis 3   Concerning types of religiosity, persons who are religious in a Samaritan-like fashion will help more frequently than those religious in a priest or Levite fashion.

Obviously, this last hypothesis is hardly operationalized as stated. Prior research by one of the investigators on types of religiosity (Batson, 1971), however, led us to differentiate three distinct ways of being religious: (a) for what it will gain one (cf. Freud, 1927, and perhaps the priest and Levite), (b) for its own intrinsic value (cf. Allport & Ross, 1967), and (c) as a response to and quest for meaning in one's everyday life (cf. Batson, 1971). Both of the latter conceptions would be proposed by their exponents as related to the more Samaritanlike "true" religiosity. Therefore, depending on the theorist one follows, the third hypothesis may be stated like this: People (a) who are religious for intrinsic reasons (Allport & Ross, 1967) or (b) whose religion emerges out of questioning the meaning of their everyday lives (Batson, 1971) will be more likely to stop to offer help to the victim.

The parable of the Good Samaritan also suggested how we would measure people's helping behavior — their response to a stranger slumped by the side of one's path. The victim should appear somewhat ambiguous — ill-dressed, possibly in need of help, but also possibly drunk or even potentially dangerous.

Further, the parable suggests a means by which the incident could be perceived as a real one rather than part of a psychological experiment in which one's behavior was under surveillance and might be shaped by demand characteristics (Orne, 1962), evaluation apprehension (Rosenberg, 1965), or other potentially artifactual determinants of helping behavior. The victim should be encountered not in the experimental context but on the road between various tasks.

METHOD

In order to examine the influence of these variables on helping behavior, seminary students were asked to participate in a study on religious education and vocations. In the first testing session, personality questionnaires concerning types of religiosity were administered. In a second individual session, the subject began experimental procedures in one building and was asked to report to another building for later procedures. While in transit, the subject passed a slumped "victim" planted in an alleyway. The dependent variable was whether and how the subject helped the victim. The independent variables were the degree to which the subject was told to hurry in reaching the other building and the talk he was to give when he arrived there. Some subjects were to give a talk on the jobs in which seminary students would be most effective, others, on the parable of the Good Samaritan.

Subjects

The subjects for the questionnaire administration were 67 students at Princeton Theological Seminary. Forty-seven of them, those who could be reached by telephone, were scheduled for the experiment. Of the 47, 7 subjects' data were not included in the analyses—3 because of contamination of the experimental procedures during their testing and 4 due to suspicion of the experimental situation. Each subject was paid $1 for the questionnaire session and $1.50 for the experimental session.

Personality Measures

Detailed discussion of the personality scales used may be found elsewhere (Batson, 1971), so the present discussion will be brief. The general personality construct under examination was religiosity. Various conceptions of religiosity have been offered in recent years based on different psychometric scales. The conception seeming to generate the most interest is the Allport and Ross (1967) distinction between "intrinsic" versus "extrinsic" religiosity (cf. also Allen & Spilka, 1967, on "committed" versus "consensual" religion). This bipolar conception of religiosity has been questioned by Brown (1964) and Batson (1971), who suggested three-dimensional analyses instead. Therefore, in the present research, types of religiosity were measured with three instruments which together provided six separate scales; (a) a *doctri-*

nal orthodoxy (D-O) scale patterned after that used by Glock and Stark (1966), scaling agreement with classic doctrines of Protestant theology; (b) the Allport-Ross *extrinsic* (AR-E) scale, measuring the use of religion as a means to an end rather than as an end in itself; (c) the Allport-Ross *intrinsic* (AR-I) scale, measuring the use of religion as an end in itself; (d) the *extrinsic external* scale of Batson's Religious Life Inventory (RELI-EE), designed to measure the influence of significant others and situations in generating one's religiosity; (e) the *extrinsic internal* scale of the Religious Life Inventory (RELI-EI), designed to measure the degree of "driveness" in one's religiosity; and (f) the *intrinsic* scale of the Religious Life Inventory (RELI-I), designed to measure the degree to which one's religiosity involves a questioning of the meaning of life arising out of one's interactions with his social environment. The order of presentation of the scales in the questionnaire was RELI, AR, D-O.

Consistent with prior research (Batson, 1971), a principal-component analysis of the total scale scores and individual items for the 67 seminarians produced a theoretically meaningful, orthogonally rotated three-component structure with the following loadings:

Religion as means received a single very high loading from AR-E (.903) and therefore was defined by Allport and Ross's (1967) conception of this scale as measuring religiosity as a means to other ends. This component also received moderate negative loadings from D-O ($-.400$) and AR-I ($-.372$) and a moderate positive loading from RELI-EE (.301).

Religion as an end received high loadings from RELI-EI (.874), RELI-EE (.725), AR-I (.768), and D-O (.704). Given this configuration, and again following Allport and Ross's conceptualization, this component seemed to involve religiosity as an end in itself with some intrinsic value.

Religion as quest received a single very high loading from RELI-I (.945) and a moderate loading from RELI-EE (.75). Following Batson, this component was conceived to involve religiosity emerging out of an individual's search for meaning in his personal and social world.

The three religious personality scales examined

in the experimental research were constructed through the use of complete-estimation factor score coefficients from these three components.

Scheduling of Experimental Study

Since the incident requiring a helping response was staged outdoors, the entire experimental study was run in 3 days, December 14–16, 1970, between 10 A.M. and 4 P.M. A tight schedule was used in an attempt to maintain reasonably consistent weather and light conditions. Temperature fluctuation according to the *New York Times* for the 3 days during these hours was not more than 5 degrees Fahrenheit. No rain or snow fell, although the third day was cloudy, whereas the first two were sunny. Within days the subjects were randomly assigned to experimental conditions.[1]

Procedure

When a subject appeared for the experiment, an assistant (who was blind with respect to the personality scores) asked him to read a brief statement which explained that he was participating in a study of the vocational careers of seminary students. After developing the rationale for the study, the statement read:

> *What we have called you in for today is to provide us with some additional material which will give us a clearer picture of how you think than does the questionnaire material we have gathered thus far. Questionnaires are helpful, but tend to be somewhat oversimplified. Therefore, we would like to record a 3–5 minute talk you give based on the following passage. . . .*

Variable 1: Message In the task-relevant condition the passage read,

> *With increasing frequency the question is being asked: What jobs or professions do seminary students subsequently enjoy most, and in what jobs are they most effective? The answer to this question used to be so obvious that the question was not even asked. Seminary students were being trained for the min-*

istry, and since both society at large and the seminary student himself had a relatively clear understanding of what made a "good" minister, there was no need even to raise the question of for what other jobs seminary experience seems to be an asset. Today, however, neither society nor many seminaries have a very clearly defined conception of what a "good" minister is or of what sorts of jobs and professions are the best context in which to minister. Many seminary students, apparently genuinely concerned with "ministering," seem to feel that it is impossible to minister in the professional clergy. Other students, no less concerned, find the clergy the most viable profession for ministry. But are there other jobs and/or professions for which seminary experience is an asset? And, indeed, how much of an asset is it for the professional ministry? Or, even more broadly, can one minister through an "establishment" job at all?

In the helping-relevant condition, the subject was given the parable of the Good Samaritan exactly as printed earlier in this article. Next, regardless of condition, all subjects were told,

> *You can say whatever you wish based on the passage. Because we are interested in how you think on your feet, you will not be allowed to use notes in giving the talk. Do you understand what you are to do? If not, the assistant will be glad to answer questions.*

After a few minutes the assistant returned, asked if there were any questions, and then said:

> *Since they're rather tight on space in this building, we're using a free office in the building next door for recording the talks. Let me show you how to get there [draws and explains map on 3 × 5 card]. This is where Professor Steiner's laboratory is. If you go in this door [points at map], there's a secretary right here, and she'll direct you to the office we're using for recording. Another of Professor Steiner's assistants will set you up for recording your talk. Is the map clear?*

Variable 2: Hurry   In the high-hurry condition the assistant then looked at his watch and said, "Oh, you're late. They were expecting you a few minutes ago. We'd better get moving. The assistant should be waiting for you so you'd better hurry. It shouldn't take but just a minute." In the intermediate-hurry condition he said, "The assistant is ready for you, so please go right over." In the low-hurry condition, he said, "It'll be a few minutes before they're ready for you, but you might as well head on over. If you have to wait over there, it shouldn't be long."

The Incident   When the subject passed through the alley, the victim was sitting slumped in a doorway, head down, eyes closed, not moving. As the subject went by, the victim coughed twice and groaned, keeping his head down. If the subject stopped and asked if something was wrong or offered to help, the victim, startled and somewhat groggy, said, "Oh, thank you [cough]. . . . No, it's all right. [Pause] I've got this respiratory condition [cough]. . . . The doctor's given me these pills to take, and I just took one. . . . If I just sit and rest for a few minutes I'll be O.K. . . . Thanks very much for stopping though [smiles weakly]." If the subject persisted, insisting on taking the victim inside the building, the victim allowed him to do so and thanked him.

Helping Ratings   The victim rated each subject on a scale of helping behavior as follows:

> 0 = *failed to notice the victim as possibly in need at all; 1 = perceived the victim as possibly in need but did not offer aid; 2 = did not stop but helped indirectly (e.g., by telling Steiner's assistant about the victim); 3 = stopped and asked if victim needed help; 4 = after stopping, insisted on taking the victim inside and then left him.*

The victim was blind to the personality scale scores and experimental conditions of all subjects. At the suggestion of the victim, another category was added to the rating scales, based on his observations of the pilot subjects' behavior:

> 5 = *after stopping, refused to leave the victim (after 3–5 minutes) and/or insisted on taking him somewhere outside experimental context (e.g., for coffee or to the infirmary).*

(In some cases it was necessary to distinguish Category 0 from Category 1 by the postexperimental questionnaire and Category 2 from Category 1 on the report of the experimental assistant.)

This 6-point scale of helping behavior and a description of the victim were given to a panel of 10 judges (unacquainted with the research) who were asked to rank order the (unnumbered) categories in terms of "the amount of helping behavior displayed toward the person in the doorway." Of the 10, 1 judge reversed the order of Categories 0 and 1. Otherwise there was complete agreement with the ranking implied in the presentation of the scale above.

The Speech   After passing through the alley and entering the door marked on the map, the subject entered a secretary's office. She introduced him to the assistant who gave the subject time to prepare and privately record his talk.

Helping Behavior Questionnaire   After recording the talk, the subject was sent to another experimenter, who administered "an exploratory questionnaire on personal and social ethics." The questionnaire contained several initial questions about the interrelationship between social and personal ethics, and then asked three key questions: (a) "When was the last time you saw a person who seemed to be in need of help?" (b) "When was the last time you stopped to help someone in need?" (c) "Have you had experience helping persons in need? If so, outline briefly." These data were collected as a check on the victim's ratings of whether subjects who did not stop perceived the situation in the alley as one possibly involving need or not.

When he returned, the experimenter reviewed the subject's questionnaire, and, if no mention was made of the situation in the alley, probed for reactions to it and then phased into an elaborate debriefing and discussion session.

Debriefing

In the debriefing, the subject was told the exact nature of the study, including the deception involved, and the reasons for the deception were explained. The subject's reactions to the victim and to the study in general were discussed. The role of situational determinants of helping behavior was explained in relation to this particular incident and to other experiences of the subject. All subjects seemed readily to understand the necessity for the deception, and none indicated any resentment of it. After debriefing, the subject was thanked for his time and paid, then he left.

RESULTS AND DISCUSSION

Overall Helping Behavior

The average amount of help that a subject offered the victim, by condition, is shown in Table 1. The unequal-N analysis of variance indicates that while the hurry variable was significantly ($F = 3.56$, $df = 2/34$, $p < .05$) related to helping be-

TABLE 1 / Means and Analysis of Variance of Graded Helping Responses

		M		
		Hurry		Sum-
Message	Low	Medium	High	mary
Helping relevant	3.800	2.000	1.000	2.263
Task relevant	1.667	1.667	.500	1.333
Summary	3.000	1.818	.700	

Analysis of variance				
Source	SS	df	MS	F
Message (A)	7.766	1	7.766	2.65
Hurry (B)	20.884	2	10.442	3.50*
A × B	5.237	2	2.619	.89
Error	99.633	34	2.930	

Note. $N = 40$.
*$p < .05$.

havior, the message variable was not. Subjects in a hurry were likely to offer less help than were subjects not in a hurry. Whether the subject was going to give a speech on the parable of the Good Samaritan or not did not significantly affect his helping behavior on this analysis.

Other studies have focused on the question of whether a person initiates helping action or not, rather than on scaled kinds of helping. The data from the present study can also be analyzed on the following terms: Of the 40 subjects, 16 (40%) offered some form of direct or indirect aid to the victim (Coding Categories 2–5), 24 (60%) did not (Coding Categories 0 and 1). The percentages of subjects who offered aid by situational variable were, for low hurry, 63% offered help, intermediate hurry 45%, and high hurry 10%; for helping-relevant message 53%, task-relevant message 29%. With regard to this more general question of whether help was offered or not, an unequal-N analysis of variance (arc sine transformation of percentages of helpers, with low- and intermediate-hurry conditions pooled) indicated that again only the hurry main effect was significantly ($F = 5.22$, $p < .05$) related to helping behavior; the subjects in a hurry were more likely to pass by the victim than were those in less of a hurry.

Reviewing the predictions in the light of these results, the second hypothesis, that the degree of hurry a person is in determines his helping behavior, was supported. The prediction involved in the first hypothesis concerning the message content was based on the parable. The parable itself seemed to suggest that thinking pious thoughts would not increase helping. Another and conflicting prediction might be produced by a norm salience theory. Thinking about the parable should make norms for helping salient and therefore produce more helping. The data, as hypothesized, are more congruent with the prediction drawn from the parable. A person going to speak on the parable of the Good Samaritan is not significantly more likely to stop to help a person by the side of the road than is a person going to talk about possible occupations for seminary graduates.

Since both situational hypotheses are confirmed, it is tempting to stop the analysis of these variables at this point. However, multiple regression analysis procedures were also used to analyze the relationship of all of the independent variables of the study and the helping behavior. In addition to often being more statistically powerful due to the use of more data information, multiple regression analysis has an advantage over analysis of variance in that it allows for a comparison of the relative effect of the various independent variables in accounting for variance in the dependent variable. Also, multiple regression analysis can compare the effects of continuous as well as nominal independent variables on both continuous and nominal dependent variables (through the use of point biserial correlations, r_{pb}) and shows considerable robustness to violation of normality assumptions (Cohen, 1965, 1968). Table 2 reports the results of the multiple regression analysis using both help versus no help and the graded helping scale as dependent measures. In this table the overall equation Fs show the F value of the entire regression equation as a particular row variable enters the equation. Individual variable Fs were computed with all five independent variables in the equation. Although the two situational variables, hurry and message condition, correlated more highly with the dependent measure than any of the religious dispositional variables, only

hurry was a significant predictor of whether one will help or not (column 1) or of the overall amount of help given (column 2). These results corroborate the findings of the analysis of variance.[2]

Notice also that neither form of the third hypothesis, that types of religiosity will predict helping, received support from these data. No correlation between the various measures of religiosity and any form of the dependent measure ever came near statistical significance, even though the multiple regression analysis procedure is a powerful and not particularly conservative statistical test.

Personality Difference among Subjects Who Helped

To further investigate the possible influence of personality variables, analyses were carried out using only the data from subjects who offered some kind of help to the victim. Surprisingly (since the number of these subjects was small, only 16) when this was done, one religiosity variable seemed to be significantly related to the kind of helping behavior offered. (The situational variables had no significant effect.) Subjects high on the religion as quest dimension appear likely, when they stop for the victim, to offer help of a

TABLE 2 / Stepwise Multiple Regression Analysis

Help vs. no help					Graded helping				
	Individual variable		Overall equation			Individual variable		Variable equation	
Step	r[a]	F	R	F	Step	r	F	R	F
1. Hurry[b]	− .37	4.537*	.37	5.884*	1. Hurry	− .42	6.665*	.42	8.196**
2. Message[c]	.25	1.495	.41	3.834*	2. Message	.25	1.719	.46	5.083*
3. Religion as quest	− .03	.081	.42	2.521	3. Religion as quest	− .16	1.297	.50	3.897*
4. Religion as means	− .03	.003	.42	1.838*	4. Religion as means	− .08	.018	.50	2.848*
5. Religion as end	.06	.000	.42	1.430	5. Religion as end	− .07	.001	.50	2.213

Note. $N = 40$. Helping is the dependent variable. $df = 1/34$.
[a] Individual variable correlation coefficient is a point biserial where appropriate.
[b] Variables are listed in order of entry into stepwise regression equations.
[c] Helping-relevant message is positive.
* $p < .05$.
** $p < .01$.

more tentative or incomplete nature than are subjects scoring low on this dimension ($r = -.53$, $p < .05$).

This result seemed unsettling for the thinking behind either form of Hypothesis 3. Not only do the data suggest that the Allport-Ross-based conception of religion as *end* does not predict the degree of helping, but the religion as quest component is a significant predictor of offering less help. This latter result seems counterintuitive and out of keeping with previous research (Batson, 1971), which found that this type of religiosity correlated positively with other socially valued characteristics. Further data analysis, however, seemed to suggest a different interpretation of this result.

It will be remembered that one helping coding category was added at the suggestion of the victim after his observation of pilot subjects. The correlation of religious personality variables with helping behavior dichotomized between the added category (1) and all of the others (0) was examined. The correlation between religion as quest and this dichotomous helping scale was essentially unchanged ($r_{pb} = -.54$, $p < .05$). Thus, the previously found correlation between the helping scale and religion as quest seems to reflect the tendency of those who score low on the quest dimension to offer help in the added helping category.

What does help in this added category represent? Within the context of the experiment, it represented an embarrassment. The victim's response to persistent offers of help was to assure the helper he was all right, had taken his medicine, just needed to rest for a minute or so, and, if ultimately necessary, to request the helper to leave. But the *super* helpers in this added category often would not leave until the final appeal was repeated several times by the victim (who was growing increasingly panicky at the possibility of the arrival of the next subject). Since it usually involved the subject's attempting to carry through a preset plan (e.g., taking the subject for a cup of coffee or revealing to him the strength to be found in Christ), and did not allow information from the victim to change that plan, we originally labeled this kind of helping as rigid—an interpre-

tation supported by its increased likelihood among highly doctrinal orthodox subjects ($r = .63$, $p < .01$). It also seemed to have an inappropriate character. If this more extreme form of helping behavior is indeed effectively less helpful, then the second form of Hypothesis 3 does seem to gain support.

But perhaps it is the experimenters rather than the super helpers who are doing the inappropriate thing; perhaps the best characterization of this kind of helping is as different rather than as inappropriate. This kind of helper seems quickly to place a particular interpretation on the situation, and the helping response seems to follow naturally from this interpretation. All that can safely be said is that one style of helping that emerged in this experiment was directed toward the presumed underlying needs of the victim and was little modified by the victim's comments about his own needs. In contrast, another style was more tentative and seemed more responsive to the victim's statements of his need.

The former kind of helping was likely to be displayed by subjects who expressed strong doctrinal orthodoxy. Conversely, this fixed kind of helping was unlikely among subjects high on the religion as quest dimension. These latter subjects, who conceived their religion as involving an ongoing search for meaning in their personal and social world, seemed more responsive to the victim's immediate needs and more open to the victim's definitions of his own needs.

CONCLUSION AND IMPLICATIONS

A person not in a hurry may stop and offer help to a person in distress. A person in a hurry is likely to keep going. Ironically, he is likely to keep going even if he is hurrying to speak on the parable of the Good Samaritan, thus inadvertently confirming the point of the parable. (Indeed, on several occasions, a seminary student going to give his talk on the parable of the Good Samaritan literally stepped over the victim as he hurried on his way!)

Although the degree to which a person was in a hurry had a clearly significant effect on his likelihood of offering the victim help, whether he was going to give a sermon on the parable or on possible vocational roles of ministers did not. This lack of effect of sermon topic raises certain difficulties for an explanation of helping behavior involving helping norms and their salience. It is hard to think of a context in which norms concerning helping those in distress are more salient than for a person thinking about the Good Samaritan, and yet it did not significantly increase helping behavior. The results were in the direction suggested by the norm salience hypothesis, but they were not significant. The most accurate conclusion seems to be that salience of helping norms is a less strong determinant of helping behavior in the present situation than many, including the present authors, would expect.

Thinking about the Good Samaritan did not increase helping behavior, but being in a hurry decreased it. It is difficult not to conclude from this that the frequently cited explanation that ethics becomes a luxury as the speed of our daily lives increases is at least an accurate description. The picture that this explanation conveys is of a person seeing another, consciously noting his distress, and consciously choosing to leave him in distress. But perhaps this is not entirely accurate, for, when a person is in a hurry, something seems to happen that is akin to Tolman's (1948) concept of the "narrowing of the cognitive map." Our seminarians in a hurry noticed the victim in that in the postexperiment interview almost all mentioned him as, on reflection, possibly in need of help. But it seems that they often had not worked this out when they were near the victim. Either the interpretation of their visual picture as a person in distress or the empathic reactions usually associated with that interpretation had been deferred because they were hurrying. According to the reflections of some of the subjects, it would be inaccurate to say that they realized the victim's possible distress, then chose to ignore it; instead, because of the time pressures, they did not perceive the scene in the alley as an occasion for an ethical decision.

For other subjects it seems more accurate to conclude that they decided not to stop. They appeared aroused and anxious after the encounter in the alley. For these subjects, what were the elements of the choice that they were making? Why were the seminarians hurrying? Because the experimenter, *whom the subject was helping,* was depending on him to get to a particular place quickly. In other words, he was in conflict between stopping to help the victim and continuing on his way to help the experimenter. And this is often true of people in a hurry; they hurry because somebody depends on their being somewhere. Conflict, rather than callousness, can explain their failure to stop.

Finally, as in other studies, personality variables were not useful in predicting whether a person helped or not. But in this study, unlike many previous ones, considerable variations were possible in the kinds of help given, and these variations did relate to personality measures — specifically to religiosity of the quest sort. The clear light of hindsight suggests that the dimension of kinds of helping would have been the appropriate place to look for personality differences all along; *whether* a person helps or not is an instant decision likely to be situationally controlled. How a person helps involves a more complex and considered number of decisions, including the time and scope to permit personality characteristics to shape them.

REFERENCES

Allen, R. O., & Spilka, B. Committed and consensual religion. A specification of religion–prejudice relationships. *Journal for the Scientific Study of Religion,* 1967, *6,* 191–206.

Allport, G. W., & Ross, J. M. Personal religious orientation and prejudice. *Journal of Personality and Social Psychology,* 1967, *5,* 432–443.

Batson, C. D. Creativity and religious development: Toward a structural-functional psychology of religion. Unpublished doctoral dissertation, Princeton Theological Seminary, 1971.

Bickman, L. B. The effect of the presence of others on bystander intervention in an emergency. Unpublished doctoral dissertation, City College of the City University of New York, 1969.

Brown, L. B. Classifications of religious orientation.

Journal for the Scientific Study of Religion, 1964, *4,* 91–99.

Burton, R. V. The generality of honesty reconsidered. *Psychological Review,* 1963, *70,* 481–499.

Cohen, J. Multiple regression as a general data-analytic system. *Psychological Bulletin,* 1968, *70,* 426–443.

Cohen, J. Some statistical issues in psychological research. In B. B. Wolman (Ed.), *Handbook of clinical psychology.* New York: McGraw-Hill, 1965.

Darley, J. M., & Latané, B. Bystander intervention in emergencies: Diffusion of responsibility. *Journal of Personality and Social Psychology,* 1968, *8,* 377–383.

Freud, S. *The future of an illusion.* New York: Liveright, 1953.

Funk, R. W. *Language, hermeneutic, and word of God.* New York: Harper & Row, 1966.

Glock, C. Y., & Stark, R. *Christian beliefs and anti-Semitism.* New York: Harper & Row, 1966.

Hartshorne, H., & May, M. A. *Studies in the nature of character.* Vol. 1. *Studies in deceit.* New York: Macmillan, 1928.

Korte, C. Group effects on help-giving in an emergency. *Proceedings of the 77th Annual Convention of the American Psychological Association,* 1969, *4,* 383–384. (Summary)

Orne, M. T. On the social psychology of the psychological experiment: With particular reference to demand characteristics and their implications. *American Psychologist,* 1962, *17,* 776–783.

Rosenberg, M. J. When dissonance fails: On eliminating evaluation apprehension from attitude measurement. *Journal of Personality and Social Psychology,* 1965, *1,* 28–42.

Schwartz, S. H., & Clausen, G. T. Responsibility, norms, and helping in an emergency. *Journal of Personality and Social Psychology,* 1970, *16,* 299–310.

Tolman, E. C. Cognitive maps in rats and men. *Psychological Review,* 1948, *55,* 189–208.

NOTES

1. An error was made in randomizing that increased the number of subjects in the intermediate-hurry conditions. This worked against the prediction that was most highly confirmed (the hurry prediction) and made no difference to the message variable tests.

2. To check the legitimacy of the use of both analysis of variance and multiple regression analysis, parametric analyses, on this ordinal data, Kendall rank correlation coefficients were calculated between the helping scale and the five independent variables. As expected τ approximated the correlation quite closely in each case and was significant for hurry only (hurry $\tau = -.38, p < .001$).

For assistance in conducting this research thanks are due Robert Wells, Beverly Fisher, Mike Shafto, Peter Sheras, Richard Detweiler, and Karen Glasser. The research was funded by National Science Foundation Grant GS-2293.

CRITICAL THINKING QUESTIONS

1. Being prompted to think of the parable of the Good Samaritan did not increase the subjects' helping behavior in this study, but being in a hurry did. Suppose that you are in the business of soliciting money for a worthy purpose. What strategies could you use to maximize the money you receive, based upon the implications of this study?

2. "Rush hour," as the name implies, describes those times of day when people are in a hurry to get to and from work. Do you think that people would be less likely to help someone in need during rush hour than at other times of the day? What about on weekends? Design a study to test this possibility, being sure to address any ethical issues that may be involved.

3. Reading about the Good Samaritan had no impact on subsequent helping behavior. Do you think that reading an article such as this one would change people's helping behavior? Specifically, now that you know that being in a hurry will decrease the likelihood of your giving help, do you think that this awareness will make you more likely to give help in the future, even if you are in a hurry? Why or why not? If simply telling someone about the Good Samaritan wasn't enough to improve people's helping behavior, what might be more effective?

ADDITIONAL RELATED READINGS

Batson, C., Cochran, P., Biederman, M., Blosser, J., Ryan, M., & Vogt, B. (1978). Failure to help when in a hurry: Callousness or conflict? *Personality and Social Psychology Bulletin, 4,* 97–101.

Rushton, J., & Sorrentino, R. (Eds.). (1981). *Altruism and helping behavior.* Hillsdale, NJ: Erlbaum.

ARTICLE 27 _____

Since the pioneering research of Darley and Latané, discussed in Article 25, a large body of research has been conducted documenting the inhibition of helping when others are present. Three main explanations account for these findings.

The first is *diffusion of responsibility,* which simply means that any one individual is less likely to assume personal responsibility for helping the more other potential helpers are present. A second explanation is *social influence effects.* Specifically, we look to others around us for information about what we are seeing and what we are doing, especially if the situation is novel or ambiguous. Standing in a group of bystanders, none of whom seems concerned or is doing anything, might convey the impression that nothing is wrong and that nothing needs to be done. Finally, the potential presence of an *audience* also might inhibit helping, such as when we want to avoid doing something potentially foolish in front of other people.

The following study by John Cacioppo and his colleagues examines audience-inhibition processes that may have an impact on helping behavior. The two experiments discussed suggest not only that people tend to attribute blame to the first person helping another person but also that people's decisions to help may be influenced by whether they think others will blame them. Further, these effects were related to the number of bystanders present. This study provides a good example of conceptual refinement of a research topic. At first, single variables, such as diffusion of responsibility, are found to affect behavior. Over time, however, other variables that may influence the behavior are discovered and the conditions under which they operate are further elaborated.

Attributions of Responsibility for Helping and Doing Harm
Evidence for Confusion of Responsibility

■ John T. Cacioppo, Richard E. Petty, and Mary E. Losch

The social inhibition of helping is well documented, and this phenomenon has been explained in terms of the general processes of audience inhibition, social influence, and diffusion of responsibility. In the present research, we adapted the paradigm used in studies of the attribution of responsibility for an accident to examine a specific audience-inhibition process that may contribute to the social inhibition of helping. Evidence from two experiments showed that an individual who adopted the perspective of a helper following an accident expected to be held increasingly responsible by arriving onlookers for the victim's plight as the number of extant bystanders increased. Results also indicated that there was an objective basis for this expectation: Subjects who adopted the perspective of a newly arriving onlooker increasingly attributed responsibility for doing harm to the individual helping the victim in the accident as the number of by-

Reprinted from the *Journal of Personality and Social Psychology,* 1986, *50,* 100–105. Copyright 1986 by the American Psychological Association. Reprinted by permission.

standers described as already at the scene increased. The distinction between confusion and diffusion of responsibility is emphasized, and limitations to confusion of responsibility for accidents are discussed.

Previous research on attributions of responsibility for accidents has focused on the victim (Howard, 1984; Walster, 1966; see review by Burger, 1981). The present focus is on the helper rather than the victim. The thesis advanced in the present research is that individuals who adopt the perspective of a helper expect to be held increasingly responsible by arriving onlookers for the victim's plight following an accident as the number of extant bystanders increases. Specifically, evidence is reported for an attributional process that appears to increase the social cost of helping as the number of bystanders increases.

SOCIAL INHIBITION OF HELPING

According to Latané and Darley (1970), a bystander in a situation in which a victim needs help is in an unenviable position. The bystander must notice the event, interpret it as an emergency, assume the responsibility to act, know an appropriate form of assistance, and act on the decision to help. Moreover, the bystander oftentimes is at risk of incurring substantial costs, personal and social, by acting on his or her decision to help (cf. I. M. Piliavin, J. A. Piliavin, & Rodin, 1975). Because these potential costs increase as the number of bystanders increases, it is perhaps less than surprising that "despite the great diversity of styles, settings, and techniques among the studies, the social inhibition of helping is a remarkably consistent phenomenon" (Latané & Nida, 1981, p. 308).

Latané and Darley specified three general social psychological processes that could short-circuit a bystander's decision to help when others were present but clarifying communications were not. The first, diffusion of responsibility, specifies that an individual who recognizes there is a need for help may fail to feel personal responsibility for helping because the individual feels incompetent

to help, the victim is viewed as being undeserving or unrelated, or the individual thinks others are present and available to help.

> *If only one bystander is present at an emergency, he carries all of the responsibility for dealing with it; he will feel all of the guilt for not acting; he will bear all of the blame that accrues for nonintervention. If others are present, the onus of responsibility is diffused, and the finger points less directly at any one person (Latané & Darley, 1970, p. 90).*

Latané and Darley's diffusion of responsibility hypothesis has stimulated considerable research both on the social inhibition of helping (cf. Latané & Nida, 1981) and on social loafing generally (e.g., Brickner, Harkins, & Ostrom, in press; Harkins & Petty, 1982; Latané, Williams, & Harkins, 1979).

Social influence was a second general process postulated by Latané and Darley (1970) to contribute to the inhibition of helping by the presence of others. A potential helper, confronted with a situation in which another may be in need of assistance, was posited to look to the reactions of others to help define the situation (cf. Schachter, 1959; Shaver & Klinnert, 1982). According to this view, a bystander would be less likely to decide that intervention was appropriate or necessary when the actions of others indicated the situation was not an emergency.

Latané and Darley (1970) also noted in their discussion of social influence that the potential cost of making an inappropriate response—such as embarrassment and shame—increases as the number of bystanders increases (pp. 37–38). This discussion of audience-inhibition processes was embedded in their discussion of social influence because of the posited interactive effects of these two processes: "If each bystander sees other bystanders momentarily frozen by audience inhibition, each may be misled into thinking the situation must not be serious" (Latané & Darley, 1970, p. 125).

Audience-inhibition processes have since become an interesting focus of research in their own right (e.g., Petty, Harkins, Williams, & Latané,

1977). In an important set of studies, for instance, Schwartz and Gottlieb (1976, 1980) argued that bystanders who believe that others are aware of their presence may be apprehensive regarding others' expectations and evaluations of their behavior; accordingly, bystanders are viewed as seeking to optimize these evaluations (cf. Schlenker, 1980). Schwartz and Gottlieb (1980) reported data consistent with the notion that bystanders' anonymity inhibited helping when they believed other bystanders thought helping to be an appropriate response, whereas anonymity enhanced helping when they believed other bystanders viewed helping as an inappropriate response.

CONFUSION OF RESPONSIBILITY

The present research probed an audience-inhibition process based on people's attributions of the helper's responsibility for doing harm. Specifically, we reasoned that an individual who adopts the perspective of a helper following an apparent accident expects to be held increasingly responsible by newcomers for the victim's misfortune as the number of extant bystanders increases. A corollary to this hypothesis is that there is a basis for this belief: An individual who is seen with a victim tends to be held responsible for the victim's misfortune, and this tendency increases as the number of bystanders increases.

The initial basis for these postulates came from the literature on the manner in which people draw inferences and on affirming the consequent in particular. For instance, because people approach things they like, they tend to infer that they like the things they approach (Triandis, 1971). Similarly, because in our society people are expected to help those they have unintentionally harmed, helpers may anticipate being held partially responsible for harming the very victim they are helping unless evidence to the contrary is present. Furthermore, if the presence of nonhelping bystanders enhances the attention drawn to the event or the uniqueness of the helper's actions in the eyes of arriving onlookers, then the perceived connection between the helper and victim should be strengthened. Consequently, people

who adopt the perspective of a helper may anticipate that the number of extant bystanders would increase the attributions of responsibility for doing harm assigned to them by arriving onlookers.

Note that the emphasis here is not on the responsibility a potential helper (e.g., a bystander) feels for helping a victim, but rather it is on the responsibility for harmdoing the potential helper believes others will attribute to him or her should he or she help the victim. In this respect, the present research is more similar to the research on attributions of responsibility for doing harm in accidents than to traditional research on social inhibition. Nevertheless, if as we have suggested people anticipate being assigned greater responsibility for doing harm when they are helping a victim and bystanders are present than when they and the victim are alone, then this "confusion of responsibility" would represent a perceived social cost to helping that would vary as a function of the number of bystanders present.

Walster's (1966) methodology for studying the attributions of responsibility for doing harm was adapted for use in the present study. Walster presented subjects with information about a stimulus person, including a description of an accident in which the person was supposedly involved. Some subjects were informed that the person's parked car rolled a short distance down a hill and struck a tree stump, resulting in minor damage. Others were informed that the car rolled all of the way down the hill and struck a tree, resulting in considerable damage. Whether the stimulus person and other people were or could have been injured was also varied. Results revealed that subjects attributed more responsibility for the accident to the stimulus person when the consequences of the accident were severe rather than mild.

In the present studies, students were informed of a realistic campus-situation in which a student was seen providing help to the victim following an apparently minor mishap. The situation was described from the point of view of a person just arriving on the scene, and the victim and helper were described either as being alone or as the focus of the attention of varying numbers of silent bystanders. In some conditions, subjects were asked to adopt the perspective of the helper, and in others subjects were asked to adopt the perspective of the arriving onlooker. Subjects were asked to attribute responsibility for doing harm (Studies 1 & 2) and helping (Study 2). To assure that the bystander information was salient to subjects, the number of existing bystanders described as being at the scene served as a within-subjects factor in both experiments — although the design of Study 2 allowed both between-subjects and within-subjects comparisons to be performed.

STUDY 1

Method

Subjects and Design   A 4 × 2 (Number of Extant Bystanders: 0, 1, 5, or 10 × Subject's Perspective: Helper or Arriving Onlooker) within-subjects factorial design was used in which 220 students in an undergraduate psychology class served as subjects. All subjects were tested during a class early in the semester while they were seated at desks in a large auditorium.

Procedure   Subjects were instructed to consider eight different scenarios. The first four scenarios involved the subjects making attributions of responsibility for another individual's behavior as the number of bystanders, who were at the scene when the subject arrived was varied. In the first, subjects were instructed:

> *Imagine that you are leaving this building alone and you see a man lying on the ground groaning in pain. You see a pair of crutches lying on the ground next to the man and an individual lifting the man to his feet. There is no one else around.*

Subjects were then asked to rate "How responsible is the individual who is lifting the man to his feet for the victim's pain and suffering?" using a 9-point scale ranging from *not at all responsible* (1) to *very responsible* (9). The next three scenarios to which subjects responded differed only in the last sentence. In the second, third, and fourth sce-

narios, respectively, subjects were instructed that there was 1 other person, 5 other people, and 10 other people standing nearby simply watching the individual lift the man. Subjects again used 9-point scales to respond to each scenario.

The remaining four scenarios were similar except that the subject was asked to imagine that he or she was the person who was lifting the man to his feet; their task was to indicate how an individual leaving the building would view his or her behavior given no one else was around (fifth scenario), 1 other person was standing nearby watching (sixth scenario), 5 other people were standing nearby watching (seventh scenario), or 10 other people were standing nearby watching (eighth scenario). Following each, subjects responded to the question: "How responsible will someone just leaving the building think you are for the man's pain and suffering?" Subjects rated their responses on a scale ranging from *not at all responsible* (1) to *very responsible* (9).

After subjects completed their ratings, they were engaged in an active discussion regarding the purpose of the study and the methods used. Features such as the use of a completely within-subjects design and the absence of counterbalancing across scenarios were noted, and sources of artifact (e.g., sensitization) were discussed to illustrate the importance of these features. Finally, an experimental design that avoided these interpretive problems was described (see Study 2).

Results

The 4 × 2 analysis of variance (ANOVA) revealed two main effects. First, a main effect for the Perspective factor indicated that the individual lifting the victim (the helper) was viewed as being more responsible for the victim's suffering when subjects adopted the perspective of the observer ($M = 5.19$) than when they adopted the perspective of the helper ($M = 3.77$), $F(1, 219) = 94.28$, $p < .001$. This finding is consistent with the operation of the fundamental attribution error (Ross, 1977).

Second, and more importantly here, the number of bystanders affected subjects' attributions of responsibility, $F(3, 657) = 76.39$, $p < .001$. Newman-Keuls pair-wise comparisons revealed that subjects rated the helper as increasingly responsible for the victim's suffering as the number of extant bystanders increased from 0 to 1, from 1 to 5, and from 5 to 10 ($Ms = 3.39, 4.12, 4.93, \&$ 5.48, respectively; all $ps < .05$). The Bystander × Perspective interaction did not approach significance ($F < 1$). Thus, subjects adopting the perspective of a newly arriving bystander not only tended to view a person engaged in a prosocial behavior as more responsible for doing harm as the number of bystanders already at the scene increased, but the attributions for harmdoing made when they adopted the perspective of the helper suggested that subjects were cognizant of this potential social cost of helping.

Although Study 1 was conducted primarily for exploratory and demonstrative purposes, analyses provided encouraging results regarding the confusion of responsibility hypothesis. A second study, therefore, was undertaken to test this hypothesis more rigorously. In addition to the counterbalancing of materials, subjects were asked to rate the extent to which the individual lifting the victim in the scenarios was (a) responsible for the victim's plight and (b) a helpful person. This was done to determine whether or not the presence of bystanders was simply enhancing any dispositional attribution subjects might form regarding the helper's behavior.

STUDY 2

Method

Subjects and Design   We used a 3 × 2 × 3 × 2 (Number of Extant Bystanders: 0, 4, or 10 × Subject's Perspective: Helper or Arriving Onlooker × Order of Scenarios × Order of Dependent Measures) mixed model factorial. The Number of Extant Bystanders factor was manipulated within subjects, the Subject's Perspective was manipulated between subjects, and the Order of the Scenarios and the Order of the Dependent Measures were counterbalanced across subjects. Subjects were 136 undergraduates who partici-

pated to obtain credit toward their grade in an introductory psychology course. Subjects were tested in groups of 40–60 in a large auditorium in which seating was arranged to assure that at least one vacant desk separated subjects. All experimental instructions and dependent measures were contained in booklets, which were placed facedown on the subjects' desk before their arrival, and conversation among subjects was not allowed following the onset of the session. In this way, each experimental condition was conducted during each of the experimental sessions.

Procedure   Following introductory materials, subjects were instructed to consider three different scenarios. Subjects who adopted the perspective of an observer were told the following:

> *Imagine that you are leaving this building alone and you see a man lying on the ground groaning in pain. There is a pair of crutches lying on the ground next to the man, and an individual is lifting the man to his feet.*

The number of bystanders was manipulated by varying the final sentence in this description, which stated that either there was no one else around, 4 other people were standing nearby simply watching, or 10 other people were standing nearby simply watching. After reading each scenario, subjects responded to two questions: "How responsible is the individual who is lifting the man to his feet for the man's fall?" (1 = *not at all responsible*, 5 = *very responsible*); and "How would you characterize the individual who is lifting the man to his feet?" (1 = *not at all helpful*, 5 = *very helpful*).

Subjects who adopted the perspective of the helper read the following paragraph:

> *Imagine that you are leaving this building alone and you see a man lying on the ground groaning in pain. There is a pair of crutches lying on the ground next to the man, and you stop to help him. As you are lifting the man to his feet, another individual leaves the building and sees that you are lifting the man.*

The number of bystanders was again manipulated by varying the final sentence of this description. Subjects read that either there was no one else around, 4 other people were standing nearby simply watching, or 10 other people were standing nearby simply watching. After reading each scenario, subjects responded to two questions: "How responsible will this individual think you are for the man's fall?" (1 = *not at all responsible*, 5 = *very responsible*); and "How do you think that individual would characterize you?" (1 = *not at all helpful*, 5 = *very helpful*).

Results

A 3 × 2 × 3 × 2 ANOVA of subjects' attributions of responsibility for doing harm revealed the expected main effect for Number of Extant Bystanders, $F(2, 248) = 5.24, p < .01$, as well as a Bystander × Perspective interaction, $F(2, 248) = 4.68, p < .05$. Cell means and Newman-Keuls pair-wise comparisons are summarized in Table 1. Briefly, subjects who adopted the perspective of the helper indicated they believed that a newcomer to the scene would hold them increasingly responsible for having harmed the victim as the number of bystanders already on the scene increased. Subjects who adopted the perspective of an arriving onlooker, however, made intermediate attributions of responsibility for doing harm regardless of group size. No other main effect or interaction was significant for this measure.

Analyses of the attributions of helpfulness revealed a main effect for the Perspective factor, reflecting the fact that subjects again tended to make more dispositional attributions to others ($M = 4.79$) than to themselves ($M = 4.18$), $F(1, 124) = 30.02, p < .001$. Importantly, however, the main effect for the Bystanders factor was not significant, and the trend revealed that subjects tended to rate the individual lifting the victim as less rather than more helpful as the number of extant bystanders increased (see Table 1).[1] In addition, the correlation between the attributions of responsibility for doing harm and the attributions of helping were significantly but negatively correlated ($r = -.23$). Thus, no evidence was found

TABLE 1 / Attributions of Helpfulness and Responsibility for Doing Harm as a Function of Number of Bystanders and Subject's Perspective

No. of extant bystanders	None	4	10
Attributions of responsibility for doing harm			
Helper	2.47$_a$	2.90$_{bc}$	3.09$_c$
Arriving onlooker	2.79$_b$	2.77$_b$	2.80$_b$
Overall	2.63$_a$	2.84$_b$	2.95$_b$
Attributions of helpfulness			
Helper	4.39$_b$	4.11$_a$	4.03$_a$
Arriving onlooker	4.79$_c$	4.81$_c$	4.78$_c$
Overall	4.58$_a$	4.46$_a$	4.40$_a$

Note. Means with differing subscripts differ by the Newman-Keuls test, $p < .05$.

for the notion that ratings of responsibility for doing harm and of helpfulness were affected similarly.

Finally, because each scenario appeared first in one of the three sets, it was possible to examine the attributions of helpfulness and of responsibility for doing harm treating the Number of Extant Bystanders as a between-subjects factor. Effects found in this analysis are informative because they cannot be ascribed to the potential contaminating effects of within-subjects manipulations (e.g., carryover, sensitization).

The analysis of the subjects' attributions of responsibility for doing harm again revealed a main effect for Number of Extant Bystanders, $F(2, 112) = 3.37, p < .04$. Subjects regarded the helper associated with a victim as the least responsible for doing harm when no bystander was present ($M = 2.42$), moderately responsible for harmdoing when 4 bystanders were already present ($M = 2.73$), and most responsible for harmdoing when 10 bystanders were already present ($M = 3.01$). Newman-Keuls pair-wise comparisons indicated that the first and third means differed significantly ($p < .05$). No other test involving attributions of responsibility for doing harm was significant, meaning that the confusion of responsibility effect held whether subjects adopted the perspective of the helper or of the arriving on-looker.

The analysis of subjects' attributions of helpfulness revealed two significant effects. Consistent with the fundamental attribution error, subjects made stronger dispositional attributions of helpfulness when they adopted the perspective of an observer ($M = 4.67$) than helper ($M = 4.29$), $F(1, 111) = 10.20, p < .01$. This main effect was qualified by a Perspective × Order of Dependent Measures interaction, $F(1, 111) = 7.52, p < .01$, which indicated that the fundamental attribution error was stronger when subjects judged the helper's responsibility for doing harm first. No other test was significant.

DISCUSSION

Results of the first study indicated that as the number of existing bystanders increased, subjects attributed increasing responsibility for doing harm to an individual who was lifting an injured man to his feet. Although an interaction in Study 2 suggested this effect was not robust when subjects adopted the perspective of a bystander, subjects who imagined they were the helper did judge that they would be held more responsible for doing harm by observers who arrived subsequently on the scene when bystanders were present than when bystanders were not. Furthermore, when analyses were performed on only the data provided in response to the first scenario, subjects attributed more responsibility for doing harm to the helper whether subjects adopted the perspective of the helper or of the arriving onlooker. Hence, the present research suggests yet another reason why groups can be a source of evaluation apprehension and inhibit people's impulse to help.

We do not however mean to suggest here that expectations regarding the confusion of responsibility are of sufficient magnitude that they alone are likely to deter an individual from helping. For instance, the attributions of helpfulness obtained in Study 2 are greater in magnitude than are the attributions for doing harm. More important, however, inspection of Table 1 indicates that the

effect of group size on the anticipated social cost of helping is not offset by expectations of corresponding benefits. That is, confusion of responsibility may represent but one small deterrent to helping, but it is a deterrent that increases in magnitude as the number of silent bystanders increase.

Moreover, the present research does not imply that group size invariably fosters nonhelping or that the confusion of responsibility for harmdoing invariably increases as group size increases. For instance, the presence of others may not inhibit but rather may actually enhance prosocial behavior in situations in which there are no ambiguities regarding the cause of an emergency (e.g., the emergency was witnessed or an individual was seen going to the aid of the victim), the motive of a helper is clear (e.g., the helper is labeled as such by a uniform), communication among bystanders facilitates the clarification rather than the diffusion or confusion responsibility (e.g., the helper is cheered by bystanders), and greater evaluation apprehension is aroused by not helping (e.g., the victim is identifiable as a dependent of the helper; cf. Schwartz & Gottlieb, 1976, 1980; Staub, 1974; cf. Latané & Nida, 1981). It remains an interesting possibility that group size in these situations would not affect, or perhaps even decrease, the attributions of responsibility for doing harm made by arriving onlookers as well.

Nevertheless, specific models of the process underlying the confusion of responsibility effect can be evaluated in light of the present data. For instance, Walster's (1966) methodology for examining the attributions of responsibility for accidents was simple to adapt and informative in its yield. Could these areas of study have more in common than methodology? That is, perhaps people's attributions in the present study were motivated by their desire to avoid being singled-out to help in a potentially embarrassing circumstance. It seems unlikely to us that ego-defensive attributional processes were operative in this setting, but it would nevertheless be interesting to examine whether factors known to affect the attributions of responsibility for victims have similar effects on the attributions of responsibility for helpers. For instance, situational and personal similarity — variables introduced by Shaver (1970) to specify the conditions under which the severity of an accident enhances attributions for responsibility to the victim (see review by Burger, 1981) could conceivably prove to be moderators of the confusion of responsibility effect as well. Should the parallels between the present results and those from studies on attributions of responsibility for victims extend to elements such as personal and situational similarity, then one would be more inclined to consider ego-defensive attributions as a likely mediator of the confusion of responsibility effect.

Several other accounts warrant discussion, however. The results from the second study clearly differentiated the confusion of responsibility effect from a simple augmenting effect on dispositional attributions. Although the helper's behavior could be viewed as increasingly unique by arriving onlookers as the number of extant bystanders increased, no evidence was obtained for the notion that dispositional attributions increased generally as the number of bystanders increased. Instead, subjects' attributions indicated that the number of bystanders simply standing about affected primarily their inferences regarding responsibility for doing harm. A variation of the principle that unique behaviors enhance dispositional attributions, however, could conceivably be operative here. Consider that the behavioral context from the perspective of the arriving onlooker is causally ambiguous and decidedly negative: A victim is encountered who has somehow experienced an unfortunate mishap. In addition, another individual is standing with the victim, and there is either no one else around or other people attending to but not associating with the individual and victim. To the extent that the presence of bystanders enhances the uniqueness of the helper's behavior, the negative, causally ambiguous context may motivate stronger dispositional attributions along hedonically consistent trait dimensions. This suggestion is consistent with the literature demonstrating the powerful influence of affect on attributional processes (e.g., Abramson, Seligman, & Teasdale, 1978; Isen, Shalker,

Clark, & Karp, 1978) but would require a revision of present notions regarding the factors governing dispositional attributions.

Alternatively, the operation of biases and heuristics that allow individuals in a complex social situation (e.g., bystanders, people passing nearby) to formulate judgments on the basis of limited information or information processing (e.g., why an individual might be next to a victim while others stand nearby) could be viewed as contributing to a confusion of responsibility. Kahneman, Slovic, and Tversky (1982) provided evidence that judgments under uncertainty are particularly susceptible to such biases. For instance, let the letter H designate the act of helping a victim and the letter R designate the responsibility for the victim's harm. For most situations, $P(H|R)$ does not equal $P(R|H)$, and to equate these probabilities (i.e., to affirm the consequent) is logically specious and generally leads to errors in human judgment. Even if people were highly likely to help someone they had harmed [e.g., $P(H|R) = .80$], observers could not logically deduce from this an individual's responsibility for having harmed a person he or she is seen helping [i.e., $P(H|R)$]. Nevertheless, to the extent that (a) the presence of bystanders renders a helping situation increasingly ambiguous to newcomers on the scene, (b) the belief that people should help those they unintentionally harm is a salient social norm, and (c) simple heuristics such as affirming the consequent are more likely to be used in an ambiguous situation, then confusion of responsibility should indeed be more likely individually and collectively as the number of bystanders increases.

Could the confusion of responsibility possibly reflect a logical judgmental process? Consider the following. The probability a helper is responsible for having harmed the victim, $P(R|H)$, is defined by the joint probability of harming and helping the victim, $P(R, H)$ divided by the probability the individual would help the victim, $P(H)$. This is decidedly different from the probability of harming and helping the victim, $P(R, H)$, divided by the probability the individual would harm the victim $P(R)$. There are two interesting observations that can be made on the basis of these formulae. First, even if it were true that when confronted with a helping situation people consider both people's probability of helping [$P(H)$] and the probability that they are involved in both doing harm and helping [$P(R, H)$], this would not provide the information one would need logically to determine the basis for $P(R|H)$—the inference that an individual who helped a person was somehow responsible for the person's plight. Second, however, these formulae and research since Latané and Darley (1970) raise the possibility that confusion of responsibility is not entirely without basis in fact. Research suggests that in many helping situations $P(H)$ decreases as the number of bystanders increases (Latané & Nida, 1981). Given this finding, the simplifying assumption that $P(R, H)$ is constant, and the conditional probability, $P(R|H) = P(R, H)|P(H)$, it can be seen that the likelihood an individual who is helping a person will be held responsible for a person's harm increases as the number of existing bystanders increases. Thus, it cannot be asserted with absolute certainty that observers are acting illogically when they attribute increasing responsibility for harmdoing to helpers as the number of bystanders increases. Of course, the nonobvious nature of the bystander effect suggests that most people believe $P(H)$ stays constant or increases as the number of bystanders increases. Hence, both the judgments of bystanders and of potential helpers, which should be guided by their beliefs rather than research facts regarding the likelihood an individual will help given the number of bystanders increase, appear even more likely to represent biased than logical information processing.

Nevertheless, the operation of a logical judgmental process cannot be completely eliminated if one considers biases that might be introduced when people try to recall the information relevant for forming their judgment regarding a helper's responsibility for doing harm. The probability an individual helps a person $P(H)$ equals the sum of the probability the individual both harms and helps the individual $P(R, H)$ plus the probability that the individual helps and does not harm the person $P(\text{not } R, H)$. If the latter term is relatively high, then $P(R|H)$ may be quite low, even though

$P(H|R)$ is high (Dawes, 1982). People may indeed feel a special responsibility for helping a person whom they have accidentally harmed (Cialdini, Darby, & Vincent, 1973; Harvey & Enzle, 1981). Despite the salience of this norm or cognitive element (i.e., the high likelihood of $P(H|R)$ in many people's view), most victims are helped by individuals not responsible for their harm. If these latter instances are less salient or memorable to people, and especially with respect to the effects of group size, then it could be argued that people are acting logically given the inaccurate information that is accessible at the time they formulated their judgment.

In sum, the present analysis of attributions of responsibility and the social inhibition of helping extends previous analyses in at least two respects. First, the emphasis is not on the responsibility a given bystander feels for helping a victim, but rather it is on the responsibility for doing harm the potential helper believes others will attribute to the person who tries to help the victim. If, as the present data suggest, people anticipate being assigned greater responsibility for doing harm when they are helping a victim when bystanders are standing about than when the helper and the victim are alone, then this expectation of a confusion of responsibility would constitute a perceived social cost to helping that varies with the number of extant bystanders. Second, most research on the social inhibition of helping has focused on bystanders who were present when the emergency occurred. Confusion of responsibility in these circumstances may be minimal, because all those present know that none was responsible for or contributed to the accident. In some situations in which a person needs help, however, observers (e.g., bystanders, onlookers, people passing by) do not know who was or was not present or responsible for the emergency or both. It may be precisely these types of situations that confusion of responsibility is likely to occur.

REFERENCES

Abramson, L., Seligman, M., & Teasdale, J. (1978). Learned helplessness in humans: Critique and reformulation. *Journal of Abnormal Psychology, 87,* 49–74.

Brickner, M. A., Harkins, S. G., & Ostrom, T. M. (in press). The effects of personal involvement: Thought provoking implications for social loafing. *Journal of Personality and Social Psychology.*

Burger, J. M. (1981). Motivational biases in the attribution of responsibility for an accident: A meta-analysis of the defensive-attribution hypothesis. *Psychological Bulletin, 90,* 496–512.

Cialdini, R. B., Darby, B. L., & Vincent, J. E. (1973). Transgression and altruism: A case for hedonism. *Journal of Experimental Social Psychology, 9,* 502–516.

Dawes, R. M. (1982). The value of being explicit when making clinical decisions. In T. A. Wills (Ed.), *Basic processes in helping relationships.* New York: Academic Press.

Harkins, S. G., & Petty, R. E. (1982). Effects of task difficulty and task uniqueness on social loafing. *Journal of Personality and Social Psychology, 43,* 1214–1229.

Harvey, M. D., & Enzle, M. E. (1981). A cognitive model of social norms for understanding the transgression-helping effect. *Journal of Personality and Social Psychology, 41,* 866–875.

Howard, J. A. (1984). Societal influences on attribution: Blaming some victims more than others. *Journal of Personality and Social Psychology, 47,* 494–505.

Isen, A. M., Shalker, T., Clark, M., & Karp, L. (1978). Affect, accessibility of material in memory and behavior: A cognitive loop? *Journal of Personality and Social Psychology, 36,* 1–12.

Kahneman, D., Slovic, P., & Tversky, A. (Eds.). (1982). *Judgment under uncertainty: Heuristics and biases.* New York: Cambridge University Press.

Latané, B., & Darley, J. M. (1970). *The unresponsive bystander: Why doesn't he help?* New York: Appleton-Century-Crofts.

Latané, B., & Nida, S. (1981). Ten years of research on group size and helping. *Psychological Bulletin, 89,* 308–324.

Latané, B., Williams, K. D., & Harkins, S. G. (1979). Many hands make light the work: The causes and consequences of social loafing. *Journal of Personality and Social Psychology, 37,* 822–832.

Petty, R. E., Harkins, S. G., Williams, K. D., & Latané, B. (1977). The effects of group size on cognitive effort and evaluation. *Personality and Social Psychology Bulletin, 3,* 579–582.

Piliavin, I. M., Piliavin, J. A., & Rodin, J. (1975). Cost, diffusion, and the stigmatized victim. *Journal of Personality and Social Psychology, 32,* 429–438.

Ross, L. (1977). The intuitive psychologist and his shortcomings: Distortions in the attribution process. In L. Berkowitz (Ed.), *Advances in experimental social psychology* (Vol. 10, pp. 174–221). New York: Academic Press.

Schachter, S. (1959). *The psychology of affiliation.* Stanford, CA: Stanford University Press.

Schlenker, B. (1980). *Impression management: The self-concept, social identity and interpersonal relations.* Monterey, CA: Brooks/Cole.

Schwartz, S. H., & Gottlieb, A. (1976). Bystander reactions to a violent theft: Crime in Jerusalem. *Journal of Personality and Social Psychology, 34,* 1188–1199.

Schwartz, S. H., & Gottlieb, A. (1980). Bystander anonymity and reactions to emergencies. *Journal of Personality and Social Psychology, 39,* 418–430.

Shaver, K. G. (1970). Defensive attribution: Effects on severity and relevance on the responsibility assigned for an accident. *Journal of Personality and Social Psychology: 14,* 101–113.

Shaver, P., & Klinnert, M. (1982). Schachter's theories of affiliation and emotion: Implications of developmental research. In L. Wheeler (Ed.), *Review of personality and social psychology* (Vol. 3, pp. 37–72). Beverly Hills, CA: Sage.

Staub, E. (1974). Helping a distressed person: Social, personality, and stimulus determinants. In L. Berkowitz (Ed.), *Advances in experimental social psychology* (Vol. 7, pp. 294–342). New York: Academic Press.

Triandis, H. C. (1971). *Attitude and attitude change.* New York: Wiley.

Walster, E. (1966). Assignment of responsibility for an accident. *Journal of Personality and Social Psychology, 3,* 73–79.

NOTE

1. The analyses of attributions of helpfulness also revealed four significant tests involving the order in which the scenarios or dependent measures were presented. Main effects were obtained for Order of Scenarios, $F(3, 124) = 3.34$, p < .05, showing that the overall judgments of helpfulness were lowest when the scenario involving no bystanders was presented first ($M = 4.33$), moderate when the scenario involving four bystanders was presented first ($M = 4.41$), and highest when the scenario involving 10 bystanders was presented first ($M = 4.70$); and Order of Dependent Measure, $F(1, 124) = 4.27$, $p < .05$, showing that the ratings of helpfulness were higher when judgments of helpfulness were sought before ($M = 4.52$) rather than following ($M = 4.43$) judgments of respon-

sibility for harmdoing. The Helper × Order of Scenarios interaction was significant, $F(2, 124) = 3.12$, $p < .05$, indicating that the fundamental attribution error was strongest when the scenario involving no bystanders was presented first and weakest when the scenario involving 10 bystanders was presented first. And a Number of Bystanders × Order of Scenarios interaction, $F(4, 248) = 2.89$, $p < .05$, revealed that the number of bystanders had no significant effect on judgments of helpfulness when the scenario involving 10 bystanders was presented first, whereas judgments of helpfulness decreased as the number of bystanders increased when the scenario involving no bystanders was presented first.

CRITICAL THINKING QUESTIONS

1. This study employed paper-and-pencil measurements to hypothetical helping situations. How generalizable are the results of such a study to real-world situations? Do you think the underlying cognitive processes are the same, or is there some fundamental difference between them?

2. Design an experiment to test the results of this study using people in real situations rather than hypothetical situations. Can it be done? How?

3. The authors of the article suggest that this "confusion of responsibility" effect does not always occur; in fact, the presence of an audience may actually increase helping behavior under certain circumstances. Elaborate on the conditions that might increase helping when an audience is present.

Chapter Ten

AGGRESSION

PICK UP A COPY of today's newspaper. How much of it concerns acts of violence, whether it be war, a terrorist bombing, homicide, or domestic violence? Aggression seems to be a fairly common part of modern life.

Now think about your own experiences. Chances are, you have not directly experienced a murder or assault. But what other types of aggressive behavior have you witnessed? Have you seen verbal aggression, where the intention was to hurt another person's feelings? Have you experienced cruelty in one form or another, where pain was experienced, even though no blood was shed?

Must aggression be a part of life? Is it simply part of human nature and consequently something that can't be changed? Or is it possible that the amount of aggression in the world could be reduced, if not actually eliminated? Two of the articles in this chapter address that question. Article 29, "Transmission of Aggression through Imitation of Aggressive Models," by Bandura and his colleagues, represents one of the earliest studies demonstrating that aggression is learned and in particular that violence portrayed on television may contribute to aggressiveness in children. Since many behavioral patterns, such as aggression, may be learned in childhood, knowledge about what contributes to aggression can be used to help reduce those very behaviors. Article 30, "The Control of Human Aggression," examines the overall issue of the inevitability of aggression. Baron's review of the literature provides a very optimistic perspective that aggression can be controlled.

Finally, an article on one specific type of aggressive act, terrorism, has been included. Article 28, "Theater of Terror," examines the motives for terrorist acts, as well as some of the ways terrorism can be handled and consequently reduced in frequency and/or intensity.

ARTICLE 28 _____

Aggression can take many different forms, ranging from verbal abuse to killing. One distinction that can be made about the cause of aggression is whether it is premeditated, a distinction that also is made in the law. Although unpremeditated aggression can be as harmful as premeditated aggression, a particular horror is held for acts of violence that were deliberate.

In this violent world, one particular form of aggression has received increasing attention over the years and is viewed with reprehension by most people: terrorism. The word evokes images of innocent people being deliberately harmed by individuals or groups who hope to accomplish a social or political agenda.

What motivates terrorists? Why do they select the targets they do? Are terrorist acts really a form of senseless violence directed at a convenient target, or are they well-planned and deliberately executed maneuvers to further some desired end? The number of terrorist incidents reported by the press seems to have escalated greatly over the years. Is terrorism a relatively recent phenomenon, a unique product of the times we live in? Or like war, has terrorism in some form always existed? Rubin and Friedland address these questions, as well as the important consideration of how terrorism should be dealt with, in the following article, "Theater of Terror."

Theater of Terror

■ Jeffrey Z. Rubin and Nehemia Friedland

Down go the houselights, up goes the curtain and then—BANG. The stage becomes alive with the sounds, the lights and the characters of a highly dramatic performance. The actors are political terrorists. They are the protagonists of much modern tragedy, and their theater is the globe.

Terrorists may explode on the scene in Teheran, Beirut or Latin America, but they soon take the show on the road via television or transportation technology, as with last year's hijacking of a TWA jet in Athens and the abortive takeover of the Italian liner *Achille Lauro*. For today's terrorists, all the world is indeed a stage. And that may be an apt metaphor to help us come to grips with and perhaps devise methods of dealing with political terrorism.

Above all else, terrorists seek leverage, a way of exercising influence beyond their actual means or strength. They are like the Wizard of Oz, menacing and frightening from out front, but behind the scenes really rather inconsequential figures pulling at a set of levers. To be believed, to be heard or to have an impact, terrorists need to be experts in the art of amplification or exaggeration—the real wizardry of theater.

A political terrorist's first job is to get and hold the attention of the audience—not only to make a big splash on Broadway but also to have an impact out in the streets, guaranteeing an SRO audience in the future. We typically think of terrorists as having short-term goals, such as obtaining the release of prisoners or some governmental admission of guilt, but their most important objective is to attract an audience and deliver a message.

Once they capture the attention of the audience, terrorists must develop the dramatic theme,

Reprinted from *Psychology Today,* 1986 (March), *20*, 23–28. Reprinted with permission from *Psychology Today Magazine.* Copyright © 1986 (PT Partners, L.P.).

Achille Lauro: *A Flop on the High Seas*

On Monday, October 7, 1985, four Palestinian terrorists seized a 23-ton Italian luxury liner, the *Achille Lauro,* off the coast of Egypt. They indicated that they would blow up the ship if their demands were not met. They demanded the release of 50 political prisoners being held in Israel in exchange for the safe release of the more than 400 passengers and crew aboard the ship. Two days later the drama came to an end when the pirates surrendered to a representative of the Palestine Liberation Front (the notorious Abul Abbas) without gaining the release of the prisoners. One American had already been murdered, but the other hostages were released safely. From the terrorists' point of view, the hijacking must have been considered something of a flop.

The theater metaphor suggests several reasons for this failure. Consider the sets and props. A huge luxury liner is indeed an unusual and costly piece of machinery to capture, but it lacks the dramatic appeal of a jet airplane. Heavier than air, fated to return to earth in a matter of hours for fuel and supplies, an airplane (and fear of its crashing) is guaranteed to stir the imagination. A ship, in contrast, can continue to bounce about on the high seas for weeks at a time. A passenger plane hijacking demands immediate attention, but the *Achille Lauro* episode gave the various governments ample time to develop a reasoned response to the terrorist demands and to resist succumbing prematurely to terrorist pressure.

The absence of time pressure also made it relatively easy for third-party negotiators to get involved in the *Achille Lauro* affair. It seems clear that Italian Prime Minister Bettino Craxi, Egyptian President Hosni Mubarak and Palestine Liberation Organization chairman Yasir Arafat were each able to make suggestions that increased the chances of the hostages being released with minimum loss of life. For third parties to intervene effectively, they need a legitimate entree into the conflict and sufficient time to have their views considered. Both of these conditions were present more strongly in the ship hijacking than they are in most skyjacking events.

A final difference, and clearly the most important one, has to do with the audience. When the TWA jet was hijacked in Athens last year, millions of people around the world saw the actors in action. The terrorists and their parent organization had exactly what they wanted: access to and attention from an extraordinarily large audience. In contrast, communications between the terrorists on the *Achille Lauro* and the news media were extremely limited.

Because there was no television access to the ship, little of the terrorists' motivation or dramatic theme could be conveyed, nor could the suffering of the hostages themselves. Even the fact that the terrorists had drawn up an execution list to kill certain hostages did not reach world attention until the drama was over. The terrorists may have been full of sound and fury, but little of its significance, or lack thereof, was heard beyond the footlights.

or message, by giving their actions clear symbolic significance. Members of the Baader-Meinhof gang of Germany, for instance, insisted that they staged their violent acts as a protest against the injustices suffered by the poor and oppressed peoples of the world. An act of terrorism without underlying political justification is as devoid of sympathetic potential as a play without an organizing theme.

Once the plot is set in motion, a convincing dramatic performance must be given. This can be done without elaborate sets or unusual lighting and props, but such devices can be highly effective. A busload of schoolchildren is a far more dramatic target than a busload of military personnel. The hijacking of a planeload of vacationers can get the juices flowing much more vigorously than can a series of letter bombs or an occasional political assassination.

At the heart of the theater metaphor, of course, is the audience. The drama is certainly not put on for the benefit of the victims. Nor are most acts of political terrorism staged solely for the benefit of the particular government involved.

The desired audience is the general public of the target country and often the world public as well. And the best way to reach and hold the interest of such a large and diverse audience is with the assistance of the media. Indeed, Ariel Merari, an Israeli psychologist and expert on terrorism, argues that the media are the focus of much terrorist activity.

In terrorist situations, media personnel are a bit like drama critics who convey information to a group much larger than the immediate theater audience. Terrorists usually do all they can to make sure television, radio and newspaper people tell about the event in sufficient detail, emphasis and color to attract and to hold the audience's attention.

The media are important to terrorists because they not only relay information but, like good drama critics, interpret it as well. The slant they give — by deciding which events to report and which to ignore, by intentionally or unintentionally expressing approval or disapproval — can create a climate of public support, apathy or anger. During the TWA hijacking, for example, American television conferred tacit legitimacy on the skyjackers by interviewing them on nationwide broadcasts.

Capturing the audience's attention may be easy, but terrorist organizations need a flair for the dramatic to sustain that interest. This requires changing acts, locations, demands and performers. Perhaps most importantly, it requires some awareness of the psychology of satiation. Even the most interesting piece of music becomes tiring after too many repetitions. And even the most ingeniously staged terrorist action can, if re-peated too often, cause the audience to turn away in boredom. To be effective, terrorists cannot strike too often in the same place or the same way.

Changes in locations, demands and even actors may give the impression that some terrorist actions are improvised, but a closer look suggests that most of them are tightly scripted, with fairly predictable moves by both the terrorists and the government.

Terrorists typically begin with some dramatic action, such as the hijacking of an airliner, and then issue threats and a set of demands. The government usually responds by testing the credibility of whatever terrorist threats have been made and by stalling for time. At this point, the terrorists may attempt to prove they mean business, perhaps by killing a hostage and imposing time limits, if that has not already been done. The government continues to stall for time, if possible, even as it continues to explore the feasibility of using force.

The government also tries to take advantage of the so-called Stockholm syndrome — the tendency for captors and prisoners to identify with each other as time passes. This growing closeness makes it less likely that the terrorists will carry out threats to destroy the hostages if their demands are not met.

These events usually end with the government either using force or conceding to one or more of the demands of the terrorists. The concessions may be made in public or behind the scenes, giving the terrorists what they want without making the government lose more face than is absolutely necessary.

One reason terrorist incidents are so heavily scripted is that both sides like being able to predict, within reason, what will happen. It is when such predictability is not possible that disasters occur, such as the "liberating assault" on the EgyptAir jet, an action that resulted in at least 57 deaths.

A government's interest in predictability is obvious, but terrorists are equally interested in predictability. Just as a theater company wants to present an event that is stimulating without being so bizarre and repulsive that it causes the show to be shut down, political terrorists want to create a stir and attract attention without inviting massive retaliation by the government.

As any theater buff can tell you, knowing the inevitable outcome of a play in no way detracts from audience involvement or appeal; if anything, predictability heightens anticipation and involvement. From the target government's point of view, scripting increases predictability and thus takes some of the destructive punch out of the terrorist production. Therefore, it makes sense to increase scripting by encouraging both sides to tacitly agree to a routine set of moves—signals that let the other side know in advance what is meant.

This analysis suggests that promises of rewards for the capture of terrorists (of the sort issued by the Reagan administration last November in the wake of the *Achille Lauro* hijacking) are likely to be both ineffectual and undesirable: ineffectual because the terrorist theater is likely to continue despite the availability of bounty and undesirable because such promises undercut the possibility of subrosa agreements between the two sides. Such agreements provide each side with greater scripting of the sort that it wants—terrorist access to an audience and governmental protection from terrorist violence.

The terrorism-theater metaphor works on a variety of levels, from audiences to actors to scripts. But the true test of any metaphor lies in the ideas it generates. Increased scripting is one example. Another suggestion that follows from our metaphor is that terrorist drama has an underlying theme. Too often it is assumed that terrorists and their parent organizations mean what they say and nothing more than that. The challenge is to move beyond the performance—what terrorists say they want—to determine what they really want. Or, as Roger Fisher and William Ury of the Program on Negotiation at Harvard Law School put it in their discussion of methods of negotiation, to move from positions to interests.

This movement doesn't guarantee that a dispute will be settled, but it often helps. Whether the dispute involves a divorcing couple trying to come to an amicable settlement, two nations trying to settle an argument or labor and management negotiating a contract, it is useful to distinguish positions from interests and then move from the former to the latter.

How does one do this? By learning to listen between the lines and by proceeding from the assumption that what terrorists really want is an opportunity to be heard rather than blind adherence to a set of demands.

This works better than simply responding to the latest set of demands because even when positions are diametrically opposed, underlying interests often are not. A demand for the release of political prisoners in exchange for civilian hostages may be irreconcilable with a governmental policy against negotiating with terrorists. But the underlying interests of each side (such as terrorist desire to be recognized as the official representative of a beleaguered minority or government desire to reduce its vulnerability to extortion tactics) may not be inconsistent at all. Addressing these interests directly may increase the chances of reaching a settlement that brings the desired benefits to both sides.

If terrorists want attention, recognition and some sense of legitimacy, and if a government wants security from violent attack, then each wants something the other is uniquely positioned to offer. Terrorists can reduce their use of violence while the government gradually confers legitimacy. If the dramatic theme of a terrorist performance is "protest against injustice," then government negotiators might be able to acknowledge their sympathy and shared concern with the issue; injustice is a shared problem that invites shared attention. Moreover, one side's terrorist may be the other side's hero, visionary or martyr.

One danger in negotiating with terrorists is the loss of face, but this usually can be avoided by moving negotiations out of the limelight into some darkened corner of the theater where neither side is in danger of being made a fool of in the eyes of the audience. Patience and restraint on the part of the media can be enormously helpful in this regard, while too aggressive coverage can sabotage such face-saving arrangements.

Such behind-the-scenes maneuvering by French attorney Christian Bourguet and Argentine businessman Hector Villalon during the Iranian hostage crisis several years ago helped the United States and Iran to reach an agreement with reduced loss of face. Similarly, during the TWA hijacking incident in Athens, Syrian President Hafez Assad moved the negotiations off the television screens and front pages and provided a face-saving formula that called for Israel to release political prisoners—but only after the TWA passengers had been released.

Keeping negotiations offstage not only helps save face, it deprives the terrorists of their audience. Another way to do this would be to simply outlaw the reporting of terrorist incidents until they are concluded. If terrorists know in advance that a planned action will go unnoticed because of a government ban on news coverage, they should find the prospect of a terrorist takeover less appealing.

This approach presents several problems, however. Aside from violating freedom of the press, such restrictions might incite terrorists to even deadlier actions to coerce audience attention. If a letter bomb or a school bus hijacking won't get into the press, how about a massive program to poison a city's water supply?

While the government can't easily get the audience to disappear by eliminating media coverage, it may be possible to take advantage of the media's unique position in another way. Being external to the dispute, news organizations may be able to intervene, identify issues and move the opposing parties toward settlement.

News organizations are already involved in most terrorist situations, if for no other reason than the desire to gather as much information as possible. Moreover, as the object of considerable interest among terrorist organizations, the media are in a position to extract concessions from terrorists in exchange for access to the public. As controllers of audience attention, the news media may be able to serve as reasonably trustworthy go-betweens, representing the interests of both terrorists and government as well as themselves.

While it is unreasonable to ask members of the media to risk their lives, we think it is reasonable to explore the usefulness of any role they could assume. Given their enormous importance and responsibility as reporters and interpreters of facts, it makes sense to enlist their assistance in understanding the underlying interests of both sides.

Governments should also try to reduce the destructiveness of terrorism by making it clear that a less dramatic performance will suffice to get the desired audience attention. Cameo appearances, for example, might be invited or encouraged as a substitute for full-scale productions. Imagine that Yasir Arafat or George Habash were to be invited to meet the press on Israeli television to express their views on what they consider to be political reality in the Middle East. Such an arrangement would provide these actors with the element of legitimacy they seek and would air issues without resorting to anything more violent than the savagery of the Israeli news media.

Governments could further encourage nonviolence by pointing out that repeated violence risks both audience apathy and severe government retaliation. The best way of sustaining audience attention may be by staging modest, nonviolent productions every now and then—perhaps with the silent partnership of the government itself. The government's message might go something like this: "Let us know when you are in need of audience attention, and let us help set a stage that can give you access to an audience without resorting to bloodshed. We guarantee a full house of interested observers if you guarantee an act that takes the terror out of terrorism."

Terrorists and terrorism have been around for many years and are likely to be with us as long as there are groups who consider themselves disenfranchised and want attention. In thinking about ways of negotiating with terrorists, therefore, we must assume that terrorism is largely inevitable.

Both terrorist organizations and governments must work to understand better the interests they share. And both must work to place their relations in the context of an ongoing drama that is likely to be around even longer than *My Fair Lady* and *A Chorus Line* combined. If they do, both sides should be more effective at meeting their underlying needs: attention and audience exposure for terrorists; decreased destructiveness for governments.

CRITICAL THINKING QUESTIONS

1. The article offered several suggestions for how to deal with terrorists and potential terrorists, including negotiating with them. Can you think of any counterarguments to the suggestions given in the article? For example, would giving in to the demands of terrorists only make it more likely that such tactics would be used again in the future?

2. The article suggested that the media plays an important role in dealing with terrorism. Currently, the U.S. television networks have a code of ethics that they follow. If you were asked to develop a set of guidelines for the media to follow in dealing with terrorism, what would they be?

3. Are all acts of terrorism as well thought out as the article seemed to suggest? Or are there different types of terrorism and terrorist groups? If so, what factors should determine how each should be dealt with?

ARTICLE 29 _____

Think of the amount of time that a typical child spends in front of the television. Do you think that what that child sees on "the tube" influences his or her behavior to a great extent? Or is television more neutral, just entertainment with no lasting effects?

A major concern of parents and social psychologists alike is the impact of one particular aspect of television on children's subsequent behavior: aggression. If you haven't done so in a long time, sit down and watch the Saturday morning cartoons or other programs shown after school or in the early evening, when children are most likely to be watching. How many of these programs involve some sort of violence? What are these shows teaching children, not only in terms of behaviors but also in terms of values?

The following article by Bandura, Ross, and Ross was one of the earliest studies to examine the impact of televised aggression on the behavior of children. In the nearly 30 years since its publication, numerous other experiments have been conducted on the same topic. In general, all of these studies strongly suggest that televised aggression does have a direct impact on the aggressive behavior of its viewers. The research by Bandura and colleagues helped initiate this important line of research.

Transmission of Aggression through Imitation of Aggressive Models[1]

■ Albert Bandura, Dorothea Ross, and Sheila A. Ross[2]

A previous study, designed to account for the phenomenon of identification in terms of incidental learning, demonstrated that children readily imitated behavior exhibited by an adult model in the presence of the model (Bandura & Huston, 1961). A series of experiments by Blake (1958) and others (Grosser, Polansky, & Lippitt, 1951; Rosenblith, 1959; Schachter & Hall, 1952) have likewise shown that mere observation of responses of a model has a facilitating effect on subjects' reactions in the immediate social influence setting.

While these studies provide convincing evidence for the influence and control exerted on others by the behavior of a model, a more crucial test of imitative learning involves the generalization of imitative response patterns to new settings in which the model is absent.

In the experiment reported in this paper children were exposed to aggressive and nonaggressive adult models and were then tested for amount of imitative learning in a new situation in the absence of the model. According to the prediction, subjects exposed to aggressive models would reproduce aggressive acts resembling those of their models and would differ in this respect both from subjects who observed nonaggressive models and from who had no prior exposure to any models. This hypothesis assumed that subjects had learned imitative habits as a result of prior reinforcement, and these tendencies would generalize to some extent to adult experimenters (Miller & Dollard, 1941).

It was further predicted that observation of subdued nonaggressive models would have a gen-

Reprinted from the *Journal of Abnormal and Social Psychology*, 1961, 63, 575–583.
    Some of the language used and views presented are indicative of the time in which the article was written. The reader should consider the article in that context.

eralized inhibiting effect on the subjects' subsequent behavior, and this effect would be reflected in a difference between the nonaggressive and the control groups, with subjects in the latter group displaying significantly more aggression.

Hypotheses were also advanced concerning the influence of the sex of model and sex of subjects on imitation. Fauls and Smith (1956) have shown that preschool children perceive their parents as having distinct preferences regarding sex appropriate modes of behavior for their children. Their findings, as well as informal observation, suggest that parents reward imitation of sex appropriate behavior and discourage or punish sex inappropriate imitative responses, e.g., a male child is unlikely to receive much reward for performing female appropriate activities, such as cooking, or for adopting other aspects of the maternal role, but these same behaviors are typically welcomed if performed by females. As a result of differing reinforcement histories, tendencies to imitate male and female models thus acquire differential habit strength. One would expect, on this basis, subjects to imitate the behavior of a same-sex model to a greater degree than a model of the opposite sex.

Since aggression, however, is a highly masculine-typed behavior, boys should be more predisposed than girls toward imitating aggression, the difference being most marked for subjects exposed to the male aggressive model.

METHOD

Subjects

The subjects were 36 boys and 36 girls enrolled in the Stanford University Nursery School. They ranged in age from 37 to 69 months, with a mean age of 52 months.

Two adults, a male and a female, served in the role of model, and one female experimenter conducted the study for all 72 children.

Experimental Design

Subjects were divided into eight experimental groups of six subjects each and a control group consisting of 24 subjects. Half the experimental subjects were exposed to aggressive models and half were exposed to models that were subdued and nonaggressive in their behavior. These groups were further subdivided into male and female subjects. Half the subjects in the aggressive and nonaggressive conditions observed same-sex models, while the remaining subjects in each group viewed models of the opposite sex. The control group had no prior exposure to the adult models and was tested only in the generalization situation.

It seemed reasonable to expect that the subjects' level of aggressiveness would be positively related to the readiness with which they imitated aggressive modes of behavior. Therefore, in order to increase the precision of treatment comparisons, subjects in the experimental and control groups were matched individually on the basis of ratings of their aggressive behavior in social interactions in the nursery school.

The subjects were rated on four five-point rating scales by the experimenter and a nursery school teacher, both of whom were well acquainted with the children. These scales measured the extent to which subjects displayed physical aggression, verbal aggression, aggression toward inanimate objects, and aggressive inhibition. The latter scale, which dealt with the subjects' tendency to inhibit aggressive reactions in the face of high instigation, provided a measure of aggression anxiety.

Fifty-one subjects were rated independently by both judges so as to permit an assessment of interrater agreement. The reliability of the composite aggression score, estimated by means of the Pearson product-moment correlation, was .89.

The composite score was obtained by summing the ratings on the four aggression scales; on the basis of these scores, subjects were arranged in triplets and assigned at random to one of two treatment conditions or to the control group.

Experimental Conditions

In the first step in the procedure subjects were brought individually by the experimenter to the experimental room and the model who was in the hallway outside the room, was invited by the experimenter to come and join in the game. The experimenter then escorted the subject to one corner of the room, which was structured as the subject's play area. After seating the child at a small table, the experimenter demonstrated how the subject could design pictures with potato prints and picture stickers provided. The potato prints included a variety of geometrical forms; the stickers were attractive multicolor pictures of animals, flowers, and western figures to be pasted on a pastoral scene. These activities were selected since they had been established, by previous studies in the nursery school, as having high interest value for the children.

After having settled the subject in his corner, the experimenter escorted the model to the opposite corner of the room which contained a small table and chair, a tinker toy set, a mallet, and a 5-foot inflated Bobo doll. The experimenter explained that these were the materials provided for the model to play with and, after the model was seated, the experimenter left the experimental room.

With subjects in the *nonaggressive condition,* the model assembled the tinker toys in a quiet subdued manner totally ignoring the Bobo doll.

In contrast, with subjects in the *aggressive condition,* the model began by assembling the tinker toys but after approximately a minute had elapsed, the model turned to the Bobo doll and spent the remainder of the period aggressing toward it.

Imitative learning can be clearly demonstrated if a model performs sufficiently novel patterns of responses which are unlikely to occur independently of the observation of the behavior of a model and if a subject reproduces these behaviors in substantially identical form. For this reason, in addition to punching the Bobo doll, a response that is likely to be performed by children independently of a demonstration, the model exhibited distinctive aggressive acts which were to be scored as imitative responses. The model laid Bobo on its side, sat on it and punched it repeatedly in the nose. The model then raised the Bobo doll, picked up the mallet and struck the doll on the head. Following the mallet aggression, the model tossed the doll up in the air aggressively and kicked it about the room. This sequence of physically aggressive acts was repeated approximately three times, interspersed with verbally aggressive responses such as "Sock him in the nose . . . ," "Hit him down . . . ," "Throw him in the air . . . ," "Kick him . . . ," "Pow . . . ," and two nonaggressive comments, "He keeps coming back for more" and "He sure is a tough fella."

Thus in the exposure situation, subjects were provided with a diverting task which occupied their attention while at the same time insured observation of the model's behavior in the absence of any instructions to observe or to learn the responses in question. Since subjects could not perform the model's aggressive behavior, any learning that occurred was purely on an observational or covert basis.

At the end of 10 minutes, the experimenter entered the room, informed the subject that he would now go to another game room, and bid the model goodbye.

Aggression Arousal

Subjects were tested for the amount of imitative learning in a different experimental room that was set off from the main nursery school building. The two experimental situations were thus clearly differentiated; in fact, many subjects were under the impression that they were no longer on the nursery school grounds.

Prior to the test for imitation, however, all subjects, experimental and control, were subjected to mild aggression arousal to insure that they were under some degree of instigation to aggression. The arousal experience was included for two main reasons. In the first place, observation of aggressive behavior exhibited by others tends to reduce the probability of aggression on the part of the observer (Rosenbaum & deCharms, 1960). Consequently, subjects in the aggressive condition, in relation both to the nonaggressive and control groups, would be under weaker instigation following exposure to the models. Second, if subjects in the nonaggressive condition expressed little aggression in the face of appropriate instigation, the presence of an inhibitory process would seem to be indicated.

Following the exposure experience, therefore, the experimenter brought the subject to an anteroom that contained these relatively attractive toys: a fire engine, a locomotive, a jet fighter plane, a cable car, a colorful spinning top, and a doll set complete with wardrobe, doll carriage, and baby crib. The experimenter explained that the toys were for the subject to play with but, as soon as the subject became sufficiently involved with the play material (usually in about 2 minutes), the experimenter remarked that these were her very best toys, that she did not let just anyone play with them, and that she had decided to reserve these toys for the other children. However, the subject could play with any of the toys that were in the next room. The experimenter and the subject then entered the adjoining experimental room.

It was necessary for the experimenter to remain in the room during the experimental session; otherwise a number of the children would either refuse to remain alone or would leave before the termination of the session. However, in order to minimize any influence her presence might have on the subject's behavior, the experimenter remained as inconspicuous as possible by busying herself with paper work at a desk in the far corner of the room and avoiding any interaction with the child.

Test for Delayed Imitation

The experimental room contained a variety of toys including some that could be used in imitative or nonimitative aggression, and others that tended to elicit predominantly nonaggressive forms of behavior. The aggressive toys included a 3-foot Bobo doll, a mallet and peg board, two dart guns, and a tether ball with a face painted on it which hung from the ceiling. The nonaggressive toys, on the other hand, included a tea set, crayons and coloring paper, a ball, two dolls, three bears, cars and trucks, and plastic farm animals.

In order to eliminate any variation in behavior due to mere placement of the toys in the room, the play material was arranged in a fixed order for each of the sessions.

The subject spent 20 minutes in this experimental room during which time his behavior was rated in terms of predetermined response categories by judges who observed the session through a one-way mirror in an adjoining observation room. The 20-minute session was divided into 5-second intervals by means of an electric interval timer, thus yielding a total number of 240 response units for each subject.

The male model scored the experimental sessions for all 72 children. Except for the cases in which he served as model, he did not have knowledge of the subjects' group assignments. In order to provide an estimate of interscorer agreement, the performances of half the subjects were also scored independently by a second observer. Thus one or the other of the two observers usually had no knowledge of the conditions to which the subjects were assigned. Since, however, all but two of the subjects in the aggressive condition performed the models' novel aggressive responses while subjects in the other conditions only rarely exhibited such reactions, subjects who were exposed to the aggressive models could be readily identified through their distinctive behavior.

The responses scored involved highly specific concrete classes of behavior and yielded high interscorer reliabilities, the product-moment coefficients being in the .90s.

Response Measures

Three measures of imitation were obtained:

Imitation of physical aggression: This category included acts of striking the Bobo doll with the mallet, sitting on the doll and punching it in the nose, kicking the doll, and tossing it in the air.

Imitative verbal aggression: Subject repeats the phrases, "Sock him," "Hit him down," "Kick him," "Throw him in the air," or "Pow."

Imitative nonaggressive verbal responses: Subject repeats, "He keeps coming back for more," or "He sure is a tough fella."

During the pretest, a number of the subjects imitated the essential components of the model's behavior but did not perform the complete act, or they directed the imitative aggressive response to some object other than the Bobo doll. Two responses of this type were therefore scored and were interpreted as partially imitative behavior.

Mallet aggression: Subject strikes objects other than the Bobo doll aggressively with the mallet.

Sits on the Bobo doll: Subject lays the Bobo doll on its side and sits on it, but does not aggress toward it.

The following additional nonimitative aggressive responses were scored:

Punches Bobo doll: Subject strikes, slaps, or pushes the doll aggressively.

Nonimitative physical and verbal aggression: This category included physically aggressive acts directed toward objects other than the Bobo doll and any hostile remarks except for those in the verbal imitation category; e.g., "Shoot the Bobo," "Cut him," "Stupid ball," "Knock over people," "Horses fighting, biting."

Aggressive gun play: Subject shoots darts or aims the guns and fires imaginary shots at objects in the room.

Ratings were also made of the number of behavior units in which subjects played nonaggressively or sat quietly and did not play with any of the material at all.

RESULTS

Complete Imitation of Models' Behavior

Subjects in the aggression condition reproduced a good deal of physical and verbal aggressive behavior resembling that of the models, and their mean scores differed markedly from those of subjects in the nonaggressive and control groups who exhibited virtually no imitative aggression (see Table 1).

TABLE 1 / Mean Aggression Scores for Experimental and Control Subjects

| Response category | Experimental Groups | | | | Control groups |
| | Aggressive | | Nonaggressive | | |
	F Model	M Model	F Model	M Model	
Imitative physical aggression					
Female subjects	5.5	7.2	2.5	0.0	1.2
Male subjects	12.4	25.8	0.2	1.5	2.0
Imitative verbal aggression					
Female subjects	13.7	2.0	0.3	0.0	0.7
Male subjects	4.3	12.7	1.1	0.0	1.7
Mallet aggression					
Female subjects	17.2	18.7	0.5	0.5	13.1
Male subjects	15.5	28.8	18.7	6.7	13.5
Punches Bobo doll					
Female subjects	6.3	16.5	5.8	4.3	11.7
Male subjects	18.9	11.9	15.6	14.8	15.7
Nonimitative aggression					
Female subjects	21.3	8.4	7.2	1.4	6.1
Male subjects	16.2	36.7	26.1	22.3	24.6
Aggressive gun play					
Female subjects	1.8	4.5	2.6	2.5	3.7
Male subjects	7.3	15.9	8.9	16.7	14.3

Since there were only a few scores for subjects in the nonaggressive and control conditions (approximately 70% of the subjects had zero scores), and the assumption of homogeneity of variance could not be made, the Friedman two-way analysis of variance by ranks was employed to test the significance of the obtained differences.

The prediction that exposure of subjects to aggressive models increases the probability of aggressive behavior is clearly confirmed (see Table 2). The main effect of treatment conditions is highly significant both for physical and verbal imitative aggression. Comparison of pairs of scores by the sign test shows that the obtained over-all differences were due almost entirely to the aggression displayed by subjects who had been exposed to the aggressive models. Their scores were significantly higher than those of either the nonaggressive or control groups, which did not differ from each other (Table 2).

Imitation was not confined to the model's aggressive responses. Approximately one-third of the subjects in the aggressive condition also repeated the model's nonaggressive verbal responses while none of the subjects in either the nonaggressive or control groups made such remarks. This difference, tested by means of the Cochran Q

test was significant well beyond the .001 level (Table 2).

Partial Imitation of Models' Behavior

Differences in the predicted direction were also obtained on the two measures of partial imitation.

Analysis of variance of scores based on the subjects' use of the mallet aggressively toward objects other than the Bobo doll reveals that treatment conditions are a statistically significant course of variation (Table 2). In addition, individual sign tests show that both the aggressive and the control groups, relative to subjects in the nonaggressive condition, produced significantly more mallet aggression, the difference being particularly marked with regard to female subjects. Girls who observed nonaggressive models performed a mean number of 0.5 mallet aggression responses as compared to mean values of 18.0 and 13.1 for girls in the aggressive and control groups, respectively.

Although subjects who observed aggressive models performed more mallet aggression ($M = 20.0$) than their controls ($M = 13.3$), the difference was not statistically significant.

TABLE 2 / Significance of the Differences between Experimental and Control Groups in the Expression of Aggression

| Response category | x^2_r | Q | p | Comparison of pairs of treatment conditions | | |
				Aggressive vs. Nonaggressive p	Aggressive vs. Control p	Nonaggressive vs. Control p
Imitative responses						
Physical aggression	27.17		<.001	<.001	<.001	.09
Verbal aggression	9.17		<.02	.004	.048	.09
Nonaggressive verbal						
responses		17.50	<.001	.004	.004	ns
Partial imitation						
Mallet aggression	11.06		<.01	.026	ns	.005
Sits on Bobo		13.44	<.01	.018	.059	ns
Nonimitative aggression						
Punches Bobo doll	2.87		ns			
Physical and verbal	8.96		<.02	.026	ns	ns
Aggressive gun play	2.75		ns			

With respect to the partially imitative response of sitting on the Bobo doll, the over-all group differences were significant beyond the .01 level (Table 2). Comparison of pairs of scores by the sign test procedure reveals that subjects in the aggressive group reproduced this aspect of the models' behavior to a greater extent than did the nonaggressive (p = .018) or the control (p = .059) subjects. The latter two groups, on the other hand, did not differ from each other.

Nonimitative Aggression

Analyses of variance of the remaining aggression measures (Table 2) show that treatment conditions did not influence the extent to which subjects engaged in aggressive gun play or punched the Bobo doll. The effect of conditions is highly significant (χ^2_r = 8.96, p < .02), however, in the case of the subjects' expression of nominative physical and verbal aggression. Further comparison of treatment pairs reveals that the main source of the over-all difference was the aggressive and nonaggressive groups which differed significantly from each other (Table 2), with subjects exposed to the aggressive models displaying the greater amount of aggression.

Influence of Sex of Model
and Sex of Subjects on Imitation

The hypothesis that boys are more prone than girls to imitate aggression exhibited by a model was only partially confirmed. t tests computed for subjects in the aggressive condition reveal that boys reproduced more imitative physical aggression than girls (t = 2.50, p < .01). The groups do not differ, however, in their imitation of verbal aggression.

The use of nonparametric tests, necessitated by the extremely skewed distributions of scores for subjects in the nonaggressive and control conditions, preclude an over-all test of the influence of sex of model per se, and of the various interactions between the main effects. Inspection of the means presented in Table 1 for subjects in the aggression condition, however, clearly suggests the possibility of a Sex × Model interaction. This interaction effect is much more consistent and pronounced for the male model than for the female model. Male subjects, for example, exhibited more physical (t = 2.07, p < .05) and verbal imitative aggression (t = 2.51, p < .05), more nonimitative aggression (t = 3.15, p < .025), and engaged in significantly more aggressive gun play (t = 2.12, p < .05) following exposure to the aggressive male model than the female subjects. In contrast, girls exposed to the female model performed considerably more imitative verbal aggression and more nonimitative aggression than did the boys (Table 1). The variances, however, were equally large and with only a small N in each cell the mean differences did not reach statistical significance.

Data for the nonaggressive and control subjects provide additional suggestive evidence that the behavior of the male model exerted a greater influence than the female model on the subjects' behavior in the generalization situation.

It will be recalled that, except for the greater amount of mallet aggression exhibited by the control subjects, no significant differences were obtained between the nonaggressive and control groups. The data indicate, however, that the absence of significant differences between these two groups was due primarily to the fact that subjects exposed to the nonaggressive female model did not differ from the controls on any of the measures of aggression. With respect to the male model, on the other hand, the differences between the groups are striking. Comparison of the sets of scores by means of the sign test reveals that, in relation to the control group, subjects exposed to the nonaggressive male model performed significantly less imitative physical aggression (p = .06), less imitative verbal aggression (p = .002), less mallet aggression (p = .003), less nonimitative physical and verbal aggression (p = .03) and they were less inclined to punch the Bobo doll (p = .07).

While the comparison of subgroups, when some of the over-all tests do not reach statistical significance, is likely to capitalize on chance differences, nevertheless the consistency of the findings adds support to the interpretation in terms of influence by the model.

Nonaggressive Behavior

With the exception of expected sex differences, Lindquist (1956) Type III analyses of variance of the nonaggressive response scores yielded few significant differences.

Female subjects spent more time than boys playing with dolls ($p < .001$), with the tea set ($p < .001$), and coloring ($p < .05$). The boys, on the other hand, devoted significantly more time than the girls to exploratory play with the guns ($p < .01$). No sex differences were found in respect to the subjects use of the other stimulus objects, i.e., farm animals, cars, or tether ball.

Treatment conditions did produce significant differences on two measures of nonaggressive behavior that are worth mentioning. Subjects in the nonaggressive condition engaged in significantly more nonaggressive play with dolls than either subjects in the aggressive group ($t = 2.67$, $p < .02$), or in the control group ($t = 2.57$, $p < .02$).

Even more noteworthy is the finding that subjects who observed nonaggressive models spent more than twice as much time as subjects in aggressive condition ($t = 3.07$, $p < .01$) in simply sitting quietly without handling any of the play material.

DISCUSSION

Much current research on social learning is focused on the shaping of new behavior through rewarding and punishing consequences. Unless responses are emitted, however, they cannot be influenced. The results of this study provide strong evidence that observation of cues produced by the behavior of others is one effective means of eliciting certain forms of responses for which the original probability is very low or zero. Indeed, social imitation may hasten or short-cut the acquisition of new behaviors without the necessity of reinforcing successive approximations as suggested by Skinner (1953).

Thus subjects given an opportunity to observe aggressive models later reproduced a good deal of physical and verbal aggression (as well as nonaggressive responses) substantially identical with that of the model. In contrast, subjects who were exposed to nonaggressive models and those who had no previous exposure to any models only rarely performed such responses.

To the extent that observation of adult models displaying aggression communicates permissiveness for aggressive behavior, such exposure may serve to weaken inhibitory responses and thereby to increase the probability of aggressive reactions to subsequent frustrations. The fact, however, that subjects expressed their aggression in ways that clearly resembled the novel patterns exhibited by the models provides striking evidence for the occurrence of learning by imitation.

In the procedure employed by Miller and Dollard (1941) for establishing imitative behavior, adult or peer models performed discrimination responses following which they were consistently rewarded, and the subjects were similarly reinforced whenever they matched the leaders' choice responses. While these experiments have been widely accepted as demonstrations of learning by means of imitation, in fact, they simply involve a special case of discrimination learning in which the behavior of others serves as discriminative stimuli for responses that are already part of the subject's repertoire. Auditory or visual environmental cues could easily have been substituted for the social stimuli to facilitate the discrimination learning. In contrast, the process of imitation studied in the present experiment differed in several important respects from the one investigated by Miller and Dollard in that subjects learned to combine fractional responses into relatively complex novel patterns solely by observing the performance of social models without any opportunity to perform the models' behavior in the exposure setting, and without any reinforcers delivered either to the models or to the observers.

An adequate theory of the mechanisms underlying imitative learning is lacking. The explanations that have been offered (Logan, Olmsted, Rosner, Schwartz, & Stevens, 1955; Maccoby, 1959) assume that the imitator performs the model's responses covertly. If it can be assumed additionally that rewards and punishments are self-administered in conjunction with the covert responses, the process of imitative learning could be accounted for in terms of the same principles that govern instrumental trial-and-error learning. In the early stages of the developmental process, however, the range of component responses in the organism's repertoire is probably increased through a process of classical conditioning (Bandura & Huston, 1961; Mowrer, 1950).

The data provide some evidence that the male model influenced the subjects' behavior outside the exposure setting to a greater extent than was true for the female model. In the analyses of the Sex × Model interactions, for example, only the comparisons involving the male model yielded significant differences. Similarly, subjects exposed to the nonaggressive male model performed less aggressive behavior than the controls, whereas comparisons involving the female model were consistently nonsignificant.

In a study of learning by imitation, Rosenblith (1959) has likewise found male experimenters more effective than females in influencing children's behavior. Rosenblith advanced the tentative explanation that the school setting may involve some social deprivation in respect to adult males which, in turn, enhances the male's reward value.

The trends in the data yielded by the present study suggest an alternative explanation. In the case of a highly masculine-typed behavior such as physical aggression, there is a tendency for both male and female subjects to imitate the male model to a greater degree than the female model. On the other hand, in the case of verbal aggression, which is less clearly sex linked, the greatest amount of imitation occurs in relation to the same-sex model. These trends together with the finding that boys in relation to girls are in general more imitative of physical aggression but do not differ in imitation of verbal aggression, suggest that subjects may be differentially affected by the sex of the model but that predictions must take into account the degree to which the behavior in question is sex-typed.

The preceding discussion has assumed that maleness-femaleness rather than some other personal characteristics of the particular models involved, is the significant variable—an assumption that cannot be tested directly with the data at hand. It was clearly evident, however, particularly from boys' spontaneous remarks about the display of aggression by the female model, that some subjects at least were responding in terms of a sex discrimination and their prior learning about what is sex appropriate behavior (e.g., "Who is that lady. That's not the way for a lady to behave. Ladies are supposed to act like ladies. . . ." "You should have seen what that girl did in there. She was just acting like a man. I never saw a girl act like that before. She was punching and fighting but no swearing."). Aggression by the male model, on the other hand, was more likely to be seen as appropriate and approved by both the boys ("Al's a good socker, he beat up Bobo. I want to sock like Al.") and the girls ("That man is a strong fighter, he punched and punched and he could hit Bobo right down to the floor and if Bobo got up he said, 'Punch your nose.' He's a good fighter like Daddy.").

The finding that subjects exposed to the quiet models were more inhibited and unresponsive than subjects in the aggressive condition, together with the obtained difference on the aggression measures, suggests that exposure to inhibited models not only decreases the probability of occurrence of aggressive behavior but also generally restricts the range of behavior emitted by the subjects.

"Identification with aggressor" (Freud, 1946) or "defensive identification" (Mowrer, 1950), whereby a person presumably transforms himself from object to agent of aggression by adopting the attributes of an aggressive threatening model so as to allay anxiety, is widely accepted as an explanation of the imitative learning of aggression.

The development of aggressive modes of response by children of aggressively punitive adults, however, may simply reflect object displacement without involving any such mechanism of defensive identification. In studies of child training antecedents of aggressively antisocial adolescents

(Bandura & Walters, 1959) and of young hyperaggressive boys (Bandura, 1960), the parents were found to be nonpermissive and punitive of aggression directed toward themselves. On the other hand, they actively encouraged and reinforced their sons' aggression toward persons outside the home. This pattern of differential reinforcement of aggressive behavior served to inhibit the boys' aggression toward the original instigators and fostered the displacement of aggression toward objects and situations eliciting much weaker inhibitory responses.

Moreover, the findings from an earlier study (Bandura & Huston, 1961), in which children imitated to an equal degree aggression exhibited by a nurturant and a nonnurturant model, together with the results of the present experiment in which subjects readily imitated aggressive models who were more or less neutral figures suggest that mere observation of aggression, regardless of the quality of the model-subject relationship, is a sufficient condition for producing imitative aggression in children. A comparative study of the subjects' imitation of aggressive models who are feared, who are liked and esteemed, or who are essentially neutral figures would throw some light on whether or not a more parsimonious theory than the one involved in "identification with the aggressor" can explain the modeling process.

SUMMARY

Twenty-four preschool children were assigned to each of three conditions. One experimental group observed aggressive adult models; a second observed inhibited nonaggressive models; while subjects in a control group had no prior exposure to the models. Half the subjects in the experimental conditions observed same-sex models and half viewed models of the opposite sex. Subjects were then tested for the amount of imitative as well as nonimitative aggression performed in a new situation in the absence of the models.

Comparison of the subjects' behavior in the generalization situation revealed that subjects exposed to aggressive models reproduced a good deal of aggression resembling that of the models, and that their mean scores differed markedly from those of subjects in the nonaggressive and control groups. Subjects in the aggressive condition also exhibited significantly more partially imitative and nonimitative aggressive behavior and were generally less inhibited in their behavior than subjects in the nonaggressive condition.

Imitation was found to be differentially influenced by the sex of the model with boys showing more aggression than girls following exposure to the male model, the difference being particularly marked on highly masculine-typed behavior.

Subjects who observed the nonaggressive models, especially the subdued male model, were generally less aggressive than their controls.

The implications of the findings based on this experiment and related studies for the psychoanalytic theory of identification with the aggressor were discussed.

REFERENCES

Bandura, A. Relationship of family patterns to child behavior disorders. Progress Report, 1960, Stanford University, Project No. M-1734, United States Public Health Service.

Bandura, A., & Huston, Aletha C. Identification as a process of incidental learning. *J. abnorm. soc. Psychol.*, 1961, *63*, 311–318.

Bandura, A., & Walters, R. H. *Adolescent aggression.* New York: Ronald, 1959.

Blake, R. R. The other person in the situation. In R. Tagiuri & L. Petrullo (Eds.), *Person perception and interpersonal behavior.* Stanford, Calif: Stanford Univer. Press, 1958. Pp. 229–242.

Fauls, Lydia B., & Smith, W. D. Sex-role learning of five-year olds. *J. genet. Psychol.*, 1956, *89*, 105–117.

Freud, Anna. *The ego and the mechanisms of defense.* New York: International Univer. Press, 1946.

Grosser, D., Polansky, N., & Lippitt, R. A laboratory study of behavior contagion. *Hum. Relat.*, 1951, *4*, 115–142.

Lindquist, E. F. *Design and analysis of experiments.* Boston: Houghton Mifflin, 1956.

Logan, F., Olmsted, O. L., Rosner, B. S., Schwartz, R. D., & Stevens, C. M. *Behavior theory and social science.* New Haven: Yale Univer. Press, 1955.

Maccoby, Eleanor E. Role-taking in childhood and its consequences for social learning. *Child Develpm.,* 1959, *30,* 239–252.

Miller, N. E., & Dollard, J. *Social learning and imitation.* New Haven: Yale Univer. Press, 1941.

Mowrer, O. H. (Ed.) Identification: A link between learning theory and psychotherapy. In, *Learning theory and personality dynamics.* New York: Ronald, 1950. Pp. 69–94.

Rosenbaum, M. E., & deCharms, R. Direct and vicarious reduction of hostility. *J. abnorm. soc. Psychol.,* 1960, *60,* 105–111.

Rosenblith, Judy F. Learning by imitation in kindergarten children. *Child Develpm.,* 1959, *30,* 69–80.

Schachter, S., & Hall, R. Group-derived restraints and audience persuasion. *Hum. Relat.,* 1952, *5,* 397–406.

Skinner, B. F. *Science and human behavior.* New York: Macmillan, 1953.

NOTES

1. This investigation was supported by Research Grant M-4398 from the National Institute of Health, United States Public Health Service.

2. The authors wish to express their appreciation to Edith Dowley, Director, and Patricia Rowe, Head Teacher, Stanford University Nursery School for their assistance throughout this study.

CRITICAL THINKING QUESTIONS

1. Notice that the children's anger was aroused prior to their being placed in the situation where their aggression would be measured. Why was this done? What might have resulted had their anger not been aroused beforehand? Were there different effects, depending on whether the children experienced prior anger arousal? If so, then what are the implications for generalizing the results of this study to how violent television affects its young viewers?

2. This study reported that the sex of the actor made a difference in how much physical aggression was imitated. It also mentioned that some of the children simply found it inappropriate for a female actor to act aggressively. Nearly 30 years have passed since publication of this study. Do you think children today would still see physical aggression by a female as inappropriate?

3. Analyze the content of television shows directed toward children (including cartoons) for aggression, examining type of aggression (physical versus verbal) and sex of the aggressive character. Relate the findings to question 2, above.

4. Examine research conducted over the last three decades that documents the impact of televised aggression on children's behavior. Given these findings, what should be done? Should laws be passed to regulate the amount of violence shown on television? Or should this form of censorship be avoided? What other alternatives might exist to reverse or prevent the potential harm of observing violence on television?

ADDITIONAL RELATED READINGS

Berkowitz, L. (1984). Some thoughts on anti- and pro-social influences of media events: A cognitive-neoassociation analysis. *Psychological Bulletin, 95,* 410–427.

Eron, L. (1987). The development of aggressive behavior from the perspective of a developing behaviorism. *American Psychologist, 42,* 435–442.

Lievert, R., & Sprafkin, R. (1988). *The early window: Effects of television on children and youth.* (3rd ed.). New York: Pergamon.

ARTICLE 30

An important area of research on aggression concerns its causes. There are three general classes of theories explaining aggression. The first class, which can be called *instinct theories,* explains aggression as somehow rooted in biology. Thus aggression stems from internally generated forces and is something that human beings are genetically programmed to do. A second type of theory, called *drive reduction,* essentially explains aggression as arising from forces outside of the individual; for instance, experiencing frustration may produce readiness to engage in aggressive behavior. *Social learning* is the third theoretical explanation of aggression. Basically, this approach maintains that aggression, like many other behaviors, is learned. It is not instinctive, nor is it simply a reaction to a specific external event. Rather, like other complex social behaviors, aggression is learned.

Each of these theoretical views attributes aggression to a different cause. It follows, then, that whichever theoretical explanation you adopt will influence how optimistic you are about the possible control of aggression. For example, if you believe that aggression is innate, a biological predisposition of sorts, then there isn't much that can be done about it. It is simply human nature to be aggressive. However, if you believe that aggression is learned, then it is not inevitable that people be aggressive. After all, if aggressive behaviors can be learned, then nonaggressive behaviors can be learned, as well.

The following article by Baron comments upon numerous studies concerning the factors influencing aggression. As the title suggests, Baron is very optimistic that aggression is a behavior that can be controlled. This article was selected not only because of the summary of research on aggression control that it contains but also because of its definitely upbeat perspective. All too often, people (including social psychologists) assume that little can be done to control aggression—it's simply a fact of life. Baron's analysis suggests otherwise.

The Control of Human Aggression
An Optimistic Perspective
■ Robert A. Baron

Several techniques for the control of human aggression are reviewed. These include punishment, catharsis, exposure to nonaggressive models, cognitive interventions, the induction of responses incompatible with anger or overt aggression, and training in basic social skills. These procedures are found to vary in their overall effectiveness, and also in terms of the conditions under which they are applicable. However, taken as a whole, existing empirical evidence suggests that when used with appropriate skill, several of the techniques reviewed may indeed prove useful in deterring overt violence under many conditions. Reasons for the persistent pessimism among behavioral scientists with respect to the possibility of controlling human aggression are considered. In general,

Reprinted with permission from *Journal of Social and Clinical Psychology,* 1983, *1,* 97–119. Copyright 1983 by Guilford Publications, Inc.

these are rejected as resting on doubtful beliefs and questionable assumptions.

Mass murder in Lebanon; chemical warfare in Afghanistan; assassinations and attempted assassinations of world leaders (including even the Pope); senseless attacks on the elderly; random violence in urban centers; child abuse; terrorism; rape—the list of human atrocities goes on and on. Faced with daily reports of such events on the evening news, it is tempting to conclude that we live at a time when human violence has risen to new and unprecedented heights. Yet even a casual inspection of the events of the past calls this conclusion into question. In the 5600 years of recorded human history, there have been some 14,600 wars—a rate of more than 2.6 per year (Montagu, 1976). And it has been estimated that only 10 of the 185 generations that have lived during this period have known the blessings of uninterrupted peace. Finally, history is literally studded with shocking instances of mass torture, murder, and even genocide. In view of such facts, it is difficult to make a convincing case for the view that violence is very much a "child" of the 20th century. Rather, each epoch appears to have endured its full share.

But given that aggression has always been with us, and is (alas!) an all too common event, a key question follows: Can anything be done to reduce or control its occurrence? The answer one offers to this question depends, to an important degree, on the theoretical perspective one adopts. If aggression is viewed as a built-in, genetically programmed aspect of human nature, a pessimistic conclusion is suggested: In all likelihood, little can be done to prevent overt aggression from occurring. At best, such behavior may be temporarily held in check, or diverted to less harmful forms and less vulnerable targets (e.g., Freud, 1933; Lorenz, 1974). In contrast, if aggression is viewed as a learned form of behavior—and thus as under the influence of a wide range of situational, social, and environmental conditions—a much more optimistic outlook follows. Presumably, if we know enough about the nature and causes of aggression, major reductions in its frequency or strength can be obtained. In short, this latter perspective—often known as the "social learning

approach"—holds that, given sufficient knowledge, we can indeed break the chain of violence binding us to previous generations.

Fortunately, most researchers concerned with aggression (including myself) favor this latter view (e.g., Bandura, 1973; Baron, 1977; Geen & Donnerstein, 1983). Indeed, it is the widespread acceptance of this optimistic perspective that lies behind the subtitle of this article. Needless to add, however, it is one thing to suggest that tactics for controlling aggression can in principle be obtained; it is quite another actually to devise them. Has measurable progress toward this goal been achieved? The answer, I believe, is an emphatic "yes." While many important gaps in current knowledge continue to exist, we already possess considerable understanding of tactics that are potentially useful in the reduction of overt aggression. It is upon such procedures that the present paper focuses. In particular, it reviews a number of strategies that appear to be effective in restraining human violence, or in reducing its intensity. As soon becomes apparent, these are highly diverse in nature, and range from traditional approaches such as punishment or catharsis on the one hand, to newer techniques involving cognitive interventions (Kremer & Stephens, in press) and training in appropriate social skills (A. P. Goldstein, 1981) on the other. For each of the strategies considered, evidence relating to its effectiveness is reviewed and conditions limiting its applicability are described. In addition, attention is directed to important gaps in current knowledge—questions and issues requiring further research and additional clarification.

PUNISHMENT: AN EFFECTIVE DETERRENT TO AGGRESSION?

Can the threat of punishment deter individuals from engaging in harmful or illegal acts? And will punishment itself discourage its recipients from repeating the acts that produced these unpleasant outcomes? Most societies have assumed that the answer to both questions is "yes." For this reason, many have established severe penalties for aggressive crimes such as murder, rape, and assault. Interestingly, a number of authorities on human aggression concur with these basic views. For example, in their famous text, *Frustration and Aggression,* Dollard and his colleagues stated: "The strength of inhibition of any act of aggression varies positively with the amount of punishment anticipated to be a consequence of that act" (Dollard, Doob, Miller, Mowrer, & Sears, 1939, p. 33). And, writing some 23 years later, Leonard Berkowitz noted: "This principle, as it stands, cannot be disputed" (1962, p. 73). In short, it has often been assumed that punishment is a highly effective technique for restraining human aggression. But is this actually the case? Is this widespread and long-standing faith in the deterrent capabilities of punishment wholly justified? Existing empirical evidence on this issue presents a complex picture. Briefly, it appears that under some conditions, punishment (or simply the threat of future punishment) can indeed inhibit acts of violence. Under other circumstances, however, it may totally fail to exert such effects; and in certain cases, it may actually tend to encourage rather than to restrain such behavior. Perhaps the best means of reviewing this very "mixed bag" of evidence is that of considering the effects of threatened and of actual punishment separately.

THREATENED PUNISHMENT: WHEN IT SUCCEEDS AND WHEN IT FAILS

Many crime films contain the following type of scene: At some point in the action, the heroine or hero "gets the drop" on a villain. She or he then orders this person to surrender. In some cases, the villain complies, and further bloodshed is averted. In others, however, this person refuses and quickly meets a predictable end. Obviously, films are not, per se, a sound basis for scientific conclusions. In this case, however, they seem to mirror events in many actual situations, for sometimes threats of punishment succeed in preventing aggressive actions, and sometimes they do not. Why is this the case? The answer yielded by several decades of empirical research is as follows: The impact of threatened punishment is strongly mediated by a number of different factors. To-

gether, these variables determine whether—and to what degree—it will succeed. A number of variables seem to play a role in this regard, but here I focus upon four that appear to be of greatest importance.

The first of these is the level of anger experienced by potential aggressors. The results of several studies suggest that when provocation is low or moderate in intensity, threats of punishment may well succeed in deterring overt aggression. In contrast, when provocation is intense, threatened punishment may totally fail in this regard (e.g., Baron, 1973; Rogers, 1980). Apparently, while experiencing powerful anger, many persons become incapable of considering the consequences of aggressive acts. Thus, they respond in what Berkowitz would describe as an "impulsive" manner, fully in accordance with their current emotional state (cf. Berkowitz, 1974). Instances of such behavior are frequent during time of war. For example soldiers who witness the mutilation or death of close comrades-at-arms often launch desperate and seemingly hopeless attacks against the hated enemy, regardless of the fact that such behavior will almost certainly result in serious injury or death. For example, consider the following description of events occurring during the bloody struggle for independence by the people of Bangladesh (Leamer, 1972); "Some of the Bengalis were so fierce in their fury, so outraged, that they could not be held back, and they ran forward into the cantonment until they were cut down by machine gun bursts, a few . . . rising again to throw their spears arching up into the sky . . ." (p. 80). Here, the persons involved were so overwhelmed with anger that they literally threw themselves into the guns of their foes, seemingly oblivious to the fact that they were courting certain death.

A second factor mediating the impact of threatened punishment on overt aggression is the instrumentality of such behavior. Briefly, when individuals have much to gain from acts of aggression (e.g., large monetary rewards, increased status), even strong threats of punishment may fail to deter them from such acts. In contrast, when individuals have relatively little to gain from such behavior, threats of punishment may be much more effective in restraining overt aggression (Baron, 1974).

Two additional variables affecting the impact of threats of punishment upon subsequent overt aggression seem obvious but are, surprisingly, often overlooked: the magnitude of the punishment involved, and the apparent probability that such aversive treatment will actually be delivered. As might be anticipated, research findings suggest that threatened punishment is more effective in deterring overt aggression when it is strong than when it is weak (e.g., Shortell, Epstein, & Taylor, 1970), and that it is more successful when the probability of its actually being delivered is high rather than low (Baron, 1971, 1974).

In sum, existing evidence indicates that the impact of threats of punishment upon aggression is strongly mediated by several different factors. As a result, such procedures will usually succeed only when (1) potential aggressors are not very angry; (2) they have relatively little to gain from such behavior; (3) the magnitude of punishment anticipated is great; and (4) the probability that such unpleasant treatment will be delivered is high. The implications of these limiting conditions for the criminal justice system are considered below.

ACTUAL PUNISHMENT: WHAT "LESSONS" DOES IT TEACH?

While threats of future punishment often fail to inhibit subsequent aggression, it seems reasonable to expect that the actual delivery of such treatment might prove more effective in this regard. After all, the use of punishment may serve to convince aggressors that society "means business" and will not tolerate aggressive outbursts. Further, if carried to relatively high levels, punishment may incapacitate aggressors or totally restrain them, and so may prevent further acts of violence (cf. Buss, 1971). In support of this reasoning, many studies suggest that punishment, even in mild forms such as verbal disapproval, can deter overt aggression (e.g., Deur & Parke, 1970). And stronger levels of such treatment have often been used with great success in clinical settings,

especially in cases where violent actions by one patient threaten the safety or well-being of others (e.g., Ludwig, Marx, Hill, & Browning, 1969). Unfortunately, however, the use of actual punishment also involves several complications.

First, the recipients of punishment often perceive it as an unjustified attack against them, especially if they observe other persons escaping such treatment after performing the same behaviors. And since attack is a strong elicitor of aggression (cf. O'Leary & Dengerink, 1973), punishing individuals for aggressive actions may sometimes increase rather than inhibit such behavior. Similarly, the individuals who deliver punishment may serve as aggressive models for those who receive it. In this way, they may actually tend to stimulate rather than discourage similar actions among recipients (see Eron, 1982).

Finally, it should be noted that recent investigations suggest that punishment will exert lasting effects upon behavior only when it is administered under certain conditions. These involve (1) a short interval between performance of the aggressive action and delivery of punishment; (2) a relatively high and aversive intensity; and (3) establishment of a clear contingency between the recipient's behavior and punishment (Bower & Hillgard, 1981). Only when punishment is administered in accordance with such principles will it produce lasting changes in behavior.

In sum, actual punishment, too, involves certain drawbacks when used as a deterrent to overt aggression. It can be perceived as an attack by those who receive it; it may provide such individuals with aggressive modeling cues; and it will succeed only when delivered in accordance with certain principles. In view of these considerations, it is far from surprising that the persons who receive various forms of punishment rarely "reform" as a result of such experiences.

PUNISHMENT AND CRIMINAL JUSTICE: POTENTIAL PARADOXES

As noted earlier, punishment lies at the heart of the criminal justice system in most societies. For this reason, it is probably the most widely used technique for controlling overt aggression. Given this fact, it might be expected that when punishment is employed, it is applied with considerable care. That is, one would hope that every step possible is taken to maximize its aggression-deterring impact. Is this actually the case? In fact, it is not. At present, conditions existing in many legal systems seem more likely to operate against the effectiveness of punishment than to promote it. This unsettling fact can be readily clarified.

First, consider the influence of threatened punishment. Several conditions seem likely to reduce its potential impact. First, in many nations, the probability of being apprehended and convicted for a given aggressive act is low. The gains provided by such behavior are often substantial. And the magnitude of punishment associated with assaults against others are uncertain at best, varying from one legal jurisdiction to another and across different courtrooms. Together, these factors seem likely to weaken the deterrent influence of threats of punishment.

Similarly, actual punishment is often administered in ways that operate against its potential impact. The delay between the performance of violent actions and punishment for them is long—often stretching into months or even years. The contingency between these actions is anything but clear, so that some persons who commit a given aggressive crime are punished, while others escape such consequences and receive only minimal chastisement. Given these conditions, it is far from surprising that those few who are actually punished often view themselves as the unfortunate victims of bad luck or an irrational system, not as the deserving recipients of society's wrath. Finally, the magnitude of punishment also varies greatly across legal jurisdictions and presiding judges. And often, it appears, it is too minimal in scope to serve as an effective deterrent to subsequent aggression.

In conclusion, existing evidence suggests that when punishment is used with appropriate care, it can indeed serve as an effective deterrent to human violence. In order for it to produce such effects, however, it must be applied systematically and in accordance with specific principles. Unfortunately, these requirements seem to be lacking or overlooked in many systems of criminal justice. The outcome, then, is readily predictable: Under such chaotic circumstances, punishment often fails to exert any appreciable restraining effects upon potential aggressors. Indeed, as its critics often charge, it may operate largely as an exercise in cruelty or retribution. It is important to note, however, that such outcomes are *not* intrinsically associated with punishment itself; on the contrary, growing evidence suggests that when used with appropriate care, it can serve as an effective technique for modifying human behavior. Whether its potential value as a deterrent to human violence will ever be realized, however, remains an open question.

CATHARSIS: DOES "GETTING IT OUT OF ONE'S SYSTEM" REALLY HELP?

Suppose that one day, you are are strongly provoked by your boss: He or she criticizes you harshly for something that was not really your fault. After the boss leaves, you pound your fist on your desk, break two pencils, and tear the morning newspaper into small irregular shreds. Would these actions be effective in reducing your anger? And would they lower your tendency to act against your boss in some aggressive fashion on future occasions? According to the well-known "catharsis hypothesis," the answer to both questions is "yes." Briefly, this view suggests that when angry persons "blow off steam" through the performance of vigorous but nonharmful actions, two effects will follow: First, their level of tension or arousal will be reduced; second, their tendencies to engage in overt acts of aggression against the persons who provoked them (or others) will be lowered.

These suggestions can be traced to the writings of Aristotle, who held that exposure to emotion-provoking stage drama could produce a vicarious "purging" of the emotions. While Aristotle himself did not refer directly to the reduction of aggressive impulses in this manner, this seemingly logical extension of his views was proposed by Freud, who suggested that such reactions could be lessened through the expression of aggression-related emotions, as well as through exposure to aggressive actions by others. While Freud accepted the existence of such catharsis, however, he was relatively pessimistic regarding its usefulness in preventing overt aggression. Indeed, he seemed to regard it as both minimal in scope and short-lived in nature. The popular acceptance of the notion of catharsis in psychology, therefore, seems to stem primarily from certain statements made by Dollard *et al.* in *Frustration and Aggression.* According to these authors, *"The expression of any act of aggression is a catharsis that reduces the instigation to all other acts of aggression"* (1939, p. 33; italics added). In short, Dollard *et al.* held that the performance of one aggressive act—whatever its nature—could serve to reduce an aggressor's tendency to engage in all other forms of violence. Largely on the basis of this and similar suggestions, generations of parents have urged their children to play with aggressive toys; thousands of psychotherapists have urged their patients to "release" their hostile feelings; and astute entrepreneurs have reaped handsome profits from the sale of foam-rubber bats and similar implements, specifically designed to induce "catharsis." Is this faith in the value of catharsis and cathartic activities justified? Once again, empirical findings offer a highly mixed picture.

First, let us consider the suggestion that in the face of strong provocation, participation in safe but vigorous activities can lead to reductions in tension or emotional arousal. Studies performed to examine this suggestion have generally yielded positive results, but also point to important limitations on this phenomenon. On the other hand, it appears that the arousal stemming from strong provocation can sometimes be reduced through the performance of physically exhausting actions (Zillmann, 1979). Thus, in a general sense, this portion of the catharsis hypothesis seems to be correct. On the other hand, however, it appears that the most effective means of producing such reductions in arousal is participation in acts that directly harm the source of one's anger (Hokanson & Burgess, 1962). That is, after being angered, individuals provided with an opportunity to do physical harm to the persons who annoyed them generally show larger and faster reductions in arousal than do persons permitted to engage in other, less dangerous kinds of activity (Hokanson, 1970). In short, tension can indeed be reduced through the performance of noninjurious actions, but acts of aggression directed toward provocateurs are much more successful in this respect.

As for the suggestion that the performance of "safe" vigorous actions can reduce the likelihood of overt aggression, the picture is perhaps even more discouraging. Research on this topic indicates that, contrary to what the catharsis hypothesis suggests, aggression is not reduced by (1) watching scenes of filmed or televised violence (Geen, 1978), (2) attacks against inanimate objects (Mallick & McCandless, 1966), or (3) verbal assaults against others (Ebbesen, Duncan, & Konecni, 1975). Indeed, there is some evidence pointing to the conclusion that aggression may actually be increased by each of these conditions. Obviously, these results cast serious doubt upon the widely credited aggression-deterring impact of catharsis. But it might still be suggested, however, that such effects take place under one special set of conditions: when angry persons can either inflict harm directly on or observe harm done to the persons who annoyed them. That is, having "evened the score" in some manner, angry persons may be less likely to engage in further attacks against their provocateurs on later occasions. In short, catharsis may well operate, but more in accordance with principles of equity or distributive justice (Greenberg & Cohen, 1982) than with principles of "emotional purging." While this suggestion seems quite reasonable, evidence concerning its accuracy, too, has been mixed. Several experiments suggest that after harming or witnessing harm to the objects of their anger, aggressors are indeed less likely to attack these persons on later occasions (Fromkin, Goldstein, & Brock, 1977; Konecni & Ebbesen, 1976). But several other studies indicate that participation in such activities fails to reduce later aggression, or may even tend to *increase* its occurrence at other times (e.g., Geen, Stonner, & Shope, 1975). One possible explanation for these latter results can be readily suggested: The infliction of harm upon one's enemy is often pleasurable and can serve as a form of reinforcement (Baron, 1979). Thus, successful assaults against such persons can strengthen, rather than weaken, aggressive tendencies. Whatever the mechanism involved, however, it is clear that the type of effects usually described as "catharsis" often fails to occur in such cases.

At present, then, evidence concerning the aggression-deterring impact of catharsis is mixed: Such effects have been observed in some investigations but not in others. And, currently, no simple or obvious explanation for these conflicting results exists. One possibility, however, is as follows: Contrary to popular belief, catharsis occurs only under highly specific conditions. Thus, it has been observed in some studies but not in others because only in certain cases were the appropriate circumstances present. But what, precisely, are these key conditions? Existing evidence offers few concrete clues. In addition, it should be noted that current literature also fails to address a related and equally crucial point: When catharsis occurs, how long does its impact persist? This question is of major importance, for only if catharsis-induced reductions in aggression persist for substantial periods of time will they be of any practical benefit. In general, it has been assumed that cathartic effects are quite long-lasting. However, recent research on social cognition — especially on person memory (e.g., Hastie, Ostrom, Ebbesen, Wyer, Hamilton, & Carlston, 1980) — calls this assumption into doubt. Such research indicates that human beings have an impressive capacity to store and retrieve social information (e.g., information about others' characteristics or behavior). In view of this ability, it is reasonable to assume that persons who have been strongly provoked often think about their real or imagined wrongs at the hands of others. To the extent that they engage in such activities, reductions in aggressive tendencies produced by catharsis may quickly dissipate. And even if such persons do not actively scan their own memories in the absence of provocateurs, these annoyers may serve as a rich source of retrieval cues when encountered "in the flesh." Thus, even cathartic

effects that have persisted for long periods of time may be quickly eradicated in face-to-face encounters, as a result of ongoing cognitive processes. At the moment, no evidence on such possibilities exists. Thus, research designed to investigate the potential relationship between basic cognitive processes and catharsis would seem to offer an exciting avenue for further investigation.

To sum up, taking the mixed research findings noted above and these additional complicating factors into account, the following generalizations seem justified: First, catharsis is not nearly as widespread or general in its occurrence as once believed. Second, while the opportunity to commit aggressive acts against persons who have been provocative sometimes reduces the tendency to aggression, this is not always the case. And third, full understanding of this phenomenon will require attention to principles of equity and social cognition, as well as to the simpler mechanisms of "emotional purging" on which much past research has been based.

EXPOSURE TO NONAGGRESSIVE MODELS: THE CONTAGION OF RESTRAINT

An impressive body of literature points to the conclusion that exposure to the actions of aggressive models — persons who behave in a highly aggressive manner — can sometimes elicit similar actions on the part of observers (e.g., Liebert, Sprafkin, & Davidson, 1982). Moreover, such effects have been observed among both adults (Baron & Bell, 1975) and children (Huesmann, 1982). One common explanation for the occurrence of this phenomenon involves the presumed impact of aggressive models upon the restraints or inhibitions of observers. Specifically, it has been suggested that witnessing the actions of such models produces sharp reductions in the strength of observers' restraints against overt acts of aggression, and in this manner facilitates the occurrence of such behavior. If this is indeed the case (and existing evidence suggests that it is), then an interesting possibility follows: Might not opposite effects, too, be induced? That is, if restraints against aggression can be weakened through exposure to highly aggressive models, might they not be strengthened as a result of exposure to nonaggressive models—persons who demonstrate restrained, calm behavior even in the face of strong provocation? Informal observation offers support for the existence of such effects. For example, many tense and threatening situations subside when one or more of the persons present demonstrate and urge restraint. Similarly, informal procedures based on such an approach have been employed—with some apparent success—to avert confrontations between police and students on several college campuses.

That nonaggressive models can be effective in reducing overt aggression has also been demonstrated in several different experiments (e.g., Baron, 1971; Baron & Kepner, 1970; Donnerstein & Donnerstein, 1976). In these investigations, angry individuals exposed to nonaggressive models prior to an opportunity to commit acts of aggression against the sources of their annoyance demonstrated significantly lower levels of aggression than did persons not exposed to such models. Moreover, such effects were produced both by exposure to nonaggressive actions (Donnerstein & Donnerstein, 1976) and verbal calls for restraint (Baron, 1972). And, impressively, they were observed even among individuals who had previously endured strong provocation at the hands of the potential targets (Baron & Kepner, 1970). Finally, additional studies have noted that exposure to the actions of nonaggressive models can go a long way toward countering the aggression-eliciting impact of highly aggressive models (Baron, 1971). Since both types of individuals are often present in settings where dangerous instances of collective violence erupt, this latter finding points to practical strategy for averting such events: Specifically, the likelihood of riots and similar tragic events may be sharply reduced through the judicious "planting" of nonaggressive models at such locations. Of course, direct evidence on the effectiveness of such procedures is lacking at present. But given the consistent pattern of findings obtained in research on this topic, the potential efficacy of such tactics seems quite feasible.

One final point concerning the aggression-reducing impact of nonaggressive models should be noted. In some cases, at least, exposure to such persons seems somewhat more effective in deterring overt aggression than do other widely used tactics for attaining this goal (e.g., threat of punishment or retaliation; see Donnerstein & Donnerstein, 1976). This may be the case because nonaggressive models tend to induce two distinct effects among potential aggressors. First, as noted earlier, they strengthen restraints or inhibitions against overt aggression. Second, they exert a calming effect upon such persons, reducing their level of emotional arousal. In contrast, other aggression-deterring tactics, such as threatened punishment, may serve only to strengthen restraints against aggression. Whatever the precise mechanisms involved, however, existing evidence suggests that restraint, as well as violence, may be socially "contagious." Thus, further research designed to specify the precise conditions under which nonaggressive models can exert such beneficial effects would seem to be well worthwhile.

COGNITIVE INTERVENTIONS: ATTRIBUTIONS AND MITIGATING CIRCUMSTANCES

Aggression often stems from or is associated with intense emotional arousal. For this reason, several techniques (e.g., catharsis, the incompatible-response strategy described in the next section) that are designed to reduce its occurrence focus on this emotional component. But emotion is far from the only element involved in human aggression. Cognitive processes, too, play a role. A number of these seem relevant and may affect the occurrence (and inhibition) of aggression in different settings. However, two appear to be of greatest importance: memory and attribution.

We have already noted the potential role of memory in the elicitation of aggression. Briefly, individuals often retain information relating to real or imagined wrongs suffered at the hands of others. When such information is retrieved from memory at later times, it may serve to reinstate anger, and so to facilitate overt aggressive outbursts (cf. Zillmann, 1979). Conversely, conditions serving to block such recall (e.g., distracting events or stimuli) or ones that actually eliminate anger-evoking information from memory (e.g., factors producing appropriate interference) may help to reduce the likelihood of aggression by the persons involved. At present, little evidence on such possibilities is available. However, existing literature on the operation of memory (Wingfield & Byrnes, 1981) suggests that interventions designed to lessen the recall of anger-inducing events or situations may prove quite effective.

A second cognitive process that plays a key role in aggression is attribution. This process involves efforts by human beings to make sense out of the behavior of the persons around them—to understand the causes behind their actions (e.g., Harvey & Weary, 1981). One major aspect of attribution, in turn, concerns the following question: Do another person's actions stem primarily from *internal* causes (e.g., his or her traits or motives), or *external* causes (e.g., situational causes, factors beyond his or her control)? The answer to this question can exert powerful effects upon social behavior in situations where individuals are exposed to annoyance or provocation from others. In such cases, they must determine whether this provocative behavior stems mainly from internal causes and is intended, or whether it stems from external causes and is unintended. Obviously, anger and aggression are more likely in the context of the former conclusion than in the context of the latter. Perhaps a specific example may help to clarify this crucial point.

Imagine that another person pours hot coffee onto your lap. If that person then offers profuse apologies and attempts to assist you in wiping off the stain, you will probably interpret his or her behavior as being unintended. Then, both anger and attempts at retaliation are unlikely. In contrast, if that person laughs sadistically at your plight and seems to relish your discomfort and embarrassment, you will probably perceive his or her action as being intended. And then you are quite likely to become angry, and to seek to pay him or her back in kind. In this and countless other situations, reactions to seemingly provocative behavior on the part of another person may be strongly mediated by attributional processes.

Direct evidence for the impact of attribution on aggression has been obtained in two distinct but related lines of investigation. The first of these has focused on the task of determining whether conditions known to promote either internal or external explanations for others' behaviors also affect aggression. In such studies (e.g., Dyck & Rule, 1978), participants have been exposed to provocation from other persons and also to information favoring either an internal or an external explanation of such actions. In general, results have supported the view that attributions are indeed of crucial importance in such cases. As predicted, both anger toward the annoyer and overt aggression against this person are stronger under conditions favoring internal attributions (e.g., "low consensus"—few other persons act in such a provocative manner) than under conditions favoring external attributions (e.g., "high consensus"—most persons behave in a similar provocative fashion). The findings of such studies, in turn, point to a possible technique for preventing or reducing aggression. Briefly, they suggest that if attributions can somehow be shifted or biased toward external causes, aggression may be reduced. But how, specifically, can this task be accomplished? How can individuals be induced to interpret provocative actions by others as unintended or as stemming from external causes?

The second line of research mentioned above offers some suggestions. This research has been concerned with the potential aggression-reducing impact of mitigating circumstances—information suggesting that provocative actions by another person stem from circumstances or events beyond that person's control, rather than from his or her traits, intentions, or motives (e.g., Zillmann & Cantor, 1976). Such information, of course, should serve to shift attributions in the direction of externality, and so reduce the likelihood or intensity of aggressive reactions to seeming provocation. Several studies have examined this possibility, and in general, results have been quite encouraging. When individuals receive information about potentially mitigating circumstances, they demonstrate significantly lower levels of aggression than when they do not. Moreover, this is true even following severe or repeated provocation (e.g., Kremer & Stephens, in press; Zillmann & Cantor, 1976). As might be expected, such effects are strongest when mitigating information either precedes or immediately follows provocation; when the information is not presented until several minutes later, its aggression-deterring impact is substantially reduced (Kremer & Stephens, in press). That information about mitigating circumstances actually exerts its influence through shifts in attributions is suggested by additional findings. Specifically, when such information is present, subjects seem to perceive the provocation they have endured as less unusual or unique than is true when such information is absent. That is, they perceive the annoyer's behavior as more typical of what most persons would do in the current situation (Kremer & Stephens, in press). Finally the results of at least one study (Zillman & Cantor, 1976) suggest that when mitigating information is presented prior to provocation, the physiological signs of arousal typically produced by such treatment may be totally eliminated. In short, when such information is presented in an appropriate manner, events or actions by others that ordinarily generate strong feelings of anger may fail to induce such emotional effects.

Taken as a whole, research of the impact of mitigating information points to the conclusion that such information can often provide an effective means of reducing overt aggression. Apparently, the cognitive processes set in motion by such input can counter the impact of even strong annoyance or provocation. Needless to add, information about mitigating circumstances is not always appropriate and will not always produce such effects. After all, in many conditions, provocations *are* intended and *do* stem from internal sources. But in many other cases, seemingly provocative actions are not intended and stem primarily from external factors or causes. In such instances, calling individuals' attention to these factors may avert unnecessary retaliation, and thus may prevent the reciprocal, escalating process that often characterizes human aggression (e.g., J. M. Goldstein, Davis, & Herman, 1975).

Before the present discussion of cognitive interventions is concluded, one additional line of investigation should be mentioned. Briefly, such research has focused on the possibility that providing individuals with certain types of information may lessen the impact of various aggression-enhancing factors upon their behavior. In short, it has examined the possibility that such information and the cognitions it induces can reduce aggression under conditions where it would ordinarily be expected to take place. Much of this work has focused on possible cognitive techniques for lessening the aggression-enhancing impact of televised violence. For example, in several related studies, Horton and Santogrossi (1978) have found that commentary by an adult expressing disapproval of the aggressive actions shown by characters in a popular police show can totally eliminate the impact of these materials on later behavior by children. Indeed, youngsters who heard such comments while watching this program did not differ in their later behavior from youngsters who never watched the aggressive program. Similarly, in more recent research, Huesmann, Eron, Klein, Brice, and Fischer (1981) found that children given information designed to assist them in discriminating televised violence from real-life events were rated as showing less aggression by their classmates several months later. These findings offer further evidence for the view that interventions focused on the cognitive processes underlying human aggression may well prove quite effective in reducing or preventing such behavior. Given the ease with which such interventions can be employed and magnitude of the effects they seem to produce, further research designed to develop and refine such procedures may well prove valuable.

THE INDUCTION OF INCOMPATIBLE RESPONSES: EMPATHY, HUMOR, AND SEXUAL AROUSAL AS DETERRENTS TO HUMAN AGGRESSION

It is a well-established principle in psychology that all organisms, including human beings, are incapable of engaging in two incompatible responses at once. To mention just two examples, it is difficult (if not impossible) both to daydream and to carry on complex cognitive activities (e.g., reading a scientific paper). Similarly, it is difficult (if not impossible) to feel both elated and depressed at once. Recently, attempts have been made to extend this basic principle to the control of aggressive behavior. Specifically, it has been suggested that any conditions serving to induce responses or emotional states among aggressors that are incompatible with anger or overt aggression will often be highly effective in reducing such behavior (e.g., Baron, 1983; Ramirez, Bryant, & Zillmann, 1982). Although many different responses might prove to be inconsistent with aggression in this manner, most research has focused on three: empathy, humor, and mild sexual arousal.

In experiments concerned with the potential aggression-inhibiting impact of such reactions, participants have generally first been angered or not angered in some fashion (e.g., through direct insult or negative evaluations of their personalities). Then they are exposed either to neutral materials such as pictures of scenery and abstract art, or to stimuli designed to induce incompatible responses (e.g., humorous cartoons, mild forms of erotica). Following these experiences, they are provided with an opportunity to commit aggressive acts against the persons who annoyed them. In general, the results of such investigations have supported the view that inducing incompatible responses among potential aggressors may sharply reduce the intensity or likelihood of their later attacks against others (e.g., Baron, 1983; Mueller & Donnerstein, 1976). Moreover, such effects have been observed in field as well as laboratory settings (Baron, 1976). It appears, then, that strategies for the reduction of aggression based upon the induction of incompatible responses among persons who have been angered or otherwise provoked to aggression may well prove effective. But how can such techniques be put to practical use? In what settings can they be used to reduce or inhibit outbursts of aggression? At present, little evidence on these crucial issues exists. However, two potential applications of such procedures can be mentioned briefly.

First, the induction of incompatible responses

may be of considerable use in certain areas of clinical practice. Many individuals experience major personal difficulties as a result of what might be described as a "short interpersonal fuse"—an inability to hold their tempers in check under conditions in which others succeed at this task. At present, such persons are often treated by means of relaxation training and related procedures (Sundel & Sundel, 1982). It seems possible that the incompatible-response strategy might provide an alternative form of treatment. Specifically, if such persons can be trained to generate appropriate humorous or sexual images at times when they experience provocation, the reactions so induced may assist them in avoiding costly aggressive actions. Considerable systematic research will be necessary to determine how such incompatible-response-generating cognitions can best be generated, and what specific types are most useful in this regard. However, given the large number of persons whose careers, marriages, and social lives suffer greatly from a lack of appropriate restraint, such efforts might well prove beneficial.

Second, it seems possible that incompatible responses can be used as one strategy for deterring an especially repugnant type of violence—rape. Reports by women who have successfully fended off such attacks suggest that they often engaged in actions that may well have served to induce incompatible reactions among their assailants. For example, some have reported telling these persons that they might soon be physically ill, or that they might lose control of their bodily functions during sex. And others have succeeded in averting sexual assaults in an even more surprising manner—by turning to their would-be assailants and asking them for help or protection. This tactic, of course, might well have induced feelings of empathy among the potential rapists. For example, consider the following incident (Groth, 1979):

one offender who had raped six women reported being deterred on one occasion; he spotted his potential victim while riding on a subway and decided that if she got off alone . . . he would rape her. She did exit alone in a rather remote area of town, but as the offender followed her, she turned to him and explained that because it was so late at night she didn't feel safe walking home alone and asked him if he would be kind enough to accompany her until she reached her house. He did so and never touched her, puzzled that his wish to rape her had suddenly disappeared. (p. 31)

Needless to add, such evidence, suggestive as it seems to be, is far from conclusive in nature. Thus, it would be folly at this point to recommend that women rely on this approach as a basic means of self-defense. The fact that such informal reports are often consistent with the findings of a large number of laboratory studies, however, underscores the possibility that strategies based upon the induction of incompatible responses may be of potential use in this crucial area.

TRAINING IN SOCIAL SKILLS: LEARNING TO AVOID TROUBLE

One major reason why many persons become involved in repeated aggressive encounters is disturbingly simple: They are severely lacking in basic social skills. For example, they do not know how to communicate effectively; moreover, to make matters worse, they often possess an unfortunate, abrasive style of self-expression. Similarly, they lack sensitivity to the emotional states of others, and so are unable to tell when they are annoying the persons around them. Finally, they do not know how to perform basic social arts in a manner viewed as "appropriate" by their culture. Making requests, engaging in negotiations, lodging complaints—all these tasks are beyond their limited repertoire of social skills. Needless to add, their ineptness in performing these basic tasks often irritates friends, acquaintances, coworkers, or total strangers. Thus, the severe social deficits shown by such persons seem to assure (1) that they will experience repeated, intense frustration, and (2) that they will frequently anger individuals with whom they have social contact.

Given their inability to satisfy their own basic needs, and their irritating impact on others, it seems only reasonable to expect that persons lacking in social skills will often serve both as sources and targets of aggressive behavior. And in fact, growing evidence suggests that this is the case. When individuals with a long history of interpersonal violence are closely and systematically studied, many demonstrate the pattern of arrested social development noted above (e.g., Toch, 1980). And while such persons are not very great in number, they contribute far more than their fair share to the overall level of violence occurring in a given society (Toch, 1980). Thus, one technique for reducing the frequency of such behavior might logically involve equipping these persons with the skills they so sorely lack. Can this be done? A large and rapidly growing body of literature suggests that indeed it can (A. P. Goldstein, 1981). During the past dozen years, several systematic programs for accomplishing this goal have been developed and put to actual use. While these efforts at training in social skills have varied greatly both in scope and content, many have made use of the following major techniques: modeling, role playing, performance feedback, and transfer of training.

Modeling involves procedures in which persons lacking in specific social skills are provided with actual examples of appropriate modes of behavior. These can be presented by means of videotape, audiotape, or even live demonstrations. The basic goal in each case, however, remains the same: to equip the persons in question with responses and behaviors not previously available to them.

Role playing is often the next step in social skills training. Here, participants pretend to be in certain situations and attempt to put the behaviors acquired through modeling into actual practice. That is, they attempt to behave in ways they have previously observed in modeling films or live demonstrations. In a sense, then, role playing gives such individuals an opportunity to practice behaving in effective ways—or, at least, in ways more effective than has been true for them in the past.

A third aspect of social skills training involves

performance feedback. During this phase (which may overlap with role playing or even with modeling), individuals receive one or more forms of feedback—typically in the form of positive reinforcement—on their behavior. Specifically, they are praised or otherwise rewarded for engaging in desired, effective behaviors. And, conversely, such praise is omitted when older, less effective patterns are demonstrated. In addition to feedback provided during training sessions, attempts are made to assure that individuals receive some appropriate feedback in other contexts as well. In this manner, generalization from training to actual life situations may be increased.

Finally, considerable attention is devoted to the transfer of what is learned in systematic training sessions to real-life settings. This can be accomplished by providing participants with general principles—ones that can be applied to real life as well as to therapy settings—by assuring that training sessions contain at least some elements that are identical to those in other contexts, and by employing a wide range of training stimuli and situations. Since practical benefits will be obtained from programs of social skills training only to the extent that the newly acquired skills are transferred to actual life situations, a great deal of care is usually employed to maximize the probability of such transfer.

These general principles are often employed in settings involving anywhere from 6 to 12 participants. Such persons are carefully selected so that all share similar levels of deficiency with respect to selected social skills. (If individuals differ too greatly in this respect, some will find the sessions too simple or repetitious, while others may be totally lost in a maze of new skills beyond their comprehension.) Sessions can vary in length and frequency, but many experts recommend two or three per week, lasting from 1 to 2 hours each.

Such procedures have been employed to produce improvements in a wide range of social skills—everything from enhanced interpersonal communication on the one hand (e.g., Guerney, 1977; Johnson, 1978) to improved ability to handle rejection (McFall & Twentyman, 1973) and stress (A. P. Goldstein, Sprafkin, & Gershaw,

1979) on the other. Moreover, social skills training has been applied to diverse groups of individuals, including highly aggressive teenagers, police officers, and child-abusing parents (cf. A. P. Goldstein, 1981). In many cases, dramatic changes in the targeted behaviors have been produced. And reductions in aggressive behavior related to these shifts have frequently been observed. Thus, taking the existing evidence into account, it appears that training in appropriate social skills offers a promising approach to the reduction of human violence. Of course, as should be apparent, it is not appropriate for use with all individuals; indeed, it is designed for application to specific and relatively small groups. Since these target individuals account for a disproportionately large share of aggression in their societies, however, its potential impact appears to be far greater than absolute numbers would suggest.

CONCLUSION: A FINAL WORD OF OPTIMISM

This paper begins with an admittedly optimistic premise: While major gaps in our knowledge remain, we already know a great deal about the prevention and control of human aggression. I sincerely hope that the intervening pages have made a convincing case for this proposal. But thoughtful readers may now be wondering: If it is true that we know so much about the control of aggression, what accounts for the persistent aura of pessimism concerning this issue? Why, in short, do so many behavioral scientists throw up their hands in despair whenever the topic of preventing human violence is mentioned? In my opinion, three major factors have contributed to this unsettling state of affairs.

First, for some unfathomable reason, many social scientists continue to believe (at least implicitly) that aggression is genetically or instinctively preordained. To the extent that one holds this view, of course, there is a basis for pessimism; after all, if aggression stems from our basic biological nature, it cannot be readily avoided. As I have tried to indicate throughout this paper, however, a vast body of empirical evidence points to a different conclusion: Aggression is largely acquired. And even if it is not wholly learned (recent research on biological constraints upon learning casts doubt upon the opinion that any form of behavior is totally acquired), it is certainly modifiable. Thus, there do not seem to be strong grounds for pessimism on this score.

Second, it is my impression that much of the present despair can be traced to the following basic fact: To date, research on aggression has failed to uncover a single, all-powerful technique highly effective in controlling such behavior in a wide range of settings. In short, many of our colleagues appear to be pessimistic because, in answer to the question "How can violence be reduced?," we are unable to offer a single, simple answer. While the attractions of possessing such a reply are obvious, I do not view its current absence as a reasonable basis for despair. Aggression, we have found, is a highly complex phenomenon. Indeed, it appears to stem from a wide range of factors and to be affected by an almost endless number of conditions. Given these facts, it does not seem reasonable to expect that such behavior can be controlled by means of a single procedure or in a straightforward manner. Rather, efforts to reduce human violence will almost certainly have to be as varied and complex as the roots of aggression themselves. Thus, once again, the current pessimism among behavioral scientists seems to rest on highly questionable grounds.

Finally, pessimism concerning the possibility of controlling human aggression derives from a third source: the persistent fear that even if we devise appropriate answers, no one "out there" will listen. That is, even if we succeed in discovering effective means for reducing aggression, this information will be largely ignored. Such concerns, of course, are not easily dismissed; society does indeed have a fairly dismal record of utilizing knowledge uncovered by behavioral scientists. Yet it is also my impression that knowledge, once acquired, has a way of being used. And in this respect, I perceive no strong *a priori* reasons why information about the control of human aggression should represent an exception to this general

rule. Thus, even here, I remain guardedly optimistic.

In sum, I believe that during the past two decades we have made substantial progress toward the goals of (1) understanding the nature and origins of human aggression, and (2) developing effective techniques for its ultimate control. From a purely scientific point of view, then, there seem to be no convincing grounds for assuming that aggression is a necessary aspect of human affairs, or that its reduction is forever beyond our grasp. On the contrary, growing evidence suggests that such behavior *can* be prevented or reduced. The knowledge base for doing so exists, or is rapidly taking shape. But will it actually be used in the years ahead? Unfortunately, this is primarily a social or political decision, largely beyond the control of researchers working in this general area. Of course, we can continue to speak out and to call for appropriate actions. But the implementation of such recommendations rests mainly in other hands. Perhaps our advice will be heeded and our knowledge used—perhaps; only time will tell. However, until all the evidence is in and we sit either among the burning ruins of our civilization or in the secure comfort of a just and peaceful world society, I suggest the following course of action: Let us reject current counsels of despair and opt instead for that most sustaining of all human emotions: hope!

REFERENCES

Bandura, A. *Aggression: A social learning analysis.* Englewood Cliffs, N.J.: Prentice-Hall, 1973.

Baron, R. A. Reducing the influence of an aggressive model: The restraining effects of discrepant modeling cues. *Journal of Personality and Social Psychology,* 1971, *20,* 240–245.

Baron, R. A. Reducing the influence of an aggressive model: The restraining effects of peer censure. *Journal of Experimental Social Psychology,* 1972, *8,* 266–275.

Baron, R. A. Threatened retaliation from the victim as an inhibitor of physical aggression. *Journal of Research in Personality,* 1973, *7,* 103–115.

Baron, R. A. Threatened retaliation as an inhibitor of

human aggression: Mediating effects of the instrumental value of aggression. *Bulletin of the Psychonomic Society,* 1974, *29,* 217–219.

Baron, R. A. The reduction of human aggression: A field study of the influence of incompatible reactions. *Journal of Applied Social Psychology,* 1976 *6,* 260–274.

Baron, R. A. *Human aggression.* New York: Plenum Press, 1977.

Baron, R. A. Effects of victim's pain cues, victim's race, and level of prior instigation upon physical aggression. *Journal of Applied Social Psychology,* 1979, *9,* 103–114.

Baron, R. A. The control of human aggression: A strategy based on incompatible responses. In R. G. Geen & E. I. Donnerstein (Eds.), *Aggression: Theoretical and empirical reviews.* New York: Academic Press, 1983.

Baron, R. A., & Bell, P. A. Aggression and heat: Mediating effects of prior provocation and exposure to an aggressive model. *Journal of Personality and Social Psychology,* 1975, *31,* 825–832.

Baron, R. A., & Kepner, C. R. Model's behavior and attraction toward the model as determinants of adult aggressive behavior. *Journal of Personality and Social Psychology,* 1970, *14,* 335 344.

Berkowitz, L. *Aggression: A social-psychological analysis.* New York: McGraw-Hill, 1962.

Berkowitz, L. Some determinants of impulsive aggression: Role of mediated associations with reinforcements for aggression. *Psychological Review,* 1974, *81,* 165–176.

Bower, G. H., & Hilgard, E. R. *Theories of learning* (5th ed.). Englewood Cliffs, N.J.: Prentice-Hall, 1981.

Buss, A. H. Aggressive pays. In J. L. Singer (Ed.), *The control of aggression and violence.* New York: Academic Press, 1971.

Deur, J. D., & Parke, R. D. Effects of inconsistent punishment on aggression in children. *Developmental Psychology,* 1970, *2,* 401–411.

Dollard, J., Doob, L., Miller, N., Mowrer, O. H., & Sears, R. R. *Frustration and aggression.* New Haven: Yale University Press, 1939.

Donnerstein, E., & Donnerstein, M. Research in the control of interracial aggression. In R. G. Geen & E. C. O'Neal (Eds.), *Perspectives on aggression.* New York: Academic Press, 1976.

Dyck, R., & Rule, B. G. The effect of causal attributions concerning attack on retaliation. *Journal of*

Personality and Social Psychology, 1978, *36,* 521–529.

Ebbesen, E. B., Duncan, B., & Konecni, V. J. Effects of content of verbal aggression on future verbal aggression: A field experiment. *Journal of Experimental Social Psychology,* 1975, *11,* 192 204.

Eron, L. D. Parent-child interaction, television violence, and aggression of children. *American Psychologist,* 1982, *37,* 197–211.

Freud, S. *New introductory lectures on psycho-analysis.* New York: Norton, 1933.

Fromkin, H. L., Goldstein, J. H., & Brock, T. C. The role of "irrelevant" derogation in vicarious aggression catharsis: A field experiment. *Journal of Experimental Social Psychology,* 1977, *13,* 239–252.

Geen, R. G. Some effects of observing violence upon the behavior of the observer. In B. A. Maher (Ed.), *Progress in experimental personality research* (Vol. 8). New York: Academic Press, 1978.

Geen, R. G., & Donnerstein, E. I. (Eds.). *Aggression: Theoretical and empirical reviews.* New York: Academic Press, 1983.

Geen, R. G., Stonner, D., & Shope, G. L. The facilitation of aggression by aggression: Evidence against the catharsis hypothesis. *Journal of Personality and Social Psychology,* 1975, *31,* 721 726.

Goldstein, A. P. Social skill training. In A. P. Goldstein, E. G. Carr, W. S. Davidson II, & P. Wehr (Eds.), *In response to aggression: Methods of control and prosocial alternatives.* New York: Pergamon Press, 1981.

Goldstein, A. P., Sprafkin, R. P., & Gershaw, N. J. *I know what's wrong but I don't know what to do about it.* Englewood Cliffs, N.J.: Prentice-Hall. 1979.

Goldstein, J. M., Davis, R. W., & Herman, D. Escalation of aggression: Experimental studies. *Journal of Personality and Social Psychology,* 1975, *31,* 162–170.

Greenburg, J., & Cohen, R. L. (Eds.), *Equity and justice in social behavior.* New York: Academic Press, 1982.

Groth, A. N. *Men who rape.* New York: Plenum Press, 1979.

Guerney, B. G., Jr. *Relationship enhancement.* San Francisco: Jossey-Bass, 1977.

Harvey, J. H., & Weary, G. *Perspectives on attributional processes.* Dubuque, Iowa: William C. Brown, 1981.

Hastie, R., Ostrom, T. M., Ebbesen, E. B., Wyer, R. S.,

Hamilton, D. L., & Carlston, D. E. (Eds.). *Person memory: The cognitive basis of social perception.* Hillsdale, N.J.: Erlbaum, 1980.

Hokanson, J. E. Psychophysiological evaluation of the catharsis hypothesis. In E. I. Megargee & J. E. Hokanson (Eds.). *The dynamics of aggression.* New York: Harper & Row, 1970.

Hokanson, J. L., & Burgess, M. The effects of status, type of frustration, and aggression on vascular processes. *Journal of Abnormal and Social Psychology,* 1962, *65,* 232–237.

Horton, R. W., & Santogrossi, D. A. The effect of adult commentary on reducing the influence of televised violence. *Personality and Social Psychology Bulletin,* 1978, *4,* 337–340.

Huesmann, L. R. Television violence and aggressive behavior. In D. Pearl & L. Bouthilet (Eds.), *Television and behavior: Ten years of scientific progress and implications for the 80's.* Washington, D.C.: U.S. Government Printing Office, 1982.

Huesmann, L. R, Eron, L. D., Klein, R., Brice, P., & Fischer, P. *Mitigating the imitation of aggressive behaviors by changing children's attitudes about media violence* (Tech. Report No. 3). Chicago: University of Illinois at Chicago Circle, 1981.

Johnson, D. W. *Human relations and your career: A guide to interpersonal skills.* Englewood Cliffs, N.J.: Prentice-Hall, 1978.

Konecni, V., & Ebbesen, E. G. Disinhibition versus the cathartic effect: Artifact and substance. *Journal of Personality and Social Psychology,* 1976, *34,* 325–365.

Kremer, J. F., & Stephens, L. Attributions and arousal as mediators of mitigation's effect on retaliation. *Journal of Personality and Social Psychology,* in press.

Leamer, L. Bangladesh in the morning. *Harper's Magazine,* August 1972, pp. 84–98.

Liebert, R. M., Sprafkin, J. N., & Davidson, E. S. *The early window: Effects of television on children and youth* (2nd ed.). New York: Pergamon Press, 1982.

Lorenz, K. *Civilized man's eight deadly sins.* New York: Harcourt Brace Jovanovich, 1974.

Ludwig, A. M., Marx, A. J., Hill, P. A., & Browning, R. M. The control of violent behavior through fa-radic shock. *Journal of Nervous and Mental Disease,* 1969, *148,* 624–637.

Mallick, S. K., & McCandless, B. R. A study of catharsis of aggression. *Journal of Personality and Social Psychology,* 1966, *4,* 591–596.

McFall, S. K., & Twentyman, C. T. Four experiments on the relative contributions of rehearsal, modeling, and coaching to assertion training. *Journal of Abnormal Psychology,* 1973, *81,* 199–218.

Montagu, A. *The nature of human aggression.* New York: Oxford University Press, 1976.

Mueller, C., & Donnerstein, E. The effects of humor-induced arousal upon aggressive behavior. *Journal of Research in Personality,* 1977, *11,* 73–82.

O'Leary, M. R., & Dengerink, H. A. Aggression as a function of the intensity and pattern of attack. *Journal of Experimental Research in Personality,* 1973, *7,* 61–70.

Ramirez, J., Bryant, J., & Zillman, D. Effects of erotica on retaliatory behavior as a function of level of prior provocation. *Journal of Personality and Social Psychology,* 1982, *43,* 971–978.

Rogers, R. W. Aggression-inhibiting effects of anonymity to authority and threatened retaliation. *Personality and Social Psychology Bulletin,* 1980, *6,* 315–320.

Shortell, J., Epstein, S., & Taylor, S. P. Instigation to aggression as a function of degree of defeat and the capacity for massive retaliation. *Journal of Personality,* 1970, *38,* 313–328.

Sundel, M., & Sundel, S. *Behavior modification in the human services: A systematic introduction to concepts and applications.* Englewood Cliffs, N.J.: Prentice-Hall, 1982.

Toch, H. *Violent men* (Rev. ed.). Cambridge, Mass.: Schenkman, 1980.

Wingfield, A., & Byrnes, D. L. *The psychology of human memory,* New York: Academic Press, 1981.

Zillman, D. *Hostility and aggression.* Hillsdale, N.J.: Erlbaum, 1979.

Zillmann, D., & Cantor, J. R. Effect of timing of information about mitigating circumstances on emotional responses to provocation and retaliatory behavior. *Journal of Experimental Social Psychology,* 1976, *12,* 38–55.

CRITICAL THINKING QUESTIONS

1. The article presented information on the control of aggression from six areas of research. Select one of them and give an example of how it might be used to help control aggression in the real world.

2. If you were a parent who wanted to prevent your child from being aggressive, how could you use the information from the article to help your parenting strategies?

3. Examine your own assumptions about aggression. Do you believe that it is part of human nature (genetically or biologically determined, that is), or is it due to learning and experience? How do these personally held assumptions influence your view of the purpose of punishment of criminals, in general, and the issue of capital punishment, in particular?

Chapter Eleven

GROUP BEHAVIOR

HOW MUCH OF your life is spent interacting with people in some sort of group? If we use the simple definition of *group* as "two or more individuals that have some unifying relationship," then most likely a significant amount of your time is spent in groups, whether informal (such as two friends trying to decide what to do on a Saturday night) or formal (a work group deciding on a course of action).

Research on group behavior has gone in many directions. The three articles selected for this chapter focus on some of the most commonly investigated topics. Article 31, "Groupthink," examines a set of circumstances found in certain types of groups that may lead them to make very poor decisions, even when they may be composed of very competent individuals. Since the conditions that may contribute to groupthink are not uncommon, the implications of the article for developing more effective groups is clearly important.

Article 32, "The Effect of Threat upon Interpersonal Bargaining," is a classic work. Think of these two possibilities: In the first situation, party 1 has the potential to inflict harm on party 2, but party 2 cannot reciprocate. In the second situation, both parties have equal threat potential—that is, if party 1 inflicts harm, party 2 can reciprocate. Which situation would yield the best outcomes for *both* parties? As the article demonstrates, the answer is not what you might think.

Article 33, "Role of Sex, Gender Roles, and Attraction in Predicting Emergent Leaders," examines another important area of research in group behavior: leadership. Specifically, the article examines some of the factors that may predict who will emerge as the leader of a group. The results of the study suggest that certain individual characteristics may be more important than others in determining leadership ability.

ARTICLE 31 ———————————

Let's suppose that you are in a position of authority. As such, you are called upon to make some very important decisions. You want to make the best possible decisions, so you turn to other people for input. You assemble the best possible set of advisors, people distinguished by their ability and knowledge. Before making a final decision, you meet with them to discuss the options.

Following such a procedure would seem to ensure that the decision you make would be a good one. After all, with your expert resources, how can you go wrong?

Actually, it's not very hard to imagine that the above procedure can go wrong. Working in a group, even when that group is composed of very competent individuals, does not guarantee quality decision making. To the contrary, as the following article by Janis explains, groups may actually make some very poor decisions. The concept of *groupthink,* a term coined by Janis, explains how and why some groups come to make poor decisions, not only failing to recognize that they are poor decisions but actually convincing themselves more and more that they are good decisions. Considering the number of decisions that are made in groups, the process of groupthink, as well as the suggestions for how it can be minimized, are important indeed.

Groupthink

■ Irving L. Janis

The idea of "groupthink" occurred to me while reading Arthur M. Schlesinger's chapters on the Bay of Pigs in *A Thousand Days.* At first I was puzzled: How could bright men like John F. Kennedy and his advisers be taken in by such a stupid, patchwork plan as the one presented to them by the C.I.A. representatives? I began wondering if some psychological contagion of complacency might have interfered with their mental alertness.

I kept thinking about this notion until one day I found myself talking about it in a seminar I was conducting at Yale on the psychology of small groups. I suggested that the poor decision-making performance of those high officials might be akin to the lapses in judgment of ordinary citizens who become more concerned with retaining the approval of the fellow members of their work group than with coming up with good solutions to the tasks at hand.

When I re-read Schlesinger's account I was struck by many further observations that fit into exactly the pattern of concurrence-seeking that has impressed me in my research on other face-to-face groups when a "we" feeling of solidarity is running high. I concluded that a group process was subtly at work in Kennedy's team which prevented the members from debating the real issues posed by the C.I.A.'s plan and from carefully appraising its serious risks.

By now I was sufficiently fascinated by what I called the "groupthink" hypothesis to start looking into similar historic fiascoes. I selected for intensive analysis three that were made during the administrations of three other American presidents: Franklin D. Roosevelt (failure to be prepared for Pearl Harbor), Harry S. Truman (the invasion of North Korea) and Lyndon B. Johnson (escalation of the Vietnam war). Each decision was

Reprinted with permission from *Yale Alumni Magazine,* 1973. Copyright 1973 by Yale Alumni Publications, Inc.

a group product, issuing from a series of meetings held by a small and cohesive group of government officials and advisers. In each case I found the same kind of detrimental group process that was at work in the Bay of Pigs decision.

In my earlier research with ordinary citizens I had been impressed by the effects—both unfavorable and favorable—of the social pressures that develop in cohesive groups: in infantry platoons, air crews, therapy groups, seminars and self-study or encounter groups. Members tend to evolve informal objectives to preserve friendly intra-group relations, and this becomes part of the hidden agenda at their meetings. When conducting research on groups of heavy smokers, for example, at a clinic established to help people stop smoking, I noticed a seemingly irrational tendency for the members to exert pressure on each other to increase their smoking as the time for the final meeting approached. This appeared to be a collusive effort to display mutual dependence and resistance to the termination of the sessions.

Sometimes, even long before the final separation, pressures toward uniformity subverted the fundamental purpose. At the second meeting of one group of smokers, consisting of 12 middle-class American men and women, two of the most dominant members took the position that heavy smoking was an almost incurable addiction. Most of the others soon agreed that nobody could be expected to cut down drastically. One man took issue with this consensus, arguing that he had stopped smoking since joining the group and that everyone else could do the same. His declaration was followed by an angry discussion. Most of the others ganged up against the man who was deviating from the consensus.

At the next meeting the deviant announced that he had made an important decision. "When I joined," he said, "I agreed to follow the two main rules required by the clinic—to make a conscientious effort to stop smoking, and to attend every meeting. But I have learned that you can only follow one of the rules, not both. I will continue to attend every meeting but I have gone back to smoking two packs a day and I won't make

any effort to stop again until after the last meeting." Whereupon the other members applauded, welcoming him back to the fold.

No one mentioned that the whole point of the meetings was to help each person to cut down as rapidly as possible. As a psychological consultant to the group, I tried to call this to the members' attention and so did my collaborator, Dr. Michael Kahn. But the members ignored our comments and reiterated their consensus that heavy smoking was an addiction from which no one would be cured except by cutting down gradually over a long period of time.

This episode—an extreme form of groupthink—was only one manifestation of a general pattern that the group displayed. At every meeting the members were amiable, reasserted their warm feelings of solidarity and sought concurrence on every important topic, with no reappearance of the unpleasant bickering that would spoil the cozy atmosphere. This tendency could be maintained, however, only at the expense of ignoring realistic challenges—like those posed by the psychologists.

The term "groupthink" is of the same order as the words in the "newspeak" vocabulary that George Orwell uses in *1984*—a vocabulary with terms such as "doublethink" and "crimethink." By putting "groupthink" with those Orwellian words, I realize that it takes on an individious connotation. This is intentional: groupthink refers to a deterioration of mental efficiency, reality testing and moral judgment that results from in-group pressures.

When I investigated the Bay of Pigs invasion and other fiascoes, I found that there were at least six major defects in decision-making which contributed to failures to solve problems adequately.

First, the group's discussions were limited to a few alternatives (often only two) without a survey of the full range of alternatives. Second, the members failed to re-examine their initial decision from the standpoint of non-obvious drawbacks that had not been originally considered. Third, they neglected courses of action initially evaluated as unsatisfactory; they almost never discussed whether they had overlooked any non-obvious gains.

Fourth, members made little or no attempt to obtain information from experts who could supply sound estimates of losses and gains to be expected from alternative courses. Fifth, selective bias was shown in the way the members reacted to information and judgments from experts, the media and outside critics; they were only interested in facts and opinions that supported their preferred policy. Finally, they spent little time deliberating how the policy might be hindered by bureaucratic inertia, sabotaged by political opponents or derailed by the accidents that happen to the best of well-laid plans. Consequently, they failed to work out contingency plans to cope with foreseeable setbacks that could endanger their success.

I was surprised by the extent to which the groups involved in these fiascoes adhered to group norms and pressures toward uniformity, even when their policy was working badly and had unintended consequences that disturbed the conscience of the members. Members consider loyalty to the group the highest form of morality. That loyalty requires each member to avoid raising controversial issues, questioning weak arguments or calling a halt to soft-headed thinking.

Paradoxically, soft-headed groups are likely to be extremely hard-hearted toward out-groups and enemies. In dealing with a rival nation, policy-makers constituting an amiable group find it relatively easy to authorize dehumanizing solutions such as large-scale bombings. An affable group of government officials is unlikely to pursue the difficult issues that arise when alternatives to a harsh military solution come up for discussion. Nor are they inclined to raise ethical issues that imply that this "fine group of ours, with its humanitarianism and its high-minded principles, could adopt a course that is inhumane and immoral."

The greater the threat to the self-esteem of the members of a cohesive group, the greater will be their inclination to resort to concurrence-seeking at the expense of critical thinking. Symptoms of groupthink will therefore be found most often when a decision poses a moral dilemma, especially if the most advantageous course requires the policy-makers to violate their own standards of humanitarian behavior. Each member is likely to become more dependent than ever on the in-group for maintaining his self-image as a decent human being and will therefore be more strongly motivated to maintain group unity by striving for concurrence.

Although it is risky to make huge inferential leaps from theory to practice, we should not be inhibited from drawing tentative inferences from these fiascoes. Perhaps the worst mistakes can be prevented if we take steps to avoid the circumstances in which groupthink is most likely to flourish. But all the prescriptive hypotheses that follow must be validated by systematic research before they can be applied with any confidence.

The leader of a policy-forming group should, for example, assign the role of critical evaluator to each member, encouraging the group to give high priority to airing objections and doubts. He should also be impartial at the outset, instead of stating his own preferences and expectations. He should limit his briefings to unbiased statements about the scope of the problem and the limitations of available resources.

The organization should routinely establish several independent planning and evaluation groups to work on the same policy question, each carrying out its deliberations under a different leader.

One or more qualified colleagues within the organization who are not core members of the policy-making group should be invited to each meeting and encouraged to challenge the views of the core members.

At every meeting, at least one member should be assigned the role of devil's advocate, to function like a good lawyer in challenging the testimony of those who advocate the majority position.

Whenever the policy issue involves relations with a rival nation, a sizable block of time should be spent surveying all warning signals from the rivals and constructing alternative scenarios.

After reaching a preliminary consensus the

policy-making group should hold a "second chance" meeting at which all the members are expected to express their residual doubts and to rethink the entire issue. They might take as their model a statement made by Alfred P. Sloan, a former chairman of General Motors, at a meeting of policymakers:

"Gentlemen, I take it we are all in complete agreement on the decision here. Then I propose we postpone further discussion until our next meeting to give ourselves time to develop disagreement and perhaps gain some understanding of what the decision is all about."

It might not be a bad idea for the second-chance meeting to take place in a relaxed atmosphere far from the executive suite, perhaps over drinks. According to a report by Herodotus dating from about 450 B.C., whenever the ancient Persians made a decision following sober deliberations, they would always reconsider the matter under the influence of wine. Tacitus claimed that during Roman times the Germans also had a custom of arriving at each decision twice—once sober, once drunk.

Some institutionalized form of allowing second thoughts to be freely expressed might be remarkably effective for breaking down a false sense of unanimity and related illusions, without endangering anyone's reputation or liver.

PEARL HARBOR: GENIALITY AND SECURITY

On the night of Dec. 6, 1941—just 12 hours before the Japanese struck—Admiral Husband E. Kimmel (Commander in Chief of the Pacific Fleet) attended a dinner party given by his old crony, Rear Admiral H. Fairfax Leary, and his wife. Other members of the in-group of naval commanders and their wives were also present. Seated next to Admiral Kimmel was Fanny Halsey, wife of Admiral Halsey, who had left Hawaii to take his task force to the Far East. Mrs. Halsey said that she was certain the Japanese were going to attack. "She was a brilliant woman," according to Captain Joel Bunkley, who described the party, "but everybody thought she was crazy."

Admiral Leary, at a naval inquiry in 1944, summarized the complacency at that dinner party and at the daily conferences held by Admiral Kimmel during the preceding weeks. When asked whether any thought had been given to the possibility of a surprise attack by the Japanese, he said, "We all felt that the contingency was remote . . . and the feeling strongly existed that the Fleet would have adequate warning of any chance of an air attack." The same attitude was epitomized in testimony given by Captain J. B. Earle, chief of staff, Fourteenth Naval District. "Somehow or other," he said, "we always felt that 'it couldn't happen here.' "

From the consistent testimony given by Admiral Kimmel's advisers, they all acted on the basis of an "unwarranted feeling of immunity from attack," though they had been given a series of impressive warnings that they should be prepared for war with Japan.

Most illuminating of the norm-setting behavior that contributed to the complacency of Kimmel's in-group is a brief exchange between Admiral Kimmel and Lieutenant Commander Layton. Perturbed by the loss of radio contact with the Japanese aircraft carriers, Admiral Kimmel asked Layton on Dec. 1, 1941, to check with the Far East Command for additional information. The next day, discussing the lost carriers again with Layton, he remarked jokingly: "What, you don't know where the carriers are? Do you mean to say that they could be rounding Diamond Head [at Honolulu] and you wouldn't know it?" Layton said he hoped they would be sighted well before that.

This exchange implies an "atmosphere of geniality and security." Having relegated the Japanese threat to the category of laughing matters, the admiral was making it clear that he would be inclined to laugh derisively at anyone who thought otherwise. "I did not at any time suggest," Layton later acknowledged at a Congressional hearing, "that the Japanese carriers were under radio silence approaching Oahu. I wish I had."

But the admiral's foolish little joke may have induced Layton to remain silent about any vague, lingering doubts he may have had. Either man would risk the scornful laughter of the other—whether expressed to his face or behind his back—if he were to express second thoughts such as, "Seriously, though, shouldn't we do something about the slight possibility that those carriers might *really* be headed this way?" Because this ominous inference was never drawn, not a single reconnaissance plane was sent out to the north of the Hawaiian Islands, allowing the Japanese to win the incredible gamble they were taking in trying to send their aircraft carriers within bombing distance of Pearl Harbor without being detected.

That joking exchange was merely the visible part of a huge iceberg of solid faith in Pearl Harbor's invulnerability. If a few warm advocates of preparedness had been within the Navy group, steamed up by the accumulating warning signals, they might have been able to melt it. But they would certainly have had a cold reception. To urge a full alert would have required presenting unwelcome arguments that countered the myth of Pearl Harbor's impregnability. Anyone who was tempted to do so knew that he would be deviating from the group norm: the others were likely to consider him "crazy," just as the in-group regarded Mrs. Halsey at the dinner party on the eve of the disaster when she announced her deviant opinion that the Japanese would attack.

ESCALATION IN VIETNAM: HOW COULD IT HAPPEN?

A highly revealing episode occurred soon after Robert McNamara told a Senate committee some impressive facts about the ineffectiveness of the bombings. President Johnson made a number of bitter comments about McNamara's statement. "That military genius, McNamara, has gone dovish on me," he complained to one Senator. To someone in his White House staff he spoke even more heatedly, accusing McNamara of playing into the hands of the enemy. He drew the analogy of "a man trying to sell his house while one of his sons went to the prospective buyer to point out that there were leaks in the basement."

This strongly suggests that Johnson regarded his in-group of policy advisers as a family and its leading dissident member as an irresponsible son who was sabotaging the family's interest. Underlying this revealing imagery are two implicit assumptions that epitomize groupthink: We are a good group, so any deceitful acts that we perpetrate are fully justified. Anyone who is unwilling to distort the truth to help us is disloyal.

This is only one of the many examples of how groupthink was manifested in Johnson's inner circle.

A PERFECT FIASCO: THE BAY OF PIGS

Why did President Kennedy's main advisers, whom he had selected as core members of his team, fail to pursue the issues sufficiently to discover the shaky ground on which the faulty assumptions of the Cuban invasion plan rested? Why didn't they pose a barrage of penetrating and embarrassing questions to the representatives of the C.I.A. and the Joint Chiefs of Staff? Why were they taken in by the incomplete and inconsistent answers they were given in response to the relatively few critical questions they raised?

Schlesinger says that "for all the utter irrationality with which retrospect endowed the project, it had a certain queer logic at the time as it emerged from the bowels of government." Why? What was the source of the "queer logic" with which the plan was endowed? If the available accounts describe the deliberations accurately, many typical symptoms of groupthink can be discerned among the members of the Kennedy team: an illusion of invulnerability, a collective effort to rationalize their decision, an unquestioned belief in the group's inherent morality, a stereotyped view of enemy leaders as too evil to warrant genuine attempts to negotiate, and the emergence of self-appointed mind-guards.

Robert Kennedy, for example, who had been constantly informed about the Cuban invasion plan, asked Schlesinger privately why he was opposed. The President's brother listened coldly and then said: "You may be right or you may be wrong, but the President has made his mind up.

Don't push it any further. Now is the time for everyone to help him all they can."

Here is a symptom of groupthink, displayed by a highly intelligent man whose ethical code committed him to freedom of dissent.

Robert Kennedy was functioning in a self-appointed role that I call being a "mind-guard." Just as a bodyguard protects the President and other high officials from physical harm, a mind-guard protects them from thoughts that might damage their confidence in the soundness of the policies which they are about to launch.

CRITICAL THINKING QUESTIONS

1. How common is groupthink? Do you think that the conditions that give rise to groupthink are relatively rare or relatively common? Cite additional examples of decisions that may have been influenced by groupthink.

2. Have you ever been involved in a group that experienced some sort of groupthink process? Describe the situation and discuss the process in terms of groupthink.

3. If groupthink is common, then it would be useful if people were made aware of how it works. Should the conditions of groupthink, as well as how it can be prevented, be taught to leaders and potential leaders? How could this be accomplished?

4. The article gave some suggestions as to how groupthink could be prevented or at least minimized. Would all leaders be equally open to following these suggestions? Or might individual characteristics influence how open various leaders might be?

ARTICLE 32 _____

Whenever two or more individuals act as a group, a central part of the interaction may involve trying to reach some agreements about an issue or activity. When the group consists of individuals or nations, reaching agreement is often a major concern.

Bargaining is one form that such negotiations take. The bargaining may be about something small and be informal in style, such as a couple deciding on which movie to see, or it may be major and formal, such as two nations trying to reach an agreement on nuclear arms control. In either case, central to the bargaining is the belief by both parties that reaching a mutually agreed upon solution will possibly benefit both of them.

Two broad approaches to bargaining are cooperation and competition. In a *competitive* situation, individuals or groups view the situation in "win-lose" terms: I want to win, and it most likely will be at your expense. In a *cooperative* arrangement, the situation is more likely to be viewed as a "win-win" opportunity: We can both get something good out of this; neither one has to lose. Other things being equal, a cooperative strategy is more likely to ensure a good outcome for all concerned. But is that the strategy most likely to be used? Or do individuals and groups tend to use competitive strategies instead, even if it might not ultimately be in their best interest to do so?

The following classic contribution by Deutsch and Krauss examines the effect of threat on interpersonal bargaining. One major finding of the study is that the presence of threat, as well as whether only one or both parties are capable of threat, has a major impact on the outcome of the bargaining situation. Common sense might suggest that if my opponent has some threat that he or she can use against me, then I would be better off having the same level of threat to use against him or her, rather than having no threat to retaliate with. The findings of the study do not confirm this expectation, however, and may suggest a rethinking of the use of threat and power in real-world negotiations.

The Effect of Threat upon Interpersonal Bargaining

■ Morton Deutsch and Robert M. Krauss

A bargain is defined in *Webster's Unabridged Dictionary* as "an agreement between parties settling what each shall give and receive in a transaction between them"; it is further specified that a bargain is "an agreement or compact viewed as advantageous or the reverse." When the term "agreement" is broadened to include tacit, infor-

mal agreements as well as explicit agreements, it is evident that bargains and the processes involved in arriving at bargains ("bargaining") are pervasive characteristics of social life.

The definition of bargain fits under sociological definitions of the term "social norm." In this light, the experimental study of the bargaining

Reprinted from the *Journal of Abnormal and Social Psychology*, 1960, *61*, 181–189.

process and of bargaining outcomes provides a means for the laboratory study of the development of certain types of social norms. But unlike many other types of social situations, bargaining situations have certain distinctive features that make it relevant to consider the conditions that determine whether or not a social norm will develop as well as those that determine the nature of the social norm if it develops. Bargaining situations highlight the possibility that, even where cooperation would be mutually advantageous, shared purposes may not develop, agreement may not be reached, and interaction may be regulated antagonistically rather than normatively.

The essential features of a bargaining situation exist when:

1. Both parties perceive that there is the possibility of reaching an agreement in which each party would be better off, or no worse off, than if no agreement were reached.

2. Both parties perceive that there is more than one such agreement that could be reached.

3. Both parties perceive each other to have conflicting preferences or opposed interests with regard to the different agreements that might be reached.

Everyday examples of bargaining include such situations as: the buyer-seller relationship when the price is not fixed, the husband and wife who want to spend an evening out together but have conflicting preferences about where to go, union-management negotiations, drivers who meet at an intersection when there is no clear right of way, disarmament negotiations.

In terms of our prior conceptualization of cooperation and competition (Deutsch, 1949) bargaining is thus a situation in which the participants have mixed motives toward one another: on the one hand, each has interest in cooperating so that they reach an agreement; on the other hand, they have competitive interests concerning the nature of the agreement they reach. In effect, to reach agreement the cooperative interest of the bargainers must be strong enough to overcome their competitive interests. However, agreement is not only contingent upon the *motivational* balances of cooperative to competitive in-

terests but also upon the situational and *cognitive* factors which facilitate or hinder the recognition or invention of a bargaining agreement that reduces the opposition of interest and enhances the mutuality of interest.[1]

These considerations lead to the formulation of two general, closely related propositions about the likelihood that a bargaining agreement will be reached.

1. Bargainers are more likely to reach an agreement, the stronger are their cooperative interests in comparison with their competitive interests.

2. Bargainers are more likely to reach an agreement, the more resources they have available for recognizing or inventing potential bargaining agreements and for communicating to one another once a potential agreement has been recognized or invented.

From these two basic propositions and additional hypotheses concerning conditions that determine the strengths of the cooperative and competitive interests and the amount of available resources, we believe it is possible to explain the ease or difficulty of arriving at a bargaining agreement. We shall not present a full statement of these hypotheses here but turn instead to a description of an experiment that relates to Proposition 1.

The experiment was concerned with the effect of the availability of threat upon bargaining in a two-person experimental bargaining game.[2] Threat is defined as the expression of an intention to do something detrimental to the interests of another. Our experiment was guided by two assumptions about threat:

1. If there is a conflict of interest and one person is able to threaten the other, he will tend to use the threat in an attempt to force the other person to yield. This tendency should be stronger, the more irreconcilable the conflict is perceived to be.

2. If a person uses threat in an attempt to intimidate another, the threatened person (if he considers himself to be of equal or superior status) would feel hostility toward the threatener and tend to respond with counterthreat and/or in-

creased resistance to yielding. We qualify this assumption by stating that the tendency to resist should be greater, the greater the perceived probability and magnitude of detriment to the other and the less the perceived probability and magnitude of detriment to the potential resister from the anticipated resistance to yielding.

The second assumption is based upon the view that when resistance is not seen to be suicidal or useless, to allow oneself to be intimidated, particularly by someone who does not have the right to expect deferential behavior, is to suffer a loss of social face and, hence, of self-esteem; and that the culturally defined way of maintaining self-esteem in the face of attempted intimidation is to engage in a contest for supremacy vis-à-vis the power to intimidate or, minimally, to resist intimidation. Thus, in effect, the use of threat (and if it is available to be used, there will be a tendency to use it) should strengthen the competitive interests of the bargainers in relationship to one another by introducing or enhancing the competitive struggle for self-esteem. Hence, from Proposition 1, it follows that the availability of a means of threat should make it more difficult for the bargainers to reach agreement (providing that the threatened person has some means of resisting the threat). The preceding statement is relevant to the comparison of both of our experimental conditions of threat, bilateral and unilateral (described below), with our experimental condition of nonthreat. We hypothesize that a bargaining agreement is more likely to be achieved when neither party can threaten the other, than when one or both parties can threaten the other.

Consider now the situations of bilateral threat and unilateral threat. For several reasons, a situation of bilateral threat is probably less conducive to agreement than is a condition of unilateral threat. First, the sheer likelihood that a threat will be made is greater when two people rather than one have the means of making the threat. Secondly, once a threat is made in the bilateral case it is likely to evoke counterthreat. Withdrawal of threat in the face of counterthreat probably in-

volves more loss of face (for reasons analogous to those discussed in relation to yielding to intimidation) than does withdrawal of threat in the face of resistance to threat. Finally, in the unilateral case, although the person without the threat potential can resist and not yield to the threat, his position vis-à-vis the other is not so strong as the position of the threatened person in the bilateral case. In the unilateral case, the threatened person may have a worse outcome than the other whether he resists or yields; while in the bilateral case, the threatened person is sure to have a worse outcome if he yields but he may insure that he does not have a worse outcome if he does not yield.

METHOD

Procedure

Subjects (*Ss*) were asked to imagine that they were in charge of a trucking company, carrying merchandise over a road to a destination. For each trip completed they made $.60, minus their operating expenses. Operating expenses were calculated at the rate of one cent per second. So, for example, if it took 37 seconds to complete a particular trip, the player's profit would be $.60 − $.37 or a net profit of $.23 for that particular trip.

Each *S* was assigned a name, Acme or Bolt. As the "road map" (see Figure 1) indicates, both players start from separate points and go to separate destinations. At one point their paths cross. This is the section of road labeled "one lane road," which is only one lane wide, so that two trucks, heading in opposite directions, could not pass each other. If one backs up the other can go forward, or both can back up, or both can sit there head-on without moving.

There is another way for each *S* to reach the destination on the map, labeled the "alternate route." The two players' paths do not cross on this route, but the alternative is 56% longer than the main route. *Ss* were told that they could expect to lose at least $.10 each time they used the alternate route.

At either end of the one-lane section there is a gate that is under the control of the player to

FIGURE 1 / Subject's road map

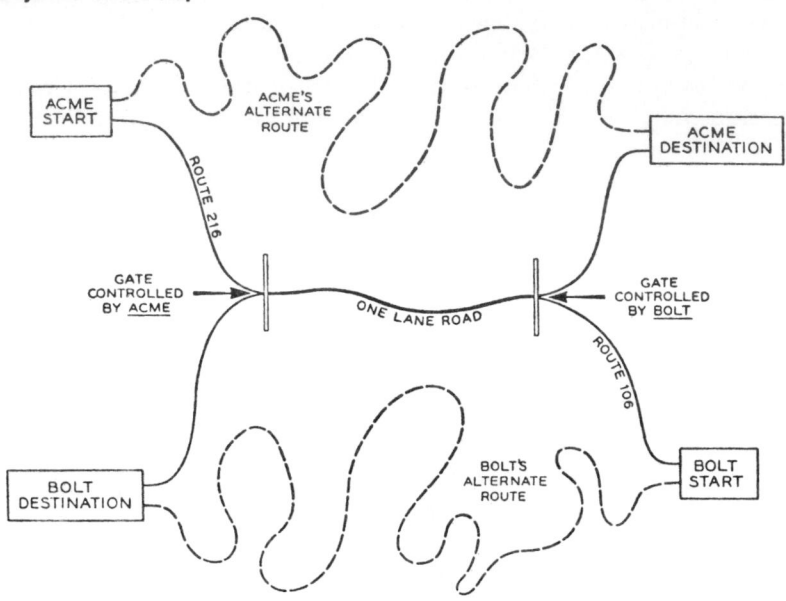

whose starting point it is closest. By closing the gate, one player can prevent the other from traveling over that section of the main route. The use of the gate provides the threat potential in this game. In the bilateral threat potential condition (Two Gates) both players had gates under their control. In a second condition of unilateral threat (One Gate) Acme had control of a gate but Bolt did not. In a third condition (No Gates) neither player controlled a gate.

*S*s played the game seated in separate booths placed so that they could not see each other but could see the experimenter (*E*). Each *S* had a "control panel" mounted on a 12″ × 18″ × 12″ sloping-front cabinet (see Figure 2). The apparatus consisted essentially of a reversible impulse computer that was pulsed by a recycling timer. When the *S* wanted to move her truck forward she threw a key that closed a circuit pulsing the "add" coil of the impulse counter mounted on her control panel. As the counter cumulated, *S* was able to determine her "position" by relating the number on her counter to reference numbers that had been written in on her road map. Similarly, when she wished to reverse, she would throw a switch that activated the "subtract" coil of her counter,

thus subtracting from the total on the counter each time the timer cycled.

S's counter was connected in parallel to counters on the other *S*'s panel and on *E*'s panel. Thus each player had two counters on her panel, one representing her own position and the other representing the other player's. Provision was made in construction of the apparatus to permit cutting the other player's counter out of the circuit, so that each *S* knew only the position of her own truck. This was done in the present experiment. Experiments now in progress are studying the effects of knowledge of the other person's position and other aspects of interpersonal communication upon the bargaining process.

The only time one player definitely knew the other player's position was when they had met head-on on the one-way section of road. This was indicated by a traffic light mounted on the panel. When this light was on, neither player could move forward unless the other moved back. The gates were controlled by toggle switches and panel-mounted indicator lights showed, for both *S*s, whether each gate was open or closed.

The following "rules of the game" were stated to the *S*s:

FIGURE 2 / Subject's control panel

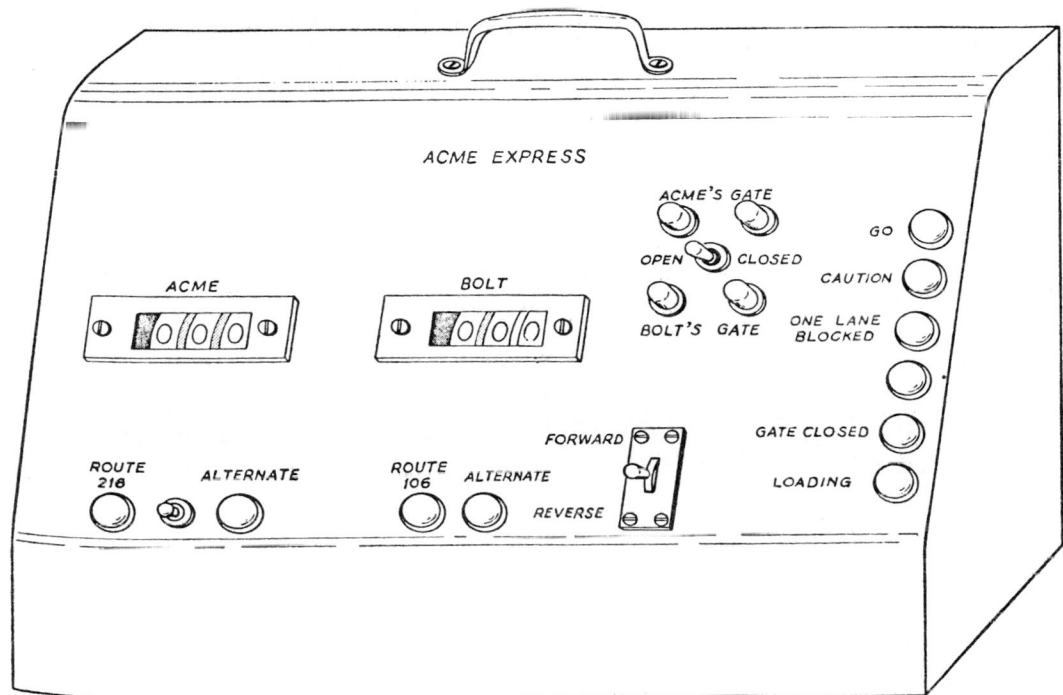

1. A player who started out on one route and wished to switch to the other route could only do so after first reversing and going back to the start position. Direct transfer from one route to the other was not permitted except at the start position.

2. In the conditions where *S*s had gates, they were permitted to close the gates no matter where they were on the main route, so long as they were on the main route (i.e., they were not permitted to close the gate while on the alternate route or after having reached their destinations). However, *S*s were permitted to open their gates at any point in the game.

*S*s were taken through a number of practice exercises to familiarize them with the game. In the first trial they were made to meet head-on on the one-lane path; Acme was then told to back up until she was just off the one-lane path and Bolt was told to go forward. After Bolt had gone through the one-lane path, Acme was told to go

forward. Each continued going forward until each arrived at her destination. The second practice trial was the same as the first except that Bolt rather than Acme backed up after meeting head-on. In the next practice trial, one of the players was made to wait just before the one-way path while the other traversed it and then was allowed to continue. In the next practice trial, one player was made to take the alternate route and the other was made to take the main route. Finally, in the bilateral and unilateral threat conditions the use of the gate was illustrated (by having the player get on the main route, close the gate, and then go back and take the alternate route). The *S*s were told explicitly, with emphasis, that they did *not* have to use the gate. Before each trial in the game the gate or gates were in the open position.

The instructions stressed an individualistic motivation orientation. *S*s were told to try to earn as much money for themselves as possible and to have no interest in whether the other player made money or lost money. They were given $4.00 in poker chips to represent their working capital and told that after each trial they would be given "money" if they made a profit or that "money" would be taken from them if they lost (i.e., took more than 60 seconds to complete their trip). The profit or loss of each *S* was announced so that both *S*s could hear the announcement after each trial. Each pair of *S*s played a total of 20 trials; on all trials, they started off together. In other words each trial presented a repetition of the same bargaining problem. In cases where *S*s lost their working capital before the 20 trials were completed, additional chips were given them. *S*s were aware that their monetary winnings and losses were to be imaginary and that no money would change hands as a result of the experiment.

Subjects

Sixteen pairs of *S*s were used in each of the three experimental conditions. The *S*s were female clerical and supervisory personnel of the New Jersey Bell Telephone Company who volunteered to participate during their working day.[3] Their ages ranged from 20 to 39, with a mean of 26.2. All were naive to the purpose of the experiment. By staggering the arrival times and choosing girls from different locations, we were able to insure that the *S*s did not know with whom they were playing.

Data Recorded

Several types of data were collected. We obtained a record of the profit or loss of each *S* on each trial. We also obtained a detailed recording of the actions taken by each *S* during the course of a trial. For this purpose, we used an Esterline-Angus model AW Operations Recorder which enabled us to obtain a "log" of each move each *S* made during the game (e.g., whether and when she took the main or alternate route; when she went forward, backward, or remained still; when she closed and opened the gate; when she arrived at her destination).

RESULTS[4]

The best single measure of the difficulty experienced by the bargainers in reaching an agreement is the sum of each pair's profits (or losses) on a given trial. The higher the sum of the payoffs to the two players on a given trial, the less time it took them to arrive at a procedure for sharing the one-lane path of the main route. (It was, of course, possible for one or both of the players to decide to take the alternate route so as to avoid a protracted stalemate during the process of bargaining. This, however, always results in at least a \$.20 smaller joint payoff if only one player took the alternate route, than an optimally arrived at agreement concerning the use of the one-way path.) Figure 3 presents the medians of the summed payoffs (i.e., Acme's plus Bolt's) for all pairs in each of the three experimental conditions over the 20 trials.[5] These striking results indicate that agreement was least difficult to arrive at in the no threat condition, was more difficult to arrive at in the unilateral threat condition, and exceedingly difficult or impossible to arrive at in the bilateral threat condition (see also Table 1).

Examination of Figure 3 suggests that learning occurred during the 20 trials: the summed payoffs for pairs of *S*s tend to improve as the number of trials increases. This suggestion is confirmed by an analysis of variance of the slopes for the summed payoffs[6] over the 20 trials for each of the 16 pairs in each of the 3 experimental treatments. The results of this analysis indicate that the slopes are significantly greater than zero for the unilateral

FIGURE 3 / Median joint payoff (Acme + Bolt) over trials

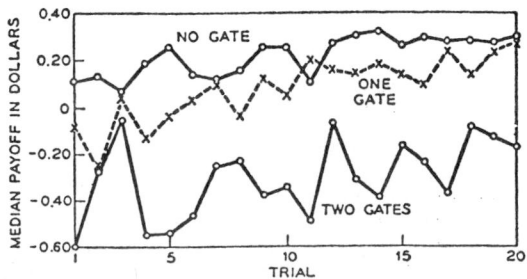

TABLE 1 / Mean Payoffs Summated Over the Twenty Trials

Variable	Means			Statistical Comparisons: p values[a]			
	(1) No Threat	(2) Unilateral Threat	(3) Bilateral Threat	Overall	(1)ᵘᵖ (2)	(1)ᵢₐᵢ(0)	(2)ᵥⱼ.(0)
Summed Payoffs (Acme + Bolt)	203.31	− 405.88	− 875.12	.01	.01	.01	.05
Acme's Payoff	122.44	− 118.56	− 406.56	.01	.10	.01	.05
Bolt's Payoff	80.88	− 287.31	− 468.56	.01	.01	.01	.20
Absolute Differences in Payoff (A − B)	125.94	294.75	315.25	.05	.05	.01	ns

[a]Evaluation of the significance of overall variation between conditions is based on an F test with 2 and 45 df. Comparisons between treatments are based on a two-tailed t test.

threat ($p < .01$) and the no threat ($p < .02$) conditions; for the bilateral threat condition, the slope does not reach statistical significance ($.10 < p < .20$). The data indicate that the pairs in the no threat condition started off at a fairly high level but, even so, showed some improvement over the 20 trials; the pairs in the unilateral threat condition started off low and, having considerable opportunity for improvement, used their opportunity; the pairs in the bilateral threat condition, on the other hand, did not benefit markedly from repeated trials.

Figure 4 compares Acme's median profit in the three experimental conditions over the 20 trials; while Figure 5 compares Bolt's profit in the three conditions. (In the unilateral threat condition, it was Acme who controlled a gate and Bolt who did

not.) Bolt's as well as Acme's outcome is somewhat better in the no threat condition than in the unilateral threat condition; Acme's, as well as Bolt's, outcome is clearly worst in the bilateral threat condition (see Table 1 also). However, Figure 6 reveals that Acme does somewhat better than Bolt in the unilateral condition. Thus, if threat-potential exists within a bargaining relationship it is better to possess it oneself than to have the other party possess it. However, it is even better for neither party to possess it. Moreover, Figure 5 shows that Bolt is better off not having than having a gate even when Acme has a gate: Bolt tends to do better in the unilateral threat condition than in the bilateral threat condition.

The size of the absolute discrepancy between the payoffs of the two players in each pair provides

FIGURE 5 / Bolt's median payoff

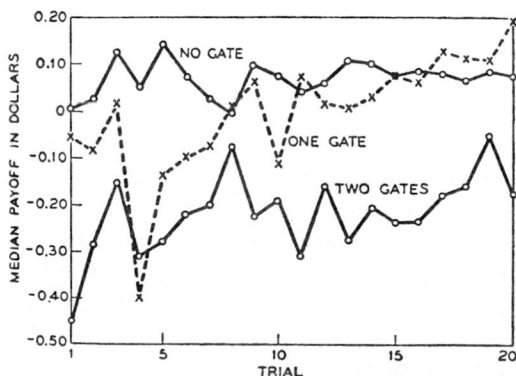

FIGURE 4 / Acme's median payoff

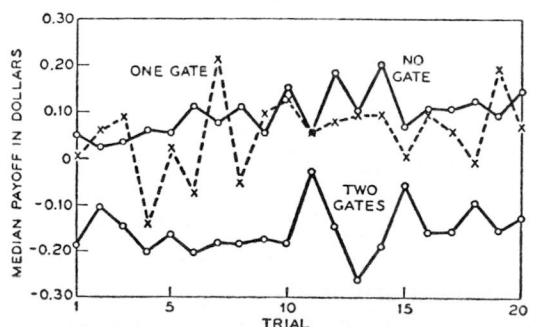

FIGURE 6 / Acme's and Bolt's median payoffs in unilateral threat condition

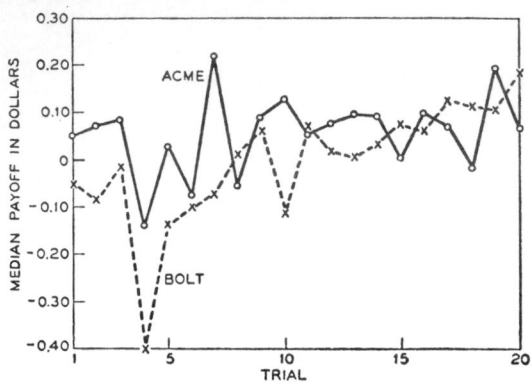

FIGURE 7 / Median absolute differences in payoff

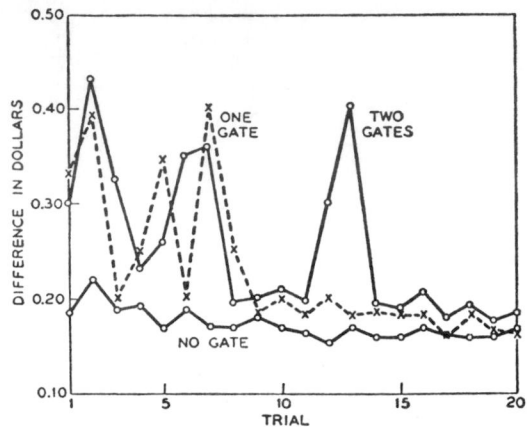

a measure of the confusion or difficulty in predicting what the other player was going to do. Thus, a large absolute discrepancy might indicate that after one player had gone through the one-way path and left it open, the other player continued to wait; or it might indicate that one player continued to wait at a closed gate hoping the other player would open it quickly but the other player did not; etc. Figure 7 indicates that the discrepancy between players in the no threat condition is initially small and remains small for the 20 trials. For the players in both the bilateral and unilateral threat conditions, the discrepancy is initially relatively larger; but it decreases more noticeably in the unilateral threat condition by the tenth trial and, therefore, is consistently smaller than in the bilateral condition.

By way of concrete illustration, we present a synopsis of the game for one pair in each of three experimental treatments.

No Threat Condition

Trial 1   The players met in the center of the one-way section. After some back-and-forth movement Bolt reversed to the end of the one-way section, allowing Acme to pass through, and then proceeded forward herself.

Trial 2   They again met at the center of the one-way path. This time, after moving back and forth deadlocked for some time, Bolt reversed to "start" and took the alternate route to her destination, thus leaving Acme free to go through on the main route.

Trial 3   The players again met at the center of the one-way path. This time, however, Acme reversed to the beginning of the path, allowing Bolt to go through to her destination. Then Acme was able to proceed forward on the main route.

Trial 5   Both players elected to take the alternate route to their destinations.

Trial 7   Both players took the main route and met in the center. They waited, deadlocked, for a considerable time. Then Acme reversed to the end of the one-way path allowing Bolt to go through, then proceeded through to her destination.

Trials 10–20   Acme and Bolt fall into a pattern of alternating who is to go first on the one-way section. There is no deviation from this pattern.

The only other pattern that emerges in this condition is one in which one player dominates the other. That is, one player consistently goes first on the one-way section and the other player consistently yields.

Unilateral Threat Condition

Trial 1   Both players took the main route and met in the center of it. Acme immediately closed the gate, reversed to "start," and took the alternate route to her destination. Bolt waited for a few seconds, at the closed gate, then reversed and took the alternate route.

Trial 2   Both players took the main route and met in the center. After moving back and forth deadlocked for about 15 seconds, Bolt reversed to the beginning of the one-way path, allowed Acme to pass, and then proceeded forward to her destination.

Trial 3   Both players started out on the main route, meeting in the center. After moving back and forth deadlocked for a while, Acme closed her gate, reversed to "start," and took the alternate route. Bolt, meanwhile, waited at the closed gate. When Acme arrived at her destination she opened the gate, and Bolt went through to complete her trip.

Trial 5   Both players took the main route, meeting at the center of the one-way section. Acme immediately closed her gate, reversed, and took the alternate route. Bolt waited at the gate for about 10 second, then reversed and took the alternate route to her destination.

Trial 10   Both players took the main route and met in the center. Acme closed her gate, reversed, and took the alternate route. Bolt remained waiting at the closed gate. After Acme arrived at her destination, she opened the gate and Bolt completed her trip.

Trial 15   Acme took the main route to her destination and Bolt took the alternate route.

Trials 17–20   Both players took the main route and met in the center. Bolt waited a few seconds, then reversed to the end of the one-way section allowing Acme to go through. Then Bolt proceeded forward to her destination.

Other typical patterns that developed in this experimental condition included an alternating pattern similar to that described in the no threat condition, a dominating pattern in which Bolt would select the alternate route leaving Acme free to use the main route unobstructed, and a pattern in which Acme would close her gate and then take the alternate route, also forcing Bolt to take the alternate route.

Bilateral Threat Condition

Trial 1   Acme took the main route and Bolt took the alternate route.

Trial 2   Both players took the main route and met head-on. Bolt closed her gate. Acme waited a few seconds, then closed her gate, reversed to "start," then went forward again to the closed gate. Acme reversed and took the alternate route. Bolt again reversed, then started on the alternate route. Acme opened her gate and Bolt reversed to "start" and went to her destination on the main route.

Trial 3   Acme took the alternate route to her destination. Bolt took the main route and closed her gate before entering the one-way section.

Trial 5   Both players took the main route and met head-on. After about 10 seconds spent backing up and going forward, Acme closed her gate, reversed, and took the alternate route. After waiting a few seconds, Bolt did the same.

Trials 8–10   Both players started out on the main route, immediately closed their gates, reversed to "start," and took the alternate route to their destinations.

Trial 15   Both players started out on the main route and met head-on. After some jockeying for position, Acme closed her gate, reversed, and took the alternate route to her destination. After waiting at the gate for a few seconds, Bolt reversed to "start" and took the alternate route to her destination.

Trials 19–20   Both players started out on the main route, immediately closed their gates, reversed to "start," and took the alternate routes to their destinations.

Other patterns that emerged in the bilateral threat condition included alternating first use of the one-way section, one player's dominating the other on first use of the one-way section, and another dominating pattern in which one player consistently took the main route while the other consistently took the alternate route.

DISCUSSION

From our view of bargaining as a situation in which both cooperative and competitive tendencies are present and acting upon the individual, it is relevant to inquire as to the conditions under which a stable agreement of any form develops. However, implicit in most economic models of bargaining (e.g., Stone, 1958; Zeuthen, 1930) is the assumption that the cooperative interests of the bargainers are sufficiently strong to insure that some form of mutually satisfactory agreement will be reached. For this reason, such models have focused upon the form of the agreement reached by the bargainers. Siegel and Fouraker (1960) report a series of bargaining experiments quite different in structure from ours in which only one of many pairs of Ss were unable to reach agreement. Siegel and Fouraker explain this rather startling result as follows:

> Apparently the disruptive forces which lead to the rupture of some negotiations were at least partially controlled in our sessions. . . .
> Some negotiations collapse when one party becomes incensed at the other, and henceforth strives to maximize his opponent's dis-

pleasure rather than his own satisfaction. . . . Since it is difficult to transmit insults by means of quantitative bids, such disequilibrating behavior was not induced in the present studies. If subjects were allowed more latitude in their communications and interactions, the possibility of an affront-offense-punitive behavior sequence might be increased (p. 100).

In our experimental bargaining situation, the availability of threat clearly made it more difficult for bargainers to reach a mutually profitable agreement. These results, we believe, reflect psychological tendencies that are not confined to our bargaining situation: the tendency to use threat (if the means for threatening is available) in an attempt to force the other person to yield, when the other is seen as obstructing one's path; the tendency to respond with counterthreat or increased resistance to attempts at intimidation. How general are these tendencies? What conditions are likely to elicit them? Answers to these questions are necessary before our results can be generalized to other situations.

Dollard, Doob, Miller, Mowrer, and Sears (1939) have cited a variety of evidence to support the view that aggression (i.e., the use of threat) is a common reaction to a person who is seen as the agent of frustration. There seems to be little reason to doubt that the use of threat is a frequent reaction to interpersonal impasses. However, everyday observation indicates that threat does not inevitably occur when there is an interpersonal impasse. We would speculate that it is most likely to occur: when the threatener has no positive interest in the other person's welfare (he is either egocentrically or competitively related to the other); when the threatener believes that the other has no positive interest in his welfare; and when the threatener anticipates either that his threat will be effective or, if ineffective, will not worsen his situation because he expects the worst to happen if he does not use his threat. We suggest that these conditions were operative in our experiment; Ss were either egocentrically or competitively oriented to one another[7] and they felt that they would not be worse off by the use of threat.

Everyday observation suggests that the tendency to respond with counterthreat or increased resistance to attempts at intimidation is also a common occurrence. We believe that introducing threat into a bargaining situation affects the meaning of yielding. Although we have no data to support this interpretation directly, we will attempt to justify it on the basis of some additional assumptions.

Goffman (1955) has pointed out the pervasive significance of "face" in the maintenance of the social order. In this view, self-esteem is a socially validated system that grows out of the acceptance by others of the claim for deference, prestige, and recognition that a person presents in his behavior toward others. Since the rejection of such a claim would be perceived (by the recipient) as directed against his self-esteem, he must react against it rather than accept it in order to maintain the integrity of his self-esteem system.

One may view the behavior of our Ss as an attempt to make claims upon the other, an attempt to develop a set of shared expectations as to what each was entitled to. Why then did the Ss' reactions differ so markedly as a function of the availability of threat? The explanation lies, we believe, in the cultural interpretation of yielding (to a peer or subordinate) under duress, as compared to giving in without duress. The former, we believe, is perceived as a negatively valued form of behavior, with negative implications for the self-image of the person who so behaves. At least partly, this is so because the locus of causality is perceived to be outside the person's voluntary control. No such evaluation, however, need be placed on the behavior of one who "gives in" in a situation where no threat or duress is a factor. Rather, we should expect the culturally defined evaluation of such a person's behavior to be one of "reasonableness" or "maturity," because the source of the individual's behavior is perceived to lie within his own control.

Our discussion so far has suggested that the psychological factors which operate in our experimental bargaining situation are to be found in many real-life bargaining situations. However, it is well to recognize some unique features of our experimental game. First, the bargainers had no opportunity to communicate verbally with one another. Prior research on the role of communication in trust (Deutsch 1958, 1960; Loomis, 1959) suggests that the opportunity for communication would have made reaching an agreement easier for individualistically-oriented bargainers. This same research (Deutsch, 1960) indicates, however, that communication may not be effective between competitively oriented bargainers. This possibility was expressed spontaneously by a number of our Ss in a post-game interview.

Another characteristic of our bargaining game is that the passage of time, without coming to an agreement, is costly to the players. There are, of course, bargaining situations in which lack of agreement may simply preserve the *status quo* without any worsening of the bargainers' respective situations. This is the case in the typical bilateral monopoly case, where the buyer and seller are unable to agree upon a price (e.g., see Siegel & Fouraker, 1960). In other sorts of bargaining situations, however, (e.g., labor-management negotiations during a strike, international negotiations during an expensive cold war) the passage of time may play an important role. In our experiment, we received the impression that the meaning of time changed as time passed without the bargainers reaching an agreement. Initially, the passage of time seemed to place the players under pressure to come to an agreement before their costs mounted sufficiently to destroy their profit. With the continued passage of time, however, their mounting losses strengthened their resolution not to yield to the other player. They comment: "I've lost so much, I'll be damned if I give in now. At least I'll have the satisfaction of doing better than she does." The mounting losses and continued deadlock seemed to change the game from a mixed motive into a predominantly competitive situation.

It is, of course, hazardous to generalize from a laboratory experiment to the complex problems of the real world. But our experiment and the theoretical ideas underlying it can perhaps serve to emphasize some notions which, otherwise, have an intrinsic plausibility. In brief, these are that there is more safety in cooperative than in competitive coexistence, that it is dangerous for bargainers to have weapons, and that it is possibly even more dangerous for a bargainer to have the capacity to retaliate in kind than not to have this capacity when the other bargainer has a weapon. This last statement assumes that the one who yields has more of his values preserved by accepting the agreement preferred by the other than by extended conflict. Of course, in some bargaining situations in the real world, the loss incurred by yielding may exceed the losses due to extended conflict.

SUMMARY

The nature of bargaining situations was discussed. Two general propositions about the conditions affecting the likelihood of a bargaining agreement were presented. The effects of the availability of threat upon interpersonal bargaining were investigated experimentally in a two-person bargaining game. Three experimental conditions were employed: no threat (neither player could threaten the other), unilateral threat (only one of the players had a means of threat available to her), and bilateral threat (both players could threaten each other). The results indicated that the difficulty in reaching an agreement and the amount of (imaginary) money lost, individually as well as collectively, was greatest in the bilateral and next greatest in the unilateral threat condition. Only in the no threat condition did the players make an overall profit. In the unilateral threat condition, the player with the threat capability did better than the player without the threat capability. However, comparing the bilateral and unilateral threat conditions, the results also indicate that when facing a player who had threat capability one was better off *not* having than having the capacity to retaliate in kind.

REFERENCES

Deutsch, M. A theory of cooperation and competition. *Hum. Relat.*, 1949, *2*, 129–152.

Deutsch, M. Trust and suspicion. *J. conflict Resolut.*, 1958, *2*, 265–279.

Deutsch, M. The effect of motivational orientation upon trust and suspicion. *Hum. Relat.*, 1960, *13*, 123–140.

Dollard, J., Doob, L. W., Miller, N. E., Mowrer, O. H., & Sears, R. H. *Frustration and aggression.* New Haven: Yale Univer. Press, 1939.

Goffman, E. On face-work, *Psychiatry,* 1955, *18*, 213–231.

Loomis, J. L. Communication, the development of trust and cooperative behavior. *Hum. Relat.*, 1959, *12*, 305–315.

Schelling, T. C. Bargaining, communication and limited war. *J. conflict Resolut.*, 1957, *1*, 19–38.

Schelling, T. C. The strategy of conflict: Prospectus for the reorientation of game theory. *J. conflict Resolut.*, 1958, *2*, 203–264.

Siegel, S., & Fouraker, L. E. *Bargaining and group decision making.* New York: McGraw-Hill, 1960.

Stone, J. J. An experiment in bargaining games. *Econometrica*, 1958, *26*, 286–296.

Zeuthen, F. *Problems of monopoly and economic warfare.* London: Routledge, 1930.

NOTES

1. Schelling in a series of stimulating papers on bargaining (1957, 1958) has also stressed the "mixed motive" character of bargaining situations and has analyzed some of the cognitive factors which determine agreements.
2. The game was conceived and originated by M. Deutsch; R. M. Krauss designed and constructed the apparatus employed in the experiment.
3. We are indebted to the New Jersey Bell Telephone Company for their cooperation in providing Ss and facilities for the experiment.
4. We are indebted to M. J. R. Healy for suggestions concerning the statistical analysis of our data.
5. Medians are used in graphic presentation of our results because the wide variability of means makes inspection cumbersome.
6. A logarithmic transformation of the summed payoffs on each trial for each pair was made before computing the slopes for a given pair.
7. A post-experimental questionnaire indicated that, in all three experimental conditions, the Ss were most strongly motivated to win money, next most strongly motivated to do better than the other player, next most motivated to "have fun," and were very little or not at all motivated to help the other player.

CRITICAL THINKING QUESTIONS

1. For many years, the Mutually Assured Destruction (MAD) policy has defined U.S. nuclear strategy. That is, nuclear war is to be prevented by the threat of assured destruction of the aggressor nation. What might be the implications of this study for the nuclear policies of nations?

2. The best performance in this study was obtained in the no-threat condition; the unilateral threat condition in turn produced better results than the bilateral threat condition, which did the worst. To what extent are these findings generalizable to other situations? In some situations, might it be best to have bilateral threat instead of unilateral threat? What variables might be important in determining when each would be preferred?

3. In an area such as international relations, how can the existence of threat be reduced? What role may communication play in the process?

ADDITIONAL RELATED READINGS

Moln, L. (1981). The conversion of power imbalance to power use. *Social Psychology Quarterly, 44,* 151–163.

Stech, F., & McClintock, C. G. (1981). Effects of communication timing on duopoloy bargaining outcomes. *Journal of Personality and Social Psychology, 40,* 664–674.

ARTICLE 33 _____

Some leaders are obviously more effective than others. What makes them so? Research has focused on many different elements of leadership and leadership effectiveness, but two lines of study stand out. The first centers around identifying characteristics of leaders that may distinguish them from nonleaders. For example, certain personality traits, such as self-confidence, may be related to achieving leadership. Some factors may be fixed and difficult to change (physical appearance, for instance); others may be more easily changed or modified.

A second line of study has focused on styles of leadership that may be most effective in given situations. What works in one situation may not work in another.

The following article by Goktepe and Schneier provides a recent look at research examining which factors may predict who emerges as leader of a group. In particular, three factors—sex, gender role characteristics, and interpersonal attractiveness—are investigated to determine if they can be used to predict emergent leadership. Before reading the article, think of the implications of the variables being studied. At least one of the variables being studied—sex—is a fixed characteristic of the person, which is frustrating for a large segment of the population. However, the other two variables, although usually thought of as individual attributes, are much more modifiable. Thus, persons wanting to emerge as leaders could potentially change their behavior or characteristics to increase their chances.

Role of Sex, Gender Roles, and Attraction in Predicting Emergent Leaders

■ Janet R. Goktepe and Craig Eric Schneier

Examined the influence of sex, gender role characteristics, and interpersonal attractiveness on the selection of emergent leaders. Data were collected on 2 occasions from 122 subjects in 28 task groups performing "sex neutral" tasks for valued rewards over many weeks of interaction. Results showed no significant difference in the proportion of men and women to emerge as leaders through intragroup sociometric choice. Regardless of sex, group members with masculine gender role characteristics emerged as leaders significantly more than *those with feminine, androgynous, or undifferentiated gender role characteristics. Emergent leaders received significantly higher interpersonal attractiveness ratings than nonleaders within groups.*

The importance of leadership to management and organizations has resulted in a significant amount of theorizing and research over the past several decades (see Bass, 1981, for review). Many theorists and researchers (e.g., Hollander & Ju-

Reprinted from the *Journal of Applied Psychology*, 1989, *74*, 165–167. Copyright 1989 by the American Psychological Association. Reprinted by permission.

lian, 1969; Stogdill, 1974) have noted the useful-ness of viewing leadership as a dynamic social process and, hence, of studying how and why individuals emerge as leaders in groups. However, this topic has received considerably less attention than that of leaders with "legitimate" authority (e.g., elected or appointed leaders). Yet, recent studies (e.g., Lord, DeVader, & Alliger, 1986) have emphasized the theoretical and methodological reasons for considering the impact that individuals' traits have on their tendency to emerge as leaders in an interacting group.

Emergent leadership has important implications for organizations in such areas as personnel selection, training, and the identification and development of women leaders. Emergent leaders function in organizations as individuals that assume leadership responsibilities in leaderless groups (e.g., informal meetings, work teams) or in groups where leaders are incompetent or have been deposed. As individuals become labeled as leaders in one group, they are readily identified as leaders in other situations and groups, improving the probability of being appointed or promoted into managerial positions.

EMERGENT LEADERSHIP RESEARCH

Leadership research is generally built on studies with appointed or elected, not emergent, leaders. Moreover, it has been conducted largely with men, but much less often with both men and women as subjects. Typically, when emergent leadership has been studied, the research has not included tasks that are "sex neutral."

Sex Effects

Laboratory experiments and field studies have examined the effects of sex on emergence as a leader with equivocal results. In laboratory experiments researchers (e.g., Carbonell, 1984; Fleischer & Chertkoff, 1986; Megargee, 1969) have found that many women had difficulty becoming the leader even when their personalities (i.e., dominant) were well suited for the role. In field studies, however, researchers (e.g., Anderson &

Schneier, 1978; Schneier & Bartol, 1980) have found no difference in the proportion of men and women to emerge as leaders.

Interpersonal Attraction

Reviews of a substantial literature (e.g., Berscheid & Walster, 1978) on attractiveness attest to its powerful influence on social attitudes, attributions, and behaviors. Research in the management and organizational literature has consistently shown that attractive individuals are perceived as leaders (e.g., Stogdill, 1974).

Gender Role Characteristics

The few empirical studies examining the relationship between an individual's gender role orientation (i.e., masculine, feminine, androgynous, or undifferentiated) as measured by such instruments as Bem's (1974) Sex Role Inventory have generally found a strong relationship between leadership status and a masculine identity (e.g., Powell & Butterfield, 1979).

The following three research questions guided this study: (a) Will sex influence the choice of emergent leaders within groups? (b) Will the most interpersonally attractive individuals within groups be chosen as emergent leaders? and (c) Will gender role influence the choice of emergent leaders within groups?

METHOD

Subjects

One hundred twenty-two subjects (62 men and 60 women) participated in the study. They were enrolled in personnel management or business policy courses at a large state university in the northeastern United States. During the first week of the study, 28 sexually heterogeneous groups were formed. Eighty-two percent of the groups had 3, 4, or 5 people, and 18% of the groups had 6 or 7 people. Because results from other studies (e.g., Stogdill, 1974, p. 240) using groups of varying sizes have shown that group size did not influence emergence as a leader, size was not expected to influence emergence in this study. The formation of the groups was unsystematic. Groups were formed by students themselves, primarily on the basis of proximity. The median age was 22 years, with a mean of 22.3 and a standard deviation of 2.2. Subjects' ages ranged from 20 to 31 years old.

Design and Procedure

Task   The groups performed a series of exercises in personnel or business policy as part of the course requirements. Group membership remained fixed throughout the entire 6-week summer session or the 15-week fall semester of the study. Although the time periods varied from 6 to 15 weeks, groups were required to complete the same number of projects and, hence, spent the same amount of time together. Most groups spent at least 10 hr together outside of class time. At least 50% of the individual's course grade was based on the group performance score.

Timing of Measures   Groups were formed during the first week of class. About halfway through their assignments, but before receiving feedback about performance, measurement of the predictors (i.e., sex, interpersonal attractiveness, and gender role orientation) was taken. Measurement of the dependent variable (i.e., leader status) was taken at the next session. This completed measurement at Time 1. Measurement of the predictors was taken again toward the end of the course, and the second measurement of the dependent variable was taken at the last class. This completed measurement at Time 2. The measures were explained to students as being used for research purposes only, with total confidentiality of responses and no relationship to the students' course grades. Participation in the study was voluntary. Data collection was supervised each time to assure independent and confidential responses by group members.

Instrumentation   Gender role orientation was assessed by having subjects describe themselves us-ing Bem's (1974) Sex Role Inventory (BSRI) and by assigning them a gender role identity accordingly (i.e., masculine, feminine, androgynous, or undifferentiated). Interpersonal attraction was assessed by asking each member of each group to rate the interpersonal attractiveness of each other member of the group by responding to six questions that were based on Byrne's (1971) Interpersonal Judgment Scale. Choice of the leader was made by asking each member of each group to write the name of the leader of his or her group on a piece of paper without consulting other group members. Sociometric choice of the leader by peer ratings and secret ballot, used repeatedly in the leadership literature, has continued to demonstrate strong predictive validities (Bass, 1981; Stogdill, 1974). The reliability coefficients and test–retest reliabilities for the instruments ranged from .74 to .89, and were consistent with those generally obtained in other studies using these measures.

Groups in which leader choice was not unanimous or clearly indicated by the majority of group members were discarded from the analysis. Of the 47 groups with complete data, 12 (about 25%) were excluded from the analysis because of lack of agreement on the choice of the group leader, and 7 (about 15%) were excluded because they were unisexual.

Collecting data on two occasions was useful in identifying any possible changes in leadership status and gender role within groups between Times 1 and 2. The results of this experimental check showed that both leadership status and gender role of leaders remained stable.

RESULTS

Leadership Status and Sex

Of 28 leaders, 17 (61%) were men and 11 (39%) were women. Table 1 shows the number of men and women gaining leadership status. Given the unequal group size and unequal sex distribution across groups, a chi-square statistic for the entire sample would not accurately reflect the differences, if any, in the proportion of men and women to emerge as leaders.

TABLE 1 / Sex Differences in Emergent Leadership between Leaders and Nonleaders within Groups

Mixed-sex groups	Men	Women	Total
Leaders (n = 28)	17	11	28
Nonleaders (n = 94)	45	49	94
Total	62	60	122

Note. N groups = 28. Calculating for each of the 28 groups separately, the Mantel–Haenszel chi-square value of 1.23 was obtained. Neither this value nor the normal test, $Z(= 1.11) < 1.64$, results was statistically significant.

We used the Mantel–Haenszel (MH) chi-square statistic (Bishop, Fienberg, & Holland, 1975) to evaluate sex effects within each of the 28 groups. A separate 2 × 2 (Leader Status × Sex) contingency table for each group was developed, and the results were combined into a single summary statistic (MH $\chi^2 = 1.23$), which was not significant. In a normal test we found the same results, $Z (= 1.11) < 1.64$, that is, no sex bias within groups.

Leadership Status and Attractiveness

Using the group as the unit of analysis, a split-split plot ANOVA design (Hicks, 1973, pp. 222–225) with repeated measures on attractiveness ratings in two dimensions (i.e., time and leader status) showed that leaders received significantly higher, $F(1, 27) = 6.22$, $p < .025$, interpersonal attractiveness ratings than nonleaders. This ANOVA design used relative, weighted averages of ratings within groups to compute one single leader-status test across all groups. In addition, attractiveness ratings of male and female leaders were compared by using average ratings between groups. Results of t tests showed a significant difference, $t(80) = -2.07$, $p < .04$ at Time 1 (when female leaders received higher ratings), but no difference between ratings of male and female leaders at Time 2.

Leadership Status and Gender Role Identity

On the basis of responses to the BSRI, we classified subjects into gender role categories by sex and

leader status. Regardless of sex, individuals with masculine gender role orientations (i.e., those who described themselves with masculine characteristics using the BSRI) emerged as leaders within groups significantly more (MH $\chi^2 = 6.24$, $p < .01$, at Time 1; MH $\chi^2 = 18.79$, $p < .0001$, at Time 2) than those with feminine, androgynous, or undifferentiated gender roles.

The group was used as the unit of analysis, because whether a person emerges as a leader is a function of the dynamics and composition of the particular group. Expected frequencies within groups were used. In the 21 groups with at least 1 person with a masculine gender role, 13 subjects with masculine gender roles emerged as leaders, significantly more than those with other gender roles given their relative proportions in the group. Results are shown in Table 2.

DISCUSSION

Using task groups working over a considerable period of time on a meaningful task that determined important consequences, this research demonstrated that sex is not a predictor of leader emergence, but that interpersonal attractiveness and sex role orientation (i.e., a masculine gender role) are associated with leader emergence. These findings are noteworthy, given that calls for the study of the process of emergent, as opposed to appointed, leadership (e.g., Bass, 1981; Lord et

TABLE 2 / Gender Role Type Differences in Emergent Leaders versus Nonleaders within Groups

Groups with at least 1 person of a particular role type	Number of groups		Emergent leaders of this type	
	Time 1	Time 2	Time 1	Time 2
Masculine role type	21	21	13[a]	13[a]
Feminine role type	19	22	6	5
Androgynous	15	17	4	4
Undifferentiated	19	18	5	5

[a]Calculating the Mantel–Haenszel chi-square on the basis of expected frequencies within groups, chi-square statistics obtained for Times 1 and 2, respectively, were 6.24 and 18.79 ($p < .01$, at Time 1; and $p < .0001$, at Time 2).

al., 1986) have gone unanswered. In addition, we observed an association between interpersonal attractiveness and leader emergence in task groups, but the causal link was not established.

The natural setting, the noncontrived nature of the groups and tasks, the importance of group performance for the course grade, and the extensive contact during the study all provided a realistic context for the study. Hence, in contrast to many other studies examining sex effects in leadership, this study did not use paper-and-pencil stimulus subjects in artificial situations. Furthermore, in collecting data on two different occasions from the same sample as an experimental check, we found that leadership status and gender role of leaders remained stable over time.

Replication of this study using groups with different demographic characteristics, in different geographical regions, or in different cultures might reveal differences in leadership emergence. Future research could benefit from addressing the issue of emergent leadership in task groups in actual organizations and including measures of other potential explanatory variables.

REFERENCES

Anderson, C. R., & Schneier, C. E. (1978). Loss of control, leader behavior and leader performance among management students. *Academy of Management Journal, 21,* 690–698.

Bass, B. M. (1981). *Stogdill's handbook of leadership.* New York: Free Press.

Bem, S. L. (1974). The measurement of psychological androgyny. *Journal of Consulting and Clinical Psychology, 43,* 155–162.

Berscheid, E., & Walster, E. (1978). *Interpersonal attraction* (2nd ed.). Reading, MA: Addison-Wesley.

Bishop, Y., Fienberg, S. E., & Holland, P. W. (1975). *Discrete multivariate analysis.* Cambridge, MA: MIT Press.

Byrne, D. (1971). *The attraction paradigm.* New York: Academic Press.

Carbonell, J. L. (1984). Sex roles and leadership revisited. *Journal of Applied Psychology, 69,* 44–49.

Fleischer, R. A., & Chertkoff, J. M. (1986). Effects of dominance and sex on leader selection in dyadic work groups. *Journal of Personality and Social Psychology, 50,* 94–99.

Hicks, C. R. (1973). *Fundamental concepts in the design of experiments.* New York: Holt, Rinehart & Winston.

Hollander, E. P., & Julian, J. W. (1969). Contemporary trends in the analysis of leadership processes. *Psychological Bulletin, 71,* 387–397.

Lord, R. G., DeVader, C. L., & Alliger, G. M. (1986). A meta-analysis of the relation between personality traits and leadership perceptions: An application of validity generalization procedures. *Journal of Applied Psychology, 71,* 402–410.

Megargee, E. I. (1969). Influence of sex roles on the manifestation of leadership. *Journal of Applied Psychology, 53,* 377–382.

Powell, G. N., & Butterfield, D. A. (1979). Sex, attributions and leadership: A brief review. *Psychological Reports, 51,* 1171–1174.

Schneier, C. E., & Bartol, K. M. (1980). Sex effects in emergent leadership. *Journal of Applied Psychology, 65,* 341–345.

Stogdill, R. M. (1974). *Handbook of leadership.* New York: Free Press.

CRITICAL THINKING QUESTIONS

1. One finding of this study was that people with masculine gender role characteristics emerged as leaders more often than people with other gender role characteristics, regardless of the sex of the individual. Suppose that you worked in a personnel setting and were asked to identify people with leadership potential. Knowing that it is relatively quick and easy to assess sex role characteristics, would this be a good technique to use in identifying potential leaders? What limitations could this approach have?

2. Examine the specific methodology employed in this study. What are the relative advantages and disadvantages of this particular method compared to those used in studies employing subjects in a laboratory setting?

3. Let's assume that parents want their children to be successful in the work world. Does this mean that parents should encourage the development of masculine sex role characteristics in their children, regardless of the sex of the child? Discuss.

4. Examine the literature on sex roles and androgyny. How do the findings of this study compare to those of other studies on the relative advantages and disadvantages of androgynous, masculine, and feminine sex role characteristics?

Chapter Twelve

ENVIRONMENTAL INFLUENCES

PEOPLE ARE INFLUENCED by the environment in which they live. However, in some ways, people can control that by adapting the environment to suit their desires and needs. This is the focus of environmental psychology, an outgrowth of social psychological research but now regarded as a discipline in its own right. Part of the attention has been directed to discovering the impact of environmental stressors, such as loud noises and high temperatures, on human behavior. As a recent example, Article 36, "Emotional, Behavioral, and Physiological Effects of Chronic Stress at Three Mile Island," examines a relatively modern environmental stressor, a nuclear power plant accident, and how it affected people even years later.

A second line of research has looked at how we can alter the physical environment to influence human behavior. Article 34, "Designing to Deter Crime," illustrates the ways in which the design of a building, an aspect of the physical environment, can influence certain behaviors, such as crime.

A third area of study in environmental psychology has concerned the social environment, such as how we use personal space and our reactions to crowding. Article 35, "Territorial Defense and the Good Neighbor," is a classic example of early research investigating territorial behavior in public spaces.

ARTICLE 34 _____

If you live in or have visited a major metropolitan area, you undoubtedly know that certain parts of the area have higher crime rates than others. Why is that? Is it due to the income levels of the residents? To their personal characteristics? To the presence or absence of police?

Each of these, as well as many other factors, may play a role in explaining this complex social behavior. Psychologists, sociologists, and criminologists all have worked on studying the nature of crime and ways to reduce it. Even a superficial review of literature in the field will indicate that there are no simple answers or solutions. However, some factors can likely be identified as having a mediating effect on crime.

In the following article, Krupat and Kubzansky examine some of the research that has been done on the relationship between the physical design of buildings and criminal activity, as well as other factors that may increase or decrease the likelihood of crime. The article does not claim that these are the only factors influencing crime but that they do play a role in it nonetheless. Some of the issues may have personal relevance for how to lessen your own chances of being victimized.

Designing to Deter Crime

■ Edward Krupat and Philip E. Kubzansky

No matter what city you live in, it is impossible to open the local paper without being bombarded by stories of fear and crime. Evidence of public vandalism and concerns about being mugged or robbed are part of daily life in the city. The causes of urban crime and its possible remedies have been debated endlessly by social reformers, from politicians to philosophers, but few have been able to do anything significant to reduce this critical social problem.

Based on the premise that slums were the breeding ground of crime, planners in the 1950s and '60s tore down entire neighborhoods of old, decaying buildings and replaced them with new high-rise housing developments. They also improved street lighting and hired extra police to patrol problem areas. Yet, to their surprise and disappointment, crime still flourished. Police presence and better lighting did little to reduce either crime or fear. In fact, people seemed more afraid to use the newly created open spaces of their housing projects at night than they had been to walk the streets of their old slum neighborhoods.

Architect Oscar Newman looked at these efforts in his controversial book, *Defensible Space,* and labeled them misguided. He claimed that crime occurred because of this new design, not in spite of it, and concluded, "the new physical form of the urban environment is possibly the most cogent ally the criminal has in his victimization of society." Better lighting, more police and stronger locks could not deter crime, Newman said, unless residents became the critical agents in their own security.

Newman believed that the proper design, one that fostered "defensible space," could arouse the strong, but latent, territorial feelings of city dwellers and stir them to action. First, it should generate opportunities for people to see and be seen

Reprinted from *Psychology Today,* 1987 (October), *21,* 58–61. Reprinted with permission from *Psychology Today Magazine.* Copyright © 1987 (PT Partners, L.P.).

continuously. Knowing that they are, or could be, watched makes residents feel less anxious, leads them to use an area more and deters criminals by making them fear being identified and caught.

Second, people must not only watch but also be willing to intervene or report crime when it occurs. Newman proposed reducing anonymity and increasing territorial feelings by dividing larger spaces into zones of influence. This can be accomplished on a small scale by clustering a few apartments around a common entrance or a common elevator. On a larger scale individual yards or areas can be demarcated by having paths and recreational areas focus around a small set of apartment units or by having each building entry serve only a limited number of apartments.

Newman and his followers tested these ideas by studying housing developments in cities across the country, from New York to San Francisco, and concluded that rates of crime, vandalism and turnover were lower in places that conformed to the principles of defensible space. In a variety of large and small cities, housing projects and urban neighborhoods have been redesigned in accord with defensible space principles. While the results have not been consistent, reductions in crime and fear and increases in a sense of community have been found in several places.

Still, many disagreed. Some have argued that the principles are too mechanistic and narrow to account for the complex issues of fear and crime. Other critics object to the concept of territoriality that forms the basis of the theory, while still others believe that Newman and his colleagues did a poor job of picking matched sites for comparison and analyzing their data.

More recent studies have looked at crime from the opposite perspective, that of the criminal. Social psychologists Ralph Taylor and Stephen Gottfredson of Temple University and other researchers believe that criminals form mental images of potential target sites in deciding where to commit a crime. They read the nonverbal cues given off by the target to pick up messages about the opportunities, risk and convenience involved.

Social psychologists Irwin Altman and Barbara Brown of the University of Utah have expanded on this idea. They suggest that burglars ask themselves five kinds of questions:

- How detectable am I? For instance, where are windows and door positioned, and how far is it from the street to the house?
- Are there any real barriers present? Does the place have strong locks, a gate or an alarm system?
- Are there any symbolic barriers present? Are there any nameplates, "Neighborhood Watch" signs or similar indicators of territoriality and vigilance?
- Are there traces of presence or activity on the part of the residents? Is the newspaper still in the driveway, and are the lights on?
- What is the social climate of the area? Are people staring at and questioning me, or can I go about my business ignored by others?

In 1984 sociologist Stephanie Greenberg, then of the University of Denver, and urban planner William Rohe of the University of North Carolina at Chapel Hill tested this "criminal opportunity" theory in three pairs of Atlanta neighborhoods. They were matched on racial and socioeconomic makeup but differed greatly in their levels of crime. The researchers found that the low-crime neighborhoods were more residential, had less public parking and had fewer through-streets.

To get a closer look into the mind of a burglar, Altman and Brown went right to the scene of the crime. The Salt Lake City Sheriff's Office gave them the locations of 102 suburban middle-class homes that had been broken into over the previous 15 months. The researchers compared these homes to similar homes that hadn't been burglarized. Their research team walked along the block coding each home—or should we say, casing it—for the presence or absence of 200 specific environmental cues that might give off a special scent of criminal attractiveness.

Several differences were clear. Burglarized homes were more likely to be on a street with signs revealing it was a public thoroughfare, where strangers might commonly be found. Non-burglarized blocks had a more private sense about them: They looked hard to enter, were clearly set off from public areas and often had large names or numbers on them. These cues, all suggesting the owners' presence, activity and territorial commitment, apparently signaled criminals to keep away.

The Southland Corporation, owner of the 7-Eleven convenience chain, has redesigned its stores with a special eye toward the criminal's aversion to surveillance. The chief architect of this plan, Ray D. Johnson, has excellent credentials. Before working for 7-Eleven, Johnson served 25 years for robbery and burglary in the California state penitentiary system. Now working on the other side of the law as a consultant on crime prevention, Johnson and his colleagues rearranged the physical design of 60 7-Elevens in southern California.

Knowing that robbers like concealment, they provided just the opposite. To allow clear sightlines from the street into the store, they moved cash registers up front and removed all advertising from the front windows. They also put bright floodlights outside the entrance, forcing potential robbers to perform where any passerby could look in and see.

They also installed special cash drawers that make it impossible to get at more than $10 every two minutes. This gives the would-be robber the choice of getting away with very little cash, waiting "onstage" to make the payoff worthwhile or simply going elsewhere. As Johnson says, "It takes too much time. With the register so visible from the street, no robber would hold a gun on anyone that long. When you're worried about getting caught—and every robber is very worried every time—two minutes is an eternity. It's just not worth it to wait that long for another $10."

Johnson's insights proved to be right on the money. The Southland Corporation found that robberies were 30 percent lower in the 60 redesigned stores than in 60 similar stores that had not been redesigned. "Our experience has been that robbers frustrated by small takes don't shoot; they leave," says Richard Nelson, security manager for Southland.

The new design has proven itself over time against other convenience stores, as well. While the average loss at convenience store holdups was $607 and the number of robberies rose 47 percent in the late 1970s and early 1980s, 7-Eleven's losses averaged $45 and its number of robberies went down 56 percent.

Anthropologist Sally Merry of Wellesley College combined the resident and criminal perspective during 18 months as a participant-observer in a low-to-moderate-income housing project in Boston, which Merry refers to as "Dover Square." Merry got to know many of her fellow residents and interviewed several young men who were responsible for much of the street crime in the neighborhood. The section Merry studied consisted of four-story buildings, built in 1965, that reflected several of the design factors later recommended by Newman. Yet it had the highest per capita robbery and assault rates in the city.

More than half Chinese and one quarter black, with a sprinkling of whites and Hispanics, Dover Square is, in Merry's words, "a neighborhood of strangers." It is a pot that simmers and boils but rarely melts or blends. Few friendships stretch across racial or cultural lines, and each of the groups harbors strong and often negative stereotypes of the others.

In Merry's interviews and surveys, she found several differences between the residents' perspective and that of the criminals. The places the residents considered most dangerous were not necessarily those where the most crime took place. They felt safest when they were familiar with an area and the people who used it and felt unsafe if the turf was unfamiliar. And although they did identify a number of architectural features that they associated with danger, these were not major concerns.

The criminals, on the other hand, equated the safety of a place with the number of crimes that took place there, and they were particularly conscious of an area's architectural features. Several of them spontaneously mentioned that they looked for places with poor surveillance, such as narrow, enclosed pathways or where windows were obstructed by fences.

One of the young criminals had a favorite spot where no one could hear or see his victims. Describing it, he explained, "Someone can back you in there, and if you scream, all you can hear is the echo." Another young robber mentioned that he carefully avoided one spot because there are "so many eyes there."

Merry's research on criminals and residents helped make a critical distinction between space that is defensible and space that is defended. She notes that a neighborhood may be architecturally designed to encourage defense against crime but still not be defended because there is little or no social cohesion. Even when buildings are low and the entrances and public spaces focus around a small set of families, people will not react to crime when they believe that they are on someone else's turf, when they do not consider the police effective or when they fear retribution.

Designing defensible space is neither the panacea that some proponents have hoped, nor is it as irrelevant to crime and fear as some detractors have contended. Environmental design does address the when and where of crime and can make people feel more secure even when they live in dangerous circumstances. But it can never eliminate crime because it does not attack its root causes; design, as some critics have suggested, may only move crime from one place to other, more vulnerable areas. It remains easier to remodel buildings than to create opportunities for teenagers who live in poverty, and until that is done the motivation for crime will not disappear.

Design also cannot generate a social environment in which people of different races and cultures understand, care for or share responsibility for one another. As Merry says, "Design can provide preconditions for effective control, but it cannot create such control if the social fabric of the community is fragmented." Environmental design is hardly the ultimate solution to the puzzle that we call urban crime, yet it does add some new and important pieces that make the picture a good deal clearer.

CRITICAL THINKING QUESTIONS

1. At one point, the article suggested that designing to deter crime may work but that unless other steps are taken to eliminate the causes of crime, it may simply shift to another location. The article also discussed the successful design changes implemented at 7-Eleven stores to reduce crime. Is it possible the design changes implemented by 7-Eleven reduced their robberies but prompted crime to shift to other stores, perhaps those without the resources to make similar changes? Reject or defend this position.

2. Environmental design does have an impact on crime, as discussed in the article. Should architects be required to study the relationship between building design and crime? Why or why not?

3. Based upon the information contained in the article, what steps would you recommend to your neighbors to reduce the likelihood of their being victimized by crime? Don't limit your suggestions to physical design features only.

4. If the funds were available, how could you construct two housing projects of varying designs and then make comparisons of criminal activity in them? What major ethical issues would be involved in such a study?

5. Can some of the design factors related to crime also be related to behaviors such as littering and vandalism? How could the principles for crime reduction be used to reduce the amount of litter in a given area?

ARTICLE 35 _____

Most people are aware that many species of animals claim and mark territory as belonging to them. Another animal, including a human, entering that territory may elicit defensive behaviors on the owner's part.

Humans also tend to claim territory as belonging to them. Some territories, such as our bedrooms, belong exclusively to us. If someone came into your bedroom and rearranged the furniture without your permission, you would most likely be unhappy, to say the least. In contrast with these private territories, we also lay claim, albeit temporarily, to semiprivate spaces. An example of this might be a seat in a classroom. You don't own it, and other people use it when you are not there, yet you most likely sit in the same seat every time you attend a particular class. If after attending the class for a semester you arrive one day to find someone else sitting in your seat, you might feel a little annoyed at whoever took your seat. Finally, there also are public spaces, which we use temporarily but over which we lay no claim other than when we actually occupy the space. Seats in a movie theater or in a restaurant are examples of this type of territory.

The following classic article by Robert Sommer and Franklin Becker concerns public space. Sometimes when occupying a public space, it becomes necessary to leave for a short time. How can we effectively indicate that the space is already taken? Also, sometimes we want to protect our space from the presence of others. How do we keep people from sitting next to us if we want to be alone? These are but two of the questions addressed in a series of studies presented in the article.

Territorial Defense and the Good Neighbor

■ Robert Sommer[1] and Franklin D. Becker

A series of questionnaire and experimental studies was designed to explore how people mark out and defend space in public areas. The use of space is affected by instructions to defend actively the area or retreat, by room density, and by the location of walls, doors, and other physical barriers. Under light population pressure, most markers are capable of reserving space in a public area, but more personal markers have the greatest effect. As room density increases, the effect of the marker is seen in delaying occupancy of the area and in holding onto a smaller subarea within the larger space. Neighbors play an important part in legitimizing a system of space ownership.

The concept of human territoriality is receiving increased attention. In addition to the popular books by Ardrey (1961, 1966), a number of social scientists have become impressed with the utility of the concept (Altman & Haythorn, 1967; Esser et al., 1965; Hall, 1966; Lipman, 1967; Lyman & Scott, 1967). Hediger (1950) defined a territory as "an area which is first rendered distinctive by its owner in a particular way and, secondly, is defended by the owner." When the term is used by social scientists to refer to human behavior, there is no implication that the underlying mechanisms are identical to those described in animal research. The major components of Hediger's defi-

Reprinted from the *Journal of Personality and Social Psychology*, 1969, *11*, 85–92. Copyright 1969 by the American Psychological Association. Reprinted by permission.

nition are *personalization* and *defense*. Roos (1968) uses the term *range* as the total area an individual traverses, *territory* as the area he defends, *core area* as the area he preponderantly occupies, and *home* as the area in which he sleeps. Goffman (1963) makes the further distinction between a territory and a *jurisdiction*, such as that exercised by a janitor sweeping the floor of an office and keeping other people away. Territories are defended on two grounds, "you keep off" and "this space is mine." Jurisdictions are controlled only on the former ground; no claim of ownership, no matter how transitory, is made.

In a previous study, the reactions to staged spatial invasions were investigated (Felipe & Sommer, 1966). There was no single reaction to a person coming too close; some people averted their heads and placed an elbow between themselves and the intruder, others treated him as a nonperson, while still others left the area when he came too close. The range of defensive gestures, postures, and acts suggested that a systematic study of defensive procedures would contribute materially to our knowledge of human spatial behavior. Following the tradition of ecological research, the studies would be undertaken in naturally occurring environments.

QUESTIONNAIRE STUDIES

During previous observations of library study halls Sommer (1967) was impressed by the heavy concentration of readers at the side-end chairs. Interviewing made it clear that students believed that it was polite to sit at an end chair. Someone who sat, for example, at a center chair of an empty six-chair table (three chairs on each side) was considered to be "hogging the table." There appeared to be two styles by which students gained privacy in the library areas. One method was avoidance, to sit as far away from other people as one could. The other method was offensive ownership of the entire area. To study the two methods of gaining privacy, a brief questionnaire was constructed which presented the student with table diagrams containing 6, 8, and 10 chairs, respectively (Sommer, 1967). Two forms to the questionnaire were

distributed randomly within a class of 45 students. Twenty-four students received avoidance instructions: "If you wanted to be as far as possible from the distraction of other people, where would you sit at the table?" Twenty-one other students in the same class were shown the same diagrams and given the offensive display instructions: "If you wanted to have the table to yourself, where would you sit to discourage anyone else from occupying it?" Even though both sets of instructions were aimed at insuring privacy, the two tactics produced a striking difference in seats chosen. Those students who wanted to sit by themselves as far as possible from other people overwhelmingly chose the *end* chairs at the table, while those students who wanted to keep other people away from the table almost unanimously chose the *middle* chair.

When the findings were discussed with architect James Marston Fitch, his first question concerned the location of the door in regards to the table. This seemed a good question, since the preferred location for retreat or active defense should be guided by the path the invaders would take or by the most accessible escape route. The previous diagrams had depicted only a table and chairs, so it seemed necessary to undertake another study in which the entrance to the room was indicated. This conception of the study suggested that additional information could be obtained on the ecology of retreat and active defense by varying the location of walls and aisles and the table size.

Method

The present study involved four diagrams, each one drawn on a separate $8^1/2 \times 11$-inch sheet.

Form G showed eight rectangular six-chair tables, with a large aisle down the center and two smaller aisles along the walls. (See Figure 1.)

Form H was the same as Form G, only the tables were set against the wall and the center aisle was wider.

Form J was a hybrid of G and H, with the right row of tables against the wall and the left row of tables away from the wall.

Form I contained one row of four-chair tables

FIGURE 1 / Arrangement of Tables and Chairs in Form G.

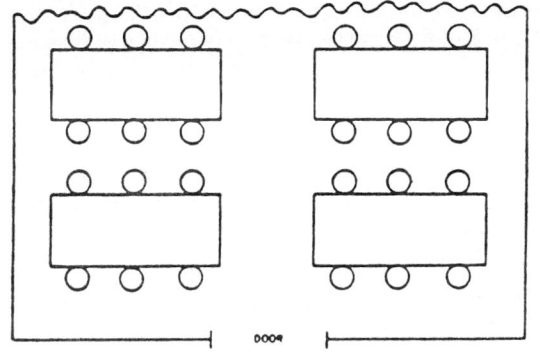

and one row of eight-chair tables, with aisles in the center and along both walls.

Four different sets of instructions were used with the forms (two defense styles and two densities), but any single subject received only one set. One form asked the subject where he would sit if he wanted to be by himself and away from other people—the retreat instructions. The other form asked where he would sit if he wanted to keep other people away from the table—the active defense instructions. In each case, the prospective room density was also indicated. On half the questionnaires, it was stated that room density was likely to be low throughout the day and very few people would be using the room, while remaining subjects were told that room density was likely to be high and many people would be using the room. All the instructions described the room as a study hall such as that already existing in the campus library, and the respondent was informed that he was the first occupant in the room, so he could take any seat he wanted. Booklets containing some combination of instructional set (Defense Style × Room Density) and two diagrams in random order were passed out randomly among 280 students in introductory psychology classes.

Results

Hypothesis 1 stated that during the retreat condition people gravitate to the end chair closest to the wall. During the active defense condition they make greater use of the center and aisle chairs. Hypothesis 1 was confirmed beyond the .01 level. During the retreat conditions 76% of the subjects occupied a wall chair compared to 48% during the active defense condition.

Hypothesis 2 stated that with the retreat instructions the subjects face away from the door, while they face towards the door with the active defense instructions. The data disclose a preference in all conditions for a subject to sit with his back to the door—60% of the subjects faced away from the door compared to 40% who faced towards it. However, the results were still in the predicted direction since 44% of the subjects in the active defense condition faced the door compared to 36% in the retreat condition ($p < .05$).

Although the authors had imagined that the use of different-sized tables and the variation in wall placement would influence seating patterns, specific hypotheses had not been formulated. In all conditions there was a marked preference for chairs towards the rear of the room. Overall, 79% selected chairs in the rear half of the room. However, occupancy of the rear was significantly higher with the retreat instructions under high room density than in any of the other conditions ($p < .05$). There was also a highly significant preference for the four-chair tables when they were paired with the eight-chair tables, with 73% selecting a small table compared with 27% selecting a large table. There was a slight trend in the active defense condition to make greater use of the small tables, but this was not statistically significant.

When tables against the wall were paired with tables with aisles on both sides, 62% of the subjects selected a table against the wall compared to 38% who chose a table with aisles on both sides ($p < .001$). As an independent variable, description of the projected room density as high or low made very little difference in where people sat. However, density interacted with the defense instructions on several of the tabulations. With high density *and* retreat instructions, there was significantly greater use of (a) the rear half of the room, (b) a wall compared to an aisle table, and (c) the chair closest to the wall. In essence, the attribution of high room density increased the degree of physical retreat. It had no observable effects on the active defense conditions.

The results make it clear that room dimension and the location of barriers must be considered if we are to understand the ecology of spatial defense. In a library reading room, the best chair for retreat is at the rear, facing away from the door, next to a wall, and at a small table if one is available. Distance from the door protects the person against people simply walking by as well as lazy intruders who are more likely to sit in the first available chair; facing away from the door tends to minimize distraction and also displays an antipathy toward social intercourse; a wall table protects a person's entire left (or right) side; and a small table reduces the number of invaders in close proximity. At this point the authors felt they had derived many useful hypotheses from the questionnaire data which they wanted to extend using an experimental approach under natural conditions. The first experimental studies took place in two soda fountains, and the remainder took place in library areas.

EXPERIMENTAL STUDIES

Most territories are marked and bounded in some clear way. In the animal kingdom, markers may be auditory (bird song), olfactory (glandular secretions by deer), or visual (bear-claw marks on a tree). Since humans rely almost exclusively on visual markers, the authors decided to test the strength of various markers ranging from the physical presence of a person to impersonal artifacts.

Study 1

The first study took place in a popular soda fountain on campus. The soda fountain was located in a converted office building which still contained a number of small rooms. Patrons would obtain their refreshments at a central counter and then repair to one of the smaller rooms to eat and chat informally. Prior to the study, the authors had

been struck by the sight of students walking up and down the corridor looking for an empty room. One of the small rooms which contained three square tables, each surrounded by four chairs, was used for the study. A 20-year-old girl who appeared to be studying stationed herself at a table facing the door. On other occasions during the same hours she stationed herself down the hall so she could observe who entered the experimental room. A session took place only when the room was unoccupied at the outset.

If an all-or-none criterion of room occupancy is applied, the experimenter's defense was not very successful. During only 1 of the 10 experimental sessions was she able to keep the entire room to herself. The average length of time before the room was occupied during the experimental sessions was 5.8 minutes compared to 2.6 minutes during the control sessions, but the difference was not statistically reliable. Although the experimenter was unable to keep the room to herself, she was able to protect the table at which she studied. The remaining three seats were occupied only once during the experimental sessions compared to 13 occupancies during the control sessions ($p < .01$). It seems clear that territorial defense in a public area is not an all-or-none affair. The defender's presence may be seen in a delay in occupancy rather than an absence of invaders and in the avoidance of a subarea within the larger area.

Study 2

The next study took place in a more traditional open-plan soda fountain and, instead of the physical presence of the experimenter, three sorts of objects were used as territorial markers—a sandwich wrapped in cellophane, a sweater draped over a chair, and two paperback books stacked on the table. In each case the experimenter located two adjacent empty tables and arbitrarily placed a marker on one with the other as a control. Seating himself some distance away, he was able to record the duration of time before each table was occupied. The sessions all took place at moderate room density. There were 8 sessions with a sandwich marker, 13 with a sweater, and 20 with the books.

The authors were interested in whether a marker would reserve an entire table as well as the marked chair. The answer for all of the markers was affirmed. The unmarked control tables were occupied significantly sooner than were the marked tables, and the difference was significant for each of the three markers. In fact, in all 41 sessions the control table was occupied sooner or at the same time as the marked table. In only three of the sessions did anyone sit at the marked *chair*. All three were occupied by males, a finding whose significance will be discussed later. It is also interesting to examine the occupancy patterns at the two sorts of tables. The marked tables were eventually occupied by 34 lone individuals and 4 groups of 2 persons, while the unmarked tables were occupied by 18 lone individuals and 20 groups. It can be noted that a group of 2 or 3 could easily be accommodated at a marked table even assuming that the marker represented one person, yet virtually all the groups sat at unmarked tables. It is clear that the markers were able to (a) protect the particular chair almost totally, (b) delay occupancy of the entire table, and (c) divert groups away from the table.

Study 3

A similar study using books and newspapers as markers was undertaken in a dormitory study hall at a time of very light room density. Virtually all the markers proved effective in reserving the marked chair. The only exceptions were two sessions when the school paper which had been used as a marker was treated as litter and pushed aside. After more than 30 individual sessions where virtually all the markers were respected, the authors decided to move the experiments to the main university library where room density was much heavier. It seemed clear that at low densities almost any marker is effective. One qualification is that the object must be perceived as a marker and not as something discarded and unwanted by its former owner. Certain forms of litter such as old newspapers or magazines may, indeed, attract people to a given location.

The locus of study was switched to the periodical room in the university library where room density was high and pressure for seats was great. This room contained rectangular six-chair tables, three chairs to a side. The experimenter arrived at one of the six seats at a designated table at 6:50 P.M., deposited a marker, and then departed to another table at 7:00 P.M. to view any occupancy at the marked position by a student seeking space. During each session, a similarly situated empty chair which was unmarked was used as the control. There were 25 experimental sessions, each lasting 2 hours. The markers included two notebooks and a textbook, four library journals piled in a neat stack, four library journals randomly scattered on the table, a sports jacket draped over the chair, and a sports jacket draped over the chair in addition to the notebooks on the table.

If one compares the average time before occupancy of the marked and the control chairs, it is apparent that all markers were effective. Seventeen of the 25 marked chairs remained vacant the entire 2-hour period, while *all* control chairs were occupied. The average interval before the control chairs were occupied was 20 minutes. Some of the markers were more potent than others. Only one student occupied a chair that was marked either by a sports jacket or a notebook-and-text. Chairs marked by the neatly-piled journals were occupied three of the five sessions, while chairs marked by the randomly placed journals were occupied all five sessions, even though the interval in each case exceeded that of the control chairs. It is clear that the personal markers, such as the sports jacket and notebooks, were able to keep away intruders entirely, while the impersonal library-owned markers (journals) could only delay occupancy of the marked chairs.

An interesting sidelight is that eight of the nine students who sat down despite the markers were males. Since there were more females than males in the control chairs at the same time, the high incidence of males is quite significant. It may be recalled in the previous study that the only three individuals who pushed aside the marker and sat at a marked chair were also males. It is likely that some sort of dominance or risk-taking factor is at work in the decision to disregard a territorial marker. The relationship between personality characteristics and the likelihood of invading someone else's space seems an exciting topic for further investigation.

Another serendipitous finding concerns the role of the neighbor, the person sitting alongside the marked chair, in defending the marked space. In all five trials with the scattered journals, the potential invader questioned the person sitting alongside the marked chair (the neighbor) as to whether the space was vacant. Early in the 2-hour session, the neighbor unknowingly served as the protector of the space. He informed all inquisitive intruders that the space was taken, since he believed the experimenter would return in view of the marker left on the table. As time passed, the neighbor's belief that the experimenter would return to the chair began to wane. At this point he would impart his new conception of the situation to potential invaders, "Yes, somebody was sitting there, but that was over an hour ago. Maybe he's not coming back."

Study 4

Since the role of the neighbor seemed an important aspect of a property-ownership system, the authors decided to investigate it experimentally. The first of such studies involved two experimenters and a person sitting alongside an empty chair. One experimenter seated himself next to a stranger (the neighbor) for 15 minutes and then departed, leaving behind an open book and an open notebook upon the table as territorial markers. After a fixed interval, the second experimenter, in the role of a student looking for a chair, came and inquired about the marked space nonverbally. The nonverbal questioning was a pantomime which included catching the neighbor's eye, pulling out the chair slightly, hesitating, looking at the place markers and at the neighbor, and then back at the markers. The authors had

very little experience with such nonverbal cues, but expected that the neighbor's reactions might include verbal defenses ("That seat is taken") and nonverbal defenses (moving the books to reinforce the marker). The independent variable was the length of time between the departure of the first experimenter and the arrival of the second—which was either a 5- or a 20-minute interval. Some sessions had to be terminated when the neighbor departed before the second experimenter arrived on the scene.

Overall the results were discouraging. In only 6 of the 55 trials did the neighbor respond to the nonverbal gestures of the second experimenter in what could be described as a space-defending manner, such as a statement that the seat was taken. Five of the six defensive acts occurred when the experimenter had been away 5 minutes, compared to only one defensive act when he had been away 20 minutes, but considering that there were 55 trials the difference was unimpressive.

Study 5

The authors decided to make another attempt to see if the neighbor could be involved in property defense on a spontaneous basis—that is, if he would defend marked space without being questioned directly. Unlike in the preceding study, the "owner" attempted to establish a relationship with the neighbor prior to the "owner's" departure. There were two phases of the study; when it seemed that the first approach was not leading anywhere, another approach was used. The markers were a neat stack of three paperback books left on the table in front of a chair. The sessions took place at six-chair tables where there was at least 1 empty seat between the marker and the neighbor. The first experimenter entered the room and found the location meeting the experimental requirements (a person sitting at the end chair of a six-person table with two empty chairs alongside him—O-O-S). The experimenter (a girl) sat down on the same side of the table but one seat away (E-O-S). There were 13 trials in each of the following conditions: (a) The experimenter sat 5 minutes and then departed from the table, leaving her books neatly stacked on the table. During this time she did not interact with her neighbor. (b) Similar to Condition *a*, the experimenter sat for 5 minutes except that during the 5-minute wait, the experimenter asked the neighbor "Excuse me, could you tell me what time it is?" (c) Similar to Condition *a*, the experimenter sat for 5 minutes except that during the 5-minute wait the experimenter engaged the neighbor in conversation four times and, while leaving and placing the stack of three paperback books on the table, declared, "See you later." Fifteen minutes later, the second experimenter (a male) entered the room, walked directly to the marked chair, pushed the books directly ahead of him, and sat down at the table.

The results were again discouraging. In none of the 39 trials involving Conditions *a*, *b*, and *c* did the neighbor inform the intruder that the seat was taken. The authors therefore decided to strengthen the conditions by having the "owner" return and directly confront the intruder. Seven of such trials were added to Condition *a*, 6 to Condition *b*, and 6 to Condition *c*, making 19 trials in all when the "owner" came back and told the intruder "You are sitting in my chair." Each time she hesitated about 30 seconds to see if the neighbor would intervene, and then she picked up her books and departed. There was no verbal response from the neighbor in any of the 19 sessions. The most that occurred would be a frown or a look of surprise on the part of the neighbor, or some nonverbal communication with someone else at the table. Stated simply, despite a flagrant usurpation of a marked space, all neighbors chose to remain uninvolved. It became clear that if one wanted to study the neighbor's role in such an informal regulatory system one would have to question him directly as to whether the seat was occupied.

Study 6

The next study employed two experimenters, a male and a female, and the same three paperback books as markers. Two different girls were used as experimenters, and the sessions occurred in two different, nearby college libraries. The experimental situation involved six-chair tables where the first experimenter (female) sat down at the same side of a table with a subject, leaving an empty chair between them (E-O-S). The goal of the study was to learn whether a greater amount of interaction between the former occupant and the neighbor would increase the neighbor's likelihood of defending the chair. Unlike in the previous study, the neighbor was questioned directly as to whether the seat was taken. There were three different instructional sets, and these took place according to a prearranged random order. In 14 trials, the first experimenter sat at the chair for 5 minutes without saying anything, deposited the marker (three paperback books), and left. Fourteen other sessions were similar except that at some time during her 5-minute stay, the first experimenter asked the neighbor for the time. Ten other sessions were similar except that the experimenter engaged the neighbor in conversation as to where to get a coke, what was happening on campus, and other minor matters. Fifteen minutes after the first experimenter departed, the second experimenter (a male) entered the room, walked over to the marked chair, and asked the neighbor "Excuse me, is there anyone sitting here?"

The results differ markedly from those in the previous study. A total of 22 out of the 38 neighbors defended the seat when questioned directly on the matter. The typical defense response was "Yes, there is" or "There is a girl who left those books."[2] However, the amount of contact between the first experimenter and the neighbor made little difference in defensive behavior. When there had been no contact, or minimal contact, between the first experimenter and neighbor the seat was protected 58% of the time, while the use of several items of conversation between the experimenter and her neighbor raised the percentage of defensive responses only to 66%. The difference between conditions is small and statistically unreliable; what is impressive is the great increase in defensive behavior when the neighbor was questioned directly. Two other parameters of the situation are (a) the time that the first experimenter remained in the seat before depositing her marker, and (b) the length of time that the first experimenter was out of room before the second experimenter approached the marked chair.

Study 7

The final study employed two experimenters, both males, and the same three paperback books. The sessions took place at six-chair tables in the library, where the first experimenter again sat down on the same side of the table with a subject, leaving an empty chair between them (E-O-S). He remained either 5 minutes or 20 minutes, depending upon the experimental condition, and then departed, leaving on the table a neat stack of three paperback books. After a designated interval of either 15 or 60 minutes, the second experimenter entered the room and asked the neighbor whether the (marked) chair was taken. The second experimenter recorded the neighbor's reply verbatim just as soon as he was able to sit down somewhere. Since both experimenters were males, it was decided to use only male neighbors in the experiment.

The independent variables were (a) the length of time the first experimenter had been seated before he left his marker and departed and (b) the length of time the first experimenter was absent before the neighbor was questioned by the second experimenter. Some sessions were unusable since the neighbor departed before the designated time and could not be interviewed. Most of the unusable sessions occurred when the experimenter had been absent for 60 minutes. The sessions took place at times of light-to-moderate room density.

Although the design had not called for comparison of marked and unmarked chairs, it is noteworthy that the markers were effective in keeping people away. Not one of the 64 marked chairs was ever occupied. Regarding the inclination of the neighbor to defend the marked space when questioned by the second experimenter, a content analysis of the neighbor's responses to the query "Is this seat taken?" into defense and non-defense categories revealed that 44 neighbors defended the marked space by indicating that it was taken, while 20 failed to do so either by pleading ignorance or by stating that the chair was empty.

The response to a direct question stands in contrast to the lack of involvement when neighbors were approached nonverbally. The length of time that the first experimenter had originally occupied the chair (his tenure period) had no effect on the willingness of the neighbor to defend the chair. However, the length of time that the previous owner was away—either 15 or 60 minutes—had a significant effect. When the former owner had been absent 15 minutes, 80% of the neighbors defended the space compared to 54% defending it when the former owner had been away a full hour ($p < .05$).

Several aspects of the results require elaboration. It is possible that initial tenure periods of 5 and 20 minutes were not sufficiently different. Yet it seems noteworthy that even with a rather impersonal marker, more than two-thirds of the neighbors defended the marked chair upon direct questioning. Most of those who didn't defend it simply pleaded ignorance ("I don't know if it's taken") rather than indicating that the seat was vacant.

After the experiments had been completed, 15 additional students in the library were interviewed on the question of how personal belongings could reserve space. Each student was asked how he would react if he saw someone intrude into a marked space, particularly if the original owner came back and claimed the space (i.e., the actual experimental situation was described to him). The replies were at variance with what the authors had actually found in such a situation. Most of the respondents maintained that they would indeed protect a marked space, although some of them added qualifications that they would defend the space only if the person were away a short time. Typical responses were: "I would protect the person's books and state (to the intruder) that the place was obviously taken by the presence of the books," and "Yes, I would mention that someone was sitting there." Although the majority mentioned specifically that they would protect a marked chair, in the actual situation no one had done so unless approached directly. The ethic regarding space ownership in the library exists, but is paid lip service, probably because institutional means of enforcement do not exist.

DISCUSSION

The present article represents a small beginning toward understanding how markers reserve space and receive their legitimacy from people in the area (neighbors) and potential intruders. Psychologists have paid little attention to boundary markers in social interaction, perhaps because such markers were regarded as physical objects relegated to the cultural system (the province of the anthropologist) rather than an interpersonal system which is the true province of the social psychologist. Generally it is the geographers and lawyers who are most concerned with boundaries and markers. Since the present studies took place in public spaces, we are dealing more with norms and customs than with legal statutes. Stated another way, the situations involve an interpersonal system where sanctions are enforced by the individuals immediately present. Goffman (1963) labels the situations the authors used in the experiments *temporary territories*. It is clear that a person placing his coat over the back of a chair desires to reserve the space, and most people in the immediate vicinity will support his claim if questioned (although they will remain uninvolved if they can); such behavior meets Hediger's (1950) definition of territory presented previously as well as the more simple one provided by Noble (1939) that a territory represents "any defended area." The phenomena the present authors have studied do not belong under other available rubrics of spatial behavior, such as home range, biotope, niche, or life space. The major differences between the experimental situations and more enduring territories is that the latter are meshed with a legal-cultural framework and supported in the end by laws, police, and armies. The marked spaces in the present authors' experiments have no legal status and are supported only by the immediate social system. Occasionally it became necessary to articulate the structure of the system by "requiring" neighbors to enter the situation.

People are now spending an increasing portion of their time in public or institutional spaces, including theaters, airport lobbies, buses, schools, and hospitals, where the use of personal belongings to mark out temporary territories is a common phenomenon. The study of territories, temporary as well as enduring ones, deserves study by psychologists. There is some danger that such work will lose much of its force if some semantic clarity is not obtained. While the ethologist's definition of a territory as "any defended area" has considerable heuristic value, there is no need to assume that the mechanisms underlying human and animal behavior are identical. The paucity of data about human territorial behavior makes it most reasonable to assume that the mechanisms are analogous rather than homologous.

In conclusion, the present series of studies suggests that further investigation of spatial markers is feasible and warranted. The physical environment has for too long been considered the background variable in psychological research. The time is past when we can have theories of man that do not take into account his surroundings. Boundary markers not only define what belongs to a person and what belongs to his neighbor, but also who he is and what it means to be a neighbor in a complex society.

REFERENCES

Altman, I., & Haythorn, W. W. The ecology of isolated groups. *Behavioral Science,* 1967, *12,* 169–182.

Ardrey, R. *African genesis.* London: Collins, 1961.

Ardrey, S. *The territorial imperative.* New York: Atheneum, 1966.

Esser, A. H. et al. Territoriality of patients on a research ward. In J. Wortis (Ed.), *Recent advances in biological psychiatry.* Vol. 8. New York: Plenum Press, 1965.

Felipe, N., & Sommer, R. Invasions of personal space. *Social Problems,* 1966, *14,* 206–214.

Goffman, E. *Behavior in public places.* New York: Free Press of Glencoe, 1963.

Hall, E. T. *The hidden dimension.* Garden City: Doubleday, 1966.

Hediger, H. *Wild animals in captivity.* London: Butterworths, 1950.

Lipman, A. Old peoples homes: Siting and neighborhood integration. *The Sociological Review,* 1967, *15,* 323–338.

Lyman, S. M., & Scott, M. B. Territoriality: A neglected sociological dimension. *Social Problems,* 1967, *15,* 236–249.

Noble, G. K. The role of dominance in the social life of birds. *Auk,* 1939, 263–273.

Roos, P. D. Jurisdiction: An ecological concept. *Human Relations,* 1968, *21,* 75–84.

Sommer, R. Sociofugal space. *American Journal of Sociology,* 1967, *72,* 654–660.

NOTES

1. The authors are grateful to Harriet Becker, Martha Connell, Ann Gibbs, Lee Mohr, Tighe O'Hanrahan, Pamela Pearce, Ralph Requa, Sally Robison, and Nancy Russo for their assistance.

2. The neighbors' replies to the intruder's question were scored separately by two coders as indicating defense of the space ("Yes, that seat is taken") or nondefense ("No, it isn't taken" or "I don't know"). There was 100% agreement between the two raters in scoring the replies into defense or nondefense categories.

CRITICAL THINKING QUESTIONS

1. The study noted that in several instances, males were much more likely to ignore territorial markers than were females. Why do you think this was the case? Design a study to determine why males treat territorial markers differently than females do.

2. This article studied various territorial markers in several different settings. What other public spaces might be interesting to study in terms of territorial defense? Besides the markers used in the article, what other ones might be examined?

3. Following the presentation of Study 7, the authors mentioned that they interviewed additional subjects on the question of how personal belongings could reserve space. These subjects' responses differed from what was found in the research. What does this suggest about the relationship between what people do and say? Does it imply that how people respond to a questionnaire also may differ from how they actually act?

ADDITIONAL RELATED READINGS

Altman, I. (1975). *The environment and social behavior.* Monterey, CA: Brooks/Cole.

Werner, C. M., Brown, B. B., & Damron, G. (1981). Territorial marking in a game arcade. *Journal of Personality and Social Psychology, 41,* 1094–1104.

Worchel, S., & Lollis, M. (1982). Reactions to territorial contamination as a function of culture. *Personality and Social Psychology Bulletin, 8,* 365–370.

ARTICLE 36 _____

Another area of research on environmental factors undertaken by psychologists is the impact of the physical environment on human behavior. For example, much research has been done on factors such as noise, crowding, and temperature, determining the conditions under which these variables negatively affect behavior and the types of effects that are produced.

One important environmental factor that also may influence behavior is disaster or the potential for disaster, either natural or humanmade. What would be the consequences of experiencing a natural disaster, such as an earthquake? What about living in the shadow of a potential earthquake? Physical, psychological, and emotional reactions are all possible outcomes of such stressful experiences.

In March 1979, there was an accident at the nuclear power plant at Three Mile Island (TMI) in Pennsylvania. Studies were done immediately following the accident on the physical and psychological effects on the people who lived near TMI. Once the immediate danger was over, did the lives of these people return to normal, at least as measured by psychological and physical indices? Or did the effects of the accident persist well beyond the immediate emergency situation? What about people who may live near a nuclear reactor that has never had a problem, although the potential for one certainly exists? Is living next to a nuclear reactor stressful? These and related questions are addressed in the following article by Baum, Gatchel, and Schaeffer.

Emotional, Behavioral, and Physiological Effects of Chronic Stress at Three Mile Island

■ Andrew Baum, Robert J. Gatchel, and Marc A. Schaeffer

The present study evaluated the psychophysiological impact of a powerful environmental stressor—the uncertainty and threat during the aftermath of the nuclear accident at Three Mile Island (TMI). TMI residents were compared with samples of people living near an undamaged nuclear power plant, people living near a traditional coal-fired power plant, and people living in an area more than 20 miles from any power plant. A number of self-report measures of psychological stress were evaluated by administering the Symptom Checklist-90 and the Beck Depression Inventory more than 1 year after the nuclear accident. In addition, two behavioral measures of stress were obtained (performances on a proofreading task and an embedded figures task). Finally, urinary catecholamine levels were assayed in order to examine chronic stress-related sympathetic arousal. Results indicated that residents of the TMI area exhibited more symptoms of stress (self-report, performance, and catecholamine levels) more than 1 year after the nuclear accident than did people living under different circumstances. Although the intensity of these problems appears

Reprinted from the *Journal of Consulting and Clinical Psychology*, 1983, *51*, 565–572. Copyright 1983 by the American Psychological Association. Reprinted by permission.

to be subclinical, the persistence of stress may be cause for some concern.

Cataclysmic phenomena, as defined by Lazarus and Cohen (1977), are sudden, powerful events that severely tax the adaptive abilities of those who are exposed. These phenomena may be acute or chronic: natural disasters usually pass quickly, whereas effects of war or imprisonment are usually more prolonged. When events are of brief duration, psychological disturbances generally subside as the event ends and social cohesiveness and effective coping increase (e.g., Quarantelli & Dynes, 1972). When more prolonged, these events are associated with longer term disturbances (e.g., Menninger, 1952; Popkin, Stillner, Osborn, Pierce, & Shurley, 1974). The present study considers a sudden and powerful stressor that had both acute and chronic components. The accident at Three Mile Island (TMI) was a relatively short-term event that required major adaptive response by area residents. The subsequent years, filled with continued uncertainty, threat, confusion, and mistrust, may be considered a chronic aftermath that has inhibited recovery from the accident and generated stress of its own.

The accident at TMI and the 2-week emergency period that followed appear to have had acute effects on area residents. Previous research at TMI has reported evidence of psychological stress and mental health problems including demoralization, fear, and emotional disturbances (e.g., Dohrenwend, Dohrenwend, Kasl, & Warheit, 1979; Flynn, 1979; Houts, Miller, Tokuhata, & Ham, 1980). Other studies have reported on the continuing effects, including increased risk for depression, anxiety, and heightened symptom reporting up to 9 months after the accident (Bromet, 1980a; 1980b; Flynn & Chalmers, 1979). These chronic problems may reflect a chronic perception of threat by area residents (e.g., Lazarus, 1966), and a number of persistent sources of threat can be identified. These include continuing concern about possible harm caused by radiation during the accident and the perception that "new" radiation exposure or radioactive contamination could occur as a result of the radioactive gas and water that remained trapped within the reactor building.

Whether residents have actually been exposed to dangerous levels of radiation or whether such exposure is still possible or likely is not as important here as whether area residents believe that these possibilities are real. The crucial role of appraisal in stress has been well-documented (e.g., Lazarus & Launier, 1978), and data suggest that many residents of the TMI area continued to perceive threats as a result of the nuclear plant's presence (Flynn & Chalmers, 1979). Given the continued presence of sources of stress in the TMI area, it was predicted that TMI residents would exhibit emotional disturbances symptomatic of stress and that these problems would be in excess of what would be expected if the TMI incident had not occurred.

The demonstration of an "excess" in psychological difficulties is elusive: preaccident data on area residents are not available, and one can never know what could have happened to them in the absence of an accident. Most studies of TMI have compared TMI residents with control populations in order to demonstrate elevations in stress or mental health problems. Typically, they compare residents living near the plant (e.g., within 5 miles) with people living relatively far from TMI (e.g., more than 40 miles). This kind of comparison does not eliminate the possibility that simply living near a power plant generates stress, whether or not an accident has occurred. Bromet (1980a) corrected for this, comparing TMI residents with people living near an undamaged nuclear plant. She did not, however, include a group living near a nonnuclear plant or a group of people living far from any type of plant. As a result, we do not know if living near an undamaged power plant is associated with greater stress than is living far from such a plant. If it is stressful living near any plant, interpretation of responses by TMI area residents must consider this.

In order to account for all levels of presence of a power plant and to determine the effects, if any, of living near an undamaged plant, the present study considered four groups. TMI residents were compared with samples of people living near an undamaged nuclear power plant, near a traditional coal-fired power plant, and in an area more than 20 miles from any power plant. An attempt was made to sample areas of comparable socioeconomic status so that comparisons would only reflect differences related to TMI and the presence of power plants. By making these comparisons, the independent effects of living near any power plant could be considered.

A number of self-report measures of psychological stress were collected, including anxiety, depression, somatic complaints, and alienation, 1 year after the accident. In addition, two behavioral measures of stress were obtained, and urinary catecholamine levels were assayed in order to examine chronic stress-related sympathetic arousal. These measures were intended not to identify major psychological or health problems associated with acute stressors but to assess subclinical disturbances more characteristic of longer term problems.

METHOD

Subjects

A total of 121 subjects participated in this study. The TMI group was composed of 38 people living within 5 miles of the damaged power plant. One control group (Frederick, Maryland) was made up of people living in an area 20 miles away from any plant, and another control group (Oyster Creek, New Jersey) consisted of 32 people living within 5 miles of an undamaged nuclear plant. The third control group (Dickerson, Maryland) was made up of 24 residents of a 5-mile area around a coal-fired plant.

Neighborhoods within each of these four communities were selected on the basis of comparability with one another on several demographic variables. Subjects were selected in a quasi-random fashion: Streets within neighborhoods were randomly sampled, and every third house on sampled streets was approached. If the person answering the door was an adult, he or she was recruited for an interview by the experimenter. Potential subjects were told that the study was

concerned with the psychological impact of events such as the accident at TMI. Control subjects were given an explanation that indicated they would serve as a comparison to the TMI sample. They were all told that the study was a scientific one and that the results would not necessarily be applicable to the decision-making process regarding future disposition of the TMI plant. Approximately 70% of those given the opportunity to participate agreed to do so, and there were no differences in response rates among the four sites. Interviews were performed in the subject's home and lasted 1 to 2 hours. Subjects were paid for their participation.

Dependent Measures

A number of self-report, behavioral and biochemical measures were evaluated. Two behavioral measures, a proofreading task and an embedded figures task, were administered to subjects. The proofreading task was similar to that used by Glass and Singer (1972) in their studies of noise stress. Subjects were given a passage to read and asked to find typographical and grammatical errors that had been inserted into the text. The other task consisted of eight complex geometric figures in which one of five simpler target figures was hidden. The object was for the subject to locate and outline the simpler figure. On each of the eight trials, time was measured in an unobtrusive manner.

The following three different self-report measures were collected:

1. The Symptom Checklist-90 (SCL-90) is a 90-item multidimensional inventory developed at Johns Hopkins University. It has been shown useful in examining subclinical levels of disturbance in a number of settings (e.g., Bromet, 1980a, 1980b; Derogatis, Rickels, & Rock, 1976). Symptoms are rated on a 5-point scale, and a measure of global symptom reporting as well as subscale indexes are obtained.
2. The Beck Depression Inventory (BDI) is an instrument that has been found to be effective in measuring symptoms of depression (Beck,

1967). The inventory consists of 21 sets of statements from which the respondent is asked to select the most self-descriptive. This instrument has been useful in discriminating depression from other psychological difficulties.

3. A background questionnaire assessing demographic and social status information was administered for the purpose of comparing the degree of similarity of the four samples.

Chronic sympathetic arousal was measured through biochemical assays of urine samples provided by subjects. These assays yielded estimates of free epinephrine and norepinephrine in the urine. These estimates have proven to be a useful measure of stress-related arousal and are particularly useful when stress is chronic (Frankenhaeuser, 1975). Studies have, for example, found associations between occupational stress and catecholamine excretion (e.g., Frankenhaeuser, Note 1) and several researchers have reported that stress increases catecholamine levels in plasma and urine (e.g., Baum, Grunberg, & Singer, 1982; Levi, 1972; Mason, 1975).

Procedure

All four groups were surveyed simultaneously by four teams of trained experimenters. This was done in August 1980, approximately 17 months after the accident at TMI. Two independent teams of 3 trained experimenters each collected data at TMI and Oyster Creek, while two independent teams of two trained experimenters each gathered information at Frederick and Dickerson. Each session began with a brief discussion of the project and an explanation that participation was voluntary. Informed consent was obtained.

The two performance measures were administered first. Subjects were allowed to work on each of the eight embedded figures as long as they wanted. Instructions stated that the subject was to work on each problem in order and to go to the next problem only when the present problem was solved or when they desired to stop working on it. It was emphasized that they could not go back and work on problems once passed. The number

of attempts, number of correct responses, and time spent on each problem were recorded. After completion of the embedded-figures exercise, the subjects were given instructions on the proofreading task. They were told that they had 5 minutes to read through the seven-page passage and to circle as many spelling, grammatical, and typographical errors as they found. Following the proofreading, subjects were asked to complete the questionnaires.

Subjects were asked to provide a 15-hour urine sample. This meant collecting all urine excreted overnight (6 p.m.–9 a.m.) following their interview. A noncaustic preservative was added to each sample to prevent oxidation, and samples were frozen immediately after collection. Assays of these samples for urinary epinephrine and norepinephrine levels were performed according to radioenzymatic COMT procedures.

RESULTS

One-way analyses of variance (ANOVAS) considering the effects of living in one or another of the research sites were performed on the data. In addition, mean contrasts were performed according to procedures suggested by Tukey (Myers, 1966). In this way, the differences (or lack thereof) between TMI and each control group and among the control groups, could be examined.

The background and demographic characteristics of the four groups were comparable, as can be seen in Table 1. All subjects were white, and roughly two thirds of each sample was female. Seventy percent of the subjects were 30 years of age or older, and less than one third had graduated from college. The Frederick sample deviated a bit in that it had more college graduates and was slightly younger than the others. Almost all subjects were married and over three quarters had children. Furthermore, nearly all of the subjects were employed in some capacity. Correlations between background variables (i.e., education, income, years married, family size, age, number of children) and behavioral and self-report measures failed to attain significance.

TABLE 1 / Background Characteristics of the Three Mile Island (TMI), Frederick, Oyster Creek, and Dickerson Samples

Characteristic	TMI	No plant (Frederick)	Undamaged nuclear plant (Oyster Creek)	Undamaged coal plant (Dickerson)
Age (M)	33.3	30.9	35.8	34.1
Sex (% female)	65	58	57	67
No. of children				
None	22	23	25	23
1–2	60	67	65	64
3	18	10	12	13
Own home	91	100	100	96
Education				
High school degree or less	78	65	80	75
College degree or more	22	35	20	25
Family income				
$15,000/year	6	6	12	8
$15,001–20,000/year	46	52	55	46
$20,001–30,000/year	33	37	31	33
> $30,000/year	15	5	12	13

Note. All values given are percentages except those for age.

Symptom Reporting

It was predicted that TMI residents would exhibit greater evidence of stress than would control subjects by reporting more symptoms of emotional distress. In addition, it was reasoned that the differences in levels of stress between TMI and comparison residents were not caused by the fact that TMI residents lived near a power plant but rather by the fact that the power plant was TMI. Generally these predictions were confirmed, as TMI residents' reports of emotional distress were greater than those of residents in each of the three control groups (see Table 2). One-way ANOVAS and subsequent mean comparisons indicated that TMI residents were significantly different from the three comparison groups for global symptom reporting, somatic complaints, anxiety, and alienation. Findings for the Beck Depression Inventory approached significance. Mean comparisons indicated that control subjects were comparable to one another on these measures, $p > .05$ and that they were all significantly different from TMI residents ($p < .05$).

Task Performance

As can be seen in Table 3, data for task performance also suggested that TMI residents experienced more difficulty than did residents of any control areas. Analyses of variance on the embedded-figures task indicated that there were significant differences among the four groups for success at solving puzzles, $F(3, 126) = 3.089$, $p < .05$, and number of attempts made on the puzzles, $F(3, 126) = 5.793$, $p < .01$. The analysis for amount of time spent on the task did not produce any significant effects. Again, there were no significant differences among the three control groups on either number of attempts or number correct, and mean comparisons indicated that TMI subjects' performance was significantly different from the three control groups' when the latter was combined ($p < .05$).

Performance on the proofreading task also showed deficits among TMI residents relative to control subjects. TMI residents appeared to find fewer of the inserted errors overall than did control subjects, $F(3, 127) = 15.804$, $p < .001$.

TABLE 2 / Group Means and Standard Deviations for Each Symptom Checklist-90 Scale and for the Beck Depression Inventory

Scale	Three Mile Island		No plant (Frederick)		Coal-fired plant (Dickerson)		Undamaged nuclear plant (Oyster Creek)		$F(3,118)$
	M	SD	M	SD	M	SD	M	SD	
Total number of symptoms reported	25.97	21.0	14.54	11.5	16.63	11.8	16.16	13.5	3.827**
Somatic distress	.55	.67	.24	.30	.29	.50	.30	.30	2.854**
Concentration problems	.52	.61	.40	.60	.37	.33	.45	.65	ns
Interpersonal problems	.22	.34	.06	.20	.15	.27	.43	.43	ns
Depression	.45	.53	.30	.38	.27	.32	.29	.51	ns
Anxiety	.47	.54	.29	.39	.18	.34	.17	.41	3.387**
Anger	.34	.44	.28	.36	.34	.47	.66	.25	ns
Fear	.20	.33	.31	.14	.08	.27	.30	1.3	ns
Suspiciousness	.38	.07	.17	.24	.16	.27	.51	1.6	ns
Alienation	.20	.36	.03	.02	.10	.10	.10	.17	3.033**
Beck Depression Inventory	6.0	6.5	3.64	3.3	3.54	3.6	3.50	4.2	2.104*

*$p < .10.$ **$p < .05.$

TABLE 3 / Group Means for the Embedded Figures and Proofreading Tasks

Measure	Three Mile Island	No plant (Frederick)	Coal-fired plant (Dickerson)	Undamaged nuclear plant (Oyster Creek)
No. of attempts	6.64	7.97	8.00	7.48
No. correct	3.79	5.64	5.10	5.00
Total time spent on each problem (sec)	789	910	940	872
% of proofreading errors found	44	73	70	74

When the amount of the passage that was completed was considered, an ANOVA also found differences among the four groups, $F(3, 127) = 13.349$, $p < .001$ (see Table 3). Mean contrasts again revealed no significant differences among control groups. They also indicated that TMI residents found fewer of the errors in the passage that they read than did each control group (*ps* < .05).

Urinary Catecholamines

Table 4 summarizes findings for epinephrine and norepinephrine levels in subjects' urine samples. Chronic sympathetic arousal among TMI subjects would be revealed in higher levels of these catecholamines, and ANOVAS indicated that there were differences among the groups in levels of ep-

TABLE 4 / Group Means for Epinephrine and Norepinephrine

Measure	Three Mile Island	No plant (Frederick)	Coal-fired plant (Dickerson)	Undamaged nuclear plant (Oyster Creek)
Epinephrine (ng/ml)	12.32	8.88	6.20	7.50
Norepinephrine (ng/ml)	25.66	21.01	15.68	13.73

inephrine, $F(3, 89) = 3.016, p < .05$, and norepinephrine, $F(3, 94) = 3.743, p < .05$. Mean comparisons indicated that both epinephrine and norepinephrine levels among TMI area residents were significantly higher than were levels exhibited by subjects living near undamaged coal and nuclear plants ($ps < .05$). These differences approached significance for the TMI–no plant comparison, $p < .10$, and there were no differences among control groups.

DISCUSSION

It is rare to have the opportunity to systematically evaluate the effects of a naturally occurring stressor. It is also unusual to be able to examine psychological reactions during a protracted stress situation, not just after the stressor has been terminated. The present study was able to evaluate the ongoing psychophysiological impact of an environmental stressor—the uncertainty and threat during the aftermath of the nuclear accident at TMI.

The results of the present investigation indicate that residents of the TMI area exhibit more symptoms of stress almost 1 1/2 years after the accident than do people living under different circumstances. Residents of the TMI area reported more symptoms overall as well as more somatic complaints, anxiety, depression, and alienation relative to residents in other areas. Moreover, task performance revealed significant differences between TMI and other residents. Both tests require concentration and a certain degree of motivation, both of which can be affected by stress. Finally, examination of catecholamine levels suggested that TMI residents experienced greater stress-

related sympathetic arousal than did control subjects.

The present study represents some degree of refinement of previous research on TMI. Only one other study evaluating the psychological impact of the TMI accident (Bromet, 1980b) considered the possibility that living near any nuclear plant, regardless of whether an accident had occurred there, could be stressful. In that study, TMI residents were compared to people living near an undamaged nuclear plant more than 100 miles away. However, no comparisons were made with people who did not live near a plant, and, as a result, the study indicates only that TMI residents exhibit some stress symptoms that people living near an undamaged nuclear plant do not. No conclusions about the stressful effects of any plant can be drawn. The present study allows for this comparison and adds a test for the possibility that any power plant may be a source of stress. The data indicate that residents of an area near an undamaged nuclear plant show no more stress effects than do people living near a fossil-fuel plant or near no plant at all. The effects observed at TMI, then, appear to be unique to TMI and not to be associated with the simple presence of a nuclear plant.

When one has multiple sources of data to draw upon, there is usually a higher degree of confidence in making a conclusive statement about the effects of a stressor than when only one type of data is available. In the present study, subjective evaluations, performance measures, and physiological markers of arousal all point to the general conclusion that there is a higher level of background or chronic stress among TMI residents relative to the other groups. As predicted, the magnitude of the psychological effects assessed in the present study suggests that the stress is mild: Symptom reporting scores for TMI residents were lower than one would expect for mental health patients, and behavioral performance deficits were on an order commonly associated with response to acute laboratory stressors (e.g., Glass & Singer, 1972). Further, average catecholamine levels among TMI area residents were in what is considered to be the normal range. Generally speaking, the degree or extent of stress experienced by TMI residents appears to resemble the low magnitude "daily hassles" described by Lazarus and Cohen (1977).

However, this does not eliminate the possibility of negative consequences for TMI area residents. These low-level stress responses persisted 17 months after the accident, and there is some research to indicate that negative effects can occur if an individual remains for an extended period of time in a situation where he or she feels threatened. Satloff (1967) and Serxner (1968) assessed groups of individuals confined in submerged submarines for 60-day periods. In these groups, approximately 5% of the men developed psychological disturbances, which appeared to be precipitated by stress. Symptoms such as anxiety, depression, insomnia, headaches, and other somatic complaints were common. In another such study, Popkin et al. (1974) examined the behavior of a team in a South Pole station during the 6-month Antarctic night. More than one half of the 22 men demonstrated "drifting" during this period. This condition was characterized by apathy, inattention, and a general reduction of cognitive functioning. Prolonged exposure to stress has also been linked to health problems (e.g., Eliot & Buell, Note 2). Exposure to stress for relatively long periods of time, even if not severe, may have significant effects on the functioning of an individual.

Given this persistent distress, some discussion of possible intervention and ameliorative effort is warranted. However, the nature of stress at TMI may make such action extremely difficult. The various sources of stress at TMI are fairly clear, and although removal of these threats is the most ob-vious step to take, such a strategy may not prove effective. Research has suggested that removal of one of these sources of stress, the radioactive gas in the reactor containment building, was associated with a temporary decrease in stress (Baum, Gatchel, Fleming, & Lake, 1981). This research also indicates, however, that even at its lowest levels, stress was still greater among TMI area residents than among control subjects and that stress levels among TMI subjects increased again after this decontamination step was completed. This probably reflects the fact that only one of several sources of stress was eliminated in this decontamination procedure. Radioactive water, for example, still remains in the reactor building, and the core has not been removed.

Ultimately, there may be sources of stress that cannot be removed. Some area residents believe that they have been exposed to radiation already, and this appears to have given rise to uncertainty as well as appraisal of harm. These psychological outcomes can evoke stress responding, and it may be neither ethical nor possible to change them. In the absence of firm evidence that residents were not exposed to any radiation and any clear information about the effects of even modest exposure levels, it may not be in anyone's interest to attempt to convince residents that their concerns are inappropriate or unwarranted. Treatment of continuing concerns presents a challenge to those interested in reducing distress among area residents.

One fruitful avenue for approaching these problems may be found in the use of behavioral or cognitive stress-management programs. Research at TMI has indicated that residents who have concentrated their coping on regulation of emotional response exhibit less stress than do those who do not (Collins, Baum, & Singer, 1982). Procedures such as those used in muscle relaxation training, biofeedback, cognitive restructuring, and the like are analogous to these self-directed attempts to reduce stress, and they may prove useful in managing the problems experienced at TMI. Stress-management programs are currently available to people living near several nuclear plants, and it would be interesting and useful to determine whether such efforts could bring about changes in psychological and physiological distress among TMI area residents.

REFERENCE NOTES

1. Frankenhaeuser, M. *Coping with job stress: A psychological approach* (Report No. 532). Stockholm, Sweden: Department of Psychology, University of Stockholm, 1978.
2. Eliot, R., & Buell, J. *Environmental and behavioral influences in the major cardiovascular disorders.* Paper presented at the annual meeting of the Academy of Behavioral Medicine Research, Snowbird, Utah 1979.

REFERENCES

Baum, A., Gatchel, R. J., Fleming, R., & Lake, C. R. *Chronic and acute stress associated with the Three Mile Island accident and decontamination: Preliminary findings of a longitudinal study* (Technical report submitted to the U.S. Nuclear Regulatory Commission.).Washington, D.C.: U.S. Government Printing Office, 1981.

Baum, A., Grunberg, N. E., & Singer, J. E. The use of psychological and neuroendocrinological measurements in the study of stress. *Health Psychology,* 1982, *1,* 217–236.

Beck, A. T. *Depression: Clinical, experimental, and theoretical aspects.* New York: Hoeber, 1967.

Bromet, E. *Preliminary report on the mental health of Three Mile Island residents.* Pittsburgh, Penn.: Western Psychiatric Institute, 1980. (a)

Bromet, E. *Three Mile Island: Mental health findings.* Pittsburgh, Pa: Western Psychiatric Institute and Clinic and the University of Pittsburgh, 1980. (b)

Collins, D. L., Baum, A., & Singer, J. E. Coping with chronic stress at Three Mile Island: Psychological and biochemical evidence. *Health Psychology.* 1983, *2,* 149–166.

Derogatis, L., Rickels, K., & Rock, A. The SCL-90 and the MMPI: A step in the validation of a new self-report scale. *British Journal of Psychiatry,* 1976, *128,* 280–289.

Dohrenwend, B. P., Dohrenwend, B. S., Kasl, S. V., & Warheit, G. J. *Report of the Task Group on Behavioral Effects to the President's Commission on the Accident at Three Mile Island.* Washington, D.C.: U.S. Government Printing Office, 1979.

Flynn, C. B. *Three Mile Island telephone survey.* Washington, D.C.: Nuclear Regulatory Commission (NUREG/CR-1093), 1979.

Flynn, C. B., & Chalmers, J. A. The social and eco-nomic effects of the accident at Three Mile Island (Prepared for the Nuclear Regulatory Commission as Document NUREG/CR-1215). Tempe, Ariz.: Mountain West Research, 1979.

Frankenhaeuser, M. Experimental approaches to the study of catecholamines and emotions. In L. Levi (Ed.), *Emotions: Their parameters and measurement.* New York: Raven Press, 1975.

Glass, D. C., & Singer, J. E. *Urban stress: Experiments on noise and social stressors.* New York: Academic, 1972.

Houts, P., Miller, R. W., Tokuhata, G. K., & Ham, K. S. *Health-related behavioral impact of the Three Mile Island nuclear accident* (Report submitted to the TMI Advisory Panel on health-related studies). Hershey, Penn.: Pennsylvania Department of Health, 1980.

Lazarus, R. S. *Psychological stress and the coping process.* New York: McGraw-Hill, 1966.

Lazarus, R. S., & Cohen, J. B. Environmental stress. In I. Attman & J. F. Wohlwill (Eds.), *Human behavior and environment* (Vol. 2). New York: Plenum Press, 1977.

Lazarus, R. S., & Launier, R. Stress-related transactions between person and environment. In L. A. Pervin & M. Lewis (Eds.), *Internal and external determinants of behavior.* New York: Plenum Press, 1978.

Levi, L. Stress and distress in response to psychosocial stimuli: Laboratory and real life studies on sympathoadrenomedullary and related reactions. *Acta Medica Scandinavia Supplement. 528,* 1972.

Mason, J. W. A historical view of the stress field. *Journal of Human Stress,* 1975, *1,* 22–36.

Menninger, W. C. Psychological reactions in an emergency. *American Journal of Psychiatry,* 1952, *109,* 128–130.

Myers, J. L. *Fundamentals of experimental design.* Boston: Allyn and Bacon, 1966.

Popkin, M. K., Stillner, V., Osborn, L. W., Pierce, C. M., & Shurley, J. T. Novel behaviors in an extreme environment. *American Journal of Psychiatry,* 1974, *131,* 651–654.

Quarantelli, E. L., & Dynes, R. R. When disaster strikes. *Psychology Today,* September 1972, 66–70.

Satloff, A. Psychiatry and the nuclear submarine. *American Journal of Psychiatry,* 1967, *124,* 547–551.

Serxner, J. An experience in submarine psychiatry. *American Journal of Psychiatry,* 1968, *125,* 25–30.

Witkin, H. A., Goodenough, D. R., & Oltman, D. K. Psychological differentiation: Current status. *Jour-*

nal of Personality and Social Psychology, 1979, *37,* 1127–1145.

This research was facilitated by research support from the Uniformed Services University of the Health Sciences (CO7216) and from the U.S. Nuclear Regulatory Commission (NRC-03-81-135). Its conclusions are those of the authors and do not necessarily reflect the opinions of these agencies.

The authors wish to thank C. R. Lake for conducting catecholamine assays and John R. Aiello, Daniel L. Collins, Raymond Fleming, Martha M. Gisriel, and Brenda Thew for their help in conducting this research. Our appreciation is also extended to Carlene S. Baum, Martha M. Gisriel, and Jerome E. Singer for their helpful comments on earlier drafts of this manuscript.

CRITICAL THINKING QUESTIONS

1. In October 1989, San Francisco experienced a major earthquake. Would you expect to see a pattern of behavioral effects in the people who experienced the earthquake similar to that found in the people who lived through the TMI experience? Or are the situations somehow different? Design an experiment to study the effects of experiencing an earthquake versus living in an area with the potential for an earthquake.

2. Besides nuclear accidents and potential earthquakes, what other situations may produce prolonged stress reactions similar to those found in the present study?

3. The present study was conducted $1\frac{1}{2}$ years after the TMI accident. Would it be worthwhile to continue to conduct similar studies over varying lengths of time (i.e., 5 years, 10 years, etc.)? Why or why not?

4. The results of the study were statistically significant but subclinical in intensity for residents of TMI. In fact, the authors suggested that "the degree or extent of stress experienced by TMI residents appears to resemble the low magnitude 'daily hassles' " described by other researchers. However, as discussed in the article, "negative effects can occur if an individual remains for an extended period of time in a situation where he or she feels threatened." Could it be that the consequences of exposure to prolonged stress experienced by TMI residents might not be different from those experienced by people facing other prolonged stress, such as long commutes in heavy traffic? What "daily hassles" could possibly cause effects similar to those found in TMI residents?

Chapter Thirteen

APPLYING SOCIAL PSYCHOLOGY I: HEALTH AND LEGAL ISSUES

BOTH OF THE LAST two chapters in this book of readings have *Applying Social Psychology* in their titles. This heading needs some explaining, since it otherwise might create the wrong impression for the reader.

Applied social psychology usually refers to the application of principles and findings generated by research in social psychology to a real-world setting. In a sense, this is where social psychology is used to help solve practical problems. But by labeling these chapters *applied,* it might seem to suggest that the preceding 12 chapters were not applied and did not have real-world applications. If you already have read through most if not all of the preceding chapters, you know that is not the case. Many of the studies in the earlier chapters have direct implications for real-world problems. Although the research may seem abstract and theoretical at times, we need only to apply those principles to various social problems to yield an applied form of social psychology.

What distinguishes the research contained in Chapters 13 and 14 is that it was specifically designed and undertaken to address significant real-world issues. Such research has been conducted in many, many areas. The issues selected here are some of the most common areas of concern but are by no means the only ones in the domain of applied social psychology.

This chapter addresses applications of social psychological research to two important areas of human endeavor. The first area is health psychology. When we think of health, often the first thing that comes to mind is the medical, biological component of illness. But what about the behaviors that are linked to illness? Obviously, people can do many things either to increase or decrease the likelihood of illness. Health psychology research examines issues such as personality factors that may be related to health, the underlying beliefs about health-related issues, and how these beliefs can be changed. Article 37 is a good example of the types of concerns addressed by social psychologists working in this field. "Private Passions and Public Health" addresses an illness that is—or should be—of concern to everyone: AIDS. Why people continue to engage in sexual behavior that puts them at risk for contracting AIDS, as well as potential ways to change such dangerous behaviors, are but two of the issues raised in the article.

The remaining two articles are drawn from the area of forensic (legal) psychology. Does the legal system, as it presently operates, guarantee an objective, unbiased outcome from its processes? Social psychologists working in this field have examined a number of factors that may influence the outcome in a legal setting. One major topic has been jury trials, since they are a common part of the U.S. judicial system. Article 38, "Beautiful but Dangerous," examines the relationship between the attractiveness of an offender and the nature of the crime and how these two factors may influence the judgments of a jury. Article 39, "Trivial Persuasion in the Courtroom," also relates to jury trials but focuses on the type and amount of information that eyewitnesses use and how this may influence the outcome of a jury's deliberations. Both of these articles have very important implications for how fair the verdicts of juries may be.

ARTICLE 37 _____

One area where research in social psychology can have a direct impact on the well-being of society is that of health psychology. Illness and wellness are not just the results of certain biological factors. Many health factors are directly related to behaviors over which people have some control. For example, lung cancer has been clearly linked to cigarette smoking. Programs that effectively get people to stop smoking or prevent people from beginning to smoke in the first place are of obvious practical importance. Social psychology has made many useful discoveries for how the health-related behavior of people may be improved.

One of the major health issues confronting the United States and much of the rest of the world today is Acquired Immune Deficiency Syndrome, or AIDS. By now, most people know something about who may contract AIDS (not only homosexuals and intravenous drug users, for example), as well as how it spreads. Yet in spite of the knowledge available for how to reduce or minimize the risk of getting AIDS, many people ignore the advice and continue in behaviors that put them at high risk. Why? Why would someone be unwilling to take even the simplest precautions to minimize the risk of getting AIDS? In "Private Passions and Public Health," Krajick examines the reasons people may engage in such risky behavior, as well as ways that such threatening behavior might be changed.

Private Passions and Public Health

■ Kevin Krajick

A few years ago, Gayle, a 29-year-old Houston woman who works in a bank, had a three-week fling with a man in her office. "The next thing I knew," she says, "some of the other guys in the office were telling me he'd been propositioning them." She became terrified that her apparently bisexual lover had infected her with the AIDS virus.

During the next two years, she worried often but was dissuaded from being tested for infection; her friends and her doctor told her she was worrying about nothing. In the meantime, she insisted that her sex partners use condoms. But the fear built to such a pitch that she would wake up two or three nights a week obsessed with the question: "Do I have it?"

Recently Gayle (all case names have been changed) decided that she had to know for sure.

She went for testing, and at the end of three agonizing weeks, she got the result: negative. "I felt like I'd been given back my life," she says. To celebrate, she treated herself to a week-long vacation at a Florida resort, where a good-looking man "came on strong" to her. After resisting for several days, she decided to go to bed with him—"no birth control, no rubber, no nothing. I just decided to let myself get swept up by the moment."

When Gayle returned home, she was stricken by mortal fear. Now she is back to waking up nights. "I feel like I'm right back where I started," she says. Gayle wants to take another test but knows she will have to wait for months before the results will be reliable.

Gayle isn't the only one who is worried. An estimated 43,000 people a month in this country are voluntarily going to public test sites to find

Reprinted from *Psychology Today*, 1988 (May), *22*, 50–58. Reprinted with permission from *Psychology Today Magazine.* Copyright © 1988 (PT Partners, L.P.).

out whether they are infected with the Human Immunodeficiency Virus (HIV), believed to be the cause of AIDS. Three times that number may be flocking to physicians' offices, family-planning clinics and other private settings. At public sites alone the monthly test rate has almost tripled since a year ago. Still, probably only 10 to 25 percent of the 1 million to 1.5 million people in the United States who may be infected know they are. Whether they know their status or not, all are capable of passing on the disease by having unprotected sex, sharing contaminated needles while using drugs or both. One-third of those now infected may develop AIDS within seven years of testing, but no one can yet predict who will become ill.

Some test-site personnel are annoyed at the flood of people coming to the centers, most of whom test negative. But a number of experts find the trend encouraging, since they see the test sites as a good place to educate and motivate people — whatever their test results — to practice "safer sex." (That term is replacing "safe sex," since condoms are only 90 percent effective in preventing pregnancy and may be somewhat less effective in preventing HIV infection.)

One such optimist is Michael Osterholm, a Minnesota state epidemiologist: "For those who come out negative, it's an added incentive to stay that way. For those who are positive, it brings home the fact that they can infect others. In either case, it's an important opportunity to educate people about how to change their behavior."

But does the combination of being tested and educated about AIDS actually help people reduce risky behavior? A handful of behavioral scientists are studying how people react once they know their test results. One of the first of these was Thomas J. Coates, a psychologist at the University of California, San Francisco. His work, like most studies so far, focuses on gay and bisexual men. Coates found that while testing and education produced a substantial reduction in risky sexual behavior among the men he studied, some continued to practice sex that might expose themselves or others to HIV.

When the study began, 40 to 50 percent of the 502 men in his study reported that they engaged in anal intercourse without using a condom. Two years later, after all the men had been informed about safer sex and many had been tested, only 12 percent of the 99 men found positive and 18 percent of the 77 men found negative were still practicing unprotected sex; among those who were not tested, 27 percent were still unprotected. Other studies of gay men have had similar results.

Coates acknowledges that the proportion of men who still are knowingly spreading the deadly disease or exposing themselves to it "sounds high, but," he says, "you have to put it in perspective." He sees the group's shift toward safer sex as "above and beyond any other health-related change we've seen. . . . We need to celebrate it while looking for ways to encourage further behavior change."

There is barely any research on how high-risk heterosexuals respond to testing and education, but what little evidence there is suggests that while many do change, a surprising number do not. In a preliminary study, researchers at the University of California, San Francisco, and California State University at Hayward recently interviewed 40 white, middle-class women who were in danger of HIV infection or reinfection because their male sex partners — bisexuals, drug users or hemophiliacs — were infected. Seven of the women were already carrying the virus themselves.

The researchers found that within six months of being tested and taught about safer sex, half of the women continued to practice unprotected sex with their partners, some occasionally, some steadily. Six months after the first test, the women were retested. Miraculously, there were no new cases of HIV infection — although the antibodies may still have been incubating.

Many mental-health professionals who deal with high-risk people say that when such people find they are infected, they usually go to great lengths to protect others. "Most overreact to their infection on the side of caution," says Steve Morin, a San Francisco psychologist who counsels HIV-positive people. "The most common early phenomenon is that they don't want to be touched. They go through elaborate things like refusing to let anyone drink out of the same glass or even sit in the same chair." Many even become celibate for awhile, he said.

But why do some people, even though they know better, continue to place themselves or others at risk of infection? It's too soon for any solid answers, but there are some clues. Some people may be overwhelmed by the raw need for sex, protected or otherwise; others may simply become careless after awhile; still others seem to develop a malicious form of dependency on their partners. Rick Reich, who is the AIDS services co-ordinator for Clark County, Nevada, says he has seen a few cases in which infected men actively try to infect their wives; only some of the women resist, mainly because most of them can't believe their partners are infected. One man even told his wife: "You better stay with me, because no one else will have you when they find out about me. This way, we can have sex forever and never use condoms."

Such men, Reich says, are "scared of being left alone. They're the ones who won't be able to find anyone else, and infecting their wives is the only way for them to make sure they'll have a companion."

Other people do try to get their behavior under control but may find it difficult to adopt a new way of life. Jonathan, a single man in his early 30s, has the easy laugh and engaging, amiable manner of a traveling salesman, which he is. In late 1985, Jonathan found out that he was carrying HIV, although he still has no symptoms of AIDS.

He says that at first, being gay, he tried to seek out other infected men—not necessarily because he wanted to be able to have sex without a condom (not a good idea, say experts; repeated exposure to the virus may hasten the onset of AIDS) but because he felt he could be closer to them. "As a positive, you have this terrible secret you can't even tell other gay men," he explains. "You're an outsider in your own community."

But Jonathan says he has always had a desperate fear of commitment—to the point that he al-

most never goes out on more than two or three dates with anyone. He says, "There's too much tension; it gets too belabored when people try to get to know one another."

Some people, once they discover they're HIV positive, may withhold that fact from their sex partners. Psychologists Susan Kegeles and Joseph Catania of the University of California, San Francisco, found that one-quarter of heterosexual and homosexual people at two test sites said they did not intend to tell casual partners if they turned out to be infected.

But Jonathan found a way to avoid the issue entirely. He returned last year to the life-style that probably infected him in the first place: hanging out in gay bookstores and cinemas, where, two or three nights a week, he has quick, anonymous liaisons with other patrons, ranging from protected to completely unshielded sex. "For me sex is a way of dealing with a lot of problems," says Jonathan, "a lot of anger and frustration. It's a high for me. When you're horny enough, you just want to get it over with, rather than ask a thousand questions and make a confession. When I feel like that, the last thing I'm willing to think about is safe sex.

"When someone comes along and says, 'How can you do that?' well, I used to think it was awful, but now I'm not so self-righteous about it. I assume any guy who comes into one of those places is already infected. . . . It's his decision to be there; I'm not his keeper. If he's there for me, he's there for a whole group of men."

Despite what Jonathan says, some of the people who agree to have sex with him may not be infected at all. Indeed, some may have tested negative but continue to press their luck. Why do they do it?

Brian Willoughby, a physician in Vancouver who has studied gay men's reactions to testing, has a theory shared by a number of other researchers: "When people test negative, some part of them seems to think they're invulnerable. They've suddenly had a big burden lifted from them, and they start thinking all is OK with the world out there."

People have other reasons, too, for behaving

somewhat carelessly after they get the good news. For example, Tom, a single, heterosexual, 29-year-old illustrator in Cincinnati, began to worry recently that he might have become infected during one of his frequent sexual encounters with women he picks up at bars. He began to envy some of his friends who were tested and came out negative because they were "sure they were clear." So a few months ago Tom went for a test. To his relief, he too came out negative. But he has "not really changed" the amount of casual sex he has, although he did "go out and buy a big box of rubbers." He uses them when the women insist.

"If anything, I'm more desperate about getting laid," he says. "There's so much fear of AIDS around that in a few years, no one will want to have sex at all. I want to get it while I can."

In explaining why women sometimes fail to protect themselves and others after getting their test results, sociologists Jane Zones and Diane Beeson say that some women they studied interpreted their reassuring test results to mean that since they weren't already infected, they weren't going to be infected later. Others, they say, "had a mystical thing: They believed if they thought positively, they wouldn't get infected." For the majority, the researchers say, "it was just passion. People were so overcome with sexual feelings that they couldn't think."

Most of the research on how gay men and heterosexual women react to testing has been done with well-educated, highly motivated people who received repeated counseling and who lived in communities such as San Francisco, where awareness of the dangers of HIV is high. What happens among people who are not part of these select groups, such as intravenous drug abusers?

Epidemiologists fear that drug addicts, most of whom are heterosexual, may be a major factor in spreading AIDS to the heterosexual population at large. But for the addicts themselves, the possibility of getting or spreading AIDS—although frightening—is just one problem among many, and often a seemingly remote one. In New York City and northern New Jersey, the center of HIV infection among drug users, as many as 60 percent of addicts may already be infected, but they are not rushing out to be tested.

Debbie, a 31-year-old addict in New York City, had to be talked into being tested by an AIDS-prevention outreach worker. At the testing center, she told a counselor she had been shooting drugs for four years and, although married, had been having sex frequently with various men and women.

Her home is in one of the impoverished Hispanic and black neighborhoods where the virus is still spreading rapidly as many intravenous drug addicts acquire it by sharing contaminated needles. Often they then transmit it to their sex partners, who may or may not be addicts themselves. Some addicts turn to prostitution to pay for their drugs.

Debbie's big, dark eyes and long, curly eyelashes, lithe figure and friendly manner do not seem to fit with the brownish track marks that form splotchy paths along her arms. When it comes time for the test itself, her eyebrow curls up. "Is it gonna hurt?" she asks. "If it's gonna hurt, forget it." The medical technician has a hard time finding an intact vein in her tortured arms and finally has to draw blood from a tiny blood vessel near the surface of her delicate left hand.

When she sees the size of the needle, Debbie gasps, but the technician slides it in quickly. Blood dribbles into the clear glass tube at an agonizingly slow pace as Debbie alternates between wincing and trying to smile. "Almost done, almost done," the technician soothes. After a long minute, with the tube only half full, Debbie moans, "Oh, oh, it really hurts." Her eyes fill with tears. "I don't know why I ever became a drug addict. I hate needles."

According to counselors at the center, there is a less-than-even chance that Debbie will bother to come back for her test results. If she does, and comes out positive, she will get an hour or so of counseling—less if she is negative. What then?

"[The positives] are handed a card with a phone number and address so they can get in line for both drug- and AIDS-related services," says Conrad Maugé, program director of AIDS outreach for New York-based Narcotic and Drug Research, Inc. His private organization uses street workers to inform addicts about the dangers of AIDS, encourage testing and hand out condoms as well as vials of bleach for sterilizing needles. "A lot of the time, they look at the piece of paper and curse you and your mother, and walk out," says Maugé. "You've told them they're positive, but you have no help to offer them. We don't have people on the street to make sure they get to the drug treatment center or the hospital."

Experts on drug addiction and AIDS say that some addicts, particularly street users, react to a positive test by going out on a heavy drug binge that lasts for weeks and may often include unprotected sex.

"Using drugs is a junkie's habitual way of dealing with bad things in life, and finding out that you're infected with HIV is very bad," says Stephan Sorrell, medical director of health services for the substance-abuse program at New York's St. Luke's/Roosevelt Hospital and at Daytop Village, a residential drug-treatment center. "No drug addict wants to infect anyone," he says, "but someone in the throes of heroin addiction doesn't give a damn about anybody else."

This situation is especially tragic because at least three studies suggest that many addicts can cut down their high-risk sex and drug behavior if they are given intensive counseling. For example, Richard G. Marlink, a physician at Harvard University's School of Public Health, has found that the intensity of counseling affects how much drug addicts will change. A group of 75 addicts in a drug treatment program were all given information on sterilizing needles and safer sex by their drug counselors during their weekly meetings. But clients who tested HIV-positive and their partners were given more intensive education about condom use than were clients who tested negative or were untested.

A year after the program began, all the clients were cleaning needles more consistently: 68 percent of those who tested positive (a fourfold increase); 82 percent of those who tested negative (a more than tenfold increase); and 50 percent of the untested (a more than sixfold increase).

Consistent condom use improved, too, but only among those who tested positive and received intense counseling; for them, the proportion using condoms every time rose from 36 to 68 percent, and the remainder used condoms most

of the time or were celibate. Among those who got less counseling about condoms, none used them all the time. "We think we've shown that mandatory education, not mandatory testing, is the key," Marlink says.

All too often, women who are sex partners of male addicts are willing to go along with unprotected sex, even when they have been educated about the risks, says Joyce Jackson, director of community support services for the New Jersey Department of Health's AIDS program, who has studied how people in the drug-using community are responding to the threat of AIDS. "Using a condom requires male participation, and in many of these communities, if a woman tells a man to use a condom, it's seen as a threat to masculinity," she says. "Such women are bound by the traditional sex roles, and they're not about to take control of the situation."

Perhaps even more powerful, says Jackson, is the women's urge to have children. Pregnant addicts in New York are being encouraged to come for testing and counseling, and some do. They usually choose to have their babies, even if they learn they are infected and are told there's a 30 to 50 percent chance their infant will be born infected. The results: A study of births in New York during November 1987 revealed that in the Bronx, where drug use is high, 1 newborn in 43 was infected with HIV.

Telling addicts that they are HIV carriers is almost a side issue, says Don Des Jarlais, a psychologist and epidemiologist who is director of AIDS research for the New York State Division of Substance Abuse Services. Getting people off drugs altogether is more to the point, he says. But there are far too few drug treatment programs; addicts often have to wait up to six months to get into one. Perhaps, Des Jarlais says, only one in seven addicts in the United States is now in a drug treatment program.

Clearly, no one has yet come up with a panacea to keep people from spreading or acquiring HIV. Finding a balance between protecting public health and preserving individual dignity and freedom of choice may be as great a challenge as the epidemic itself (see "Arresting the Epidemic: What Will it Take?" this article). Both drug abuse

A Date with ELISA

As part of the research for this article, I volunteered to take a Human Immunodeficiency Virus (HIV) test at a public testing site in New York City. When I arrived, there were five other people, men and women, in the tiny waiting room. One man was obviously very nervous; he sighed every few seconds and shifted back and forth in his chair.

When my turn came, a counselor invited me into an even tinier room where she spent half an hour explaining how HIV is transmitted and how the test works and encouraging me to engage only in "safer sex" if I have casual partners. She was very explicit in discussing the specifics of my future social life; richly illustrated pamphlets were avaliable in the waiting room, as well. Most public testing sites consider the test as much an educational experience as a medical procedure, and such counseling is required; private physicians may or may not offer it. After my blood was drawn, I was given a card with a six-digit number; no one ever asked my name. The counselor told me I could pick up my results in three weeks.

As a single, relatively nonpromiscuous straight man who doesn't use drugs, I thought I had little to worry about. (The HIV rate among heterosexuals with no identified risks is estimated at 1 in 5,000.) But when the blood was being drawn, I flashed back on some past relationships with a spark of fear. "What if, by some chance. . . ." And more seriously, I thought about the terrible ramifications of a false-positive result.

Before one is declared positive, three separate tests are usually done: a so-called ELISA, which detects antibodies to the virus; a second ELISA, if the first is positive; and then a Western Blot, which detects antibodies to the major proteins that make up the virus. If the

first ELISA is negative, no further test is made.

The tests are highly accurate but not perfect: According to the federal Centers for Disease Control, 1 person in 135,000 in a low-risk group will be a false positive due to labeling or handling errors.

When I returned for my results, I spent a long half hour waiting for the counselor. I was called in, and she opened the folder with my number on it. She smiled. "OK, you're negative." I shrugged, trying to seem as if I had expected that. "Let's keep it that way," she said. After she reviewed information about condoms, needles and various body fluids that might transmit HIV, I thanked her and got up to leave. As we shook hands, she said, "Now be careful, and you won't have to go through this again."

For people who are truly worried, there are more than 1,000 federally funded HIV test sites where testing is free and, in most states, anonymous. Or one can get a test from a doctor, medical clinic or other private setting, where charges range from $50 to about $300. In most cases, the sample will be sent to the same labs used by public test sites. In addition, a private physician or clinic may keep a record of the test; this could conceivably leak out and later cause a problem with an insurance company or employer, even if the test results are negative. By contrast, most HIV test sites refuse even to take anyone's name. However, six states — Montana, Idaho, Colorado, Minnesota, South Carolina and Wisconsin — ban anonymous tests and require that anyone who is infected be reported to health authorities.

Local health departments can supply the name of the nearest test site, as can the toll-free National AIDS Hotline: 800-342-AIDS.

Arresting the Epidemic: What Will it Take?

Fear of AIDS has stimulated a rash of proposals to stop the epidemic. They range from giving drug addicts free needles, disinfectant and condoms, to making universal testing mandatory and even quarantining carriers of the AIDS virus (the latter suggestion made by North Carolina Sen. Jesse Helms). At least five states have made knowing transmission of HIV a crime. Most states already have quarantine measures for infectious disease on the books but may find them hard to enforce.

So far, most of the very restrictive measures have hardly ever been used, although Florida public-health officials are now looking for state funding to set up a special locked therapeutic ward for knowing spreaders of HIV. William F. Buckley Jr. has made the less drastic, but still startling, suggestion that anyone with AIDS be "tattooed, discreetly, to protect against nonchalant spreading of the disease."

Most AIDS experts warn that mandatory tests will drive the most highly infected groups further underground. Even tattoos would do little to deter people willing to expose themselves to infection anyway.

Many behavioral researchers believe that voluntary testing and counseling can put a substantial brake on the epidemic, and they cite the drop in new infections among gay men as a case in point. But they acknowledge that for some people, counseling will probably have to go beyond mere education about AIDS and safer sex and provide more guidance and support.

The research of psychologist Albert Bandura of Stanford University, for example, has shown that people are more likely to change their behavior if they believe that they can change, are shown specific examples of what to do and are given a chance to practice their new skills so they build confidence in their ability. Training programs based on these principles have been used effectively in community campaigns to reduce the risks of cardiovascular disease and might be applicable to AIDS prevention as well. But this kind of counseling—or any other that goes much beyond the basic facts of life and death about AIDS—has yet to be offered at most testing sites.

People such as those described in the main article probably need much more than a test and a lecture to behave responsibly in this age of AIDS. But so far, while we threaten them or their partners with tattoos, imprisonment and quarantine, we're offering very little else that can help them save their own lives and those of other people.

and sex are driven by powerful motivation. And they are embedded in life-styles, psychological traits and cultural values that are not easily altered. Given that, the wonder may be that so many people have changed their behavior simply as a result of voluntary testing and education—not that some have not.

CRITICAL THINKING QUESTIONS
1. One of the researchers quoted in the article stated that "mandatory education, not mandatory testing, is the key." Is it possible to establish a mandatory AIDS education program? How would you do it? Who would be the target of the education? What would be taught?

2. Most testing done for the HIV (Human Immuno-deficiency Virus) infection is now anonymous, although some states require that people who test positive be reported to public health authorities. What are the issues involved in anonymous versus identified testing procedures? Which type of testing is most likely to reduce the spread of the AIDS virus?

3. Some of the more extreme suggestions to combat the spread of AIDS range from mandatory quarantine of infected individuals to tattooing them to mark them as carriers. What do you think of these proposals? What other suggestions can you think of?

4. The article suggested many different reasons for why people who may be at risk for AIDS do nothing to alter their behavior. Does this suggest that different educational or other strategies may be needed for different groups? Select two of the groups discussed in the article and show how the intervention programs for these groups may need to differ based on the characteristics of the individuals involved.

5. What are the parallels between programs designed to prevent or eliminate smoking behavior and those targeted at preventing AIDS? In recent years, the number of people smoking in most groups has decreased. What has accounted for these reductions in smoking? How might that information be applied to reducing the spread of AIDS?

ARTICLE 38 _____

One cornerstone of the U.S. legal system is jury trial by one's peers. Perhaps you have already served as a juror. If not, you may very well have that opportunity some time in the future. As a juror, you are expected to make a conscientious effort to determine a defendant's guilt or innocence based upon the weight of evidence presented in the trial. Hopefully, you would not let irrelevant characteristics of the individual—such as his or her physical appearance, race, or sex—affect your judgment. But is it really possible to be totally objective in such situations? Or do irrelevant factors play a role in our beliefs about guilt or innocence?

The following article by Sigall and Ostrove is a classic piece of research that investigated the impact of the defendant's physical attractiveness on the severity of sentences given to her. Earlier studies had indicated that physically attractive individuals often have great advantages over less attractive people in a variety of situations. This study not only examined the role of physical attractiveness in a triallike setting but also how the nature of the crime and attractiveness interacted to influence judgments about the defendant. The article also tests two different models that may explain why this particular effect occurs.

Beautiful but Dangerous
Effects of Offender Attractiveness and Nature of the Crime on Juridic Judgment

■ Harold Sigall and Nancy Ostrove

The physical attractiveness of a criminal defendant (attractive, unattractive, no information) and the nature of the crime (attractiveness-related, attractiveness-unrelated) were varied in a factorial design. After reading one of the case accounts, subjects sentenced the defendant to a term of imprisonment. An interaction was predicted: When the crime was unrelated to attractiveness (burglary), subjects would assign more lenient sentences to the attractive defendant than to the unattractive defendant; when the offense was attractiveness-related (swindle), the attractive defendant would receive harsher treatment. The results confirmed the predictions, thereby supporting a cognitive explanation for the relationship between the physical attractiveness of defendants and the nature of the judgments made against them.

Research investigating the interpersonal consequences of physical attractiveness has demonstrated clearly that good-looking people have tremendous advantages over their unattractive counterparts in many ways. For example, a recent study by Miller (1970) provided evidence for the existence of a physical attractiveness stereotype with a rather favorable content. Dion, Berscheid, and Walster (1972) reported similar findings: Compared to unattractive people, better-looking people were viewed as more likely to possess a variety of socially desirable attributes. In addition, Dion et al.'s subjects predicted rosier futures for the beautiful stimulus persons—attractive people were expected to have happier and more successful lives in store for them. Thus, at least in the eyes of others, good looks imply greater potential.

Since physical attractiveness hardly seems to

Reprinted from the *Journal of Personality and Social Psychology*, 1975, *31*, 410–414. Copyright 1975 by the American Psychological Association. Reprinted by permission.

provide a basis for an *equitable* distribution of rewards, one might hope that the powerful effects of this variable would occur primarily when it is the only source of information available. Unfair or irrational consequences of differences in beauty observed in some situations would cause less uneasiness if, in other situations given other important data, respondents would tend to discount such "superficial" information. Unfortunately, for the vast majority of us who have not been blessed with a stunning appearance, the evidence does not permit such consolation. Consider, for example, a recent study by Dion (1972) in which adult subjects were presented with accounts of transgressions supposedly committed by children of varying physical attractiveness. When the transgression was severe the act was viewed less negatively when committed by a good-looking child, than when the offender was unattractive. Moreover, when the child was unattractive the offense was more likely to be seen as reflecting some enduring dispositional quality: Subjects believed that unattractive children were more likely to be involved in future transgressions. Dion's findings, which indicate that unattractive individuals are penalized when there is no apparent logical relationship between the transgression and the way they look, underscore the importance of appearance because one could reasonably suppose that information describing a severe transgression would "overwhelm the field," and that the physical attractiveness variable would not have any effect.

Can beautiful people get away with murder? Although Dion (1972) found no differences in the punishment recommended for offenders as a function of attractiveness, Monahan (1941) has suggested that beautiful women are convicted less often of crimes they are accused of, and Efran (1974) has recently demonstrated that subjects are much more generous when assigning punishment to good-looking as opposed to unattractive transgressors.

The previous findings which indicate a tendency toward leniency for an attractive offender can be accounted for in a number of ways. For ex-

ample, one might explain such results with the help of a reinforcement-affect model of attraction (e.g., Byrne & Clore, 1970). Essentially, the argument here would be that beauty, having positive reinforcement value, would lead to relatively more positive affective responses toward a person who has it. Thus we like an attractive person more, and since other investigators have shown that liking for a defendant increases leniency (e.g., Landy & Aronson, 1969), we would expect good-looking (better liked) defendants to be punished less than unattractive defendants. Implicit in this reasoning is that the nature of the affective response, which influences whether kind or harsh treatment is recommended, is determined by the stimulus features associated with the target person. Therefore, when other things are equal, benefit accrues to the physically attractive. A more cognitive approach might attempt to explain the relationship between physical appearance and reactions to transgressions by assuming that the subject has a "rational" basis for his responses. It is reasonable to deal harshly with a criminal if we think he is likely to commit further violations, and as Dion's (1972) study suggests, unattractive individuals are viewed as more likely to transgress again. In addition, inasmuch as attractive individuals are viewed as possessing desirable qualities and as having relatively great potential, it makes sense to treat them leniently. Presumably they can be successful in socially acceptable ways, and rehabilitation may result in relatively high payoffs for society.

There is at least one implication that follows from the cognitive orientation which would not flow readily from the reinforcement model. Suppose that situations do exist in which, because of his high attractiveness, a defendant is viewed as more likely to transgress in the future. The cognitive approach suggests that in such instances greater punishment would be assigned to the attractive offender. We might add that in addition to being more dangerous, when the crime is attractiveness related, a beautiful criminal may be viewed as taking advantage of a God-given gift. Such misappropriation of a blessing may incur animosity, which might contribute to severe judgments in attractiveness-related situations.

In the present investigation, the attractiveness of a defendant was varied along with the nature of the crime committed. It was reasoned that most offenses do not encourage the notion that a criminal's attractiveness increases the likelihood of similar transgressions in the future. Since attractive offenders are viewed as less prone to recidivism and as having greater potential worth, it was expected that under such circumstances an attractive defendant would receive less punishment than an unattractive defendant involved in an identical offense. When, however, the crime committed may be viewed as attractiveness-related, as in a confidence game, despite being seen as possessing more potential, the attractive defendant may be regarded as relatively more dangerous, and the effects of beauty could be expected to be cancelled out or reversed. The major hypothesis, then, called for an interaction: An attractive defendant would receive more lenient treatment than an unattractive defendant when the offense was unrelated to attractiveness; when the crime was related to attractiveness, the attractive defendant would receive relatively harsh treatment.

METHOD

Subjects and Overview

Subjects were 60 male and 60 female undergraduates. After being presented with an account of a criminal case, each subject sentenced the defendant to a term of imprisonment. One-third of the subjects were led to believe that the defendant was physically attractive, another third that she was unattractive, and the remainder received no information concerning appearance. Cross-cutting the attractiveness variable, half of the subjects were presented with a written account of an attractiveness-unrelated crime, a burglary, and the rest with an attractiveness-related crime, a swindle. Subjects were randomly assigned to condition, with the restriction that an equal number of males and

females appeared in each of the six cells formed by the manipulated variables.

Procedure

Upon arrival, each subject was shown to an individual room and given a booklet which contained the stimulus materials. The top sheet informed subjects that they would read a criminal case account, that they would receive biographical information about the defendant, and that after considering the materials they would be asked to answer some questions.

The case account began on the second page. Clipped to this page was a 5 × 8 inch card which contained routine demographic information and was identical in all conditions.[1] In the attractive conditions, a photograph of a rather attractive woman was affixed to the upper right-hand corner of the card; while in the unattractive conditions, a relatively unattractive photograph was affixed. No photograph was presented in the control conditions.

Subjects then read either the account of a burglary or a swindle. The burglary account described how the defendant, Barbara Helm, had moved into a high-rise building, obtained a pass key under false pretenses, and then illegally entered the apartment of one of her neighbors. After stealing $2,200 in cash and merchandise she left town. She was apprehended when she attempted to sell some of the stolen property and subsequently was charged with breaking and entering and grand larceny. The swindle account described how Barbara Helm had ingratiated herself to a middle-aged bachelor and induced him to invest $2,200 in a nonexistent corporation. She was charged with obtaining money under false pretenses and grand larceny. In both cases, the setting for the offense and the victim were described identically. The information presented left little doubt concerning the defendant's guilt.

The main dependent measure was collected on the last page of the booklet. Subjects were asked to complete the following statement by circling a number between 1 and 15: "I sentence the defendant, Barbara Helm, to — years of imprisonment." Subjects were asked to sentence the defendant, rather than to judge guilt versus innocence in order to provide a more sensitive dependent measure.

After sentencing had been completed, the experimenter provided a second form, which asked subjects to recall who the defendant was and to rate the seriousness of the crime. In addition, the defendant was rated on a series of 9-point bipolar adjective scales, including physically unattractive (1) to physically attractive (9), which constituted the check on the attractiveness manipulation. A post-experimental interview followed, during which subjects were debriefed.

RESULTS AND DISCUSSION

The physical attractiveness manipulation was successful: The attractive defendant received a mean rating of 7.53, while the mean for the unattractive defendant was 3.20, $F(1, 108) = 184.29$, $p < .001$. These ratings were not affected by the nature of the crime, nor was there an interaction.

The criminal cases were designed so as to meet two requirements. First, the swindle was assumed to be attractiveness-related, while the burglary was intended to be attractiveness-unrelated. No direct check on this assumption was made. However, indirect evidence is available: Since all subjects filled out the same forms, we obtained physical attractiveness ratings from control condition subjects who were not presented with a photograph. These subjects attributed greater beauty to the defendant in the swindle condition ($\bar{X} = 6.65$) than in the burglary condition ($\bar{X} = 5.65$), $F(1, 108) = 4.93$, $p < .05$. This finding offers some support for our contention that the swindle was viewed as attractiveness-related. Second, it was important that the two crimes be viewed as roughly comparable in seriousness. This was necessary to preclude alternative explanations in terms of differential seriousness. Subjects rated the seriousness of the crime on a 9-point scale extending from not at all serious (1) to extremely serious (9). The resulting responses indicated that the second requirement was met: In the swindle

TABLE 1 / Mean Sentence Assigned, in Years (n = 20 per cell)

Offense	Defendant condition		
	Attractive	Unattractive	Control
Swindle	5.45	4.35	4.35
Burglary	2.80	5.20	5.10

condition the mean seriousness rating was 5.02; in the burglary condition it was 5.07 ($F < 1$).

Table 1 presents the mean punishment assigned to the defendant, by condition. Since a preliminary analysis demonstrated there were no differences in responses between males and females, subject sex was ignored as a variable. It can be seen that our hypothesis was supported: When the offense was attractiveness-unrelated (burglary), the unattractive defendant was more severely punished than the attractive defendant; however, when the offense was attractiveness-related (swindle), the attractive defendant was treated more harshly. The overall Attractiveness × Offense interaction was statistically significant, $F(2, 108) = 4.55$, $p < .025$, and this interaction was significant, as well, when the control condition was excluded, $F(1, 108) = 7.02$, $p < .01$. Simple comparisons revealed that the unattractive burglar received significantly more punishment than the attractive burglar, $F(1, 108) = 6.60$, $p < .025$, while the difference in sentences assigned to the attractive and unattractive swindler was not statistically significant, $F(1, 108) = 1.39$. The attractive-swindle condition was compared with the unattractive-swindle and control-swindle conditions also, $F(1, 108) = 2.00$, *ns.* Thus, strictly speaking, we cannot say that for the swindle attractiveness was a great liability; there was a tendency in this direction but the conservative conclusion is that when the crime is attractiveness-related, the advantages otherwise held by good-looking defendants are lost.

Another feature of the data worth considering is that the sentences administered in the control condition are almost identical to those assigned in the unattractive condition. It appears that being unattractive did not produce discriminatory responses, per se. Rather, it seems that appearance had its effect through the attractive conditions: The beautiful burglar got off lightly, while the beautiful swindler paid somewhat, though not significantly, more. It can be recalled that in the unattractive conditions the stimulus person was seen as relatively unattractive and not merely average looking. Therefore, the absence of unattractive-control condition differences does not seem to be the result of a weak manipulation in the unattractive conditions.

Perhaps it is possible to derive a small bit of consolation from this outcome, if we speculate that only the very attractive receive special (favorable or unfavorable) treatment, and that others are treated similarly. That is a less frightening conclusion than one which would indicate that unattractiveness brings about active discrimination.

As indicated earlier, previous findings (Efran, 1974) that attractive offenders are treated leniently can be interpreted in a number of ways. The results of the present experiment support the cognitive explanation we offered. The notion that good-looking people usually tend to be treated generously because they are seen as less dangerous and more virtuous remains tenable. The argument that physical attractiveness is a positive trait and therefore has a unidirectionally favorable effect on judgments of those who have it, would have led to accurate predictions in the burglary conditions. However, this position could not account for the observed interaction. The cognitive view makes precisely that prediction.

Finally, we feel compelled to note that our laboratory situation is quite different from actual courtroom situations. Most important, perhaps, our subjects made decisions which had no consequences for the defendant, and they made those decisions by themselves, rather than arriving at judgments after discussions with others exposed to the same information. Since the courtroom is not an appropriate laboratory, it is unlikely that actual experimental tests in the real situation would ever be conducted. However, simulations constitute legitimate avenues for investigating person perception and interpersonal judgment,

and there is no obvious reason to believe that these processes would not have the effects in trial proceedings that they do elsewhere.

Whether a discussion with other jurors would affect judgment is an empirical, and researchable, question. Perhaps if even 1 of 12 jurors notes that some irrelevant factor may be affecting the jury's judgment, the others would see the light. Especially now when the prospect of reducing the size of juries is being entertained, it would be important to find out whether extralegal considerations are more likely to have greater influence as the number of jurors decreases.

REFERENCES

Byrne, D., & Clore, G. L. A reinforcement model of evaluative responses. *Personality: An International Journal,* 1970, *1,* 103–128.

Dion, K. Physical attractiveness and evaluation of children's transgressions. *Journal of Personality and Social Psychology,* 1972, *24,* 207–213.

Dion, K., Berscheid, E., & Walster, E. What is beautiful is good. *Journal of Personality and Social Psychology,* 1972, *24,* 285–290.

Efran, M. G. The effect of physical appearance on the judgment of guilt, interpersonal attraction, and severity of recommended punishment in a simulated jury task. *Journal of Research in Personality,* 1974, *8,* 45–54.

Landy, D., & Aronson, E. The influence of the character of the criminal and victim on the decisions of simulated jurors. *Journal of Experimental Social Psychology,* 1969, *5,* 141–152.

Miller, A. G. Role of physical attractiveness in impression formation. *Psychonomic Science,* 1970, *19,* 241–243.

Monahan, F. *Women in crime.* New York: Washburn, 1941.

NOTE

1. This information as well as copies of the case accounts referred to below, can be obtained from the first author.

This study was supported by a grant from the University of Maryland General Research Board.

CRITICAL THINKING QUESTIONS

1. This article used pictures of females only to show defendants of varying attractiveness. Would the same results be obtained if male defendants were used? In other words, do you think that attractiveness stereotypes operate in the same way for females and males?

2. As the authors of the article noted, the methodology of the study differed from real-life jury trials in several ways. For example, subjects made their decisions alone and were presented with a paper description of the person and deed, not a real-life person. Design a study that would investigate the same variables studied in the article in a more natural environment.

3. Would the results of this study be generalizable to situations other than jury trials? Think of a situation where the attractiveness of a person making a request or performing a certain action may result in his or her being treated differentially as a result of his or her attractiveness.

4. What implications do these findings have for our legal system? How could the effects of irrelevant factors such as attractiveness somehow be minimized in the real-world courtroom? For example, would telling the jurors beforehand about the tendency to let attractiveness influence their judgments make any difference? Why or why not?

ADDITIONAL RELATED READINGS

Baumeister, R., & Darley, J. (1982). Reducing the biasing effect of perpetrator attractiveness in jury simulation. *Personality and Social Psychology Bulletin, 8,* 286–292.

Michelini, R., & Snodgrass, S. (1980). Defendant characteristics and juridic decisions. *Journal of Research in Personality, 14,* 340–350.

ARTICLE 39 _____

One central feature of many jury trials is the use of witnesses. The accuracy of eyewitness testimony is a topic that has been investigated by social psychologists for years. A significant body of literature suggests that such accuracy is highly questionable. Whether the witness sits on the stand and recounts events or selects a person from a police lineup, the findings regarding accuracy are discouraging.

If eyewitness testimony is not necessarily accurate, does that mean that jurors know this and accept such testimony with some reservation? Unfortunately, the answer is once again discouraging. Research suggests that jurors place a great deal of weight on eyewitness testimony in making their own judicial decisions.

The following article by Bell and Loftus examines trivial persuasion in the courtroom. By *trivial persuasion*, Bell and Loftus mean "the persuasive impact of trivial details on decisions." As the article suggests, these trivial details, even when totally irrelevant to the case being judged, still may influence the decisions reached by a jury. Besides demonstrating the impact of these trivial details in influencing judgments, as well as the specific conditions under which they operate, this article helps clarify the underlying cognitive mechanisms that may account for the observed processes.

Trivial Persuasion in the Courtroom
The Power of (a Few) Minor Details

■ Brad E. Bell and Elizabeth F. Loftus

Investigated the influence of trivial testimonial detail on judgments of 424 undergraduates who served as mock jurors. Ss read a summary of a court case involving robbery and murder. In Experiment 1, detailed testimony influenced judgments of guilt, even when the detail was unrelated to the culprit. In Experiment 2, detailed testimony was especially powerful when an opposing witness testified that she could not remember the trivial details. Subsequent analyses suggest that the impact of detailed testimony on guilt judgments is mediated by inferences about the eyewitnesses. When eyewitnesses provided more detail, they were generally judged to be more credible, to have a better memory for the culprit's face and for details, and to have paid more attention to the culprit.

John Dean, former counsel to President Richard Nixon, testified before the Watergate committee of the United States Senate in 1973. Dean's testimony contained details about dozens of meetings and conversations that took place over a period of several years. Some of Dean's testimony was specific and concrete, as, for example, in the following description of a conversation with Robert Haldeman:

> *I felt I should tell Haldeman that I was going to meet with the prosecutors personally so I called him in California on the morning of April 8 before they departed for Washington. I made the call from Mr. Shaffer's office and when I told him this he said that I should not meet with the prosecutors because, as he*

Reprinted from the *Journal of Personality and Social Psychology*, 1989, 56, 669–679. Copyright 1989 by the American Psychological Association. Reprinted by permission.

said, "once the toothpaste is out of the tube, it's going to be very hard to get it back in."
(Select Committee on Presidential Campaign Activities, 1973, 1010)

When Dean first testified, some writers were so impressed by his memory for detail that they called him the "human tape recorder" (Neisser, 1981). This anecdote about John Dean raises several important questions. Does the amount of detail a person provides influence listeners' decisions? If so, why are people impressed by detail? The present research addresses these questions using a jury simulation paradigm.

Recent research suggests that people are persuaded by testimony that contains trivial details. In one experiment (Bell & Loftus, 1988, Experiment 2) subjects read a summary of a court case involving a man who was accused of murdering a store clerk during a robbery. Two eyewitnesses to the shooting testified at the trial. The prosecution eyewitness was positive that the defendant had shot the clerk, while the defense eyewitness was positive that the defendant had not. As part of their testimony, each eyewitness described the store items that the culprit requested as either "a few store items" (low detail), or "Kleenex, Tylenol, and a six-pack of Diet Pepsi" (high detail). This study involved a 2 x 2 design in which the detail in the prosecution testimony was either high or low and the detail in the defense testimony was either high or low. One important effect on judgments of guilt was found: Mock jurors who read highly detailed prosecution testimony were more likely to find the defendant guilty than those who read the less detailed prosecution testimony.

The power of detailed information in the context of mock trials has also been investigated by researchers who couched their findings in terms of "vividness" (Reyes, Thompson, & Bower, 1980; Shedler & Manis, 1986). In the experiment of Reyes et al., subjects read a summary of a drunk driving trial. Ten summaries of argument (both circumstantial evidence and witness accounts) were provided for each side. Each argument had a vivid version (more detailed) and a pallid version

(less detailed). For example, in a pallid version of a prosecution argument, the defendant was described as staggering against a serving table, knocking a bowl to the floor. In the vivid version, the defendant was described as staggering against a serving table and knocking a "bowl of guacamole dip to the floor, splattering guacamole all over the white shag carpet." Some subjects read the vivid versions of the prosecution arguments and the pallid versions of the defense arguments, while other subjects read the pallid versions of the prosecution arguments and the vivid versions of the defense arguments. The trivial details in the vivid versions were designed to be irrelevant to the issue of the defendant's guilt. Subjects made judgments of the defendant's guilt immediately after reading the court case and 2 days later. The results suggest that arguments that are presented vividly are more persuasive than those that are presented pallidly, but only after a delay of 2 days.

Shedler and Manis (1986) used a similar design as that used by Reyes et al. (1980), but subjects heard a tape recording of a child custody case. The vivid versions in their study included colorful details that were designed to be irrelevant to the issue of the mother's fitness as a parent. For example, some subjects read the following pallid version of a favorable argument: "Mrs. Johnson [mother] sees to it that her child washes and brushes his teeth before bedtime." The vivid version added, "He uses a Star Wars toothbrush that looks like Darth Vader." Shedler and Manis found that the vividness of the arguments influenced mock judge decisions immediately after the case was read, and also two days later.

We refer to the persuasive impact of trivial details on decisions as *trivial persuasion*. The phenomenon suggests that communicators should choose their words very carefully, because the minor details that a communicator reports might be as influential as information that has genuine significant value.

Why does trivial persuasion occur? Several studies have addressed this question. One possibility is that information is easier to remember when it contains trivial details. This may be because details make information vivid. Nisbett and Ross (1980) have suggested that vividly presented information has a greater impact on judgments than pallidly presented information because it is easier to remember. Although Shedler and Manis (1986) also found that vividness (degree of detail) influenced subjects' memory for arguments, their causal modeling results indicated that the influence of vividness was not mediated by subjects' memory for the arguments.

Could the power of trivial detail be due to inferences about the person reporting these details? Some empirical evidence suggests that the answer is yes. The results of Bell and Loftus (1988) suggest that the persuasive impact of highly detailed testimony on judgments of a defendant's responsibility was due to inferences about the credibility of the witnesses. Witnesses were generally perceived to be more credible when they provided more trivial detail.

What general beliefs related to eyewitness credibility might mediate the impact of testimonial detail on judgments of a defendant's guilt? We hypothesize that general beliefs about memory and attention (e.g., an eyewitness who remembered trivial details must have really been paying attention) mediate the impact of testimonial details on jurors' judgments about a defendant. Unfortunately, in our prior work we did not have subjects rate the witnesses on dimensions other than credibility. Consequently, we did not obtain a conclusive answer to the proposed hypothesis.[1] In the present research we addressed this hypothesis. Jurors may infer that the amount of detail *reported* reflects a witness's memory for details. The juror may, in turn, reason that a witness who remembers details must have a good memory for central objects. Having a good memory for trivial details may imply a good memory for central objects because the witness is perceived to have paid a substantial amount of attention to the central objects (perhaps because the trivial details are perceived to be more difficult to remember). On the basis of this inferential model, we hypothesize that a witness who provides more trivial detail will be judged to be more credible (as previously demonstrated), to have a better

memory for a central object (culprit) and for details, and to have paid more attention to the central object.

Trivial persuasion might be characterized as involving what Chaiken (1980) called *heuristic information processing.* In this mode of persuasion people rely primarily on simple and general rules (e.g., about source credibility) that may be based on past experiences or unfounded assumptions, and they de-emphasize detailed processing of the message content. This mode of persuasion contrasts with what Chaiken (1980) referred to as *systematic information processing,* in which people engage in detailed processing of the message content. This distinction between heuristic and systematic information processing is similar to the distinction made by Petty and Cacioppo (1981) between the *peripheral route* and *central route* to persuasion.

It can be argued, however, that trivial persuasion in the courtroom may not be completely characteristic of the heuristic mode of persuasion. The difference between the two modes of persuasion has to do with the degree of issue-relevant thinking. Systematic information processing involves substantial issue-relevant thinking, whereas heuristic information processing does not. In a courtroom, the evaluation of a witness's credibility is a natural and important component in evaluating the message and making a decision. In order to determine the validity of the message, the juror must often evaluate the witnesses' honesty, memory, and attention paid to the crime or accident. This is especially true when there is contradictory testimony. It can be argued that drawing inferences about the witnesses' memory and attention paid is issue-relevant thinking because the substance of the witnesses' testimony is their memory for an event. Thus, in the courtroom communicator-associated thoughts and message-associated thoughts are closely related. In short, trivial persuasion in the courtroom might be best characterized as a blend of systematic and heuristic information processing.

There is some evidence that trivial persuasion may involve overgeneralized and fallacious reasoning. Although the results of Schooler, Gerhard, and Loftus (1986) suggest that a good memory for sensory details of an object (yield sign) is more likely to be characteristic of a real, as opposed to an unreal, memory for the object, other evidence suggests that this relation is not always true. A good memory for details may not imply that a witness is highly credible or has a good memory for a culprit's face. In the experiment of Wells and Leippe (1981), people were exposed to a staged theft and were later asked to make an identification of the culprit. People who were less likely to remember peripheral details (e.g., pictures on the wall) were more likely to have made an accurate identification. Interestingly, mock judges evaluated the credibility of the subject-witnesses to the theft as though they believed the opposite to be true. Moreover, other research has found no significant relation between identification accuracy and accuracy of prior descriptions about a suspect (Pigott & Brigham, 1985).

It is important to gain an understanding of the generality of trivial persuasion. In our prior work, the details were related to a central person involved in the crime or accident. For example, in one study (Bell & Loftus, 1988, Experiment 2), the details pertained to the store items that the culprit requested. In the present Experiment 1, we varied the relatedness of the detailed information to the culprit. The details were either related to the culprit (store items the culprit dropped) or unrelated to him (store items a customer dropped prior to the crime). Our prior mock jurors might have inferred that a witness who gave a highly detailed account paid a substantial amount of attention to the culprit at this particular time but was not necessarily the kind of person who paid a great deal of attention to people or who had an exceptional memory ability. If this was what our prior mock jurors inferred, it stands to reason that trivial details unrelated to the culprit may not have any influence on judgments of guilt. This would be true because the amount of attention paid to another person would not necessarily be indicative of memory for, and attention paid to, the culprit.

On the other hand, if people draw inferences about a witness's abilities or dispositions from the degree of detail in the testimony, then unrelated detail should also have an impact on judgments of guilt. People may infer that a witness who pays close attention to an insignificant prior event, such as a customer dropping a box of Milk Duds and a can of Diet Pepsi, is the kind of person who pays close attention to people in general and who is therefore likely to have paid a considerable amount of attention to the culprit. People may also infer that having a good memory for unrelated details implies a good memory in general, particularly when the details remembered are rather insignificant. We predicted that unrelated detail would influence judgments because people would draw inferences about the witness's abilities and dispositions from the amount of reported detail in the witness's testimony.

Another concern of ours was whether trivial persuasion would be limited to a particular type of witness testimony. In our prior work the specificity of defense testimonial detail did not significantly affect judgments of a defendant's guilt. We suspected that there might have been a floor effect. In the present research, we attempted to remedy this problem. We wished to demonstrate that trivial persuasion occurs regardless of whether the trivial details are contained in the testimony of a prosecution witness or a defense witness.

EXPERIMENT 1

The purpose of Experiment 1 was (a) to find out whether trivial details unrelated to the culprit would have an influence on judgments similar to trivial details related to the culprit, (b) to address the plausibility of the inferential model proposed, and (c) to find out whether the degree of detail in defense testimony can influence judgments of a defendant's guilt. In order to confirm that the persuasive impact of highly detailed testimony was not due to the information in the testimony's being easier to remember, we had subjects recall the information in the testimony and we performed analyses that ruled out this possibility.

Method

Subjects   Subjects were 302 students from lower division psychology courses at the University of

Washington (129 males and 173 females). They received course credit upon completion of the experiment. Subjects participated in groups of 15 to 32 and were randomly assigned to conditions.

Design The experiment involved a 2 × 2 × 2 between-subjects design. We varied the degree of detail of the prosecution eyewitness testimony (high vs. low), the degree of detail of the defense eyewitness testimony (high vs. low), and the relatedness of the critical detailed information to the culprit (related vs. unrelated). The detail was the same for prosecution and defense witnesses. There were 37 or 38 subjects in each of the eight cells.

Materials and Procedure At the beginning of the experiment subjects received a four-page booklet containing a synopsis of a criminal court case. The case was presented in the third person narrative. The entire case (excluding jury instructions and introductory paragraph) contained about 800 words. Subjects worked on the materials individually. Subjects were instructed to assume the role of a juror and to read the materials in the order presented. Finally, subjects were informed that they would make judgments on the case and that they should read through the materials as many times as needed.

The court case was the same as that used by Bell and Loftus (1988), with a few exceptions. Certain details pertaining to the culprit's clothing were added to the eyewitness testimony. The clothing of the culprit, described by both eyewitnesses, matched the clothing that the defendant was wearing when he was stopped by the police on the night of the crime. This was done to make the case more evenly balanced in terms of guilt versus innocence than it had been shown to be in our prior work.

Subjects first read a few paragraphs describing the events leading to the defendant's arrest. Subjects learned that a man walked into a small grocery store, pulled out a handgun, and demanded that the clerk give him the money in the cash register. The man shot and killed the clerk and then fled. The police stopped a car that matched the description given by the eyewitnesses. The man was positively identified by the prosecution eyewitness in a lineup.

Following the description of the events leading to the defendant's arrest, subjects read brief jury instructions. They were informed that the prosecution must prove each element of the crime beyond a reasonable doubt. Moreover, they were informed that they were to find the defendant "not guilty" if they had reasonable doubt about any of the elements of the crime.

The prosecution's case was presented first. Each side had seven or eight summaries of circumstantial evidence and one eyewitness account. The eyewitness account provided by each side was similar in length and wording. The primary difference was that the prosecution eyewitness testified that she was positive that the defendant was the man who shot the clerk, whereas the defense eyewitness was positive that defendant did not do it. Each eyewitness stated her age, occupation, vision and hearing ability, distance from the culprit when he shot the clerk, and the events that took place on the night of the crime.

The manipulations involved one sentence contained in each eyewitness description. The precise wording and location of the sentence depended upon the condition of the experiment in which the subject participated. Each eyewitness description contained a variation of a sentence that ended with "and stumbled and dropped them on his way out the door." In related-high-detail versions, the sentence began with the words "The man went and got a box of Milk Duds and a can of Diet Pepsi." In unrelated-high-detail versions, the sentence began with the words "She saw a boy purchase a box of Milk Duds and a can of Diet Pepsi." In all low-detail versions the words "a box of Milk Duds and a can of Diet Pepsi" were replaced with the words "a few store items." The sentences for the related and unrelated conditions were placed in the appropriate temporal sequence of events described by each eyewitness. The unrelated sentence preceded the description of the culprit and his actions, because the boy came into the store and left prior to the robbery.

After a subject finished reading the court case, the booklet was taken away and a response booklet was provided. On the first page subjects made judgments about the defendant's guilt and the credibility of the eyewitnesses. Subjects rendered a verdict in the case by circling *not guilty* or *guilty*. Subjects next made a judgment of the defendant's guilt in a more detailed fashion by circling a number on an 11-point scale anchored at *not guilty beyond doubt* (1) and *guilty beyond doubt* (11). After that, subjects rated the relative credibility of the two eyewitnesses by dividing 100 points between them. Finally, subjects judged the credibility of each eyewitness separately on an 11-point scale anchored at *low* (1) and *high* (11).

On the second page, subjects rated the memory and attention of the eyewitnesses on 11-point scales. Subjects first rated the memory of each eyewitness for the culprit's face. The scale was anchored at *very poor* (1) and *very good* (11). Subjects judged the memory of each eyewitness for details (in general) on a scale anchored in the same way as for the other memory judgments. The last two judgments on the second page pertained to the attention paid by each eyewitness to the culprit and his actions on the night of the crime. The scale for these judgments was anchored at *a very small amount* and *a very large amount*.

On the third page, subjects wrote down, in any order, all they could recall about the testimony of the eyewitnesses. After each remembered item, they had to place in parentheses the source (prosecution and/or defense) of that item. Next, subjects provided reasons for their relative credibility judgments.

On the last page of the response booklet, subjects made judgments about the description of the crime given by each eyewitness. Subjects made judgments of the amount of information, followed by concreteness and then vividness, on 11-point scales. Finally, subjects were debriefed and dismissed.

Results

Although 302 subjects participated in the experiment, several subjects failed to complete the set of dependent measures. These subjects were re-tained for other analyses to which they contributed data.

Judgments of Guilt   We hypothesized that greater detail in prosecution testimony would result in higher judgments of guilt and more guilty verdicts and that greater detail in defense testimony would lead to lower judgments of guilt and fewer guilty verdicts. Analyses showed that the main effects of prosecution detail and defense detail on the guilt measures supported the hypothesized pattern (see Table 1). Overall, subjects were more likely to select the guilty verdict option when the prosecution detail was high, as opposed to low, 33% versus 21%; logistic regression, $z = 2.2$, $p < .05$. Moreover, they were more likely to give a rating of the defendant's guilt in the direction of being *guilty beyond doubt* when the prosecution detail was high, rather than low, 5.6 versus 5.1, $F(1, 293) = 4.4$, $p < .05$. When the defense eyewitness gave a highly detailed account, as opposed to a less detailed account, subjects were marginally less likely to believe that the defendant was guilty. Overall, they were marginally less likely to select the guilty verdict option, 23% versus 31%; logistic regression, $z = 1.7$, $p = .10$. Moreover, they were marginally less likely to give a rating of the defendant's guilt in the direction of *guilty beyond doubt*, 5.2 versus 5.6, $F(1, 293) = 2.6$, $p = .107$.

TABLE 1 / Mean Judgments of Guilt

Judgments	Low-detail prosecution		High-detail prosecution	
	High-detail defense	Low-detail defense	High-detail defense	Low-detail defense
Verdict[a]				
Related	.13	.32	.32	.32
Unrelated	.22	.18	.24	.43
11-point guilt[b]				
Related	4.4	5.5	5.6	5.4
Unrelated	5.2	5.2	5.4	6.1

[a] Proportion of guilty verdicts.
[b] Higher numbers indicate greater guilt.

No other main effects or two-way interactions were significant (all *p*s > .25). The absence of a Prosecution Detail × Relatedness interaction indicates that the size of the impact of related prosecution detail was not larger than that of unrelated prosecution detail.

There was, however, a three-way interaction between prosecution detail, defense detail, and the relatedness of the detail on both judgments of guilt, $F(1, 293) = 4.1$, $p < .05$; logistic regression, $z = 2.0$, $p < .05$. As Table 1 shows, related prosecution detail influenced judgments of guilt when defense detail was high, whereas unrelated prosecution detail influenced judgments of guilt when defense detail was low.

Mediation: Mock Jurors' Memory for the Testimony   Subjects were asked to write down all the information that they could recall from the testimony of the prosecution eyewitness and defense eyewitness, indicating whether the source was the prosecution, defense, or both. Each of the 12 sentences in the eyewitness testimony contained a basic idea, and thus each sentence was counted as an item of recall. Because the volume of recall protocols was large, each of three independent raters scored a separate sample of the 302 recall protocols. Interrater correlations were computed for the total number of correct items (prosecution + defense) for the data of 28 subjects. These correlations were .86, .93, and .97. Although each rater did not score an equal number of recall protocols from each cell, the differences were minor.

We examined the recall of the manipulated sentence (concerning the store items). Separate measures of recall of the manipulated sentence in the prosecution and defense testimony were used. Finally, we computed the proportion of total items that were correctly indicated by the subject as being from the prosecution eyewitness testimony, number of prosecution items/(number of prosecution items + number of defense items).

Analyses of variance (ANOVAS) performed on the three recall measures yielded only two significant effects. Subjects who read highly detailed prosecution testimony were more likely to recall

the manipulated sentence in the prosecution testimony than subjects who read a prosecution account of low detail, 70% versus 56%, $F(1, 288) = 6.3$, $p < .02$. Moreover, there was a significant Defense Detail × Relatedness interaction on the recall of the manipulated sentence in the defense testimony, $F(1, 288) = 4.9$, $p < .03$. This interaction indicated that high defense-detail subjects were more likely to recall the manipulated sentence than low defense-detail subjects when the detail was related (74% vs. 59%). When the detail was unrelated, the opposite pattern was observed (56% vs. 66%).

Analyses of covariance (ANCOVAS) were performed on judgments of guilt (11-point) with each recall measure used as a covariate in a separate analysis. None of the recall covariates were significant when controlling for the condition effects *(p*s > .14). Moreover, the main effect of prosecution detail and the three-way interaction still remained at least marginally significant when controlling for each recall covariate (all *p*s < .07). Thus, no conclusive evidence was obtained for the notion that subjects' memory for the testimony mediated the detail effects observed.

Mediation: Inferences about the Witnesses   Next, we examined the possibility that the effects of detail on judgments of guilt were mediated by inferences about the eyewitnesses. First we asked what effect the detail manipulations had on these mediational measures. The means for each judgment for each cell are listed in Tables 2 and 3. As expected, there were significant main effects of prosecution detail and defense detail on judgments. When the prosecution detail was high, as opposed to low, the prosecution witness was judged (a) to have higher relative credibility, 53.9 versus 47.0, $F(1, 294) = 28.3$, $p < .001$; (b) to be more credible, 7.0 versus 6.4, $F(1, 293) = 6.3$, $p < .05$; (c) to have a better memory for details in general, 7.5 versus 6.3, $F(1, 291) = 29.4$, $p < .001$; (d) to have a better memory for the culprit's face, 6.6 versus 5.9, $F(1, 291) = 10.1$, $p < .01$; and (e) to have devoted more attention to the culprit and his actions, 7.4 versus 6.4, $F(1, 291) =$

TABLE 2 / Mean Judgments of Credibility

	Low-detail prosecution		High-detail prosecution	
Judgments	High-detail defense	Low-detail defense	High-detail defense	Low-detail defense
Relative credibility[a]				
Related	40.7	50.5	51.7	56.7
Unrelated	45.2	51.6	51.1	56.0
Prosecution witness[b]				
Related	6.1	6.7	7.1	7.5
Unrelated	6.0	6.8	6.4	6.8
Defense witness[b]				
Related	7.8	6.5	7.1	6.7
Unrelated	7.1	6.8	6.4	5.8

[a] Points assigned to the prosecution eyewitness.
[b] Higher numbers indicate greater credibility.

TABLE 3 / Mean Judgments of Eyewitness Memory and Attention

	Low-detail prosecution		High-detail prosecution	
Judgments	High-detail defense	Low-detail defense	High-detail defense	Low-detail defense
Prosecution witness				
Memory for face				
Related	5.5	5.7	6.8	6.8
Unrelated	5.5	6.7	6.1	6.7
Attention paid				
Related	6.0	6.5	7.5	8.0
Unrelated	6.2	7.0	6.5	7.5
Memory for details				
Related	5.5	6.6	7.5	7.8
Unrelated	5.8	7.1	6.8	7.8
Defense witness				
Memory for face				
Related	6.9	5.4	6.7	6.1
Unrelated	6.3	6.3	6.0	5.4
Attention paid				
Related	7.9	6.5	7.5	6.5
Unrelated	7.0	6.7	6.2	6.2
Memory for details				
Related	7.9	6.6	7.2	5.8
Unrelated	7.6	6.8	6.6	6.2

Note. Higher numbers indicate better memory or more attention paid.

20.4, $p < .001$. When the defense detail was high (vs. low), the defense witness was judged (a) to have higher relative credibility, 52.8 versus 46.3, $F(1, 294) = 25.4$, $p < .001$; (b) to be more credible, 7.1 versus 6.5, $F(1, 293) = 11.9$, $p < .001$; (c) to have a better memory for details in general, 7.3 versus 6.3, $F(1, 291) = 19.3$, $p < .001$; (d) to have a better memory for the culprit's face, 6.5 versus 5.8, $F(1, 291) = 9.3$, $p < .01$; and (e) to have devoted more attention to the culprit and his actions, 7.2 versus 6.5, $F(1, 291) = 11.3$, $p < .001$.

The degree of detail in the testimony of one witness also influenced judgments about the opposing witness. Several main effects were found on these judgments. When the defense detail was high, as opposed to low, the prosecution witness was judged (a) to be less credible, 6.4 versus 7.0. $F(1, 293) = 6.6$, $p < .05$; (b) to have a poorer memory for details, 6.4 versus 7.3, $F(1, 291) = 16.8$, $p < .001$; (c) to have devoted less attention to the culprit, 6.6 versus 7.3 $F(1, 291) = 11.6$, $p < .001$; and (d) to have a poorer memory for the culprit's face, 6.0 versus 6.5, $F(1, 291) = 4.2$, $p < .05$. When the prosecution detail was high, rather than low, the defense witness was judged (a) to be less credible, 6.5 versus 7.0, $F(1, 293) =$

6.6, $p < .05$; (b) to have a poorer memory for details, 6.5 versus 7.2, $F(1, 291) = 11.6$, $p < .001$; and (c) to have devoted less attention to the culprit, 6.6 versus 7.0 $F(1, 291) = 3.8$, $p < .05$. The main effect of prosecution detail on judgments of the defense witness' memory for the face of the culprit was not significant (6.0 vs. 6.2, $F < 1$).

A few unexpected interactions emerged. There was a significant interaction between prosecution detail and detail relatedness for judgments of the attention paid by the prosecution eyewitness, $F(1,$

291) = 7.1, p < .01. Moreover, there was a significant interaction between defense detail and detail relatedness on judgments of the attention paid by the defense eyewitness, $F(1, 291) = 6.6$, p < .01. These interactions basically demonstrate that a witness who provided more detail was judged to have paid more attention to the culprit only when the detail was related. No other interactions were significant.[2]

In determining a defendant's guilt, jurors must compare the strength of the prosecution's case against that of the defense's case. Thus, relative measures comparing the prosecution witness against the defense witness were computed for each of the four judgments about the witnesses. Relative measures of credibility, memory for the face of the culprit, attention paid, and memory for detail were computed for each subject by subtracting the defense witness rating from the prosecution witness rating. The ANOVAS performed on these four relative measures yielded expected main effects of prosecution detail and defense detail. When the prosecution detail was high, as opposed to low, the prosecution witness was judged (a) to have relatively higher credibility, $F(1, 294) = 20.5$, p < .001; (b) to have a relatively better memory for details, $F(1, 294) = 90.2$, p < .001; (c) to have a relatively better memory for the face of the culprit, $F(1, 294) - 15.3$, p < .001; and (d) to have paid relatively more attention to the culprit, $F(1, 294) = 50.3$, p < .001. When the defense detail was high, rather than low, the defense witness was judged (a) to have relatively higher credibility, $F(1, 294) = 26.4$, p < .001; (b) to have a relatively better memory for details, $F(1, 294) = 83.1$, p < .001; (c) to have a relatively better memory for the culprit's face, $F(1, 294) = 23.2$, p < .001; and (d) to have paid relatively more attention to the culprit, $F(1, 294) = 54.3$, p < .001. There was a significant Defense Detail × Relatedness interaction on the relative attention paid measure, $F(1, 294) = 4.3$, p < .05. This interaction indicates that the effect of defense detail was greater when the detail was related. No other interactions were significant.

To further explore whether the significant effects of detail on judgments of guilt (main effect of prosecution detail and three-way interaction) were mediated by inferences about the eyewitnesses, ANCOVAS were performed on the 11-point judgments of guilt with each of the nine judgments about the eyewitnesses and four relative measures used as a covariate in a separate analysis. All witness judgments and relative measures were reliably related to judgments of guilt when controlling for the condition effects (all ps < .01) except for judgments about the defense witness's attention paid and memory for details (ps > .10). When controlling for each prosecution witness judgment, judgments of relative credibility, and the four relative measures, the main effect of prosecution detail was not significant (Fs < 1). When controlling for each defense witness judgment, however, the main effect of prosecution detail was still marginally significant (all ps < .07). Moreover, the three-way interaction still remained at least marginally significant when controlling for each witness judgment and relative measure (all ps < .09), except for the relative measures of credibility and memory for the face of the culprit (ps = .12 and .13). In summary, these results are compatible with the notion that inferences about the eyewitnesses, particularly the prosecution witness, contributed to the main effect of prosecution detail on judgments of guilt.

Discussion

The results of Experiment 1 demonstrate that the degree of detail in prosecution eyewitness testimony had a modest, but reliable, main effect on judgments of guilt. This finding is consistent with our prior research (Bell & Loftus, 1988).

Conclusions about the influence of defense detail on judgments of guilt must be made more cautiously, however, because the main effect only approached significance. In our prior work the main effect of defense detail on judgments of a defendant's guilt was not significant. One possible reason for the weaker effects of defense detail is that the strength of the case for the prosecution in the present research and our prior research was low to begin with. Some mock jurors may have been sufficiently convinced that the burden of proof had not been met without the added detail. Alternatively, the prosecution eyewitness testimony may have received more weight in the judgment of guilt than the defense eyewitness testimony because it was presented first. Some subjects may have assumed that the defense witness simply heard the details provided by the prosecution witness and did not remember the details on her own. It should be pointed out, however, that differences in the size of the effect of prosecution detail versus defense detail were small for judgments of guilt and most of the judgments about the eyewitnesses (see Tables 1, 2, and 3).

The significant three-way interaction on judgments of guilt suggests that related detail and unrelated detail influenced juror judgments in different situations. The three-way interaction is difficult to interpret because there were no other significant three-way interactions on any of the judgments about the eyewitnesses or on any of the recall measures. Moreover, the pattern found for related detail on judgments of guilt is inconsistent with our prior research (Bell & Loftus, 1988), in which prosecution detail had the same impact on judgments of guilt regardless of whether defense detail was high or low. However, we speculate that the three-way interaction might be partly due to differences in whether the judgment of guilt is primarily based on weaknesses in the prosecution testimony or defense testimony. Mock jurors exposed to related prosecution detail may have made their decision primarily on the basis of whether the prosecution witness appeared to have a poorer memory than the defense witness and not on whether the defense witness appeared to have a poorer memory than the prosecution witness. This would explain why related prosecution detail had an effect only when defense detail was high. Only when defense detail was high did the prosecution witness report less detail than the defense witness. Moreover, mock jurors exposed to unrelated detail may have made their decision primarily on the basis of whether the defense witness, but not the prosecution witness, had a poorer memory than the opposing witness. Only

when the defense detail was low was there an influence of unrelated prosecution detail on judgments of guilt. It is unclear, however, why the relatedness of the detail should shift the decision rule from weaknesses in the prosecution testimony to weaknesses in the defense testimony. At best, the three-way interaction suggests that a reliable impact of testimonial detail on inferences about the eyewitnesses may not always lead to a concomitant effect on judgments of guilt.

The influence of detailed testimony on judgments of guilt appeared not to be due to subjects' being better able to remember testimony that is detailed. Previous research has not found conclusive support for the notion that the influence of detailed testimony is mediated by subjects' memory for the testimony (e.g., Shedler & Manis, 1986). This finding suggests that perhaps judgments were made on-line (see Hastie & Park, 1986). Memory for and judgments about information are more likely to be related when there is a substantial demand on people's attention (Bargh & Thein, 1985) or when people are not aware that a judgment will be requested (Hastie & Park, 1986). Neither of these situations was present in Experiment 1.

Our mediational analyses support the notion that the effects of detail specificity on judgments of guilt were partly due to inferences about the eyewitnesses. The results of our prior research suggest that the effects of detail were mediated by judgments about the credibility of the eyewitnesses. The present research extends this finding by showing specifically that inferences about the attention an eyewitness paid to the culprit and an eyewitness's memory for the face of the culprit contributed to the persuasive impact of detailed testimony on judgments of guilt. Witnesses were generally judged to have paid more attention to the culprit and to have a better memory for the culprit's face when they provided more detail.

In some situations, unrelated detail influenced judgments about the eyewitnesses' memory and attention paid. In some cases, there were main effects of testimonial detail on these judgments, but no interaction with relatedness. This suggests that it is likely that our mock jurors drew inferences about the eyewitnesses' dispositions and abilities from the degree of detail in the testimonies.

It is unclear how our mock jurors interpreted the low-detail report of "a few store items." The testimony in Experiment 1 was presented in third person narrative. Subjects were informed that the eyewitness "testified to the following." They then read a paragraph description of the crime without any explicit indication of questions asked by the attorneys. Some subjects may have wondered about the specific questions that were asked at the trial. Some mock jurors may have inferred that the low-detail witness was probably asked to be explicit about the details of the crime or related events, and thus the report of low detail implied that the witness could not remember the store items. Other mock jurors may have inferred that the low-detail witness was probably not asked to be explicit about the details and might possibly be able to recall them if asked. Perhaps the effects of detail on judgments of guilt were weak because some mock jurors had doubts about what the low-detail witness could remember. Perhaps if our mock jurors were explicitly informed that a low-detail witness could not remember the details provided by the high-detail witness, trivial persuasion would be substantially more significant. Experiment 2 addressed this hypothesis.

EXPERIMENT 2

In Experiment 2 some mock jurors learned that a low-detail witness (prosecution witness) was never asked if she could remember the specific store items reported by the high-detail witness (store items that the culprit dropped on his way out). Other mock jurors were informed that a low-detail witness was asked about the store items but could not remember them. We chose to manipulate only the detail in the defense witness testimony (as opposed to the prosecution witness testimony) because we felt that it was important to demonstrate a significant effect of defense detail (which had not been demonstrated previously). Thus, the detail in the prosecution witness testimony was always low (a few store items), but this witness was either explicitly asked or not asked about these store items (and the defense witness was never asked).

This manipulation of the verification of a low-detail witness's memory for details allowed us to determine conditions in which the detail in defense testimony would have a substantial or a minimal impact on judgments. It also allowed us to garner stronger evidence for the notion that inferences about the witnesses' memory mediates the effects of degree of detail on judgments of guilt. Specifically, if the effects of detail on these judgments are mediated by inferences about the witnesses' memory, defense detail should have a greater effect when the prosecution witness specifically testifies that she cannot remember the store items than when she does not. This would be borne out if mock jurors were less certain that the prosecution witness actually has a poor memory for details when she is not asked about the store items than when she is asked. Such uncertainty regarding the prosecution witness would affect the relative credibility of the defense witness.

Method

Subjects   Subjects were 122 students (males and females) from lower-division psychology courses at the University of Washington. Subjects received course credit upon completion of the experiment. There were 28 to 32 subjects in each cell.

Materials and Design   The court case materials were the same as in Experiment 1, except that the eyewitness testimony for both sides was presented in a question–answer format. (Thus, there were some minor changes of wording in the testimonies.) Subjects were informed that the court case summary contained all the questions asked by the attorneys and the answers given by the eyewitnesses. The prosecution eyewitness testimony was always low detail (a few store items). The degree of detail in the defense testimony contained the same related detail as in the first experiment. Moreover, the verification of the prosecution witness's memory for the store items was manipulated. In the no-verification condition the prosecution eyewitness is not asked whether she can remember the store items. In the verification condition the prosecution eyewitness is asked if she can remember the store items, and the eyewitness replies, "I, uh, no, I can't remember what they were, sorry."

Procedure   The procedure followed was the same as in the first experiment, with a few exceptions. Although subjects were asked to make judgments of guilt, credibility, attention paid, memory for the culprit's face, and memory for details, they were not asked to recall the testimony, to give reasons for relative credibility judgments, or to make judgments abut the eyewitness descriptions. In addition, subjects had their court case materials with them while making judgments on the case.

Results

The main effects of defense detail on judgments paralleled those found in Experiment 1 (see Table 4). Specifically, when the defense witness gave a highly detailed, as opposed to a less detailed, account, the defendant was judged to be less guilty on the 11-point scale, $F(1, 118) = 4.6, p < .05$; fewer guilty verdicts were rendered (logistic regression, $z = 2.3, p < .05$); and the prosecution witness was judged to have lower relative credibility, $F(1, 118) = 19.8, p < .001$. Furthermore, when the defense witness gave a highly detailed account, she was judged to have a better memory for details, $F(1, 118) = 23.4, p < .001$; to have paid more attention to the culprit, $F(1, 118) = 31.3, p < .001$; and to have a better memory for the culprit's face, $F(1, 118) = 9.1, p < .01$. The effect of defense detail on judgments of defense witness credibility was marginally significant $F(1, 118) = 3.2, p < .08$. The impact of defense detail on the prosecution witness judgments was opposite on these dimensions. The main effects were significant for judgments of memory for details, $F(1, 118) = 9.3, p < .01$, credibility, $F(1, 118) = 13.0, p < .001$, but nonsignificant for judgments of attention paid to the culprit and memory for the culprit's face *(Fs < 1)*.

TABLE 4 / Mean Judgments of Guilt, Credibility, Memory, and Attention Paid

Judgments	Verification		No verification	
	High detail	Low detail	High detail	Low detail
Verdict	.06	.47	.31	.25
11-point guilt	4.0	6.1	5.3	4.8
Relative credibility	40.3	54.4	47.9	52.9
Prosecution witness				
Credibility	5.5	7.3	6.4	7.0
Memory for face	5.3	5.7	6.3	5.3
Attention paid	5.9	6.9	6.3	5.9
Memory for details	4.9	6.5	5.9	6.3
Defense witness				
Credibility	7.4	6.7	7.0	5.8
Memory for face	6.5	5.0	6.1	5.1
Attention paid	7.8	6.3	7.6	5.8
Memory for details	7.9	6.2	7.8	6.3

Note. The scales are the same as for Tables, 1, 2, and 3.

The main effects of defense detail on prosecution witness judgments, relative credibility, and judgments of guilt were qualified by interactions with the verification manipulation. When there was no verification of the prosecution witness's memory for the store items, there was little or no impact of defense detail on these judgments. In contrast, when it was made known to the mock jurors that the prosecution witness could not remember the store items, there were substantial effects on most of these judgments. Specifically, there were significant interactions on verdicts (logistic regression, $z = 2.9, p < .01$); 11-point guilt judgments, $F(1, 118) = 10.8, p < .001$; judgments of attention paid to the culprit, $F(1, 118) = 5.0, p < .05$; and relative credibility judgments, $F(1, 118) = 4.5, p < .05$. The interaction effects were marginally significant for judgments about the prosecution witness's memory for details, credibility, and memory for the face of the culprit (all $ps < .09$).

Further analyses of simple effects revealed that there were no significant effects of defense detail on judgments of guilt and judgments about the prosecution witness in the no-verification condition (all *p*s > .20). The simple main effect of defense detail, did, however, approach significance for judgments of relative credibility and memory for the culprit's face (.10 < *p*s < .12). In contrast, the effects of defense detail in the verification condition were significant for all judgments (all *p*s < .05), except for the prosecution witness's memory for the face of the culprit (*p* > .20).

As in Experiment 1, relative measures of credibility, memory for the culprit's face, attention paid, and memory for details were computed for each subject by subtracting the rating for the defense witness from the rating for the prosecution witness. ANOVAS performed on these measures yielded expected main effects of defense detail. When the defense witness provided an account of high detail, as opposed to low, the defense witness was judged to have relatively higher credibility, $F(1, 118) = 16.9$, $p < .001$; to have a relatively better memory for the culprit's face, $F(1, 118) = 4.8$, $p < .05$; to have paid relatively more attention to the culprit, $F(1, 118) = 35.8$, $p < .001$; and to have a relatively better memory for details, $F(1, 118) = 54.4$, $p < .001$. The Defense Detail × Verification interaction was significant for the relative measure of memory for the culprit's face, $F(1, 118) = 5.8$, $p < .05$; marginally significant for the relative measure of memory for details, $F(1, 118) = 3.6$, $p < .06$; and nonsignificant for the other relative measures (.11 < *p*s < .15). The effect of defense detail was larger in the verification condition than in the no-verification condition.

The ANCOVAS were performed on the 11-point judgments of guilt with each of the nine judgments about the eyewitnesses and four relative measures used as a covariate in a separate analysis. When controlling for the condition effects, all judgments about the eyewitnesses and relative measures were reliably related to judgments of guilt (all *p*s < .01), except for judgments about the defense witness' memory for details and memory for the face of the culprit (*F*s < 1). When controlling for judgments of relative credibility, prosecution credibility, the two judgments about memory for details, and the four relative measures, the main effect of defense detail was nonsignificant (all *p*s > .20, except for

defense memory for details). The main effect of defense detail was marginally significant or significant when controlling for the two judgments of memory for the culprit's face, the two attention paid judgments, and defense credibility (all *p*s < .10). Finally, the Defense Detail × Verification interaction remained significant when controlling for each witness judgment and relative measure (all *p*s < .05). These results are compatible with the notion that the main effect of defense detail on judgments of guilt was mediated by judgments of the eyewitness's relative credibility, memory, and attention paid.

In light of the finding that memory for a culprit's face can be negatively related to memory for peripheral details (Wells & Leippe, 1981), correlations were computed between judgments of memory for a culprit's face and memory for details to see how these correlations compared with this finding. Correlational analyses revealed that judgments of the prosecution witness's memory for details and memory for the culprit's face were positively related in the verification condition ($r = .38$, $p < .001$) and the no-verification condition ($r = .43$, $p < .001$). Moreover, judgments of the defense witness's memory for details and memory for the face of the culprit were positively correlated in the verification condition ($r = .46$, $p < .001$) and the no-verification condition ($r = .52$, $p < .001$).

Discussion

The results of Experiment 2 are important for several reasons. First, they demonstrate that the specificity of defense detail can actually have a substantial effect on judgments of guilt when there is a definite weakness in the testimony of the prosecution witness (e.g., cannot remember store items the culprit dropped). It stands to reason that if the defense witness could not remember details, the degree of detail in the prosecution testimony would also have a substantial impact. Second, the difference in the impact of defense detail in the two verification conditions may help explain the weak effects on judgments of guilt in Experiment 1. It is possible that some mock jurors who participated in Experiment 1 simply were not sure that the opposing witness's report of "a few store items" indicated that the witness could not remember the store items. Third, the results of Experiment 2 provide stronger evidence that the effects of testimonial detail on judgments of a defendant's guilt are partly mediated by inferences about the eyewitnesses' memory. Only when subjects explicitly learned that the prosecution witness could not remember the store items was there a reliable and substantial impact of defense detail on judgments of guilt.[3]

In Experiment 2, the impact of reporting trivial details on judgments of guilt and on the prosecution witness judgments was generally smaller (and nonsignificant) in the no-verification condition than in the comparable condition in Experiment 1. This may have been because subjects in Experiment 2, but not Experiment 1, explicitly learned that the prosecution witness was never asked whether she could remember the store items. It must be noted, however, that Experiment 2 also differed from Experiment 1 in that subjects had their case materials with them while making judgments. It is not entirely clear what role this difference played in contributing to the nonsignificant results in the no-verification condition. In our prior research (Bell & Loftus, 1988), however, subjects also had their court case summaries with them while making the judgments, and there still were some reliable effects of testimonial detail on judgments. Thus, it seems unlikely that the fact that subjects had their case summaries with them while making their judgments led to an attentuation of the effect in the no-verification condition.

GENERAL DISCUSSION

This jury simulation research provides further support for a phenomenon we call trivial persuasion. We have shown that detailed information need not be related to persons directly involved in the incident in question in order to be powerful. Thus, even seemingly insignificant and irrelevant information, such as the store items a customer

dropped prior to a crime, can influence mock juror judgments. The effect of reporting trivial details appears to be especially powerful when an opposing witness testifies that he or she cannot remember the same details. In the context of a jury trial, trivial persuasion seems to be mediated by inferences about the eyewitnesses' credibility, memory, and attention paid.

Systematic versus Heuristic Information Processing

Prior work suggests that source cues play a major role in persuasion when people are relatively uninvolved in their task, but they play a minor or negligible role when people are highly involved in their task (e.g., Chaiken, 1980; Petty, Cacioppo, & Goldman, 1981). Chaiken interpreted her findings in terms of a systematic versus heuristic information-processing view of persuasion. In the heuristic mode of persuasion, people primarily rely on simple and general rules (e.g., about source credibility) and de-emphasize detailed processing of the message content. In contrast, systematic information processing involves considerable processing of the message content. Chaiken's results suggest that highly involved people are more likely to engage in systematic information processing, whereas less involved people are more likely to engage in heuristic information processing.

Trivial persuasion resembles the heuristic information processing model in that it seems to involve the utilization of simple and general rules about source credibility. Our results suggest that trivial persuasion might involve the heuristic "people who remember trivial details have a really good memory." However, trivial persuasion may not be completely compatible with the heuristic information-processing model. Our mock jurors may have been fairly involved in their task and engaged in detailed processing of the message content. Several arguments can be made in support of this notion. First, subjects would need to read each testimony carefully to notice the minor differences in the amount of detail reported. Second, it appears that the effects of reporting trivial details were mediated by issue-relevant inferences. It seems that our subjects drew inferences about the witnesses' memory for the culprit and crime. Third, in Experiment 1, most subjects appeared to have fairly adequate recall of the eyewitness testimony.

We speculate that our findings suggest a situation in which superficial source cues may have a substantial impact on persuasion regardless of how involved people are in the task. Thus, these superficial source cues may play a role even when people engage in considerable processing of the message content. In our experiments, subjects received a two-sided communication with contradictory information provided by an opposing communicator. The prosecution eyewitness testified that the defendant was the man who shot the clerk, whereas the defense witness testified to the contrary. It may be difficult to predicate a judgment on the basis of argumentation alone when presented with conflicting or contradictory information. Under such conditions, people may feel that it is necessary to resolve the contradiction by evaluating the relative credibility of the communicators. The minimal impact of source factors (e.g., expertise) among high-involvement subjects in the experiments of Chaiken (1980) and Petty et al. (1981) might be attributed to the fact that their subjects received a one-sided communication presented by a single communicator. Highly involved people may be substantially affected by source-related factors when presented with two-sided communications involving conflicting or contradictory information.

In short, we suggest that trivial persuasion may best be characterized as a blend of systematic and heuristic information processing. Trivial persuasion can be characterized as involving appreciable issue-relevant thinking and the utilization of simple and general rules about source credibility. Other research has found that both message-related thoughts and perceptions of the communicator (expertise) were significant predictors of persuasion in some situations (Chaiken & Eagly, 1983).

Validity of Juror Beliefs

We found that mock jurors believe that memory for trivial detail is positively related to memory for the culprit's face. Is this belief warranted? The answer may be no. Although memory for details of a face has been shown to be positively related to identification accuracy (Wells, 1985), this does not appear to be true for peripheral details. In fact, the relation between memory for peripheral details and a culprit's face can be negative (Cutler, Penrod, & Martens, 1987; Wells & Leippe, 1981). If processing resources are limited, then allocating attention to the processing of peripheral details may result in insufficient resources allocated to the culprit's face (see Kahneman, 1973).

It is conceivable that a witness who has a good memory for the store items that a robber picked up may be less likely to accurately remember the culprit's face. This could occur if the attention paid to what the culprit had in his hands took away from attention to the culprit's face. This notion would not, however, apply to a witness who had a better memory for details unrelated to the crime, because the unrelated details would not be in competition for resources with the encoding of the culprit's face. Thus, we still need to learn whether people who are better at remembering trivial details in general are better, or not better, at remembering a culprit's face. We need to learn more about the relation between eyewitness memory for the culprit's face and details that pertain to another event. This line of research would better allow us to assess the validity of the notion that jurors make inaccurate inferences about the memorial processes involved in eyewitness events.

Future Research

The present experiments involved contradictory information provided by opposing witnesses. It seems reasonable to ask whether trivial persuasion is limited to conditions in which people are presented with two-sided communications involving contradictory information. It would be interesting to find out whether the effect of trivial details is attenuated when people receive only a one-sided communication, or no contradictory information.

To what extent does trivial persuasion depend on the vividness of the detailed information? In the vividness studies of Reyes et al. (1980) and Shedler and Manis (1986), the vivid versions contained more detail than the pallid versions. Thus, it is unclear whether the effects found were due to the amount of detail or the vividness of the detailed information (see Taylor & Thompson, 1982, for a review of the vividness effect). Subsequent research could address whether testimony that was equivalent in amount of detail would be more persuasive if the detail in the testimony was vivid than if it was pallid.

The assessment of an eyewitness's credibility involves two inferences: perceived honesty and perceived memory. It could be that inferences about honesty also mediate the influence of reporting trivial details. It is possible that in contexts outside the courtroom, perceived honesty, rather than perceived memory, mediates trivial persuasion.

How powerful are trivial details that are completely irrelevant? If people draw inferences about a witness's abilities and dispositions from the degree of detail in the witness's testimony, it stands to reason that even detailed information that seems totally irrelevant may be persuasive. For example, if a witness interjected into an account of the crime some details about another crime that was previously witnessed, the witness could conceivably be perceived as highly credible because these details imply that the witness is one of those persons who has an exceptional memory. The notion that John Dean was a human tape recorder seems to suggest that people do draw inferences about a witness's memory from the amount of detail reported. Future research could profitably address this issue.

Concluding Remarks

We believe that our findings demonstrate a general phenomenon: The specificity of trivial details in a communication can be an important variable for persuasion, and this persuasion may occur through a process in which people form inferences about the communicator. Trivial persuasion is most likely to occur when there is good reason to question the credibility of the communicator, for example, when there is contradictory information provided by an opposing communicator. Trivial details may be powerful in other decision contexts as well, such as employment or helping a stranger.

Our research not only adds to our knowledge of factors influencing perceived eyewitness credibility and memory (see Erickson, Lind, Johnson, & O'Barr, 1978; O'Barr & Conley, 1976; Wells, Lindsay, & Ferguson, 1979) but also suggests another case in which inferences about memory processes involved in eyewitness events are likely to be incongruent with actual memory processes (see Wells, 1984). We hope that future research will further illuminate the subject of trivial persuasion and its relation to inferred and actual memory processes.

REFERENCES

Bargh, J., & Thein, R. D. (1985). Individual construct accessibility, person memory, and the recall-judgment link: The case of information overload. *Journal of Personality and Social Psychology, 49,* 1129–1146.

Bell, B. E., & Loftus, E. F. (1988). Degree of detail of eyewitness testimony and mock juror judgments. *Journal of Applied Social Psychology, 18,* 1171–1192.

Chaiken, S. (1980). Heuristic versus systematic information processing and the use of source versus message cues in persuasion. *Journal of Personality and Social Psychology, 39,* 752–766.

Chaiken, S., & Eagly, A. H. (1983). Communication modality as a determinant of persuasion: The role of communicator salience. *Journal of Personality and Social Psychology, 45,* 241–256.

Cutler, B. L., Penrod, S. D., & Martens, T. K. (1987). The reliability of eyewitness identification: The role of system and estimater variables. *Law and Human Behavior, 11,* 233–258.

Erickson, B. E., Lind, A., Johnson, B. C., & O'Barr, W. M. (1978). Speech style and impression formation in a court setting: The effects of "powerful" and "powerless" speech. *Journal of Experimental Social Psychology, 14,* 266–279.

Hastie, R., & Park, B. (1986). The relationship between memory and judgments depends on whether the judgment task is memory-based or on-line. *Psychological Review, 93,* 258–268.

Kahneman, D. (1973). *Attention and effort.* Englewood Cliffs, NJ: Prentice-Hall.

Neisser, U. (1981). John Dean's memory: A case study. *Cognition, 9,* 1–22.

Nisbett, R., & Ross, L. (1980). Human inference: Strategies and shortcomings of social judgment. Englewood Cliffs, NJ: Prentice-Hall.

O'Barr, W. M., & Conley, J. M. (1976). When a juror watches a lawyer. *Barrister, 3,* 8–11.

Petty, R. E., & Cacioppo, J. T. (1981). *Attitudes and persuasion: Classic and contemporary approaches.* Dubuque, IA: Wm. C. Brown.

Petty, R. E., Cacioppo, J. T., & Goldman, R. (1981). Personal involvement as a determinant of argument-based persuasion. *Journal of Personality and Social Psychology, 41,* 847–855.

Pigott, M., & Brigham, J. C. (1985). Relationship between accuracy of prior description and facial recognition. *Journal of Applied Psychology, 70,* 547–555.

Reyes, R. M., Thompson, W. C., & Bower, G. H. (1980). Judgmental biases resulting from differing availabilities of arguments. *Journal of Personality and Social Psychology, 39,* 2–12.

Schooler, J. W., Gerhard, D., & Loftus, E. F. (1986). Qualities of the unreal. *Journal of Experimental Psychology: Learning, Memory, and Cognition, 12,* 171–181.

Select Committee on Presidential Campaign Activities (1973). *Hearings before the Select Committee on Presidential Campaign Activities of the United States Senate,* Ninety-third Congress, First Session.

Shedler, J., & Manis, M. (1986). Can the availability heuristic explain vividness effects? *Journal of Personality and Social Psychology, 51,* 26–36.

Taylor, S. E., & Thompson, S. C. (1982). Stalking the elusive "vividness" effect. *Psychological Review, 89,* 155–181.

Wells, G. L. (1984). The adequacy of human intuition for judging testimony. In G. L. Wells & E. L. Loftus. *Eyewitness testimony: Psychological perspectives* (pp. 256–272). Cambridge, England: Cambridge University Press.

Wells, G. L. (1985). Verbal descriptions of faces from memory: Are they diagnostic of identification accuracy? *Journal of Applied Psychology, 70,* 619–626.

Wells, G. L., & Leippe, M. R. (1981). How do triers of fact infer the accuracy of eyewitness identifications? Using memory for peripheral detail can be misleading. *Journal of Applied Psychology, 66,* 682–687.

Wells, G. L., Lindsay, C. L., & Ferguson, T. J. (1979). Accuracy, confidence, and juror perceptions in eyewitness identifications. *Journal of Applied Psychology, 64,* 440–484.

NOTES

1. In our prior research (Experiment 2) the specificity of detail was varied on both sides of a criminal court case. In two cells the specificity of detail was equivalent on each side. Subjects were asked to give reasons for their judgments of the relative credibility of the eyewitnesses (they divided 100 points between the eyewitnesses). Subjects mostly gave reasons for why they gave more points to one witness than the other. Consequently, in two of the cells subjects did not mention anything related to the details in the testimony. For these subjects we had no indication of subjects' inferences about the relation between detail specificity and memory. Moreover, we found that subjects gave reasons related to memory for defense witnesses even though defense detail had no effect on judgments.

2. There were marginal interactions between prosecution detail and relatedness for judgments of both prosecution and defense witnesses' credibility and memory for the face of the culprit ($ps < .10$). The interactions for the prosecution witness demonstrate that the effect of prosecution detail was attenuated when the detail was unrelated. The interactions for the defense witness indicate that the effect of prosecution detail was attenuated when the detail was related. The lack of interactions with relatedness on the relative measures of credibility and memory for the culprit's face suggests that related detail did not have a greater influence on judgments of the two witnesses overall. Rather, related detail primarily influenced judgments about the prosecution witness, whereas unrelated detail primarily influenced judgments about the defense witness.

3. An alternative explanation for the Defense Detail × Verification interaction is that subjects who learned that the prosecution witness was asked about the store items were more aware of differences in the detailed descriptions provided by the two eyewitnesses than subjects who did not read the question about the store items. If this explanation were true, there should have been a greater effect of defense detail on the defense witness judgments. However, there was no Defense Detail × Verification interaction on the defense witness judgments, which argues against this explanation.

This research was supported in part by grants from the National Science Foundation and the National Institute of Mental Health. The article is based on a master's thesis completed by Brad E. Bell.

We thank Robin Ashley, Lavonne Dorsey, Lisa Hopkins, Traci Sammeth, Cynthia Nielson, and Susan Shriener for assistance with the experiments and manuscript preparation. We also thank Robert Josephs for help with this research, and Harriet Shaklee, Kipling Williams, and seven anonymous reviewers for their comments on earlier versions of this article.

CRITICAL THINKING QUESTIONS

1. The section of the article labeled "Future Research" contained several possible directions for further studies in the area. Select one of the possibilities and design a study to investigate it.

2. The authors of the article tentatively suggested that trivial persuasion may operate in settings other than the courtroom. Give examples of where else you might expect to find this effect.

3. Considering the practical implications of this study, if you were a lawyer, what would you tell your client to do or not to do when on the witness stand? Explain.

4. The findings of this study, combined with the previous classic selection (Article 38), cast some serious doubt on how objective juries can be in evaluating evidence. Given these potential shortcomings, how can their effects be minimized? Alternatively, if the shortcomings can't be minimized, does that suggest that jury trials might not be the most effective way to administer justice?

Chapter Fourteen

APPLYING SOCIAL PSYCHOLOGY II: WORK ISSUES

A MAJOR PART of your life will be spent at work. When you think of what type of work you may be doing now or in the future, you may have many concerns. You may be concerned about how much money you will make, for one thing. But you also may be concerned about whether you will enjoy what you are doing. If you are a manager and responsible for other people's behavior, you also may be concerned with how to best utilize the human resources available, both for the benefit of the organization as well as that of the individual employee.

Questions of what motivates people, what factors are involved in job satisfaction, and what factors influence productivity are but a few of the areas examined by social psychologists working in the area of organizational behavior. As you may already have noticed in reading articles in other chapters, many of the topics addressed have implications for the world of work. In fact, the applied contributions of social-psychological research are perhaps nowhere greater than in the area of work-related issues.

Each of the three articles selected for this chapter concerns a different area of interest in organizational psychology. Article 40, "The Question of Quality Circles," looks at a particular technique that may potentially increase employee job satisfaction and productivity. Article 41, the classic selection, is entitled "One More Time: How Do You Motivate Employees?" Your beliefs about what motivates people to work may not be the same after you read the article. Finally, the last selection, Article 42, "Conflict between Managers and Workers," looks at conflict in the workplace and how it can be handled to the mutual benefit of all parties involved.

ARTICLE 40 ─────────────────────────

For several decades, business has focused on ways to maximize productivity and hence profits for the organization. Beginning in the 1970s, there was an increasing feeling that American industry was losing its competitive edge to other nations. The quality of American-made goods came to be viewed as inferior to that of imported goods. This feeling of inferiority led to an increased effort by business to discover ways to improve quality and productivity of goods and services. In searching for answers, it seemed logical to look to the country whose productivity and quality were increasing just as rapidly as American productivity and quality were declining: Japan.

In an attempt to learn from the competition, American businesses began to study Japanese industrial and management techniques. One technique widely used in Japan for improving both job satisfaction and organizational productivity is something called *quality circles* (QCs). The following article by Marks discusses what quality circles are, what they hope to accomplish, and how successful they have been when implemented in American work settings. Although quality circles may not be a panacea for lagging productivity and poor quality, they may at least help improve the situation under certain circumstances.

The Question of Quality Circles

■ Mitchell Lee Marks

Blue Cross of Washington and Alaska reports that more efficient employee procedures have saved $430,000 in less than three years, improved service to customers and increased communication between departments. A better method for checking coating thickness of floppy disks has saved $100,000 for the Verbatim Corporation in Sunnyvale, California. Sales agents at Hertz Rent a Car in Oklahoma City now get information about car availability 27 seconds faster using computers rather than microfiche.

Neither industrial engineers nor human factors analysts developed these innovations. Rather, they came directly from the workers themselves—sales agents, clerks and factory workers participating in Quality Circles (QC's, as they are often called), an employee-participation technique popularized in Japan and now widely applied in the United States.

Many business people, management experts and organizational psychologists dispute the savings claimed by QC adherents and say that QC's fail more often than they work. These critics describe the technique as management snake oil, a quick fix too often aimed at generating short-term profits rather than addressing the real problems underlying poor productivity, quality and employee morale.

A major reason for these sharp differences of opinion is that until recently the benefits of QC's have been studied and touted chiefly by people with a vested interest in QC success: managers whose bonuses and career advancement are at stake and consultants looking for ways to impress

Reprinted from *Psychology Today*, 1986 (March), *20*, 36–46. Reprinted with permission from *Psychology Today Magazine*. Copyright © 1986 (PT Partners, L.P.).

and sell new clients. There have been few rigorously collected data on how QC's affect the attitudes and productivity of employees and the effectiveness and financial performances of their organizations.

Several such evaluations have been made in the last few years. Before examining what they found, it will be useful to look at how QC's work and the reasons—aside from any accomplishments—for their tremendous growth in popularity.

Although QC programs vary from site to site most share a basic format: Small groups of people who perform similar work meet voluntarily on a regular basis, usually once a week, to analyze work-related problems and propose solutions to them. QC's are usually led by the supervisor or manager of the work unit in which they are located. Members receive training in problem solving, quality control and group dynamics to help them function well.

Discussions are limited to issues directly related to the quantity or quality of work, such as paperwork and material waste, machine maintenance, cooperation between departments and productivity. Pay, benefits, hiring or promotion decisions and factors restricted by labor-relations contracts are out of bounds. Members of QC's have no power to implement ideas directly. Instead, they present them to the person in charge of the operation involved, usually a middle-level manager, who is free to accept or reject the recommendations.

The QC process draws substantially upon psychological theory and research for its rationale. The technique, consistent with the work of theorists such as Abraham Maslow, assumes that employees become more motivated if jobs meet their need for growth. Proponents claim that QC's accomplish this by giving workers opportunities to identify and solve real problems, make presentations to company management and operate successfully in groups. They also contend that QC's offer the advantages of group decision-making—advantages that include, according to psychologist Norman R. F. Maier of the University of Michigan, higher-quality decisions and increased commitment to implementing them.

QC's are a major part of a broader current movement toward greater employee participation in decision-making. Robert E. Cole, a sociologist at the University of Michigan and former director of that school's Center for Japanese Studies, notes, "In the early 1970s there were extensive discussions in America . . . about the need to 'humanize work' and raise the quality of work life. By increasing employee participation in workplace decisions, increasing job variety, and making more effective use of worker potential, it was argued, not only would the quality of work life be enhanced, but organizational efficiency and worker productivity would be improved."

Cole recalls, "Japan scared the pants off U.S. business in the 1970s. People were desperately looking for something to try." The media, as well as many academics, attributed Japan's success in the late 1970s to its superior approach to management, and QC's were seen as the easiest part of the Japanese approach to implement. QC programs were accessible, well packaged and aggressively marketed by management consultants. Additionally, American business leaders saw them as a low-risk method for increasing worker involvement without changing the organization. Finally, QC usage also became a fad. Many managers jumped on the bandwagon simply because the technique symbolized modern management.

QC proponents argue that their technique is much more than a fad, that it is part of a trend that is permanently changing managerial assumptions and practices in the United States. Donald Dewar, president of Quality Circle Institute, the largest QC consulting firm in the United States, insists, "You don't have quality control without quality circles. Of all the participative management techniques, this is the first time it went below supervisory levels and down to the people who actually do the work. Many managers have been surprised that people could learn the problem-solving techniques. It is changing not only the quality of work, but also how managers regard their people."

Many American management scholars and practitioners, including executives who refuse to use QC's in their organizations, view these claims with caution. They contend that the technique is a poor fit with American management styles. Tai K. Oh, a management professor at California State University at Fullerton and a consultant to businesses in the United States on Japanese management techniques, says that QC programs have failed in more than 60 percent of the American organizations in which they have been tried.

At the core of these failures are the very reasons that QC programs are so popular in this country: their availability as easy-to-implement packages and the perception by many managers that the technique is a simple way to solve a firm's personnel problems. Oh likens the effects of QC's to those of aspirin or Valium: They treat symptoms and provide some immediate relief but don't touch the underlying issues of management-employee tensions, lack of respect and underutilization of workers that cause the problems in the first place.

Three recent studies provide some light to supplement the heat of the debate over the value of QC's. In one of them, psychologists Philip H. Mirvis and James F. Grady, sociologist Edward J. Hackett and I examined the claims that QC's improve participants' quality of work life and job performance. Specifically, we studied whether QC's actually increase decision-making opportunities, change employees' attitudes toward their work by convincing them that their jobs are challenging and satisfy their needs for growth. We also examined whether participating in a QC program improves productivity and lessens absenteeism.

We conducted our study in the manufacturing department of a decentralized manufacturing firm that was about to start a QC program. About half of the machine operators eligible for the program chose to participate. Working independently of the program, we developed an employee-attitude survey and administered it twice to all the machine operators, immediately before the program started and 20 months later. We also collected raw data directly from company records to assess any changes in employee behavior during the QC program. We used these data to

compare rates of productivity and attendance for a 30-month period, starting six months before the QC program began.

Looking first at employee attitudes, we found that participation in the QC had a strong impact only in work-life areas directly related to QC activity — decision-making opportunities, group communication and opportunities and skills needed for advancement. Participation did not, however, contrary to the usual claims of QC proponents, affect worker attitudes toward communication through the entire organization, job challenge, personal responsibility for getting work done and overall job satisfaction.

We also found, unexpectedly, that being in a QC did not make machine operators more satisfied with any facets of their work situation, even those directly related to their QC work. Their ratings of the quality of their work life didn't change during the 30-month period. I suspect that this was due to factors separate from the QC program. During the 20 months between the two surveys, the division we studied was merged with a much larger division and the local economy experienced a severe recession. Rumors abounded about cutbacks and layoffs; these, combined with the poor economic news, could well have depressed the operators' outlook on work and life in general.

This interpretation is strengthened by the fact that the work satisfaction of machine operators who did not participate in the QC program decreased during the same 20-month period. Perhaps taking part in QC's provided satisfaction and social support that lessened some of the stress and negative feelings produced by the rumors and the bad economic news.

Unlike the mixed nature of these attitudinal findings, our analysis of the behavioral data is quite positive: Participation in QC's raised machine operators' productivity and reduced absenteeism. Before the program started, the participants and nonparticipants had similar records of productivity, percentage of paid hours actually spent on production, quality, efficiency and monthly attendance. Over the course of the QC program, participants showed steady increases in each of these areas while nonparticipants stayed about the same.

In another study, a professor of organizational behavior, James W. Dean Jr. of Pennsylvania State University, examined why employees chose to join QC programs in the electronic equipment division of a large manufacturing corporation and how their participation affected job satisfaction. He interviewed and administered questionnaires to members of 15 QC's in both the engineering and assembly functions and to a group of similar employees who were not QC members. The QC program had been in place for two years when he did his research.

Dean found several factors that distinguish QC participants from nonparticipants. Those who join QC's want greater involvement at work and believe that a QC will address this need. They also believe that the QC process can really change things by improving their jobs and the overall organization. Factors such as age, tenure and wanting a break from work did not affect the decision to participate.

Dean concluded that employees who join a QC see it as a way to accomplish real change at work and usually choose problems that are likely to be successfully solved and implemented. Workers are satisfied by the experience if they see a direct link between QC activities and organizational change and if their QC has capable and productive people.

Commenting on this last point, Dean suggests that QC successes, both in terms of employee satisfaction and effective problem solving, can be increased through appropriate training. In his observations of QC programs, however, he finds that "training is largely pro forma in most applications and not taken very seriously. Most people who go through training are bored to death because much of what is covered does not relate to their personal work situation. Training should be differentiated for engineers, blue-collar or clerical workers and others."

Dean attributes the training problem to the fact that most QC's use the very detailed problem-solving model originally adopted by Lockheed in the early 1970s (see "Quality Circles" box.) Unfortunately, as Dean sees it, most problems addressed by QC's do not require that approach. "It is like using a tank to kill a fly," he says.

In a third study, a team from the University of Southern California (USC) Center for Effective Organizations focused on the factors that influence QC success. Organizational behaviorist Susan A. Mohrman and psychologists Edward E. Lawler III and Gerald E. Ledford Jr. studied QC's in nine separate units of a large conglomerate, using interviews, questionnaires and company data such as internal reports, newsletters and training material. The nine units varied greatly in the amount of training provided, membership criteria and use of rewards.

The researchers found that most QC's that succeed in changing the organization share several characteristics. They include sufficient training of members and direct efforts to improve group process dynamics; access to useful information inside and outside the organization; accurate record-keeping, including the establishment of measurable goals for the QC; and creation of QC's from intact work teams. However, while such QC's usually prompt some technical changes in an organization, the researchers found little evidence that they change corporate culture or improve individual work satisfaction and productivity.

The USC team also found reason to doubt the extent of the financial savings claimed for QC's. Mohrman cautions that while changes proposed by QC's often seem likely to save a great deal of money, "In many cases, the change is not implemented well, is not implemented at all, or is implemented and just does not save the money projected."

This is largely because the people who propose the changes are usually not the ones who actually implement them. The workers who do may resist the change because they do not understand the need for it or because they give priority to their regular work responsibilities. Moreover, since recognition and rewards are given only to people who develop the ideas, those who must implement them have little incentive to do so.

Quality Circles: From America to Japan and Back Again

The QC technique began in the late 1940s with H. Edwards Deming, an American who lectured in post-World War II Japan about statistical methods for quality control. He stressed that production quality must involve both workers and management; the Japanese combined these ideas with a philosophy of bringing workers together in groups to solve problems. At the heart of the Japanese program was the assumption that the person who performs a job is the one who best knows how to identify and correct its problems.

This was a radical departure from the traditional American approach to management, in which quality was the responsibility of special departments called quality assurance or quality control. All workers had to do was work. This task specialization reflected a managerial attitude that workers were incapable of performing more than a few well-defined tasks, motivated exclusively by economic rewards and indifferent to organizational needs. With this attitude prevailing in the United States, it is not surprising that QC's were ignored here.

In post-World War II Japan, QC's quickly became an integral part of a collaborative effort by government and industry leaders to improve the quality of the country's manufactured goods. By the late 1970s, "made in Japan," once a stigma, had come to represent the epitome of product quality and technological advancement to consumers worldwide. Simultaneously, American productivity stagnated. A new generation of workers, better educated and more financially secure than their older colleagues, began demanding jobs that were more psychologically rewarding and a greater say in decisions that affected their work.

In November 1973, the Lockheed Corporation sent six employees to Japan to study QC's. They were impressed by how the QC technique led to major improvements and by the excitement and involvement of Japanese workers in QC meetings and in their jobs. The visiting Americans were especially taken with the thoroughness of the problem-solving process: a nearly invariable sequence of problem generation and selection, causal analysis, solution generation and analysis, presentation to management, trial implementation, monitoring and feedback and, ultimately, full implementation.

The Lockheed people brought the Japanese technique back to the United States and, with very few changes, established the first QC's in this country one year later. The technique spread slowly at first, starting with other aerospace firms that had noticed Lockheed's success. By 1977, only five companies had QC programs. Then, as the recession forced business leaders to find new ways to increase employee productivity and as companies lost sales to high-quality Japanese products, QC's took off. The most recent national survey, conducted by the New York Stock Exchange in 1982, reported that 44 percent of all companies with more than 500 employees had QC programs. Three out of every four had been started within the previous two years.

The International Association of Quality Circles—composed of QC members, managers and consultants—has grown in membership from 100 in 1978 to more than 7,000 in 1985. QC's are now found in virtually every sector, from transportation, entertainment and finance to the military and government, and involve workers of all types and shades of collar.

The USC team identified several other problems that limit QC success. One is resistance by middle-level managers, who have no direct involvement until they are called upon to approve or implement a QC suggestion. Many are uncomfortable with getting ideas from subordinates and either reject them out of hand or respond slowly and unenthusiastically.

Either response may discourage QC participants; they may feel that the program is a waste of time or a management trick and eventually stop meeting. Other QC's become victims of their own success. Having successfully dealt with key issues, they have no major problems left to solve and disband. Sometimes, as QC's become less productive, the company scales down the resources provided for their activities. Participants become less enthusiastic, begin to meet less often and finally stop completely.

Despite these problems, Mohrman, Lawler and Ledford conclude that QC's can be valuable under the right conditions. They recommend three effective ways to use them. First, QC's may operate as group suggestion programs to improve communications and raise employee consciousness about quality and productivity. Second, QC's may be used for special projects when organizations must deal with temporary or critical issues, such as introducing a new technology, retooling for a new product line or solving a major quality problem. Third, QC's may help in making the transition toward more participative management systems. This can take place when a company, recognizing limitations of the QC approach, moves on to make the basic managerial and organizational changes needed to create a more participative organization.

Taken together, the three studies verify that QC's may have a positive impact on organizations and employees. But they do not support the larger claims of some QC proponents that the technique routinely improves employee productivity, morale and growth as well as overall organizational effectiveness. QC's can improve employee productivity and have a limited impact on morale and work satisfaction but only when programs are backed by sufficient training and genuine management commitment to them.

As Mohrman points out, the QC technique "does not take the huge financial commitment of some other programs and does rally people, but it clearly is not the stable long-term organizational change that some people make it out to be. The technique does not go far enough, it is not strong enough to promote real organizational change. For that, you need to go further and rethink the design of jobs, decision making processes, and organizational structures."

Clearly, much more research is needed to evaluate QC's accurately. We should compare, for example, how well they work in various kinds of organizations and why they work better in some than in others. In Japan, a government-sponsored association oversees QC activity. A similar industry-sponsored organization in the United States could support the necessary studies and at the same time promote a national commitment to quality and to participative management.

Bill Courtright, a corporate manager of QC's for Hughes Aircraft, has no doubts about why QC's have grown so rapidly: "It is a spiritual reason—people want to work together. They are more effective as a team. It increases their knowledge. It increases their communication. It increases their security. It increases their dignity. If handled properly, with a serious commitment on the part of management, then quality circles can do nothing but succeed."

However, as the many failed QC programs show, that's an awfully big "if." Implementing some of the suggestions made by the researchers mentioned in this article, as changed and supplemented by future research, could help QC's remove the "fad" label and more fully live up to the claims made by their advocates. They might then clearly improve the design and management of organizations, help make American companies more competitive and enhance the quality of their employees' work life.

CRITICAL THINKING QUESTIONS

1. As noted in the article, because participation in quality circles (QCs) is voluntary, not all employees participate. What would be the advantages or disadvantages of requiring all employees to participate in QCs? What might the differences be between workers who join QCs and those who don't? Might these differences be related to the eventual outcomes of QCs?

2. QCs are widely used in Japan. Although they are being used more frequently in the United States, they are not as readily accepted as they are in Japan, where they were first implemented. Based on your understanding of the QC concept, do you think that cultural differences would make QCs more accepted in Japan than in the United States? What differences may be influential?

3. Not all organizations that have implemented QCs have found them to be useful. What factors might determine success? What role would management attitudes toward QCs play in their eventual success or failure?

4. The underlying rationale of QCs is that the person who performs a given job is in the best position to give feedback on how the situation may be improved. How useful would QCs be in an academic setting? What similarities and differences do you see between workers who produce something for a company and students who produce something for a class or a degree? How could you set up an academic-setting QC? What would you expect it to accomplish?

ARTICLE 41 _____

Why do people work? Is it just to earn a living (or in some cases, to make a lot of money), or are there other reasons, too? If you look at the number of references in American culture to the "Monday morning blues" and "TGIF," you might get the impression that people would rather not work, if given a choice. Many people would consider it distinctly odd if someone expressed joy at the prospect of returning to work after a weekend off. Do most workers really feel that way? Is that the way it *should* be?

The question of what motivates people to work has been of major interest to industrial/organizational psychologists for quite some time. Ultimately concerned with productivity and profits, business has an obvious interest in trying to discover ways to increase employee motivation, since increased motivation is often viewed as synonymous with increased output. Different theories of motivation have been drawn from areas in the behavioral sciences, ranging from learning theory to humanistic theories of motivation. All seek to identify the factors that motivate people and how to implement these factors to increase motivation levels.

One person who has made significant contributions to the understanding of motivation in the workplace is Frederick Herzberg. In the following classic article, he presents an analysis of commonly used methods of motivation and why they don't work, followed by his own theory and research. Whether you fully accept the tenets and suggestions found in the article, it will most likely get you to reexamine your own assumptions about what motivates people to work.

One More Time:
How Do You Motivate Employees?

■ Frederick Herzberg

KITA—the externally imposed attempt by management to "install a generator" in the employee—has been demonstrated to be a total failure, the author says. The absence of such "hygiene" factors as good supervisor-employee relations and liberal fringe benefits can make a worker unhappy, but their presence will not make him want to work harder. Essentially meaningless changes in the tasks that workers are assigned to do have not accomplished the desired objective either. The only way to motivate the employee is to give him challenging work in which he can assume responsibility.

Frederick Herzberg, who is Professor and Chairman of the Psychology Department at Case Western Reserve University, has devoted many years to the study of motivation in the United States and abroad. He is the author of Work and Nature of Man *(World Publishing Company, 1966).*

How many articles, books, speeches, and workshops have pleaded plaintively, "How do I get an employee to do what I want him to do?"

The psychology of motivation is tremendously complex, and what has been unraveled with any

Reprinted by permission of *Harvard Business Review.* "One More Time: How Do You Motivate Employees?" by Frederick Herzberg, January/February 1968. Copyright © 1968 by the President and Fellows of Harvard College; all rights reserved.

degree of assurance is small indeed. But the dismal ratio of knowledge to speculation has not dampened the enthusiasm for new forms of snake oil that are constantly coming on the market, many of them with academic testimonials. Doubtless this article will have no depressing impact on the market for snake oil, but since the ideas expressed in it have been tested in many corporations and other organizations, it will help—I hope—to redress the imbalance in the aforementioned ratio.

"MOTIVATING" WITH KITA

In lectures to industry on the problem, I have found that the audiences are anxious for quick and practical answers, so I will begin with a straightforward, practical formula for moving people.

What is the simplest, surest, and most direct way of getting someone to do something? Ask him? But if he responds that he does not want to do it, then that calls for a psychological consultation to determine the reason for his obstinacy. Tell him? His response shows that he does not understand you, and now an expert in communication methods has to be brought in to show you how to get through to him. Give him a monetary incentive? I do not need to remind the reader of the complexity and difficulty involved in setting up and administering an incentive system. Show him? This means a costly training program. We need a simple way.

Every audience contains the "direct action" manager who shouts, "Kick him!" And this type of manager is right. The surest and least circumlocuted way of getting someone to do something is to kick him in the pants—give him what might be called the KITA.

There are various forms of KITA, and here are some of them:

Negative Physical KITA   This is a literal application of the term and was frequently used in the past. It has, however, three major drawbacks: (1) it is inelegant; (2) it contradicts the precious image of benevolence that most organizations cher-

ish; and (3) since it is a physical attack, it directly stimulates the autonomic nervous system, and this often results in negative feedback—the employee may just kick you in return. These factors give rise to certain taboos against negative physical KITA.

The psychologist has come to the rescue of those who are no longer permitted to use negative physical KITA. He has uncovered infinite sources of psychological vulnerabilities and the appropriate methods to play tunes on them. "He took my rug away"; "I wonder what he meant by that"; "The boss is always going around me"—these symptomatic expressions of ego sores that have been rubbed raw are the result of application of:

Negative Psychological KITA   This has several advantages over negative physical KITA. First, the cruelty is not visible; the bleeding is internal and comes much later. Second, since it affects the higher cortical centers of the brain with its inhibitory powers, it reduces the possibility of physical backlash. Third, since the number of psychological pains that a person can feel is almost infinite, the direction and site possibilities of the KITA are increased many times. Fourth, the person administering the kick can manage to be above it all and let the system accomplish the dirty work. Fifth, those who practice it receive some ego satisfaction (one-upmanship), whereas they would find drawing blood abhorrent. Finally, if the employee does complain, he can always be accused of being paranoid, since there is no tangible evidence of an actual attack.

Now, what does negative KITA accomplish? If I kick you in the rear (physically or psychologically), who is motivated? I am motivated; you move! Negative KITA does not lead to motivation, but to movement. So:

Positive KITA   Let us consider motivation. If I say to you, "Do this for me or the company, and in return I will give you a reward, an incentive, more status, a promotion, all the quid pro quos that exist in the industrial organization," am I motivating you? The overwhelming opinion I receive from management people is, "Yes, this is motivation."

I have a year-old Schnauzer. When it was a small puppy and I wanted it to move, I kicked it in the rear and it moved. Now that I have finished its obedience training, I hold up a dog biscuit when I want the Schnauzer to move. In this instance, who is motivated—I or the dog? The dog wants the biscuit, but it is I who want it to move. Again, I am the one who is motivated, and the dog is the one who moves. In this instance all I did was apply KITA frontally; I exerted a pull instead of a push. When industry wishes to use such positive KITAs, it has available an incredible number and variety of dog biscuits (jelly beans for humans) to wave in front of the employee to get him to jump.

Why is it that managerial audiences are quick to see that negative KITA is *not* motivation, while they are almost unanimous in their judgment that positive KITA *is* motivation? It is because negative KITA is rape, and positive KITA is seduction. But it is infinitely worse to be seduced than to be raped; the latter is an unfortunate occurrence, while the former signifies that you were a party to your own downfall. This is why positive KITA is so popular: it is a tradition; it is in the American way. The organization does not have to kick you; you kick yourself.

Myths about Motivation

Why is KITA not motivation? If I kick my dog (from the front or the back), he will move. And when I want him to move again, what must I do? I must kick him again. Similarly, I can charge a man's battery, and then recharge it, and recharge it again. But it is only when he has his own generator that we can talk about motivation. He then needs no outside stimulation. He *wants* to do it.

With this in mind, we can review some positive KITA personnel practices that were developed as attempts to instill "motivation":

1. *Reducing time spent at work*—This represents a marvelous way of motivating people to

work—getting them off the job! We have reduced (formally and informally) the time spent on the job over the last 50 or 60 years until we are finally on the way to the "6½-day weekend." An interesting variant of this approach is the development of off-hour recreation programs. The philosophy here seems to be that those who play together, work together. The fact is that motivated people seek more hours of work, not fewer.

2. *Spiraling wages*—Have these motivated people? Yes, to seek the next wage increase. Some medievalists still can be heard to say that a good depression will get employees moving. They feel that if rising wages don't or won't do the job, perhaps reducing them will.

3. *Fringe benefits*—Industry has outdone the most welfare-minded of welfare states in dispensing cradle-to-the-grave succor. One company I know of had an informal "fringe benefit of the month club" going for a while. The cost of fringe benefits in this country has reached approximately 25% of the wage dollar, and we still cry for motivation.

People spend less time working for more money and more security than ever before, and the trend cannot be reversed. These benefits are no longer rewards; they are rights. A 6-day week is inhuman, a 10-hour day is exploitation, extended medical coverage is a basic decency, and stock options are the salvation of American initiative. Unless the ante is continuously raised, the psychological reaction of employees is that the company is turning back the clock.

When industry began to realize that both the economic nerve and the lazy nerve of their employees had insatiable appetites, it started to listen to the behavioral scientists who, more out of a humanist tradition than from scientific study, criticized management for not knowing how to deal with people. The next KITA easily followed.

4. *Human relations training*—Over 30 years of teaching and, in many instances, of practicing psychological approaches to handling people have resulted in costly human relations programs and, in the end, the same question: How do you motivate workers? Here, too, escalations have taken place. Thirty years ago it was necessary to request,

"Please don't spit on the floor." Today the same admonition requires three "please"s before the employee feels that his superior has demonstrated the psychologically proper attitudes toward him.

The failure of human relations training to produce motivation led to the conclusion that the supervisor or manager himself was not psychologically true to himself in his practice of interpersonal decency. So an advanced form of human relations KITA, sensitivity training, was unfolded.

5. *Sensitivity training* — Do you really, really understand yourself? Do you really, really, really trust the other man? Do you really, really, really, really cooperate? The failure of sensitivity training is now being explained, by those who have become opportunistic exploiters of the technique, as a failure to really (five times) conduct proper sensitivity training courses.

With the realization that there are only temporary gains from comfort and economic and interpersonal KITA, personnel managers concluded that the fault lay not in what they were doing, but in the employee's failure to appreciate what they were doing. This opened up the field of communications, a whole new area of "scientifically" sanctioned KITA.

6. *Communications* — The professor of communications was invited to join the faculty of management training programs and help in making employees understand what management was doing for them. House organs, briefing sessions, supervisory instruction on the importance of communication, and all sorts of propaganda have proliferated until today there is even an International Council of Industrial Editors. But no motivation resulted, and the obvious thought occurred that perhaps management was not hearing what the employees were saying. That led to the next KITA.

7. *Two-way communication* — Management ordered morale surveys, suggestion plans, and group participation programs. Then both employees and management were communicating and listening to each other more than ever, but without much improvement in motivation.

The behavioral scientists began to take another look at their conceptions and their data, and they took human relations one step further. A glimmer of truth was beginning to show through in the writings of the so-called higher-order-need psychologists. People, so they said, want to actualize themselves. Unfortunately, the "actualizing" psychologists got mixed up with the human relations psychologists, and a new KITA emerged.

8. *Job participation* — Though it may not have been the theoretical intention, job participation often became a "give them the big picture" approach. For example, if a man is tightening 10,000 nuts a day on an assembly line with a torque wrench, tell him he is building a Chevrolet. Another approach had the goal of giving the employee a *feeling* that he is determining, in some measure, what he does on his job. The goal was to provide a *sense* of achievement rather than a substantive achievement in his task. Real achievement, of course, requires a task that makes it possible.

But still there was no motivation. This led to the inevitable conclusion that the employees must be sick, and therefore to the next KITA.

9. *Employee counseling* — The initial use of this form of KITA in a systematic fashion can be credited to the Hawthorne experiment of the Western Electric Company during the early 1930's. At that time, it was found that the employees harbored irrational feelings that were interfering with the rational operation of the factory. Counseling in this instance was a means of letting the employees unburden themselves by talking to someone about their problems. Although the counseling techniques were primitive, the program was large indeed.

The counseling approach suffered as a result of experiences during World War II, when the programs themselves were found to be interfering with the operation of the organizations; the counselors had forgotten their role of benevolent listeners and were attempting to do something about the problems that they heard about. Psychological counseling, however, has managed to survive the negative impact of World War II experiences and today is beginning to flourish with renewed sophistication. But, alas, many of these programs, like all the others, do not seem to have lessened the pressure of demands to find out how to motivate workers.

Since KITA results only in short-term movement, it is safe to predict that the cost of these programs will increase steadily and new varieties will be developed as old positive KITAs reach their satiation points.

HYGIENE VS. MOTIVATORS

Let me rephrase the perennial question this way: How do you install a generator in an employee? A brief review of my motivation-hygiene theory of job attitudes is required before theoretical and practical suggestions can be offered. The theory was first drawn from an examination of events in the lives of engineers and accountants. At least 16 other investigations, using a wide variety of populations (including some in the Communist countries), have since been completed, making the original research one of the most replicated studies in the field of job attitudes.

The findings of these studies, along with corroboration from many other investigations using different procedures, suggest that the factors involved in producing job satisfaction (and motivation) are separate and distinct from the factors that lead to job dissatisfaction. Since separate factors need to be considered, depending on whether job satisfaction or job dissatisfaction is being examined, it follows that these two feelings are not opposites of each other. The opposite of job satisfaction is not job dissatisfaction but, rather, *no* job satisfaction; and, similarly, the opposite of job dissatisfaction is not job satisfaction, but *no* job dissatisfaction.

Stating the concept presents a problem in semantics, for we normally think of satisfaction and dissatisfaction as opposites—i.e., what is not satisfying must be dissatisfying, and vice versa. But when it comes to understanding the behavior of people in their jobs, more than a play on words is involved.

Two different needs of man are involved here. One set of needs can be thought of as stemming from his animal nature—the built-in drive to avoid pain from the environment, plus all the learned drives which become conditioned to the basic biological needs. For example, hunger, a basic biological drive, makes it necessary to earn money, and then money becomes a specific drive. The other set of needs relates to that unique human characteristic, the ability to achieve and, through achievement, to experience psychological growth. The stimuli for the growth needs are tasks that induce growth; in the industrial setting, they are the *job content*. Contrariwise, the stimuli inducing pain-avoidance behavior are found in the *job environment*.

The growth or *motivator* factors that are intrinsic to the job are: achievement, recognition for achievement, the work itself, responsibility, and growth or advancement. The dissatisfaction-avoidance of *hygiene* (KITA) factors that are extrinsic to the job include: company policy and administration, supervision, interpersonal relationships, working conditions, salary, status, and security.

A composite of the factors that are involved in causing job satisfaction and job dissatisfaction, drawn from samples of 1,685 employees, is shown in Exhibit I. The results indicate that motivators were the primary cause of satisfaction, and hygiene factors the primary cause of unhappiness on the job. The employees, studied in 12 different investigations, included lower-level supervisors, professional women, agricultural administrators, men about to retire from management positions, hospital maintenance personnel, manufacturing supervisors, nurses, food handlers, military officers, engineers, scientists, housekeepers, teachers, technicians, female assemblers, accountants, Finnish foremen, and Hungarian engineers.

They were asked what job events had occurred in their work that had led to extreme satisfaction or extreme dissatisfaction on their part. Their responses are broken down in the exhibit into percentages of total "positive" job events and of total "negative" job events. (The figures total more than 100% on both the "hygiene" and "motivators" sides because often at least two factors can be attributed to a single event; advancement, for instance, often accompanies assumption of responsibility.)

EXHIBIT I / Factors Affecting Job Attitudes, as Reported in 12 Investigations

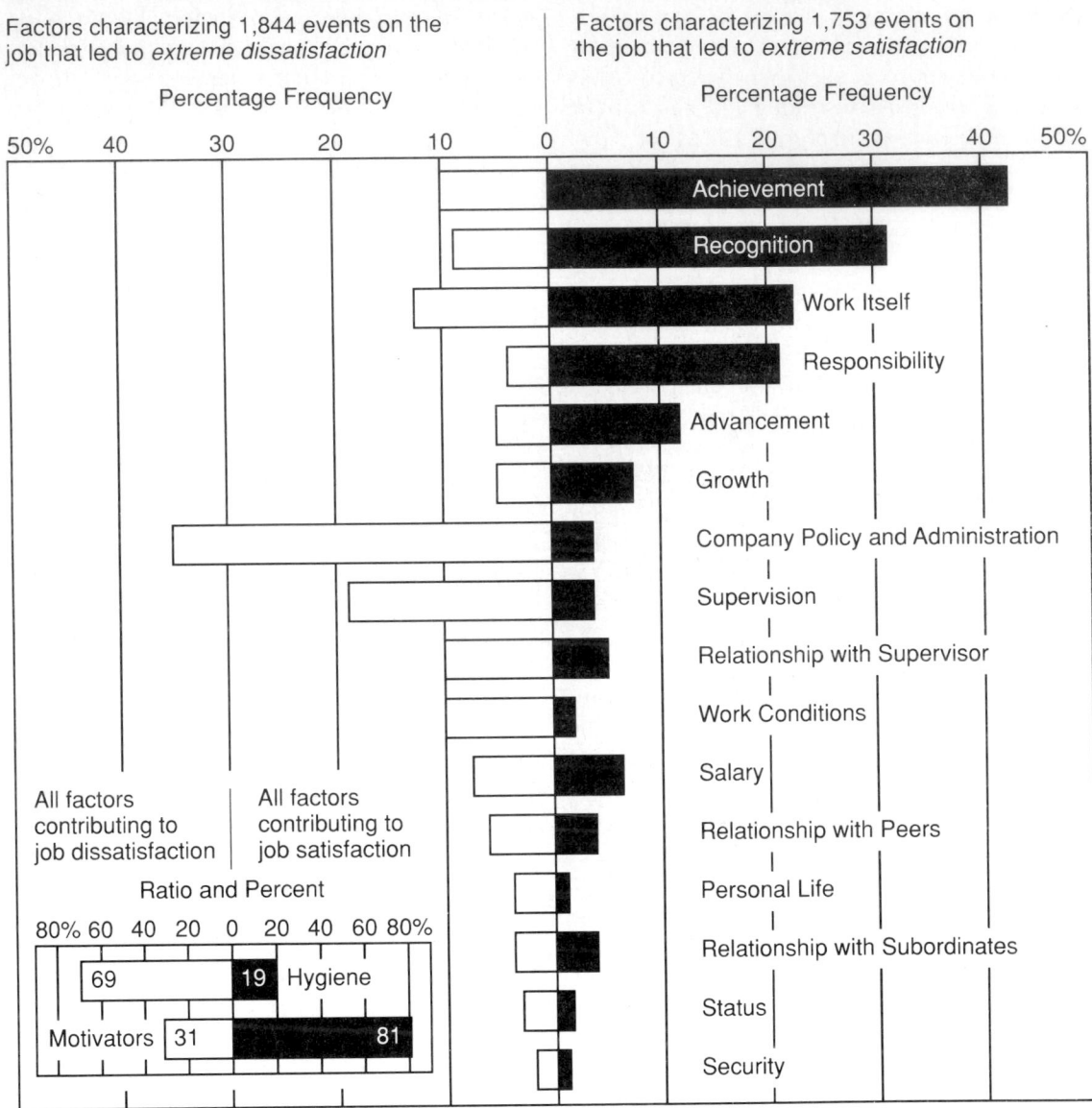

To illustrate, a typical response involving achievement that had a negative effect for the employee was, "I was unhappy because I didn't do the job successfully." A typical response in the small number of positive job events in the Company Policy and Administration grouping was, "I was happy because the company reorganized the section so that I didn't report any longer to the guy I didn't get along with."

As the lower right-hand part of the exhibit shows, of all the factors contributing to job satisfaction, 81% were motivators. And of all the factors contributing to the employees' dissatisfaction over their work, 69% involved hygiene elements.

Eternal Triangle

There are three general philosophies of personnel management. The first is based on organizational theory, the second on industrial engineering, and the third on behavioral science.

The organizational theorist believes that human needs are either so irrational or so varied and adjustable to specific situations that the major function of personnel management is to be as pragmatic as the occasion demands. If jobs are organized in a proper manner, he reasons, the result will be the most efficient job structure, and the most favorable job attitudes will follow as a matter of course.

The industrial engineer holds that man is mechanistically oriented and economically motivated and his needs are best met by attuning the individual to the most efficient work process. The goal of personnel management therefore should be to concoct the most appropriate incentive system and to design the specific working conditions in a way that facilitates the most efficient use of the human machine. By structuring jobs in a manner that leads to the most efficient operation, the engineer believes that he can obtain the optimal organization of work and the proper work attitudes.

The behavioral scientist focuses on group sentiments, attitudes of individual employees, and the organization's social and psychological climate. According to his persuasion, he emphasizes one or more of the various hygiene and motivator needs. His approach to personnel management generally emphasizes some form of human relations education, in the hope of instilling healthy employee attitudes and an organizational climate which he considers to be felicitous to human values. He believes that the proper attitudes will lead to efficient job and organizational structure.

There is always a lively debate as to the overall effectiveness of the approaches of the organizational theorist and the industrial engineer. Manifestly they have achieved much. But the nagging question for the behavioral scientist has been: What is the cost in human problems that eventually cause more expense to the organization—for instance, turnover, absenteeism, errors, violation of safety rules, strikes, restriction of output, higher wages, and greater fringe benefits? On the other hand, the behavioral scientist is hard put to document much manifest improvement in personnel management, using his approach.

The three philosophies can be depicted as a triangle, as is done in Exhibit II, with each persuasion claiming the apex angle. The motivation-hygiene theory claims the same angle as industrial engineering but for opposite goals. Rather than rationalizing the work to increase efficiency, the theory suggests that work be *enriched* to bring about effective utilization of personnel. Such a systematic attempt to motivate employees by manipulating the motivator factors is just beginning.

The term *job enrichment* describes this embryonic movement. An older term, job enlargement, should be avoided because it is associated with past failures stemming from a misunderstanding of the problem. Job enrichment provides the opportunity for the employee's psychological growth, while job enlargement merely makes a job structurally bigger. Since scientific job enrichment is very new, this article only suggests the principles and practical steps that have recently emerged from several successful experiments in industry.

EXHIBIT II / "Triangle" of Philosophies of Personnel Management

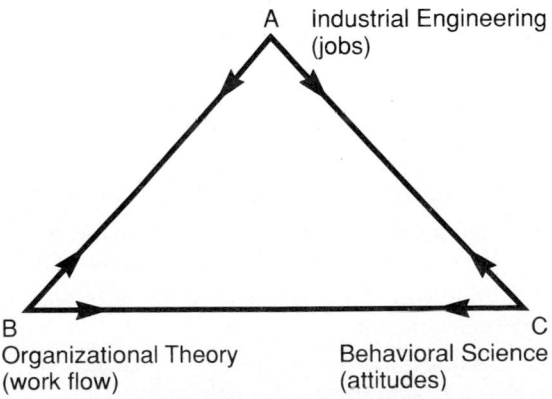

A   Industrial Engineering (jobs)

B   Organizational Theory (work flow)

C   Behavioral Science (attitudes)

Job Loading

In attempting to enrich an employee's job, management often succeeds in reducing the man's personal contribution, rather than giving him an opportunity for growth in his accustomed job. Such an endeavor, which I shall call horizontal job loading (as opposed to vertical loading, or providing motivator factors), has been the problem of earlier job enlargement programs. This activity merely enlarges the meaninglessness of the job. Some examples of this approach, and their effect, are:

- Challenging the employee by increasing the amount of production expected of him. If he tightens 10,000 bolts a day, see if he can tighten 20,000 bolts a day. The arithmetic involved shows that multiplying zero by zero still equals zero.
- Adding another meaningless task to the existing one, usually some routine clerical activity. The arithmetic here is adding zero to zero.
- Rotating the assignments of a number of jobs that need to be enriched. This means washing dishes for a while, then washing silverware. The arithmetic is substituting one zero for another zero.

- Removing the most difficult parts of the assignment in order to free the worker to accomplish more of the less challenging assignments. This traditional industrial engineering approach amounts to subtraction in the hope of accomplishing addition.

These are common forms of horizontal loading that frequently come up in preliminary brainstorming sessions on job enrichment. The principles of vertical loading have not all been worked out as yet, and they remain rather general, but I have furnished seven useful starting points for consideration in Exhibit III.

A Successful Application

An example from a highly successful job enrichment experiment can illustrate the distinction between horizontal and vertical loading of a job. The subjects of this study were the stockholder correspondents employed by a very large corporation. Seemingly, the task required of these carefully selected and highly trained correspondents was quite complex and challenging. But almost all indexes of performance and job attitudes were

EXHIBIT III / Principles of Vertical Job Loading

Principle	Motivators involved
A. Removing some controls while retaining accountability	Responsibility and personal achievement
B. Increasing the accountability of individuals for own work	Responsibility and recognition
C. Giving a person a complete natural unit of work (module, division, area, and so on)	Responsibility, achievement, and recognition
D. Granting additional authority to an employee in his activity; job freedom	Responsibility, achievement, and recognition
E. Making periodic reports directly available to the worker himself rather than to the supervisor	Internal recognition
F. Introducing new and more difficult tasks not previously handled	Growth and learning
G. Assigning individuals specific or specialized tasks, enabling them to become experts	Responsibility, growth, and advancement

low, and exit interviewing confirmed that the challenge of the job existed merely as words.

A job enrichment project was initiated in the form of an experiment with one group, designated as an achieving unit, having its job enriched by the principles described in Exhibit III. A control group continued to do its job in the traditional way. (There were also two "uncommitted" groups of correspondents formed to measure the so-called Hawthorne Effect — that is, to gauge whether productivity and attitudes toward the job changed artificially merely because employees sensed that the company was paying more attention to them in doing something different or novel. The results for these groups were substantially the same as for the control group, and for the sake of simplicity I do not deal with them in this summary.) No changes in hygiene were introduced for either group other than those that would have been made anyway, such as normal pay increases.

The changes for the achieving unit were introduced in the first two months, averaging one per week of the seven motivators listed in Exhibit III. At the end of six months the members of the achieving unit were found to be outperforming their counterparts in the control group, and in addition indicated a marked increase in their liking for their jobs. Other results showed that the achieving group had lower absenteeism and, subsequently, a much higher rate of promotion.

Exhibit IV illustrates the changes in performance, measured in February and March, before the study period began, and at the end of each month of the study period. The shareholder service index represents quality of letters, including accuracy of information, and speed of response to stockholders' letters of inquiry. The index of a current month was averaged into the average of the two prior months, which means that improvement was harder to obtain if the indexes of the previous months were low. The "achievers" were performing less well before the six-month period started, and their performance service index continued to decline after the introduction of the motivators, evidently because of uncertainty over their newly granted responsibilities. In the third month, how-

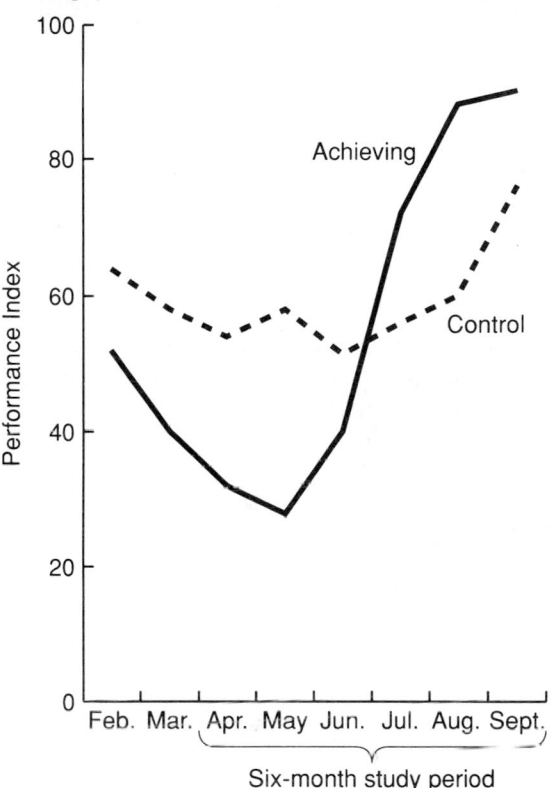

EXHIBIT IV / Shareholder Service Index in Company Experiment (Three-Month Cumulative Average)

ever, performance improved, and soon the members of this group had reached a high level of accomplishment.

Exhibit V shows the two groups' attitudes toward their job, measured at the end of March, just before the first motivator was introduced, and again at the end of September. The correspondents were asked 16 questions, all involving motivation. A typical one was, "As you see it, how many opportunities do you feel that you have in your job for making worthwhile contributions?" The answers were scaled from 1 to 5, with 80 as the maximum possible score. The achievers became much more positive about their job, while the attitude of the control unit remained about the same (the drop is not statistically significant).

How was the job of these correspondents restructured? Exhibit VI lists the suggestions made

EXHIBIT V / Changes in Attitudes toward Tasks in Company Experiment (Changes in Mean Scores over Six-Month Period)

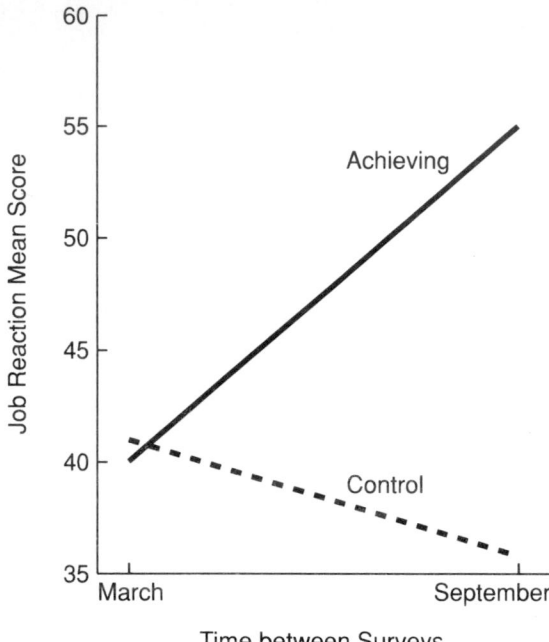

that were deemed to be horizontal loading, and the actual vertical loading changes that were incorporated in the job of the achieving unit. The capital letters under "Principle" after "Vertical loading" refer to the corresponding letters in Exhibit III. The reader will note that the rejected forms of horizontal loading correspond closely to the list of common manifestations of the phenomenon in Exhibit III, left column.

STEPS TO JOB ENRICHMENT

Now that the motivator idea has been described in practice, here are the steps that managers should take in instituting the principle with their employees:

1. Select those jobs in which (a) the investment in industrial engineering does not make changes too costly, (b) attitudes are poor, (c) hygiene is becoming very costly, and (d) motivation will make a difference in performance.

2. Approach these jobs with the conviction

that they can be changed. Years of tradition have led managers to believe that the content of the jobs is sacrosanct and the only scope of action that they have is in ways of stimulating people.

3. Brainstorm a list of changes that may enrich the jobs, without concern for their practicality.

4. Screen the list to eliminate suggestions that involve hygiene, rather than actual motivation.

5. Screen the list for generalities, such as "give them more responsibility," that are rarely followed in practice. This might seem obvious, but the motivator words have never left industry; the substance has just been rationalized and organized out. Words like "responsibility," "growth," "achievement," and "challenge," for example, have been elevated to the lyrics of the patriotic anthem for all organizations. It is the old problem typified by the pledge of allegiance to the flag being more important than contributions to the country—of following the form, rather than the substance.

6. Screen the list to eliminate any *horizontal* loading suggestions.

7. Avoid direct participation by the employees whose jobs are to be enriched. Ideas they have expressed previously certainly constitute a valuable source for recommended changes, but their direct involvement contaminates the process with human relations *hygiene* and, more specifically, gives them only a *sense* of making a contribution. The job is to be changed, and it is the content that will produce the motivation, not attitudes about being involved or the challenge inherent in setting up a job. That process will be over shortly, and it is what the employees will be doing from then on that will determine their motivation. A sense of participation will result only in short-term movement.

8. In the initial attempts at job enrichment, set up a controlled experiment. At least two equivalent groups should be chosen, one an experimental unit in which the motivators are systematically introduced over a period of time, and the other one a control group in which no changes are made. For both groups, hygiene should be allowed to follow its natural course for the duration of the experiment. Pre- and post-installation tests of performance and job attitudes are necessary to

EXHIBIT VI / Enlargement vs. Enrichment of Correspondents' Tasks in Company Experiment

Horizontal loading suggestions (rejected)	Vertical loading suggestions (adopted)	Principle
Firm quotas could be set for letters to be answered each day, using a rate which would be hard to reach.	Subject matter experts were appointed within each unit for other members of the unit to consult with before seeking supervisory help. (The supervisor had been answering all specialized and difficult questions.)	G
The women could type the letters themselves, as well as compose them, or take on any other clerical functions.	Correspondents signed their own names on letters. (The supervisor had been signing all letters.)	B
All difficult or complex inquiries could be channeled to a few women so that the remainder could achieve high rates of output. These jobs could be exchanged from time to time.	The work of the more experienced correspondents was proofread less frequently by supervisors and was done at the correspondents' desks, dropping verification from 100% to 10%. (Previously, all correspondents' letters had been checked by the supervisor.)	A
The women could be rotated through units handling different customers, and then sent back to their own units.	Production was discussed, but only in terms such as "a full day's work is expected." As time went on, this was no longer mentioned. (Before, the group had been constantly reminded of the number of letters that needed to be answered.)	D
	Outgoing mail went directly to the mailroom without going over supervisors' desks. (The letters had always been routed through the supervisors.)	A
	Correspondents were encouraged to answer letters in a more personalized way. (Reliance on the form-letter approach had been standard practice.)	C
	Each correspondent was held personally responsible for the quality and accuracy of letters. (This responsibility had been the province of the supervisor and the verifier.)	B, E

evaluate the effectiveness of the job enrichment program. The attitude test must be limited to motivator items in order to divorce the employee's view of the job he is given from all the surrounding hygiene feelings that he might have.

9. Be prepared for a drop in performance in the experimental group the first few weeks. The changeover to a new job may lead to a temporary reduction in efficiency.

10. Expect your first-line supervisors to experience some anxiety and hostility over the changes you are making. The anxiety comes from their fear that the changes will result in poorer performance for their unit. Hostility will arise when the employees start assuming what the supervisors regard as their own responsibility for performance. The supervisor without checking duties to perform may then be left with little to do.

After a successful experiment, however, the supervisor usually discovers the supervisory and managerial functions he has neglected, or which were never his because all his time was given over to checking the work of his subordinates. For example, in the R&D division of one large chemical company I know of, the supervisors of the laboratory assistants were theoretically responsible for their training and evaluation. These functions, however, had come to be performed in a routine, unsubstantial fashion. After the job enrichment program, during which the supervisors were not merely passive observers of the assistants' performance, the supervisors actually were devoting their time to reviewing performance and administering thorough training.

What has been called an employee-centered style of supervision will come about not through education of supervisors, but by changing the jobs that they do.

CONCLUDING NOTE

Job enrichment will not be a one-time proposition, but a continuous management function. The initial changes, however, should last for a very long period of time. There are a number of reasons for this:

- The changes should bring the job up to the level of challenge commensurate with the skill that was hired.
- Those who have still more ability eventually will be able to demonstrate it better and win promotion to higher-level jobs.
- The very nature of motivators, as opposed to hygiene factors, is that they have a much longer-term effect on employees' attitudes. Perhaps the job will have to be enriched again, but this will not occur as frequently as the need for hygiene.

Not all jobs can be enriched, nor do all jobs need to be enriched. If only a small percentage of the time and money that is now devoted to hygiene, however, were given to job enrichment efforts, the return in human satisfaction and economic gain would be one of the largest dividends that industry and society have ever reaped through their efforts at better personnel management.

The argument for job enrichment can be summed up quite simply: If you have someone on a job, use him. If you can't use him on the job, get rid of him, either via automation or by selecting someone with lesser ability. If you can't use him and you can't get rid of him, you will have a motivation problem.

Readers of this article may be interested in "What Job Attitudes Tell About Motivation," by Lyman W. Porter and Edward E. Lawler, III, *Harvard Business Review,* Vol. 46, January/February 1968, pp. 118–126.

Author's note: I should like to acknowledge the contributions that Robert Ford of the American Telephone and Telegraph Company has made to the ideas expressed in this paper, and in particular to the successful application of these ideas in improving work performance and the job satisfaction of employees.

CRITICAL THINKING QUESTIONS

1. Suppose we change the topic of the article from how to motivate employees to how to motivate students. Can Herzberg's principles of employee motivation be used in the academic environment? How? As part of this question, conduct a survey of students to identify what school factors lead to extreme satisfaction and extreme dissatisfaction. Classify these as hygiene or motivation factors.
2. Would the principles of successful job enrichment outlined by Herzberg apply equally to all employees in all situations? What individual- or work-related factors might mediate whether the principles will work?
3. Conduct an informal survey of people you know who work full time, asking them the same questions about job satisfaction and dissatisfaction outlined in the ar-

ticle. How well do your observations correspond with the information presented by Herzberg?

4. After reading an article such as this, why might some managers still be reluctant to undertake such changes? Are any of these concerns legitimate? Why or why not?

ADDITIONAL RELATED READINGS

Berkowitz, L., Fraser, C., Treasure, F., & Cochran, S. (1987). Pay, equity, job gratifications, and comparisons in pay satisfaction. *Journal of Applied Psychology, 72,* 544–551.

Lawler, E. E. (1982). Strategies for improving the quality of work life. *American Psychologist, 37,* 324–334.

ARTICLE 42 _____

Conflict is a natural and common occurrence in everyday life. This most certainly includes work settings, where the conflict may be about goals, issues, or personalities, to name but a few. Before reading this article, stop and think for a second about what the term *conflict* means to you. Most likely, it implies something negative, something you would be better off without.

Is conflict always about opposing goals and interests, where what one person wants is different from and presumably incompatible with what another person wants? For example, one spouse may want children, and the other may not. How do they resolve the conflict? Have half a child? Or can conflict arise over common goals and interests about which people agree? For example, the couple may both want to raise happy, well-adjusted children (their interests and goals are common) but disagree as to how to accomplish that end. Although both types of conflict are possible, as well as common, many people consider only the former example as conflict, not the latter. Perhaps a better distinction is whether the goals and interests are *competitive* (the first case) or *cooperative* (the second case).

The following article by Tjosvold and Chia examines one theory of cooperative and competitive goals on the outcomes of conflict in a business setting. The article is of interest for several reasons. First, it applies a theory that had been experimentally tested in a laboratory setting to a real-world business environment. Second, the study was conducted in a business environment very different than one that might be found in the United States, providing a cross-cultural perspective. Finally, and perhaps most importantly, the results of the study suggest some ways that conflict might be managed more productively in business settings.

Conflict between Managers and Workers
The Role of Cooperation and Competition

■ Dean Tjosvold and Lai Cheng Chia

Deutsch's (1973) theory of cooperative and competitive goals was tested on the dynamics and outcomes of conflict in a field study involving two organizations in Singapore. Cooperative goals, effective interaction during the conflict, and prior strong work relationships were associated with positive outcomes. The results suggest reasons for cooperative versus competitive goals in conflicts, types of issues that provoke conflicts, and the role of procedures in conflicts. Deutsch's theory generalized to organizations in a non-Western society.

Executives, managers, supervisors, and workers repeatedly cope with conflict. Managers dispute with employees about how the work can be most effectively completed; employees may be irritated when their manager denies their requests. Conflict occurs throughout an organization, but con-

From *Journal of Social Psychology*, 129, 235–247, 1989. Reprinted with permission of the Helen Dwight Reid Educational Foundation. Published by Heldref Publications, 4000 Albermarle St., NW, Washington, DC 20016. Copyright © 1989.

flicts between managers and workers are particularly important, because if poorly handled, they can disrupt an organization's labor relations and productivity (Katz, Kochan, & Gobeille, 1983; Katz, Kochan, & Weber, 1985). Organizational behavior and industrial-relations researchers have increasingly recognized the importance of conflict (Bazerman & Lewicki, 1982; Pfeffer, 1981; Tjosvold & Johnson, 1983). Deutsch's (1973) theory of the role of goal interdependence has been little used in the analysis of organizational conflict, however. The present study used that theory to analyze the dynamics and outcomes of conflicts between workers and managers.

Deutsch (1973, 1980) defined conflict as incompatible activities: One person's behavior harms, obstructs, opposes, interferes, or in some way makes another's behavior less effective. This definition differs from the widely accepted position that organizational conflict derives from opposing interests and mixed-motive situations (Bacharach & Lawler, 1981; Commons, 1934; Kochan & Verma, 1982; Walton & McKersie, 1965). Conflict certainly occurs in situations of opposing interest, such as a wage dispute between managers and workers. Conflict also occurs when interests overlap and goals are common, however. A manager and worker may both wish to provide high-quality service to the customer but present opposing proposals because they disagree about what the customer wants. Thus, conflict may occur without opposing interests.

Because both competitive and cooperative goals may engender conflict, the definition of *conflict* should be distinguished from *opposing interests* (i.e., competition). Conclusions that goals are competitive rather than cooperative have been found to affect conflict management (Deutsch, 1973; Tjosvold, 1985). Competition occurs when goals are negatively related so that one's goal attainment makes it less likely that others reach their goals (Deutsch, 1949, 1973). In cooperation, goals are positively correlated because movement toward one's goal facilitates others in reaching their goals. Managers and

workers in conflict over how to proceed may believe their goals are cooperative: They want the best plan possible for both of them. Or, the manager and worker may conclude their goals are competitive: Each wants a plan that works for him- or herself, and not the other.

Deutsch theorized that cooperative goals contribute to productive conflict management. Those who cooperate prefer that others pursue their own interests and behave effectively because it is in their own interest for others to be successful. Those who cooperate are expected to pursue mutual benefits, use collaborative influence rather than try to dominate, and integrate opposing views into a solution. These behaviors in turn are expected to result in mutually advantageous agreements, high morale, and the confidence that future difficulties can be resolved. For the competitive, self-interests clash. People are threatened when others succeed because they are less likely to reach their own goals.

Considerable research supports the role of goal interdependence in resolving conflicts (Deutsch, 1973, 1980; Pruitt & Syna, 1983; Rubin & Brown, 1975; Tjosvold, 1982, 1985; Tjosvold & Johnson, 1983). In particular, conflict participants who believe their goals are cooperative rather than competitive have been found to express their opinions openly, exchange information and ideas, explore and understand each other's perspective, work for mutually acceptable solutions, influence and be open to influence, integrate their positions to create solutions, and develop commitment to their agreement. Persons who believe their goals are competitive try to win the conflict; they are suspicious, make unreasonable demands, pursue their own interests at the expense of others, and often fail to reach an agreement.

Nearly all the research supporting Deutsch's theory is experimental; few studies have been conducted in organizational settings. The present study investigated conflicts between managers and workers to test the generalizability of the theory and suggest the strength of the relationship among cooperative goals, interaction, and outcomes of conflict in organizations.

An additional purpose was to explore how organizational actors conclude that their goals are cooperative or competitive. Weick (1979), Burrell and Morgan (1979), and others have argued that organizational members enact their environment through social construction and interaction. They use cognitive schemas to interpret their experiences and develop meanings (Bartunek, 1984; Gioia & Manz, 1985). This perspective suggests the importance of the reasons people use to reach their conclusions about how their goals are linked. Previous work has focused on the effects of goal interdependence, but it is theoretically and practically important to understand what leads people to conclude they are cooperatively or competitively interdependent.

Deutsch (1973) proposed that the major conditions that create an interdependence are in turn created by it. Cooperative and competitive goals form causal loops; the effects of cooperation strengthen the belief that goals are cooperatively linked. According to Deutsch, the prior relationship is a significant antecedent for concluding that goals are cooperative or competitive. Relationships characterized by typical effects of cooperation, namely, openness, trust, and mutual assistance, are expected to encourage people in conflict to believe that they still have cooperative goals. They have the confidence and orientation that they will be able to resolve the conflict for mutual benefit.

This study also explored the procedures and specific ways used to handle conflict. Managers have been advised to confront the other person directly rather than procrastinate and avoid an open discussion. Team meetings, quality circles, and other regular group meetings have recently become more popular in part because they are thought to be useful in discussing conflicts. Procedures and settings can be used to manage or to wage conflict, however. Cooperative goals and effective interaction are needed to make productive use of procedures (Deutsch & Krauss, 1962).

The prominence of conflict in organizations is much more widely appreciated, but research is needed to document the issues over which employees conflict. This study also sampled and classified the issues that provoked organizational conflict.

On the basis of Deutsch's reasoning, the following hypotheses were proposed:

1. Managers and workers who conclude that their goals are cooperative rather than competitive interact effectively as they deal with the conflict and resolve the conflict to improve their work and strengthen their relationship.
2. Managers and workers who have developed a strong work relationship prior to the conflict believe their goals are cooperative, interact effectively within the conflict, and resolve their conflict to improve their work and strengthen their relationship.

This study also explored the reasons that managers and workers use to conclude that their goals are cooperative or competitive. The procedures to try to handle the conflict and issues that provoke the conflict were also investigated. Finally, the data were collected in Singapore, and thus the study tests the generalizability of Deutsch's theory not only to organizations but also to another society with a different culture.

METHOD

Participants

The management of three hotels in Singapore (two were used in the study and one in the pilot) and the Food, Drinks, and Allied Workers Union agreed to sponsor the study. Lai Cheng Chia met with the personnel managers and the branch union chairman in each hotel to ensure that both management and union supported the research. They identified the persons eligible to participate. Twenty-five managers and 22 workers participated (26 people from Company 1 and 21 from Company 2). The interviews were conducted in 1984.

Subordinates chosen were at the highest level of "unionizable" staff to ensure that the conflicts they reported involved those with a line manager and not a supervisor. The workers had to give their free consent to participate and be fluent in English because the interviews were conducted in English, the language of business in Singapore. The sample, although not randomly selected, is probably reasonably representative of the population.

Interview

The critical incident method was used (Flanagan, 1954). Interviewees were informed that the purpose of the research was to study conflict in their organization, that both the management and union of their company supported the research, and that their responses would be kept confidential. The interviews were not designed to evaluate their performance but to understand how they handled their conflicts.

The participants were told that conflict occurs whenever their actions and those of their superior (or subordinate) are in the way of each other and go in opposite directions. Interviewees were then asked to think of two specific conflicts that had occurred recently and that they remembered clearly. They were told that one conflict should have been effective and brought benefits and the other should have been less effective with few benefits and several costs.

Interviewees then described each conflict incident in detail to refresh their memories and inform the interviewer. On occasion, interviewees needed prompting to give sufficient information. Then the interviewees were asked specific questions to analyze the incident. They were asked to identify their own goals (what they wanted in the situation) and the other's goals. They were asked to indicate whether these two goals went together and whether both could be reached. Those who indicated that their goals did go together were rated as concluding their goals were cooperative, and those who indicated that their goals did not go together were rated as believing their goals were competitive.

The participants were asked specific questions, given in Table 1, to assess their prior relationship with the other person, interaction during the conflict, and outcomes of the conflict. They were told

to focus on their relationship before the conflict in answering the prior-relationship questions, and then they answered the interaction and outcomes questions. Analysis indicated that the scales had sufficient reliability to test the hypotheses. Specifically, the Cronbach alphas were .78 for prior relationship, .90 for interaction, .76 for work outcomes, .80 for relationship outcomes, and .86 for combined outcomes.

Interviewees were thanked for their contributions and reminded that the information would be kept confidential. Interviews lasted about 90 min. A total of 85 cases were obtained.

Coding

Lai Cheng Chia wrote brief descriptions about the issue, the major reason given for cooperative or competitive goals, and the method of handling each incident. Previous research and a preliminary examination of the cases led to proposed categories in which to sort these incidents. The final categories for antecedents to cooperative and competitive goals, conflict procedures, and conflict issues are given in Tables 3 through 5.

Two groups, each with two people, worked independently to classify the descriptions. The groups agreed in 88% of the classifications and were usually able to resolve their differences. The consensus classifications were used in the analysis. However, the descriptions did not always provide the coders with enough information to resolve their differences. Ten incidents from the analysis of reasons for cooperative and competitive goals, five incidents from procedures, and three from conflict issues were dropped because of insufficient information and inability to reach agreement.

After all the data were collected and tabulated, the general findings were shared with the personnel departments of each company as well as with union officials. The confidentiality promised the interviewees was strictly maintained. This feedback data to the participating companies helped them assess the impact of previous training programs and suggested other training and skills

TABLE 1 / Relationship, Interaction, and Outcome Scales

Scale	Item
Prior Relationship	1. He (superior, subordinate) is approachable.
	2. He (superior) encourages us to go and talk to him if we have problems. He (subordinate) comes to talk to me if he has problems.
	3. He helps me in my work.
	4. We take part in activities other than work.
	5. We know each other.
	6. We work like a team.
Interaction During Conflict	1. I worked for the benefit of both of us.
	2. I expressed my views and feelings fully.
	3. I feel that as a person I was respected.
	4. I used give and take.
	5. I tried to understand his point of view and his feelings.
	6. I tried to put the best of my ideas with his to come up with an agreement.
	7. He worked for the benefit of both of us.
	8. He expressed his views and feelings fully.
	9. He feels that as a person he was respected.
	10. He used give and take.
	11. He tried to understand my point of view and my feelings.
	12. He tried to put the best of his ideas with mine to come up with an agreement.
Work-Related Outcomes	1. I worked harder because of the conflict.
	2. It was a good agreement for me.
	3. Everyone involved accepted the agreement.
	4. In general there were positive changes.
Relationship Outcomes	5. The conflict helped me to know my boss (subordinate) better.
	6. I am more willing to help him.
	7. I am able to work better with him.
	8. I think this conflict and the way it was handled helped to make our relationship stronger.

that could help employees manage their conflicts productively.

RESULTS

Goal Interdependence and Interaction

Results support the major hypotheses of the study (Table 2). In particular, cooperative goals were significantly correlated with effective interaction, work outcomes, relationship outcomes, and combined outcomes. Prior work relationships were also significantly correlated with interaction, work outcomes, and combined outcomes. Unexpectedly, prior relationships were not significantly correlated with cooperative goals or relationship outcomes.

Separate analyses conducted on the data from each company indicated that the correlations among prior relationships, goal interdependence, interaction, and outcomes were similar for both companies.

Also in support of the major hypothesis, 32 incidents that had cooperative goals were described as effective (Table 3); of the incidents with competitive goals, 18 were ineffective, and only 4 were

TABLE 2 / Correlations among Variables

Variable	1	2	3	4	5
1. Goal interdependence					
2. Interaction	39**				
3. Prior relationship	12	35**			
4. Work outcomes	48**	65**	30*		
5. Relationship outcomes	39**	50**	21	69**	
6. Combined outcomes	47**	63**	27*	92**	91**

*p < .05. **p < .01.

effective. It should be noted, however, that 17 ineffective conflicts were characterized by cooperative goals.

Reasons for Goal Interdependence

The most prevalent reason given for cooperative goals was that interviewees believed they could work out the issue to the benefit of both persons (Table 3); it was clear that both persons could be satisfied. Improved information and understanding were also important for cooperative goals. For example, a manager thought that feedback to an employee was welcomed because it helped the employee understand his job and work more effectively and the manager would also reach his goal. The attempt to create or maintain a positive relationship also led managers and workers to believe their goals were cooperative. Having the same objective was also a reason for cooperative goals; they were working to accomplish a common task.

Scarce resources — whereby the more one received the less the other could get — was a reason for deciding goals were competitive. Goals were also thought to be competitive when interviewees concluded that their goals were directly opposite and could not both be satisfied. People indicated that the fact that a problem was unsolved was also evidence that goals were competitive. Hostility, biases, and revenge were also cited as reasons for competition.

Conflict Procedures

Four conflict procedures were identified (Table 4). Many effective conflicts were handled through direct discussion. Many ineffective conflicts were also handled this way, however. The option of avoiding discussion of the conflict was associated with ineffective conflict. Workers at times brought the conflict up at their work group meeting for general discussion. (The Singapore government has been promoting work teams for several years.)

TABLE 3 / Reasons for Cooperative and Competitive Goals

Reason	Effective	Ineffective	Worker	Superior	Total
Cooperative Goals					
Mutual benefit	19	10	15	14	29
Information and understanding	9	6	5	10	15
Positive relationship	5	1	1	5	6
Same objective	4	0	3	1	4
Competitive Goals					
Opposing goals	2	10	7	5	11
Emotional antagonism	2	7	5	4	9
Scarce resources		1	1	0	1

Note. Based on 75 incidents.

TABLE 4 / Conflict Procedures

Procedure	Effective	Ineffective	Worker	Superior	Total
Direct discussion with other	29	20	20	29	49
Avoid discussion	2	10	7	5	12
Group discussion	5	4	5	4	9
Third party	5	5	6	4	10

Note. Based on 80 incidents.

Group discussions, as well as asking a third party (usually a union official), were used in both effective and ineffective conflicts. Superiors recounted conflicts in which they used direct discussions very frequently, but they, like workers, also avoided discussions.

Conflict Issues

The most prevalent conflict issue was scheduling and rostering (Table 5). Managers and workers also disputed the quality of work performed and whether they had been treated with consideration and respect. They reported conflict over rules and procedures, the fairness of their evaluations and performance appraisals, insufficient resources, and opposing views. The data suggest the quality-of-work issues were difficult to resolve effectively, whereas disputes over rules and procedures were more easily resolved. Superiors more than workers recounted conflicts that involved quality of work and rules and procedures. Workers reported on conflicts that involved work schedules.

DISCUSSION

Deutsch's theory proved useful in analyzing conflict between managers and workers and identifying constructive ways to manage it. Cooperative goals were related to effective interaction and productive outcomes, whereas competitive goals were associated with ineffective interaction and undesirable outcomes. The correlation between goal interdependence and outcomes was not only statistically significant, but high enough to suggest that the relationship is strong. In addition, cooperative goals were more frequent in effective conflicts but still existed in many ineffective conflicts. Overall, these results support the hypothesized role of cooperative and competitive goals and extend this hypothesis by suggesting that, although cooperative goals do not ensure constructive conflict, their absence makes it difficult to manage conflict constructively.

Cooperative goals were not themselves sufficient for constructive conflict. Interaction during conflict was found to be more strongly correlated with constructive outcomes than with goal inter-

TABLE 5 / Conflict Issues

Issue	Effective	Ineffective	Worker	Superior	Total
Scheduling and rostering	9	11	12	8	20
Quality of work	5	12	6	11	17
Personal treatment	9	7	7	9	16
Rules and procedures	9	3	2	10	12
Insufficient resources	4	3	5	2	7
Performance evaluation	4	1	3	2	5
Opposing views	2	3	4	1	5

Note. Based on 82 incidents.

dependence. Communicating that one is working for mutual benefit, discussing the problem fully, feeling accepted as persons, influencing collaboratively, trying to understand each other's perspective, and integrating each other's ideas were all found to be highly related with each other and with positive outcomes. Results support experimental findings that these dynamics develop from cooperation, reinforce each other, and contribute to constructive conflict management (Tjosvold, 1985).

Prior relationship was also related to constructive outcomes, but not as highly as interdependence and interaction. An open, helpful relationship was found to be a relatively weak antecedent to constructive conflict. Personal relationship was cited as a reason for cooperative goals, but not very frequently. Emotional antagonism was one of the two most frequently cited reasons for competitive goals. These results, when taken together, suggest that a strong work relationship did not guarantee constructive conflict; cooperative goals and effective interaction were still needed. Hostility and suspicion can make conflict management difficult, however.

Employees indicated their reasons for concluding that their goals were cooperative or competitive. The most often cited reason was that they understood that the problem at hand could be solved to the satisfaction of both persons. They realized that, though in conflict, their interests were not opposing and that the conflict could be mutually beneficial. Managers and workers were also confident that communication would be useful; by sharing information people would understand the issues, learn and broaden their perspectives, and resolve the conflict. Having the same goal was also cited as a major reason, but it certainly was not necessary to conclude goals were cooperative.

Procedures themselves did not appear to determine how conflicts were managed. Consistent with common advice, open discussion was often used for effective conflicts, and avoiding discussion characterized ineffective conflicts. Nevertheless, open discussion was frequently used in unproductive conflicts as well. Group discussions and third parties were also used in both effective and ineffective conflicts. The results point to the potential value of open discussion and underline the potential harm of avoiding discussions of conflict. The overall results, however, support the idea that procedures themselves do not ensure productive conflict and that managers and workers should develop cooperative goals and interact effectively to make productive use of them.

The type of issue involved may make effective conflict more or less easy. Conflicts over quality of work seemed to be more difficult to resolve effectively, whereas conflicts over procedures were more easily resolved. In general, though, type of issue did not appear to have been a strong antecedent of effective or ineffective conflict.

Results of this study reaffirm the importance of distinguishing conflict from goal interdependence. Conflict does not derive solely or even mostly from opposing interests and scarce resources. Not all, and maybe not even most, organizational conflict is competitive. Persons with highly compatible, mutual goals are often in conflict. Indeed, in this study about 60% of the conflicts were over cooperative goals. Because this study did not attempt to take a random sample of all conflict situations, however, future research is needed to determine more adequately the frequency of conflict within cooperation and competition. Nevertheless, this study clearly demonstrated that conflict should not be assumed to be competitive.

Equating conflict with opposing interests and competitive goals appears to impede the understanding and managing of conflict. People who conclude that their goals are competitive have much more difficulty in managing conflict constructively. Believing that goals are cooperative contributes significantly to productive conflict management in organizations.

Although developed in North America, the theory of cooperation and competition appears to apply quite well to conflict in the Southeast Asian culture of Singapore. The conditions and approaches found in North America to be productive for conflict were also facilitative in Singapore. These findings do not, however, imply that there are no cultural differences between North American and Singaporean modes of conflict management. The issues that become embroiled in conflict, the intensity and frequency of conflict, the frequency of goal interdependence, and the use of different strategies could all vary, and the results of this study do not indicate the extent of these differences between Singapore and North America.

The present results are, of course, limited by this study's operations and sample. The data are self-reported and correlational, but these limitations should be considered in the context of considerable experimental research with supportive findings.

If replicated, the present results have important practical implications. The ability of managers and workers to handle their daily conflicts affects collective bargaining and other traditional industrial relations issues (Katz et al., 1983; Kochan, 1980). Results indicate that training programs should concentrate on helping managers and workers identify their conflicts, conclude that their goals are cooperative, interact effectively within the conflict, and develop their relationships (Tjosvold, 1986).

Cooperation and competition were found useful for understanding and predicting constructive conflict in two companies in Singapore. Employees with compatible goals and interests do conflict, but they are more apt to manage the conflict constructively. Cooperative goals appear to support effective interaction, which in turn is a powerful antecedent to constructive outcomes. A strong work relationship prior to the conflict also predicted constructive conflict. Productive relationships between workers and management, and others in the organization, do not depend on eliminating conflict but on developing cooperative goals and interaction to manage conflicts successfully.

REFERENCES

Bacharach, S. B., & Lawler, E. J. (1981). *Bargaining: Power, tactics, and outcomes*. San Francisco: Jossey-Bass.

Bartunek, J. (1984). Changing interpretive schemes and organizational restructuring: The example of a religious order. *Administrative Science Quarterly, 29*, 355–372.

Bazerman, M. H., & Lewicki, R. J. (Eds.). (1982). *Negotiating in organizations*. Beverly Hills, CA: Sage.

Burrell, G., & Morgan, G. (1979). *Sociological paradigms and organizational analysis*. London: Heinemann.

Commons, J. R. (1934). *Institutional economics: Its place in the political economy*. New York: Macmillan.

Deutsch, M. (1949). A theory of cooperation and competition. *Human Relations, 2*, 129–152.

Deutsch, M. (1973). *The resolution of conflict*. New Haven, CT: Yale University Press.

Deutsch, M. (1980). Fifty years of conflict. In L. Festinger (Ed.), *Retrospections on social psychology* (pp. 46–77). New York: Oxford University Press.

Deutsch, M., & Krauss, R. M. (1962). Studies in interpersonal bargaining. *Journal of Conflict Resolution, 6*, 52–76.

Flanagan, J. C. (1954). The critical incident technique. *Psychological Bulletin, 51*, 327–358.

Gioia, D., & Manz, C. C. (1985). Linking cognition and behavior: A script processing interpretation of vicarious learning. *Academy of Management Review, 10*, 527–539.

Katz, H. C., Kochan, T. A., & Gobeille, K. R. (1983). Industrial relations performance, economic performance, and QWL programs: An interplant analysis. *Industrial and Labor Relations Review, 37*, 3–17.

Katz, H. C., Kochan, T. A., & Weber, M. R. (1985). Assessing the effects of industrial relations systems and efforts to improve the quality of working life on organizational effectiveness. *Academy of Management Journal, 28*, 509–526.

Kochan, T. A. (1980). *Collective bargaining and industrial relations*. Homewood, IL: Irwin.

Kochan, T. A., & Verma, A. (1982). Negotiations in organizations. Blending industrial relations and organizational behavior approaches. In M. Bazerman & R. Lewicki (Eds.), *Negotiating in organizations* (pp. 13–32). Beverly Hills, CA: Sage.

Pfeffer, J. (1981). *Power in organizations*. Boston: Pittman.

Pruitt, D. G., & Syna, H. (1983). Successful problem solving. In D. Tjosvold & D. W. Johnson (Eds.), *Productive conflict management: Perspectives for organizations* (pp. 62–81). New York: Irvington.

Rubin, J., & Brown, B. (1975). *The social psychology of bargaining*. New York: Academic Press.

Tjosvold, D. (1982) Effects of the approach to controversy on superiors' incorporation of subordinates' information in problem-solving. *Journal of Applied Psychology, 67,* 189–193.

Tjosvold, D. (1985). Implications of controversy research for management. *Journal of Management, 11,* 21–37

Tjosvold, D. (1986). *Working together to get things done: Managing for organizational productivity.* Lexington, MA: Heath.

Tjosvold, D., & Johnson, D. W. (Eds.). (1983). *Productive conflict management: Perspectives for organizations.* New York: Irvington.

Walton, R. E., & McKersie, R. B. (1965). *A behavioral theory of labor negotiations.* New York: McGraw-Hill.

Weick, K. (1979). Cognitive processes in organizations. In B. Staw (Ed.), *Research in organizational behavior* (Vol. 1, pp. 41–74). Greenwich, CT: JAI.

We thank the Social Sciences and Humanities Council of Canada for its financial support and Choy Wong for her able assistance.

CRITICAL THINKING QUESTIONS

1. The data used in the study were based upon people's self-reports of events that happened to them, their and the other person's goals at the time of the incident, and their relationship prior to the incident. What are the potential problems with using data like these?
2. Is it possible to experimentally test the hypotheses of this study in a real-world setting? How would you do it?
3. How can the results of this study be used to design programs for organizations to help managers and workers more effectively resolve conflicts?
4. The study specifically pertained to the roles of cooperation and competition in determining the outcomes of conflict in a business setting. Could the findings derived from the study apply to other situations that involve conflict, such as in marriage counseling? How could you test this?

Author Index

Subject Index